D1613910

BRITISH COMMENT ON THE UNITED STATES

British Comment
on the United States

A Chronological Bibliography, 1832–1899

Ada B. Nisbet

Edited by Elliot J. Kanter

With a Foreword by Asa Briggs

UNIVERSITY OF CALIFORNIA PRESS
Berkeley • Los Angeles • London

UNIVERSITY OF CALIFORNIA PUBLICATIONS:
CATALOGS AND BIBLIOGRAPHIES

Editorial Board: Roger B. Berry, Lynda Corey Claassen,
Robert D. Harlan, John V. Richardson, Jr., John W. Tanno

Volume 15

UNIVERSITY OF CALIFORNIA PRESS
BERKELEY AND LOS ANGELES, CALIFORNIA

UNIVERSITY OF CALIFORNIA PRESS, LTD.
LONDON, ENGLAND

Library of Congress Cataloging-in-Publication Data

Nisbet, Ada B. (Ada Blanche), 1907–
    British comment on the United States : a chronological bibliography,
1832–1899 / Ada B. Nisbet ; edited by Elliot J. Kanter.
        p. cm. — (University of California publications. Catalogs and
bibliographies ; v. 15)
    Includes bibliographical references and indexes.
    ISBN 0-520-09811-0 (cloth : alk. paper)
        1. United States—Foreign public opinion, British—Bibliography.
2. United States—Relations—Great Britain—Bibliography. 3. Great Britain—
Relations—United States—Bibliography. 4. National characteristics,
American—Bibliography. 5. United States— Civilization—19th century—
Bibliography. 6. Public opinion—Great Britain—History—19th century—
Bibliography. I. Kanter, Elliot J. (Elliot Jay) II. Title. III. Series.

Z6465.U5 N58 2001
[E183.8.G7]
016.9735—dc21   00-067622

Contents

Foreword

It has been a privilege to be associated with the last stages of this great project that Ada Nisbet, a memorable scholar, conceived of so many years ago. I first learned of it from Ada herself while I was at the University of Sussex helping to create a new university while at the same time pursuing my own interests in Victorian studies, then at a very different stage of development from now. I had been involved from the inception, in 1957, of the periodical *Victorian Studies*, published from Bloomington, Indiana, the product of a generation of new Victorian scholars very different in background and, to a lesser extent, in preoccupations, from my own.

With Ada, as with me, different generations always coexist, even when there is a sense of clash. They continue to explore new scholarly interests, but draw on similar sources, written, visual and oral, published and unpublished. Their range has widened since the 1960s. We already knew then, however, that the sources included not only books but periodicals, and that in Victorian Britain, when there was usually social continuity as well as change, influential periodicals flourished which focused on the issues that united and divided. This was an age of discussion, but it was also an age when class divides were manifest. The themes and moods of late-Victorian Britain were markedly different from those of the mid-Victorian years, and the rise at the same time of popular and specialized periodicals reflected this.

Through periodicals—and through newspapers, including new popular newspapers, which for me were an essential source—I became interested too both in ephemera, including advertising, an interest that was to grow, and in the structures and dynamics of publishing. Ada herself was to state in 1969, when she was recollecting her initiation into bibliography, that "some of the nineteenth century's best commentary on the United States is based on [book] reviews and is often more significant than the works reviewed." So, too, as this Bibliography demonstrates throughout, are its publishing history and its contextual surround. Ada always bracketed literary and historical scholarship, paying special attention to her likely "users," a word not in much use during the 1960s. They mattered as much to her as the students she taught in the classroom. She knew long before the Internet was conceived that scholars already constituted an international network and that she herself was contributing directly not only to bibliographical scholarship, her starting point being with Louis B. Wright, but also to literary and historical scholarship. And since both literary and historical scholarship were changing, often rapidly, her work acquired increasing significance.

The result of it, this volume, completed with tender care by Elliot Kanter, who followed in her wake before and after her death in 1994, contains much essential biographical information about Ada herself, not only charting the origins and development of this daunting project, worthy of the Victorians themselves, but also probing the motives that led Ada to begin it and continue it in the midst of a busy life of institutional obligations. These included service as secretary of UCLA's Academic Senate and (more agreeably, perhaps) as president of UCLA's Faculty Women's Association and of the UCLA chapter of Phi Beta Kappa. Teaching was a necessary obligation for her by will as much as by a sense of duty, and among the scholars she inspired was Kanter, who became her research assistant in 1978 upon entering the graduate program in United States history at UCLA.

By then Ada was well known on both sides of the Atlantic, particularly for her pioneering Dickens scholarship. *Dickens and Ellen Ternan,* her first book, had appeared in 1952, documenting the previously concealed relationship between Dickens and the young actress Ellen Ternan, and she had gone on to serve as an advising editor of the multivolume Pilgrim Edition of Dickens's letters published by Oxford University Press under its Clarendon Press imprint. She also served as an associate editor of *Nineteenth Century Fiction,* which brought her into touch with many scholars in the network (including me), and in 1964 produced an authoritative survey of Dickens scholarship for *Victorian Fiction: A Guide to Research,* edited by Lionel Stevenson for Harvard University Press.

The year 1870, when Dickens died, has been singled out by historians of literature and society not only for the National Education Act, a belated achievement, but also because it opened a decade that has been called "the watershed" in Victorian intellectual and cultural history. The centenary year 1970 must be singled out too in Ada's life. She lectured on Dickens that year in more than a dozen countries, some behind the Iron Curtain, learning at first hand of a variety of educational traditions and becoming fascinated by the challenge to compare them. Having met her at UCLA before the memorable year began, I know how much this exciting but exhausting year meant to her. In a sense it was a watershed in her own life. Four years later she retired from UCLA, continuing work on an international bibliography of Dickens, and on her death her invaluable collection of books on Dickens—and her bibliographical notes on them—were housed in the Dickens Project at the University of California, Santa Cruz, in an Ada B. Nisbet Archive and Library. Once again, more was involved than the handing over of a collection. For Ada collecting had been a labor of love, and as Ada's contemporary and friend Blake Nevius put it, Dickens would have loved Ada more confidently than he loved America, which played such an important part in his life.

For me the most remarkable detailed entry in this Bibliography—and the place for people picking it up to begin—is that relating to Dickens's two-volume *American Notes for General Circulation* (1842), introductions to which have been written by writers as different as Andrew Lang (1898), G.K. Chesterton (1908), Sacheverell Sitwell (1957), Christopher Lasch (1961), and Angus Wilson (1975). At the time the notes inspired what Ada called "a retaliatory volume," sometimes attributed erroneously to Edgar Allen Poe, *English Notes, Intended for Very Extensive Circulation,* published in Boston in 1842. Of Boston Dickens himself wrote, as no one else did, that "every thoroughfare looked exactly like a scene in a pantomime." He "never turned a corner without looking for a clown or a pantaloon."

There are many accounts of Dickens's trip to the United States in 1842 listed in this Bibliography, which may be compared with his American trip of 1867–78. Ada, who leaves out novels containing only "incidental" American scenes, nonetheless refers to *Martin Chuzzlewit* (1843). The information given in what she called the "annotation" to this entry—and most entries were given one—is indispensable to the Dickens scholar. It encourages further exploration leading to re-evaluation. In my own work on cities I was deeply impressed by what Dickens had to say about both Washington and, above all, New York. In Bayrd Still's *Mirror for Gotham: New York as seen by Contemporaries from Dutch Days to the Present* (1956), a pioneering study of urban impressions and perceptions which I found immensely rewarding, Dickens is singled out for his descriptions of New York as "the beautiful metropolis of America."

It is not for the most part great names that constitute the authors who figure in Ada's complete Bibliography, which is devoted to separately published works about the United States, written by British subjects or (an important addition) subjects of the British Empire. Some of the topics treated were inconspicuous; more dealt in stereotypes than in original perceptions. My favorite title in the Bibliography is Thomas Brothers, *The United States of North America as they are; not as they are generally described* (London, 1840), although its subtitle, "being a cure for radicalism," gives it away. A close runner-up is Fred Kerr [i.e., Frederick Grinham Keen], *Recollections of a Defective Memory* (London, 1930), published well after 1899, but describing various tours in America during the 1880s and 1890s. Titles, as Ada noted, could be totally misleading. Thus, a book called *A Visit to the Wild West* proved to be a book not on the United States but on Ireland.

The incorporation of bibliographical material from outside Britain is important given that the British Empire grew conspicuously in size and significance between 1832, where the Bibliography begins, and 1899, where it ends. The period is different in length (and deliberately so) from Queen Victoria's reign. Ada chose 1832 as her starting point since it was the year of what is still often called the Great Reform Bill, giving as her reason for doing so that in the movement for reform, radicals and conservatives drew lessons, though different ones, from American experience. "The passage of the Reform Bill was an alarm to both Conservatives and Radicals: to the Conservatives, a signal for increased effort to discountenence any further movement toward democracy; to the Radicals, a signal that efforts at further movement be increased. The youthful American experiment supplied ammunition for reactionaries, radicals, and middle-of-the-roaders alike in the battle for democracy in Britain." The case for 1899, fin de siècle, is less strong. It seemed "a neater and more logical changing date than the death of Victoria in 1901." Yet it was the death of the Queen, who had never referred to the century's end in her diary, that for most Britons marked the end of an era or epoch, something more momentous than the end of a century.

The last entry in the Bibliography, Sir George Younghusband's *The Philippines and Round About,* refers to an American rather than to a British war: it includes a chapter on "The American Soldier." Near the beginning of the Bibliography, the fourth entry looks at a different combat and the creation of a distinctive American colony, Liberia. It is not merely a matter of publishing that such a high proportion of early entries relate to slavery and the fate of black slaves. Exploration is as much of a recurring topic as slavery, and the sixth entry takes us to California, the botanist Thomas Coulter's *Notes on Upper California, A Journey from Monterey to the Colorado River in 1832.* That was nearly twenty years before the Gold Rush, which was a subject for both action best-sellers and practical guide books. Henry Vizetelly's *Four Months among the Gold Finders in Alta California* is the best example of the first. Written under a pseudonym, J. Tyrrwhitt Brooks, M.D., it was published in 1849 and translated into several languages. Vizetelly, with an interesting and controversial history ahead of him, wrote it in ten days without leaving England. Two of the most useful guide books appeared in the same year. One, by George Alexander Thompson, described eight different routes by sea and the ports reached by steamers of the Royal Mail Steam Packet Company; the other, by William Thurston, looking inside California, was entitled *Guide to the Gold Regions of Upper California. With a map, and scientific designs of native gold, mode of working &c., &c.*

For Ada, internationalist though she was in her travels and contacts, twentieth-century California was the hub of the universe. She first graduated from the Dominican College in San Rafael before moving to UCLA, and her archives and library were deposited, as has been noted, at Santa Cruz. I have been fortunate enough to visit both UCLA and Santa Cruz on several occasions, meeting future friends in literature and history at UCLA when I was a young scholar, and I subsequently shared the experiences in the 1960s of helping to create a new university with the founders of the University of California at Santa Cruz, discussing "new universities" as a group—and the ideas that inspired them—with Chancellor McHenry, who gave his name to the library building where the Nisbet collection is housed. I have given seminars at the University of California, San Diego, and in 1999 visited the University of California, Santa Barbara, with Robert Nisbet, Ada's brother, a wonderful companion, who was deeply anxious to see this Bibliography appear.

I have had other Californian connections too. Professor Alexander Welsh, then a professor at UCLA, now at Yale, who took part with me in the 1967 *Victorian Studies* conference on Victorian Cities, published as his first book *The City of Dickens* (1971), and in 1976 attended a Festschrift conference given me by the University of Sussex when I left Brighton for Oxford. An edition of my *Victorian Cities,* a book that owes a great debt to my months at the University of Chicago, was published by University of California Press in 1993, and I have subsequently been a visiting professor in Communications at the University of Southern California. I was also one of the invited platform speakers on the occasion of the Jubilee of the California Institute of Technology.

Travel, the subject of many books in this Bibliography, beginning with one of the most famous of all, Mrs. Trollope's *Domestic Manners of the Americans* (1832), has not been reduced by the growth of new communications technologies: indeed, it has been fostered, at least for the academic community. I have enjoyed more than once the delights of the Huntington Library, where, in 1969, Ada held a seminar to recall the history of her venture—an occasion that she called an "epiphany."

At this seminar, Ada spoke of the difficulties that she had faced as a bibliographer. "All the contempt" that she had felt as a graduate student for the carelessness of other bibliographers had long since disappeared, and she quoted the Canadian bibliographer Lawrence Burpee who had once remarked that "if you are troubled with conceit of accuracy, and would have it completely taken out of you, prepare a bibliography." Between the 1960s and the 1990s the bibliographical strand in the history of the book became only one of many different strands, and in several countries, beginning with France, new approaches were followed, as they were later in Britain and the United States. Ada herself had singled out among her predecessors the historian Alan Nevins, who was in no sense a bibliographer, but who pioneered both business history and oral history, and various writers on the Anglo-American connection, who might have included Henry Steele Commager in the United States and in Britain Frank Thistlethwaite, first vice-chancellor of the new University of East Anglia, whose book on the connection in the early nineteenth century was based on lectures delivered at the University of Pennsylvania. His second lecture was called "British Political Radicals and the United States" and the fourth "Freedom for Slaves and Women."

These were themes on which Ada lectured, and she also paid her tribute to Joseph Sabin for his massive multivolume *Dictionary of Books Relating to America from its Discovery to the Present Time.* The last volume that he himself completed, volume 19, was followed up by ten more. In Britain a new version of *The Cambridge Bibliography of English Literature,* volume 4, 1800–1900, edited by Joanne Shattock, appeared in 1999, but section 12 on travel includes only a short list of travel books relating to the United States. There is a useful section on newspapers and magazines, and the first section deals with book production and distribution. My favorite entry in it is an 1889 publication that did not last for a whole year, *Books, A Weekly Journal for those who Buy them, Sell them and Read them.* Publishers are omitted, as they are in Ada's Bibliography. Dickens gets an exceptionally long entry, however, and Ada's contribution to the Lionel Stevenson volume, *Victorian Fiction: A Guide to Research,* is among the books noted.

Perhaps the biggest change since the year when Ada started her project relates not to literary, historical, or economic and sociological scholarship but to technology. When Kanter took over as her research assistant in 1978, she placed in his hands a massive file of bundles of 3-

by-5 inch cards and slips filling twelve wooden drawers and seven shoeboxes. They had to be patiently handled: she herself had described her materials in 1969 as "bibliolunacy in 29 shoeboxes." Checking all entries against the *National Union Catalog* and the *British Library Catalogue* (and their supplements) was a time-consuming project. Yet better times lay ahead. A landmark date in Britain was the introduction of a computer-based eighteenth-century titles catalog in 1982, and this was followed later by a nineteenth-century catalog. These catalogs not only facilitate cross reference but simplify statistical classification and comparative analysis. They also make it easier to find out where particular books (and related materials) can be found. With the Internet there is a further unprecedented opportunity for networking scholarship from below.

Whatever the technology, love of books is at the heart of the scholarship that this Bibliography represents. Ada's shoeboxes were instrumental, and I hope they will survive.

ASA BRIGGS
Lewes, Sussex

Acknowledgments

My sister Professor Ada Nisbet's tireless dedication to research is no more evident than in this Bibliography. Needless to say, such an exhaustive compilation could not have been accomplished without the assistance of many others. First and foremost was Elliot Kanter, whose great effort, skill, and personal sacrifice resulted in the completion of this Bibliography following Professor Nisbet's untimely illness and death in 1994. Mr. Kanter, therefore, is really co-author as well as editor of this work. I personally observed his patient checking of Ada's raw notes and library slips contained in 29 shoeboxes in my basement. (Ada's handwriting was akin to the proverbial physician's prescription scrawl.)

Also high on the acknowledgment list is Page Ackerman, Professor Emeritus of the Graduate School of Library and Information Science at UCLA and UCLA's University Librarian from 1973 to 1977. As a close personal friend of Ada's and a consistent liaison between Elliot Kanter and the University of California Press, Professor Ackerman has been a key player for many years in keeping this project alive. She deserves great credit for her work.

In the early 1980s, Page Ackerman and former UCLA University Librarian Robert Vosper (1961–1973), together with Professor Blake Nevius, brought the Bibliography to the attention of the University of California Press. Thereafter they served as an informal liaison committee between the Press, Mr. Kanter, and myself in the joint and finally successful effort to publish this work. They played an essential role in that success.

Contributing moral as well as financial support were Joan Palevsky and former UCLA Chancellor Franklin Murphy.

The Research Committee at UCLA provided funds over the years for continuation of work on the Bibliography. Financial assistance in the form of grants also came from the American Association of University Women, the Fulbright Committee, and the Guggenheim Foundation.

Louis B. Wright of the Huntington and Folger Libraries was an early mentor of Ada's with respect to this work. (The first 900 items were filed with the Huntington Library in 1939!)

Grateful acknowledgment must also be made for the loyal support of Ada's long-time friend, Ruth McGuire, and our mother, Bessie Nisbet, who lived with Ada much of the time.

Lord Asa Briggs of Oxford University, Florence Ridley, Teona Schley, Ada's nephew Professor Kirk Smith, and many others also contributed in various ways to the completion of this Bibliography.

ROBERT NISBET
Berkeley, California

Editor's Note

I have been involved with Ada Nisbet's Bibliography since September 1978, when as an incoming UCLA graduate student in United States history I began work as her research assistant. At that time she placed in my hands the final phase of library research and checking of what was still a massive file of bundled 3-by-5 inch cards and slips, filling twelve wooden drawers and seven shoeboxes. Each of more than 3,000 major entries was to be checked against the newly published *National Union Catalog,* the *British Library Catalogue,* and their supplements to confirm bibliographic accuracy and verify the earliest edition; to identify all subsequent editions incorporating new material by author or editors; and to locate, where not yet found, at least one library in North America and the United Kingdom holding a copy of each work.

Several hundred entries were either incomplete or missing entirely; years of use of the card-file bibliography by scholars and a 1964 theft of some of Professor Nisbet's papers had taken their toll. These gaps in main entries or annotations were discovered by cross-checking from a card-file index, and the entries had to be completed or fully reconstructed. In the process, scores of additional entries were identified and added. Finally, the annotations for each entry had to be updated to reflect scholarship up to a final cutoff point of 1980.

Although Professor Nisbet was unable to prepare an introduction specifically for this published volume, the Introduction that follows is substantially based on a talk she gave at the Huntington Library in May 1969, entitled "Bibliolunacy in 29 Shoeboxes." It also includes material from preliminary introductions and reports on the project written in the 1960s and 1970s.

ELLIOT J. KANTER
Librarian and Bibliographer
University of California, San Diego

Introduction

Ada B. Nisbet

A RECOLLECTION

I would like all of you to know that being invited to give a seminar here at the Huntington Library is a very special moment for me—a kind of Joycean epiphany, with the mixture of pleasure and guilt that usually accompanies such moments. For it was here at the Huntington, nearly thirty years ago, that I began the work I am about to describe, and the then-leading spirit of the Library, Louis B. Wright, was its "onlie begetter."

Louis Wright taught, for a time, a class in bibliography at UCLA. I enrolled in that class with a light heart, little knowing how it would change my life by turning me into a bleary-eyed bibliographer, spending my days standing long hours at catalogs and in chairless (and cheerless) library stacks and my nights wheezing into my typewriter keys. The course was one of the finest, best-planned, thorough, grueling, soul-crushing courses ever devised, and during it were planted the seeds of my future career.

My term project for the course was the compilation of a bibliography, and in ignorance and naiveté I chose the topic "British Comment on America." By the time I found out the difficulties of compiling a list of books on a topic that could not be culled swiftly from ordinary subject catalogs and standard bibliographies, it was too late for retreat. At the end of a semester I turned in 900 items typed in blood, knowing that I had merely scratched behind the ear of the megalosaur. I also knew I was trapped by the excitement and challenge of the chase.

That was in 1940. Now the Bibliography includes roughly 3,000 major entries [3,211 in 2001—Editor], and perhaps 20,000 others in the annotations. I have pored through all of the major bibliographies and scholarly studies of Americana; haunted libraries large and small on both sides of the Atlantic, including almost every major collection in Great Britain, Ireland, Canada, and the United States; corresponded with scholars and librarians on at least two continents; and drawn on the talents of successive research assistants. I realize, of course, that I could spend *another* thirty years and not have everything. Nor would I have solved every problem such as location of elusive first editions, identification of anonymous works, positive determination of nationality, and so on. All the contempt I had felt as a graduate student for the perceived carelessness of other bibliographers has long since faded, as I have struggled with the immense difficulties facing any scholar taking on such a task. As the Canadian bibliographer Lawrence Burpee once remarked, "if you are troubled with conceit of accuracy, and would have it completely taken out of you, prepare a bibliography."

This then is my epiphany—recognizing at last my conceit of perfection for the illusion it is. And recognizing that the time has come at last to declare that the "project" has reached its completion.

THE BIBLIOGRAPHY

Perhaps the best way to clarify just what the Bibliography includes and excludes—and to describe the kinds of problems and exceptions with which I have had to wrestle in the course of its compilation—is to explicate in detail the title: *British Comment on the United States: A Chronological Bibliography, 1832–1899.*

1. **British:** "British" has been taken to include any citizen of Great Britain or its colonies in the nineteenth century. Entries include, therefore, authors from England, Scotland, Ireland, Wales, Canada, Australia, India, New Zealand, and other parts of the British Empire.

My major problem in the matter of nationality has been verification of authors as "British" and not American. Since many items are anonymous or were written by individuals who never ascended to the notice of biographical dictionaries, a close reading of the work itself was frequently necessary before inclusion or exclusion. Sometimes even such a reading was insufficient, and other forms of detection became necessary. For example, after unsuccessful searches through biographical dictionaries for any reference to John Mortimer Murphy, correspondence with a librarian in Oregon, where one of Murphy's books was published, turned up documentation of British nationality in a local Oregon newspaper. In another case, neither the British Library nor the Library of Congress could identify the anonymous author of the two-volume *Visit to the United States: A Reprint of Letters from the Special Correspondent of the Times.* But inquiries to the offices of the London *Times* brought the revelation that this often-quoted sourcebook for the study of British attitudes toward the United States in the 1880s was in fact written by a well-known U.S. journalist, Joel Cook.

Other perplexing questions were posed by British authors who eventually became United States citizens (or, much less frequently, by U.S. citizens who became British citizens). Many of these hybrids are listed in both the *Dictionary of American Biography* and the *Dictionary of National Biography,* and are thus claimed by both countries. Some British writers, although settling permanently in the United States, never became American citizens and sometimes continued to think of themselves as loyal servants of the Crown. In the end, I decided to include those authors who seemed to write from an obviously "British" point of view, with notes calling attention to the fact of their immigration. Frequently I have included the *early* works of writers who settled in the United States, reflecting their impressions as new arrivals; their later works, written after many years of residence in the United States, have been left out or referred to only in the annotations. And, finally, I have included writers of *other* national origins when, like the Russian Ivan Golovin, they became British citizens and thereafter wrote as British authors.

2. **Comment:** "Comment" I have taken to mean any kind of *factual* comment published in books, pamphlets, or even leaflets. Articles in periodicals, however, have *not* been included as main entries unless they were reprinted in separate pamphlet form with independent pagination or as part of a book of collected essays. Entries have *not* been limited to travel accounts, and so comment embracing all areas of interest has been included—ranging from history, economics, political science, law, literature, and the theater, to agriculture, anthropology, and the natural sciences.

The major exclusions from "comment" have been poetry, works of fiction, accounts of the pre-nineteenth-century United States, works on *individual* Americans, critiques of American books, and such purely technical publications as geographical dictionaries, sailing guides, maps, and the like. However, exceptions in each of these categories have been admitted whenever I decided that the work reflected actual observation of or attitudes toward the United States.

When fictional works were clearly semifictionized travel experiences or fictionized satire of the United States, even in verse, I have generally admitted them as valuable reflections of British attitudes, with a note indicating the fictional nature of the item. However, novels containing only incidental American scenes or characters have been left out, although I direct attention to such works in the annotations attached to entries for factual works by their authors, *if* any such works could be found.

When *histories* have included accounts of the United States in the period 1832–1899 (e.g., those on the Civil War), they have been included as representative of contemporary reactions and opinion; otherwise, general histories have been excluded. Works on individual American figures or on particular books by Americans have been left out *except* when such publications (e.g., about a figure such as Lincoln or a work such as *Uncle Tom's Cabin*) reflected significant attitudes toward American affairs. Such works would also be included if they recorded actual visits to the United States, as did several books on Walt Whitman. Handbooks and guidebooks have in general been included, except when they were little more than dictionaries or when they drew exclusively from American sources.

Finally, I have generally excluded official parliamentary and diplomatic publications; these are usually accessible to scholars in other ways and represent such a large body of documents that they would swamp the rest of the bibliography. Nevertheless, when speeches, reports, official correspondence, etc., appeared as separate nonofficial pamphlet reprints, they *have* been included. I have also included a select number of especially important "official" publications, such as James Fraser's report on education in the United States, George Tucker's report on insane asylums (including 600 pages on the United States), and the 1835 Mondelet and Neilson report on American penitentiaries. Such valuable items have often been overlooked by scholars simply because they were buried bibliographically in the mass of official correspondence and reports. However, such rescues are limited to major book-length reports of a nondiplomatic nature.

3. *On the United States:* I have included only comment on U.S. affairs in general, on the United States geographically as a whole, or on any portion of the *continental* United States. Thus comment limited to Alaska, Hawaii, the Panama Canal, etc., has been excluded, while comment on such areas as California, Oregon, or Texas has been retained, even though made prior to their annexation. This geographic focus required examination of each item, even when the title included "America," since many such works proved to be exclusively about Latin America or Canada. There were also other misleading titles, such as *A Visit to the Wild West*—in fact, a book about Ireland.

In general, entries are devoted in their entirety to the United States or to American affairs; any other works by the same author which are only in part about the United States are relegated to the annotations. But when an author wrote no major work on the United States, but did publish a round-the-world tour including a chapter or chapters on the United States, or if substantial portions of an author's memoirs or biography or published letters concerned a visit to, or consecutive and substantial comment on the United States, such works are listed as major entries, with the pertinent portion or portions indicated in the notes.

4. *A Chronological:* Entries are arranged chronologically under the date of the first edition (and alphabetically for each year by author, or if anonymous, by title). This arrangement is for the convenience of scholars interested in any given year or period of United States or British history, or in noting the fluctuations in volume, character, and tone of British interest in the United States over the 68-year span covered. Users interested in individual commentators may, of course, consult the fully cross-referenced index for a complete guide to various publications of any given author as well as to all persons cited in the annotations. If a given work is not found under the date expected, the user is advised also to use the index, which will allow for little-known first editions or for incorrect listings in standard bibliographies and catalogs. The annotations will then clarify the relation between the first edition, as listed, and the edition more commonly sought.

5. ***Bibliography:*** I have made no attempt to describe each item in rigorous bibliographic detail or fully to summarize or annotate each work. The exact wording of each title page is given in full, except for the publisher's name, epigraphical quotations, and the repetition of the author's name, unless it appears on the title page in a form different from that given at the head of the entry. Wherever possible, anonymous and pseudonymous authors have been identified and full names furnished for initials. In general, Library of Congress cataloging practice has been followed for authors' names, e.g., listing ennobled authors by title rather than family name.

I have made every effort to locate at least one library in North America and the United Kingdom which holds the first edition of each work (using the standardized library symbols developed for the *National Union Catalog*). In every case, where the work is owned by the Library of Congress (DLC) or the British Library (Uk), only those symbols are provided. If the first edition is not owned by either or both, I have tried to provide *at least* one library on both sides of the Atlantic (or in a few cases, such distant shores as New Zealand or Australia). The annotations then indicate the earliest edition, if any, which *is* owned by DLC or Uk. In those instances where *no* copy could be located, in spite of intensive personal search, examination of printed library catalogs, and inquiries among major British and American libraries—and when there was reasonable assurance that the item was not a "ghost"—the work is listed with a note giving the grounds for its inclusion.

[In a few cases, documentation of the entry's legitimacy was lost before the final editing process had commenced; such items are listed with the simple notation "No locations found." A concerted effort was made to locate these entries in the *National Union Catalog, Pre-1956 Imprints,* which covers thousands of North American libraries, and included many catalog records not yet available in electronic form. A final search for the "No locations" entries was carried out in 1999 using two major online union catalogs: OCLC, representing more than 41 million records from 12,000 libraries of all types, largely in the United States but also in Europe; and RLIN, linking more than 140 major research libraries in the United States and including about 30 million records.—Editor]

Annotations have been made with the scholar's, rather than the bibliographer's, interests in mind. My research turned up so much material related to individual works that I decided to pass such information along for whatever use the researcher could make of it. Thus, notes call attention to earlier publications in periodicals, to later editions appearing under a changed title or with substantial corrections or additions, and to subsequent critical editions or studies of the authors' experiences in, or attitudes toward, the United States. Contemporary satires of or answers to the works in question have also been noted whenever found. The notes frequently direct attention to other writings by the author which touch upon the United States, including periodical articles, works of fiction, or other books concerned with the United States only in part, such as volumes of letters, biographies, collected essays, or diaries. Where necessary, the notes are also used to explain seeming exceptions to the general criteria for selecting works for inclusion in the Bibliography.

Finally, reviews in both the British and American press are cited for many of the entries, although no claim is made to be exhaustive or comprehensive. Some of the nineteenth century's best commentary on the United States is buried in these reviews and is often more significant than the works reviewed. John Stuart Mill, for example, wrote no major study of the United States. He did, however, publish lengthy reviews of such books by his contemporaries, beginning with his probing review of Tocqueville's *Democracy in America,* a book that very powerfully influenced Mill's later work. Without reference to those reviews in the annotations, Mill would otherwise have been omitted from the Bibliography entirely.

6. ***1832–1899:*** I chose 1832 as a starting point because it represents the beginning of the Victorian period, with the passage of the first Reform Bill. It was also the publication year of perhaps the most famous (or infamous) of all English books on the United States: Frances Trollope's *The Domestic Manners of the Americans.* The passage of the Reform Bill was an

alarm bell to both Conservatives and Radicals: to the Conservatives, a signal for increased effort to discountenance any further movement toward democracy; to the Radicals, a signal that efforts at further movement be increased. The youthful American experiment supplied ammunition for reactionaries, radicals, and middle-of-the-roaders alike in the battle for democracy in Britain. The year 1899, popularly viewed as closing out the nineteenth century, seemed a neater and more logical closing date than the death of Queen Victoria in 1901.

Items in the Bibliography are entered by date of publication of the first book edition, even when that first edition was a pirated one. (In those few cases where no record of the first edition could be found, the date of the earliest known is used.) Within each of the 68 years covered, the entries are arranged alphabetically. Naturally, this order by date means that the chronological entry is not always a guide to the exact period of the observations recorded, since many works were not published until years after the events described.

Once again, a number of inconsistencies had to be worked through. Works published on the United States from 1832 to 1899 were excluded if they were concerned entirely with the eighteenth century or earlier; but they were *included* if they focused on nineteenth-century America before 1832. For example, Sir Augustus John Foster's *Notes on the U.S.,* published in 1841 but descriptive of Foster's experiences between 1804 and 1812, was used; but Francis Baily's 1856 book *Journal of a Tour in Unsettled Parts of North America in 1796 & 1797,* was omitted. In a few instances, later editions of works first published earlier than 1832 were included when they contained *substantial* changes or additions based on post-1832 observations.

Finally, a number of works published after 1900 have been included as main entries *if* they contained accounts of visits to the United States made within the period 1832–1899 and if the author had *not* published any pre-1900 books on the United States. (Otherwise, the later works would have been included only as annotations.) These exceptions include travel books, memoirs, autobiographies, collections of letters, and diaries. Some were eventually published by the observer during early decades of the twentieth century; others represent nineteenth-century manuscripts rescued and published during the twentieth century by scholars or descendants of the original author. In all cases, such twentieth-century entries are arranged chronologically in the bibliography according to the ending date of the actual visit or visits, so that they may appear in the context of books actually published in the same year.

WHY IS SUCH A BIBLIOGRAPHY NEEDED?

I have described just *what* it is that I have constructed over the past several decades. I'd like now to turn to *why* I have searched so widely and persevered for so long. As my work progressed, my irritation with the inadequacy of many of the bibliographical sources consulted extended to many learned publications by scholars working in fields related to the scope of the Bibliography. I found myself racing to the library for each newly announced study of Anglo- or Canadian-American relations, or of the American Civil War, or of slavery, emigration, the American West, the California Gold Rush, the Mormons, and so on—with the expectation of picking up bibliographic pearls from hitherto uncombed oyster beds. Time and again I was disappointed—not because in every case these studies were not sound or comprehensive in their scholarship or in the coverage of their particular subject, but because so frequently the observation and comment of *British* writers on each subject appeared to receive such short shrift. This frequently led, whenever British comment on any American subject was wanted, to quoting from the same old group of shop-worn British travelers whose favorite passages had long since become clichés.

Of course I have had predecessors in the bibliographical field. Most important are Alan Nevins's *American Social History as Recorded by British Travellers* (1923; reissued in 1948 with additions as *America Through British Eyes*), with its bibliography of 300 items; Jane Mesick's

The English Traveller in America, 1785–1835 (1922); Max Berger's *British Traveller in America, 1836–1860* (1943); and Richard Rapson's *Britons View America: Travel Commentary, 1860–1935* (1971). Yet as the titles indicate, these works have been limited to the comment of travelers. They therefore leave out by definition the mass of commentators who did not choose to cross the Atlantic, but whose analyses of the American scene and whose transmission of varied perspectives to their countrymen had an impact frequently far more significant than that of their traveling compatriots. These bibliographies are also selective, including only the better known and more widely publicized travelers. For both reasons they tend to perpetuate certain stock generalizations about British attitudes toward the United States.

It is, of course, in the jokes of each generation that the old clichés are perpetuated, as in that most popular Anglo-American jest of World War I: the Britisher's complaint about American servicemen that "they are overpaid, oversexed, and over here," which in fact is simply Charles Dickens's *Martin Chuzzlewit* brought into the twentieth century. As English traveler David Macrae observed:

> The old popular notion of an American was that of a man who wore nankeen trousers, carried a bowie-knife, sat with his feet on a mantlepiece [sic], and squirted tobacco-juice on the carpet. There may be some people still possessed with this idea of Cousin Jonathan, just as there are probably some Cockneys who still imagine that Scotsmen wear kilts [and] live on porridge and whiskey.
> — *The Americans at Home: Pen and Ink Sketches of American Men, Manners and Institutions* (Edinburgh, 1870)

Twenty years later, a reviewer complaining of the dullness and sameness of travel books on the United States remarked of the 1881 book by Lady Duffus Hardy, *Through Cities and Prairie Lands. Sketches of an American Tour* (reprinted in 1890), "We scarcely hoped to live long enough to see any writer in good faith again describe Chicago as 'rising Phoenix-like from its ashes.'" Few, certainly, have been as candid as Dean Arthur Penrhyn Stanley who, when asked in 1879 whether he had been surprised at anything on his visit to the United States the previous year, replied, "chiefly by my own ignorance." (See Stanley's comments during the visit, published in 1879, *Addresses and Sermons, Delivered During a Visit to the United States and Canada in 1878*). More seriously, as lampooned by Sam Slick, that delightful Yankee creation of Nova Scotian author Thomas Haliburton, it often seemed that every British traveler came to the United States with a thesis in his pocket:

> First comes a great high Tory. . . . He sees no established church, and he swears there's no religion; and he sees no livery helps and he says it's all vulgar; and if he sees a citizen spit, he jumps a one side as scared as if it wor a rifle agoin' off. Then comes a radical. . . . sour as vinegar, and lookin' as hungry as a bear gist starved out in the spring . . . and *they* say as we have the slavery of opinion here; that our preachers want moral courage, and that our great cities are cursed with the aristocracy of wealth. . . . They think they know everything. . . . Then out comes a book. If it's a Tory writes it, then the Tory paper says it's the best pictur' they have seen—lively, interestin', intelligent. If a radical, then radical papers say it's a very philosophical work. . . . statesman-like-view, able work, throws great light on the politics of the day.
> — "Travelling in America," in *The Clockmaker; or,*
> *The Sayings and Doings of Sam Slick, of Slickville* (2nd series, London, 1838)

But what of other travelers and of observers who never traveled at all, and whose writings touched on subjects far more varied and concrete than "what I saw in America"? What of the impact, year after year, of such a widely circulated magazine as *Field,* its pages filled with accounts of all sectors of the United States—reviewing the prospects in agriculture, industry, mining, sports, cattle and sheep raising, and so on, written for the benefit of visitor and emigrant and investor? And what about slavery? Certainly the attitudes of the English working class at the time of the Civil War, spoken of by John Bright [see his speeches listed in the Bibliography, 1862, 1864, 1865—Editor] cannot be understood without taking into account the flood of anti-slavery literature disseminated by innumerable evangelical and dissenting groups. Following the British emancipation act of 1833, these groups turned their attention with a vengeance upon the United States. Similarly, the many virulent anti-Mormon publications by British clergy and other critics included in the Bibliography (appearing as early as 1840) suggests that enticing invitations to a land of milk and honey on the shores of Utah's Great Salt Lake may have been finding a positive response from the impoverished masses in great cities like Liverpool. Comparable examples could be multiplied from almost every area of commentary—economic, political, scientific, religious, educational, sociological, industrial.

The long-enduring impressions—and stereotypes—formed by travel accounts should not be minimized. Yet nor should it be forgotten that such books were more often than not written for a select public with leisure to read, money to pay, and often prejudices to be catered to. There was also a concurrent, steady flood of cheap publications in shilling pamphlets, emigration literature, workingmen's lectures, etc. And it is through this less remembered, and often less visible, body of publication that we may find a quieter, cumulative effect on British views of the United States. The resulting mosaic of varied and sustained impressions can only enhance our vision of the nineteenth century—of the United States, of Great Britain, and of their ongoing, trans-Atlantic relationship.

I have saved for the end my acknowledgment of indebtedness to Joseph Sabin and his monumental *A Dictionary of Books Relating to America from its Discovery to the Present Time* (published from 1868 to 1936). As I checked through the 106,413 items in Sabin's 29 volumes, my astonishment at one man's temerity in setting out to climb a bibliographical Mount Everest—no less than a list of *everything* in *every* language written about the whole Western Hemisphere since the beginning of printing—was matched only by my respect for his accomplishment and my gratitude as a fellow laborer in a small peripheral vineyard. When I came to the end of volume 19, the last that Sabin lived to complete—and took up volume 20, continued by other men after a lapse of 37 years—I found myself meditating on how one initiates canonization procedures for a bibliographer.

Were I to choose an epigraph for my bibliography, I should borrow one that appears on the title page of every one of the 29 volumes of Sabin's *Dictionary,* one that *he* borrowed from an earlier bibliographer, Anthony à Wood:

> A painful work it is I'll assure you, and more than difficult, wherein what toyle hath been taken, as no man thinketh so no man believeth, but he hath made the triall.

As a postscript I should also borrow the epigraph with which librarian and historian R.W.G. Vail brought the project begun by Sabin in 1868 to its final conclusion, seventy years later, in 1938:

> Some Tyme an ende there is of every dede.

Guide to the Bibliography

SCOPE

The Bibliography includes separately published works (books or pamphlets) about the United States, written by British subjects or other subjects of the British Empire, and published between 1832 and 1899. Some exceptions to the date range include works published later than 1899, but concerning earlier visits to the United States, and earlier manuscripts discovered and published in the twentieth century.

ORGANIZATION

Entries are arranged chronologically by date of first known edition or, in the case of works published after 1899, by date of last visit to the United States. Within each year from 1832 to 1899, entries are in alphabetical order by name of author or, for anonymous works, by title.

FORM OF ENTRY

Each entry contains the following elements for the first edition: author's full name, with anonymous and pseudonymous authors identified wherever possible; full and exact title, as taken from the title page; city of publication; date of publication; pagination (or with multivolume works, number of volumes); identification (if possible) of at least one British and one U.S. or Canadian library holding the first edition (using *National Union Catalog* symbols). If held by the British Library (Uk) and the Library of Congress (DLC), only those locations are noted.

ANNOTATIONS

Where needed and appropriate, annotations provide the following information:
  — earliest edition held by the Library of Congress and British Library, if it is *not* the first edition
  — subsequent editions containing additional material by the author or by subsequent editors
  — significant title variations in later editions
  — original sources, if the work was first published in periodicals
  — pages containing material on the United States (if the whole book is not on the United States)

— other writings by the author about the United States which would not qualify as
main entries
— secondary sources commenting on the work or on the author's experiences in, or
opinions of, the United States
— discussion of any controversies generated by the work
— any other information needed to clarify inclusion in the Bibliography

Following the annotation, known contemporary reviews of the book are listed, including authors
of reviews, where known.

Library Abbreviations

Abbreviations are based on the system of location symbols used in the eleventh edition of the *National Union Catalog (NUC)*. The country is indicated only for libraries outside the United States; otherwise, only U.S. states are noted. The first one or two letters of the abbreviation represent state or country, e.g., N for New York and Nc for North Carolina. Alphabetical order of abbreviations below is therefore modified to group them geographically, e.g., NN, for New York Public Library, precedes NcU, for University of North Carolina.

A

AuCNL	National Library of Australia (formerly known as the Commonwealth National Library), Canberra, Australia
AuSM	Mitchell Library, Sydney, Australia

C

C	California State Library, Sacramento, CA
C-S	California State Library, Sutro Branch, San Francisco, CA
CBGTU	Graduate Theological Union, Berkeley, CA
CCC	Honnold Library, Claremont, CA
CCSC	School of Theology at Claremont, Claremont, CA
CL	Los Angeles Public Library, Los Angeles, CA
CLSM	Southwest Museum, Los Angeles, CA
CLSU	University of Southern California, Los Angeles, CA
CLU	University of California, Los Angeles, CA
CLU-C	William Andrews Clark Memorial Library, University of California, Los Angeles, CA
CS	Sacramento City-County Library System, Sacramento, CA
CSbC	California State College, San Bernardino, CA
CSmH	Henry E. Huntington Library, San Marino, CA
CSt	Stanford University, Stanford, CA
CU	University of California, Berkeley, CA
CU-BANC	Bancroft Library, University of California, Berkeley, CA

CU-S	University of California, San Diego, CA
CaAEU	University of Alberta, Edmonton, Alb., Canada
CaBVa	Vancouver Public Library, Vancouver, B.C., Canada
CaBVaU	University of British Columbia, Vancouver, B.C., Canada
CaBViP	British Columbia Provincial Library, Victoria, B.C., Canada
CaNBFU	University of New Brunswick, Fredericton, N.B., Canada
CaNSHD	Dalhousie University, Halifax, N.S., Canada
CaNSHL	Legislative Library, Halifax, N.S., Canada
CaNSWA	Acadia University, Wolfville, N.S., Canada
CaOKQ	Queens University, Kingston, Ont., Canada
CaOLU	University of Western Ontario, London, Ont., Canada
CaOOA	Public Archives of Canada, Ottawa, Ont., Canada
CaOONL	National Library of Canada, Ottawa, Ont., Canada
CaOOP	Library of Parliament, Ottawa, Ont., Canada
CaOTP	Toronto Public Library, Toronto, Ont., Canada
CaOTU	University of Toronto, Toronto, Ont., Canada
CaQMBM	Bibliothèque de la Ville de Montréal, Montréal, Que., Canada
CaQMBN	Bibliothèque nationale du Québec, Montréal, Que., Canada
CoD	Denver Public Library, Denver, CO
CoDI	Iliff School of Theology, Denver. CO
CoDU	University of Denver, Denver, CO
CtY	Yale University, New Haven, CT
CtY-D	Yale University, Divinity School, New Haven, CT
CtY-M	Yale University, Medical School, New Haven, CT
CtY-Mus	Yale University, School of Music, New Haven, CT

D

DAU	American University, Washington, DC
DBRE	Association of American Railroads, Economics and Finance Department Library, Washington, DC
DHEW	U.S. Department of Health, Education, and Welfare, Washington, DC [with evolution of a separate Education Department, locations may have changed]
DHU	Howard University, Washington, DC
DL	U.S. Department of Labor Library, Washington, DC
DLC	Library of Congress, Washington, DC
DN	U.S. Department of the Navy Library, Washington, DC
DNAL	U.S. National Agricultural Library, Beltsville, MD
DNLM	U.S. National Library of Medicine, Bethesda, MD
DNW	U.S. National War College, Washington, DC
DS	U.S. Department of State Library, Washington, DC
DSI	Smithsonian Institution, Washington, DC
DeU	University of Delaware, Newark, DE

F

FU   University of Florida, Gainesville, FL

G

GU   University of Georgia, Athens, GA

I

ICHi   Chicago Historical Society, Chicago, IL
ICJ   John Crerar Library, Chicago, IL
ICN   Newberry Library, Chicago, IL
ICRL   Center for Research Libraries, Chicago, IL
ICU   University of Chicago, Chicago, IL
IEN   Northwestern University, Evanston, IL
IHi   Illinois State Historical Library, Springfield, IL
IU   University of Illinois, Urbana, IL
IaAS   Iowa State University of Science and Technology, Ames, IA
IaHi   State Historical Society of Iowa, Iowa City, IA
IaU   University of Iowa, Iowa City, IA
InU   Indiana University, Bloomington, IN
IreDNL   National Library of Ireland, Dublin, Ireland
IreDT   Trinity College, University of Dublin, Dublin, Ireland

K

KEmT   Kansas State Teachers College, Emporia, KS
KU   University of Kansas, Lawrence, KS

L

LNT   Tulane University, New Orleans, LA
LU   Louisiana State University, Baton Rouge, LA

M

MB   Boston Public Library, Boston, MA
MBAt   Boston Athenaeum, Boston, MA
MH   Harvard University, Cambridge, MA
MH-A   Harvard University, Arnold Arboretum, Cambridge, MA

MH-AH	Harvard University, Andover-Harvard Theological Library, Cambridge, MA
MH-BA	Harvard University, Graduate School of Business Administration, Boston, MA
MH-L	Harvard University, Law School, Cambridge, MA
MHi	Massachusetts Historical Society, Boston, MA
MU	University of Massachusetts, Amherst, MA
MWA	American Antiquarian Society, Worcester, MA
MdBE	Enoch Pratt Free Library, Baltimore, MD
MdBJ	Johns Hopkins University, Baltimore, MD
MeU	University of Maine, Orono, ME
MiD	Detroit Public Library, Detroit, MI
MiD-B	Detroit Public Library, Burton Historical Collection, Detroit, MI
MiU	University of Michigan, Ann Arbor, MI
MiU-C	University of Michigan, William L. Clements Library, Ann Arbor, MI
MnHi	Minnesota Historical Society, St. Paul, MN
MnU	University of Minnesota, Minneapolis, MN
MoKU	University of Missouri at Kansas City, Kansas City, MO
MoU	University of Missouri, Columbia, MO
MsU	University of Mississippi, University, MS
MtU	University of Montana at Missoula, Missoula, MT

N

NUC	National Union Catalog
N	New York State Library, Albany, NY
NB	Brooklyn Public Library, Brooklyn, NY
NBLiHi	Long Island Historical Society, Brooklyn, NY
NBuG	Grosvenor Reference Division, Buffalo and Erie County Public Library, Buffalo, NY
NCaS	Saint Lawrence University, Canton, NY
NHi	New York Historical Society, New York, NY
NIC	Cornell University, Ithaca, NY
NN	New York Public Library, New York, NY
NNC	Columbia University, New York, NY
NNEC	Explorers' Club, New York, NY
NNUT	Union Theological Seminary, New York, NY
NRU	University of Rochester, Rochester, NY
NSbSU	State University of New York at Stony Brook, Stony Brook, NY
NSchU	Union College, Schenectady, NY
NSyU	Syracuse University, Syracuse, NY
NcD	Duke University, Durham, NC
NcU	University of North Carolina, Chapel Hill, NC
NhM	Manchester City Library, Manchester, NH
NjP	Princeton University, Princeton, NJ
NzDOt	University of Otago, Dunedin, New Zealand
NzWTu	Turnball Library, Wellington, New Zealand

O

OC	Public Library of Cincinnati and Hamilton County, Cincinnati, OH
OCl	Cleveland Public Library, Cleveland, OH
OClW	Case Western Reserve University, Cleveland, OH
OClWHi	Western Reserve Historical Society, Cleveland, OH
OKentU	Kent State University, Kent, OH
OO	Oberlin College, Oberlin, OH
OU	Ohio State University, Columbus, OH
Or	Oregon State Library, Salem, OR
OrHi	Oregon Historical Society, Portland, OR
OrP	Library Association of Portland (Public Library for Portland and Multnomah County), Portland, OR

P

PGC	Gettysburg College, Gettysburg, PA
PHC	Haverford College, Haverford, PA
PHi	Historical Society of Pennsylvania, Philadelphia, PA
PPAN	Academy of Natural Sciences of Philadelphia, PA
PPFr	Friends' Free Library of Germantown, Philadelphia, PA
PPL	Library Company of Philadelphia, Philadelphia, PA
PPPrHi	Presbyterian Historical Society, Philadelphia, PA
PPT	Temple University, Philadelphia, PA
PPULC	Union Library Catalogue of Pennsylvania, Philadelphia, PA
PPWa	Wagner Free Institute of Science, Philadelphia, PA
PSC	Swarthmore College, Swarthmore, PA 19081
PSt	Pennsylvania State University, University Park, PA
PU	University of Pennsylvania, Philadelphia, PA
PU-L	University of Pennsylvania, Biddle Law Library, Philadelphia, PA

R

RP	Providence Public Library, Providence, RI
RPB	Brown University, Providence, RI

T

T	Tennessee State Library and Archives, Nashville, TN
TNF	Fisk University, Nashville, TN
TU	University of Tennessee, Knoxville, TN
Tx	Texas State Library and Historical Commission, Austin, TX
TxDaM	Southern Methodist University, Dallas, TX

TxFTC	Texas Christian University, Fort Worth, TX
TxU	University of Texas, Austin, TX

U

USl	Salt Lake City Public Library, Salt Lake City, UT
USlC	Church of Jesus Christ of Latter-Day Saints, Historian's Office, Salt Lake City, UT
UU	University of Utah, Salt Lake City, UT
Uk	British Library, London, United Kingdom
UkCU	Cambridge University, Cambridge, United Kingdom
UkENC	New College, Edinburgh, United Kingdom
UkENL	National Library of Scotland, Edinburgh, United Kingdom
UkEU	University of Edinburgh, Edinburgh, United Kingdom
UkLFO	Foreign Office Library, London, United Kingdom
UkLGl	Gladstone Library, London, United Kingdom
UkLL	London Library, London, United Kingdom
UkLNiip	National Institute of Industrial Psychology, London, United Kingdom
UkLRC	Reform Club, London, United Kingdom
UkLRSS	Royal Statistical Society Library, London, United Kingdom
UkLSE	London School of Economics, London, United Kingdom
UkLU	University of London, London, United Kingdom
UkLU-C	University College, University of London, London, United Kingdom (according to the "Note to Users" in the London Bibliography of the Social Sciences, located in the Hume, Ricardo, or other special economic and political collections)
UkLU-G	Goldsmith's Library of Economic Literature, University of London, London, United Kingdom
UkMa	Manchester Public Libraries, Manchester, United Kingdom
UkOxU	Oxford University, Oxford, United Kingdom
UkRCS	Royal Commonwealth Society (formerly Royal Empire Society), London, United Kingdom

V

Vi	Virginia State Library, Richmond, VA
ViU	University of Virginia, Charlottesville, VA

W

WHi	State Historical Society of Wisconsin, Madison, WI
WU	University of Wisconsin, Madison, WI
WaS	Seattle Public Library, Seattle, WA
WaT	Tacoma Public Library, Tacoma, WA
WaU	University of Washington, Seattle, WA

1832

1   ADVICE TO EMIGRANTS, who intend to settle in the United States of America. Bristol [1832?]. 24 p.   **UkLU-G**

DLC, NN have 2d ed., "greatly enlarged and improved", Bristol, [1832?].

2   AMERICA AND ENGLAND CONTRASTED, in a series of letters, from settlers in the United States & Canada. With an introduction, comprising all necessary information for persons desirous to emigrate. London, 1832. 52 p.   **CSmH**

Uk has 1845 ed. Later eds. carry variant titles.

3   BELL, JAMES. A system of geography, popular and scientific, or a physical, political, and statistical account of the world and its various divisions . . . Illustrated by a complete series of maps, and other engravings. Glasgow, 1832. 6 vols.   **CtY CU Uk**

Uk ed. has 1831 on t.p. of vol. V, although cover page has 1832; CtY copy has all six vols. dated 1832. DLC has Glasgow, 1834 ed. On U.S., V, pp. 324–502, 509–513; VI, pp. 597–611. Later eds. added more material on the U.S.

4   [BEVAN, JOHN]. A vindication of the American colonization society, and the colony of Liberia. Extracted from the Herald of Peace. [London, 1832]. 20 p.   **DLC Uk**

Caption title: "A reply to the attack of Charles Stuart"; original article in the *Herald of Peace*, VIII, n.s., 252–269.

5   CARR, GEORGE KIRWAN. A short tour through the United States & Canadas, October 10th to December 31st, 1832, the journal of Lieut. George Kirwan Carr; edited, with notes, by Deoch Fulton. New York, 1937. 34 p.   **DLC Uk**

Repr. from the *Bull. N.Y. Pub Lib.*, XLI (Oct. 1937), 743–774.

6   COULTER, THOMAS. Notes on upper California: a journey from Monterey to the Colorado river in 1832. Los Angeles, 1951. 39 p.   **DLC**

Early California Travel Series, No. 1, adds "Letters from Thomas Coulter to Sir W. J. Hooker." Originally appeared in the *J. Royal Geog. Soc.*, V (1835), 59–70; repr. in French in *Nouvelles annales des voyages, et des sciences geographiques*, LXXV (1837), 30–52. See Frederick V. Colville's "The botanical explorations of Thomas Coulter in Mexico and California," in the *Botanical Gazette.*, XX (Dec. 1895), 519–531; and the *Calif. Hist. Soc. Quar.*, II, 227.

7   CROPPER, JAMES. A letter to Thomas Clarkson, by James Cropper, and Prejudice vincible; or, The practicability of conquering prejudice by better means than by slavery and exile; in relation to the American colonization society — by [Charles] Stuart. Liverpool, 1832. 24 p.   **DLC Uk**

Repr. as a supp. to the *Emancipator*, New York, 1833, 15 pp.; also in *Anti-Slavery Reporter*, I, No. 1, and in *British opinions of the American colonization society*, Boston, 1833, below.

Review: [Leonard Bacon], *Review of pamphlets on slavery and colonization. First published in the Quarterly Christian spectator, for March, 1833*, New Haven, 1833, pp. 14–22.

8   DYKE, THOMAS, *jun*. Advice to emigrants; or, An impartial guide to the Canadas, New Brunswick, Nova Scotia, the United States, New South Wales, Van Dieman's Land, the Swan River, and the Cape of Good Hope; pointing out the advantages and disadvantages of the several locations, with the latest government instructions. London, 1832.   **Uk**

Chap. 4, "The United States," pp. 45–59; other refs., passim.

9   THE EMIGRANT'S GUIDE; containing practical and authentic information, and copies of original and unpublished letters from emigrants, to their friends in the counties of Mayo, Galway and Roscommon. Westport, 1832. 136 p.   **Uk**

Contains 14 pp. of letters from settlers in the U.S.; the rest on Canada.

10   FERGUSON, ADAM. On the agricultural state of Canada, and part of the United States of America. Cupar [Scotland], 1832. 37 p.   **MH**

DLC has 2d ed.: *Practical notes made during a tour in Canada and a portion of the United States in MDCCCXXXI*, Edinburgh, 1833; an 1834 ed. added subtitle, "to which are now added notes made during a second visit to Canada in 1833." The work appeared originally in the *Quar. J. Agric.*, Mar.–Sept., 1832, under title "Notes made during a visit to the United States and Canada in 1831."

Reviews: *Knickerbocker*, II, 283; *Monthly Rev.*, CXXX, 298; *Eclectic Rev.*, (April 1833), 338.

11   FERRALL, SIMON ANSLEY. A ramble of six thousand miles through the United States of America. London, 1832. 360 p.   **DLC Uk**

DLC catalogs under O'Ferrall.

Review: *Monthly Rev.*, CXXXIX, 57.

12   HIGGINSON, EDWARD. Liberia philanthropically and economically considered. Hull, [1832?]. 24 p.   **NN**

13   HINTON, JOHN HOWARD, *ed*. The history and topography; of the United States: ed. by John Howard Hinton, A.M. Assisted by several literary gentlemen in America and England, illustrated with a series of views, drawn on the spot, and engraved on steel, expressly for this work. London, 1830–32. 2 vols.   **DLC Uk**

Vol. I: history; vol. II: geography, manners, institutions, etc. First pub. in monthly parts; very popular work that went into many eds.; a Boston ed. [1834] appeared "with additions and corrections by Samuel L. Knapp."

Reviews: *Eclectic Rev.*, V, (April 1831), 281; *Monthly Rev.*, CXXVIII, 347; *Westmin. Rev.*, XVII, 168.

14   HORE, MAURICE P. Sketches, miscellaneous, descriptive, and statistical . . . of that part of the United States of America, comprising the seat of the Federal Government, the States of Virginia, Maryland, Pennsylvania, Delaware, New Jersey, New York, New Hampshire, Connecticut, Vermont and Massachusetts, etc. Cork, 1832. 95 p.   **Uk**

15   HOWELLS, H. C. Letters from Ohio; containing advice to emigrants. . . Also, America as they find it: or letters from America. London, 1832. 2 vols. in 1.

No locations found.

16   [LORIMER, JOHN GORDON]. Church establishments defended; being a review of the speeches, delivered in Dr. Beattie's chapel, on Monday evening, the 12th November, 1832,

by the leading men of the Voluntary Church Association. By a churchman. Glasgow, 1832. 31 p. **DLC**

Uk has 1833 ed.

17   MARTIN, ROBERT MONTGOMERY. The past and present state of the tea trade of England, and of the continents of Europe and America; and a comparison between the consumption, price of, and revenue derived from tea, coffee, sugar, wine, tobacco, spirits, &c. London, 1832. 222 p. **DLC Uk**

Includes many refs. to the U.S.

18   NOTES ON THE ARMY of the United States of America. London, 1832. **NHi**

Signed "A." Repr. from *United Service Mag.*, (Oct. 1832), 154–161.

19   OUSELEY, *SIR* WILLIAM GORE. Remarks on the statistics and political institutions of the United States, with some observations on the ecclesiastical system of America, her sources of revenues, &c. London, 1832. 208 p. **DLC Uk**

Philadelphia ed., 1832, "to which are added statistical tables", 226 p. See also author's *Notes on the slave-trade, etc.*, London, 1850, for incidental comment on America.

Reviews: *Am. Monthly Rev.*, II, 457; *Edinb. Rev.* (by W. Empson), LV, 479; *Monthly Rev.*, CXXVIII, 347; *Penny Mag.*, I, 133; *Quar. Rev.*, XLVIII, 507; *Westmin. Rev.*, XVII, 168.

20   PICKEN, ANDREW. The Canadas, as they at present commend themselves to the enterprise of emigrants, colonists, and capitalists. Comprehending a variety of topographical reports [concerning the quality of the land, etc., in different districts]; and the fullest general information: compiled and condensed from original documents furnished by John Galt., esq., late of the Canada company, and now of the British land association, and other authentic sources. London, 1832. 349 p. **DLC Uk**

2d ed. appeared anonymously as *The Canadas: comprehending topographical information, etc.*, London, 1836. Contains description of New York state in "Travelling to the Canadas: Pt. II," pp. 225–249; other comment on U.S. in appendix, pp. li–lxii.

21   PICKERING, JOSEPH. Inquiries of an emigrant; being the narrative of an English farmer from the year 1824 to 1830; during which period he traversed the United States and Canada, with a view to settle as an emigrant. Containing observations on the manners, soil, climate, and husbandry of the Americans; estimates of outfit charges of voyage, and travelling expenses. London, 1832. 207 p. **DLC**

3d ed., with additions, of work first pub. in 1830, under title: *Emigration or no emigration, etc.* Uk has 4th ed. which carried subtitle, "With the author's additions to March, 1832, during which period he traversed the United States and Canada."

22   REPUBLICS AND MONARCHIES: a dialogue between the President of the United States and John Bull. London, 1832.

No locations found; advertised in *America and England contrasted*, 1832, above.

23   SAWBRIDGE, H. B. A letter addressed to Michael Thomas Sadler, Esq., M.P. on the subject of emigration. London, 1832. 49 p. **CaOOA Uk**

Discusses advantages offered in the U.S.

24   STRACHAN, JOHN, *Bishop of Toronto*. A letter to the Rev. Thomas Chalmers, D.D., professor of divinity in the University of Edinburgh, on the life and character of the Right

Reverend Dr. Hobart, Bishop of New-York, North-America. New York, 1832. 56 p.

NN NNUT Uk

Compares Episcopal church of Canada with that of U.S.

25　　STUART, *CAPT*. CHARLES. A letter on the American colonization society, addressed to the editor of the "Herald of Peace." December 1st, 1831. Birmingham, 1832, 14 p.

MB NN

See Fred Landon, "Captain Charles Stuart, Abolitionist," *Western Ontario Hist. Nuggets*, XXIV (1956), 1–19.

26　　STUART, *CAPT*. CHARLES. Remarks on the colony of Liberia and the American colonization society, with some account of the settlement of coloured people, at Wilberforce, Upper Canada. London, 1832. 16 p.　　**CaOLU NNUT**

See also collection of letters to Stuart from the U.S. and U.S. newspaper items about the American colonization society in: *Liberia unmasked; or, the incompatibility of the views and schemes of the American colonization society with those of the real friends of the immediate abolition of slavery proved by facts*, Edinburgh, 1833.

27　　THOMPSON, DAVID. History of the late war between Great Britain and the United States of America; with a retrospective view of the causes from whence it originated; collected from the most authentic sources. To which is added an appendix, containing public documents &c., relating to the subject. Niagara, U.C., 1832. 300 p.　　**DLC Uk**

28　　TROLLOPE, *MRS*. FRANCES [MILTON]. Domestic manners of the Americans. London, 1832. 2 vols.　　**DLC Uk**

Many later eds. including English, American, French, German and Dutch. The 5th English ed. (Bentley's Standard Library of Popular Modern Literature, vol. IV), London, 1839, contains new notes by Mrs. Trollope. More recent editions with notes and commentary include those ed. by Harry Thurston Peck, New York (1894), New York, 1901; by Michael Sadleir, New York, 1927; most valuable of all, by Donald Smalley, New York, 1949, which prints for the first time selections from Mrs. Trollope's notebooks and rough draft; by James E. Mooney, Barre, Mass., 1969; and by Herbert Vanthal, London, 1974.

Mrs. Trollope was in America, 1827–1831. See also the account of her son, Thomas Adolphus Trollope, who accompanied his mother to America, in his *What I remember*, London, 1888, I, pp. 105–131; and the account by her daughter-in-law Frances Eleanor (Ternan) Trollope, *Frances Trollope, her life and literary works from George II to Victoria*, London, 1895, 2 vols. See also accounts in Una Pope-Hennesy, *Three English women in America*, London, 1929; and in various biographies, including: *The Trollopes: the chronicle of a writing family*, by Lucy Poate Stebbins and Richard Poate Stebbins, New York, 1947; Monique Parent Frazee, *Mrs. Trollope and America*, Caen, 1969; Marcus Conliff, "Frances Trollope," in *Abroad in America: visitors to the new nation, 1776–1914*, ed. by Marc Pachter, Reading, Mass., 1976, pp. 33–42; Johanna Johnston, *The life, manners, and travels of Fanny Trollope*, New York, 1978, esp. "American manners: 1827–1831," pp. 55–124; and Helen Heineman, *Mrs. Trollope: the triumphant feminine in the nineteenth century*, Athens, Ohio, 1979, esp. pp. 37–106, 143–149, 161–167. See also Peter Conrad, *Imagining America*, Oxford, 1980, pp. 30–38.

Of special interest are the author's novels based on her American experiences, such as *The refugee in America*, London, 1832, 3 vols.; *The life and adventures of Jonathan Jefferson Whitlaw, or scenes on the Mississippi*, London, 1836, 3 vols.; *The Barnabys in America;*

or adventures of the widow wedded, London, 1843, 3 vols.; and *The old world and the new*, London, 1849. See below the verse-satire, *The Trollopiad; or, Travelling gentlemen in America* [By Frederick William Shelton], New York, 1837. See also *The Americans. By an American in London* [pref. signed by Calvin Colton], London, 1833; and the extended attack in the introd. to the anonymous novel, *Bellegarde, the adopted Indian boy. A Canadian tale*, London, 1832, 3 vols.

Reviews: *Am. Monthly Rev.*, II, 158; *Am. Quar. Observer*, I, 270; *Am. Quar. Rev.*, XII, 109; *Blackwood's Edinb. Mag.*, XXXI, 829; *Cincinnati Mirror & Ladies' Parterre*, I, 188; *Edinb. Rev.* (by W. Empson), LV, 479; *Fraser's Mag.*, V, 336; *Illinois Monthly Mag.*, II, 505; *Knickerbocker*, II, 283; *Method. Quar. Rev.*, (by J.T. Crane), XXVIII (3rd ser., 6), 508; *Monthly Rev.*, CXXVII, 540; *New Eng. Mag.*, III, 144; *New Monthly Mag.*, XXXV, 446; *N.Y. Mirror*, X, 223; *Niles' Register*, VII (4th ser.), 67; *No. Am. Rev.* (by E. Everett), XXXVI, 1; *Penny Mag.*, I, 83; *Quar. Rev.*, XLVII, 39; *Tait's Edinb. Mag.*, I, 229. See also the collection of reviews in book form: *American criticisms on Mrs. Trollope's Domestic manners of the Americans*, London, 1833; and D. C. Johnson, "Trollopania," in *Scraps*, No. 4, for the year 1833, Boston, 1833.

29   VIGNE, GODFREY THOMAS. Six months in America. London, 1832. 2 vols.   **DLC Uk**

Reviews: *Edinb. Rev.* (by W. Empson), LV, 479; *Monthly Rev.*, CXXVIII, 117.

30   WORK, JOHN. The journal of John Work, a chief-trader of the Hudson bay co., during his expedition from Vancouver to the Flatheads and Blackfeet of the Pacific Northwest, edited, and with an account of the fur trade in the Northwest, and life of Work, by William S. Lewis and Paul C. Phillips. Cleveland, 1923. 209 p.   **DLC Uk**

Journal, Aug. 18, 1831–July 27, 1832. For later journals, see his entries for 1833 and 1835, below.

1833

31   ALEXANDER, *SIR* JAMES EDWARD. Transatlantic sketches, comprising visits to the most interesting scenes in North and South America, and the West Indies. With notes on Negro slavery and Canadian emigration. London, 1833. 2 vols.   **DLC Uk**

See also the poem based on Alexander's account of Francis Abbott, in James Bird, *Francis Abbott, the recluse of Niagara: and Metropolitan sketches; second series*, London, 1837, pp. 3–93.

32   [BOARDMAN, JAMES]. America and the Americans. By a citizen of the world. London, 1833. 430 p.   **DLC Uk**

Author's name sometimes given as "James Broadhead"; work has also been attributed to Charles Simpson, of Newcastle-on-Tyne.

Reviews: *Eclectic Rev.*, LVII, 233; *Monthly Rev.*, CXXX, 84.

33   BRITISH AND FOREIGN TEMPERANCE SOCIETY. A brief view of the operations and principles of temperance societies; with a sketch of their origin and progress in America. London, [1833]. 4 p.   **MB UkLU-C**

34   BRITISH OPINIONS of the American colonization society. Boston, 1833. 36 p.   **DLC**

Includes the following pamphlets: 1) *A letter to Thomas Clarkson by James Cropper; and Prejudice vincible, or the practicability of conquering prejudice by better means than by slavery and exile: in relation to the American colonization society*, by C[harles] Stuart (see Cropper, 1832, above). 2) *Facts designed to exhibit the real character and tendency of the American colonization society*, by "Clericus" [i.e. George Smith] (see Smith, 1833, below). 3) Extracts from the *Anti-Slavery Reporter*. 4) Extract from the Liverpool *Mercury*.

35   CAMPBELL, ROBERT. Two journals of Robert Campbell, Chief Factor, Hudson's Bay Company, 1808 to 1853; early journal, 1808 to 1851, later journal, Sept. 1850 to Feb. 1853. Seattle, 1958. 151 p.   **DLC**

Contains a "Journey to Kentucky for sheep," (1832–33), pp. 11–27; originally pub. separately in *Annals of Iowa* (3rd ser.), XV (Apr. 1926), 242–253. Campbell was commissioned by Sir George Simpson to secure sheep for the Red River colony.

36   COKE, EDWARD THOMAS. A subaltern's furlough: descriptive of scenes in various parts of the United States, Upper and Lower Canada, New Brunswick, and Nova Scotia, during the summer and autumn of 1832. London, 1833. 485 p.   **DLC Uk**

Various eds. appeared under slightly different titles; a New York ed., 1833, appeared in 2 vols., a 1 vol. Philadelphia ed. came out the same year. The illustrations (12 plates) were pub. separately in 1833, under title *Views in North America*, but no copy has been located.

Reviews: *Method. Quar. Rev.* (by J. T. Crane), XXVIII (VI, 3d ser.). 508; *Monthly Rev.*, (Aug. 1833), 466.

37   CONDER, JOSIAH. Wages or the whip. An essay on the comparative cost and productiveness of free and slave labour. London, 1833. 91 p.   **DLC Uk**

Contains many refs. to the U.S.

Review: *Monthly Rev.* (June 1833), 231.

38   CROPPER, JAMES. The extinction of the American Colonization Society the first step to the abolition of American slavery. London, 1833. 24 p.   **MnU NcD**

39   DAVIS, STEPHEN. Notes of a tour in America, in 1832 and 1833. Edinburgh, 1833. 150 p.   **DLC Uk**

A Baptist minister, author toured U.S. to raise funds for missionary work in Ireland; critical of slavery.

40   DEFENCE OF THE AMERICAN ECCLESIASTICAL STATISTICS, put forth by the Voluntary Church Magazine; in a letter to the Rev. J[ohn] G[eorge] Lorimer. Glasgow, 1833. 60 p.   **CtY**

41   DUHRING, HENRY. Remarks on the United States of America, with regard to the actual state of Europe. London, 1833. 209 p.   **DLC Uk**

42   [FAIRPLAY, FRANCIS]. The Canadas as they now are. Comprehending a view of their climate, rivers, lakes, canals, government, laws, taxes, towns, trade, &c. With a description of the soil and advantages or disadvantages of every township in each province: derived from the reports of the inspectors made to the justices at quarter-sessions, and from other authentic sources, assisted by local knowledge. With a map, showing the position of each township, a point of the utmost consequence to the settler; compiled without reference to

the particular interest of any land company or association. By a late resident. London, 1833. 116 p. **DLC Uk**

On U.S., pp. 1–18.

43   FIDLER, ISAAC. Observations on professions, literature, manners, and emigration, in the United States and Canada, made during a residence there in 1832. London, 1833. 434 p. **DLC Uk**

See Asa Green's parody, pub. anonymously: *Travels in America. By George Fibbleton, esq., ex-barber to His Majesty, the King of Great Britain*, New York, 1833.

Reviews: *Am. Monthly Rev.*, IV, 216; *Am. Quar. Observer*, I, 270; *Knickerbocker*, II, 283; *Monthly Rev.*, CXXXI, 317; *No. Am. Rev.* (by A. H. Everett), XXVII, 273.

44   FINCH, JOHN. Travels in the United States of America and Canada, containing some account of their scientific institutions, and a few notices of the geology and mineralogy of those countries. To which is added, an essay on the natural boundaries of empires. London, 1833. 455 p. **DLC Uk**

The essay, "The natural boundaries of empires," was pub. separately, London, 1844.

Review: *Monthly Rev.*, CXXXII, 72.

45   GOUGE, W[ILLIA]M. The curse of paper money and banking; or, A short history of banking in the United States of America, with an account of its ruinous effects on landowners, farmers, traders, and on all the industrious classes of the community . . . . Introduction by William Cobbett. London, 1833. 200 p. **DLC Uk**

Gouge was American. See Cobbett's introd., pp. v–xxii. See also Cobbett's earlier works: *Cobbett's address to the Americans*, London, 1817; and *A year's residence in the United States of America*, New York 1818–19.

46   [HAMILTON, *CAPT*. THOMAS]. Men and manners in America. By the author of "Cyril Thornton," etc. Edinburgh, 1833. 2 vols. **DLC Uk**

1843 ed. (Edinburgh & London) includes "a portrait of the author and letters written by him during his journey through the United States."

Reviews: *Am. Quar. Rev.*, XIV, 520; *Blackwood's Edinb. Mag.* (by Sidney Smith), XXXIV, 285, 548, XXXV, 342; *Chr. Examiner* (by S. A. Eliot), XV, 219; *Dublin Univ. Mag.*, II, 444, 558; *Fraser's Mag.*, IX, 42; *Knickerbocker*, II, 283; *Method. Quar. Rev.* (by J. T. Crane), XXVIII (VI, 3rd ser.), 508; *N.Y. Mirror*, XI, 73; *No. Am. Rev.*, XXXVIII, 210; *Select J. of Foreign Periodical Lit.* (by Andrews Norton), III, 81; *Spectator*, VI, 717; *Tait's Edinb. Mag.*, III, 679; *Westmin. Rev.* (by J. S. Mill), XXX, 365. The review in *No. Am. Rev.* was repr. in pamphlet form, London, 1834. DLC has a pamphlet containing a series of 6 numbered articles dated Philadelphia, Sept 15, 1833 to Oct. 2, 1833 and all signed M. C.; the caption title reads, "Review of 'Men and Manners in America, by Mr. Hamilton, author of Cyril Thornton,' &c. &c.," [Philadelphia? 1833?].

47   HODGKIN, THOMAS. An inquiry into the merits of the American Colonization Society: and a reply to the charges brought against it. With an account of the British African Colonization Society. London, 1833. 62 p. **DLC Uk**

48   HODGKIN, THOMAS. Liberia; or, the American colonization scheme. Glasgow, 1833.

No locations found.

49   HODGKIN, THOMAS. On Negro emancipation and American colonization. London, [1833?]   **MB Uk**

50   LORIMER, *REV*. JOHN GORDON. The past and present condition of religion and morality in the United States of America, an argument, not for voluntary, but for established churches. Part I. An exposure of the religious statistics of America put forth by the Voluntary Church Magazine. Glasgow, 1833. 19 p.   **CtY NN Uk**

    Pub. separately from Part II, below.

51   LORIMER, *REV.* JOHN GORDON. The past and present condition of religion and morality in the United States of America, an argument not for voluntary, but for established churches. Part II. Showing, on the testimony of Americans themselves, the deplorable destitution of the means of grace, the immense progress of error, and the extensive prevalence of other great moral and religious evils, which obtain in the United States. Glasgow, 1833. 110 p.   **CLU Uk**

52   [LORIMER, *REV*. JOHN GORDON]. A second defence of church establishments: being a second review of the speeches, delivered in Dr. Beattie's chapel, on Monday evening, the 12th of November, 1832, by leading men of the Voluntary church association; in which the argument against establishments drawn from the state of religion in the United States of America is fully considered, and ample information of the subject adduced. By a churchman, author of the former review of the speeches, etc. Glasgow, 1833. 71 p.   **NN Uk**

53   MACKENZIE, WILLIAM LYON. Sketches of Canada and the United States. London, 1833. 504 p.   **DLC Uk**

    See also Thomas Jefferson Sutherland: *A canvas of the proceedings on the trial of W. L. MacKenzie for an alleged violation of the neutrality laws of the United States, with a report of the testimony, etc.*, New York, 1840. Also see, "A contemporary account of the rebellion in upper Canada, 1837. By the late George Coventry, esq., with notes by the Hon. William Renwick Riddell," *Ontario Hist. Soc. Papers*, XVII (1919), 113–174. For a further account of MacKenzie's relations with America, see Charles Lindsey, *The Life and times of Wm. Lyon MacKenzie*, Toronto, 1862, passim.

    Review: *Monthly Rev.*, CXXXI, 411.

54   MISSIONARY RECORDS. North America. London [1833?]. 423 p.   **DLC**

    Pub. by The Religious Tract Society, London.

55   REFLECTIONS ON THE DOMESTIC and foreign policy of Great Britain since the war. By a British merchant long resident abroad. London, 1833. 236 p.   **DLC Uk**

    Includes an account of trade relations with the U.S.

56   [RODGER, ALEXANDER?] The emigrant's friend; a complete manual of plain practical directions, drawn up for the benefit of persons emigrating to North America. By Ellik Rosier [*pseud.*]. London, 1833. 81 p.

    Uk has earliest located ed., 3d., "improved and enlarged," Glasgow, 1834; many later eds.

57   [SMITH, GEORGE]. Facts designed to exhibit the real character and tendency of the American colonization society. By Clericus [*pseud.*] Liverpool, 1833. 19 p.   **DLC**

    Repr. in *British opinions of the American colonization society*, 1833, above.

58   SPEECHES DELIVERED at the anti-colonization meeting in Exeter hall, July 13, 1833, by James Cropper, esq., William Lloyd Garrison, Rev. Nathaniel Paul, Daniel O'Connell, esq., M.P., George Thompson, esq., etc., etc. Boston, 1833. 39 p.   **DAU MB OO**

O'Connell's speech repr. in his *Daniel O'Connell Upon American Slavery*, 1860, below.

59   STRICTURES ON DR. [THOMAS] HODGKIN'S pamphlet on Negro emancipation and American colonization. London, 1833. 8 p.   **DLC**

"From the Imperial Magazine, July, 1833".

60   STUART, CHARLES. The American colonization scheme further unravelled. Bath [1833?]. 30 p.   **MB NNUT**

61   STUART, CHARLES. Letter addressed to Elisha Bates, esq., minister of the Society of Friends, by Captain Stuart. [Bath? 1833?]. 3 p.   **MH**

Signed, C. Stuart, 17th December, 1833, Bathwick Hill, Bath.

62   STUART, CHARLES. Liberia, or the American colonization scheme examined and exposed. A report of a lecture at a meeting in Glasgow, 15th April, 1833. Glasgow, 1833. 24 p.   **MH**

63   STUART, JAMES. Three years in North America. Edinburgh, 1833. 2 vols.   **DLC Uk**

3rd ed. rev. Edinburgh, 1833, 2 vols. See *Letters by Major Norman Pringle, late of the 21st Royal Scots fusiliers, vindicating the character of the British army, employed in North America in the years 1814–15, from aspersions cast upon it in Stuart's "Three years in North America,"* Edinburgh, [1834?]; the first of these letters originally appeared in the Edinburgh *Evening Courant*, Oct. 31, 1833. See also Stuart's answer, *Refutation of aspersions on "Stuart's Three years in North America,"* London, 1834.

Reviews: *Eclectic Rev.*, IX, 233; *Edinb. Rev.*, (by J. R. McCulloch), LVI, 460; *Knickerbocker*, II, 283; *Monthly Rev.*, CXXX, 298 (mispaging in *Monthly Rev.*); *Penny Mag.*, II, 38; *Taits Edinb. Mag.*, II, 636, *Westmin. Rev.* (by T. P. Thompson), XVIII, 317.

64   TREMBLE, WILLIAM. The Liberian Crusade. Louth, 1833. 8 p.   **NN**

65   [WAKEFIELD, EDWARD GIBBON]. England and America. A comparison of the social and political state of both nations. London, 1833. 2 vols.   **DLC Uk**

An anonymous reviewer in the *Am. Quar. Rev.*, XV, 243, states this work is "a republication with additions and modifications" of the pamphlet: *A statement of the principles and objects of a proposed national society for the cure and prevention of pauperism, by means of systematic colonization*, London, 1830. But examination of both confirms this is an entirely new work. Repr. in *The collected works of Edward Gibbon Wakefield*, ed. with an introd. by M. F. Lloyd Prichard, Glasgow and London, 1968, pp. 311–636.

66   WORK, JOHN. Fur brigade to the Bonaventura; John Work's California expedition, 1832–1833, for the Hudson's bay company, edited by Alice Bay Maloney from the original manuscript journal in the provincial archives of British Columbia; with a foreword by Herbert Eugene Bolton, and a hitherto unpublished letter of John Work from the archives of the Hudson's bay company. San Francisco, 1945. 112 p.   **DLC**

Repr. from the *Calif. Hist. Soc. Quar.*, XXII (Sept. 1943), 193–222, (Dec. 1943), 323–348; XXIII (Mar. 1944), 19–40, (June 1944), 123–146.

67   BLOMFIELD, CHARLES JAMES, *Bishop of London*. The uses of a standing ministry, and an established church. Two sermons, preached at the consecration of churches. London, 1834. 63 p.   **NN Uk**

Appendix contains a reply to Calvin Colton's *Church and state in America, Part I* (London, 1834), which took issue with some of Blomfield's comments on the U.S.; for Colton's answer see *Church and state in America, Part II. Review of the Bishop of London's reply*, London, 1834. For an answer to Colton, see John Gordon Lorimer, *Church establishments defended. . . .*, 1835, below.

68   BRYDONE, JAMES MARR. Narrative of a voyage, with a party of emigrants, sent out from Sussex, in 1834, by the Petworth emigration committee, to Montreal, thence up the River Ottawa and through the Rideau Canal, to Toronto, Upper Canada, and afterwards to Hamilton; also of the journey from Hamilton to the Township of Blandford, where the families were settled: and of a journey through a large portion of the London and Gore districts, with a map, showing the route: a description of the state of the country generally, and the nature of the soil. To which is added a comparison of the route to Upper Canada by Quebec, with that by New York; and observations on the proper mode of fitting out emigrant ships. Petworth [Eng.], 1834. 66 p.   **DLC UkLRC**

Ed. by Thomas Sockett. Description of the U.S., pp. 48–66.

69   BUCHANAN, JAMES. Facts and observations in relation to the extension of state prisons in England: also bearing on poverty and crime. New York, 1834. 84 p.   **MH-BA Uk**

British consul at New York, Buchanan includes description of conditions in the U.S., based on 14 years' observations. Portions from these reports were also pub. in the appendix of the author's pamphlet: *Project for the formation of a depot in Upper Canada, with a view to receive the whole pauper population of England, etc.*, New York, 1834.

70   BURFORD, ROBERT. Description of a view of the city of New York, now exhibiting at the Panorama, Leicester square. Painted by the proprietor, Robert Burford, from drawings taken by him in the autumn of 1832. London, 1834. 12 p.   **DLC**

See also incidental comment in *Description of a view of the Falls of Niagara, now exhibiting at the Panorama, Leicester square. Painted by the proprietor, Robert Burford, from drawings taken by him in the autumn of 1832*, London, 1833, (also held by DLC).

71   CONDER, JOSIAH. A dictionary of geography, ancient and modern: comprising a succinct description of all the countries of the globe, their physical and political geography, the several races of their inhabitants, and their ancient as well as modern denominations, together with a brief notice of all the capitals and principal towns; also of seas, rivers, and mountains; and a glossary of geographical terms. London, 1834. 724 p.   **DLC Uk**

Includes data on U.S., pp. 15–18, 687–691, with no comment. For earlier account, see author's *The United States of America and Canada*, London, 1830.

72   CRAWFORD, WILLIAM. Penitentiaries (United States). Report of William Crawford, esq., on the penitentiaries of the United States, addressed to His Majesty's principal secretary of state for the Home department. Ordered, by the House of Commons, to be printed, 11 August, 1834. [London, 1834]. 229 p.   **DLC Uk**

73   THE EMIGRANT'S INFORMANT; or, A guide to upper Canada, containing reasons for emigration, who should emigrate, necessaries for outfit, and charges of voyage, travelling expences, manners of the Americans; qualities, and capabilities, of the soil, price current of the country for 1833, rates of wages, and an estimate of the amount necessary for the purchase of 80 acres of land, building on, and stocking the same; interspersed with reflections on the happiness of a cottage life. By a Canadian settler, late of Portsea, Hants. London, 1834. 237 p.   **NN**

74   FOUR MONTHS IN AMERICA. By a young Englishman. Olney, [1834]. 87 p.   **DLC**

75   HEYWOOD, ROBERT. A journey to America in 1834. [Cambridge, Eng.], 1919. 112 p.   **DLC Uk**

    100 copies priv. pr.; ed. by Mrs. Mary (Heywood) Haslam. Travelled between Boston and Baltimore, west to Louisville.

76   [HODGKIN, THOMAS]. On the British African colonization society. To which are added, some particulars respecting the American colonization society; and a letter from Jeremiah Hubbard, addressed to a friend in England, on the same subject. [London], 1834. 32 p.   **DLC Uk**

77   HOWE, JOSEPH. An address delivered before the Halifax mechanics' institute, on the 5th November, 1834. Published by request of the Institute. Halifax, 1834. 23 p.   **MH**

    Includes an appeal to patrolmen of Nova Scotia against enticements of the U.S.

78   MATHER, JAMES. The constitutions of Great Britain, France, and the United States of America. Consisting of Magna Charta, Bill of Rights, and coronation oath; French Declaration of Rights, Charter of Louis XVIII, and Constitution of 1830; American Declaration of Independence, Constitution of the United States, Constitutions of Pennsylvania, Maryland, etc., from the most authentic sources. London, 1834. 76 p.   **DLC Uk**

    A brief pref. followed by the documents themselves.

79   [MATHISON, JOHN, *ed. and pub.*]. Counsel for emigrants, and interesting information from numerous sources; with original letters from Canada and the United States. Aberdeen, 1834. 140 p.   **DLC Uk**

    DLC and Uk catalog under title. 2d "enlarged" ed., Aberdeen, 1835, contains a bibliography of books on the U.S.

    Review: *Monthly Rev.*, (May 1835), 145.

80   [MATHISON, JOHN, *ed. and pub.*]. Sequel to the counsel for emigrants, containing interesting information from numerous sources; with original letters from Canada and the United States. Aberdeen, 1834. 72 p.   **ICU Uk**

    Review: *Monthly Rev.*, (May 1835), 145.

81   MORISON, JOHN. The day-star of the world's freedom; or, the British lion trampling on the neck of slavery: an Ebenezer for the first day of August, 1834. Third edition. London, 1834. 96 p.   **Uk**

    No locations found for 1st ed.

82   NUTTALL, THOMAS. A manual of the ornithology of the United States and of Canada. Boston, 1832–34. 2 pts. 627 p.   **DLC Uk**

Part I: The land birds; Part II: The water birds. A later ed. carried the title, *A popular hand-book of the ornithology of the United States and Canada, based on Nuttall's manual*, by Montague Chamberlain, Boston, 1891. Nuttall was in America from 1808–1841 with two return visits to England. See also his "Remarks and inquiries concerning the birds of Massachusetts," *Memoirs Am. Acad. of Arts & Sciences.*, I, n.s. (1833), 91–106; "Descriptions of new species and genera of plants in the natural order of the Compositae, collected in a tour across the continent to the Pacific, a residence in Oregon, and a visit to the Sandwich islands and Upper California, during the years 1834 and 1835 . . . Read Oct. 2, 1840," *Trans. Am. Phil. Soc.*, VII, n.s. (1841), 283–453; "Description and notices of new or rare plants in the natural orders Lobeliacese, Campanulacese, Vacciniese, Ericacese, col-lected in a journey over the continent of North America, and during a visit to the Sandwich islands, and Upper California . . . Read December 3, 1841," ibid., VIII, n.s. (1843), 251–272; "On Simmondsia, a new genus of plants from California," *London J. Botany*, III (1844), 400–401; "Description of plants collected by William Gambel, M.D., in the Rocky mountains and Upper California," *J. Acad. Nat. Sciences* (Philadelphia), I, n.s. (Aug. 1848), 149–189; "A catalogue of a collection of plants made chiefly in the valleys of the Rocky mountains or northern Andes, towards the sources of the Columbia river, by Nathaniel B. [sic] Wyeth, and described by Thomas Nuttall," ibid., VII (1834), 1–60.

See also the following comments on Nuttall: John Kirk Townsend, *Narrative of a journey across the Rocky mountains, to the Columbia river, and a visit to the Sandwich islands, Chili, &c.; with a scientific appendix*, Philadelphia, 1839; Frederick Vernon Coville, "The botanical explorations of Thomas Nuttall in California," *Proc. Biol. Soc.* (Washington), XIII (1899), 109–121; Willis Linn Jepson, "The overland journey of Thomas Nuttall," *Madrono*, II (1934), 143–147; two items by Francis W. Pennell: "Travels and scientific col-lections of Thomas Nuttall," *Bartonia* (Philadelphia), No. 18 (1936), 1–64, and "An English obituary account of Thomas Nuttall," ibid., No. 19, 50–53; and Susan Delane McKelvey's *Botanical exploration of the Trans-Mississippi west, 1790–1850*, Jamaica Plain, Mass., 1955, pp. 586–626. See also Jeannette E. Graustein, *Thomas Nuttall, natu-ralist; explorations in America, 1808–1841*, Cambridge, Mass., 1967.

83   O'KELLY, PATRICK B. Advice and guide to emigrants, going to the United States of America. Dublin, 1834. 96 p.   **DLC**

84   SHORT, RICH. Travels in the United States of America, through the states of New York, Pennsylvania, Ohio, Michigan Territory, Kentucky, Virginia, Maryland, Columbia, North Carolina, Rhode-Island and Massachusetts; with advice to emigrants. London [1834?].

       DLC has 2d ed., London [183–?], 24 p. Travels cover 1831–1833.

85   [SIMPSON, JAMES]. On the American scheme of establishing colonies of free Negro emigrants on the coast of Africa, as exemplified in Liberia. [Edinburgh? 1834]. 16 p.
                                                                                        DLC

       Caption title is preceded by: "From The Phrenological Journal, No. XXXV". (Edinburgh). Article originally appeared under title, "Liberian Controversy," in the *Phrenological J.*, VIII, (Dec. 1832–June 1834), 145–160.

86   THOMPSON, GEORGE. An address, &c. upon the subject of an anti-slavery mission to the United States of America: delivered before the ladies of Edinburgh and its vicinity, assembled in Rose street chapel, Edinburgh, Monday, 11th Nov. 1833. Edinburgh, 1834. 22 p.   **PU**

87   [THORBURN, GRANT]. Men and manners in Britain; or, A bone to gnaw for the Trollopes, Fidlers, &c. being notes from a journal, on sea and on land in 1833–4. New York, 1834. 187 p.   **DLC Uk**

Glasgow ed., 1835, has a pref. by "A Scots gentleman in New York", possibly John Galt, denouncing Thorburn's pro-American answer to British critics. Thorburn was the Scottish seedsman made famous as "Lawrie Todd" by John Galt. Other works on the U.S. by Thorburn are not listed here because he emigrated in 1794; however, such works as his *Forty years' residence in America*, London, 1833, maintain the perspective of a Scotsman. See also the *Life and writings of Grant Thorburn: prepared by himself*, New York, 1852; and Charles E. Shain, "John Galt's America," *Am. Quar.*, VIII (Fall 1956), 254–263.

Reviews: *London Rev.*, II, 365; *Westmin. Rev.* (by J. S. Mill), XXX, 365.

88   TUDOR, HENRY. Narrative of a tour in North America; comprising Mexico, the mines of Real del Monte, the United States, and the British colonies: with an excursion to the Island of Cuba. In a series of letters, written in the years 1831–32. London, 1834. 2 vols.   **DLC Uk**

89   WILMOT-HORTON, *SIR* ROBERT JOHN. A letter addressed to the anonymous author of "England and America." Colombo, Ceylon, 1834.

No locations found; Sabin (#33076) describes as priv. pr. and "very scarce."

90   YOUNG, GEORGE RENNY. The British North American colonies. Letters to the Right Hon. E.G.S. Stanley, M.P., upon the existing treaties with France and America, as regards their "rights of fishery" upon the coasts of Nova Scotia, Labrador and Newfoundland; the violations of these treaties by the subjects of both powers, and their effect upon the commerce, equally of the mother country and the colonies; with a general view of the colonial policy, showing that the British dependencies are now prepared to pay the expenses of their local governments; that the military expenditure, if chargeable to them, is fully counter-balanced by the commercial advantages derived from them; and that their preservation, as integral parts of the empire, is essential to the commercial prosperity and political supremacy of the British nation. London, 1834. 193 p.   **DLC Uk**

1835

91   ABDY, EDWARD STRUTT. Journal of a residence and tour in the United States of North America, from April, 1833, to October, 1834. London, 1835. 3 vols.   **DLC Uk**

Reviews: *Athenaeum* (Aug. 25, 1835), 638; *Monthly Rev.*, CXXXVII, 326; *Quar. Rev.*, LIV, 392; *Tait's Edinb. Mag.*, II, n.s., 715; *Westmin. Rev.*, XXIV, 224, and (by J. S. Mill), XXX, 365.

92   [AMES, FISHER]. The influences of democracy on liberty, property, and the happiness of society, considered. By an American, formerly member of Congress. To which is prefixed, an introduction by Henry Ewbank, esq. London, 1835. 199 p.   **DLC Uk**

Ames was an American, but Ewbank's introd. is a 24 p. denunciation of U.S. democracy.

93   BAINES, *SIR* EDWARD, *jun*. History of the cotton manufacture in Great Britain; with a notice of its early history in the East, and in all quarters of the globe; a description of the great mechanical inventions, which have caused its unexampled extension in Britain; and a view of the present state of the manufacture, and the condition of the classes engaged in its several departments. London, [1835]. 544 p.   **DLC Uk**

Includes history of cotton culture in the U.S. and a comparison of manufacturing conditions in England and the U.S., passim. The 2d ed., London, 1966, includes a bibliographical introd. by W. H. Chaloner.

94   [BRABAZON, WALTER]. Autobiography of an Irish traveller. London, 1835. 3 vols.   **PPL**

In the U.S. in the 1820's and 1830's: I, pp. 90–285; III, pp. 21–39.

95   [COBDEN, RICHARD]. England, Ireland, and America. By a Manchester manufacturer. London, 1835. 160 p.   **DLC Uk**

Repr. in his *Political writings*, London, 1867, I, pp. 5–153. See also the accounts of visits to the U.S. in 1835 and 1859 in his *American diaries*, 1859, below.

96   COLERIDGE, SAMUEL TAYLOR. Specimens of the table talk of the late Samuel Taylor Coleridge. London, 1835. 2 vols.   **DLC Uk**

DLC also has New York ed., 2 vols. in 1, 1835. Ed. by H. N. Coleridge. See esp. entries for May 28, 1830, Aug. 14, 1831, Jan. 4, 1833, Apr. 10, 1833.

Review: *Monthly Rev.*, (June 1835), 250.

97   COOKE, *SIR* JOHN HENRY. A narrative of events in the south of France, and of the attack on New Orleans, in 1814 and 1815. By Captain John Henry Cooke, (late of the 43d regiment of light infantry). London, 1835. 319 p.   **DLC Uk**

On U.S., pp. 124–308.

98   [COOKE, W. B.]. Colonial policy, with hints upon the formation of military settlements. To which are added observations on the boundary question now pending between this country and the United States. London, 1835. 49 p.   **CaOOA Uk**

DLC has 2d ed., London, 1835. Pref. signed W. B. C.

99   DEMOCRACY. Its influence on liberty, property, and social happiness. London, 1835.   **NN**

100   FEATHERSTONHAUGH, GEORGE WILLIAM. Geological report of an examination made in 1834 of the elevated country between the Missouri and Red rivers. Washington, D.C., 1835. 97 p.   **DLC Uk**

101   GLASGOW EMANCIPATION SOCIETY. First (—second) annual report of the G-E-S; with an appendix, etc. 2 pt. Glasgow, 1835, [36 p.]   **Uk**

Each part has a distinct title page and pagination.

102   GRIFFITHS, D., *jun*. Two years' residence in the new settlements of Ohio, North America: with directions to emigrants. London, 1835. 197 p.   **DLC Uk**

103   JOURNAL OF AN EXCURSION to the United States and Canada in the year 1834: with hints to emigrants; and a fair and impartial exposition of the advantages and disadvantages attending emigration. By a citizen of Edinburgh. Edinburgh, 1835. 168 p.   **DLC Uk**

Uk catalog lists under U.S. Variously ascribed to John Reid, James Inches, and Richard Weston; probably by Reid. Relates chiefly to New York State.

104   KEMBLE, FRANCIS ANNE (BUTLER). Journal of F. A. Butler. London, 1835. 2 vols.
DLC Uk

Brussels ed., 1835, carried title: *Journal of a residence in America*. The journal describes a theatrical tour of the Atlantic states, Aug. 1, 1832–July 17, 1833. For accounts of later visits to and residence in the U.S., see below, *Journal of a residence on a Georgian plantation, 1838–1839*, 1863. See also the following American retorts and parodies: *My conscience: Fanny Thimble Cutler's journal of a residence in America whilst performing a profitable theatrical engagement: beating the nonsensical Fanny Kemble journal all hollow*, Philadelphia, 1835; and *Outlines illustrative of the Journal of F***** A*** K***** drawn and collected by Mr._____* , Boston, 1835; also [Lucy Kenney], *Description of a visit to Washington, treating of the public, patriotic feelings which pervade the citizens in the public buildings . . . with a stricture on Miss Kemble's journal . . . concluded with a general view of the present course of the administration . . . .*, [n.p., 1835]. See also, Clifford Ashby, "Fanny Kemble's 'vulgar' journal," *Penn. Mag. of Hist. & Biog.*, XCXVIII (1974), 58–66.

Reviews: *Athenaeum* (1835), 404; *Edinb. Rev.*, LXI, 379; *Niles' Register*, XLVIII, 379; *No. Am. Rev.*, XLI, 109; *Quar. Rev.*, LIV, 39: *So. Lit. Mess.*, (by E. A. Poe), I, 524, (by S. W.), III, 433; *Westmin. Rev.*, XXX, 194. See also: *Fanny Kemble in America: or, The journal of an actress reviewed. With remarks on the state of society in America and England. By an English lady, four years resident in the United States*, Boston, 1835

105   LATROBE, CHARLES JOSEPH. The rambler in North America: MDCCCXXXII–MDCCCXXXIII. London, 1835. 2 vols.   **DLC Uk**

Extracts appeared under title, "A River Trip in 1833," in *Palimpsest*, II (1921), 24–263. Sections on Oklahoma ed. and annotated by Muriel H. Wright and George H. Shirk, under title *The rambler in Oklahoma: Latrobe's tour with Washington Irving*, Oklahoma City, 1955.

Reviews: *Athenaeum* (Aug. 22, 1835), 638; *Quar. Rev.*, LIV, 392; *So. Lit. Mess.* (by E. A. Poe), II, 121; *Westmin. Rev.* (by J. S. Mill), XXX, 365.

106   LETTER FROM A TRADESMAN, recently arived from America, to his brethren in trade. London, 1835. 23 p.   **DLC**

107   LETTER TO A MEMBER OF THE CONGRESS of the United States of America, from an English clergyman; including a republication, with considerable additions, of the tract entitled, "Every man his own property." London, 1835. 30 p.   **DLC Uk**

108   LORIMER, *REV.* JOHN GORDON. Church establishments defended; or, "Church and State in America" [by Calvin Colton], exposed and answered. London, 1835. 62 p.
DLC Uk

Repr. of eight papers originally pub. in the *Church of Scotland Mag.*, nos. 3–6, 9, 11, 14, 16. Colton was an American whose *Church and State in America* was an answer to Blomfield, see 1834, above.

109   M., W. T. Reminiscences of a trans-Atlantic traveller. Being a sketch of fourteen months' residence in North America, in the years 1831–32. Interspersed with statistical and topographical observations. Dublin, 1835. 188 p.   **CSmH**

Review: *Dublin Penny J.*, III, 402.

110 [MONDELET, DOMINIQUE]. Report of the commissioners appointed under the lower Canada act., 4th William IV. Cap. 10, to visit the United States penitentiaries. Hon. D. Mondelet and J. Neilson, esquires, commissioners. Quebec, 1835. 75 p.   **CaOOA**

111 MURRAY, JOHN, *of Montreal*. The emigrant and traveller's guide to and through Canada, by way of the river St. Lawrence, as well as by way of the United States of America. London, 1835. 63 p.   **DLC Uk**

112 THE NEW ROAD TO RUIN, or, Intended railroad from Boston, Portland, and Portsmouth, three principal naval arsenals of the United States to Quebec, the principal British garrison of North America. Quebec, 1835. 11 p.   **CaOTU**

In verse.

113 REED, ANDREW, *the elder*. A narrative of the visit to the American churches, by the deputation from the Congregational union of England & Wales. By Andrew Reed and James Matheson. London, 1835. 2 vols.   **DLC Uk**

See also Reed's poem, *Washington*, pub. as a broadside in 1836. An account of Reed's U.S. visit is given in: *Memoirs of the life and philanthropic labours of Andrew Reed, D.D., with selections from his journals*. Ed. by his sons, Andrew Reed . . . and Charles Reed, London, 1863.

Reviews: *Eclectic Rev.*, LXI, 421; *Fraser's Mag.*, XII, 464, 575; *Monthly Rev.*, CXXXVII, 277; *No. Am. Rev.*, XLI, 489; *Quar. Rev.*, LIV, 392.

114 SENIOR, NASSAU WILLIAM. Statement of the provision for the poor, and of the condition of the labouring classes, in a considerable portion of America and Europe. Being the preface to the foreign communications contained in the appendix to the poor-law report. London, 1835. 238 p.   **DLC Uk**

The first 20 p. discuss conditions in the U.S. as reported by various British consuls.

115 SHIRREFF, PATRICK. A tour through North America; together with a comprehensive view of the Canadas and United States. As adapted for agricultural emigration. By Patrick Shirreff, farmer. Edinburgh, 1835. 473 p.   **DLC Uk**

Reviews: *Westmin. Rev.*, XXIII, 319; *Monthly Rev.*, (March 1835), 351.

116 A SHORT AND INTERESTING account of America. By English settlers. Chester [Eng.], 1835. 56 p.   **DLC**

Letters, etc. from Mrs. _____, Philipsburg, Pennsylvania, 1823–32.

117 [TODD, HENRY COOK]. Notes upon Canada and the United States of America: in the year MDCCCXXXV. By a traveler. Toronto, 1835. 95 p.   **DLC**

Uk has a much-enlarged 2d ed. under title: *Notes upon Canada and the United States. From 1832 to 1840. Much in a small space, or a great deal in a little book. By a traveller*, Toronto, 1840, 184 p.

118 T[OWERS], I[SABELLA] J[ANE]. Perils in the woods, or, The emigrant family's return; a tale. By the author of 'the children's fire-side'; 'the wanderings of Tom starboard'; 'the wanderer's care'; and other tales. With engravings. London [1835]. 344 p.   **Uk**

Although a work of juvenile fiction, it is based on factual accounts of emigration to the U.S. The final 40 p. comprise an appendix entitled "Scrapbook."

119   TRELAWNY, EDWARD JOHN. Letters of Edward John Trelawny, edited . . . by H. Buxton Forman, C.B. London, 1910. 306 p.   **DLC Uk**

In the U.S., 1833–1835; see pp. 178–191. See also Margaret Neilson Armstrong's *Trelawny, a man's life*, New York, 1940, pp. 337–344.

120   WORK, JOHN. The journal of John Work, January to October, 1835. With an introduction and notes by Henry Drummond Dee. Victoria, B.C., 1945. 98 p.   **DLC**

Archives of British Columbia: memoir no. 10; appeared earlier in *Brit. Col. Hist. Quar.*, VIII, (Apr.–July 1944), 127–146; 227–244, under title, "The journal of John Work, 1835; being an account of his voyage northward from the Columbia river to Fort Simpson and return in the brig *Lama*, January–October, 1835." For earlier journal, see entry for 1832, above; also, Leslie M. Scott, ed., "John Work's journey from Fort Vancouver to Umpqua river, and return, in 1834," *Oregon Hist. Quar.*, XXIV (Sept. 1923), 238–268. See also account in Henry Drummond Dee, "An Irishman in the fur trade; the life and journals of John Work," *Brit. Col. Hist. Quar.*, VII (Oct. 1943), 229, 270.

1836

121   [BAYLEY, DIANA]. Henry; or, the juvenile traveller. A faithful delineation of a voyage across the Atlantic, in a New York packet; a description of a part of the United States—manners and customs of the people; a journey to Canada; with an account of the colonies—emigration—sketches of society—expenses of travelling—scenery, etc. etc. By the wife of a British officer, resident in Canada. London, 1836. 136 p.   **CSmH NN PSC**

Semi-fictionized account, but "the details recorded may be depended upon as fact" (p. 135).

122   BLACHFORD, MICHAEL. Sailing directions for the coast and harbours of North America, comprehending the entire navigation from Nova Scotia to the Gulf of Florida; to which is added, a table of the latitudes, time of high water on the full and change of the moon, and setting of the tide. Carefully compiled from the approved surveys of Messrs. Des Barres, Holland, Lockwood, De Mayne, Monteath, &c. and much improved by the introduction of many original documents, by M. Blachford. London, 1836. 75 p.   **MB MH MHi**

123   BUCHANAN, JAMES. Reasons submitted in favour of allowing a transit of merchandize through Canada to Michigan, without payment of duties: with observations as to the importance of the River St. Lawrence for extending the trade of the Canadas and British commerce generally. Toronto, 1836. 16 p.   **CaOTP Uk**

A rev. version later appeared as *A letter to the right honorable the Earl of Durham, K.G.B. Lord high commissioner and governor in chief of Her Majesty's North American possessions, &c. &c. &c. calling his lordship's attention to the advantages to be derived by allowing a free transit of merchandize through Canada to the state of Michigan and Wisconsin territory; as a means of preserving our friendly relations with the United States. With observations as to the River St. Lawrence, for extending the commerce of the empire and enriching the Canadas, by James Buchanan, esq., Her Majesty's consul for the state of New York,* [n.p.], 1838.

124   [BURLEIGH, CHARLES CALISTUS]. Reception of George Thompson in Great Britain. Boston, 1836. 238 p.   **DLC Uk**

An American compilation from various British publications of speeches of George Thompson on slavery in the U.S., together with responses, etc.

125   CASWALL, HENRY. An epitome of the history of the American Episcopal church. Lexington, 1836. 24 p.   **NN Tx Uk**

126   COX, FRANCIS AUGUSTUS, *the elder*. Suggestions designed to promote the revival and extension of religion, founded on observations made during a journey in the United States of America, in the spring and summer of 1835. London, 1836. 24 p.   **Uk**

127   COX, FRANCIS AUGUSTUS, *the elder* and JAMES HOBY. The Baptists in America; a narrative of the deputation from the Baptist Union in England, to the United States and Canada. By the Rev. F. A. Cox . . . and the Rev. J[ames] Hoby . . . New York, 1836. 476 p.   **DLC Uk**

2d ed., rev. and enlarged., London, 1836; 3d ed., "carefully revised," appeared under the title: *Religion in America; a narrative of the deputation from the Baptist Union in England, to the United States and Canada*, London, 1837.

Reviews: *Chr. Rev.*, I, 455; *Method. New Connexion Mag.* (Aug. 1836), 313.

128   D'ARUSMONT, FRANCES WRIGHT. Course of popular lectures, historical and political, as delivered . . . in various cities, towns, and counties of the United States: being introductory to a course on the nature and object of America's political institutions. Philadelphia, 1836. Vol. II. 90 p.   **NHi NN**

Contains 3 lectures on U.S. affairs; Vol. I was pub. in 1829. Famous for her *Views of society and manners in America*, London, 1821, Mrs. D'Arusmont was a contributor to the *Free Enquirer*, the New Harmony *Gazette*, the Boston *Investigator*, and the editor in Philadelphia of a little paper, *Manual of American Principles*, which produced 7 issues in 1837 (CtY has 2 nos.). Author also pub. under Frances Wright. See her address on Tom Paine in Cincinnati, Ohio, Feb. 29, 1838, printed in *The Beacon*, Mar. 17, 1838; and *Tracts on republican government and national education*, London, 1840, by Robert Dale Owen and Frances Wright. For comment on her life to 1828, see *Biography, notes and political letters of Frances Wright D'Arusmont* (From the Dundee *Northern Star*, 1844), Boston, 1848, 48 p. For the period 1835 until her death in 1852, see Alice J. G. Perkins and Theresa Wolfson, *Frances Wright: free enquirer. The study of a temperament*, New York, 1939, pp. 327–384; Wm. Randall Waterman, *Frances Wright*, New York, 1924, pp. 240–256; and accounts in Mrs. Trollope's *Domestic Manners*, 1832, above, of her visit to Nashoba and her lectures in Cincinnati. Also see Margaret Lane, *Frances Wright and the "great experiment,"* Manchester, N.H., 1972.

129   THE DOMESTIC MANNERS OF THE AMERICANS; or, Characteristic sketches of the people of the United States, by recent travellers. Glasgow, 1836. 60 p.   **MH PHC Uk**

DLC has [Glasgow, 1839] ed., issued as part of a general compilation entitled: *Five hundred curious and interesting narratives and anecdotes. Comprising the wonderful book, the anecdote book, sailors' yarns, Salmagundi, and the domestic manners of the Americans*, ed. by John Gibson Lockhart. This popular compilation of excerpts from the travel books of Hall, Trollope, Hamilton, et al. went into a number of editions and reprints during the next two decades.

130   [EDINBURGH EMANCIPATION SOCIETY]. A voice to the United States of America, from the metropolis of Scotland; being an account of various meetings held in Edinburgh on the subject of American slavery, upon the return of Mr. George Thompson, from his mission to that country . . . Edinburgh, 1836. 51 p.   **DLC Uk**

131   EDWARD, DAVID B[ARNETT]. The history of Texas; or, The emigrant's, farmer's, and politician's guide to the character, climate, soil and productions of that country: geographically arranged from personal observation and experience. Cincinnati, 1836. 336 p.   **DLC**

Written by a Scottish schoolmaster residing three years in Texas, this was a basis for many subsequent accounts in the 1830s and 1840s.

132   EYRE, JOHN. The beauties of America. Buffalo, 1836. 72 p.   **NBLiHi**

Completely separate from his *Christian Spectator* (1838, below), erroneously described by Howes as a reprint of this work.

133   FEATHERSTONHAUGH, GEORGE WILLIAM. Report of a geological reconnaissance made in 1835, from the seat of government, by way of Green bay and the Wisconsin territory to the Coteau de Prairie, an elevated ridge dividing the Missouri from the St. Peter's river. Washington, 1836. 168 p.   **DLC Uk**

134   GLASGOW EMANCIPATION SOCIETY. Address by the committee of the Glasgow emancipation society, to the ministers of religion in particular, and the friends of Negro emancipation in general, on American slavery. Glasgow, 1836. 8 p.   **NIC Uk**

135   HILL, BENSON EARLE. Recollections of an artillery officer: including scenes and adventures in Ireland, America, Flanders, and France. London, 1836. 2 vols.   **DLC Uk**

On adventures during War of 1812, I, pp. 298–342, II, pp. 1–95.

Review: *Monthly Rev.* (Sept. 1836), 45.

136   HODING, SARAH. The land log-book; a compilation of anecdotes and occurrences extracted from the journal kept by the author, during a residence of several years in the United States of America. Containing useful hints to those who intended to emigrate to that country. London, 1836. 278 p.   **DLC Uk**

137   [HOOKER, *SIR* WILLIAM JACKSON]. Companion to the Botanical magazine; being a journal, containing such interesting botanical information as does not come within the prescribed limits of the magazine; with occasional figures. London, 1835–36. 2 vols.   **DLC Uk**

Uk indexes under Periodical Publications—London. See II, pp. 79–182, for the first printing of Hooker's "A brief memoir of the life of Mr. David Douglas." Also includes letter from California, dated Nov. 20, 1831; repr. as "A David Douglas letter," *Calif. Hist. Soc. Quar.* (Oct. 1923), 223–227. Douglas spent 20 months in California, 1829–32. For another account of Douglas's visit to California, see Susan Delano McKelvey, *Botanical exploration of the Trans-Mississippi West*, Jamaica Plains, Mass., 1955, pp. 393–427.

138   MCINTOSH, JOHN. The discovery of America by Christopher Columbus; and the origin of the North American Indians. By J. Mackintosh [sic.] Toronto, 1836. 152 p.   **DLC**

Uk has enlarged ed., *The Origin of the North American Indians; with a faithful description of their manners and customs, both civil and military, their religions, language, dress, and ornaments, etc.*, New York, 1843.

139   [MILL, JOHN STUART]. A review of M. de Tocqueville's work on Democracy in America. Extracted from the London Review, No. III., published, October, 1835. New York, 1836. 46 p.   **DLC**

In *Foster's Cabinet Miscellany,* New York, 1836, vol. IV. Pref. by Theodore Foster, American publisher. See *Correspondence & conversations of Alexis de Tocqueville with Nassau William Senior from 1834 to 1859,* edited by M. C. M. Simpson, London, 1872, 2 vols.; esp. see letters, I, pp. 2–11. For Mill's complete review of *Democracy in America,* Part I, see his "De Tocqueville on Democracy in America", *London Rev.,* (Oct. 1935), 85–129; repr. in *Collected works of John Stuart Mill.* ed. by J. M. Robson, et al., Toronto, 1963– , vol. XVIII, pp. 49–90. Other British reviews of Part I: *Blackwood's Edinb. Mag.* XXXVII, 758; *Monthly Rev.* (Nov. 1835); *London Quar. Rev.* (by John Gibson Lockhart), (Sept. 7, 1836), 132–162. Mill's review of Part II of *Democracy in America* appeared in *Edinb. Rev.,* LXXII (Oct. 1840), 1–47, repr. with revisions in Mill's *Dissertations and discussions: political, philosophical and historical,* 2d ed., London, 1859–1875, vol. II, pp. 1–83, and in his *Collected works,* vol. XVIII, pp. 153–204. Other British reviews of Part II: see *Blackwood's Edinb. Mag.* XLVIII, 463; *Tait's Edinb. Mag.,* VII, 506. See also James Bryce, *The predictions of Hamilton and De Tocqueville,* 1887, below.

140   NEWCASTLE UPON TYNE SOCIETY for Abolishing Slavery All over the World. Declaration of the objects. Newcastle, 1836. 12 p.   **Vi**

141   O'BRYAN, WILLIAM. A narrative of travels in the United States of America, with some account of American manners and polity, and advice to emigrants and travellers going to that interesting country. London, 1836. 419 p.   **DLC**

142   POWER, TYRONE. Impressions of America, during the years 1833, 1834, and 1835. London, 1836. 2 vols.   **DLC Uk**

According to Sabin, the 1st American ed., Philadelphia, 1836, was corrected and prepared for the press by the author. Excerpts appeared in *The Scenery of the Catskill Mountains as described by Irving, Cooper, Bryant, Willis Gaylord Clark, N.P. Willis, Miss Martineau, Tyrone Power, Parks Benjamin, Thomas Cole, Bayard Taylor, and other eminent writers,* New York (184–?), a work which went into many eds. See also the serial biography of Power in the *Dublin Univ. Mag.,* XL (1852): see esp. the account of Power's trips to America, signed by J. W. C., (Nov. 1852), 572–581, (Dec. 1852), 722–723, 727–729. Power's full name was William Grattan Tyrone Power.

Review: *Monthly Rev.,* CXXXIX, 297.

143   ROBERTS, THOMAS. The cruel nature and injurious effects of the foreign slave trade, represented in a letter addressed to the Right Hon. Lord Brougham and Vaux. Bristol, 1836. 40 p.   **ICN NN Uk**

Mainly concerned with conditions in the U.S. See also Robert Baird's: *A letter to Lord Brougham on the subject of American slavery. By an American,* London, 1835. 44 p.

144   ROEBUCK, JOHN ARTHUR, *ed.* Pamphlets for the people. London, 1835–36. 2 vols.   **DLC Uk**

Pamphlets, paged separately, include: "The American ballot-box," and "The fallacies of the House of Commons on the ballot in America," by H. S. Chapman; "Democracy in America," and "The English in America," by J. A. Roebuck; other comment on the U.S. in various pamphlets, passim.

145 ROLPH, THOMAS. A brief account, together with observations, made during a visit in the West Indies, and a tour through the United States of America, in parts of the years 1832–3; together with a statistical account of Upper Canada. Dundas, U.C., 1836. 272 p. **DLC Uk**

Chaps. 7–9 on the U.S., pp. 69–101. 2d ed., London, 1841, carried the title: *A descriptive and statistical account of Canada: showing its great adaptation for British emigration. Preceded by an account of a tour through portions of the West Indies and the United States.*

146 THOMPSON, GEORGE. Lectures of George Thompson, with a full report of the discussion between Mr. Thompson and Mr. [Peter] Borthwick, the pro-slavery agent, held at the Royal amphitheatre, Liverpool, (Eng.), and which continued for six evenings with unabated interest: compiled from various English editions.—Also, a brief history of his connection with the anti-slavery cause in England, by Wm. Lloyd Garrison. Boston, 1836. 190 p. **DLC Uk**

Mostly on slavery in the West Indies, but much on conditions in the U.S. See esp., "Mr. Thompson's speech, delivered at the great anti-colonization meeting, in Exeter hall, London, July 1833. James Cropper, esq. in the chair," pp. 175–190. See C. Duncan Rice, "Antislavery mission of George Thompson to the United States, 1834–1835," *J. Am. Stud.*, II (Apr. 1968) 13–31.

147 THOMPSON, GEORGE. Report of the discussion on American slavery, in Dr. Wardlaw's chapel, between Mr. George Thompson, and the Rev. R[obert] J. Breckinridge, of Baltimore, United States, on the evenings of the 13th, 14th, 15th, 16th, and 17th June, 1836. Taken from the Glasgow Chronicle. Glasgow, 1836. 86 p. **MB NN Uk**

The U.S. ed., Boston, 1836, carried title: *Discussion on American slavery, between George Thompson, esq., agent of the British and foreign society for the abolition of slavery throughout the world, and Rev. Robert J. Breckinridge, delegate from the general assembly of the Presbyterian church in the United States, to the Congregational union of England and Wales: holden in the Rev. Dr. Wardlaw's chapel, Glasgow, Scotland; on the evenings of the 13th, etc. . . . with an appendix.* The 24 p. appendix added commentary by Charles C. Burleigh. The second U.S. ed. carried the same title but dropped the comments by Burleigh and added notes by William Lloyd Garrison in the separately paginated appendix (1–23), Boston, 1836.

148 [UNITED SECESSION CHURCH, SCOTLAND]. An address on Negro slavery to the Christian churches in the United States of America, by the United associate synod. Edinburgh, 1836. 18 p. **NHi TNF**

Signed by David Wilson, moderator, and Wm. Kidston, clerk.

149 URE, ANDREW. The cotton manufacture of Great Britain systematically investigated and illustrated by 150 original figures, engraved on wood and steel; with an introductory view of its comparative state in foreign countries, drawn chiefly from personal survey. London, 1836. 2 vols. **DLC Uk**

On the U.S., pp. xxxviii–liii; 96–168. An enlarged ed., London, 1861, added to the above title: *To which is added, a supplement, completing the statistical and manufacturing information to the present time,* by P. L. Simmonds, 2 vols. See esp. pp. 360–367, 431–449.

150 WESTON, RICHARD. A visit to the United States and Canada in 1833; with the view of settling in America. Including a voyage to and from New York. Edinburgh, 1836. 312 p. **DLC Uk**

151 [WOODCOCK, THOMAS SWANN]. New York to Niagara, 1836. The journal of Thomas S. Woodcock; edited, with notes, by Deoch Fulton. New York, 1938. 22 p. **DLC Uk**

Repr. from the *Bull. N.Y. Pub. Lib.*, XLIV, (Sept. 1938), 676–694.

1837

152 [AMES, JULIUS RUBENS, *ed.*]. "Liberty" . . . the image and superscription on every coin issued by the United States of America . . . Proclaim liberty throughout all the land unto all the inhabitants thereof. The inscription on the bell in the old Philadelphia statehouse, which was rung July 4, 1776, at the signing of the Declaration of Independence. [New York], 1837. 231 p. **DLC**

Includes excerpts from comment on slavery in the U.S. by James Birney, Edward Bulwer Lytton, Harriet Martineau and Daniel O'Connell as well as many other U.S. and European sources. 2d ed. appeared under title, *The legion of liberty! and force of Truth, containing the thoughts, words and deeds of some prominent apostles, champions and martyrs*, New York, 1843. (not the same as *The legion of liberty! Remonstrance. . . .*, Albany, N.Y., 1843, below; also ed. by Ames).

153 BIGGS, JOSEPH. To America in thirty-nine days before steamships crossed the Atlantic. Idbury, 1926. 26 p. **NcD Uk**

DLC has 2d ed., Oxford, 1927. Contains extracts from a diary written in 1837, ed. by Maude A. Biggs.

154 BUCKINGHAM, JAMES SILK. Address to the people of the United States. [New York, 1837]. 4 p. **DLC Uk**

Uk gives title as *Mr. Buckingham's address to the people of the United States*. Letter dated Oct. 25, 1837; repr. from *Knickerbocker*, XI, 80.

155 CATHER, THOMAS. Voyage to America; the journals of Thomas Cather, ed. with an introduction by Thomas Yoseloff. Illustrated with contemporary drawings by Harry Tyler. New York, [1961]. 176 p. **DLC Uk**

"Records a sight-seeing trip to America by a young Irish aristocrat and his friend in 1836–37." Also see the Rodale Press miniature book, *Journal of a voyage to America in 1836*, [London, 1955].

156 CLIBBORN, EDWARD. American prosperity. An outline of the American debit or banking system; to which is added a justification of the veto of the late president: also an explanation of the true principles of banking, with a paper currency in the United Kingdom. By a late resident in America. London, 1837. 44 p. **DLC Uk**

Review: *Monthly Rev.*, CXLIV, 127.

157 DAVIS, ROBERT. The Canadian farmer's travels in the United States of America, in which remarks are made on the arbitrary colonial policy practiced in Canada, and the free and equal rights, and happy effects of the liberal institutions and astonishing enterprise of the United States. Buffalo, 1837. 107 p. **CaOTP CtY InU**

158 DUNCOMB, JOHN. The British emigrant's advocate: being a manual for the use of emigrants and travellers in British America and the United States, containing a concise view

of the state and prospects of the colonists; an accurate description of the main routes; a detail of present and projected improvements; and a variety of information necessary to the emigrant, and interesting to the general reader. By Thomas Duncomb, from notes by John Duncomb. London, 1837. 362 p. **CaOTP**

159 [ENDERBY, CHARLES]. The metallic currency. The cause of the present crisis in England and America. By the author of "Money, the representative of value." London, 1837. 33 p. **DLC Uk**

Uk catalog lists under England-Appendix-Currency. 2d ed., London, 1839, has title *Metallic currency the cause of the money crisis in England and America.*

160 ENQUIRY INTO THE CIRCUMSTANCES that have occasioned the present embarrassments in the trade between Great Britain and the United States of America. London, 1837.

No locations found.

Review: *Edinb. Rev.* (by J. R. McCulloch), LXV, 221.

161 FAIRHOLME, GEORGE. New and conclusive physical demonstrations, both of the fact and period of the Mosaic deluge and of its having been the only event of its kind that has ever occurred upon the earth. London, 1837. 443 p. **DLC Uk**

On Niagara, etc., pp. 157–203, 304–305. See also his "On the falls of Niagara; with some observations on the distinct evidence which they bear to the geological character of the North American plains," *London, Edinb. & Dublin Phil. Mag.*, V, ser. 3 (July, 1834), 11–25.

162 GILBART, JAMES WILLIAM. The history of banking in America: with an inquiry how far the banking institutions of America are adapted to this country; and a review of the causes of the recent pressure on the money market. London, 1837. 207 p. **DLC Uk**

Review: *Monthly Rev.*, (July 1837), 455.

163 GLASGOW EMANCIPATION SOCIETY. Britain and America united in the cause of universal freedom: being the third annual report of the Glasgow emancipation society: containing important information relative to the working of the apprenticeship system in the West Indies; progress of the emancipation cause in the United States; history of the revolution in Texas; interesting movements of religious bodies in Great Britain, during the past year; the speeches delivered at the annual meeting, &c. &c. &c. Glasgow, 1837. 144 p. **DLC**

164 GLASGOW LADIES' AUXILIARY EMANCIPATION SOCIETY. Three years' female anti-slavery effort, in Britain and America: being a report of the proceedings of the Glasgow Ladies' Auxiliary Emancipation Society, since its formation in January, 1834: containing a sketch of the rise and progress of the American female anti-slavery societies; and valuable communications addressed by them, both to societies and individuals in this country. Glasgow, 1837. 71 p. **DLC**

165 [GREG, ROBERT HYDE]. The factory question, considered in relation to its effects on the health and morals of those employed in factories, and the "Ten hours Bill," in relation to its effects upon the manufacturers of England and those of foreign countries. London, 1837. 151 p. **KU MH NNC Uk**

Appendix, pp. 140–143, is a questionnaire contrasting English and U.S. working children.

166   MARTINEAU, HARRIET. Society in America. London, 1837. 3 vols.   **DLC Uk**

New York and Paris (in English) eds. in 2 vols. appeared the same year; Brussels, Leipzig and Paris (in French) eds. in 1838; Stockholm ed. in 1843–4, and many other eds. Also see 1962 abridged ed., with an introd. essay by Seymour Martin Lipset, Garden City, N.Y., 1962, 357 p. Partially repr. in *Views of slavery & emancipation; from "Society in America,"* New York, 1837. See also Samuel Bower, *Competition in peril; or, The present position of the Owenites or nationalists considered; together with Miss Martineau's account of communities in America,* Leeds, 1837, pp. 7–10, for extracts from Martineau's work interspersed with Bower's comments. Also of interest is the author's *Autobiography,* ed. by Maria Weston Chapman, London, 1877. For accounts of Martineau in the U.S., see Una Pope-Hennessy's *Three English women in America,* London, 1929; Narola Elizabeth Rivenburg's *Harriet Martineau: an example of Victorian conflict,* Philadelphia, 1932, pp. 84–95; R. K. Webb, *Harriet Martineau: a radical Victorian,* London, 1960, pp. 134–174; Margharita Laski, "Harriet Martineau", in *Abroad in America: visitors to the new nation, 1776–1914,* ed. by Marc Pachter, Reading, Mass., 1976, pp. 62–71; and Valerie Kossew Pichanick, *Harriet Martineau: the woman and her work,* Ann Arbor, 1980, pp. 73–103. See also Bertha-Monica Stearns, "Miss Sedwick observes Harriet Martineau," *New Eng. Quar.,* VII, (Sept. 1934), 533–541; and Stephen Bloore, "Miss Martineau speaks out," *New Eng. Quar.,* XI (Sept. 1936), 403–416.

Reviews: *Am. Monthly Mag.,* IV, n.s., 88, 190; *Am. Quar. Rev.,* XXII, 21 (repr. in pamphlet form, Philadelphia, 1837); *Chr. Examiner* (by Caleb Stetson), XXIII, 226; *Fraser's Mag.,* XIX, 557; *Gentleman's Mag.,* I, 76; *Liberator* (June 30, July 14, 1837); *Lit. & Theol. Rev.,* IV, 455; *Lit. Gazette,* CCLXXIX, 297; *Maine Monthly Mag.,* I, 561; *Method. Quar. Rev.* (by J. T. Crane), XXVIII, (3d ser., VI), 508; *Natl. Quar. Rev.,* I, 350; *New Yorker,* III, 212, 221; *No. Am. Rev.* (by J.G. Palfrey), XLV, 418; *So. Lit. Mess.* (by W. G. Simms), III, 641; *Tait's Edinb. Mag.,* IV, n.s., 404, V, 219; *Westmin. Mess.,* IV, 225; and *Westmin. Rev.,* XXVII, 478. See also James Boyle, *A review of Miss Martineau's work on "Society in America,"* Boston, 1837. Review by Simms in *So. Lit. Mess.* repr. in pamphlet form as *Slavery in America, being a brief review of Miss Martineau on that subject, by a South Carolinian,* Charleston, 1838; again repr. in *The pro-slavery argument, as maintained by the most distinguished writers of the Southern states,* Charleston, 1852.

167   NYE, THOMAS. Journal of Thomas Nye, written during a journey between Montreal & Chicago in 1837, edited by Hugh McLellan. Champlain [N.Y.], 1932. 30 p.   **DLC**

Former American, who settled in Canada in 1822. Journal covers Oct.–Dec., 1837.

168   NYE, THOMAS. Two letters of Thomas Nye, relating to a journey from Montreal to Chicago in 1837. Edited by Hugh McLellan. Champlain [N.Y.], 1931. 15 p.   **CSmH NN**

169   A PERSONAL NARRATIVE of events by sea and land, from the year 1800 to 1815; including the expeditions to Ferrol and Egypt; the sieges of Gaeta, Col de Balaguer and Tarragona; mutiny of Fribourg's regiment at Malta, in 1806; battle of Trafalgar, with extracts from the log of H. M. Ship Neptune, 98 guns, on that day; two trips to the army of Lord Wellington in 1811 and 1812; concluding with a narration of some of the principal events in the Chesapeake and South Carolina, in 1814 and 1815; interspersed with anecdotes, and embellished with four engravings, also a map of the river Patuxent, where the British army landed, when they marched to Washington. By a captain of the navy. Portsmouth [Eng.], 1837. 186 p.   **MH**

Operations in the War of 1812 discussed, pp. 149–186.

170   PORTER, GEORGE RICHARDSON. A brief memoir of the growth, progress, and extent of the trade between the United Kingdom and the United States of America, from the beginning of the 18th century to the present time. London, 1837. 16 p.   **UkLRSS**

A tract, dated 1837, and "presented to the statistical section of the British Association for the Advancement of Science, on 11th September, 1837."

171   REMONSTRANCE ON THE SUBJECT of American slavery, by the inhabitants of Dumbarton and the Vale of Leven. [Glasgow, 1837]. 8 p.   **DLC**

172   RING, WILLIAM B. A guide to mechanics and working men wishing to emigrate to the United States of America. With the most useful information necessary on their arrival at New York, etc. London, [1837]. 24 p.   **DLC**

173   SALMONS, *SIR* DAVID. The monetary difficulties of America, and their probable effects on British commerce considered. London, 1837. 45 p.   **DLC Uk**

174   [SHELTON, FREDERICK WILLIAM]. The Trollopiad; or, Travelling gentlemen in America. A satire, by Nil Admirari, esq. [*pseud.*]. New York, 1837. 151 p.   **DLC Uk**

An American answer in verse to Mrs. Trollope, Butler, Fidler, Hamilton, Martineau, et al.

175   A SKETCH OF WESTERN VIRGINIA: for the use of British settlers in that country. London, 1837. 117 p.   **DLC**

176   TEXAS. An English question. London, 1837. 40 p.   **DLC**

177   THOMPSON, GEORGE. An appeal to the abolitionists of Great Britain, in behalf of the cause of universal emancipation. . . . Recommended to the special attention of the anti-slavery females of Great Britain. Edinburgh, 1837. 32 p.   **MB NIC**

Originally a pref. to Angelina E. Grimke's *Appeal to the Christian women of the South* [New York, 1836], which was also later pub. under the title: *Slavery in America. A reprint of an appeal to the Christian women of the slave states of America. By Angelina E. Grimke, of Charleston, South Carolina. With introduction [pp. i–xx], notes and appendix by George Thompson.* . . . Edinburgh, 1837, 56 p. DLC and Uk have both works by Grimke.

178   THOMPSON, GEORGE. Letters and addresses by George Thompson, during his mission in the United States, from October 1st, 1834, to November 27, 1835. Boston, 1837. 126 p.   **DLC Uk**

Ed. by Wm. Lloyd Garrison.

179   THOMPSON, GEORGE. The speeches delivered at the soiree in honour of George Thompson, esq., in the Renfrewshire Tontine Inn, Paisley, on the evening of Wednesday 25th January, 1837. With an appendix, containing a remonstrance on the subject of slavery, by the Paisley emancipation society. Paisley [1837]. 24 p.   **NNUT**

180   WILKIE, DAVID. Sketches of a summer trip to New York and the Canadas. Edinburgh, 1837. 293 p.   **DLC**

181   WOOD, *REV.* SAMUEL. Letters from Boston, U.S., on Harvard University. [n.p.], 1837. 12 p.   **DLC**

From the *Chr. Reformer*, Nov. 1837.

182   WOOD, *REV.* SAMUEL. Letters from the United States. [London, 1837]. 11 p.   **DLC**

From the *Chr. Reformer*, Dec. 1837.

183   WOOD, *REV.* SAMUEL. The present state and future prospects of Unitarian Christianity in the United States. [London, 1837]. 19 p.   **DLC**

From the *Chr. Reformer*, Sept. 1837.

1838

184   [BELL, ANDREW]. Men and things in America; being the experience of a year's residence in the United States, in a series of letters to a friend. By A. Thomason [*pseud.*] London, 1838. 296 p.   **DLC Uk**

In U.S. 1835–36.

Review: *Athenaeum* (March 24, 1838), 211.

185   THE CANADIAN CRISIS, and Lord Durham's mission to the North American colonies: with remarks, the result of personal observations in the colonies and the United States, on the remedial measures to be adopted in the North American provinces. London, 1838. 56 p.   **DLC Uk**

Pamphlet is signed, "M. N. O."; Uk lists under those initials.

186   [CHIPMAN, WARD]. Remarks upon the disputed points of boundary under the fifth article of the Treaty of Ghent, principally compiled from the statements laid by the government of Great Britain before the King of the Netherlands, as arbiter. Saint John, [N. B.], 1838. 81 p.   **DLC Uk**

187   D'ARUSMONT, FRANCES [WRIGHT] "MME. PHIQUEPEL-DARUSMONT." What is the matter? A political address as delivered in Masonic hall, October 28th, 1838. New York, 1838. 21 p.   **DLC Uk**

188   EYRE, JOHN. The Christian spectator: being a journey from England to Ohio, two years in that state, travels in America, &c. Albany, 1838. 72 p.   **DLC Uk**

Many later eds. under variant titles. Rev. ed. containing additional material resulting from a visit in 1847 appeared under title, *Travels: comprising a journey from England to Ohio, two years in that state, travels in America, &c. To which are added the foreigner's protracted journal, letters, &c.*, New York, 1851.

189   FELTON, *MRS.* Life in America. A narrative of two years' city & country residence in the United States. Hull, 1838. 120 p.   **DLC Uk**

Later eds., e.g., London, 1842, and Bolton Percy [Eng.]: 1843, appeared under title: *American life, a narrative of two years' city and country residence in the United States.*

190   HAWKSHAW, *SIR* JOHN. Reminiscences of South America: from two and a half years' residence in Venezuela. London, 1838. 260 p.   **DLC Uk**

Visit to eastern U.S., pp. 247–260.

191   HEAD, *SIR* FRANCIS BOND. Governor Head's message to the assembly on the subject of the steamer "Caroline." Toronto, 1838.

No locations found; Sabin listing #31140.

192   JAMESON, *MRS.* ANNA BROWNELL [MURPHY]. Winter studies and summer rambles
        in Canada. London, 1838. 3 vols.   **DLC Uk**

        New York ed., 2 vols., 1839. 20th century eds: James J. Talman and Elsie McLeod Murray,
        eds., Toronto, 1943; and abridged, with an introd. by Clara Thomas, Toronto, 1965.
        Includes comment on Buffalo, Detroit, Niagara, and other portions of the U.S. Portions
        repr. in *Sketches in Canada, and rambles among the red men*, London, 1852; and in *Mich.
        Hist. Mag.*, VIII (1924), 51–76, 140–169, 349–391, and 486–533. See also accounts of
        Mrs. Jameson in America in Geraldine Macpherson, *Memoirs of the life of Anna Jameson*,
        London, 1878; Mrs. Steuart Erskine, *Anna Jameson, letters and friendships (1812–1860)*,
        London, [1915], chaps. 6 and 7; and Clara Thomas, *Love and work enough, the life of Anna
        Jameson*, Toronto, 1967.

        Review: *Tait's Edinb. Mag.*, VI, (n.s.), 69.

193   JOPLIN, T[HOMAS]. Articles on banking and currency. From "The Economist" newspa-
        per. [London], 1838. 108 p.   **DLC UkCU**

        Pages 41–87 and 90–93 deal with banking in the U.S., with emphasis upon criticisms of
        Pres. Andrew Jackson's fiscal policies.

194   K., J. Plain reasons for loyalty, addressed to plain people. Coburg [U.C.], 1838. 8 p.
                                                                              CaOOA

195   KERR, HUGH. A poetical description of Texas, and narrative of many interesting events
        in that country, embracing a period of several years, interspersed with moral and political
        impressions: also, an appeal to those who oppose the union of Texas with the United States,
        and the anticipation of that event. To which is added The Texas Heroes, no. 1 and 2. New
        York, 1838. 122 p.   **DLC**

        Factual commentary, although in verse.

196   LINDSEY, E. G. A history of the events which transpired during the Navy Island cam-
        paign: to which is added the correspondence of different public officials, with the affidavits
        of individuals in the United States and Canada. Lewiston, [N.Y.], 1838. 40 p.   **PPL**

        DLC has mutilated copy, missing 16 pp.

197   LOGAN, JAMES. Notes of a journey through Canada, the United States of America, and
        the West Indies. Edinburgh, 1838. 259 p.   **DLC Uk**

        Review: *Athenaeum* (Jan. 27, 1838), 67; *Monthly Rev.* (Feb. 1838), 310.

198   MACQUEEN, JAMES. A general plan for a mail communication by steam between Great
        Britain and the eastern and western parts of the world; also to Canton and Sydney, west-
        ward by the Pacific, to which are added geographical notices of the Isthmus of Panama,
        Nicaragua, etc. London, 1838. 132 p.   **DLC Uk**

        On the U.S. pp. 18–23, 101–108.

199   MARTINEAU, HARRIET. Retrospect of western travel. London, 1838. 3 vols.   **DLC Uk**

        See refs. to this visit to the U.S. in the author's *Autobiography*, ed. by Maria Weston
        Chapman, London, 1877, 3 vols. See also William R. Seat, "A rebuttal to Mrs. Trollope:
        Harriet Martineau in Cincinnati," *Ohio Hist. Quar.*, LXVIII (July, 1959), pp. 276–289.

        Reviews: *Am. Monthly Mag.*, XII, n.s., 89; *Chr. Examiner.* (by M. L. Hurlbut), XXIV, 386;
        Eclectic Rev., LXVII, 277; *Edinb. Rev.*, LXI, 180; *Fraser's Mag.*, XIX, 557;

Knickerbocker, XI, 474; *Ladies Companion*, IX, 48; *Ladies Mag. & Lit. Gazette*, XVI, 239; *Method. Quar. Rev.* (by J. T. Crane), XXVIII (VI, 3d ser.), 508; *Monthly Rev.*, CXLV, 361; *N.Y. Rev.*, III, 129; *New Yorker*, V, 29; *No. Am. Rev.*, XLV, 418; *So. Lit. Mess.* (by W. G. Simms), IV, 342; *Westmin. Rev.*, XXVIII, 470. Review by Simms in the *So. Lit. Mess.* repr. in pamphlet form under title: *Slavery in America: being a brief review of Miss Martineau on that subject, by a South Carolinian*, Richmond, 1838; again repr. in *The pro-slavery argument, as maintained by the most distinguished writers of the Southern states, etc.*, Charleston, 1852.

200   PEARCE, CHARLES E. Madame Vestris and her times. London [1923]. 314 p. **DLC Uk**
Describes Madame Vestris' tour of the U.S. in 1838, pp. 223–228.

201   SLEIGH, WILLIAM WILLCOCKS. Abolitionism exposed! Proving that the principles of abolitionism are injurious to the slaves themselves, destructive to this nation, and contrary to the express commands of God; with strong evidence that some of the principal champions of abolitionism are inveterate enemies to this country, and are taking advantage of the "Anti-slavery war-whoop" to dissever, and break up, the Union. Philadelphia, 1838. 93 p.   **DLC Uk**
Sleigh was a British professor of anatomy and surgery. For American answers, see *The Little Western against the Great Eastern, or Brother Jonathan vs. John Bull. Being a review by a plebian of the western hemisphere of abolitionism as exposed by Dr. Sleigh*, Philadelphia, 1838, 12 p.; also: [Origen Bacheler], *The veil removed, or W. W. Sleigh unmasked*, New York, 1836.

202   SMITH, JOSHUA TOULMIN. Journal in America, 1837–1838; ed., with introd. and notes by Floyd Benjamin Streeter. Metuchen, N.J., 1925. 54 p.   **DLC Uk**
Heartman's Historical Ser., no. 41. Smith was a Birmingham lawyer and phrenologist who later settled in New Jersey.

203   STEVENSON, DAVID. Sketch of the civil engineering of North America; comprising remarks on the harbours, river and lake navigation, light houses, steam-navigation, water-works, canals, roads, railways, bridges, and other works in that country. London, 1838. 320 p.   **DLC Uk**
Reviews: *Monthly Rev.*, CXLV (III, n.s.), 305; *United Service Mag.*, (by Captain Basil Hall), 1839, Pt. I, 40–47, 202–208, 340–348.

204   THE STRANGER'S GUIDE through the United States and Canada. Edinburgh, 1838. 143 p.   **NHi NN**

205   [STUART, ANDREW]. Succinct account of the treaties and negociations between Great Britain and the United States of America, relating to the boundary between the British possessions of Lower Canada and New Brunswick, in North America, and the United States of America. [London, 1838]. 206 p.   **DLC Uk**
See also author's *Notes upon the south western boundary line of the British provinces of Lower Canada and New Brunswick, and the United States of America*, Montreal, 1839, which was pub. anonymously and to which DLC adds the note: "First edition, Quebec, 1830, 63 p."

206   WOOD, *REV*. SAMUEL. Letters from the United States. [n.p.], 1838.   **DLC**
From the *Chr. Reformer*, Feb., 1838.

207   WOOD, T. KENNETH, *ed.* Journal of an English emigrant farmer. A record of the journey of an unknown Englishman to America in the year 1838 and his sojourn for a summer among the early pioneer settlers of Muncy Valley. Williamsport [Pa.], 1928. 38 p.   **ICN**

Proc. & Papers Lycoming Hist. Soc., no. 6.

208   YULE, PATRICK. Remarks on the disputed north-western boundary of New Brunswick, bordering on the United States of North America, with an explanatory sketch. By Capt. [later Major] P. Yule. London, 1838. 28 p.   **DLC Uk**

1839

209   ARCHER, THOMAS. Memories of America, and Reminiscences at home and abroad. A series of tales, by Thomas Archer, comedian. London [1839]. 96 p.   **Uk**

The work is largely fiction, based on experiences in the United States.

210   [BECHERVAISE, JOHN]. Thirty-six years of a seafaring life. By an old quarter-master. "The Simple Truth." Portsea, 1839. 336 p.   **CSmH MH NN Uk**

For refs. to the U.S., see pp. 14–16, 213–222, 245–259.

211   CASWALL, HENRY. America, and the American Church. London, 1839. 368 p. **DLC Uk**

The 2d ed., London, 1851, was completely rewritten and enlarged; a short selection was pub. under the title *Samuel Gunn, the lay-reader*, New York, 1861.

212   [CHATTO, WILLIAM ANDREW]. A paper: — of tobacco; treating of the rise, progress, pleasures, and advantages of smoking. With anecdotes of distinguished smokers, mems. on pipes and tobacco-boxes, and a tritical [sic] essay on snuff. By Joseph Fume, [*pseud.*]. London, 1839. 165 p.   **DLC Uk**

A 2d ed., "with additions," London, 1839.

213   CLAXTON, TIMOTHY. Memoir of a mechanic. Being a sketch of the life of Timothy Claxton, written by himself. Together with miscellaneous papers. Boston, 1839. 179 p.
    DLC

A master mechanic, and advocate of working class self-improvement, Claxton lived in Boston, 1823–36, then returned to England. For U.S. experiences, see chaps. 7–11.

214   DAUBENY, CHARLES GILES BRIDLE. Sketch of the geology of North America, being the substance of a memoir read before the Ashmolean Society Nov. 26, 1838. Oxford, 1839. 73 p.   **DLC Uk**

Also pub. in the *Trans. Ashmolean Soc.*, Oxford, vol. II (separate pagination). See also Daubney's articles, "On the climate of North America," *Rep. Brit. Assn. Adv. of Science* (1838, pt. 2), 29–32; "Notice of the thermal springs of North America," *Am. J. Science and Arts*, XXXVI, 88–93.

215   DURHAM, JOHN GEORGE LAMBTON, *1st earl*. Report on the affairs of British North America from the Earl of Durham, Her Majesty's high commissioner. Ordered by the House of Commons to be printed, February 11, 1839. London, 1839. 218, 60, 214 p.
    CtY NIC Uk

DLC has the *Report*, appendices omitted, in *The report and despatches of the Earl of Durham* . . . , London, 1839, pp. 1–245, and the first Canadian ed., Montreal, 1839. The controversial report, based upon Durham's 1838 mission to Canada and recommending structural changes in imperial relationships, was officially pub. after first being leaked to the London *Times*, which began printing major sections on Feb. 8, 1839; it was quickly reprinted, entirely and in part, in England and Canada. Authorship is sometimes ascribed to Charles Buller. Considerable comment on influence of and relationship with U.S. See the standard, 3 vol. ed. by Sir C. P. Lucas, Oxford, 1912, esp. the vol. 1 introd.: "References to the United States," pp. 257–265, and passim. (see index). Other 20th century eds., with introds. and notes by: Sir Reginald Coupland, Oxford, 1945 (abridged); Marcel-Pierre Hamel, Quebec, 1948 (in French); Gerald M. Craig, Toronto, 1963 (abridged); and Denis Bertrand and Andre Lavallee, Montreal, 1969 (in French).

For contemporary criticism of the *Report* see [Thomas Chandler Haliburton], *A reply to the Report of the Earl of Durham. By a colonist*, London, 1839; and L. J. Papineau, *Histoire de l'insurrection du Canada . . . en refutation du rapport de Lord Durham*, Burlington, Vt., 1839. On background of Durham's mission and report, see: F. Bradshaw, *Self-government in Canada and how it was achieved; the story of Lord Durham's report*, London, 1903; Leonard Cooper, *Radical Jack; the life of John George Lambton, first Earl of Durham*, London, 1959, pp. 217–276; Ged Martin, *The Durham report and British policy; a critical essay*, Cambridge, 1972; and Chester W. New, *Lord Durham; a biography of John George Lambton, first Earl of Durham*, Oxford, 1929, pp. 320–552, and on the question of authorship of the *Report*, pp. 565–577.

216 EUROPE AND AMERICA IN 1839. London, 1839. 32 p. **TxU**

217 EYRE, JOHN. The European stranger in America. New York, 1839. 84 p. **DLC Uk**

Describes travels between New York and Ohio. Was originally intended as a continuation of author's *The Christian spectator*, Albany, 1838, above. It was later added as Part III to *Travels* . . . , 1851, below.

218 FORBES, ALEXANDER. California: a history of Upper and Lower California from their first discovery to the present time, comprising an account of the climate, soil, natural productions, agriculture, commerce, &c. A full view of the missionary establishments and condition of the free and domesticated Indians. With an appendix relating to steam navigation in the Pacific. Illustrated with a new map, plans of the harbours, and numerous engravings. London, 1839. 352 p. **DLC Uk**

San Francisco, 1919, ed. by Thomas C. Russell; San Francisco, 1937 ed. with an introd. by Herbert I. Priestly; both added new indexes. See discussion of Forbes in Lester G. Engelson, "Proposals for the colonization of California by England in connection with the Mexican debt to British bondholders, 1837–1846," *Calif. Hist. Soc. Quar.*, XVIII (1939), 136–148.

Reviews: *Athenaeum*, (Feb. 23, 1839), 151; *Chambers's J.*, VII, 171; *Monthly Rev.* XXV, 4th ser., 476; *Niles' Register*, LVIII, 70; London *Times*, Sept. 6, 1839, 6.

219 [GURNEY, JOSEPH JOHN]. Free and friendly remarks on a speech lately delivered to the Senate of the United States, by Henry Clay, of Kentucky, on the subject of the abolition of North American slavery. New York, 1839. 24 p. **DLC**

Repr. in appendix of Gurney's later vol., *A winter in the West Indies, described in familiar letters to Henry Clay, of Kentucky*, London, 1840, below.

220 [HOWE, *HON.* JOSEPH]. Responsible government. Letters to the Right Honorable Lord John Russell &c. &c. &c. on the right of British Americans to be governed by the principles of the British constitution. Halifax, 1839. 40 p. **CaBVaU MH UkLU-C**

CaOTP, MH have another Halifax, 1839 ed., 48 p. Four letters, containing discussion of U.S., repr. in the author's *Speeches and public letters*, 1872, below, I, pp. 221–266. See also Howe's later letters to Russell, *Letters to the right honourable Lord John Russell, on the government of British America*, 1846, below.

221 JAMES, GEORGE PAYNE RAINSFORD. A brief history of the United States boundary question. Drawn up from official papers. London, 1839. 32 p. **DLC Uk**

See also Stewart Marsh Ellis, *The Solitary horseman; or, The life and adventures of G. P. R. James*, Kensington, 1927; esp., pp. 122–214. James was in U.S. 1850–58, as British consul in Massachusetts and Norfolk, Va.

Review: *Quar. Rev.*, (by J. W. Croker), LXVII, 501.

222 LLOYD, WILLIAM. Letters from the West Indies, during a visit in the autumn of MDC-CCXXXVI, and the spring of MDCCCXXXVII. London [1839]. 263 p. **DLC Uk**

Last chap. on New York.

223 MADDEN, RICHARD ROBERT. A letter to W. E. Channing, D.D., on the subject of the abuse of the flag of the United States in the Island of Cuba, and the advantage taken of its protection in promoting the slave trade. Boston, 1839. 32 p. **ICN NNC Uk**

This letter, and a 2d addressed to Ferdinand Clark of Havana, dated Sept. 6, 1839, appeared in the New Orleans *True American* and was repr. in the *Emancipator*, Dec. 19, 1839. See also the answer: *A letter to Wm. E. Channing, D.D., in reply to one addressed to him by R. R. Madden on the abuse of the flag of the United States in the island of Cuba, for promoting the slave trade. By a calm observer*, Boston, 1840.

224 MARRYAT, *CAPT.* FREDERICK A. A diary in America, with remarks on its institutions. London, 1839. 3 vols. Part second. London, 1839. 3 vols. **DLC Uk**

Issued originally in two parts, each in 3 vol. sets. Other complete eds., 1839 and 1840, in 1 or 2 vols., pub. in Paris, Philadelphia and New York. 20th century editions: ed., with a forward by Jules Zanger, Bloomington, [1960]; ed., with notes and introd. by Sydney Jackman, New York, 1962. See also the American parody, *Lie-ary on America! With Yarns on its institutions. By Capt. Marry-it, C.B. (Common Bloat)*, Boston, 1840. See also Marryat's novel, *The travels and romantic adventures of Monsieur Violet among the Snake Indians and wild tribes of the great western prairies*, London, 1843, 3 vols. (with several later eds. issued under variant titles). See also the following accounts of Marryat's travels in America: Florence (Marryat) Church Lean, *Life and letters of Captain Marryat*, London, 1872, II, pp. 1–73; David Hannay, *Life of Frederick Marryat*, London, 1889, pp. 98–113, 120; Arno L. Bader, "Captain Marryat in Michigan," *Mich. Hist. Mag.*, XX (1936), pp. 163–175; John T. Flanagan, "Captain Marryat at old St. Peters," *Minn. Hist.*, XVIII (1937), pp. 152–164; and Christopher Lloyd, *Captain Marryat and the old navy*, London, [1939], pp. 264–268.

Reviews: *Athenaeum*, (Jan. 4, 1840), 11; *Dublin Rev.* VII, 399; *Dublin Univ. Mag.*, XIV, 513; *Eclectic Rev.*, LXX, 422, LXXI, 271; *Edinb. Rev.* (by W. Empson), LXX, 123; *Gentleman's Mag.* (Philadelphia), VI, 103; *Monthly Rev.*, CXLIX, 497, CLI, 214; *N.Y. Rev.*, V, 142; *Quar. Rev.* (by John Gibson Lockhart), LXIV, 308; *So. Lit. Mess.*, VII, 253; *Tait's Edinb. Mag.*, VI, 553; *U.S. Mag. and Democratic Rev.*, VI, 255.

225   M[ARTINEAU], H[ARRIET]. The martyr age of the United States. Boston, 1839. 84 p.
DLC

Uk has 1840 ed. Pub. originally as a review of *Right and wrong in Boston in 1835, 1836, 1837, the annual reports of the Boston female antislavery society*, in *Westmin. Rev.*, XXXII, 1–59. Later eds. (e.g., Newcastle upon Tyne, 1840) carried title, *The martyr age of the United States of America, with an appeal on behalf of the Oberlin institute in aid of the abolition of slavery*. See also Martineau's introductory letter in John A. Collins, *Right and wrong amongst the abolitionists of the United States*, Glasgow, 1841.

226   MATHEWS, *MRS.* ANNE [JACKSON]. Memoirs of Charles Mathews, comedian. By Mrs. Mathews. [London, 1838–39]. 4 vols.   **DLC Uk**

Account of tours in the U.S.: 1822–23, III, 301–413; 1834–35, IV, 284–355. See also other works: *A continuation of the memoirs of Charles Mathews. By Mrs. Mathews. Including his correspondence and an account of his residence in the United States*, Philadelphia, 1839, 2 vols.; *The life and correspondence of Charles Mathews, the elder, comedian. By Mrs. Mathews. A new edition, abridged and condensed, by Edmund Yates*, London, 1860. See also Mathews' dramatization, "A trip to America," performed after his return to England following his first tour of 1822–23, discussed in the *Memoirs*, III, 427–429, 516–549. For Mathews' views on the earlier trip see Francis Hodge, "Charles Mathews reports on America," *Quar. J. Speech*, XXXVI (1950), 492–499.

227   MATTHEW, PATRICK. Emigration fields. North America, the Cape, Australia, and New Zealand; describing these countries, and giving a comparative view of the advantages they present to British settlers. Edinburgh, 1839. 237 p.   **DLC Uk**

On North America, pp. 25–61 and 70–74, both U.S. and Canada.

228   MATTHEWS, C. J. How do you like our country? or an autumn in America. London, 1839.

No locations found; Sabin listing, #46885.

229   MURRAY, *SIR* CHARLES AUGUSTUS. Travels in North America during the years 1834, 1835, & 1836. Including a summer residence with the Pawnee Tribe of Indians, in the remote prairies of the Missouri, and a visit to Cuba and the Azore Islands. London, 1839. 2 vols.   **DLC Uk**

3d ed. rev., with a new introd., London, 1854. Excerpted in, "A visit to Dubuque in 1835," *Annals of Iowa*, XXII, 3d ser. (1940), 410–411; and A. B. Aulbert, ed., *Pioneer Roads and Experiences of Travelers*, Vol. II, Cleveland, 1904. Also see Murray's novel, *The prairie bird*, London, 1844, 3 vols.; in the pref. he states: "One of my chief aims has been to afford correct information respecting the habits, condition, and character of the North American Indians." See also Walter Harry Green Armytage, "Charles A. Murray among the Pawnees, 1835," *Mid-America*, XXXII (July, 1950), 189–201.

Reviews: *Athenaeum* (1839), 572; *Dublin Rev.*, VII, 399; *Edinb. Rev.*, LXXIII, 77; *Gentleman's Mag.* (by E. A. Poe?), V, 227; *Knickerbocker*, XIV, 280; *N.Y. Rev.*, V, 490, VI, 142; *Quar. Rev.* (by John Gibson Lockhart), LXIV, 308; *So. Lit. Mess.*, VI, 72.

230   ON THE PRESENT DERANGEMENT of the Currency of the United States, with suggestions for its better regulation. London, 1839. 25 p.   **CtY MH-BA NNC Uk**

231 PEACE OR WAR? The question considered with special reference to the differences exist-ing between the United States of America and Great Britain. By a clergyman of the Church of England, lately resident in America. London, 1839. 47 p.   **CaOOA UkLRC**

232 PROCTOR, MICHAEL. Notes and observation on America, and the Americans: including considerations for emigrants. Lincoln. [1839]. 116 p.   **DLC**

233 REMARKS ON THE WESTERN states of America or valley of the Mississippi: with sug-gestions to agricultural emigrants, miners, &c. London, 1839. 45 p.   **DLC Uk**

Uk catalog lists under U.S.A—Misc. Institutions—Western States.

234 ROBERTS, MARY. Sketches of the animal and vegetable productions of America. London, 1839. 285 p.   **PU Uk**

235 SCOBLE, JOHN. Texas: its claims to be recognized as an independent power by Great Britain; examined in a series of letters. London, 1839. 56 p.   **DLC Uk**

Pub. by the British and foreign anti-slavery society.

236 SHILLITOE, THOMAS. Journal of the life, labours, and travels of Thomas Shillitoe, in the service of the gospel of Jesus Christ. London, 1839. 2 vols.   **NcD PHC Uk**

Account of a visit to U.S., 1826–29, II, 133–391. Also pub. in the *Friends' Library,* III (1839), 78–484.

237 [STOKES, C.]. A few notes respecting the United States of North America, in relation to their Constitution, their progress, and the stocks of the different states. Comp. from vari-ous authentic sources. London, 1839. 23 p.   **DLC**

Statistical information, without comment.

238 TAWSE, JOHN. Report to the society in Scotland for propagating Christian knowledge, of a visit to America, by their appointment, in reference to the fund under their charge for the education of native Indians. By John Tawse, advocate, secretary—and George Lyon, W. S., agent of the society. With an introduction by the directors. Edinburgh, 1839. 68 p. **CSmH**

239 TOWNLEY, *REV.* ADAM. Ten letters on the church and church establishments; addressed to the Hon. W. H. Draper, M.P.P., &c. &c. &c. By an Anglo-Canadian. Toronto, 1839. 79 p.   **DLC**

4 letters concern the U.S.: pp. 14–20, 44–60, 70–79.

240 TROTTER, ALEXANDER. Observations on the financial position and credit of such of the states of the North American Union as have contracted public debts: comprising an account of the manner in which the sums raised by each state have been applied, and a con-sideration of the probable effects of such application upon the general wealth and prosper-ity of the country. London, 1839. 455 p.   **DLC Uk**

Review: *N.Y. Rev.,* VII, 186.

241 [URQUHART, DAVID]. Exposition of the causes and consequences of the boundary dif-ferences between Great Britain and the United States, subsequently to their adjustment by arbitration . . . Addressed to the Chamber of commerce of Sheffield, 12th April, 1839. Liverpool [1839]. 95 p.   **DLC**

Priv. pr. 1st ed.; Uk has under title: *Exposition of the boundary differences between Great Britain and the United States, etc.,* Glasgow, 1840.

1840

242   ADDRESS OF THE CONGREGATIONAL union in Scotland to their fellow Christians in the United States, on the subject of American slavery. New York, 1840. 12 p.   **MH NN**

Pub. by the American and foreign anti-slavery society; signed by James R. Campbell, Ralph Wardlaw, and David Russell.

243   AMERICAN SLAVERY. Review of Wayland on Human Responsibility. Reprinted from the *Eclectic Review* for June, 1840, London. [London, 1840]. 15 p.   **NHi NNC**

Erroneously listed by Sabin as pub. in 1846. Reviews Francis Wayland's *The limitations of human responsibility*, Boston, 1838, and Theodore Weld's *American slavery as it is: testimony of a thousand witnesses*, New York, 1839.

244   BARCLAY, ALEXANDER. Remarks on emigration to Jamaica: addressed to the coloured classes of the United States. London, 1840. 16 p.   **Uk**

DLC has New York, 1840 ed., under Jamaica. Commissioner of emigration.

245   [BARING BROTHERS & CO. Statement of their transactions with S. Jaudon, agent of the Bank of the United States. London? 1840?] 70 p.   **MB**

No t.p. Bound with *The present crisis, and its remedy: being a system for the equalisation of British and foreign prices . . .* , London, 1841.

246   BRITISH AND FOREIGN ANTI-SLAVERY SOCIETY, LONDON. A report of the proceedings of the great meeting in Exeter hall, June 3, [24], 1840. London, [1840]. 32 p.

     MB UkMa

247   BROTHERS, THOMAS. The United States of North America as they are; not as they are *generally* described: being a cure for radicalism. London, 1840. 517 p.   **DLC Uk**

248   CAMPBELL, *LIEUT.-COL.* JAMES. A British army, as it was, is, and ought to be: illustrated by examples during the Peninsular war: with observations upon India, the United States of America, Canada, the boundary line, the navy, steam warfare, & c. London, 1840. 337 p.   **DLC Uk**

On U.S., pp. 264–337.

249   CHIDLAW, *REV.* BENJAMIN WILLIAMS. Yr American, yr hwn sydd yn cynnwys Nodau ar daith o dffryn Ohio i Gymru, Golweg ar dalaeth Ohio; Hanes sefydliadau Cymreig yn America; Cyfarwyddiadau i ymofynwyr cyn y daith, ar y daith, ac yn y wlad. Gan y parch. Llanrwst, 1840. 48 p.   **DLC Uk**

See *Translation of Yr American, a Welsh pamphlet, by the Rev. B. W. Chidlaw*, Cincinnati, [1911], 41 p. (*Quar. Pub. Hist. Phil. Soc. Ohio*, VI, (1911), no 1.)

250   CLARKSON, THOMAS. Speech of Thomas Clarkson, esq., as originally prepared by him in writing, and intended to have been delivered at the opening of the general anti-slavery convention. London [1840?]. 3 p.   **CSmH Uk**

The following words appear inside t.p.: "distinguishing those passages which were omitted, but which are now published by Mr. Clarkson's permission."

251   [DUER, JOHN]. A vindication of the public faith of New York & Pennsylvania, in reply to the calumnies of the "Times." To which is appended a report, made to the senate of New York, in relation to the debt, revenue, and financial policy of the state [by Gulian C. Verplanck]. London, 1840. 55 p.   **DLC**

Quotes from and discusses the London *Times* article. Duer was an American.

252   EVERSHAW, MARY. Five years in Pennsylvania. London, 1840. 227 p.   **DLC**

253   FLEMING, WILLIAM. Four days at Niagara falls in North America. Manchester, 1840. 30 p.   **NBuG**

Journal, June 29–July 2, 1835.

254   GENERAL ANTI-SLAVERY CONVENTION, 1st, London, 1840. Minutes of the proceedings of the General Anti-Slavery Convention, called by the committee of the British and Foreign Anti-Slavery Society, held in London on the 12th of June 1840 and continued by adjournment to the 23rd of the same month. London, 1840. 32 p.   **DLC Uk**

255   GLASGOW EMANCIPATION SOCIETY. Report of the annual meeting of the Glasgow emancipation society, held Aug. 8, 1840; containing, with other matter, I. Speech of William Dawes, giving information respecting Oberlin institute, a most interesting seminary in Ohio, U.S. in aid of the abolition of slavery; II. Speech of the Rev. J. Keep; III. Speech of L. Remond; and IV. Speech of the Rev. Alex. Harvey, prescribing the duty of British Christian churches towards their Christian brethern in the United States. Reprinted from the Glasgow Argus. Glasgow, 1840. 23 p.   **OO**

Most speeches by Americans, but British comment also included, passim.

256   GLASGOW EMANCIPATION SOCIETY. Report of the speeches, and reception of the American delegates, at the great public meeting of the Glasgow Emancipation Society, held in Dr. Wardlaw's chapel on the evening of Monday, the 27th July, 1840. Glasgow, 1840. 24 p.   **MH NHi Uk**

Repr. from the Glasgow *Argus*. Reception of W. L. Garrison and others.

257   GLASGOW EMANCIPATION SOCIETY. Sixth annual report of the Glasgow emancipation society: with an appendix, list of subscribers, &c . . . Glasgow, 1840.   **NHi**

258   GODWIN, *REV*. BENJAMIN. On the essential sinfulness of slavery, and its direct opposition to the precepts and spirit of Christianity. Paper presented to the General Anti-Slavery Convention. London, 1840. 11 p.   **DHU NIC**

259   GURNEY, JOSEPH JOHN. A winter in the West Indies, described in familiar letters to Henry Clay, of Kentucky. London, 1840. 282 p.   **DLC Uk**

New York ed. of same year carried title: *Familiar letters to Henry Clay of Kentucky, describing a winter in the West Indies*. The letters include comment on slavery in the U.S., and were also pub. in the *Am. Intelligencer*, I, May 1841. See William Ellery Channing's *Emancipation*, Boston, 1840, written after reading Gurney's work.

Reviews: *Am. Intelligencer*, I, No. 2 (by W. E. Channing); *Monthly Rev.*, III, n.s., 536.

260   [HERRING, CHARLES]. Comparative statement with reference to a British claim against the United States, for the illegal seizure and condemnation of the ship "Francis & Eliza," and an American claim against Her Majesty's government for the seizure and liberation of

slaves on board two American vessels stranded upon the Bahamas, for which the latter claim the proprietors of the slaves have lately received a large compensation from her Majesty's government. London, 1840. 15 p. **NN**

261 HEYS, *REV.* ROBERT. Address to the members of the Wesleyan societies and congregation in Douglas and its vicinity, on the subject of Mormonism. [Douglas, Isle of Man? 1840?].

No locations found. See reply in John Taylor, *An answer to some false statements and misrepresentations made by the Rev. Robert Heys, Wesleyan minister, in an address to his society in Douglas and its vicinity, on the subject of Mormonism*, Douglas [Isle of Man], 1840, 11 p.

262 HOOKER, *SIR* WILLIAM JACKSON. Flora Boreali-americana; or The botany of the northern parts of British America: Comp. principally from the plants collected by Dr. Richardson and Mr. Drummond on the late northern expeditions, under command of Capt. Sir John Franklin, R.N.. To which are added those of Mr. Douglas, from north-west America, etc. London, 1840. 2 vols. **DLC Uk**

See also "A collection of Douglas' Western plants," by John Thomas Howell, in *Leaflets of Western Botany*, II, nos. 4–10, Nov. 1937 to Apr. 1939; and *Journal kept by David Douglas in North America*, 1823–1827, London, 1914.

263 JEREMIE, JOHN. A letter to T. Fowell Buxton, Esq., on negro emancipation and African civilization. London, 1840. 52 p.

No locations found. See also Sir Thomas Fowell Buxton's *The African slave trade*, London, 1839–40, pp. 40–45, and passim.

264 [KNIGHT, CHARLES, ed.]. The British mechanic's and labourer's hand book, and true guide to the United States; with ample notices respecting various trades and professions. London, 1840. 288 p. **DLC Uk**

Pref. signed "C. K." [i.e., Charles Knight]. NHi has "new and improved edition," London, 1843. London, 1847 ed. appeared under title *British emigrant's guide to the United States*, London, 1847. Knight edited London, 1844 ed. of *The Lowell Offering*, a miscellany wholly composed by the factory girls of an American city; his introd. includes discussion of the model New England textile city and a letter by Harriet Martineau.

265 [KNOX, CHARLES H.]. Remarks on a war with America, and its probable consequences to that country. London, 1840. 24 p. **DLC**

DLC gives no author; Uk has 2d ed., London, 1841, under Knox.

266 LANG, JOHN DUNMORE. Religion and education in America: with notices of the state and prospects of American Unitarianism, popery, and African colonization. London, 1840. 474 p. **DLC Uk**

See author's *The moral and religious aspect of the future America of the Southern hemisphere; or, A letter to the members of the Presbyterian churches, . . . in the United States of America*, London, 1840; and his *View of the origin and migrations of the Polynesian nation; demonstrating their ancient discovery and progressive settlement of the continent of America*, London, 1834 (2d ed., rev., Sydney, 1877). For an account of Lang's tours in the U.S., in 1840 and 1874, see *John Dunmore Lang: chiefly autobiographical, 1799–1878. Cleric, writer, traveller, statesman, pioneer of democracy in Australia; an assembling of contemporary documents compiled and edited by Archibald Gilchrist,*

[Limited ed.] Melbourne, 1951, 2 vols.; see esp. I, pp. 240–290; II, 712–716, 750, and 767–771.

Review: *Monthly Rev.*, III, n.s., 307.

267   MACKENZIE, W[ILLIAM] L[YON]. . . . Who began the Frontier troubles? Who broke the Treaty? To the Hon. members of the Senate and House of Representatives in Congress. [n.p., 1840]. 24 p.   **NRU**

From *MacKenzie's Gazette*, April 18, 1840.

268   MATHER, JAMES. Two lectures delivered at Newcastle-upon-Tyne, on the constitutions and republican institutions of the United States . . . from data procured on a visit to that country. Newcastle-upon-Tyne, 1840. 90 p.   **DLC**

General discussion of U.S., including anti-slavery comments.

269   MONTGOMERY, JAMES. A practical detail of the cotton manufacture of the United States of America; and the state of the cotton manufacture of that country contrasted and compared with that of Great Britain; with comparative estimates of the cost of manufacturing in both countries. Glasgow, 1840. 219 p.   **DLC Uk**

See answer to Montgomery by "Justitia," 1841, below.

Review: *Monthly Rev.*, III, n.s., 519.

270   MOTT, LUCRETIA. Slavery and "the woman question"; Lucretia Mott's diary of her visit to Great Britain to attend the World's Anti-slavery Convention of 1840. Edited by Frederick B. Tolles. Haverford, Pa. 1952, 86 p.   **DLC Uk**

Supp. no. 23 to the *J. Friends Hist. Soc.* Contains letters to Lucretia Mott from H. Martineau, Richard D. Webb and Elizabeth Pease, pp. 79–81; the diary comments on meetings with English abolitionists, etc. See Douglas H. Maynard's "The World's anti-slavery convention of 1840," *Miss. Valley Hist. Rev.*, LXVII (Dec. 1960), 452–471.

271   PRESTON, T. R. Three years' residence in Canada, from 1837 to 1839. With notes of a winter voyage to New York, and journey thence to the British possessions: to which is added, a review of the condition of the Canadian people. London, 1840. 2 vols.   **DLC Uk**

Review: *Athenaeum*, (June 6, 1840), 451.

272   [R., W. H.]. A picture of New York; containing a topographical description of the city and its environs, with useful information respecting its commerce, society, climate, &c., and a description of the falls of Niagara. London, 1840. 60 p.   **DLC Uk**

273   REPORT OF THE BRITISH COMMISSIONERS appointed to survey the territory in dispute, between Great Britain and the United States of America, on the North-eastern of the United States; with an appendix. London, 1840.   **UkLFO**

Report title: *North American boundary. Part I. Correspondence relating to the boundary between the British possessions in North America and the United States of America, under the treaty of 1783. Presented to both houses of Parliament by command of Her Majesty. July, 1840.* Both the report and appendix are signed by Rich. Z. Mudge and G. W. Featherstonhaugh, commissioners. See articles based on this report in *Fraser's Mag.*: "The Ashburton Treaty," XXVI (Nov. 1842), 579–594; "The Ashburton Treaty again," XXVII (Mar. 1843), 272–289; "The Northwest (American) boundary question," XXVII (Apr. 1843), 484–502.

274   ROLPH, THOMAS. The emigrant's manual: particularly addressed to the industrious classes and others who intend settling abroad; together with "The memoranda of a settler in Canada." Being an account of his first settlement; his daily occupation, the prices of labour, provisions, travelling, &c. London [1840]. 98 p.   **MH**

275   [ST. CLAIR, DAVID LATIMER]. To the followers of the "Latter Day Saints." [Chiltenham, 1840]. 4 p.   **NN**

Signed, D. L. St. Clair, Captain Royal Navy, Slaverton Court, Oct. 14th, 1840.

276   SHERIDAN, FRANCIS CYNRIC. Galveston Island; or, A few months off the coast of Texas: the journal of Francis C. Sheridan, 1839–1840, edited by Willis W. Pratt. Austin, 1954. 172 p.   **DLC Uk**

277   TAYLOR, THOMAS. An account of the complete failure of an ordained priest of the "Latter Day Saints," to establish his pretensions to the gift of tongues, which took place on Monday evening, October 12th, 1840: with an address to men of reason and religion warning them not to be deceived by the craftiness of such low imposters. Manchester, [1840?]. 13 p.   **NN**

278   TURNBULL, DAVID. Travels in the west. Cuba; with notices of Porto Rico, and the slave trade. London, 1840. 574 p.   **DLC Uk**

On U.S. relations with Cuba, pp. 435–472.

279   WILLIS, NATHANIEL PARKER. American Scenery; or, Land, lake, and river illustrations of transatlantic nature. From drawings by W[illiam] H[enry] Bartlett. London, 1840. 2 vols.   **DLC Uk**

Willis was American, but extensive illustrations by the English Bartlett.

280   WOOD, JAMES. The adventures, sufferings and observations of James Wood, containing amongst other things, a description of various places lying between the Gulfs of Darien and St. Lawrence, with an account of the manners of the inhabitants of the places described. Interspersed with remarks and cautions to those who intend to emigrate. London, 1840. 68 p.   **Uk WHi**

On the U.S., pp. 58–62, and passim.

1841

281   ADAMS, GEORGE J. A few plain facts shewing the folly, wickedness and imposition of the Rev. Timothy R. Matthews; also a short sketch of the rise, faith, and doctrine of the Church of Jesus Christ of Latter day saints. Bedford, [Eng.], 1841. 16 p.   **CtY MH NN**

282   BAILEY, JAMES NAPIER. Sketches of Indian character: being a brief survey of the principal features of character exhibited by the North American Indians; illustrating the aphorism of the socialists, that "man is the creature of circumstances." Leeds, 1841. 64 p.

    DLC

See also author's *Essays on miscellaneous subjects: historical, moral, and political*, Leeds, 1842, which includes additional comment on the North American Indian; pp. 13–20, 170–171, 180.

283   BELFAST ANTI-SLAVERY SOCIETY. To the Christian churches of the United States. The address of the Belfast anti-slavery society. Belfast, 1841. 12 p.   **NIC**

284   BRITISH AND FOREIGN ANTI-SLAVERY SOCIETY. The second annual report . . . for the abolition of slavery and the slave-trade, throughout the world, presented to the general meeting held in Exeter hall, on Friday, May 14th, 1841. William Allen, esq., in the chair. With an appendix, list of contributions, &c. &c. &c. London, 1841. 142 p.   **CSmH Uk**

    Uk has the annual reports, 1840–64, cataloged under London—Misc. Societies; OO has reports on microfilm, 1840–1908. Appendix includes: VII, "Texas"; IX, "Case of the Amistad"; X, "On the condition of the colored population of upper Canada, &c. &c."; XVIII, "United States."

285   BRITISH AND FOREIGN ANTI-SLAVERY SOCIETY. Slavery and the internal slave trade in the United States of North America; being replies to questions transmitted by the committee of the British and foreign anti-slavery society, for the abolition of slavery and the slave trade throughout the world. Presented to the general anti-slavery convention, held in London, June 1840. By the executive committee of the American anti-slavery society. London, 1841. 280 p.   **DLC Uk**

    Uk catalogs under London—Misc. Societies. See also the Society's *Anti-Slavery Reporter*, 1840–?, and their Proceedings and annual reports.

286   BUCKINGHAM, JAMES SILK. America, historical, statistic, and descriptive. London, [1841]. 3 vols.   **DLC Uk**

    Extracts appeared in the *Colonial Mag.*, V, 433; VI, 197, 316 and 473. For a condensed narrative of his visit to the U.S. (1837–1840), see "Mr. Buckingham's travels in the eastern and western world," *Colonial Mag.*, IV, 417–32. Also see author's *Autobiography . . . including his voyages, travels, adventures, speculations, successes and failures, faithfully and frankly narrated; interspersed with characteristic sketches of public men with whom he has had intercourse, during a period of more than fifty years*, London, 1855, 2 vols. For additional comment on his visits to the U.S., see Ralph E. Turner, *James Silk Buckingham, 1786–1855, a social biography*, London, 1934, esp. pp. 346–386. Edgar Allen Poe introduced Buckingham into a story, "Some words with a mummy," *Whig Rev.*, I (Apr. 1845), 363.

    Reviews: *Arcturus*, II, 169; *Athenaeum* (June 1841), 437, 456; *Colonial Mag.*, V, 326; *Eclectic Rev.*, LXXIV, 388; *Natl. Quar. Rev.*, I, 350; *Quar. Rev.*, LXVIII, (by John Gibson Lockhart) 281; *Spectator*, XV, 302; *Tait's Edinb. Mag.*, VIII, n.s. 465; *Westmin. Rev.*, XL, 21.

287   CATLIN, GEORGE, *comp.* Opinions of the English and the United States press on Catlin's North American Indian museum; exhibiting in the Egyptian Hall, Picadilly, London. London, 1841. 24 p.   **DLC Uk**

288   CLARKSON, THOMAS. A letter to the clergy of various denominations, and to the slave-holding planters, in the southern parts of the United States of America. London, 1841. 6 p.   **DLC Uk**

    See also *Two letters on slavery in the United States, addressed to Thomas Clarkson, esq., by J. H. Hammond*, Columbia [S.C.], 1845. Five more letters, dated Jan. 28–Mar. 24, 1845, by Gov. James Henry Hammond, who quotes much from Clarkson in order to refute, are reprinted in *Gov. Hammond's letters on southern slavery: addressed to Thomas Clarkson, the English abolitionist*, [Charleston, 1845].

289   COMBE, GEORGE. Notes on the United States of North America, during a phrenological visit in 1838–40. Edinburgh, 1841. 3 vols.   **DLC Uk**

Later eds. carried variant titles, e.g., *American Notes*, London, 1894. See also accounts of Combe's visit to the U.S. in Charles Gibbon, *The life of George Combe*, London, 1878, II, pp. 29–97; and in Nahum Capen, *Reminiscences of Dr. Spurzheim and George Combe . . .* New York, 1881, pp. 125–138. Combe also comments on U.S. education in his *Education, its principles and practice*, London, 1879, pp. 187–193, 518–522, 607–622, and with an account of Laura Bridgman's education, pp. 710–717.

Reviews: *Arcturus*, I, 374; *No. Am. Rev.*, LIII, 534; *Quar. Rev.* (by John Gibson Lockhart), LXVIII, 281; *Spectator*, CIV, 568; *Tait's Edinb. Mag.*, VIII, n.s., 241.

290   COX, FRANCIS AUGUSTUS, *the elder*. The scriptual duty of churches in relation to slaveholders professing Christianity. London, 1841. 24 p.   **RPB**

291   DAVIES, RICHARD. Mormonism unmasked; being a statement of facts relating to the self-styled "Latter Day Saints" and the Book of Mormon; compiled from well authenticated records. Burnley, [1841]. 24 p.   **NN**

NUC shows with 1834 pub. date, but NN later corrected to 1841.

292   DAY, WILLIAM. Slavery in America shown to be peculiarly abominable, both as a political anomaly and an outrage on Christianity. London, 1841. 84 p.   **MH NIC Uk**

293   DUDGEON, THOMAS. A nine years' residence, and a nine months' tour on foot, in the states of New York and Pennsylvania, for the use of labourers, farmers and emigrants. Edinburgh, 1841. 52 p.   **CtY MiD NN**

294   FOSTER, *SIR* AUGUSTUS JOHN. Notes on the United States. London, 1841. 57 p.   **DLC**

Caption title: "Clippings from the Quarterly's Review, vol. 68, 1841." Account of Foster's experiences as American consul, 1804–06, 1811–12. Excerpts in *Wm. & Mary Quar.*, Jan., 1951 and Apr., 1952; *Penn. Mag. Hist. & Biog.*, Oct., 1951; *Maryland Hist. Mag.*, Dec., 1952. In 1954 the Huntington Library pub. the complete text, ed. by Richard Beale Davis, *Jeffersonian America. Notes on the United States of America collected in the years 1805–6–7 and 11–12 by Sir Augustus John Foster, Bart.*

Review: *Quar. Rev.* (by Lockhart), LXVIII, 20; this review included numerous selections from Foster's unpub. notes.

295   GENERAL ANTI-SLAVERY CONVENTION, *1st, London, 1840*. Proceedings of the General Anti-Slavery Convention, called by the committee of the British and Foreign Anti-Slavery Society, and held in London, from Friday, June 12th, to Tuesday, June 23rd, 1840. London, 1841. 597 p.   **DLC Uk**

296   GLASGOW EMANCIPATION SOCIETY. Report of the discussion at the first meeting of the members of the Glasgow emancipation society; conducted, on the one side, by the Rev. Drs. Heugh & King, and Wm. P. Paton, esq.; and, on the other, by Messrs. Smeal, Wright, & Anderson. Also the discussion among the members, the speakers being the Rev. P. Brewster, Messrs. [W?] Robson, J. Anderson, and others. Monday evening, May 31, 1841. Glasgow, 1841. 26 p.   **DLC**

297   GLASGOW EMANCIPATION SOCIETY. Resolution of public meeting of the members and friends of the Glasgow emancipation society; correspondence of the secretaries; and

minutes of the committee of said society, since the arrival in Glasgow of Mr. John A. Collins, the representative of the American Anti-slavery society, in reference to the divisions among American abolitionists. Glasgow, 1841. 43 p. **OCIWHi PPL**

298 GLASGOW FEMALE ANTI-SLAVERY SOCIETY. An appeal to the ladies of Great Britain, in behalf of the American slave, by the committee of the Glasgow female anti-slavery society. With the constitution of the society. Glasgow, 1841. 16 p. **DLC**

Appendix contains a letter from George Thompson.

299 GURLEY, *REV*. RALPH RANDOLPH. Mission to England, in behalf of the American colonization society. Washington, 1841. 264 p. **DLC Uk**

Includes extensive addresses, and comment by the British Gurley meets in England, passim; much of the same material is also included in author's *Letter to the Hon. Henry Clay, President of the American colonization society, and Sir Thomas Fowell Buxton, Chairman of the general committee of the African civilization society, on the colonization and civilization of Africa. With other documents on the same subject,* London, 1841.

300 GURNEY, JOSEPH JOHN. A journey in North America, described in familiar letters to Amelia Opie. Norwich [Eng.], 1841. 414 p. **DLC Uk**

Priv. pr. See also account of this trip to U.S., 1837–40, in *Memoirs of Joseph John Gurney, with selections from his journal and correspondence,* Joseph Bevan Braithwaite, ed., Norwich, 1854, II, pp. 92–235. Also see *A letter from James Cannings Fuller, of Skaneateles, State of New York, to Joseph John Gurney; being some animadversions upon J. J. Gurney's insinuations against the American abolitionists, contained in a work entitled "Familiar letters to Amelia Opie,"* recently printed for private circulation in England, Dublin, 1843.

301 [H., C.]. Letters on emigration: containing a few remarks on the benefits likely to be derived by the adoption of a national system of emigration. London, 1841. 47 p. **ICU MH-BA NNC**

302 IKIN, ARTHUR. Texas: its history, topography, agriculture, commerce, and general statistics. To which is added a copy of the treaty of commerce entered into by the republic of Texas and Great Britain. Designed for the use of the British merchant, and as a guide to emigrants. By Arthur Ikin, Texan Consul. London, 1841. 100 p. **DLC Uk**

New ed. with an introd. by James M. Day, Waco, Tex., 1964.

303 THE IMPOSTURE UNMASKED; or, A complete exposure of the Mormon fraud; being a critical review of the Book of Mormon, and an expose of the character of Joseph Smith, Sidney Rigdon, Martin Harris, Parley Pratt, and other leading actors in the Latter-Day Saint delusion. Second edition. Isle of Man, 1841. 32 p. **CtY NN**

"Reprinted from the Mona's Herald and Central Advertiser for the British Empire, by R. Fargher." No 1st ed. located; title-page indicates that this may have been the 1st ed. in book form.

304 JOHNSTON, ROBERT, *of Dublin*. Four letters to the Reverend James Caughey, on the participation of the American Methodist Episcopal Church in the sin of American slavery. Three from Robert Johnston, and one from Richard Allen. Dublin, 1841. 28 p. **MB OCIWHi**

Johnston was a member of the Methodist Society, Dublin; Allen was secretary of the Hibernian Anti-slavery Society.

305 JUSTITIA [*Pseud.*]. Strictures on Montgomery on the cotton manufacturers of Great Britain and America. Also a practical comparison of the cost of steam and water power in America. Newburyport, 1841. 75 p. **DLC Uk**

Reply to Montgomery, 1840, above.

306 KENNEDY, WILLIAM. Texas: the rise, progress, and prospects of the republic of Texas. London, 1841. 2 vols. **DLC Uk**

Partially repr. with additions, under the title, *Texas: its geography, natural history, and topography*, New York, 1844.

Reviews: *Edinb. Rev.*, LXXIII, 241; *N.Y. Rev.*, IX, 188; *No. Brit. Rev.*, XXXIII, 419.

307 KENNEDY, WILLIAM. Texas and California. Correspondence, through the "Times" newspaper, of William Kennedy and Nicholas Carter, esquires, and Richard Hartnel, showing the danger of emigrating to Texas, and the superior advantages of the British colonies. London, 1841. 48 p. **CSmH CtY**

Kennedy was British consul at Galveston. See also his letters under Charles Elliot and William Kennedy, *British diplomatic correspondence*, 1846, below.

308 LONG, GEORGE, *ed.* The geography of America and the West Indies. London, 1841. 648 p. **DLC Uk**

From Pref.: "Written by Wilhelm Wittich, George R. Porter, George Tucker, and George Long." Uk catalogs under publisher: London—Society for the Diffusion of Useful Knowledge. London, 1845 ed. has title: *America and the West Indies geographically described*. Long was the University of Virginia's first professor of ancient languages (1825–28), and maintained contact by correspondence after his return to England. See Thomas Fitzhugh, ed., *Letters of George Long*, Charlottesville, 1917, esp. pp. 35–65, for letters written 1850–78.

309 MACGREGOR, JOHN. Commercial and financial legislation of Europe and America; with a pro-forma revision of the taxation and the customs tariff of the United Kingdom. London, 1841. 320 p. **DLC Uk**

Repr. in the author's *Commercial tariffs and regulations of the several states of Europe and America, etc.*, 13 vols., London, 1841–[1850?]; and in *The progress of America*, 1847, below.

310 MASON, A. J. Lectures on the United States. London, [1841?].

No locations found; cited in Henry T. Tuckerman, *America and her commentators*, New York, 1864, p. 219.

311 MAXWELL, *LT. COL.* ARCHIBALD MONTGOMERY. A run through the United States, during the autumn of 1840. London, 1841. 2 vols. **DLC Uk**

Reviews: *Blackwood's Edinb. Mag.*, (by Geo. Croly), L, 814; *New World*, III, 342; *Tait's Edinb. Mag.*, VIII, n.s., 782.

312 MOTT, JAMES. Three months in Great Britain. Philadelphia, 1841. 84 p. **DLC Uk**

Includes letters, addresses, etc. from Daniel O'Connell, Thomas and Mary Clarkson, William Howitt, Harriet Martineau, *et al.*

313 NEWHALL, JOHN B. Sketches of Iowa, or, The emigrant's guide; containing a correct description of the agricultural and mineral resources, geological features and statistics of the territory of Iowa, a minute description of each county, and of the principal towns and

Indian villages, prairie and timbered lands, a view of the rapid increase and future prospects of the people, moral and physical, traits of Indian character, with sketches of Black Hawk, and others: being the result of much observation and travel during a continuous residence of several years. New York, [1841]. 252 p.   **DLC Uk**

Newhall emigrated to the U.S. in 1834. See Jacob Van der Zee, *The British in Iowa*, Iowa City, 1922.

314   [PLAYFAIR, HUGO, R.N., *pseud.?*]. Brother Jonathan; or, the "Smartest nation in all creation." Sketches of American life and manners, selected from the papers of Mr. Hugo Playfair . . . Edited by Paul Paterson. London, 1840–41. 3 vols.   **CSmH**

Issued in monthly parts, with color prints by Robert Cruikshank; semi-fictitious account. DLC has the 2d ed.: *The Playfair papers; Brother Jonathan, the smartest nation in all creation*, London, 1841, 3 vols.; a later ed. carried title, *Brother Jonathan, the smartest nation in all creation*, by Hugo Playfair, London, 1844. "Hugo Playfair" would appear to be a pseudonym; Paul Paterson may have been the author.

315   SAMPSON, M[ARMADUKE] B[LAKE]. Criminal jurisprudence considered in relation to mental organization. Letters originally published in the *Spectator*. London, 1841. 29 p.   **DLC Uk**

A 2d ed., with additions, appeared under the title, *Criminal jurisprudence considered in relation to cerebral organization*, London, 1843, 147 p.; and the New York, 1846 ed. carried the title, *Rationale of crime, and its appropriate treatment; being a treatise on criminal jurisprudence considered in relation to cerebral organization . . . With notes and illustrations. By E[liza] W[oodson] Farnham, matron of Mount Pleasant state prison*. Includes a discussion of the eastern state penitentiary of Pennsylvania.

316   SCRIVENOR, HARRY. A comprehensive history of the iron trade, throughout the world, from the earliest records to the present period. With an appendix, containing official tables, and other public documents. London, 1841. 453 p.   **DLC Uk**

For comments on the U.S. see esp. chaps. 4 and 11 and the appendix. A later ed. carried title, *History of the iron trade, from the earliest records to the present period*, London, 1854.

317   STEVENSON, DAVID. On the building materials of the United States of North America. [Edinburgh, 1841]. 18 p.   **ICRL**

No t.p. Read before the Society of Arts for Scotland in session, 1841, and ordered to be printed in the society's Transactions. Repr. from the *Edinb. New Phil. J.* (July 1841).

318   STUART, *CAPT.* CHARLES. Oneida and Oberlin, or a call, addressed to British christians and philanthropists affectionately inviting their sympathies, their prayers and their assistance in favour of the christians and philanthropists of the United States of North America, for the extirpation, by our aid, of that slavery which we introduced into those states, while they were under our power. Bristol, 1841. 20 p.   **DHU OCIWHi**

See *Letters of Theodore Dwight Weld, Angelina Grimke Weld, and Sarah Grimke, 1822–1844.*, ed. by Gilbert H. Barnes and Dwight L. Dumond, 2 vols., New York [1934]; contains a great many letters from Capt. Charles Stuart.

319   STURGE, JOSEPH. To the members of the religious Society of friends in the United States of America. [New York, 1841]. 3 p.   **CLU MH PHC**

Facsimile of the original letter, dated New York, July 17, 1841. The broadsheet was repr. with an added postcript dated London, May 25, 1842, London, 1842.

320 THOMPSON, GEORGE. Christianity versus slavery; or, A report, published in the "Glasgow Argus" newspaper, November 8, 1841, of a lecture, delivered at an anti-slavery meeting in that city. Dublin, 1841. 84 p. **OCIWHi**

Lecture delivered at Relief Church in Glasgow, Nov. 1, 1841, pp. 9–43

321 THOMPSON, GEORGE. Speech on the divisions among American abolitionists, delivered at the annual meeting of the Glasgow Emancipation Society, 2d. Aug., 1841. [n.p., 1841?]. 8 p. **NIC OCIWHi**

Repr., with corrections, from the Glasgow *Argus*.

322 URQUHART, DAVID. Case of Mr. McLeod, in whose person the crown of Great Britain is arraigned for felony. London, 1841. 138 p. **CaOOA NCaS**

Uk has 2d ed., Southampton, 1841 and 4th ed., London, 1841. DLC has 3d ed., rev., Southampton, 1841. Urquhart objects to the arrest of Alexander McLeod by the New York state police. Also see the following articles on the McLeod case: Alastair Watt, "The case of Alexander McLeod," *Canadian Hist. Rev.*, XII, (June 1931), 145–167; A. B. Corey, "Public opinion and the McLeod Case," *Canadian Hist. Assn. Ann Rep.*, (1936), 53–64; and Milledge L. Bonham, Jr., "A. M.: bone of contention," *N.Y. Hist.*, XVIII, (Apr. 1937), 189–217.

323 [WELCH, ANDREW]. A narrative of the early days and remembrances of Oceola Nikkanochee, Prince of Econchatti, a young Seminole Indian; son of Econchatti-Mico, king of the Red Hills, in Florida; with a brief history of his nation, and his renowned uncle, Oceola, and his parents; and amusing tales, illustrative of Indian life in Florida. Written by his guardian. London, 1841. 228 p. **DLC Uk**

1842

324 [ABBOTT, *REV*. JOSEPH]. The emigrant to North America. Being a compendium of useful practical hints to emigrants. Selected from an unpublished narrative of the adventures of a large family from the north of England, which emigrated to America in 1818, and settled in various parts of the Canadas, and the western states, as farmers, &c. Together with an account of every day's doings upon a farm for a year. By an immigrant farmer, of twenty years experience. Montreal, 1842. 80 p. **CaNSWA CaOTP**

Portions appeared in the *Quebec Mercury*, 1841–42. MH, NIC have rev. 2d ed., Montreal, 1843, 116 p.; Uk, MnHi have 3rd ed., Edinburgh & London, 1844, 120 p. Sometimes attributed to William Kemble. Also known as *Memoranda of a settler in lower Canada*. Contains scattered comment on the U.S.; Abbott's brother settled at Carlisle, Ill. See also author's handling of the same material in fictional form in *Philip Musgrave; or, Memoirs of a Church of England missionary in the North American colonies*, London, 1846.

325 ABDY, EDWARD STRUTT. American whites and blacks, in reply to a German orthodermist. London, 1842. 50 p. **DLC**

Reply to an article by F. Murchard of Cassel in *Bulau's Annual*, May, 1840, "on American slavery viewed as a question of highest interest for humanity."

326 AIKEN, PETER FREEDLAND. A comparative view of the constitutions of Great Britain and the United States of America, in six lectures. London, 1842. 192 p. **DLC Uk**

327   ALEXANDER, GEORGE WILLIAM. Letters on the slave-trade, slavery, and emancipation; with a reply to objections made to the liberation of the slaves in the Spanish colonies; addressed to friends on the continent of Europe, during a visit to Spain and Portugal. By G. W. Alexander. London, 1842. 176 p.   **DLC Uk**

See esp. pp. 110–144, for comment on U.S.

328   [ALLARDICE, ROBERT BARCLAY]. Agricultural tour in the United States and upper Canada, with miscellaneous notices. By Captain Barclay of Ury. Edinburgh, 1842. 181 p.   **DLC Uk**

Dedication signed, R. Barclay-Allardice. Repr. in the *New World,* IV (Mar. 4, 1843), 251–265.

329   BANDINEL, JAMES. Some account of the trade in slaves from Africa as connected with Europe and America; from the introduction of the trade into modern Europe, down to the present time; especially with reference to the efforts made by the British government for its extinction. London, 1842. 323 p.   **DLC Uk**

330   BARBER, JAMES HENRY. James Henry Barber: a family memorial, edited by H. M. Doncaster. Sheffield, 1905. 2 vols.   **DLC**

Diary of travel in the U.S. in 1842: I, pp. 148–237. See also *A memoir, mainly autobiographical, edited by H. M. Doncaster*, London, 1903, pp. 33–36.

331   BRITISH AND FOREIGN ANTI-SLAVERY SOCIETY. An epitome of anti-slavery information: or, A condensed view of slavery and the slave-trade, &c. &c. London, 1842.
ICN MB Uk

332   [BROWN, GEORGE]. The fame and glory of England vindicated, being an answer to "The glory and shame of England." By Libertas. London, 1842. 306 p.   **DLC Uk**

DLC erroneously ascribes to Peter Brown. An answer to Charles Edwards Lester's *The glory and shame of England*, New York, 1841. Lester retaliated with a second book, *The condition and fate of England*, New York, 1842.

333   BUCKINGHAM, JAMES SILK. The eastern and western states of America. London [1842]. 3 vols.   **DLC Uk**

Reviews: *Athenaeum* (Dec. 31, 1842), 1134; *Colonial Mag.*, IV, 417; *Eclectic Rev.*, XIII, n.s., 377; *Monthly Rev.*, CLX, 115; *Westmin. Rev.*, XL, 20.

334   BUCKINGHAM, JAMES SILK. The slave states of America. London [1842]. 2 vols.
DLC Uk

See Ralph E. Turner, *James Silk Buckingham*, London, 1934.

Reviews: *Athenaeum* (March 26, 1842), 268; *Eclectic Rev.*, LXXV, 485; *Tait's Edinb. Mag.*, IX, n.s., 303.

335   CASWALL, HENRY. The city of the Mormons; or, Three days at Nauvoo, in 1842. London, 1842. 82 p.   **CU IU MH Uk**

DLC has 2d ed., rev. and enlarged, London, 1843, 87 p.

Reviews: *English Rev.*, XIII, 399; *Irish Eccles. J.*, II (Pt. 1), 2; *Quar. Rev.*, CXXII, 450.

336   COBDEN, RICHARD. Speech of R. Cobden, Esq., M.P., on Thursday, October 6, 1842, at a meeting of members of the Anti-Corn-Law League held in the large room, Newall's-

Buildings; showing the true causes for the passing of the American tariff, and proving that Sir R. Peel's tariff is not the cause of the present low prices of food in England. London, 1842. 12 p. **NN NNC**

337   COX, FRANCIS AUGUSTUS, *the elder*. History of the Baptist missionary society, from 1792 to 1842. . . . To which is added a sketch of the general Baptist mission. London, 1842. 2 vols. **DLC Uk**

According to Uk, the added sketch was "communicated chiefly by the Rev. J. Peggs."

338   CRAWFORD, JOHN. Employment for the million; or, Emigration & colonization on a national or extended scale, the remedy for national distress; in a letter addressed to Her Majesty's ministers. London, 1842. 12 p. **ICU MH-BA UkLU-G**

339   DICKENS, CHARLES. American notes for general circulation. London, 1842. 2 vols.
DLC Uk

Many later eds., frequently bound with *Pictures from Italy*; occasionally with *The commercial traveler* or *A child's history of England*. Both the *New World* and *Brother Jonathan* issued pirated American eds. in 1848. Subsequent later eds. with introd. and critical material include: introd. by Charles Dickens, Jr., London, 1893; introd. and notes by Andrew Lang, London, 1898; introd. by G. K. Chesterton, London, 1908; introd. by Sacheverell Sitwell, London, 1957; introd. by Christopher Lasch, Greenwich, Conn., 1961; and introd., notes and bibliog. by John S. Whitley and Arnold Goldman, Harmondsworth, 1972 (added introd. to this ed. by Angus Wilson, Avon, Conn., 1975).

See also the dramatization, *Yankee notes for English circulation*, by E. Stirling, London, n.d.; and the parody, *Current American notes, by 'Buz'*. London, n.d. Also of interest are two works that anticipated Dickens: *Pickwick in America! Detailing all the remarkable adventures of taat [sic] illustrious individual and his learned companions, in the United States, extraordinary Jonathanisms, collected by Mr. Snodgrass, and the sayings, doings, and mems, of the facetious Sam Weller, edited by "Bos"*, London, [1840?] (variously ascribed to Thomas Peckett Prest and George W. M. Reynolds); and Sir Theodore Martin's "Duggins's impressions of America," by Bon Gaultier (*pseud.*), *Tait's Edinb. Mag.*, (May 1842), 329–339. See also the retaliatory volumes: *English notes, intended for very extensive circulation*, Boston, 1842 (sometimes erroneously ascribed to Edgar Allen Poe; see critical ed. by Joseph Jackson and George H. Sargent, New York, 1920); *Change for the American notes: in letters from London to New York. By an American lady*, [i.e., Henry Wood], London, 1843; and Thomas Greaves Cary, *Letter to a lady in France, etc.*, London, 1843, q.v., below.

For accounts of Dickens' famous trip to the U.S. in 1842, see William Glyde Wilkins, *Charles Dickens in America*, London, 1911; Edward F. Payne, *Dickens days in Boston*, Boston, 1927; and H. W. L. Dana, "Longfellow and Dickens," *Cambridge Hist. Soc. Pubs.*, XXVIII (Cambridge, Mass., 1943). See also the accounts of this visit, and that of 1867–68, in the standard biography by John Forster, *The life of Charles Dickens*, London, 1872–74; in Edgar Johnson, *Charles Dickens: his tragedy and triumph*, New York, 1952; and in innumerable other volumes and unpub. dissertations on Dickens' life and work. Also see Philip Collins' chapter on Dickens in *Abroad in America: visitors to the new nation, 1776–1914*, ed. by Marc Pachter and Frances Weir, Reading, Mass., 1976, pp. 82–91; and *Dickens on America and the Americans*, ed. by Michael Slater, Austin, Tx., 1978, which includes a 65 p. critical introd., and excerpts from *American Notes* and *Martin Chuzzlewit*, as well as letters and speeches covering both visits to the U.S. Also see accounts of the visits in the Nonesuch ed. of Dickens' letters, ed. by Walter Dexter, Bloomsbury, 1938; the much more extensive Pilgrim edition, ed. by Madeline House and Graham Storey, Oxford,

1965– (esp. vol. 3, which covers 1842–43). Also see *Speeches of Charles Dickens*, Oxford, 1960, pp. 15–36 (1842 visit) and 368–383 (1867 visit).

The *American Notes* comprise the bulk of Dickens' criticisms of the U.S., but special notice should be taken of the novel, *Martin Chuzzlewit*, London, 1843, a number of chapters of which deal with Martin's adventures in America. Mention of the U.S. and Americans is also to be found in many other novels and short stories of Dickens, as well as in articles appearing in *Household Words* and *All the Year Round*, the two magazines Dickens edited. For accounts of Dickens' second visit to the U.S., in 1867–68, see George Dolby, 1885, below. Also see the following articles on Dickens' visits and his views on America and Americans: Arthur A. Adrian, "Dickens in Cleveland, Ohio," *Dickensian*, XLIV, 48–50, and "Dickens on American Slavery: a Carlylean slant," *P.M.L.A.*, LXII, 315–329; Gail Platt Altman, "Dickens' journey to Pittsburgh on the Pennsylvania Canal," *Western Penn. Hist. Mag.*, LIX, 370–373; David D. Anderson, "Charles Dickens on Lake Erie," *Inland Seas*, XVII, 25–30; Peter Bracher, "The New York *Herald* and *American Notes*," *Dickens Stud.*, V, 81–85; Philo Calhoun, "Charles Dickens in Maine," *Colby Lib. Quar.*, Ser. VI, 137–148; William J. Carlton, "Dickens's Debut in America, "*Dickensian*, LV, 55–56; Philip Collins, "Dickens in America, 1867–68, " *Dickens Stud. Newsletter*, IV, 48–50; Louie Crew, "Charles Dickens as a critic of the United States," *Midwest Quar.*, XVII, 42–50; Paul B. Davis, "Dickens and the American press, 1842," *Dickens Stud.*, IV, 32–77; Ray F. Fleming, "Charles Dickens visits the Great Lakes," *Inland Seas*, XII, 301–303; Robert Giddings, "A Cockney in the court of Uncle Sam," *Dickens Stud. Newsletter*, VI, 47–55; Mabel F. Hale, "Boz bewitched Boston," *New-Eng. Galaxy*, X, 22–30.

Also see Robert B. Heilman, "The New World in Charles Dickens's writings," *Trollopian*, I, No. 3, 25–43, no. 4, 11–26; Michael Hollington, "Dickens in Pittsburgh: a stereoscopic view," *Dickensian*, LXXIV, 33–41; Louise H. Johnson, "Source of the chapter on American slavery in Dickens's *American Notes*," *Am. Lit.*, XIV, 427–430; James Louis, "Pickwick in America!" *Dickens Stud. Ann.*, I, 65–80; Edward Payne, "Dickens in Boston," *Dickensian*, XXII, 87–91, and "Dickens's first look at America," *Dickensian*, XXXVIII, 7–13; Noel C. Peyrouton, "Re: Memoir of an *American Notes* original," *Dickens Stud.*, IV, 23–31; James D. Rust "Dickens and the Americans: an unnoticed letter," *Nineteenth Cent. Fict.*, XI, 70–72; Harry Stone, "Dickens' use of his American experiences in *Martin Chuzzlewit*," *P.M.L.A.*, LXXII, 464–478; Frederick Trautmann, "Philadelphia bowled clean over: public readings by Charles Dickens," *Penn. Mag. Hist. & Biog.*, XCVIII, 456–468; John O. Waller, "Charles Dickens and the American Civil War," *Stud. in Philology*, LVII, 535–548; and Arnold Whitridge, "Dickens and Thackeray in America," *N.Y. State Hist. Soc. Quar.*, LII, 219–237;

Reviews: *Ainsworth's Mag.*, II, 470; *Athenaeum* (1842), 899, 927; *Atlantic* (by E. P. Whipple), XXXIX, 462, and (by C. C. Felton), LVI, 216; *Atlas*, XVII, 698; *Blackwood's Edinb. Mag.* (by S. Warren), LII, 783; *Chr. Remembrancer*, IV, 679; *Dublin Mag.*, II, 317; *Dublin Rev.*, XIV, 255; *Edinb. Rev.* (by J. S. Spedding), LXXVI, 497; *Fraser's Mag.*, XXVI, 617; *Knickerbocker*, XX, 580; *Lit. Gazette*, (Oct. 22, 1842), 721; *London Univ. Mag.*, I, 378; *Method. Quar. Rev.* (by J. T. Crane), XXVIII (3d ser., VI), 508; *Mirror*, XXVIII, 284; *Monthly Rev.* CLIX, 392; *Natl. Quar. Rev.*, I, 350; *New Monthly Mag.* (by T. Hood), LXVI, 396; *No. Am. Rev.* (by C. C. Felton), LVI, 212; *New Englander* (by J. P. Thompson), I, 64; *Pioneer* (Boston) (by J. R. Lowell), I, 45; *Quar. Rev.* (by J. W. Coker), LXXI, 502, LXXIII, 129; *So. Lit. Mess.* (by E. A. Poe?), IX, 58; *Tait's Edinb. Mag.*, IX, 737; *Westmin. Rev.* (by H. London), XXXIX, 146. See Dickens' reply to Warren's review in *Blackwood's Edinb. Mag.*, London *Times*, July 16, 1843, p. 5. See also K. J. Fielding, " 'American Notes' and some English reviewers", *Mod. Lang. Rev.*, LIX, 527–537.

340   FALCONER, THOMAS. Expedition to Santa Fe. An account of its journey from Texas through Mexico, with particulars of its capture. New Orleans, 1842. 12 p.

CLSM ICN TxFTC

Repr. in: *Letters and notes on the Texan Santa Fe expedition, 1841–1842, by Thomas Falconer, with an introduction and notes by F. W. Hodge*, New York, 1930, pp. 31–64. The latter vol. also contains reprints of other Falconer commentary, including his "Diary of the Santa Fe expedition," pp. 104–120 (pub. for the first time in the 7th ed. of George Wilkins Kendall, *Narrative of the Texan Santa Fe expedition*, New York, 1856, I, pp. 437–451); his *Notes of a journey through Texas and New Mexico, in the years 1841 and 1842* (see 1844, below), pp. 65–103, an account which appeared originally in the *J. Royal Geog. Soc.*, XIII, pt. 2 (1844), 199–222; his note on the Louisiana controversy, pp. 223–266; and other unpub. material.

341   GRAHAME, JAMES. Who is to blame? or, Cursory review of "American apology for American accession to Negro slavery." London, 1842. 112 p.   **DLC Uk**

Contains a repr. of Robert Baird's *A letter to Lord Brougham, on the subject of American slavery*, London, 1835.

342   GREENLAGH, JAMES. Narrative of James Greenlagh, cotton-spinner, Egerton, Bolton-Le-Moors. Liverpool [1842]. 4 p.   **USIC**

Describes a 23-week trip in 1842, from England to the Mormon settlement in Nauvoo, Illinois. Originally pub. in a free-trade political organ, *The Struggle* (1842–46), ed. by Joseph Livesey: nos. 36 & 37, (1842).

343   HAMILTON, WILLIAM RICHARD. No mistake; or, A vindication of the negotiators of the treaty of 1783, respecting the north eastern boundary of the United States. In a conversation between John Bull and Jonathan. London, 1842. 20 p.   **DLC Uk**

344   IS THE SYSTEM OF SLAVERY sanctioned or condemned by Scripture? To which is subjoined an appendix, containing two essays upon the state . . . London, 1842. 92 p.   **OO**

OO catalog transposes date as 1824.

345   [LORING, GEORGE BAILEY]. England opposed to slavery, or some remarks upon "An examination into the real causes of the war against the United States, and an appeal to the other powers of Europe against the purposes of England." Boston, 1842. 55 p.   **MH**

346   MAILLARD, N. DORAN. The history of the republic of Texas, from the discovery of the country to the present time; and the cause of her separation from the republic of Mexico. London, 1842. 512 p.   **DLC Uk**

U.S.-born author who settled in England and became violently anti-American.

347   MORLEIGH [*pseud.*]. Life in the West: back-wood leaves and prairie flowers: rough sketches on the borders of the picturesque, the sublime, and ridiculous. Extracts from the note book of Morleigh in search of an estate. London, 1842. 363 p.   **DLC**

Last 5 chaps. repr. by the State Historical Society of Wisconsin under title: *A merry Briton in pioneer Wisconsin; a contemporary narrative reprinted from Life in the West: back-wood leaves . . . published in London in the year 1842*, ed. by Livia Appel, [Madison], 1950, 108 p.

Reviews: *Monthly Rev.*, CLIX (n.s., III), 403; *Tait's Edinb. Mag.*, IX, 754.

348   [OUSELEY, *SIR* WILLIAM GORE]. Reply to an "American's examination" of the "right
       of search": with observations on some of the questions at issue between Great Britain and
       the United States, and on certain positions assumed by the North American government.
       By an Englishman. London, 1842. 111 p.   **DLC Uk**

       An answer to *An examination of the question, now in discussion between the American and
       British governments, concerning the right of search*, by an American [Lewis Cass], Paris,
       1842.

349   PALMERSTON, HENRY JOHN TEMPLE, *3d viscount*. Lord Palmerston on the Treaty of
       Washington. [London? 1842?]. 31 p.   **DLC Uk**

       Repr. of unsigned articles that had appeared in the London *Morning Chronicle*, Sept. 19
       and Oct. 3, 1842. More denunciatory than Palmerston's parliamentary speech on the treaty,
       1843, below. Also see the following works: Anthony Evelyn Melbourne Ashley, *The life
       and correspondence of Henry John Temple*, London, 1879, I, pp. 404–409, 421–425, and
       II, pp. 404–412; Charles Francis Adams, Jr., *Life of Charles Francis Adams. By his son*,
       Boston, [1900], "A bout with the Premier," pp. 240–260, and other comment, passim;
       Herbert C. F. Bell, *Lord Palmerston*, London, 1936, esp. chaps. 11 and 31; and two books
       by Philip Guedalla, *Palmerston, 1784–1865*, New York, 1927, pp. 462–468, 473–480, and
       *Gladstone and Palmerston; being the correspondence of Lord Palmerston with Mr.
       Gladstone*, New York, 1928, pp. 60–70, 194–197, 230–235, 266–267.

350   PHILLIMORE, *SIR* ROBERT JOSEPH. The case of the Creole considered, in a second let-
       ter to the Right Hon. Lord Ashburton, &c. &c. &c. London, 1842. 51 p.   **NIC Uk**

351   PHILLIMORE, *SIR* ROBERT JOSEPH. A letter to the Right Hon. Lord Ashburton, sug-
       gested by the questions of international law, raised in the message of the American presi-
       dent. London, 1842. 83 p.   **CLU Uk**

       Appendix contains two letters and a speech by Sir Francis Bond Head on American affairs,
       pp. 51–74. See also John Stuart Mill's letter to the editor of the London *Morning Chronicle*
       (signed "A"), Oct. 4, 1842, p. 3; and the publication by the U.S. Dept. of State,
       Correspondence between Mr. Webster and Lord Ashburton, [Washington? 1842?]. For a
       good discussion of Ashburton and the treaty, see Ephraim Douglass Adams, "Lord
       Ashburton and the Treaty of Washington," *Am. Hist. Rev.*, XVII (July 1912), 764–782.

352   PROPOSED NEW PLAN of a general emigration society. By a Catholic gentleman.
       London, 1842. 32 p.   **DLC**

353   RICHARDSON, [*MAJOR*] JOHN. War of 1812. First series. Containing a full and detailed
       narrative of the operations of the right division, of the Canadian army. [Brockville], 1842.
       182 p.   **DLC**

       Pub. originally in *The New Era a Canadian Chronicle*, a short-lived weekly newspaper
       edited by Richardson; appeared between March 2 and July 15, 1842. Also see fictional
       accounts by author in *Hardscrabble; or, The fall of Chicago. A tale of Indian warfare*, New
       York, 1850; and *Wau-nan-gee; or, The Massacre at Chicago. A romance of the American
       Revolution*, New York, [1852]. See also Alexander Clark Casselman, *Richardson's War of
       1812. With notes and a life of the author*, Toronto, 1902.

       Review: *Canadian Mag.* (by J. S. Carstairs), XIX, 72.

354   ROLPH, THOMAS. Comparative advantages between the United States and Canada, for
       British settlers, considered in a letter addressed to Capt. Allardyce Barclay, of Ury.
       London, 1842. 32 p.   **CaOOA Uk**

See also article quoting Rolph and Sir Francis Bond Head, "Comparison between the United States and Canada," *Colonial Mag.*, VIII, 145–152.

Review: *Colonial Mag.*, VIII, 80.

355   SMITH, J[AMES] GRAY. A brief historical, statistical, and descriptive review of east Tennessee, United States of America: developing its immense agricultural, mining, and manufacturing advantages. With remarks to emigrants. Accompanied with a map and lithographed sketch of a Tennessee farm, mansion house, and buildings. By J. Gray Smith, a naturalized citizen of the U.S.A. London, 1842. 71 p.   **DLC Uk**

Concludes with an 11 p. quotation from J. S. Buckingham's description of east Tennessee.

356   SOME PARTICULARS of the late Boston anti-slavery bazaar: with a sketch of the anti-slavery movement in the United States. Dublin, 1842. 21 p.   **DHU MB**

Reflects the interest of the Irish in the abolition of slavery.

357   STEWART, SAMUEL. Travels and residence in the free states of America, during the years 1840–41, illustrating the circumstances, condition, and character of the people: or, The emigrant's hand-book. Belfast, 1842. 24 p.   **DLC**

358   STURGE, JOSEPH. A visit to the United States in 1841. London, 1842. 192 p.

CU MH NN Uk

DLC has Boston, 1842 ed., 235 p. For an account of Sturge's visit, see Henry Richard, *Memoirs of Joseph Sturge*, London, 1864, pp. 220–249; also contains much on Sturge's anti-slavery activity, on U.S., passim. See also Sturge's letter in the *Brit. Friend*, I (1843), 60, and his letters to Binney in *Letters of James Gillespie Binney*, New York, [1938], II, pp. 613, 615.

Reviews: *Athenaeum* (Feb. 19, 1848), 158; *Chambers's J.*, XI, 116; *Eclectic Rev.*, XI (4th ser.), 414; *Tait's Edinb. Mag.*, IX, 363.

359   TASISTRO, LOUIS FITZGERALD. Random shots and southern breezes, containing critical remarks on the southern states and southern institutions, with semi-serious observations on men and manners. New York, 1842. 2 vols.   **DLC**

See also author's *Etiquette of Washington: setting forth the rules to be observed in social intercourse*, Washington, 1866, 30 p. (held by DLC).

Tasistro, an actor, settled in the U.S., but Tuckerman lists this work as representative of British commentary at the time; see Henry T. Tuckerman, *America and her commentators*, New York, 1864, p. 219n.

360   THOMSON, WILLIAM. A tradesman's travels, in the United States and Canada, in the years 1840, 41, & 42. Edinburgh, 1842. 228 p.   **PPL**

Travelled through the South and Middle West, esp. Ohio.

Reviews: *Chambers's J.*, XI, 382; *Monthly Rev.*, CLX, 177; *Tait's Edinb. Mag.*, XII, 593.

361   WHEELER, DANIEL. Memoirs of the life and gospel labours of the late Daniel Wheeler, a minister of the society of Friends. London, 1842. 793 p.   **DLC Uk**

Ed. by Daniel Wheeler, the younger. DLC also has the 1st U.S. ed., (repr. from the London ed.), Philadelphia, [n.d.], and the abridged ed., London, 1852. The memoirs also appeared in the *Friends' Lib.*, VII, (1843), 1–341. Accounts of several visits to the U.S. are included in the memoirs, esp. his visit of 1838–39.

362   AN ADDRESS FROM THE UNDERSIGNED, Unitarian ministers of Great Britain and Ireland, to their ministerial brethren of the Unitarian churches in the United States. Bristol, Eng., 1843. 3 p.   **MB**

363   THE ASHBURTON CAPITULATION. Supplement to Mr. Featherstonhaugh's pamphlet. [London, 1843]. 28 p.   **DLC**

Caption title: "Extracts from the Morning chronicle, the Farmer's journal, the Colonial gazette, etc." See below Featherstonhaugh's *Observations upon the Treaty of Washington*, London, 1843. Also see Ephraim Douglass Adams, "Lord Ashburton and the Treaty of Washington," *Am. Hist. Rev.*, XVII (July 1912), 764–782; and Wilbur Devereux Jones, "Lord Ashburton and the Maine boundary negotiations," *Miss. Valley Hist. Rev.*, XL (Dec. 1953), 477–490.

364   BELCHER, *SIR* EDWARD. Narrative of a voyage round the world, performed in Her Majesty's ship Sulphur, during the years 1836–1842, including details of the naval operations in China, from Dec. 1840, to Nov. 1841. Published under the authority of the Lords Commissioners of the Admiralty. By Captain Sir Edward Belcher, R.N., C.B., F.R.A.S., &c. Commander of the expedition. London, 1843. 2 vols.   **DLC Uk**

In Oregon and California in 1837 and 1839, I, pp. 116–137, 288–328.

Review: *Monthly Rev.* (April 1843), 468.

365   BRITISH AND FOREIGN ANTI-SLAVERY SOCIETY. Memorial presented to the Right Hon. the Earl of Aberdeen, by the committee of the British and foreign anti-slavery society, on the 22nd of February, 1843. [London? 1843?]. 2 p.   **CSmH**

Signed by Thomas Clarkson. Followed by resolution adopted Feb. 27, 1843, and signed by George Stacey, chairman. Contains objections to certain articles of the Treaty of Washington.

366   BRITISH TEMPERANCE EMIGRATION SOCIETY AND SAVING FUND. Description of the Wisconsin territory, and some of the states and territories adjoining to it, in the western parts of the United States of America. Published by the committee of the British temperance emigration society and saving fund. Liverpool, [1843.] 20 p.   **DLC**

Cover title: *The emigrant's instructor on Wisconsin and the western states of America.* 2d, enlarged ed., Liverpool, 1844, 48 p.

367   [BROUGHAM AND VAUX, HENRY PETER BROUGHAM, *1st baron*]. Lord Brougham's speech upon the Ashburton treaty, delivered in the House of Lords on Friday, 7th April, 1843. London, 1843. 70 p.   **DLC Uk**

See answer: *Comments on Lord Brougham's attack upon General Lewis Cass. By Americanus. With introductory remarks*, Harrisburg, Pa., 1843. See also the following by Brougham: "American statesmen," in his *Contributions to the Edinburgh Review*, London, 1856, III, pp. 443–482 (a review of George Tucker's *The Life of Thomas Jefferson*, from *Edinb. Rev.*, Oct. 1837); "Foreign relations of Great Britain," ibid., II, pp. 136–141, 162–168 (a review of M. Gore's *Some remarks on the foreign relations of England at the present crisis*, from *Edinb. Rev.*, Jan. 1839); 3 speeches on "Maltreatment of the North American colonies," in *Speeches of Henry Lord Brougham, upon questions relating to pub-*

lic rights, duties, and interests; with historical introductions, and a critical dissertation upon the eloquence of the ancients, Edinburgh, 1838, IV, pp. 181–304; speeches on Negro slavery in vol. X of his *Works*, London, 1855–61 (vol. title: *Speeches on social and political subjects with historical introductions*, London, 1857); "Government of the United States," in his *Political philosophy*, Part III, London, 1849 (2d ed.), pp. 329–340, and in his *The British Constitution, its history, structure, and working*, London, 1861 (2d. ed. only), pp. 408–423. See also *Letter to Lord Brougham, on the subject of American slavery, by an American* [Robert Baird], London, 1834, 44 p.; and James William's Feb. 1861 "Letter to Lord Brougham on the John Brown Raid," *Letters on slavery from the old world*, Nashville, 1861, pp. 249–276.

368   BUCHANAN, JAMES. Addresses and testimonials to James Buchanan, esq., ex-consul of New York, upon his retirement from the consulate of that city with his respective replies. [N.p.], 1843. 8 p.   **CaOOA**

369   BUCKINGHAM, JAMES SILK. Canada, Nova Scotia, New Brunswick, and the other British provinces in North America; with a plan of national colonization. London, 1843. 540 p.   **NB Uk**

Last of author's books on America; scattered comment comparing Canada and U.S.

Review: *Monthly Rev.*, CLXI, 250.

370   BULLER, CHARLES. Systematic colonization. Speech of Charles Buller, esq., M.P., in the House of Commons, on Thursday, April 6, 1843. London, 1843. 61 p.   **ICJ NN Uk**

Comparison of conditions in the U.S. and Great Britain.

371   [BUTLER, SAMUEL, *of Australia*]. The emigrant's handbook of facts, concerning Canada, New Zealand, Australia, Cape of Good Hope, etc., with the relative advantages each of the colonies offers for emigration and practical advice to intending emigrants. Glasgow, 1843. 240 p.   **CaOTP MnHi Uk**

Written to discourage emigration to U.S.; not much direct comment, but important on attitudes toward all things American.

372   CASWALL, HENRY. The prophet of the nineteenth century; or, The rise, progress, and present state of the Mormons, or Latter-day Saints: to which is appended an Analysis of the Book of Mormon. London, 1843. 277 p.   **CSmH Uk**

Reviews: *English Rev.*, XIII, 399, *Quar. Rev.*, CXXII, 450.

373   COBDEN, RICHARD. The new emigration scheme. Speech of R. Cobden in the Theatre Royal, Drury Lane, London, March 29, 1843. [Manchester, 1843]. 8 p.   **NN**

374   DAUBENY, CHARLES GILES BRIDLE. Journal of a tour through the United States, and in Canada, made during the years 1837–38. Oxford, 1843. 231 p.   **DLC Uk**

Printed for priv. circ. The *Dictionary of National Biography* mentions Daubeny as the author of a work entitled *Notes of a tour in North America* (priv. pr., 1838), but no trace of such a volume has been found.

375   DOUGLAS, *SIR* HOWARD, *bart*. Speech following Lord Palmerston's motion on the Treaty of Washington, 21 March 1843. In Great Britain Parliament. The parliamentary debates. 3d ser., vol. 67. London, 1843.   **DLC Uk**

Hansard's parliamentary debates, pp. 1267–1285.

376 EMIGRATION. Who should go; where to go; how to get there, and what to take. London, [1843?]. 22 p. **Uk**

LU has microfilm copy from original in Uk.

377 FEATHERSTONHAUGH, GEORGE WILLIAM. Observations upon the Treaty of Washington, signed August 9, 1842; with the treaty annexed. Together with a map, to illustrate the boundary line as established by the treaty between Her Majesty's colonies of New Brunswick and Canada and the United States of America. London, 1843. 119 p. **DLC Uk**

See also *The Ashburton capitulation. Supplement to Mr. Featherstonhaugh's pamphlet*, London, 1843, above.

Review: *Quar. Rev.*, LXXI, 560.

378 GENERAL ANTI-SLAVERY CONVENTION, 2d, London, 1843. Proceedings of the general anti-slavery convention, called by the committee of the British and Foreign anti-slavery Society, and held in London, from Tuesday June 13th, to Tuesday, June 20th, 1843. By J. F. Johnson, short hand writer [ed.]. London, [1843]. 360 p. **CU MB OU Uk**

379 [GRATTAN, THOMAS COLLEY]. The boundary question revised; and Dr. Franklin's red line shown to be the right one. By a British subject. New York, 1843. 24 p.
DLC UkLU-C

Repr. in author's *Civilized America*, 1859, below, I, 410–440. Also see his article, "The Irish in America," *No. Am. Rev.*, LII, (Jan. 1841), 191–234; and "Observations of a British consul, 1839–1846," in Alan Nevins, ed., *American social history as recorded by British travellers*, New York, 1923, pp. 247–261.

380 JOHNES, ARTHUR JAMES. Philological proofs of the original unity and recent origin of the human race. Derived from a comparison of the languages of Asia, Europe, Africa, and America. Being an inquiry how far the differences in the languages of the globe are referrible [sic] to causes now in operation. London, 1843. 103 p. **DLC Uk**

381 JONES, GEORGE, *M.R.S.* The history of ancient America, anterior to the time of Columbus; proving the identity of the aborigines with the Tyrians and Israelites; and the introduction of Christianity into the western hemisphere by the apostle St. Thomas. London, 1843. 461 p. **DLC Uk**

Despite table of contents, apparently only 1 vol. pub.

382 LEECH, SAMUEL. Thirty years from home, or A voice from the main deck: being the experience of Samuel Leech, who was for six years in the British and American navies: was captured in the British frigate Macedonian: afterwards entered the American navy, and was taken in the United States brig Syren, by the British ship Medway. Boston, 1843. 305 p. **DLC Uk**

Went into innumerable eds.; CsmH has copy of the 16th ed. with title, *A voice from the main deck: being a record of the thirty years adventures of Samuel Leech. With an introduction*, ed. by R. H. Dana, Boston, 1857. Repr. in *Mag. of Hist. with Notes & Queries*, III, Extra no. 9 (1909). Chiefly about the War of 1812, but account comes down to 1841 and includes a trip to England during which conditions in England and the U.S. are contrasted.

Review: *Fisher's Colonial Mag.*, I, n.s. (1844), 115.

383   [MOGRIDGE, GEORGE]. The Indians of North America. London [1843?]. 296 p.

NN Uk

Pub. by the Religious Tract Society; a fictionized account in dialogue, for children. Repr. without credit to the author, under the title *The book of the Indians of North America: illustrating their manners, customs, and present state. Edited by John Frost*, New York, 1845. 283 p.

384   MORMONISM; OR, SOME OF THE FALSE DOCTRINES and lying abominations of the so-called Latter-Day Saints confuted by the Bible. Ormskirk, [1843?]. 4 p.   **Uk**

385   O'CONNELL, DANIEL. Liberty or slavery? Daniel O'Connell on American slavery. Reply to O'Connell by Hon. S[almon] P. Chase. [Cincinnati? 1843?]. 15 p.

MB MH UkLSE

NUC entry for this ed. dated 1842, but the exchange of letters are dated Dublin, Oct. 11, 1843 and Cincinnati, Nov. 30, 1843. DLC and Uk hold reprint. [Cincinnati? 1864].

386   O'CONNELL, DANIEL. Speeches of Daniel O'Connell and Thomas Steele, on the subject of American slavery, delivered before the Loyal national repeal association of Ireland, in reply to certain letters received from repeal associations in the United States. Philadelphia, 1843. 8 p.   **ICN OO PHC**

Also repr. the letters, appearing originally in the Dublin *Freeman's Journal*, Aug. 23, 1843, and the Dublin *Evening Post*, Aug. 29, 1843.

387   OLIVER, WILLIAM. Eight months in Illinois; with information to emigrants. Newcastle-upon-Tyne, 1843. 141 p.   **DLC**

Repr., with index, Chicago, 1924, 260 p.

388   PALMERSTON, HENRY JOHN TEMPLE, *3d viscount*. Speech of Viscount Palmerston, in the House of Commons, on Tuesday the 21st of March, 1843, on the Treaty of Washington, of the 9th of August, 1842. London, 1843. 95 p.   **DLC Uk**

See also Palmerston's "Reply to inquiry as to American ship 'Caroline' by Sir Robert Inglis," delivered Feb. 2, 1858; in *Hansard's*, 3d ser., vol. 40, p. 715.

389   PROSPECTUS FOR A LOAN of £80,000, secured by a pledge of real estate in America. London, 1843. 32 p.   **PPL**

Description, based mainly on U. S. sources, of coal lands in Maryland and Virginia.

390   [SMITH, JAMES GRAY]. Description of improved farms in the state of Tennessee, in the United States of America, describing the number of acres of arable, meadow, pasture, orchard, and wood land, the mansion and dwelling-houses, farm-buildings, mills, and water-power; with the manufacturing and other advantages of each locality. London [1843]. 58 p.   **NN**

Smith was a naturalized U. S. citizen.

391   SMITH, *REV*. SYDNEY. Letters on American debts. London, 1843. 24 p.   **DLC**

Uk has 2d ed., London, 1844. Originally in the London *Morning Chronicle*, Nov., 1843. See also Smith's caustic "Humble petition to the house of congress at Washington" in the London *Times*, May 19, 1843, and the American answer in the pamphlet, *The Americans defended, by an American*, London, 1844.

392   [STUART, GEORGE OKILL]. Mertoriana; or, A series of communications published in the Kingston Herald between the years 1839 and 1844 [sic], on the subject of the statute law of the provinces, or law of the land, establishing the true boundaries and lines of survey on a permanent basis, and thereby securing the rights of land in the original patents, to the loyalists and their heirs. Kingston, 1843. 62 p.   **CaOTP MH**

393   [TAYLOR, JOHN]. The monetary policy of England and America. London, 1843. 44 p.
CSmH ICJ NjP NN

394   TEXAS EMIGRATION AND LAND COMPANY. Emigration to Texas. Texas:-being a prospectus of the advantages offered to emigrants by the Texan emigration and land company. London [1843]. 24 p.   **DLC Uk**

1844

395   BAYLEY, GEORGE. Tables shewing the progress of the shipping interest of the British Empire, United States, and France, compiled from parliamentary papers and other sources. London, 1844. 78 p.   **MBAt Uk**

Tables only, except for 1 p. introd. Tables referring to U.S. shipping and trade, pp. 72–75.

396   BOLLAERT, WILLIAM. William Bollaert's Texas, edited by W. Eugene Hollon and Ruth Lapham Butler, with an introduction by Stanley Pargellis. Norman, Okla., 1956. 423 p.
DLC Uk

Consists of six diaries and notebooks and two vols. of journals, from Dec., 1841 to April 11, 1844; Bollaert was in U.S. 1842–44. See also the following articles by Bollaert: "Notes on the coast region of the Texas territory; taken during a visit in 1842," *J. Royal Geog. Soc.*, XIII (1843), 226–244; "Observations on the geography of Texas," ibid, XX, pt. 1 (1850), 113–135; "Observations on the natural history of Texas," *Sporting Rev.*, XXVI (Oct. & Nov. 1851), 166–176, 268–277; "Observations on the Indian tribes of Texas," *J. Ethnol. Soc., London*, II (1850), 262–283; "On the botany of Texas," *Trans. Linnean Soc.*, II (1855), 97–98; "History of Texas. By a traveller," *United Service Mag.*, (1847), 70–80, 516–527; "Arrival in Texas in 1842, and cruise of the Lafitte. By a traveller," ibid, (1846) Pt. III, 341–355; "Hunting in Western Texas, and visit to San Antonio de Bejar, in 1843," *Sporting Rev.*, XX (Dec. 1848), 431–443. Also see Bollaert's contributions in *Memoirs read before the Anthropological society of London*, I (1863–64), "Observations on the past and present populations of the new world," 72–119; "Some account of the astronomy of the red man of the new world," 210–280; II, "Contributions to an introduction to the anthropology of the new world," 92–152; "Introduction to the palaeography of America," 169–194.

397   [BROWN, JAMES BRYCE]. Views of Canada and the colonists: embracing the experience of a residence; views of the present state, progress and prospects of the colony; with detailed and practical information for intending emigrants. By a four years' resident. Edinburgh, 1844. 266 p.   **DLC Uk**

DLC and Uk also have enlarged and improved ed., Edinburgh, 1851, no longer anonymous; also included is chap. on the U.S. not found in the 1844 ed., pp. 441–449. Other comment on U.S., passim.

398   CAMPBELL, JOHN. Memoirs of David Nasmith: his labours and travels in Great Britain, France, the United States, and Canada. By John Campbell, D.D., author of the "Martyr of Erromanga," "Jethro," "Maritime Discovery," etc. London, 1844. 476 p.   **DLC Uk**

Visit to U.S., Sept. 1830 to Dec. 1831, pp. 206–272.

399   CANADA: REMARKS ON THE COMPARATIVE advantages to settlers in Upper Canada or the United States in obtaining the aid of capital for individual enterprize or local improvements; and on the means of equalizing those advantages. London, 1844.   **UkRCS**

400   CLARKSON, THOMAS. A letter to such professing Christians in the Northern states of America, as have had no practical concern with slave holding, and have never sanctioned it by defending it; and to such, also, as have never visited the Southern states. London, 1844. 24 p.   **Uk**

See answer by James Henry Hammond, *Two letters on slavery in the United States, addressed to Thomas Clarkson, esq. By J. H. Hammond. Late governor of South Carolina. From the South Carolinian*, [Columbia, S.C.], 1845. See also Henry C. Wright, *American slavery proved to be theft and robbery; with a letter to Dr. [William] Cunningham containing the doctor's apologies for slavery . . . and also the opinions of T. Clarkson and Dr. A. Thomson*, 1845, below.

401   CLARKSON, THOMAS. On the ill treatment of the people of colour in the United States, on account of the colour of their skin. A letter to a friend, by Thomas Clarkson. Intended to be printed and circulated in America. [N.p., 1844]. 8 p.   **CSmH GU IHi MH**

No t.p.; above title at top of 1st page; at end, Thomas Clarkson, Playford Hall, England, Feb. 14, 1844. MB has tract no. 10 of the New England Anti-slavery Tract Assn.: *Letter to a friend on the ill-treatment of the people of color in the United States, on account of the color of their skin. By Thomas Clarkson of England. Playford Hall, Suffolk, February 15, 1844*, no t.p. [Boston, n.d.], 8 p. See also *Gerrit Smith and Thomas Clarkson. Published by Jackson & Chaplin. To the public*, [N.p., n.d.], which includes the above pamphlet in full and a letter from Smith to Clarkson, May 4, 1844, and a letter by Clarkson to Smith, Feb. 20, 1844. For incidental comment see the following: Thomas Taylor, *A biographical sketch of Thomas Clarkson*, London, 1847; James Elmes, *Thomas Clarkson: a monograph*, London, 1854.

402   [CLARKSON, THOMAS]. To the Christian and well-disposed citizen of the Northern states of America. [London? 1844?].   **CSmH**

A broadside. Signed at end, Aug. 30, 1844.

403   COLLYER, ROBERT HANHAM, *M.D.* Lights and shadows of American life. Boston, [1844?]. 40 p.   **MH Uk**

Sometimes erroneously listed as pub. in 1836 because it describes a visit made in that year, this book is referred to as a "forthcoming" volume in the review in *Brother Jonathan*, Dec. 23, 1843; also, the mention of works of James Silk Buckingham on America would place the book later than 1836.

404   COWELL, JOSEPH. Thirty years passed among the players in England and America: interspersed with anecdotes and reminiscences of a variety of persons, directly or indirectly connected with the drama during the theatrical life of Joe Cowell, comedian. Written by himself. New York, 1844. 2 pts. 103 p.   **DLC Uk**

Tours in the U.S., Part II, pp. 55–103, passim.

405　DUNN, JOHN. History of the Oregon territory and British North American fur trade; with an account of the habits and customs of the principal native tribes on the northern continent. By John Dunn, late of the Hudson's Bay Company; eight years a resident in the country. London, 1844. 359 p.　**DLC Uk**

Repr. in *Smith's Weekly Vol.* for June 11, 18, and 25, 1845.

Reviews: *Edinb. Rev.*, (by N. W. Senior), LXXXII, 238; *Foreign Quar. Rev.*, XXXV (by T. Falconer?), 489; *Spectator*, XVII, 639; *Topic*, Apr. 18, 1846, repr. *Oregon Hist. Quar.*, XXXVI (Sept. 1935), 265–294.

406　FALCONER, THOMAS. Notes of a journey through Texas and New Mexico, in the years 1841 and 1842. [London, 1844?]. 28 p.　**CtY Uk**

Appeared originally in *J. Royal Geog. Soc.*, XIII, 199–224. CSmH has repr. with original *Journal* pagination, incorrectly dated [1842?]. Repr. in *Letters and notes on the Texan Santa Fe expedition, 1841–1842* (see 1842 entry, note, above).

407　FALCONER, THOMAS. On the discovery of the Mississippi, and on the south-western, Oregon, and north-western boundary of the United States. With a translation from the original manuscript of memoirs, etc. relating to the discovery of the Mississippi, by Robert Cavelier de La Salle and the Chevalier Henry de Tonty. London, 1844. 99 p.　**DLC Uk**

Mainly translation of French documents, but includes comment on current boundary dispute.

Reviews: *Edinb. Rev.* (by N. W. Senior), LXXXII, 238; *Portfolio*, V, 123.

408　FEATHERSTONHAUGH, GEORGE WILLIAM. Excursion through the slave states, from Washington on the Potomac, to the frontier of Mexico; with sketches of popular manners and geological notices. London, 1844. 2 vols.　**DLC Uk**

Philadelphia, 1844 ed., 168 p., apparently abridged.

Reviews: *Athenaeum* (June 8, 1844), 518: *Foreign Quar. Rev.*, (by John Forster?), XXXIV, 104.

409　FRIENDS, SOCIETY OF. *LONDON YEARLY MEETING. Meetings for sufferings. Aborigines' committee.* Some of the account of the conduct of the Religious Society of Friends towards the Indian tribes in the settlement of the colonies of East and West Jersey and Pennsylvania: with a brief narrative of their labours for the civilization and Christian instruction of the Indians, from the time of their settlement in America, to the year 1843. London, 1844. 247 p.　**DLC**

410　GODLEY, JOHN ROBERT. Letters from America. London, 1844. 2 vols.　**DLC Uk**

Also see his *An answer to the question What is to be done with the unemployed labourers of the United Kingdom?* London, 1847, which contains comments on the U.S. See also C[harles] E[dmund] Carrington, *John Robert Godley of Canterbury*, London, 1950, pp. 1–2, 16–23.

Reviews: *Dublin Univ. Mag.*, XXIX, 224; *Eclectic Rev.*, LXXIX, 698; *Monthly Rev.*, CLXIV, 93; *Spectator*, XVII, 255; *Tait's Edinb. Mag.*, XI, 317, 435.

411　GOURLAY, ROBERT FLEMING. Plans for beautifying New York, and for enlarging and improving the city of Boston. Being, studies to illustrate the science of city building. Boston, 1844. 42 p.　**DLC Uk**

412   HINDS, RICHARD BRINSLEY, *ed.* The botany of the voyage of H. M. S. Sulphur, under the command of Captain Sir Edward Belcher . . . during the years 1836–42. Published under the authority of the lords commissioners of the Admiralty. Edited and superintended by Richard Brinsley Hinds, esq., surgeon, R.N., attached to the expedition. The botanical descriptions by George Bentham, esq. London, 1844. 2 vols.   **CCC MH TxU Uk**

     NUC entries under Bentham. Section on "California" deals mostly with lower Calif., but also includes San Diego.

413   HINDS, RICHARD BRINSLEY, *ed.* The zoology of the voyage of H. M. S. Sulphur, under the command of Captain Sir Edward Belcher . . . during the years 1836–42. Published under the authority of the lords commissioners of the Admiralty. Ed. and superintended by Richard Brinsley Hinds, esq., surgeon . . . London, 1844. 2 vols.   **DLC Uk**

     Vol. I: Mammalia, by J. E. Gray . . . Birds, by J. Gould . . . Fish, by J. Richardson . . . Vol. II: Mollusca, by R. B. Hinds. Issued in 10 parts, 1843–45. The expedition covered the Pacific Coast and inland on the Sacramento River in Calif.

414   HISTORY OF THE MORMONS, or Latter-Day Saints, with an account of their persecutions in Missouri and Illinois. From an authentic source. Whitehaven [Eng], 1844. 8 p.   **CtY**

415   HOUSTOUN, *MRS.* MATILDA CHARLOTTE (JESSE) FRASER. Texas and the Gulf of Mexico; or, Yachting in the new world. By Mrs. Houstoun. London, 1844. 2 vols.   **DLC Uk**

     Also ran in *Smith's Weekly Volume*, Vol. I (Feb. 12, 19, and 26, 1845), 99–112, 115–128, 131–140. Facsimile repr. of Philadelphia 1845 ed., with an introd. by Dorman H. Winfrey, Austin, Tx., 1968.

     Review: *Quar. Rev.*, LXXXVI, 98.

416   JAMIESON, ANNIE STRAITH. William King, friend and champion of slaves. Toronto, [1925]. 209 p.   **DLC**

     Semi-fictionalized but based on King's autobiography, still in manuscript. King was the original for Edward Clayton in Mrs. Stowe's *Dred, a tale of the dismal swamps*, Boston, 1856; he was in the U.S. from 1833–1844, and from 1846–1895 in Canada. During the latter period he frequently visited the U.S. in underground work. See two articles by William H. and Jane H. Pease: "Opposition to the founding of the the Elgin Settlements," *Canadian Hist. Rev.*, XXXVIII (Sept. 1957), 202–218; and "Uncle Tom and Clayton: fact, fiction and mystery," *Ontario Hist.*, L (Spring 1958), 61–73.

417   JOURNAL OF A WANDERER: being a residence in India, and six weeks in North America. London, 1844. 250 p.   **DLC**

     On U.S. visit, pp. 115–250.

418   LETTERS FROM THE UNITED STATES of America, exhibiting the workings of democracy in that country for the last twenty years, both politically and morally. By an Anglo-American, of several years' residence. London, 1844. 58 p.   **DLC**

419   [LOWER, RICHARD]. Jan Cladpole's trip to 'Merricur; giving an account of the white, black, and yellow folks wot he met wud in his travels in search for dollar trees; and how he got rich enough to beg his way home; written all in rhyme by his father, Tim Cladpole (pseud.). Hailsham [Eng.], [1844]. 32 p.   **CLU ICN Uk**

     Uk lists under Tim Cladpole. Author's name sometimes given as "Tower." Written in Sussex doggerel; intended to discourage those who were thinking of emigrating to the U.S.

420 [LUMSDEN, JAMES]. American memoranda, by a mercantile man, during a short tour in the summer of 1843. Glasgow, 1844. 60 p. **DLC Uk**

Priv. pr.; pref. signed J. L.

421 MURRAY, HUGH. The United States of America; their history from the earliest period; their industry, commerce, banking transactions, and national works; their institutions and character, political, social, and literary; with a survey of the territory, and remarks on the prospects and plans of emigrants. By Hugh Murray, F.R.S.E. With illustrations of the natural history, by James Nicol. Portraits and other engravings by Jackson. Edinburgh, 1844. 3 vols. **DLC Uk**

Later ed. appeared under title, *Pictorial history of the United States of America, from the earliest period to the close of President Taylor's administration . . . with additions and corrections by Henry C. Watson*, Boston, 1851.

Review: *No. Brit. Rev.*, (by William Cunningham), II, 136; this long review was repr. in *Littel's Living Age*, III, 387, and *Eclectic Mag.*, IV, 1.

422 [PAYNE, G. P.] Uncle Sam's peculiarities. By Uncle Sam. London, [1844]. 2 vols. **CtY DeU OU PGC**

Repr. of a very popular series of sketches that ran serially in *Bentley's Misc.*, 1838–40. Payne wrote a series of sketches under the same pseudonym for *Ainsworth's Mag.* (1842–43), including: "Series of sketches on things American by 'Uncle Sam', the author of 'Uncle Sam and his peculiarities'," I, 26–29 (interview with editor); "An aristocratic dinner party in New York," II, 14–20; "Grocery orders and 'Taking the benefit'," II, 148–151; "An American caucus," II, 553–556; "Whitehall and the battery," III, 162–167; "The loquacious Kentuckian," IV, 237–243.

423 SAMPSON, MARMADUKE BLAKE. Slavery in the United States. A letter to the Hon. Daniel Webster. New York, 1844. 87 p. **DLC**

424 A SHORT HISTORY AND DESCRIPTION of the Ojibbeway Indians now on a visit to England. With correct likenesses, engraved from daguerreotype plates, taken by M. Claudet. London, 1844. 30 p. **DLC**

Contains a letter from Charles Stuart describing rescue in Ohio of a fugitive slave by Arthur Rankin, who accompanied the Indians to England, pp. 21–30. Stuart also comments on American slavery.

425 SLIGHT, BENJAMIN. Indian researches; or, Facts concerning the North American Indians; including notices of their present state of improvement, in their social, civil, and religious condition; with hints for their future advancement. Montreal, 1844. 79 p. **DLC Uk**

426 SOME THOUGHTS ON THE INFLUENCE which the misgovernment of Ireland, and the political agitation produced by that misrule, are likely to exert on the political relations of the great powers of Europe, with each other and with the United States of America. Conveyed in the form of a letter, addressed, without permission, to the Earl of Shrewsbury and Waterford. By an Anglo-Irishman. London, 1844. **PPL**

427 THOM, ADAM. The claims to the Oregon territory considered. London, 1844. 44 p. **DLC Uk**

An answer to the U.S. claims as presented by Robert Greenhow. For further debate on Oregon between Greenhow and Thomas Falconer, see entries for Falconer, 1845, below.

428   URQUHART, DAVID. Annexation of the Texas, a case of war between England and the United States. London, 1844. 104 p.   **DLC Uk**

Appeared originally in *Portfolio*, III (1844), 435–510. Also pub. in author's *Reflections on thoughts and things, moral, religious, and political*, London, 1844, pp. 119–220.

429   URQUHART, DAVID. England in the western hemisphere: the United States and Canada. [From the Portfolio of March 1st, 1844].   **NN Uk**

London, 1844. 74 p.

430   WILBERFORCE, SAMUEL. A history of the Protestant Episcopal church in America. London, 1844. 456 p.   **DLC Uk**

Vol. 27 in the Englishman's Library; U.S. ed., New York, 1849; an extract pub. under title, *A reproof of the American church*, New York, 1846, and repr. in London, 1853. See also Wilberforce's "Letter to William Lloyd Garrison," in *Facts and opinions touching the real origin, character, and influence of the American colonization society: views of Wilberforce, Clarkson, and others, and opinions of the free people of color in the United States*, by G. B. Stebbins, Boston, 1853, pp. 215–224. See also Phillip Berry, *A review of the Bishop of Oxford's counsel to the American clergy, with reference to the institution of slavery. Also supplemental remarks on the relation of the Wilmot proviso to the interests of the colored class*, Washington, 1848. See also appendix to *American anti-slavery conventions: a series of extracts illustrative of the proceedings and principles of the "Liberty Party" in the United States; with the bearings of the anti-slavery cause or mission*, [John Dunlop, ed.], Edinburgh, 1846, which quotes at length from Wilberforce.

1845

431   AITKEN, W. A journey up the Mississippi River, from its mouth to Nauvoo, the city of the Latter-day saints. Ashton-under-Lyne [1845]. 56 p.   **IHi**

CtY has 2d ed., 58 p. Pref. dated Feb. 8, 1845.

432   AMERICA AND HER SLAVE-SYSTEM. London, 1845. 60 p.   **CtY Uk**

Review: *Westmin. Rev.*, XLV, 259.

433   B_____, *Lord*. A moral picture of Philadelphia. The virtues and frauds and follies of the city delineated. By Lord B _____, formerly of England, now a naturalized citizen and resident of Philadelphia. Philadelphia, 1845. 24 p.   **DLC**

434   BRITISH AND FOREIGN ANTI-SLAVERY SOCIETY. On the duty of promoting the immediate and complete abolition of slavery. London, 1845.

No locations found.

435   [CLARKSON, THOMAS]. Reply to the assertions of the clergy of the southern states of America, "that Abraham was the founder of slavery." [n.p., 1845?]

No locations found for published version. CSmH has galley proof sheets. Signed at end: Thomas Clarkson, Playford Hall, near Ipswich, March 26, 1845. Mostly on the Bible and slavery, but with a number of references to slavery in the U.S.

436   COMBE, GEORGE. Notes on the new reformation in Germany, and on national education, and the common schools of Massachusetts. Edinburgh, 1845. 37 p.   **MH NN Uk**

Repr. from the *Scotsman*. See also Combe's "Education in America: state of Massachusetts," *Edinb. Rev.*, LXXIII (July, 1841), 487–502.

437   COMPARATIVE CHRONOLOGICAL STATEMENT of the events connected with the rights of Great Britain and the claims of the United States to the Oregon territory. [London, 1845?]. 15 p.   **DLC**

Pol. Pamphlets, vol. 82, no.3.

438   DELIVERANCE OF THE REFORMED PRESBYTERY of Edinburgh on American slavery and church-fellowship with slave-holders. [Edinburgh? 1845?]. 4 p.   **NHi NNC**

Pamphlet signed: Joseph Wilson, Moderator; Wm. Anderson, Clerk.

439   ENGLAND AND AMERICA CONTRASTED, or, The evils of taxation; in which the superiority of America, as regards climate, produce, commercial facilities, &c. &c., is clearly demonstrated. By a cotton manufacturer. London, 1845. 38 p.   **DLC**

440   FALCONER, THOMAS. The Oregon question: or, A statement of the British claims to the Oregon territory, in opposition to the pretensions of the government of the United States of America. London, 1845. 46 p.   **DLC UK**

Started a pamphlet war with Robert Greenhow. See Greenhow's *An answer to the strictures of Mr. Thomas Falconer of Lincoln's Inn on the history of Oregon and California*, London, 1845; also Falconer's two 1845 "postscripts", pub. in pamphlet form, listed below. Also see "The Oregon question," *Knight's Penny Mag.*, XVI (3d ser., II), (1846), 139–144: an unsigned article by Falconer.

Reviews: *Am. Rev.*, III, 113; *Edinb. Rev.* (by Nassau Wm. Senior; repr. in his *Historical and Philosophical Essays*, London, 1865, II, pp. 1–44), LXXXII, 238; *Quar. Rev.* (by J.W. Croker), LXXVII, 563; *Westmin. Rev.*, XLV, 219; *Foreign Quar. Rev.*, XXXV, 489. (Also see the spirited reply to the reviews, "The Edinburgh and Foreign Quarterly on the Oregon," *U.S. Mag. and Democratic Rev.* (by D.D.F.), XVII (Nov. 1845), 323–331.)

441   FALCONER, THOMAS. Postscript to the second edition of a pamphlet entitled The Oregon Question &c. London, 1845. 4 p.   **CaOTP**

DLC and UK have repr. in *Mr. Falconer's reply to Mr. Greenhow's answer: with Mr. Greenhow's rejoinder*, [Washington?, 1845]; Greenshaw's rejoinder appeared in the Washington *Union*, June 24, 1845.

442   FALCONER, THOMAS. Second postscript to a pamphlet entitled "The Oregon question," by Thomas Falconer, esq., in reply to the "Rejoinder" of Mr. Greenhow, and to some observations in the 'Edinburgh Review, Aug. 7, 1845.' London, 1845. 12 p.   **CSmH NN Uk**

443   GLASGOW EMANCIPATION SOCIETY. The American board of commissioners for foreign missions, and the Rev. Dr. [Thomas] Chalmers, on Christian fellowship with slave-holders: an address, by the Glasgow emancipation society, to Christians of all denominations, but especially to members of the Free church of Scotland. Glasgow, 1845. 11 p.

DLC

Address is signed by John Murray and William Smeal, secretaries.

444 GOODMAN, W.F. Seven years in America; or, A contrast of British America, namely, Canada, New Brunswick, Prince Edward Island, Nova Scotia, Cape Breton, and Newfoundland, with the United States and Texas, shewing the superiority of the former over the latter, for the British emigrant. London, 1845. 32 p. **DLC Uk**

DLC lists under Goodmane.

445 GOUGH, JOHN BARTHOLOMEW. Autobiography. Boston, 1845. 172 p. **DLC**

Uk has London, 1855 ed. A tremendously popular work that went into many thousands of printings. Later eds. were extended and brought up to date, e.g., *Autobiography and personal recollections of John B. Gough, with twenty-six years' experience as a public speaker*, Springfield, Mass., 1869. Gough came as a boy to the U.S. in 1831; he later settled and returned to England only for lecture tours. However, he was generally thought of as English and is listed in the *Dictionary of National Biography*. The *Autobiography* gives an account of the U.S. at the time of his arrival; his other works, such as *Platform echoes* and *Sunlight and shadow* are not listed here because they include only accounts of his travels after many years in the U.S. For other comment on Gough's life in America see Carlos Martyn's *John B. Gough: the apostle of cold water*, New York, 1893, and Rev. William Reid's *Sketch of the life and oratory of John B. Gough*, Glasgow, 1854.

446 GREVILLE, ROBERT KAYE. Slavery and the slave trade in the United States of America; and the extent to which the American churches are involved in their support. Drawn up at the request of the committee of the Edinburgh emancipation society. Edinburgh, 1845. 24 p. **DLC**

447 JARVIS, PETER ROBINSON. Memoirs of P.R. Jarvis. [Ottawa, n.d.]. 133 p. **CaOOA MH TxU**

Trip to New Orleans and Boston, 1844–45, pp. 22–61. Pub. after 1900.

448 LEWIS, *REV.* G[EORGE]. Impressions of America and the American churches: from journal of the Rev. G. Lewis, one of the deputation of the Free church of Scotland to the United States. Edinburgh, 1845. 432 p. **DLC UK**

Excerpts under title, *Slavery and slaveholders in the United States of America*, Edinburgh, 1846.

Review: Edinburgh *Advertiser* (by J.M. Buffum), May 8, 1846.

449 LYELL, *SIR* CHARLES. Travels in North America, with geological observations on the United States, Canada, and Nova Scotia. London, 1845. 2 vols. **DLC Uk**

New York ed., 1845, carried title: *Travels in North America in the years 1841–2; with geological observations*, etc., 2 vols. in 1; many later eds., with variant titles. See account of his U.S. experiences in: *Life, letters and journals of Sir Charles Lyell, bart . . .* Ed. by his sister-in-law, Mrs. Lyell, London, 1881, II, 53–104, 176–190, and passim.; also pp. 392–400, containing his answer to Thomas S. Spedding in a letter dated March 12, 1865. See also Lyell's "A memoir on the recession of the Falls of Niagara," *Proc. Geol. Soc. London*, III (1842), 595–602; and "Summary of Mr. Lyell's memoir on the Falls," IV, 19–22.

Reviews: *Eclectic Rev.*, LXXXII, 464; *Edinb. Rev.*, LXXXIII, 129; *English Rev.*, IV, 72; *No. Am. Rev.* (by A. Gray), LXI, 498; *No. Brit. Rev.*, (by David Brewster), XIV, 541; *Tait's Edinb. Mag.*, XII, n.s., 599; *U.S. Mag. & Democratic Rev.*, XVII, 199.

450 MACLEOD, ALEXANDER. To the Honorable Sir Allan Napier MacNab, Knight, Speaker of the Legislative Assembly of Canada. [N.p., 1845]. 22 p. **CaOTP Uk**

No t.p. Letter is signed, Alexander McLeod, Niagara, 4th January, 1845. Claims compensation for imprisonment by U.S.

451   MERRITT, WILLIAM HAMILTON. A brief review of the revenue, resources, and expenditures of Canada compared with those of the neighboring state of New-York: with an examination into the causes which have produced the present extravagant system, and suggesting a remedy. Designed to relieve the inhabitants of this province wholly from direct taxation, and afford a large annual surplus for the improvement of the country. St. Catharines, 1845. 22 p.   **CaOTP MH**

452   MOORE, GEORGE. Journal of a voyage across the Atlantic: with notes on Canada & the United States; and return to Great Britain, in 1844. London, 1845. 96 p.   **DLC Uk**

Includes comment on business methods in the U.S.

453   PEASE, JOHN. Address of John Pease to friends in America. New York, 1845. 16 p.
                                                                                    DLC

Uk has above title followed by "From the New York edition, with corrections, York, 1845", 16 pp. Sermon in letter form is dated at end "Boston, seventh-month 1st, 1845."

454   [PHILLIPS, GEORGE SPENCER (JOHN DIX, *pseud.*)]. Local loiterings, and visits in the vicinity of Boston. By a looker-on. Boston, 1845. 147 p.   **DLC**

Uk has Boston, 1846 ed. *Dictionary of National Biography* lists Dix as author of this and other books on America, q.v. Author came to the U.S. in 1845 and remained; he used various pseudonyms, e.g., "John Ross," "John Ross Dix," etc. Authorship of all items ascribed to John Dix has been attributed to George Spencer Phillips, although the *DNB* article would seem to refute this. Another ed. of the above item carried title, *Loiterings in America, by the author of "Pen and ink sketches,"* London, 1850. See also author's *Amusing and thrilling adventures of a California artist, while daguerreotyping a continent, amid burning deserts, savages, and perpetual snows. And a poetical companion to the Pantoscope of California, Nebraska & Kansas, Salt Lake & the Mormons. From 1500 daguerreotypes. By J. Wesley Jones, esq., detailing the startling adventures of an overland journey of 8,000 miles. Written by John Ross Dix,* Boston, 1854 (on inside t.p. "Written by John Ross Dix, esq. Editor Waverly Magazine, author of Pen and ink sketches, &c.").

455   RAWLINGS, THOMAS. Emigration; an address to the clergy of England, Ireland, Scotland and Wales, on the condition of the working classes, with a few suggestions as to their future welfare. Also, an address to persons about emigrating to America . . . New York, 1845. 31 p.   **NN**

NHi and Uk have 2d ed., Liverpool, 1846. Rawlings, formerly editor of the Cheltenham *Chronicle* in England, had become editor of the *Oldcountryman* in New York.

456   SCORESBY, *REV.* WILLIAM. American factories and their female operatives; with an appeal on behalf of the British factory population. London, 1845. 122 p.   **DLC UK**

457   [SENIOR, NASSAU WILLIAM]. The Oregon question. [Edinburgh, 1845]. 28 p.
                                                                              CSmH MB MdBJ

Repr. of an article in the *Edinb. Rev.*, LXXXII (July 1845), 238–265, reviewing Falconer, Dunn, Simpson, et al., q.v. Repr. in *Historical and Philosophical Essays*, London, 1865, II, 1–44. Also see Frederick Merk's articles in the *Am. Hist. Rev.*: "British Politics and the Oregon Treaty," XXXVII, 653–677; "British government propaganda and the Oregon Treaty," XL (Oct. 1934), 38–62.

Review: *U.S. Mag. & Democratic Rev.*, XVII n.s. (Nov. 1845; by D.D.F.), 323.

458   SLAVERY IN AMERICA. [Edinburgh, 1845]. 32 p.   **DLC**

No. 27 of *Chamber's miscellany of useful and entertaining tracts.* DLC lists under Chambers. No. 19 of the series, "History of the slave trade," contains some comment on the U.S.

459   [STURGE, JOSEPH]. To the members of the meeting for sufferings. [N.p., 1845?]. 2 p.
       CSmH

Signed, Joseph Sturge, Birmingham, 4th Month, 19th, 1845. Comment on the Indiana yearly meeting and the split among American Friends on the slavery question.

460   [TAPSCOTT, WILLIAM and J.T.]. Tapscott's emigrants' travelling guide through the United States & Canada, showing the distance from New York, time by rail road and steam boat, and steam boat and canal boat, rate of passage, and charge for extra baggage, during the period the navigation remains open. [Liverpool? 1845]. 15 p.   **CaQMBN CSmH**

CtY has 4th ed., *Tapscott's emigrants' guide to the United States, Canada and California: containing a brief description of the United States, their government, climate, soil, and productions, with particular notice of Ohio, Indiana, Illinois, and Missouri, and a general description of Canada, California, and the Oregon territory; also, instructions to emigrants concerning the voyage, tables of travelling routes, distances, railroad and steamboat fares, etc.*, Liverpool, 1851.

461   WRIGHT, HENRY CLARKE. American slavery proved to be theft and robbery; with a letter to Dr. Cunningham containing the doctor's apologies for slavery, an account of eight human beings sold by a theological seminary, and of the sale of a young woman, and also the opinions of T[homas] Clarkson and A[ndrew] Thomson. Edinburgh, 1845. 24 p.

UK has 2d ed., Edinburgh, 1845. MiU, NIC and NNC have 3d ed., Edinburgh, 1845.

462   [WYLIE, ALEXANDER HENRY]. American corn and British manufactures. London, 1845. 36 p.   **ICU NjP NN Uk**

NUC and Uk both list under A. H. Wylie.

1846

463   "ACKNOWLEDGED SLANDER" AGAIN! Free church assembly and slavery contrasted with the Irish assembly and slavery; and "acknowledged slander" against Mr. Frederick Douglass, by the Rev. Dr. Smyth, of Charleston. Reprinted from the Glasgow *Argus.* Glasgow, 1846.   **NHi**

Includes "Letter from the general assembly of the Presbyterian church in Ireland, to the general assembly of the Presbyterian church in the United States of America."

464   AMERICAN SLAVERY. Report of a public meeting held at Finsbury chapel, Moorfields, to receive Frederick Douglass, the American slave, on Friday, May 22, 1846. 24 p.
       CSmH MH

465   ANTI-SLAVERY SOIREE. Report of the speeches delivered at a soiree in honour of Messrs. Douglass, Wright, & Buffum, Dundee, 10th March, 1846. By the reporter of the Dundee *Courier.* Dundee, 1846. 32 p.   **MB**

466   BEAVEN, JAMES. Recreations of a long vacation, or A visit to Indian missions in upper Canada. By James Beavan, D.D., Professor of divinity in the university of King's college, Toronto. London, 1846. 196 p.   **DLC UK**

Includes comment on U.S.; see esp. pp. 90–150.

467   BONNYCASTLE, *SIR* RICHARD HENRY. Canada and the Canadians, in 1846. London, 1846. 2 vols.   **DLC Uk**

Includes caustic comment on the U.S.: I, pp. 200–216, 241–257; II, 109–124, 171–193.

468   A BRIEF NOTICE OF AMERICAN SLAVERY, and the abolition movement. Bristol, 1746 [i.e. 1846]. 40 p.   **DLC**

Review: *Fraser's Mag.* (by F. W. Newman), XIX, n.s. (Feb. 1879), 170.

469   BRITISH AND FOREIGN ANTI-SLAVERY SOCIETY. American slavery. Address of the committee of the British and foreign anti-slavery society to the moderator, office bearers, and members of the general assembly of the Free church of Scotland. [London, 1846]. 12 p.   **DLC**

Signed: John Scoble, secretary.

470   BROTHERTON, EDWARD. Mormonism; its rise and progress, and the prophet Joseph Smith. Manchester, [1846]. 36 p.   **ICN MH**

471   BUCHANAN, JAMES. Letter on free trade, and navigation of the St. Lawrence, addressed to the Earl of Elgin and Kincardine, governor-general of Her Majesty's North American possessions; by James Buchanan, esq., late Her Majesty's consul at New York; with an appendix showing that it is contrary to the laws of England, to raise a revenue from the manufacture of spirituous liquors, as abetting crime. Toronto, 1846. 31 p.   **CaOTU NN**

472   [CAMERON, ANDREW]. The free church and her accusers in the matter of American slavery; being a letter to Mr. George Thompson, regarding his recent appearances in this city. Edinburgh, 1846. 35 p.   **CSmH ICN UkEU**

Signed: "A Free Churchman." See George Thompson, below. CSmH gives Cameron as "supposed" author.

473   CHALMERS, THOMAS. Letter on American slaveholding, with remarks, by the Belfast anti-slavery committee. Belfast, 1846. 16 p.   **NN**

See also Chalmer's "Letter to Rev. Dr. Smyth of Charleston, Edinburgh, 25 Sept., 1844," printed in *The character of the late Thomas Chalmers, D.D., LL.D. and the lessons of his life, from personal recollection*, Charleston, 1848; comment on Chalmer's pro-slavery position, pp. 14–19. Repr. in William Hanna, *Memoirs of the life and writings of Thomas Chalmers*, New York, 1850–52, 4 vols. See also appendix I, "Matured expression of Dr. Chalmer's sentiments on the subject of slavery in America," IV, pp. 566–575; also pp. 443–444. For a defense of Chalmers, and others, see *The exodus of the Church of Scotland and the claims of the Free church of Scotland to the sympathy and assistance of American Christians*. By Thomas Smyth, Charleston, S.C., 1843. See also George Shepperson, ed., "Thomas Chalmers, the Free church of Scotland, and the South," *J. Southern Hist.*, XVII (Nov. 1951), 517–537.

474   [DUNLOP, JOHN]. American anti-slavery conventions: a series of extracts illustrative of the proceedings and principles of the "Liberty party" in the United States; with the hearings of the anti-slavery cause on missions. By J. D. Edinburgh, 1846. 47 p.
                    NNC OCIWHi

475   [DUNLOP, JOHN]. American slavery, organic sins: or the iniquity of licensed injustice. Edinburgh, 1846. 31 p.   **MB NNC OCIWHi**

476   EDINBURGH LADIES' EMANCIPATION SOCIETY. Report . . . for the last year, passed at their annual meeting, held May 27th, 1846. With an appendix containing their remonstrance to the assembly of the Free church of Scotland; resolutions passed at a public meeting of ladies held in the Waterloo rooms, May 1st, 1846; resolutions passed at a public meeting of the British and foreign anti-slavery society, held in Finsbury chapel, London, May 22, 1846. Together with some account of the Twelfth Boston anti-slavery bazaar. Edinburgh, [1846]. 15 p.   **NHi NNC**

       See entry for the Society, 1848, below.

477   EGAN, CHARLES. The law of extradition, comprising the treaties now in force between England and France, and England and America, for the mutual surrender, in certain cases, of persons fugitive from justice; with the recent enactments and decisions relative thereto. London, [1846]. 62 p.   **DLC Uk**

478   ELLIOT, *SIR* CHARLES and KENNEDY, WILLIAM. British diplomatic correspondence concerning the republic of Texas—1836–46. Ed. by Ephraim Douglass Adams. Austin, [1918?]. 636 p.   **DLC**

       Repr. from *Texas State Hist. Assn. Quar.*, XV, nos. 3 and 4, and from the *Southwestern Hist. Quar.*, XVI, no. 1, XXI, no. 2. Consists mainly of letters and reports to the British government, hitherto unpub., by Charles Elliot, charge d'affairs, and William Kennedy, consul at Galveston. For more letters and views by Kennedy on Texas, and on Calif., see his 1841 entries, above. See also Adams' *British interests and activities in Texas, 1838–1846,* Baltimore, 1910; and Clagette Blake, *Charles Elliot R.N., 1801–1875: A servant of Britain overseas*, London, 1960, pp. 64–109.

479   ESTLIN, JOHN BISHOP. A brief notice of American slavery, and the abolition movement. Bristol, [1846]. 40 p.   **MB NN**

       DLC has 2d ed., rev., London, [1853], 54 p.

480   FREE CHURCH OF SCOTLAND. *General Assembly*. Report of the proceedings of the general assembly on Saturday, May 30, and Monday, June 1, 1846. Regarding the relations of the Free church of Scotland, and the Presbyterian churches of America. Revised. Edinburgh, 1846. 52 p.   **DLC UkEU**

       See George Shepperson, "The Free Church and American slavery," *Scottish Hist. Rev.,* XXX (1951), 126–143.

481   FREE CHURCH OF SCOTLAND. Report of the proceedings at a meeting of the members, held at Dundee the 8th of May, 1846, for the purpose of petitioning the General Assembly to disown fellowship with the slave-holding churches of America . . . ; appended, the remonstrance of the American anti-slavery society. Dundee, 1846. 28 p.   **MB**

482   FRIENDLY INTERNATIONAL ADDRESSES recommended, being a brief narrative of the origin and early progress of an already rapid movement in the cause of national arbitration, unfettered commerce, and universal peace. Manchester, [1846].

       No locations found.

483   GLASGOW EMANCIPATION SOCIETY. The Evangelical alliance. Will slaveholders be admitted to membership in it? And will its influence go to support and perpetuate slavery? Letter from the committee of the Glasgow emancipation society, to the Rev. John Angell James, the Rev. Dr. King, the Rev. Dr. Candlish, and other members of the committee, appointed by the Liverpool conference on Christian union, to make arrangements for the great meeting to be held in London, in June, 1846. Glasgow, 1846. 16 p.

MH NHi OCIWHi

Signed by John Murray and William Smeal, Secs.

484   GLASGOW EMANCIPATION SOCIETY. Memorial from the Glasgow emancipation society, in public meeting assembled, to the general assembly of the Free church of Scotland, regarding Christian fellowship with slaveholders, and imploring them to send back the money, a large number of those comprising said meeting being members of the Free church. Glasgow, 1846. 7 p.   **MB NHi**

Signed, James Turner, chairman.

485   GREAT BRITAIN. FOREIGN OFFICE. Correspondence relative to the negotiation of the question of disputed right to the Oregon territory, on the north-west coast of America; subsequent to the treaty of Washington of August 9, 1842. Presented to both houses of Parliament by command of Her Majesty. London, 1846. 71 p.   **DLC**

A British government Blue Book.

486   HEAD, *SIR* FRANCIS BOND. The emigrant. London, 1846.   **UkLL**

MB, CLU have 2d ed., London, 1846; Uk and DLC, 5th ed., London, 1847. Visit to the U.S. in 1838, pp. 275–287; and comment on Canadian-U.S. relations, passim. See also Head's *A narrative*, London, 1839, for incidental comment on his handling of difficulties with the U.S. during the troubled times of the Canadian rebellion; also see his "The red man," in *Descriptive essays contributed to the Quarterly Rev.*, London, 1857, I, pp. 307–367.

Review: *Dublin Univ. Mag.*, XXIX, 224.

487   [HOWE, *HON.* JOSEPH]. Letters to the right honourable Lord John Russell, on the government of British America. [Nova Scotia, 1846]. 41 p.   **DLC**

Two letters written in Oct. 1846; different from Howe's *Responsible government. Letters to the Right Hon. Lord John Russell*, 1839, above. Repr. in Howe's *Speeches and public letters*, 1872, below, I, pp. 609–631.

488   INTERESTING MEMOIRS and documents relating to American slavery, and the glorious struggle now making for complete emancipation. London, 1846. 286 p.   **DLC**

Mostly statements taken from American sources, but with an English preface and some comment by English clergymen.

489   IRISH UNITARIAN CHRISTIAN SOCIETY. Address of the Irish Unitarian Christian society to their brethren in America. Boston, 1846. 7 p.   **DLC**

Signed by Daniel Hutton, president; W. H. Drummond, George A. Armstrong, James Haughton, members of committee; Robert Andrews, secretary.

490   [JAMES, THOMAS HORTON]. Rambles in the United States and Canada during the year 1845, with a short account of Oregon. By Rubio [*pseud.*]. London, 1846. 259 p. **DLC Uk**

Reviews: *Foreign Quar. Rev.*, XXXVI, 518 (very short); *Westmin. Rev.*, XLV, 275.

491   LETTER TO THE REV. WILLIAM CUNNINGHAM . . . regarding communion with slaveholding churches. By a minister of the Gospel. Edinburgh, 1846. 2 p.   **MB NIC**

492   LEVINGE, *SIR* R[ICHARD] G[EORGE] A[UGUSTUS]. Echoes from the backwoods; or, Sketches of transatlantic life. By Captain R. G. A. Levinge. London, 1846. 2 vols.

DLC Uk

Chaps. 1–7, on Canada only, appeared in *Anglo Am.*, VI. Also printed in *New Monthly Mag.*, LXXVI–LXXVII. Includes 4 chaps. on U.S., and passim. Levinge was in America 1835–38.

Review: *Dublin Univ. Mag.*, XXIX, 224.

493   LEWIS, ISRAEL. Crisis in North America! Slavery, war, balance of power, and Oregon. By Israel Lewis, Colored Man! Montreal, 1846. 15 p.   **CaOTU**

494   MACBETH, *REV*. JAMES. No fellowship with slaveholders: a calm review of the debate on slavery, in the full assembly of 1846; addressed respectfully to the assembly of 1847, and to the members and Irish sessions of the Free Church. Glasgow, 1846. 29 p.   **MH-AH**

NIC has expanded pamphlet, . . . *with a recommendatory notice by the celebrated Thomas Clarkson, Esq.; and deliverance of the Irish Presbyterian assembly of July, 1846*, Edinburgh, 1846, 34 p.; a May anti-slavery pamphlet, vol. 181.

495   MCLOUGHLIN, JOHN. The letters of John McLoughlin from Fort Vancouver to the governor and committee . . . edited by E. E. Rich . . . with an introduction by W. Kaye Lamb . . . Toronto, 1941–44. 3 vols.   **DLC Uk**

1st ser., 1825–38; 2d ser., 1839–44; 3d ser., 1844–46. A publication of the Champlain Society Hudson's Bay Company Series, vols. IV, VI, VII; much on California, Oregon and the Pacific northwest, 1825–46, passim. See other collections of letters: Burt Brown Barker, ed., *Letters of Dr. John McLoughlin, written at Fort Vancouver, 1829–1832*, Portland, Oregon, [1948]; T. C. Elliott, ed., "Letters of John McLoughlin, 1835–37, to Edward Ermalinger, *Oregon Hist. Soc. Quar.*, XXIII (1922), 365–371; Jane Lewis Chapin, ed., "Letters of John McLoughlin, 1805–1849," ibid, XXXVI (1935), 320–337, XXXVII (1936), 45–75, 293–300; Katherine B. Judson, "Dr. John McLoughlin's last letter to the Hudson's Bay Company, as chief factor, in charge at Fort Vancouver, 1845," *Am. Hist. Rev.*, XXI (Oct. 1915), 104–134. See also Fred V. Holman, *Dr. John McLoughlin, the father of Oregon*, Cleveland, 1907; Robert C. Johnson, *John McLoughlin: patriarch of the northwest*, Portland, 1935; Richard E. Montgomery, *The White-headed Eagle; John McLoughlin, builder of an empire*, New York, 1935; Eva Emery Dye's semi-fictionized account, *McLoughlin and old Oregon: a chronicle*, Chicago, 1900; and Anson S. Blake, "The Hudson's Bay Company in San Francisco," *Calif. Hist. Soc. Quar.*, XXVIII (June 1949), 97–112.

496   MACNAUGHTAN, *REV*. J. The Free church and American slavery. Slanders against the free church met and answered, in a speech delivered by the Rev. J. Macnaughtan, at the south church soiree, Paisley, April 1846. Paisley, 1846. 8 p.   **DLC**

497   MARCUS, *REV*. MOSES. Address to the members of the "United church of England and Ireland," and of the Protestant Episcopal church in the United States of America, on the subject of emigration, more especially in reference to the spiritual condition of British subjects, and certain proposed measures for their future benefit. New York, 1846. 40 p.

DLC Uk

498   MEREDITH, EDMUND ALLEN. An essay on the Oregon question, written for the Shakespeare club. Montreal, 1846. 43 p.   **CaNSWA CSmH CtY**

499   MODERN GEOGRAPHY . . . with brief notices of European discovery and colonization. By a member of the Society of Friends. London, 1846. 230 p.

No locations found; Sabin #49806.

500   MORTON, A. C. St. Lawrence and Atlantic rail-road. Proceedings of a special general meeting of proprietors, held in Montreal, on the 30th July, 1846, and report of A. C. Morton, esquire, chief engineer. Montreal, 1846. 18 p.   **CaOOA**

DBRE lists only Morton's report, dated 29th July, 1846.

501   NARRATIVE OF VOYAGES to New South Wales and the East Indies, in 1840, 1841, 1842, and 1843, and to New York and the West Indies, in 1843 and 1844. London, 1846. 71 p.   **ICN**

On U.S., pp. 47–63.

502   NATIONAL ASSOCIATION FOR PROMOTING the Political and Social Improvement of the People. An address . . . to the working classes of America on the war spirit that is sought to be excited between the two countries. London, 1846. 8 p.   **CtY Uk**

Uk catalogs under England—misc. Signed: W[illiam] Lovett, sec.

503   NICOLAY, *REV.* C[HARLES] G[RENFELL]. The Oregon territory: a geographical and physical account of that country and its inhabitants, with outlines of its history and discovery. London, 1846. 226 p.   **DLC Uk**

Widely cataloged as also bound with London, 1846 ed. of Catharine Parr Traill, *Backwoods of Canada*, but that work is actually *The Oregon territory*, 1846, below. However Nicolay's 2d ed., with supp., London, 1860, is in fact bound with Traill's work. CSmH has a copy in original paper cover reading "Knight's weekly volume for all readers, LXXXIX."

Review: *Quar. Rev.* (by J. W. Croker), LXXVII, 563.

504   THE OREGON TERRITORY, consisting of a brief description of the country and its productions; and of the habits and manners of the native Indian tribes. London, 1846. 78 p.   **DLC**

Also bound with Catharine Traill, *Backwoods of Canada*, London, 1846. (See note under Nicolay, 1846, above).

505   OREGON: THE CLAIM of the United States to Oregon, as stated in the letters of the Hon. J. C. Calhoun and the Hon. J. Buchanan, (American secretaries of state,) to the Right Hon. R[ichard] Pakenham, Her Britannic Majesty's plenipotentiary. With an appendix, containing the counter statement of Mr. Pakenham to the American secretaries of state. And a map, showing the boundary line proposed by each party. London, 1846. 71 p.   **CaOOA CU ICU Uk**

NUC holdings listed under John C. Calhoun.

506   P., S. Plan for a philanthropic institution for emigration. London, 1846. 32 p.   **NN**

Deals with emigration to and recognition of Texas.

507   PEÑA Y REYES, ANTONIO DE LA. Lord Aberdeen, Texas y California; coleccion de documentos precedida de una introduccion por Antonio de la Peña y Reyes. Mexico, 1925. 72 p.   **DLC Uk**

Archivo historico diplomatico mexicano, num. 15. Covers the Aberdeen correspondence concerning Texas, 1844–46. For further discussion of Lord Aberdeen's relations with the U.S., see: *The life of George, fourth earl of Aberdeen*, by Lady Frances Balfour, London, 1922, I, 125–143; *Incidente diplomatico con Inglaterra en 1843*, Mexico, 1923; and Wilbur D. Jones, *Lord Aberdeen and the Americas*, Athens [Ga], 1958. See also Charles Elliot and William Kennedy, *British diplomatic correspondence concerning the Republic of Texas, 1838–1846*, 1846, above. Also see the following articles: Robert C. Clark, "Aberdeen and Peel on Oregon, 1844," *Oregon Hist. Quar.*, XXXIV (1933), 236–240; "Letter of Aberdeen to Palsenhan, Mar. 4, 1844, concerning the Oregon question," ibid., XXXIX (1938), 74–76; and Julius W. Pratt, "James K. Polk and John Bull," *Canadian Hist. Rev.*, XXIV (Dec. 1943), 341–349.

508   PROCEEDINGS AT THE PUBLIC meeting of the Glasgow anti-war society, held in the city hall, 23d April, 1846. Containing the speeches delivered, by Andrew Paton, Robert Reid, H. C. Wright, and George Thompson, Esq. of London; and address to the citizens of the United States. Glasgow, 1846.   **IreDNL**

509   RAWLINGS, THOMAS. Emigration to the United States. An address on emigration, delivered by Thomas Rawlings, late editor of "The old countryman and emigrants' friend", New York; at Bethesda, in Wales, July 21, 1846. Liverpool, 1846. 8 p.   **NN**

510   RELATION OF THE FREE CHURCH to the American churches: speeches delivered in the Free synod of Angus and Mearns, on Tuesday the 28th April 1846. Dundee, 1846. 24 p.   **MB NN**

Speeches by Mr. [Edward John?] Nixon, et al.

511   RUXTON, GEORGE FREDERICK AUGUSTUS. The Oregon question. A glance at the respective claims of Great Britain and the United States to the territory in dispute. London, 1846. 43 p.   **CtY Uk**

512   SAMPSON, MARMADUKE BLAKE. The Oregon question, as it stands. London, 1846. 15 p.   **CU-BANC Uk**

Review: *Quar. Rev.* (by J. W. Croker), LXXVII, 563.

513   SHOULD THE FREE CHURCH hold fellowship with slave-holders? And, should the money lately received from slave-holding churches be sent back? Respectfully addressed to the members of the Free church of Scotland, by a Member of the Free Church. Linlithgow, 1846. 24 p.   **MB NHi**

514   [SIBBALD, THOMAS]. A few days in the United States and Canada, with some hints to settlers. London [1846?]. 48 p.   **CaOTP MiD Uk**

515   SIMPSON, ALEXANDER. The Oregon territory. Claims thereto of England and America considered; its conditions and prospects. By Alexander Simpson, esq., a late British resident there. London, 1846. 60 p.   **CSmH NN Uk**

Review: *Quar. Rev.* (by J. W. Croker.), LXXVII, 564.

516   SINNETT, JANE, "*MRS*. PERCY SINNETT." Hunters and fishers; or, Sketches of primitive races in the lands beyond the sea. London, 1846. 146 p.   **DLC Uk**

"The wild Indians of the prairies," pp. 114–146.

517   SLAVERY AND THE CHRISTIAN WITNESS: Dr. Campbell and William Lloyd Garrison. Kilmarnock, 1846.   **MB**

A broadside: on slavery in the U.S. Repr. from the *Chr. News*, Nov. 25, 1846.

518   [STEWART, *SIR* WILLIAM GEORGE DRUMMOND]. Altowan; or, Incidents of life and adventure in the Rocky mountains. By an amateur traveller. Ed. by J. Watson Webb. London, 1846. 2 vols.   **DLC**

Semi-fictionized sketches described as "drawn from nature." Also of interest is Stewart's fictionized autobiography, *Edward Warren*, London, 1854, which contains a descriptive account of his travels in western North America. See also *Prairie and mountain sketches, by Mathew C. Field*, collected by Clyde and Mae Reed Porter, ed. by Kate L. Gregg and John Francis McDermott, Norman [Okla.], 1957. (Field accompanied Stewart on his transcontinental hunting trip in 1843.) See also Elizabeth Everitt Russel, "Hunting buffalo in the early forties," *J. Am. Hist.*, XVIII (1924), 137–148 (Russel's father was a member of Stewart's 1842 expedition from St. Louis to and from Yellowstone); and Mae Reed Porter and Odessa Davenport, *Scotsman in buckskin; Sir William Drummond Stewart and the Rocky Mountain fur trade*, New York, 1963. Other items of interest: Marvin C. Ross, ed., *The West of Alfred Jacob Miller (1837), from the notes and water colours in The Walters art gallery*, Norman [Okla.], 1951 (an American artist, Miller travelled with Stewart); and account of Stewart in Bernard De Voto's *Across the wide Missouri*, Boston, 1947; See also reports on Stewart's expedition of 1843 in *Niles' Register*, LXIV (5th ser., XIV), Apr. 1, 1843, p. 80; Apr. 29, p. 134; May 27, p. 195; June 10, p. 234; June 24, p. 262; July 8, p. 297; July 15, p. 320; July 22, p. 323; LXV (5th ser., XV), Sept. 30, pp. 70–71; Nov. 4, p. 160; Nov. 18, p. 192; Nov. 25, p. 208; Dec. 2, p. 214; Dec. 9, p. 240.

519   THOMPSON, GEO[RGE]. The Free church and her accusers: the question at issue. A letter from Geo. Thompson to Henry C. Wright; and one from Henry C. Wright to ministers and members of the Free Church of Scotland. Glasgow, 1846. 12 p.   **MB NN**

Also see *Free Church alliance with manstealers. Send back the money. Great anti-slavery meeting in the city hall, Glasgow, containing speeches by Messers Wright, Douglass, and Buffum, from America, and by George Thompson, esq. of London*, Glasgow, 1846.

520   THOMPSON, GEORGE. The free church of Scotland and American slavery. Substance of speeches delivered in the Music hall, Edinburgh, during May and June 1846, by George Thompson, esq., and the Rev. Henry C. Wright. With an appendix, containing the deliverances of the Free church on the subject of slavery, 1844, 1845, and 1846, and other valuable documents. Edinburgh, 1846. 104 p.   **DLC Uk**

521   TUKE, JAMES HACK. The common and free schools of the United States of America; a paper read at the annual meeting of the Friends' Educational Society, 1846. York, 1846. 31 p.   **ICJ Uk**

522   TWISS, *SIR* TRAVERS. The Oregon question examined, in respect to facts and the law of nations. London, 1846. 391 p.   **DLC Uk**

U.S. ed. carried title, *The Oregon territory, its history and discovery, etc.*, New York, 1846. Refutes Robert Greenhow's position on the boundary dispute; see notes to Thomas Falconer, *The Oregon Question*, 1845, above.

Reviews: *Athenaeum* (1846), 701; *Knight's Penny Mag.* (by T. Falconer), XVI (3d ser., II), 139; *New Monthly Mag.*, LXXVI, 488; *Quar. Rev.* (by J. W. Croker), LXXVII, 536; *Westmin. Rev.*, XLV, 279.

523 VERITAS [*pseud*]. Slavery and the Free church, being a remonstrance with the members of the free church upon their connexion with the slave holders of America, and their duty at the present time. Edinburgh, [1846]. 8 p. **NN**

524 WALLACE, EDWARD J. The Oregon question determined by the rules of international law. London, 1846. 39 p. **DLC Uk**

Reviews: *Knight's Penny Mag.* (by T. Falconer), XVI (3d ser. II), 139; *Quar. Rev.* (by J. W. Croker), LXXVII, 563; *Westmin. Rev.* (by T. Falconer), XLV, 219.

525 [WARBURTON, GEORGE DROUGHT]. Hochelaga; or, England in the new world. Ed. by Eliot Warburton. London, 1846. 2 vols. **DLC Uk**

Vol. II is devoted to the U.S.

Reviews: *Blackwood's Edinb. Mag.*, LX, 464; *Dublin Univ. Mag.*, XXIX, 224; *No. Am. Rev.* (by W. B. C. Peabody), LXIV, 237.

526 WAUGH, ALFRED S. Travels in search of the elephant: the wanderings of Alfred S. Waugh, artist, in Louisiana, Missouri, and Santa Fe, in 1845–46. Edited and annotated by John Francis McDermott. St. Louis, 1951. 153 p. **DLC**

Appendix includes repr. of Waugh's pub. articles: "A trip to Mexico," *So. Lit. Mess.*, XII (Dec. 1846), 755–762; "Mora Valley," *Western J. & Civilian*, VII (Oct. 1851), 33–38.

527 WAYLEN, EDWARD. Ecclesiastical reminiscences of the United States. London, 1846. 542 p. **DLC UK**

In U.S., 1834–45; an Episcopal missionary in Maryland.

528 [WILLIAMS, SAMUEL B.]. Thoughts on finance and colonies, by Publius [*pseud*.]. London, 1846. 141 p. **DLC Uk**

Uk and DLC lists under Publius. Chap. 4 on the Oregon question, pp. 117–134.

529 WOOLLAM, J. G. Useful information for emigrants to the western states of America. Manchester, 1846.

No locations found.

530 WYSE, FRANCIS. America, its realities and resources: comprising important details connected with the present social, political, agricultural, commercial, and financial state of the country, its laws and customs, together with a review of the policy of the United States that led to the war of 1812, and peace of 1814 — the "right of search," the Texas and Oregon questions, etc., etc. London, 1846. 3 vols. **DLC Uk**

Spent several years in U.S., beginning 1841.

1847

531 [ADAMSON, JOHN]. An account of Texas; with instructions for emigrants. [London, 1847]. 12 p. **CtY**

532 ADDRESS TO FRIENDS IN NORTH AMERICA, from the committee of the Society of Friends in London, appointed on the subject of the distress existing in Ireland, 2nd of 1st month, 1847. London, 1847. 16 p.

No locations found; Sabin #86026.

533 BARHAM, WILLIAM. Descriptions of Niagara; selected from various travellers; with original additions. Gravesend, [Eng.], [1847]. 180 p. **DLC**

Includes descriptions by Mrs. Trollope, Dickens, and Mrs. Jameson and Charles Latrobe, et al.

534 BROWN, FRANCIS CARNAC. Free trade & the cotton question with reference to India, being a memorial from the British merchants of Cochin, to the Right Hon. Sir John Hobhouse, with a letter and appendix. London, 1847. 126 p. **PPL MH-BA Uk**

Uk lists under Cochin. On U.S. cotton trade, pp. 60–68; scattered references to slavery, pp. 44, 45, 48.

535 COULTER, JOHN, *M.D.* Adventures on the western coast of South America, and the interior of California: including a narrative of incidents at the Kingsmill Islands, New Ireland, New Britain, New Guinea, and other islands in the Pacific Ocean; with an account of the natural productions, and the manners and customs, in peace and war, of the various savage tribes visited. London, 1847. 2 vols. **DLC Uk**

Includes 7 chaps. on California, which Coulter claimed to have visited. However see Willard O. Waters, "Franciscan Missions of upper California as seen by foreign visitors and residents," *Bookman's Holiday*, New York, 1943, p. 137: "it is doubtful if he ever saw California."

536 DOUGLASS, FREDERICK. Farewell speech of Mr. Frederick Douglass, previously to embarking upon the Cambria, upon his return to America, delivered at the valedictory soiree given to him at the London Tavern, on March 30, 1847. Published, by order of the council of the Anti-Slavery league, from the short-hand notes of Mr. W. Farmer. London, [1847]. 24 p. **NN NNC OClWhi**

Uk lists *Report of proceedings at the soiree given to F.D., March 30, 1847*, London, 1847. Pp. 21–24 contain British comment on slavery in the U.S.

537 EDINBURGH EMANCIPATION SOCIETY. Statement of the principles and proceedings of the Edinburgh emancipation society, instituted in 1833. Edinburgh, 1847. **NHi**

538 FEATHERSTONHAUGH, GEORGE WILLIAM. A canoe voyage up the Minnay Sotor; with an account of the lead and copper deposits in Wisconsin; of the gold region in the Cherokee country: and sketches of popular manners; &c. &c. &c. London, 1847. 2 vols. **DLC Uk**

Extracts repr. in *Tenn. Hist. Mag.*, 2d ser., III (1932), 45–58. St. Paul, 1970 ed., with introd. and refs. by William E. Lass. Featherstonhaugh was also the author of many geological reports in connection with boundary disputes between England and the U.S. Also see his *Observations on the application of human labour under different circumstances, when employed on reproductive industry, or for national objects, in various parts of the British Empire, by a field officer*, London, 1847.

539 FREE CHURCH ANTI-SLAVERY SOCIETY. An address to the office-bearers and members of the Free church of Scotland, on her present connexion with the slave-holding churches of America. From the committee of the Free church anti-slavery society. Edinburgh, 1847. 16 p. **CtY MH NIC NN**

540 FREE CHURCH ANTI-SLAVERY SOCIETY. The sinfulness of maintaining Christian fellowship with slave-holders. Strictures on the proceedings of the last general assembly of the Free church of Scotland, regarding communion with the slave-holding churches of America, respectfully addressed to the office-bearers and members of that church. From the committee of the Free church anti-slavery society. Edinburgh, 1847. 32 p. **MH NIC NN UkMa**

541   [GALT, *SIR* ALEXANDER TILLOCH]. The Saint Lawrence and Atlantic railroad. A letter to the chairman [James Dowie] and deputy chairman [Robert Harrison] of the North American Colonial Association. London, 1847. 40 p.   **CaNSWA MH-BA Uk**

See Oscar Douglas Skelton, *The life and times of Sir Alexander Tilloch Galt,* Toronto, 1920; chap. 11, "Canada and the U.S." (esp. Galt's visit to Wash., D.C. in 1861–62), pp. 284–322; and chap. 16, "The Halifax Commission," pp. 493–514; other comment, passim. Also see Fred Landon, "Canadian Opinion of Abraham Lincoln," *Dalhousie Rev.*, II (Oct., 1922), 329–334.

542   GILFILLAN, GEORGE. The debasing and demoralizing influence of slavery on all and on everything connected with it. Edinburgh, 1847. 15 p.   **UkLSE**

Pub. by Free church anti-slavery society of the Free church of Scotland, Edinburgh.

543   HAUGHTON, JAMES. Slavery immoral; being a reply to a letter in which an attempt is made to prove that slavery is not immoral. Dublin, 1847. 23 p.   **MH NIC**

544   HOOTON, CHARLES. St. Louis' Isle, or Texiana; with additional observations made in the United States and in Canada. London, 1847. 204 p.   **DLC Uk**

See also author's "The emigrants to Texas — a true story," the *Anglo Am.*, I (Aug. 19, 1843), 398–400; and "Rides, rambles and sketches in Texas," *Simmonds Colonial Mag.*, VIII (May–Aug 1846), 39–54, 198–210, 315–365, 416–428.

545   HORNSBY, JAMES. Account of a visit to America, with many interesting particulars respecting the country, the condition of the people, etc. [Wortley, near Leeds, 1847?]. 24 p.   **MB**

In America 1845–47.

546   JEFFREY, GEORGE. The pro-slavery character of the American churches, and the sin of holding Christian communion with them. A lecture . . . delivered at the request of the Free Church anti-slavery society. Edinburgh, 1847. 19 p.   **DHU NIC UkLSE**

Pub. by the Free church anti-slavery soc.

547   LETTER FROM THE INHABITANTS of Bridgewater, Somersetshire, England, to the inhabitants of Bridgewater, Massachusetts, New-England, America, dated Sept. 10, 1846; with the reply of the latter, dated Feb. 10, 1847. Boston, 1847. 39 p.   **MH NIC**

548   MACGREGOR, JOHN. The progress of America, from the discovery by Columbus to the year 1846. London, 1847. 2 vols.   **DLC Uk**

This work gathers together all the material relating to the U.S. which had appeared earlier in author's other works, and also included material pub. in later works. Portions will be found in the following: *Commercial tarriffs and regulations of the several states of Europe and America,* London: 1841–[1850?], 13 vols.; *Commercial statistics. A digest of the productive resources, commercial legislation . . . of all nations,* London, 1844–50, 5 vols.; *Sketches of the progress of civilization and public liberty, with a view of the political condition of Europe and America in 1848,* London, 1848; *Commercial statistics of America: a digest of her productive resources, commercial legislation, etc.,* London, [1847], which included the earlier *The commercial and financial legislation of Europe and America,* London, 1841.

Reviews: *Athenaeum,* (June 5, 1847), 591; *Hunt's Merch. Mag.,* XV, 60; *Littel's Living Age,* XV, 385.

549   MAURY, SARAH MYTTON [HUGHES], "*Mrs.* William Maury." The progress and influence of the Catholic church in the United States of America; described in a memoir of John [Hughes], Bishop of New York. London, 1847. 40 p.   **DLC Uk**

Review: *Dublin Rev.,* XXIII, 526.

550   MAURY, SARAH MYTTON [HUGHES], "*Mrs.* William Maury." The statesmen of America in 1846. London, 1847. 548 p.   **DLC Uk**

Sketches of individual Americans includes one of James Hughes, Bishop of New York (see preceding entry); also included are chaps. on "The president and people of the United States," "Note on the corps diplomatique at Washington," "Essay on free trade," "The Catholic church in Oregon," "Notes on the Mexican war," etc. Pref. states this vol. will be succeeded by Opinions of an Englishwoman in America (see *An Englishwoman in America,* 1848, below.)

Reviews: *Church of Eng. Quar. Rev.,* XXI, 423; *Littel's Living Age,* XII, 566; *No. Am. Rev.,* LXIV, 513; *Spectator,* XX, 90.

551   MERRITT, W[ILLIAM] HAMILTON. Letters addressed to the inhabitants of the Niagara district. On free trade, &c. By W. Hamilton Merritt, Esq., M.P. Niagara, 1847. 32 p.   **CaOTP**

Six letters dated St. Catherines, Apr.–May, 1847; manuscript notes throughout the text.

552   NELSON, *REV.* ISAAC. Slavery supported by the American churches and countenanced by recent proceedings in the Free church of Scotland. A lecture by Rev. Isaac Nelson, Belfast, delivered at the request of the Free church anti-slavery society. Edinburgh, 1847. 20 p.   **DHU FU NIC MH**

Pub. by the Free church anti-slavery soc.

553   [O'CONNELL, DANIEL]. Address from the people of Ireland to their countrymen and countrywomen in America. [N.p., 1847]. 32 p.   **DLC**

Introduction signed, "Daniel O'Connell, Theobald Mathew, and sixty thousand other inhabitants of Ireland." Extracts from O'Connell's speeches, pp. 5–30.

554   RICHARDSON, *MAJOR* JOHN. Eight years in Canada; embracing a review of the administrations of Lords Durham and Sydenham, Sir Chas. Bagot, and Lord Metcalfe; and including numerous interesting letters from Lord Durham, Mr. Chas. Buller, and other well-known public characters. By Major Richardson, Knight of the military order of St. Ferdinand, author of "Ecarte," "Wacousta," "The Canadian Brothers," &c. &c. &c. Montreal, 1847. 232 p.   **DLC Uk**

On U.S., pp. 10–22, 30–33, 128–150, 161–177. Also see author's *The Canadian brothers; or the prophecy fulfilled. A tale of the late American War,* Montreal, 1840; contains a chap. on the battle of Queenston and a glorification of British arms; republished as *Matilda Montgomerie: or, the Prophecy fulfilled. A tale of the late American War. Being the sequel to "Wacousta,"* New York, [c. 1851], omitting the Queenston episode. Also see *The guards in Canada, or the point of honor; being a sequel to Major Richardson's "Eight years in Canada,"* Montreal, 1848. See also William Renwick Riddell, *John Richardson,* Toronto, [1923].

555   RUXTON, GEORGE FREDERICK AUGUSTUS. Adventures in Mexico and the Rocky mountains. London, 1847. 332 p.   **DLC Uk**

New York, 1915, ed. by Horace Kephart. Portions also pub. under title, *Wild life in the Rocky mountains*, New York, 1916, ed. by Horace Kephart, and in *Mountain men; George Frederick Ruxton's first hand accounts of fur trappers and Indians in the Rockies*, ed. and illust. by Glen Rounds, New York, [1966]. Chaps. 21–36 describe travels in southwestern U.S. See accounts in *Ruxton of the Rockies*, collected by Clyde and Mae Reed Porter, ed. by LeRoy R. Hafen, Norman, [Okla.], 1950; and *Some heroes of travel; or, Chapters from the history of geographical discovery and enterprise*, compiled and rewritten by William Henry Davenport Adams, London, 1880, pp. 49–89. See also Ruxton's articles, pub. anonymously: "Sketches of the Mexican war," *Fraser's Mag.*, XXXVIII, 91–102.

Reviews: *Brit. Quar. Rev.*, XI, 154; *Eliza Cook's J.*, I, 234; *Knickerbocker*, XXXI, 258.

556   SIMPSON, *SIR* GEORGE. Narrative of a journey round the world, during the years 1841 and 1842. London, 1847. 2 vols.   **DLC Uk**

U.S. ed., Philadelphia, 1847, with title: *An overland journey round the world during the years 1841 and 1842*. Contains four chaps. on California and one on Boston. Portions on California repr. in: *California: its history, population, climate, soil, productions, and harbors. From Sir George Simpson's "Overland journey round the world." An account of the revolution in California, and conquest of the country by the United States, 1846–7*. By John T. Hughes, Cincinnati, 1848; portions also repr., with additional material, in *Narrative of a voyage to California ports in 1841–42 together with voyages to Sitka, the Sandwich islands & Okhotsk, to which are added sketches of journeys across America, Asia, & Europe, from the Narrative of a voyage around the world by Sir George Simpson . . . This edition edited, corrected typographically, with sketches of visits and journeys made outside of California, and with a foreward, new division synopses, and an ample index*, by Thomas C. Russell, San Francisco, 1930. According to Gagnon the above work was prepared by Adam Thom from Simpson's notes. See also Joseph Schafer, ed., "Letters of Sir George Simpson, 1841–1843," *Am. Hist. Rev.*, XIV (Oct. 1908), 70–94. Frank E. Ross, "Sir George Simpson at the Department of State," *Brit. Col. Hist. Quar.*, II (Apr. 1938), 131–55, includes text of letter, dated Jan. 20, 1855, describing conference in Washington, D.C., on Hudson's Bay Co. fur trade rights on U.S. soil. See also the account in *Sir George Simpson, overseas governor of the Hudson's bay company, a pen picture of a man of action*, by Arthur S. Morton, [Toronto, 1944]. Reviews: *Blackwood's Edinb. Mag.* (by Geo. Croly), LXI, 653; *New Monthly Mag.*, LXXX, 219.

557   SPRAGUE, WILLIAM BUELL. A discourse commemorative of the Rev. Thomas Chalmers. With a letter from Dr. Chalmers to an American clergyman. Albany, [N.Y.], 1847. 47 p.   **DLC Uk**

Chalmer's letter, pp. 45–47 discusses gradual emancipation versus abolition.

558   TUKE, JAMES HACK. A visit to Connaught in the autumn of 1847. A letter addressed to the Central relief committee of the Society of Friends, Dublin. London, 1847. 67 p.

MH-BA

Uk has 2d ed., London, 1848. Includes account of the U.S. in 1845. See also extended discussion of U.S., esp. in connection with emigration, in *James Hack Tuke: a memoir*, comp. by the Right Hon. Sir Edward Fry, London, 1899, pp. 19–40 and passim.

559 WARR, G[EORGE] W[INTER]. Canada as it is; or, The emigrant's friend and guide to Upper Canada, being a sketch of the country, climate, inhabitants, professions, trades, etc., taken during a residence in 1843, 1844, 1845, 1846, together with important instructions to persons of all classes who purpose becoming inhabitants of the colony. London, 1847. 108 p. **ICN MiD Uk**

DLC has 3d ed., Dublin, 1849. Mostly on Canada, but see pp. 28–33 for description of New York, including hotels and boarding houses, American manners and opinions of England.

560 WILLIS, MICHAEL. Slavery indefensible; showing that the relation of slave and slave-holder has no foundation either in the law of nature nor of Christianity. Glasgow, 1847. 23 p. **UkLSE**

Pub. by Free church anti-slavery society.

561 [WILTON, JOHN HENRY.] The deserters; a narrative founded on facts of recent occurrence. By the author of "Scenes in a soldier's life." Montreal, [1847?].

CaOTP has 3d ed., Montreal, 1847, 7 p. Describes various U.S. army posts and the life of British deserters in them. Prepared for circulation in the Canadian army.

562 YOUNG, *REV*. DAVID. Slavery forbidden by the Word of God. A lecture . . . delivered at the request of the Free church anti-slavery society. Edinburgh, 1847. 17 p. **NHi**

Pub. by the Free church anti-slavery society. On the U.S.

1848

563 APPEAL IN BEHALF of the proposed church and hospital for British emigrants arriving at the port, and in the city of New York. [London, 1848?]. 16 p. **DNLM Uk**

Uk catalogs under New York (Appendix) and credits Rev. Moses Marcus as editor.

564 [BURLEND, *MRS*. REBECCA]. A true picture of emigration; or Fourteen years in the interior of North America; being a full and impartial account of the various difficulties and ultimate success of an English family who emigrated from Barwick-in-Elmet, near Leeds, in the year 1831. London, [1848]. 62 p. **DLC Uk**

The Burlends remained in the U.S., but this is an account of their early experiences as British emigrants in Pikes County, Ill. as related by the author to her son, Edward Burlend, and recorded by him. Repr. with illust., ed. by Milo Milton Quaife, Chicago, 1936, 167 p.

Review: *Sidney's Emig. J.*, I, 3.

565 BURNS, *REV*. JABEZ. Notes of a tour in the United States and Canada, in the summer and autumn of 1847. London, 1848. 180 p. **DLC Uk**

Repr. of articles pub. in the *Chr. Record* (Jersey, Eng.); see later account of this visit in Burns' *A retrospect of forty-five years*, London, 1875, below. See also author's "Missions among the American Indians," in his *Missionary enterprises in many lands*, London, 1845, pp. 33–68.

566 COFFIN, WILLIAM FOSTER. Three chapters on a triple project. The canal and the rail. Montreal, 1848. 26 p. **CaOTU MH**

567   [D'ARUSMONT, FRANCES WRIGHT]. England, the civilizer; her history developed in its principles; with reference to the civilizational history of modern Europe (America inclusive) and with a view to the denouement of the difficulties of the hour. By a woman. London, 1848. 470 p.   **MH NN Uk**

Listed in Uk catalog under "Woman." For references to the U.S., after 1832, see from pp. 377, passim.

568   DICK, DAVID. In favour of the Free Church, and also of the abolition cause; or, On American slavery and the Free Church of Scotland, inclusive of the wrongfulness of all modern slavery. By one not of the Free Church, but who is desirous of her welfare, and for the success of the cause of abolition of all modern slavery, and would not that the cause of the one should be so managed as to be injurious to the other. Edinburgh, 1848. 43 p.
UkENL

569   [DUNLOP, ALEXANDER]. American confessions of a layman, as connected with the workings of democracy in the United States; with their application to the present condition of Europe. Edinburgh, 1848.   **UkENC**

Third of a series, the first two being *Confessions of a layman*, Edinburgh, 1867 [i.e., 1847] and *Continental confessions of a layman*, Edinburgh, [1847]. Copies of the *American confessions* are very scarce.

570   EDINBURGH LADIES' EMANCIPATION SOCIETY. Annual report for the year ending June 1848. Edinburgh, 1848.   **NHi**

Reports continued through 1870, with varying titles and formats, and continuing coverage of the U.S. NHi has annual reports for 1848–1854, 1855–57, 1858 and 1859. Title change in 1860 to *Annual report of the Edinburgh ladies' emancipation society, and a sketch of anti-slavery events during the year ending 1st March 1860*; 1864 title again changes: . . . . *anti-slavery events and the condition of the freedmen* . . . No report was pub. in 1869.

571   EDWARDS, EDWARD. A statistical view of the principal public libraries in Europe and America. [London], 1848.   **Uk**

ICJ has bound with three other pamphlets by Edwards, with title *Papers on public libraries*. DLC has 3d ed., corr., with additional tables, and illustrative plans, London, 1849, 48 p. Priv. pr.; repr. from *J. Stat. Soc. London*, Aug., 1848. A debate over accuracy of Edward's statistics continued for several months; see esp., *Athenaeum* (1849), pp. 877, 902, 926, 1156, 1179, 1242, 1336, (1850), pp. 19, 74. See also Edward's *Free town libraries, their formation, management, and history; in Britain, France, Germany, & America*, London, 1869, below.

572   EMIGRANTS' HAND BOOK to the United States. London, 1848.

No locations found; Sabin #22487.

573   THE EMIGRATION CIRCULAR; or, Complete hand-book and guide to the United States; being England and America contrasted. London, 1848. 33 p.   **CaOOA**

574   EMIGRATION FOR THE MILLIONS: directions where to go, and how to get there. Containing the government information, and all other particulars necessary for emigrants proceeding to Cape of Good Hope, Australia, Van Dieman's Land, New Zealand, Canada, America, &c. London, 1848. 16 p.   **NjP**

MB has 2d ed. with slightly different title: *Emigration: directions where*. . . . , London, 1848. On U.S., pp. 10–11.

575   [EVANS, WILLIAM]. Rules and regulations of the Potters' joint-stock emigration society and savings fund. Enrolled under act of Parliament established April 18, 1844. Shelton, [1848]. 44, 12 p.   **NN**

NN catalogs under the Society. Society formed for land purchase in Wisconsin, under leadership of Evans, editor of *Potters' Examiner and Workman's Advocate*. See Grant Foreman, "Settlement of English potters in Wisconsin," *Wisc. Mag. of Hist.*, XXI (June 1938), 375–396.

576   GRAY, M. WILSON. Self-paying colonization in North America: being a letter to Captain John P. Kennedy. Dublin, 1848. 64 p.   **UkLU-G**

LU has microfilm.

577   [GREATREX, CHARLES BUTLER]. Whittlings from the West. By Abel Log [*pseud.*]. London, 1848. 5 pts.   **CSmH**

DLC and Uk have in book form under title, *Whittlings from the West: with some account of Butternut Castle*, Edinburgh, 1854. Appeared in 5 monthly parts, issued separately March–July 1848. Semi-fictional account of a trip to the U.S. Sketches also ran serially in *Hogg's Instructor* (July–Dec. 1851), VI (ser. 2), 216, etc.—IX (ser. 2), 10, etc.

Review: *Dublin Univ. Mag.*, XLIV, 721.

578   LEON, JOHN A. On sugar cultivation in Louisiana, Cuba, &c., and the British possessions. By an European and colonial sugar manufacturer. London, 1848. 2 pts.   **DLC Uk**

579   MAURY, SARAH MYTTON [HUGHES], "Mrs. William Maury." An Englishwoman in America. London, 1848. 251, 204, 16 p.   **DLC Uk**

Pref. discusses reviews of earlier works, *Progress and influence of the Catholic Church in the United States*, and *Statesmen in America*, both 1847, above. Appendix contains history of emigrant surgeon bill.

Review: *Dublin Rev.* (by W. B. McCabe), XXIV, 317.

580   MISSIONS TO THE North American Indians. London [1848?]. 244 p.   **ICN OCIWHi**

Uk copy destroyed. Pub. by the Religious Tract Society. A sketch of missionary activity in the U.S. and Canada from colonial days to 1844.

581   NORTH AMERICA VIEWED as to its eligibility for British emigration. Giving ample details to meet the inquiries of all classes. By an Englishman. London, 1848. 48 p.   **OCIWHi Uk**

Part I of *Information for emigrants: in three parts. I.— North America. II.—New South Wales, Port Phillip, Cooksland, South Australia, and New Zealand. III.—The Cape of Good Hope, Algoa Bay, and Port Natal; also, A view of Canada, etc. Comprising, an impartial account of the present state, prospects, and capabilities of each; their principal settlements; and the advantages they present to different classes of settlers; together with much useful information on all matters essential to the intending emigrant*, London, 1848.

582   NORTH TEXAN COLONIZATION COMPANY. A freehold farm of 25 acres, a free passage to America, a dwelling house, and other advantages, secured for £30, payable in weekly instalments [sic] to the artizans and labourers of Great Britain and Ireland. [London, 1848]. 4 p.   **CtY**

583   NORTH TEXAN COLONIZATION COMPANY . . . Texas; its resources, climate, and advantages for colonization. With a detailed prospectus of the "North Texan Colonization Company" for the emigration of the industrious classes, on the associative principle. [London, 1848]. 8 p.   **CtY**

584   PRENTICE, ARCHIBALD. A tour in the United States. London, 1848. 156 p.   **DLC Uk**

Later ed., London, 1849, added the subtitle, *With two lectures on emigration, delivered in the Mechanics' institution, Manchester*, 217 p. Prentice, editor of the Manchester *Times*, visited the U.S. in 1843.

585   [RUSSELL, ROBERT W.]. America compared with England. The respective social effects of the American and English systems of government and legislation; and the mission of democracy. London, 1848. 289 p.   **DLC Uk**

The 2d ed., 1849, added the words "By R. W. Russell, of Cincinnati, United States, Councellor-at-large," but he definitely wrote as an Englishman—see introd. Also see pp. 162–176, "The testimony of European writers on America," which evaluates 10 different books on the U.S.

586   SLAVERY AT WASHINGTON. Narrative of the heroic adventures of Drayton, an American trader, in "The Pearl," coasting vessel, which was captured by American citizens, near the mouth of the Potomac, having on board seventy-seven men, women, and children, endeavouring to escape from slavery in the capitol of the American republic. (In a letter from Dr. S. G. Howe, U.S.) together with the proceedings upon Captain Drayton's trial and conviction. Printed by order of the council of the Anti-slavery league. London, [1848?]. 24 p.   **NHi UkLSE**

Includes comment [by George Thompson?] on the Howe letter and the Drayton trial. Also see the *Personal memoir of Daniel Drayton, for four years and four months a prisoner (for charity's sake) in Washington jail. Including a narrative of the voyage and capture of the schooner Pearl . . .* , Boston, 1855, 122 p. (held by DLC).

587   SMITH, *LIEUT.-COL.* CHARLES HAMILTON. The natural history of the human species, its typical forms, primaeval distribution, filiations, and migrations. Illustrated by thirty-four coloured plates with portrait and vignette by Lieut.-Col. Chas. Hamilton Smith, K.H. and K.W., F.R. and L.S., President of the Devon and Cornwall natural hist. soc., etc., etc. Edinburgh, 1848. 464 p.   **DLC Uk**

On America, pp. 85–87, 89–91, 232–261; plus three plates on the American Indians, XXIII, XXIV, XXV. The U.S. ed. added *With a preliminary abstract of the views of Blumenbach, Prichard, Backman, Agassiz, and other authors of repute on the subject*, by S. Kneeland, jr., M.D., Boston, 1851.

588   TEXAS: ITS SOIL, climate and advantages. London, 1848.

No locations found; pub. by E. Wilson.

589   TO THE EMIGRANT FARMER. A view of the advantages of climate, soil, product, government, and institutions of Texas; the central maritime portion of the United States of America; comprising a candid statement of privations and difficulties to be encountered, and of the mode of culture and expenditure of labour conducive to success. With remarks on other fields of emigration. By a practical farmer. London, [1848?]. 24 p. **CtY TxU Uk**

Uk lists under Texas.

590   VERNON, B. J. Early recollections of Jamaica, with the particulars of an eventful passage home, via New York and Halifax, at the commencement of the American war in 1812; to which are added, trifles from St. Helena relating to Napoleon and his suite. London, 1848. 200 p.   **DLC Uk**

See esp. pp. 43–87 and 91–112.

591   WARRE, *SIR* H[ENRY JAMES]. Sketches in North America and the Oregon territory. By Captain H. Warre. [London, 1848]. 20 plates.   **DLC Uk**

Consists mainly of 20 magnificent color plates. New ed., with introd. by Archibald Hanna, Jr., Barre [Mass.], 1970, 26 p. See also the "Secret mission of Warre and Vavasour," *Wash. Hist. Quar.*, III (Apr. 1912), 131–153, which contains original letters by Warre, Vavasour, George Simpson and Peter Skene Ogden; and *Overland to Oregon in 1845: impressions of a journey across North America*, ed. with introd. by Madelaine Major-Fregeau, Ottawa, 1976, which selects and arranges Warre's observations as commentary on reproductions of his sketches from the Public Archives of Canada.

592   A WORD ON BEHALF of the slave; or, A mite cast into the treasury of love. London, 1848. 113 p.   **DLC**

Addressed to all ministers but "more particularly" to those of the U.S.; consists of a series of prayers about slavery. By the author of *Bread upon the waters*, 1853, below.

1849

593   ALEXANDER, *SIR* JAMES EDWARD. L'Acadie; or, Seven years' explorations in British America. London, 1849. 2 vols.   **DLC Uk**

On the U.S., I, 68–122, 288–292, II, 254–259, 272–276. See also Alexander's "A pursuit into the United States after British deserters charged with felony," *United Service Mag.*, (1844, pt. III), 530–545.

594   ANSTED, DAVID THOMAS. The gold-seeker's manual. London, 1849. 172 p. **DLC Uk**

New York ed., 1849, carried title, *The gold-seeker's manual; being a practical and instructive guide to all persons emigrating to the newly-discovered gold regions of California*, 96 p. See also Ansted's *Scenery, science and art; being extracts from the note-books of a geologist and mining engineer*, London, 1854; pp. 243–311 on the U.S.

Reviews: *Athenaeum* (1849), 157; *Quar. Rev.*, LXXXVII, 396.

595   BARROW, JOHN. Facts relating to north-eastern Texas, condensed from notes made during a tour through that portion of the United States of America, for the purpose of examining the country, as a field for emigration. Embracing the climate – topography – soil – wood – water – roads – rivers – present and future commercial prosperity – farming operations – produce – returns – haulage – locations – land titles – laws – education, and other matters – together with advice to the emigrant – his plan of proceeding – prices of passage and numerous articles of utility. With a map revised from the last authentic survey. By John Barrow, civil engineer. London, 1849. 68 p.   **DLC Uk**

596   BERRY, GEORGE. The gold of California: a short inquiry into its probable effects on currency, commerce, property, prices, taxation, and labour. London, 1849. 16 p.   **DLC**

597 BRITISH AMERICAN LEAGUE. Minutes of the proceedings of the second convention of delegates of the British American league, held at Toronto, C. W., on Thursday, November 1, and by adjournment on the 2nd, 3rd, 5th, 6th and 7th of November, 1849. Toronto, 1849. 24, lix p. **CSmH NNC**

Cover title adds "With an appendix, containing a report of the debates," concerning annexation issue and U.S.

598 BROWN, WILLIAM, [*of Leeds*]. America: a four years' residence in the United States and Canada; giving a full and fair description of the country, as it really is, with the manners, customs, & character of the inhabitants; anecdotes of persons and institutions, prices of land and produce, state of agriculture and manufactures. Leeds, 1849. 108 p. **DLC Uk**

Author's experiences as a tavern-keeper in Cleveland and Toronto.

599 BUCHANAN, ISAAC. Legislation on gold . . . The question of money — how it will be affected by large imports of gold from California. To the editor of the Weekly register. [Edinburgh, 1849]. **CtY**

600 [BYTOWN, UPPER CANADA. *LUMBERMEN*]. Proceedings of public meetings held at Bytown, October 3rd and 10th, 1849, relative to the St. Lawrence & Lake Champlain canal, with report and evidence thereon. Bytown, 1849. 16 p. **CaOTP**

Discusses U.S.-Canadian relations, particularly with respect to potential U.S. markets for Canadian lumber.

601 CANADA. PARLIAMENT. LEGISLATIVE ASSEMBLY. SELECT COMMITTEE ON CAUSES OF EMIGRATION. Report of the Select committee of the Legislative assembly, appointed to inquire into the causes and importance of the emigration which takes place annually, from Lower Canada to the United States. Montreal, 1849. 83 p. **DLC**

Appended are the answers of various persons to questions on the subject of emigration submitted by the committee.

602 CAVE, *SIR* STEPHEN. A few words, on the encouragement given to slavery and the slave trade, by recent measures, and chiefly by the Sugar Bill of 1846. [London], 1849. 34 p.
Uk

ICN, MH, TxU have 2d ed., London, 1849. Includes comment on the U.S., made as result of a visit in 1846–48.

603 [CHISHOLME, DAVID]. Annals of Canada for 1837 and 1838. [Montreal, 1849?]. 186? p. **CaOTP**

Repr. from anon. articles in the Montreal *Gazette*, Jan. 1838–Feb. 1840. Includes comment on Caroline incident, etc. F. H. Severance, ed. of *Bibliography of upper Canadian Rebellion*, p. 438, says, "The only copy seen is an incomplete volume in the Toronto Public Library. Mr. James Bains, Jr., librarian of that institution, is of the opinion that the printing of the work was never completed, the Toronto copy being inferred to be the gathered sheets as far as the work was carried. It is obviously one of the greatest rarities of all the literature relating to the Niagara region."

604 THE CLIMAX OF PROTECTION and free trade, capped by annexation. Montreal, 1849. 18 p. **CaOOA**

605   CRUIKSHANK, PERCY. Hints to emigrants; or, Incidents in the emigration of John Smith of Smith-town, designed & etched by Percy Cruikshank. London, [1849]. 9 plates.

CU-BANC NN Uk

Humorous satire in the form of illust. in color.

Review: *Bentley's Misc.*, XXV, 562 (brief notice).

606   DAVIES, EBENEZER. American scenes and Christian slavery; a recent tour of four thousand miles in the United States. London, 1849. 324 p.   **MB Uk**

First pub. in the *Patriot*. Davies in U.S. Jan.–Apr., 1848.

Review: *Eclectic Rev.*, LXXXIX, (XXV, n.s.), 438.

607   DIXON, JAMES. Methodism in America: with the personal narrative of the author, during a tour through a part of the United States and Canada. London, 1849. 498 p.   **CSmH Uk**

DLC has New York, 1849 ed., with title, *Personal narrative of a tour through a part of the United States and Canada: with notices of the history and institutions of Methodism in America*; this 2d ed. is slightly rev. Other eds. held by many libraries.

Review: *Method. Quar. Rev.*, XXXI, 653.

608   THE EMIGRANT'S GUIDE to the United States. Who should, and who should not, emigrate; being plain practical advice to intending emigrants. London, 1849. 92 p.   **UkENL**

609   THE EMIGRANT'S HAND-BOOK and guide to the United States; or England and America contrasted: comprising information respecting the best fields for agricultural and manufacturing employment, wages, climate, shipping, letters from emigrants, etc. London, [1849?]. 48 p.   **NN**

610   EMIGRATION TO CALIFORNIA. California: its situation and resources, from authentic documents; with a few practical hints to intending emigrants. London, 1849. 31 p.

CtY CU

611   [FORRESTER, ALFRED HENRY]. A goodnatured hint about California, by Alfred Crowquill [*pseud.*]. [London, 1849]. 8 p.   **DLC Uk**

612   FOX, WILLIAM JOHNSON. Lectures addressed chiefly to the working classes. London, 1845–49. 4 vols.   **CtY Uk**

Contains "Reports of lectures . . . on the common interests of Great Britain and America," IV, 162–180, an article which appeared originally in the *People's J.*, I (Mar. 28, 1846), 172–179. See also later comment: "On American indifference to the great European struggle" (letter pub. originally under the signature of "Publicola" in the *Weekly Dispatch*, Sept. 23, 1855), in *Memorial edition of collected works of W. J. Fox*, London, 1865–68, V, pp. 269–271.

613   FRENCH DOMINATION. [Hamilton? 1849?].   **CaOTP**

Broadside. Arguments against annexation to the U.S. as a means of avoiding French domination.

614   FRIENDS, SOCIETY OF. LONDON YEARLY MEETING. Address on the slave trade and slavery to sovereigns, and those in authority in the nations of Europe, and other parts of the world where the Christian religion is professed. From the yearly meeting of Friends in London, held in 1849. Richmond, Ind., [1849]. 8 p.   **NN OO**

615   GUIDE TO CALIFORNIA. (With a map.) Containing an account of the climate, soil, and natural productions of upper California, with authentic particulars respecting the gold region, derived from the official documents of the government of the United States; also, a complete description of the various routes, and all other information useful to intending emigrants. London, 1849. 36 p.   **CLU**

Uk has 2d ed., London, 1849. Effingham Wilson, pub., sometimes given as author.

616   KEILY, RICHARD. A brief description and statistical sketch of Georgia, United States of America: developing its immense agricultural, mining and manufacturing advantages, with remarks on emigration. Accompanied with a map & description of lands for sale in Irwin County, State of Georgia. London, 1849. 32 p.   **DLC Uk**

617   [KIRBY, WILLIAM]. Counter manifesto to the annexationists of Montreal. By Britannicus [*pseud.*] Niagara, 1849. 16 p.   **DLC**

Originally pub. in Niagara *Mail*, Oct. 29, 1849; an answer to an "Address to the people of Canada," with which it is repr. in William Weir, *Sixty years in Canada*, 1898, below. See also Kirby's "Stuart's raid. An incident in the siege of Richmond," Niagara *Mail*, June 12, 1862. See also his *Annals of Niagara*, 1896, below.

618   [LANCELOT, D.?]. The digger's hand-book, and truth about California; containing practical observations from researches made in the gold regions of the country, during a lengthened and extensive topographical and exploratory expedition. By D***L*** . . . comprehending all matters worthy of consideration by the digger, the merchant, the employer, or the labourer. With a map of the bay and port of San Francisco, and the surrounding country, in which are shewn the diggings on the Sacramento, San Joachim, Mercedes, &c. &c. Sydney, New South Wales, 1849. 106 p.   **CU-BANC**

Inserted by cataloger over initials (D***L***) are words "damn liar."

619   LYELL, SIR CHARLES. A second visit to the United States of North America. London, 1849. 2 vols.   **DLC Uk**

See Lyell's *Travels in North America*, 1845, above.

Reviews: *Chambers's J..*, XII, 38; *Chr. Observer*, L, 630; *Eclectic Rev.*, XC, 349; *Edinb. Rev.*, XCII, 339; *Eliza Cook's J.*, V, 342; *Fraser's Mag.*, XLI, 564; *Method. Quar. Rev.*, XXXI, 667; *No. Am. Rev.* (by F. Bowen), LXIX, 325; *No. Brit. Rev.* (by Sir David Brewster), XIV, 541; *Quar. Rev.* (by H. H. Milman), LXXXV, 183; *Spectator*, XXII, 563.

620   MACKAY, ALEXANDER. The Western world; or, Travels in the United States in 1846–47: exhibiting them in their latest development, social, political and industrial; including a chapter on California. London, 1849. 3 vols.   **CU-S NNC OU Uk**

DLC has 2d ed., London, 1849.

Reviews: *Am. Whig. Rev.*, XI, 110; *Athenaeum* (Feb. 24, March 3, 1849), 191, 220; *Edinb. Rev.*, XCII, 339; *New Monthly Mag.*, LXXXV, 472.

621   MADDEN, RICHARD ROBERT. The island of Cuba: its resources, progress, and prospects, considered in relation especially to the influence of its prosperity on the interests of the British West India colonies. London, 1849. 252 p.   **DLC Uk**

"American influence in Cuba and Texian policy," pp. 82–96; other comment on U.S., passim. See also author's *The shrines and sepulchres of the old and new world, etc.*, 1851, below.

622 MCLEAN, JOHN. Notes of a twenty-five years' service in the Hudson's Bay territory. By John M'Lean. London, 1849. 2 vols. **DLC Uk**

Repr., ed. by W. S. Wallace, Toronto, 1932 (Champlain society pubs., vol. XIX). Chaps. 12 and 13 of vol. I are on U.S.; see esp. pp. 291–304.

623 MONTREAL. ANNEXATION ASSOCIATION. Circular of the committee of the Annexation association of Montreal. Montreal, [1849]. 16 p. **CaOOA Uk**

Dated Dec. 7, 1849; signed by R. Mackay and A. A. Dorion, secretaries. See also *The annexation manifesto of 1849. Reprinted from the original pamphlet with the names of the signers*, Montreal, 1881, 31 p. Pp. 1–8 also repr. in *Sixty years in Canada*, by William Weir, Secretary of the Tariff reform association of 1858, pp. 52–79 (see under 1898, below). For the original letters to and from signers see Arthur G. Penny, "The Annexation movement, 1849–50," *Canadian Hist. Rev.*, V (Sept. 1924), 236–261. For reaction to the movement see "Canada," the *Dublin Univ. Mag.*, XXXV (Feb. 1850), 151–168.

624 MORTON, A. C. Report on the York and Cumberland railroad, the advantages of probable revenue, with statistics of the cost and traffic of various roads in the United States. By A. C. Morton, consulting engineer. Portland, 1849. 28 p. **CaOOA DLC**

DLC lists under York and Cumberland railroad.

625 MORTON, A. C. Report on the St. Lawrence and Atlantic rail-road; its influence on the trade of the St. Lawrence, and statistics of the cost and traffic of the New York and Massachusetts rail-roads. By A. C. Morton, civil engineer. Montreal, 1849. 47 p. **DLC**

626 MOUNTAIN, GEORGE JEHOSHAPHAT, *bishop of Quebec.* Thoughts on "Annexation," in connection with the duty and the interest of members of the Church of England; and as affecting some particular religious questions. Intended originally for publication as a pastoral letter, to the clergy and laity of the Church of England, in the diocese of Quebec. Quebec, [1849]. 28 p. **CaOOA**

627 NORTH TEXAN COLONIZATION COMPANY . . . Texas, its climate, physical features, and advantages for colonization, with the amended prospectus of the north Texan Colonization Company. No. I. January 1, 1849. [London? 1849]. 8 p. **CtY**

628 NUTTALL, THOMAS. The North American sylva; or, A description of the forest trees of the United States, Canada, and Nova Scotia, not described in the work of F. Andrew Michaux, and containing all the forest trees discovered in the Rocky mountains, the territory of Oregon, down to the shores of the Pacific and into the confines of California, as well as in various parts of the United States. Philadelphia, 1842–49. 3 vols., 122 plates. **CaBVa DNAL OrP Uk**

Pub. as vols. IV–VI of Michaux' *The North American sylva*, etc., Philadelphia, 1841–49. See also Nuttall's *Manual of the ornithology of the United States*, 1834, above.

629 ROEBUCK, JOHN ARTHUR. The colonies of England: a plan for the government of some portion of our colonial possessions. London, 1849. 248 p. **DLC Uk**

On U.S., see esp. pp. 186–248.

630 [ROSE, A. W. H.]. The emigrant churchman in Canada. By a pioneer of the wilderness. Edited by the Rev. Henry Christmas. London, 1849. 2 vols. **DLC Uk**

Usually cataloged under Christmas or "Churchman". Later ed. appeared under title, *Canada in 1849. Pictures of Canadian life, or, The emigrant churchman. By a pioneer of the wilderness*, London, 1850. Includes description of two visits to the U.S.: I, pp. 135–156; II, pp. 21–131.

631   ROSS, ALEXANDER. Adventures of the first settlers on the Oregon or Columbia River: being a narrative of the expedition fitted out by John Jacob Astor, to establish the "Pacific fur company"; with an account of some Indian tribes on the coast of the Pacific. London, 1849. 352 p.   **DLC Uk**

Repr. as one of the Lakeside classics, ed., with introd. and notes by Milo Milton Quaife, Chicago, 1923. Describes Ross' adventures while connected with the Pacific Fur Co., 1810–13. See account of this work in Geo. Bird Grinnell, *Beyond the Old Frontier*, New York., 1913, pp. 3–38. Also see Cecil Dryden, *Up the Columbia for furs*, Caldwell, Idaho, 1949.

632   RUXTON, GEORGE FREDERICK AUGUSTUS. Life in the far West. Edinburgh, 1849. 312 p.   **DLC Uk**

Appeared originally in *Blackwood's Edinb. Mag.* (June–Nov. 1848), LXIII, 713–732, LXIV, 17–30, 129–144, 293–314, 429–443, 573–590; vol. LXIV also carried a memoir of the author, 591–594. The book was repub. under the title, *In the old West*, New York, 1915; then reissued under original title, ed. by Leroy R. Hafen, Norman [Okla.], 1951. Also repr. in *Mountain men; George Frederick Ruxton's first hand accounts of fur trappers and Indians in the Rockies*, ed. and illust. by Glen Rounds, New York, [1966], together with portions of *Adventures in Mexico and the Rocky mountains*. Semi-fictionized handling of real experiences; Ruxton is cited as having said, "It is not fiction," in the *Blackwood's* memoir cited above, p. 594 and in the introd. to the 1851 ed., p. xi. CSmH possesses a unique copy of the 1st ed., with inserted handpainted sketches by Ruxton. See the account of Ruxton's adventures in *Ruxton of the Rockies*, ed. Leroy R. Hafen, Norman [Okla.], 1950. Also see Geo. Bird Grinnell's *Beyond the Old Frontier*, N.Y., 1913, pp. 193–234.

Reviews: *Brit. Quar. Rev.*, XI, 154; *Eliza Cook's J.*, I, 234; *Littel's Living Age*, XXII, 286.

633   SEXTON, GEORGE. A Portraiture of Mormonism, or animadiversions on the doctrines and pretensions of the Latter-day saints; a review of the history and contents of the Book of Mormon; and a sketch of the career of Joseph Smith, and various other notorious fanatics and imposters; being lectures delivered by Dr. Geo. Sexton, honorary member of various scientific, medical, and literary societies, British and continental, etc. London, 1849. 113 p.   **CLU CtY ICN Uk**

634   SMITH, CHARLES H. The Mormonites: their origin, history, & pretensions; being an exposure of the blasphemous doctrines of the Latter-day saints; the deception and falsehood practiced upon ignorant emigrants—specimens of their hymns of praise to Joseph Smith; and the ridiculous absurdities of the Book of Mormon: with a notice of their recent sufferings in America, through their own violence and folly. Bristol, 1849.   **NN OO**

635   SMITH, EDWARD. Account of a journey through northeastern Texas, undertaken in 1849, for the purpose of emigration. Embodied in a report: to which are appended letters and verbal communications, from eminent individuals; lists of temperature; of prices of land, produce, and articles of merchandize; in several parts of the western and southern states; and the recently adopted constitution of Texas, with maps from the last authentic survey. London, 1849. 188 p.   **DLC Uk**

Dr. Smith came to Texas with John Barrow, q.v.

Review: *Colonial Mag.* (by Thomas Falconer), XVIII (1850), 352.

636 SMITH, SIDNEY. The settler's new home; or, the emigrant's location, being a guide to emigrants in the selection of a settlement, and the preliminary details of the voyage. . . . British America—Canada: embracing Nova Scotia, New Brunswick, Cape Breton, Prince Edward's Island, eastern Canada, western Canada. The United States: including New England, the western states, the slave states, Texas, California, Hudson's bay settlement, comprehending Oregon, and Van Couver's island. London, 1849. 106 p. **DLC**

Later eds. carried variant titles, e.g., *The settler's new home; or, Whether to go, and whither? Being a guide to emigrants in the selection of a settlement, and the preliminary details of the voyage. Embracing the whole fields of emigration, and the most recent information relating thereto*, London, 1850, 106 p. The work made free use of earlier accounts, by Flower, Stuart, Shirreff, Dudgeon, et al.

637 THOMPSON, GEORGE ALEXANDER. Hand book to the Pacific and California, describing eight different routes, by sea, Central America, Mexico, and the territories of the United States, particularly with reference to the ports frequented by the steamers of the Royal mail steam packet company. London, 1849. 108 p. **DLC Uk**

638 THURSTON, WILLIAM. Guide to the gold regions of Upper California. With a map, and scientific designs of native gold, mode of working, &c., &c. London, 1849. 70 p. **DLC Uk**

639 [VIGER, DENIS BENJAMIN]. Policy of free trade, in a series of letters addressed to the Honorable L. H. Lafontaine, Attorney general for Canada East. . . . Letter I. Montreal, 1849. 20 p. **CaOOP**

Signed "D. V."

640 [VIZETELLY, HENRY]. Four months among the gold finders in Alta California: being the diary of an expedition from San Francisco to the gold districts. By J. Tyrwhitt Brooks, M.D. [*pseud*]. London, 1849. 207 p. **DLC Uk**

This best-seller of the gold-rush books went into numerous eds. and was translated into several languages. Paris ed., 1849, carries title, *California. Four months among the gold-finders, being the diary of an expedition from San Francisco to the gold districts. By J. Tyrwhitt Brooks, M.D. What I saw in California, a description of its soil, climate, productions, and gold mines; with the best routes and latest information for intending emigrants. By Edwin Bryant, late alcade [sic] of San Francisco. To which is annexed, an appendix containing official documents and letters authenticating the accounts of the quantities of gold found, with its actual value*. The work was long accepted as an authentic travel account until Vizetelly admitted authorship and confessed he wrote it in ten days without ever leaving England; see his *Glances back through seventy years*, London, 1893, I, pp. 343–347. See also Douglas E. Watson's account in *Calif. Hist. Soc. Quar.*, XI, no. 1 (1932), 65–68, and William P. Courteney's *Secrets of our national literature*, London, 1908, p. 110.

Reviews: *Athenaeum*, (1849), 157; London *Times*, Apr. 11, 1849; *Quar. Rev.*, XCI, 504.

641 WALPOLE, *LIEUT. HON.* FREDERICK. Four years in the Pacific. In Her Majesty's ship "Collingwood." From 1844 to 1848. London, 1849. 2 vols. **DLC Uk**

Visit to Monterey, California in 1846, II, pp. 204–219.

Review: *Littel's Living Age*, XXII, 607.

642   [WARD, JAMES, ed.?]. Perils, pastimes and pleasures in Australia, Vancouver's Island and California. London, 1849. 404 p.   **CLU CtY Uk**

Dedication to James Wyld (in Calif. at the time) signed "J. W."; introd. signed by editor, "J. W." i.e., James Ward. Section on Calif., repr. in Ward's *A history of gold as a commodity and as a measure of value. Its fluctuations both in the ancient and modern times, with an estimate of the probable supplies from California and Australia*, London, [1852], pp. 92–116. In the later, Ward describes the material on California as a "friend's" experiences, leaving ambiguous whether authorship should be attributed to Ward or Wyld.

643   WILLSON, HUGH BOWLBY. Canada and the United States: [A letter] to the editor of the National Intelligencer. [Washington, D.C., 1849].   **Uk**

644   [WYLD, JAMES]. Geographical & mineralogical notes, to accompany Mr. Wyld's map of the gold regions of California. London, 1849. 32 p.   **DLC Uk**

Map by Wyld, but authorship of notes uncertain, though item is generally attributed to him.

Review: *Athenaeum*, (Feb. 17, 1849), 157.

645   WYLD, JAMES. A guide to the gold country of California. An authentic and descriptive narrative of the latest discoveries in that country, comp. from the official dispatches of Colonel Mason, Lieutenant-Colonel Fremont, and other government authorities. Illustrated with a map of Mexico, California, and the United States. With the various sea and land routes, and their distance from each other in the number of days distinctly marked thereon. London, [1849?]. 62 p.   **DLC**

Not certain whether more than map is by Wyld, but item is generally attributed to him; Howes states that Wyld "compiled North American official documents."

Review: *Athenaeum*, (Feb. 17, 1849), 157.

1850

646   BAIRD, ROBERT. Impressions and experiences of the West Indies and North America in 1849. Edinburgh, 1850. 2 vols.   **DLC Uk**

Both DLC and Uk mistakenly list this work as by the American writer, Robert Baird, D.D., author of *Religion in the United States of America*, *View of the valley of the Mississippi*, etc. This travel account is by a British author, undoubtedly a different Robert Baird.

647   BIGSBY, JOHN JEREMIAH. The shoe and canoe; or, Pictures of travel in the Canadas. Illustrative of their scenery and of colonial life; with facts and opinions on emigration, state policy, and other points of public interest. With numerous plates and maps. By John J. Bigsby, M.D., hon. mem. American geological society, late secretary to the boundary commission under Art. VI. and VII. Treaty of Ghent. London, 1850. 2 vols.   **DLC Uk**

"Excursion the fifth, Lake Erie and the River Detroit," I, 242–294; also other comment on the U.S., passim.

648   [BILL, JOHN]. The English party's excursion to Paris, in Easter week 1849. To which is added, a trip to America, etc. etc. etc., by J. B., esq., barrister-at-law. London, 1850. 557 p.   **DLC Uk**

Extracts from an American journal "revised in 1849" (July 16, 1827–July 16, 1828), pp. 152–400. Portion about the U.S. was supposedly pub. separately under title, *A trip to America*, London, 1850; no copy located.

649   BOTTOMLEY, EDWIN. An English settler in pioneer Wisconsin: the letters of Edwin Bottomley, 1842–1850. Ed. with introd. and notes by Milo M. Quaife. Madison, 1918. 250 p.   **DLC**

Pubs. of the State Hist. Soc. of Wisconsin. Collections, Vol. XXV.

650   BOWES, JOHN, [*of Cheltenham*]. Mormonism exposed, in its swindling and licentious abominations, refuted in its principles, and in the claims of its head, the modern Mohammed, Joseph Smith, who is proved to be a deceiver and no prophet of God. London, [1850?]. 71 p.   **CtY NN Uk USIC**

2d ed., London, [1854?], 83 p., with additional material and longer title: . . . *Addressed to the serious consideration of the "Latter-day saints," and also to all the friends of mankind.*

651   BROWN, *SIR* WILLIAM, [*of Liverpool*]. Protectionism in the United States. To the secretary of the treasury of the United States. [Liverpool? 1850].   **Uk**

ICN has U.S. ed., with title: *Letter from William Brown . . . to the secretary of the treasury . . . of the United States*, New York, 1850, 10 p.

652   BURGESS, J. M. The book of Mormon contradictory to common sense, reason, and revelation; or, The Mormon hierarchy founded upon a fiction. Liverpool, 1850. 30 p.   **MH NN USIC**

653   CALIFORNIA: its present condition and future prospects; with an interesting account of the gold regions. By a scientific gentlemen, several years resident in California. Adelaide [Australia], 1850. 52 p.   **CSmH**

Preface signed, "B. Ross," but he is not the author.

654   CARLISLE, GEORGE WILLIAM FREDERICK HOWARD, *7th earl*. Two lectures, on the poetry of Pope, and on his own travels in America, by the right honourable the Earl of Carlisle. Delivered to the Leeds Mechanics' institution and literary society, December 5th and 6th, 1850. Leeds, 1850. 44 p.   **MH Uk**

DLC has copy, "eighth thousand," "revised and corrected by the author"; also has a copy of U.S. ed., *Travels in America. The poetry of Pope, etc.*, New York, 1851. The "Lecture on America" was repr. in the author's *Lectures and addresses in aid of popular education*, London, 1856. The Earl of Carlisle, then Lord Morpeth, travelled in the U.S. 1841–42.

Reviews: *Eliza Cook's J..*, IV, 205; London *Times*, Dec. 10, 1851; *New Monthly Mag.*, XCVI, 229; *No. Am. Rev.* (by E. L. Chandler), LXXIV, 197; *Quar. Rev.*, LXXXIX, 57.

655   [CARMICHAEL-SMYTH, ROBERT]. A letter to the Right honourable Earl Grey on the subjects of transportation and emigration, as connected with an imperial railway communication between the Atlantic and Pacific. London, 1850. 27 p.   **CSmH CU CtY**

Signed Robert Carmichael-Smyth. On possible U.S. routes, pp. 12–19.

656   CHAMBERS'S PAPERS FOR THE PEOPLE. Volume IV. Edinburgh, 1850.   **DLC Uk**

Pamphlet on "California" bound as number 26 in this collection of separately pub. pamphlets; 32 p. No location or pub. information found for the original pamphlet.

657   EMIGRANTS' LETTERS: being a collection of recent communications from settlers in the British colonies. London, 1850. 130 p.   **ICU Uk**

At head of title: "Published for the committee of the emigrants' school fund." Includes a letter from California, pp. 120–122.

658 ESTLIN, JOHN BISHOP. Reply to a circular issued by the Glasgow association for the abolition of slavery, recommending a discontinuance of British support to the Boston anti-slavery bazaar. Paris, 1850. 8 p. **DHU MH NIC**

659 FITZGERALD, JOHN, *M.A.* Manstealing by proxy; or, The guilt of our countrymen in upholding slavery and the slave trade, by the purchase of slave grown produce. London, 1850. 23 p. **NIC Uk**

660 [FLEMING, G.A.]. California: its past history; its present position; its future prospects; containing a history of the country from its colonization by the Spaniards to the present time; a sketch of its geographical and physical features: and a minute and authentic account of the discovery of the gold region, and the subsequent important proceedings. Including a history of the rise, progress, and present condition of the Mormon settlements. With an appendix, containing the official reports made to the government of the United States. London, 1850. 270 p. **DLC Uk**

Includes hand-colored illust.

661 FOSS, A[NDREW] T. Facts for Baptist churches, collected, arranged, and reviewed. By A[ndrew] T. Foss, of New Hampshire, and E[dward] Mathews, of Wisconsin. Utica, [N.Y.], 1850. 408 p. **DLC**

Includes many letters from English abolitionists, boards, committees, etc. Although identified as from Wisconsin, Mathews was an English clergyman who later returned to England; see his other works, 1860, 1864 and 1869, below.

662 FRERE, *REV*. JOHN. A short history of the Mormonites; or, Latter Day Saints. With an account of the real origin of the Book of Mormon. Compiled from various sources. London, 1850. 24 p. **CSmH NN Uk**

663 GOULD, JOHN. A monograph of the *Odontophorinae*, or partridges of America. London, 1850. 23 p. **DLC**

Contains 32 colored plates. Uk has only parts 1 and 2, London, 1844.

664 HAW, *REV*. WILLIAM. Fifteen years in Canada; being a series of letters on its early history and settlement; its boundaries, divisions, population, and general routes; its agricultural progress and wealth compared with the United States; its religious and educational institutions; and its present political condition and relations; together with the advantages it affords as a desirable field of emigration. Edinburgh, 1850. 120 p. **DLC Uk**

665 HOUSTOUN, *MRS*. MATILDA CHARLOTTE (JESSE) FRASER. Hesperos; or, Travels in the West. London, 1850. 2 vols. **DLC Uk**

Author's second trip to the U.S. See also her *Texas and the Gulf of Mexico*, 1844, above.

666 HUNTLEY, *SIR* HENRY VERE. Anglo-Californian gold mining company. Report of Capt. Sir Henry Vere Huntley, R.N., chief superintendent. London, [1850?]. **CSmH**

CSmH catalog, and both DLC and Uk (for other works), give Huntley's name as Henry Veel Huntly, but this title page of his earliest publication gives "Vere," as does the account in *DNB*.

667 KEEFER, THOMAS COLTRIN. Philosophy of railroads. Published at the request of the directors of the Montreal and Lachine railroad. Montreal, 1850. 39 p. **DLC**

Uk only has French-language 4th ed., Montreal, 1853. DLC also has English 4th ed., rev. and enlarged, *Philosophy of railroads, published by order of the directors of the St. Lawrence and Ottawa grand junction railway company*, Montreal, 1853, 47 p. Also included in *Philosophy of railroads and other essays*, ed. with an introd. by H. V. Nelles, Toronto, [1972].

668   KEEFER, THOMAS COLTRIN. The canals of Canada: their prospects and influence. Prize essay. Written for a premium offered by His Excellency the Earl of Elgin and Kincardine, K.T., governor general of British North America, etc., etc., etc. Toronto, 1850. 111 p.   **DLC Uk**

Discussion of trade with U.S., etc., passim. A portion repr. under title, *Free trade, protection, and reciprocity. From "The canals of Canada,"* Ottawa, 1876, 20 p. See also Keefer's *"Montreal:" and "The Ottawa:" Two lectures delivered before the Mechanics institute of Montreal, in January, 1853 and 1854*, Montreal, 1854.

669   KNOX, ROBERT. The races of men: a fragment. By Robert Knox, M.D., Lecturer on anatomy, and corresponding member of the National academy of medicine of France. London, 1850. 479 p.   **DLC**

Uk has later ed., *The races of men. A philosophical enquiry into the influence of race over the destinies of nations*, London, 1862, which includes a supp., pp. 481–600. Scattered comment on the U.S. throughout.

670   LARDNER, DIONYSIUS. Railway economy: a treatise on the new art of transport, its management, prospects, and relations, commercial, financial, and social, with an exposition of the practical results of the railways in operation in the United Kingdom, on the Continent, and in America. London, 1850. 528 p.   **DLC Uk**

Chap. 16, "Inland transport in the United States," pp. 308–348. A reorganized version of the chap. appeared as "Locomotion by river and railway in the United States," in *The museum of science and industry*, London, 1854, II, pp. 17–64. Lardner was in America, 1840–45; see his description of this visit in the pref. to his *Popular lectures on science and art; delivered in the principal cities and towns of the United States*, New York, 1846.

671   LATHAM, ROBERT GORDON. The natural history of the varieties of man. By Robert Gordon Latham, M.D., F.R.S., late fellow of King's College, Cambridge; one of the vice-presidents of the Ethnological society, London; corresponding member to the ethnological society, New York, etc. London, 1850. 574 p.   **DLC Uk**

On North American Indians, pp. 287–405. For additional comment on the American Indian see author's *Man and his migrations*, New York, 1852, pp. 129–133.

672   MACBETH, *REV.* JAMES. The church and the slave-holder; or, Light and darkness; an attempt to prove, from the word of God and from reason, that to hold property in man is wholly destitute of divine warrant, is a flagrant crime, and demands excommunication. Earnestly and respectfully addressed to the members of the approaching assembly of the Free church of Scotland, and to the churches generally. Edinburgh, [1850?]. 36 p.
    DLC Uk

673   [MANN, ALICE]. Mann's emigrant's complete guide to the United States of America: containing a description of the country and the several states, with their comparative suitableness for emigrants; the prices of land in the different states; the wages of labour and prices of living; the best and cheapest routes to the different parts of the Union: with a large amount of information of much importance to the intending emigrant. London, 1850.

AuSM, IaHi, have 4th ed., London, 1850. Sabin lists under William Mann. Later included in *The Emigrant's complete guide to the United States, Australia, Port Stephens, Van Dieman's Land, New Zealand, the Cape of Good Hope and Natal; Canada, New Brunswick, and Nova Scotia; and the Auckland Islands*, [London, n.d.].

674   MASON, [W. B.]. Mason's handbook to California; its gold and how to get it; a description of the country, etc. London, [1850?]. 16 p.

No locations found; in Sabin, #45421.

675   MELVIN, JAMES W. The emigrant's guide to the colonies. London, 1850. 134 p.
CtY ICN ICU

On Texas, pp. 36–48; California, pp. 59–81; "America," pp. 82–93; "New Orleans," pp. 93–95.

676   [MONTAGU, MONTAGU]. California broadsides. [London, 1850]. 16 p.   **DLC Uk**

Poetic satire on the rush from London to California.

677   MOONEY, THOMAS. Nine years in America . . . in a series of letters to his cousin, Patrick Mooney, a farmer in Ireland. Dublin, 1850. 154 p.

DLC, IreDT have 2d ed., Dublin, 1850. Mooney travelled as far west as Wisconsin.

678   [NETTLE, GEORGE]. A practical guide for emigrants to North America, including the United States, Lower and Upper Canada, and Newfoundland; with full information respecting the preparations necessary for the voyage, instructions on landing, travelling routes, capabilities and price of land, farming operations, price of labour, and all other matters requisite for the emigrant to become acquainted with before embarking; by a seven years' resident in North America. London, 1850. 57 p.   **DLC Uk**

On outside cover: "By George Nettle, (late of Devonport,) seven years resident in North America. London, 1850."

679   RYAN, WILLIAM REDMOND. Personal adventures in Upper and Lower California, in 1848–9; with the author's experience at the mines. London, 1850. 2 vols.   **DLC Uk**

Dutch ed., Haarlem, 1850. A mimeographed index to the work, ed. by Joseph Gaer, was issued by the SERA project, California literary research, [1935], no. 17.

Reviews: *Athenaeum*, (May 18, 1850), 527; *Brit. Quar. Rev.*, XII, 56; *Eclectic Mag.*, XXI, 289; *Quar. Rev.*, LXXXVII, 396.

680   SLAVE HOLDERS AND THE Great Exhibition. [n.p., 1850?]   **MB**

Broadside; urges obstracism of slaveholders from U.S. visiting England for the Exhibition.

681   SMITH, WILLIAM. An emigrant's narrative; or, A voice from the sterrage [sic]. Being a brief account of the sufferings of the emigrants in the ship India, on her voyage from Liverpool to New York, in the winter of 1747[i.e.,1847]–8; together with an account of the cruelties practiced upon them in the Staten Island hospital. New York, 1850. 34 p.   **MH**

682   STATEMENT AS TO THE IRON trade of Scotland, and the exports of iron to foreign parts, particularly with reference to the United States of America. Glasgow, 1850. 6 p.
NNC Uk

Uk lists under Scotland—Appendix—Agriculture, etc.

683   STEAM POSTAL INTERCOURSE & traffic with the Americas and Austral-Asia. Comparative merits of the existing and proposed mail routes. London, [1850?]. 16 p.
DLC

On back of t.p. is printed, "Official report to the American congress, on the communications between Atlantic and Pacific," but clearly of British authorship. Repr. with corrections from the *Colonial Mag.*, XVIII (April 1850), 352–365.

684 THORNTON, *MAJOR* JOHN. Diary of a tour through the northern states of the Union, and Canada. London, 1850. 120 p. **DLC Uk**

Tour made June–Oct., 1849.

685 WILSON, F. A. Britain redeemed and Canada preserved. By F. A. Wilson . . . and Alfred B. Richards . . . London, 1850. 556 p. **DLC Uk**

Chap. 4, "United States," Part I, pp. 77–102; also incidental comment on the U.S., passim.

686 WORDSWORTH, WILLIAM. Wordsworth & Reed; the poet's correspondence with his American editor: 1836–1850, and Henry Reed's account of his reception at Rydal mount, London, and elsewhere in 1854, edited by Leslie Nathan Broughton. Ithaca, New York, 1933. 288 p. **DLC Uk**

Comment on American affairs, esp. repudiation of debts in the 1840's, passim.

1851

687 AMERICAN SLAVERY. Report of a meeting of members of the Unitarian body, held at the Freemasons' tavern, June 13th, 1851, to deliberate on the duty of English Unitarians in reference to slavery in the United States. Rev. Dr. Hutton in the chair. London, 1851. 23 p. **DLC**

688 ANDERSON, WILLIAM WEMYSS. Jamaica and the Americans. New York, 1851. 30 p. **DLC Uk**

A lecture read at Kingston, before the Colonial literary society, January 17, 1850. A former member of the Jamaica legislature, Anderson visited U.S. in 1849; describes life and, esp., productivity.

689 ASHLEY, *REV.* FRANCIS BUSTEED. Mormonism: an exposure of the impositions adopted by the sect called "The Latter-Day Saints." London, 1851. 32 p. **CSmH NN**

Uk has London, 1851 ed., rev. and with additions, 36 p.

690 BRODIE, WALTER. Pitcairn's Island, and the islanders in 1850. . . . Together with extracts from his private journal, and a few hints upon California; also, the reports of all the commanders of H.M. ships that have touched at the above island since 1800. London, 1851. 260 p. **DLC**

Uk has 2d ed., London, 1851. Account of California, pp. 217–241. Unclear whether this is the W. Brodie who authored "Transatlantic Sketches," *Bentley's Misc.*, LIII, 469–475, 613–619; LIV, 185–188, 278–283.

691 BROWN, PAOLA. Address intended to be delivered in the City Hall, Hamilton, February 7, 1851, on the subject of slavery. Hamilton, 1851. 64 p. **CaOTP**

692 CASWALL, *REV.* HENRY. A brief account of the method of synodical action in the American church; a paper presented to the provisional committee of the synodal consultative meeting at Derby. London, 1851. 14 p. **CtY Uk**

693 CASWALL, *REV* HENRY. Mormonism and its author; or, A statement of the doctrines of the "Latter-Day Saints." London, 1851. 16 p. **IHi MH**

Uk has London, 1852 ed. Extension of comments on his visit to Nauvoo in 1842, described in *The City of the Mormons*, London, 1842, above, and *The Prophet of the 19th Century*, London, 1842.

694 CUNYNGHAME, *SIR* ARTHUR AUGUSTUS THURLOW. A glimpse at the great western republic. By Lieut.-Col. Arthur Cunynghame. London, 1851. 337 p. **DLC Uk**

Reviews: *Athenaeum*, (May 31, 1851), 575; *Lit. Gazette*, (June 7, 1851), 389; *Quar. Rev.*, LXXXIX, 57.

695 THE EMIGRANT'S MANUAL. British America and the United States of America. Edinburgh, 1851. 133 p. **DLC**

Uk, various U.S. libraries, have as part of *The emigrant's manual; Australia, New Zealand, America, and South Africa. With a preliminary dissertation, by John Hill Burton*, Edinburgh, 1851, 485 p. (in the 26 vol. series, *Chambers instructive and entertaining library*, Edinburgh, 1848–52). Burton's essay pub. separately under title, *Emigration in its practical application to individuals and communities*, Edinburgh, 1851, 93 p.; on U.S., passim.

696 THE EMIGRANT'S NEWEST GUIDE to the United States. Dublin, 1851. 31 p. **ICU**

697 ENGLAND'S WESTERN, or America's eastern shore? Old Ireland a new state? With their various complexities and perplexities discussed. By an old and almost obsolete loyalist. Dublin, 1851. 47 p. **DLC**

698 EVANS, HENRY SMITH, *comp*. A guide to the emigration colonies: including Australia, Tasmania, New Zealand, Cape of Good Hope, Natal, Canada, and the other British possessions of North America, also the United States and California. Compiled from official documents: being the substance of a lecture delivered at the Mechanics' institution, Southampton buildings. London, 1851. 28 p. **CSt NNC Uk**

1852 ed. carries same title, but with cover title: *The emigrant's map of the world and guide to the colonies. . . .* London, 1855 ed. changed title to *A map and guide to all the emigration colonies of Great Britain and America*.

699 EYRE, JOHN. Travels: comprising a journey from England to Ohio, two years in that state, travels in America, &c. To which are added, the foreigner's protracted journal, letters, &c. 4th thousand. New York, 1851. 360 p. **CSmH MH OCIWHi**

Part I. Travels from England to Ohio, 1832; Part II. Two years in Ohio, 1833–35; Part III. The European stranger in America, (1837), and The foreigner's protracted journal, 1847–48. The first two parts comprise, with additions, *The Christian spectator: being a journey from England to Ohio, two years in that state, travels in America, &c.*, Albany, 1838, above. The first part of part III, *The European stranger in America*, 1837, above, was issued separately. The pref. dated 1838 is the same as that in *The Christian spectator*.

700 FINDLAY, ALEXANDER GEORGE. A directory for the navigation of the Pacific Ocean; with description of its coasts, islands, etc., from the Strait of Magalhaens to the Arctic Sea, and those of Asia and Australia; its winds, currents and other phenomena. London, 1851. 2 vols. **DLC Uk**

On California and Oregon, vol. I, pp. 313–388.

701 FOSTER, VERE [HENRY LEWIS]. Diary of my voyage. Printed by order of the House of Commons. London, 1851. 9 p. **Uk**

In *Papers and records*, vol. 10, no 198. Account of Foster's voyage as a steerage passenger in the "Washington," one of three such trips to investigate harsh conditions on U.S. immigrant ships. Includes correspondence between Lord Hobart and U.S. authorities on those conditions. See also Foster's *Work and wages, or the penny emigrant's guide to the United States and Canada. . . .* , 1854, below.

702　GUTHRIE, *REV*. JOHN. Garrisonian infidelity exposed: in two letters from the Rev. John Guthrie, Greenock, in reply to George Thompson, esq., M.P. Glasgow, 1851.　**MB**

703　HALIBURTON, THOMAS CHANDLER. The English in America. London, 1851. 2 vols.
DLC Uk

1st ed. has been erroneously listed as 1841, 1843, etc. Work came out almost immediately under another title: *Rule and misrule of the English in America*, London, 1851. Haliburton is mainly concerned with events of the colonial period, but comments on contemporary Anglo-American affairs can be found in the final chap., "Application of the facts contained in this work," II, pp. 285–372. Haliburton is chiefly famed for his creation of "Sam Slick" who made a first appearance in the anonymously pub. *The clockmaker; or, The sayings and doings of Samuel Slick, of Slickville*, Halifax, 1836. Although fiction, it is noted here because perhaps no other work had so much influence in fixing the stereotype of the Yankee in the minds of British readers. A 2d series appeared in 1838, a 3d in 1840, followed by various combined and miscellaneous series. See Sten Bodvar Liljegren, *Canadian history and Thomas Chandler Haliburton: some notes on Sam Slick*, Upsala, 1969. See also Haliburton's other fictional works: *The letter bag of the Great Western; or, Life in a steamer*, London, 1840; *The attache; or, Sam Slick in England*, London, 1843 (2d ser., 1844); *The season ticket*, London, 1860. The author's *Americans at home; or, Byeways, backwoods, and prairies*, London, 1854, is a compilation of stories by American authors.

Reviews: *Acadiensis*, II, 15; *Albion*, Sept. 27, 1851; *Church Rev.*, IV, 523; *Irish Quar. Rev.*, I, 523; *New Monthly Mag.*, XCIII, 27; *Quar. Rev.*, XCIV, 565. For lists of reviews of Haliburton's other works, see V. L. O. Chittick, *Thomas Chandler Haliburton*, New York, 1924, pp. 665 ff.

704　HIND, HENRY YOULE. A comparative view of the climate of western Canada, considered in relation to its influence upon agriculture. Toronto, 1851. 38 p.　**CaOTU**

On U.S., passim. See also his "North West British America—The great American desert— Comparison between a route to the Pacific in the United States and in British America," *Brit.-Am. Mag.*, I, (July 1863), pp. 268–272.

705　HINTON, JOHN HOWARD. The test of experience; or, The voluntary principle in the United States. London, 1851. 124 p.　**CSmH ICU Uk**

Sabin lists only 1857 ed., no place of pub.

706　HOWE, JOSEPH. England's interest in colonization. Extracts from a letter. London, [1851]. 12 p.　**MH**

Caption title: "England's interest in colon. [Extracts from a letter addressed by the Hon. Joseph Howe, Provincial secretary of Nova Scotia, to the Right honourable the secretary of state of the colonies, on the 16th of Jan. 1851.]" Some comparison is made of development of the U.S. in contrast to that of Canada, etc.

707　[JEFFREY, JOHN]. Botanical expedition to Oregon. Extract from minutes of committee, held 29th September, 1851 . . . . [Edinburgh, 1851]. 3 p.　**CtY**

Caption title: "Letter from Jeffrey to J. H. Balfour, Prof. of Botany, Univ. of Edinburgh, dated Apr. 7, 1851."

708　JOHNSTON, JAMES FINLAY WEIR. Notes on North America, agricultural, economical, and social. Edinburgh, 1851. 2 vols.　**DLC Uk**

Reviews: *Blackwood's Edinb. Mag.*, LXX, 699; *Eclectic Mag.*, IV, 48, 98; *Edinb. Rev.*, XCIV, 46; *Lit. Gazette*, (1851), 277; *No. Am. Rev.*, LXXIII, 210; *Quar. Rev.*, LXXXIX, 57.

709 KELLY, WILLIAM. An excursion to California over the prairie, Rocky mountains, and the great Sierra Nevada. With a stroll through the diggings and ranches of that country. London, 1851. 2 vols. **DLC Uk**

Reissued, London, 1852, as vols. I and IV of the Bookcase series, with different titles for the two vols.: *Across the Rocky mountains, from New York to California; with a visit to the celebrated Mormon colony at the Great Salt Lake*; and *A stroll through the diggings of California*. The latter repr. as a California centennial ed., with paintings by Charles Nahl and foreword by Joseph A. Sullivan, Oakland, 1950.

Reviews: *Athenaeum* (April 26, 1851), 449; *Lit. Gazette* (by Edward Forbes), (May 24, 1851), 357; *New Monthly Mag.*, (May 1851), 345; *Quar. Rev.* (June–Sept. 1851), 504.

710 KINGSFORD, WILLIAM. History, structure, and statistics of plank roads, in the United States and Canada. By W. Kingsford . . . With remarks on roads in general, by F. G. Skinner; and a letter on plank roads, by the Hon. Charles E. Clarke. Philadelphia, 1851. 40 p. **DLC**

Uk has Philadelphia, 1852 ed. Kingsford was a Canadian engineer employed by the Hudson River railroad.

711 LATTER-DAY SAINTS. The dupes of a foolish and wicked imposture. London, [1851?]. 2 parts. **CtY USIC**

Capetown, 1853 ed., repr. "with slight alterations," 32 p.

712 [LEWIS, JOHN DELAWARE]. Across the Atlantic. By the author of "Sketches of Cantabs." London, 1851. 274 p. **DLC Uk**

Defense of Mrs. Trollope, et al.

Reviews: *Brit. Quar. Rev.*, XV, 112; *Lit. Gazette*, (1851), 35.

713 LINFORTH, JAMES. The Rev. C. W. Lawrence's "Few words from a pastor to his people on the subject of the Latter-day saints," replied to and refuted by James Linforth. [Liverpool, 1851?]. 8 p. **CSmH CtY ICN MH**

714 LONDON. GREAT EXHIBITION OF THE WORKS OF INDUSTRY OF ALL NATIONS, 1851. Offical description and illustrated catalogue. By authority of the Royal commission . . . London, 1851. 3 vols. **DLC Uk**

Ed. by Robert Ellis; introd. signed by [Sir] Henry Cole; on the U.S., III, pp. 1431–1469. See also [John Tallis]; *Tallis's history and description of the Crystal palace, and the exhibition of the world's industry in 1851; illustrated by beautiful steel engravings from original drawings and daguerreotypes, by Beard, Mayall, etc., etc.*, London, [1852]; on U.S., I, pp. 67–70, 160–162. For other comments on the U.S. exhibit in the Crystal Palace exhibit of 1851 see: *Littel's Living Age*, XXX (July 1851), 34; *Chambers's J.*, XV (May 31, 1851), 399; *Eclectic Rev.*, XCIII (June 1851), 746; XCIV (Nov. 1851), 663; *Westmin. Rev.*, LX (July 1851), 198. See also Robert F. Dalzell, *American participation in the Great Exhibition of 1851*, Amherst, Mass., 1980 (Amherst College honors thesis no. 1).

715 LOWE, JOSIAH BEATSON. "Mormonism." Delivered at the Concert hall, Liverpool, on Thursday evening, November 13th, 1851. Liverpool, [1851?]. [63]–98 p. **MH USIC**

Liverpool Church of England institution, lectures. Second course—No. 3.

716 [LUCATT, EDWARD]. Rovings in the Pacific, from 1837 to 1849; with a glance at California. By a merchant long resident at Tahiti. London, 1851. 2 vols. **DLC**

717   MCGEE, THOMAS D'ARCY. A history of the Irish settlers in North America, from the earliest period to the census of 1850. Boston, 1851. 180 p.   **DLC**

Uk has 2d ed., Boston, 1852.

718   MADDEN, RICHARD ROBERT. The shrines and sepulchres of the Old and New world; records of pilgrimages in many lands and researches connected with the history of places remarkable for memorials of the dead, or monuments of a sacred character; including notices of the funeral customs of the principal nations, ancient and modern. London, 1851. 2 vols.   **DLC Uk**

"Ancient tombs and tumuli of America," II, pp. 1–29. For account of Madden's three visits to America, 1833–1840, see: *The memoirs (chiefly autobiographical) from 1798 to 1886 of Richard Robert Madden . . .* ; Edited by his son, Thomas More Madden, London, 1891, pp. 86–108.

719   [MALEY, ANDREW JOHN.] Suggestions for the immediate establishment of a direct communication by steam navigation between Ireland and the United States of North America, without the aid of the British government. Dublin, [1851?].

No locations found.

720   [MAYHEW, HENRY]. The Mormons; or Latter-day saints. With memoirs of the life and death of Joseph Smith, the "American Mohamet." Illustrated with forty engravings. London, [1851]. 326 p.   **DLC Uk**

Charles Mackay often given as author, but Sabin and the *Dictionary of National Biography* attribute to Mayhew; ed. by MacKay. Portions appeared earlier in the London *Morning Chronicle*. Many later eds., with variant titles. New York, 1856 ed. appeared with title, *The religious, social and political history of the Mormons, or Latter-day saints, from their origin to the present time, containing full statements of their doctrines, government and condition, and memoirs of their founder, Joseph Smith. Edited, with important additions, by Samuel M. Smucker*, New York, 1856, 460 p. Yet another editor, H. L. Williams, ascribed authorship to Smucker and added new material, under title, *Life among the Mormons; or The religious, social. . . .* , New York, 1860, 466 p.

Reviews: *Brit. & For. Evang. Rev.*, I, 556; *Chr. Examiner* (by W. J. A. Bradford), LIII, 201; *Dublin Rev.* (by E. Walford), XXXIII, 77; *Edinb. Rev.*, CCII, 319 (part of a long review article by W. J. Conybeare, later repr. under the title, *Mormonism*, 1854, below); *London Quar. Rev.*, II, 95; *Quar. Rev.*, CXXII, 450; *Westmin. Rev.*, III, n.s., 196.

721   O'HANLON, *REV*. JOHN. The Irish emigrant's guide for the United States. Boston, 1851. 224 p.   **ICN NN NjP**

Lived in U.S. 1842–1853, then returned to Ireland. Reissued as a critical ed., with introd. and commentary by Edward J. Maguire, New York, 1976.

722   RECOLLECTIONS OF A RAMBLE from Sydney to Southampton; via South America, Panama, the West Indies, the United States, and Niagara. London, 1851. 340 p.   **DLC**

Uk has under title *Odds and ends of travel; or, Adventures, rambles, and recollections, of a trip from Sydney; via South America, etc.*, London, 1851; on U.S., pp. 241–340.

Review: *Lit. Gazette* (by Edward Forbes), (1851), 576; repr. in *Literary papers by the late Professor Edward Forbes, F.R.S. Selected from his writing in "The Literary Gazette,"* London, 1855, chap. 8.

723   ROWCROFT, CHARLES. An emigrant in search of a colony. London, 1851. 464 p.
CSt ICU Uk

On t.p. at head of title, "Parlour Library LXV." On U.S., pp. 151–206; fictionized account of personal experiences.

724   ROYLE, JOHN FORBES. On the culture and commerce of cotton in India, and elsewhere; with an account of the experiments made by the Hon. East India company up to the present time. Appendix: Papers relating to the great industrial exhibition. By J[ohn] Forbes Royle, M.D., F.R.S. London, 1851. 607 p.   **DLC Uk**

On U.S., pp. 12–17, 98–116, 117, 153–154, 171–181, and 216–235.

725   RYERSON, *REV.* ADOLPHUS EGERTON. A few remarks on religious corporations, and American examples of them. Toronto, 1851. 8 p.   **CaNSWA CaOTU**

726   SHAW, WILLIAM. Golden dreams and waking realities; being the adventures of a gold-seeker in California and the Pacific islands. London, 1851. 316 p.   **CtY ICN NN Uk**

Reviews: *Athenaeum*, (Oct. 11, 1851), 1064; *Blackwood's Edinb. Mag.*, LXX, 470; *Brit. Quar. Rev.*, XV, 107.

727   STARK, JAMES. Vital statistics of New Orleans. By James Stark, M.D., F.R.S.E., F.R.S.S.A., Fellow of the Royal college of physicians, Edinburgh. Edinburgh, 1851. 16 p.   **DNLM NHi**

Article appeared in the *Edinb. Med. & Surg. J.* (Jan. 1851), I, 130.

728   [STEVENS, HENRY]. An account of the proceedings at the dinner given by Mr. George Peabody to the Americans connected with the Great exhibition, at the London coffee house, Ludgate Hill, on the 27th October, 1851. London, 1851. 114 p.   **DLC Uk**

Opening remarks signed by "Henry Stevens of Vermont, Morley's Hotel, London. Nov. 20, 1851." Includes speeches by Lord Grenville and Sir Henry Bulwer-Lytton. See also *Mr. Peabody's gift to the poor of London. Statement of the trustees*, London, 1865; "George Peabody," the *Leisure Hour*, II, no. 571 (Dec. 6, 1862), pp. 776–778; and the lead article in the London *Times*, Oct. 25, 1856. Peabody was an American; he lived in England from 1846–1869.

729   STUART-WORTLEY, *LADY* EMMELINE CHARLOTTE ELIZABETH (MANNERS). Travels in the United States, etc., during 1849 and 1850. London, 1851. 3 vols.   **DLC Uk**

About 1/3 concerns U.S.; the remainder on Mexico and Panama. See account in Mrs. Henry Cust, *Wanderers: episodes from the travels of Lady Emmeline Stuart-Wortley and her daughter, Victoria, 1849–1855*, London, [1928].

Reviews: *Athenaeum* (May 10, 1851), 496; *Am. Whig. Rev.*, XIV, 178; *Chambers's J.*, XVI, 236; *Lit. Gazette* (by Edward Forbes), (May 17, 1851), 340; *Natl. Quar. Rev.*, I, 350; *No. Am. Rev.* (by Mrs. J. Ware), LXXIV, 197.

730   SUMNER, JOHN BIRD. Letter . . . to the bishops of the reformed church in America, on occasion of the third jubilee of the Society for the propagation of the gospel, with the answers . . . received from the American Bishops. London, 1851.   **Uk**

731   TAYLOR, JOHN GLANVILLE. The United States and Cuba: eight years of change and travel. London, 1851. 328 p.   **DLC UK**

Reviews: *Blackwood's Edinb. Mag.*, LXIX, 545; *Westmin. Rev.*, (by W.E.), LV, 170.

732   THOMPSON, GEORGE. Speech of George Thompson delivered at the anti-slavery meeting, Broadmead, Bristol, September 4th, 1851. Bristol, [1851]. 39 p.   **MH NIC TxU**

733   THOMPSON, GEORGE. Speech of George Thompson, member of the British House of Parliament, at Toronto, May 1851. Cincinnati, 1851. 14 p.   **CtY MiU OO**

734   TOCQUE, PHILIP. A peep at Uncle Sam's farm, workshop, fisheries, &c. Boston, 1851. 229 p.   **DLC**

Author visited the U.S., esp. Massachusetts, in 1849–50.

735   TRANSATLANTIC RAMBLES; or, A record of twelve months' travel in the United States, Cuba & the Brazils. By a Rugbaean. London, 1851. 168 p.   **DLC UK**

Catalog entry states that author's presentation copy is signed "Dixon"; i.e., Henry Hall Dixon.

Review: *Lit. Gazette* (by Edward Forbes), (1851), 576; repr. in *Literary papers by the late Professor Edward Forbes, F.R.S. Selected from his writing in "The Literary Gazette,"* London, 1855, chap. 8.

736   TYSON, JOB R[OBERT]. Letters, on the resources and commerce of Philadelphia; from Job R. Tyson to W. Peter . . . With Mr. Peter's answer prefixed. Philadelphia, 1851. 83 p.   **DLC**

Uk has Philadelphia, 1852 ed. William Peter was appointed the British consul to Pennsylvania and New Jersey in 1840.

1852

737   ADAM, WILLIAM PATRICK. Thoughts on the policy of retaliation, and its probable effect on the consumer, producer, and ship-owner. London, 1852. 125 p.   **DLC Uk**

See esp. Chap. 5, "California trade," pp. 83–97.

738   AMERICAN SLAVERY. English opinions of "Uncle Tom's cabin." Evils of slavery—method of its removal—dangers of agitation—colonization, &c. From the London Times, Friday, September 3. [n.p., 1852?]. 8 p.   **NSchU**

No. 27 in a volume of pamphlets with binder's title: Pamphlets. Slavery. vol. 4.

739   BAZLEY, *SIR* THOMAS. Cotton as an element of industry, its confined supply, and its extending consumption by increasing and improving agencies. [London, 1852]. 146 p.   **DLC Uk**

"Society of arts, London. Lectures on the results of the great exhibition of 1851. Ser. 2, no. XVI." Another ed. carries title, *A lecture upon cotton as an element of industry, delivered at the rooms of the Society of arts, London, in connexion with the exhibition of 1851. His Royal Highness Prince Albert . . . president, in the chair*. London, 1852.

740   BELFAST. Ireland and America, via Galway. Memorial to the Right Hon. Lord John Russell, from the Town council, Harbour commissioners, and Chamber of commerce of Belfast, and statement in support thereof from the deputation from these bodies. London, 1852. 16 p.   **DLC Uk**

741   BOSTON. *CITY COUNCIL*. The railroad jubilee. An account of the celebration commem-
        orative of the opening of railroad communication between Boston and Canada, September
        17th, 18th, and 19th, 1851. Boston, 1852. 288 p.   **DLC Uk**

        Includes addresses by Lord James Bruce Elgin, Francis Hincks, Joseph Howe, et al.

742   BRISTOL AND CLIFTON LADIES' ANTI-SLAVERY SOCIETY. Special report of the
        Bristol and Clifton ladies' anti-slavery society, during eighteen months, from January 1851
        to June 1852; with a statement of the reasons of its separation from the British and foreign
        anti-slavery society. London, 1852. 68 p.   **ICN MBAt NN Uk**

743   BRISTOL AND CLIFTON LADIES' ANTI-SLAVERY SOCIETY. Statements respecting
        the American abolitionists; by their opponents and their friends: indicating the present
        struggle between slavery and freedom in the United States of America. Comp. by the
        Bristol and Clifton ladies' anti-slavery society. Dublin, 1852. 24 p.   **DLC Uk**

744   THE CANADAS: SHALL THEY "Be lost or given away?" A question to be decided by the
        people of England in choosing between free trade or protection. An essay on the harmony
        of interests which subsisted between these colonies & the Mother Country under the
        protective system, showing the value of their trade & shipping, the rapid transference of
        these to the U.S., since the adoption of free trade, & the inevitable loss of these colonies,
        if that commercial policy be persisted in. Colonial ed. Toronto, 1852. 44 p.   **CaOOA**

745   CARPENTER, RUSSELL LANT. Observations on American slavery, after a year's tour in
        the United States. London, 1852. 69 p.   **DHU MH NIC**

746   CASEY, CHARLES. Two years on the farm of Uncle Sam. With sketches of his location,
        nephews, and prospects. London, 1852. 311 p.   **DLC Uk**

        Review: *Athenaeum*, (Aug. 21, 1852), 886.

747   [CASSELL, JOHN]. The emigrants' handbook: being a guide to the various fields of emi-
        gration in all parts of the globe. With an introductory essay, on the importance of emigra-
        tion, and the danger to which emigrants are exposed. London, 1852. 66 p.   **CSt Uk**

        On U.S., pp. 19–27, passim. Another London, 1852 ed., has slightly different title plus an
        additional guide to the gold fields of Australia. Unlike the later guides issued by Cassell's
        publishing house (e.g., *Cassell's emigrant's handy guide to California*, 1865, below), this
        appears to have been written by Cassell himself. For an account of Cassell's visits to the
        U.S. in 1853 and 1859, see *The story of the house of Cassell*, London, 1922, pp. 43–53.

748   CHALMER, *REV*. EDWARD BOTELER. Mormonism, a delusion. A lecture, delivered in
        the Tintwhistle church school, on Thursday, August 26, 1852. London, 1852. 47 p.
                                                                            CtY MH Uk

        On Mormonism in the U.S.

749   CLAY, *REV*. EDMUND. Tracts on Mormonism. London, 1851–1852. 4 nos. in 1 vol.
                                                                               CtY NN

        Uk has London, 1853 ed. under title *The doctrines and practices of "The Mormons," and
        the immoral character of their prophet Joseph Smith, delineated from authentic sources.*
        Individual tract titles: No. 1, "A brief account of the life and character of Joseph Smith, the
        'prophet' of Mormonism," London, 1851; No. 2, "The Book of Mormon: its history, and an
        analysis of its contents," London, 1851; No. 3, "The Book of Mormon proved to be a blas-
        phemous and impudent forgery," London, 1852; No. 4, "A review of the book of doctrine
        & covenants of the Church of Jesus Christ of Latter-day saints; selected from the Revelation
        of God by Joseph Smith, president. Second European edition. Liverpool, 1849."

750 COKE, HENRY JOHN. A ride over the Rocky mountains to Oregon and California. With a glance at some of the tropical islands, including the West Indies and the Sandwich isles. By the Hon. Henry J. Coke. London, 1852. 388 p. **DLC Uk**

Repr. with some additions under title, *Tracks of a rolling stone*, London, 1905.

Reviews: *Athenaeum*, (Jan. 31, 1852), 138; *Blackwood's Edinb. Mag.*, LXXI, 187; *Brit. Quar. Rev.*, XV, 350; *Quar. Rev.*, XCI, 504.

751 DAKIN, SUSANNA BRYANT. A Scotch paisano. Hugo Reid's life in California, 1832–1852, derived from his correspondence. Berkeley, 1939. 312 p. **DLC Uk**

752 DAVIES, ARTHUR. An outline of the empire of the West; including the United Kingdom, the United States, and the British colonies, shadowed in a correspondence between the Hon. R. J. Walker . . . [late Secretary of the treasury of the United States] . . . and Arthur Davies, Commander, R.N. London, 1852. 34 p. **DLC Uk**

Pref. and introd. are by Davies.

753 DE QUINCEY, THOMAS. California and the gold mania . . . ; illustrated with sketches from "Punch." San Francisco, 1945. 63 p. **CU NN NNC**

Originally an article, "California," in *Hogg's Instructor*, IX, n.s., (1852), 1–5; repr. in De Quincey's *Letters to a young man, and other papers*, Boston, 1854. This first separately pub. ed. is no. 3 of Colt press series, "California classics."

754 DODD, GEORGE. The curiosities of industry and the applied sciences. London, 1852. 384 p. **DLC Uk**

Also pub. under variant titles, e.g., *Dodd's curiousities*. Composed of separate parts, each with separate pagination. Includes following on the U.S.: "Gold: in the mine, the mint, and the workshop," pp. 1–24; "Iron and its manufacture," pp. 21–24; "Calculating and registering machines," p. 11; "Industrial applications of electricity," passim; "Cotton and flax: a contrast," pp. 2–4; "Corn and bread: what they owe to machinery," pp. 10–11, 19–24.

755 [DOWNES, S. T.?]. Journal of a voyage from Callao to San Francisco, California, and back to Panama, in the steamer "Ecuador." Kept by Long Tom. [Liverpool], 1852. 5 p. **CSmH**

DLC's presentation copy, signed "S. T. Downes," is missing. In verse.

756 [DUNCAN, *MRS*. MARY (GREY) LUNDIE]. America as I found it. By the author of "A memoir of Mary Lundie Duncan." London, 1852. 380 p. **DLC Uk**

T.p. of the New York ed., 1852, 440 p., reads: "By the mother of Mary Lundie Duncan."

757 GAMBLE, J. W. Mr. Gamble's speech on the commercial policy of the country, in the House of assembly, Thursday, October 28, 1852. [Toronto, 1852]. 8 p. **CaOTP**

References to the U.S. throughout.

758 GRAY, *REV*. J[OSEPH] H[ENRY]. The substance of two lectures on Mormonism: delivered in Sutton Bonnington and Muskham, Notts, by the Rev. J. H. Gray. London, 1852. 32 p. **UU UkLL**

DLC has 2d ed., "considerably enlarged": *Principles and practices of Mormons, tested in two lectures: delivered before the Religious and useful knowledge society of Douglas, on November 24th, and December 1st, 1852, and published by request*, Douglas, 1853, 78 p. Latter ed. contains a letter, pub. originally in the Swansea and Glamorgan *Herald*, giving information about Mormons in California, pp. 67–78; other comments on Mormonism in U.S., passim.

759 HELPS, *SIR* ARTHUR. A letter on "Uncle Tom's Cabin." By the author of "Friends in council." Cambridge, 1852. 29 p. **DLC**

CSmH catalogs as *Letter to an American friend*. Priv. pr. Dated July, 1852, and first pub. in *Fraser's Mag.*, Aug. 1852.

760 HEPBURN, ANDREW BALFOUR. An exposition of the blasphemous doctrines and delusions of the so-called Latter-day saints, or Mormons, containing an authentic account of the impositions, spiritual wife doctrine, and the other abominable practices of Joseph Smith, the American Mahomet, and his twelve apostles, elders, and followers to the present time. Sheffield, 1852. 68 p. **CU-BANC**

761 HURSTHOUSE, CHARLES FLINDERS, *Jun.* Emigration: WHERE to go, and WHO should go. New Zealand & Australia (as emigration fields) in contrast with the United States & Canada. Canterbury and the diggings. London, [1852]. 135 p. **DLC Uk**

762 JOHNSON, ANDREW. Some observations on the recent supplies of gold; with remarks on Mr. Scheer's letter to Sir F. Baring. London, 1852. 35 p. **CtY Uk**

On California gold supplies: pp. 1–17. See also Scheer's letter, 1852, below.

763 LANDMANN, GEORGE THOMAS. Adventures and recollections of Colonel Landmann, late of the corps of Royal engineers. London, 1852. 2 vols. **DLC Uk**

Uk catalog omits author's middle name. Visits to the U.S., I, pp. 207–222; II, 37–51, 151–153.

764 LEE, *REV*. CHARLES. Mormonism: a sketch of its rise and progress. A lecture delivered to the Derby Young Men's Christian Association. Derby, England, 1852. 31 p. **NN**

See also *Slave life in Virginia and Kentucky; or, Fifty years of slavery in the southern states of America, by Francis Fedric, an escaped slave. With preface, by the Rev. Charles Lee* . . . , London, 1863.

765 LEVI, LEONE. Commercial law, its principles and administration; or, The mercantile law of Great Britain compared with the codes and laws of commerce of the following mercantile countries: Anhalt, Austria . . . Wurtemburg. And the institutes of Justinian. London, 1850–52. 2 vols. in 4. **DLC Uk**

Paragraphs on U.S., passim., under each category of law. Rev. 2d ed., London, 1863, under title: *International commercial law. Being the principles of mercantile law of the following and other countries.* . . . .

766 LOWE, *REV*. JOSIAH BEATSON. Mormonism exposed; being a lecture on the doctrines and practices of "The Latter-Day Saints," delivered in the music hall, Bold Street. Liverpool, 1852. 50 p. **CSmH MH NN**

Lowe considers Mormonism historically and doctrinally and relates it to U.S.

767 LYTTON, EDWARD ROBERT BULWER-LYTTON, *1st earl*. Personal & literary letters of Robert, first earl of Lytton; ed. by Lady Betty Balfour. London, 1906. 2 vols. **DLC Uk**

See letters of 1850–52, covering Lytton's service as an attache in Washington, D.C. See also the account in *Owen Meredith; a critical biography of Robert, first Earl of Lytton*, by Aurelia Brooks Harlan, New York, 1946, pp. 28–39. Lytton used American experiences in his novel, *The disappearance of John Ackland*.

768 MACKINNON, LAUCHLAN BELLINGHAM. Atlantic and transatlantic sketches, afloat and ashore. By Captain Mackinnon. London, 1852. 2 vols. **DLC Uk**

Reviews: *Chambers's J.*, XVIII, 166; *New Monthly Mag.*, XCVI, 235.

769 [MACLAREN, JAMES]. Observations on the effect of the Californian & Australian gold: and on the impossibility of continuing the present standard, in the event of gold becoming seriously depreciated. London, 1852. 32 p. **DLC Uk**

770 MARRYAT, F[RANCIS SAMUEL]. Gold quartz mining in California. Practical observations during a residence of two years, 1850–51, and 52 in the mining districts of that country. By Frank Marryat. London, 1852. **Uk**

771 MARTIN, WILLIAM CHARLES LINNAEUS. A general history of humming-birds, or the Trochilidae: with especial reference to the collection of J. Gould, F.R.S. etc. . . . now exhibiting in the gardens of the zoological society of London. London, 1852. 232 p. **DLC Uk**

Accounts of American birds based mainly on Audubon.

772 MASSIE, JAMES WILLIAM. Slavery the crime and curse of America: an expostulation with the Christians of that land. London, 1852. 61 p. **CtY MB NIC Uk**

See also author's novel, *The slave: hunted, transported, and doomed to toil; a tale of Africa*, Manchester, 1846.

773 MATHEWS, EDWARD. Statistical account of the connection of the religious bodies in America with slavery; together with a notice of various anti-slavery secessions. Presented by the Rev. Edward Mathews, of Wisconsin, (Delegate of the American Baptist free mission society) to the committee of the Bristol and Clifton ladies' anti-slavery society. March, 1852. [Bristol, 1852]. 4 p. **MB**

No t.p.

774 MCALL, SAMUEL. Slavery a curse and a sin. A speech delivered at Bradford, Yorkshire, on Wednesday, October 20, 1852, at the autumnal meeting of the Congregational Union of England and Wales, under the presidency of Dr. Harris, author of Mammon, etc. London, [1852]. 12 p. **CtY MH NIC NcD**

775 MODERN GEOGRAPHY SIMPLIFIED: to which are appended, brief notices of European discovery, with select sketches of the ruins of ancient cities. 2d ed., rev. London, 1852. 155 p. **Uk**

1st ed. pub. in 1811. On U.S.: pp. 37–39, 95–99, 129–132, 135–142.

776 MORMONISM OR THE BIBLE? A question for the times. By a Cambridge clergyman. Cambridge [Eng.], 1852. 32 p. **NN Uk**

777 THE MORMONITES; or Latter-day saints. A country clergyman's warning to his parishioners. London, [1852?]. 16 p. **CtY NN**

778 MURDOCK, JOHN. Persecutions of the Latter-Day Saints. Sydney, 1852.

No locations found.

779 PAE, DAVID. A popular history of the discovery, progress, and present state of America; to which is added, a description of the principal states in the Union, and their respective merits as fields of emigration. Edinburgh, 1852. 164 p. **DLC**

780 PERKINS, WILLIAM. Three years in California. William Perkins' journal of life at Sonora, 1849–1852. Introduction and annotations by Dale L. Morgan and James R. Scobie. Berkeley & London, 1964. 424 p. **DLC Uk**

Perkins was born in Canada, 1827.

781   [PHILLIPS, GEORGE SPENCER]. A hand-book of Newport, and Rhode Island. By the author of "Pen and ink sketches," "Life of Chatterton," "Preachers and politicians," "Lions, living and dead," etc., etc., Newport, 1852. 170 p.   **DLC Uk**

Usually cataloged under John Dix. For account of Phillips and the pseudonym John Dix, see entry for 1845. A later work, *A hand book for Lake Memphremagog, with route list*, Boston, [1860], was written after Phillips had lived in the U.S. for 15 years and is not included as a main entry here.

782   REGAN, JOHN. The emigrant's guide to the western states of America; or, Backwoods and prairies: containing a complete statement of the advantages and capacities of the prairie lands—full instructions for emigrants in fitting out; and in selecting, purchasing, and settling on, land—with particulars of farming and other business operations, pictures of the home manners of the people, successes of emigrants, &c., &c. By John Regan, formerly teacher, Ayrshire; now of Peoria, Illinois. 2d ed., rev. and enlarged Edinburgh, [1852]. 408 p.   **DLC Uk**

Sabin and Phillips list Edinburgh, [1842] ed., also 408 p., but no copy of this or any 1st ed. can be located; internal evidence in "2d ed." points to 1852. Howes states this is termed 2d ed. because of previous pub. in the columns of the Ayrshire *Advertiser*, but a search of complete back issues cannot locate any trace. Reissued under the title, *The western wilds of America, or, Backwoods and prairies; and scenes in the valley of the Mississippi*, Edinburgh, 1859.

783   REPORT OF THE TRANSATLANTIC packet station committee, appointed at a meeting held on the 21st August, 1851, at the Mansion house, Dublin, the Right Hon. the Lord Mayor in the chair. Dublin, 1852.   **CLU**

Signed by Benjamin Lee Guinness, Chairman, et al. Appendix A, "Lord Monteagle to the Right Hon. Lord Mayor"; Appendix B, a report by James Whiteside.

784   SCHEER, FREDERICK. A letter to Thomas Baring, esq., M.P., on the effects of the Californian and Australian gold discoveries. London, 1852. 40 p.   **CtY CU**

Uk has 3d ed., London, 1852. See also Andrew Johnson, *Some observations . . . with remarks on Mr. Scheer's letter . . .* , 1852, above.

785   [SHAW, ARTHUR N.]. The cultivation of cotton. Can India grow cotton of a sufficiently good quality to compete with the produce of the United States? London, 1852. 24 p.

CU NN

Signed by Art Shaw; at end of work, "A. N. Shaw."

786   SLAVERY PAST AND PRESENT; or, Notes on *Uncle Tom's Cabin*. Edited by a Lady. London, 1852. 47 p.   **ICU MH Uk**

787   SOME ACCOUNT of the so-called Church of the Latter-day saints. London, 1852. 24 p.   **CtY PU UU**

788   SULLIVAN, *SIR* EDWARD ROBERT. Rambles and scrambles in North and South America. London, 1852. 424 p.   **DLC Uk**

Travelled as far west as Ft. Snelling, and down the Mississippi to New Orleans. See also Sullivan's "Uncle Sam to John Bull," No. 34 in *Stray Shots*, 2d ser., London, 1888; and *Free trade bubbles*, London, 1883, chap. 13 and passim.

Reviews: *Anti-Slavery Advocate*, I, 301; *Athenaeum*, (Oct. 2, 1852), 1060; *Bentley's Misc.*, XXXII, 405; *Blackwood's Edinb. Mag.* (by Wm. E. Y. Aytoun), LXXII, 680.

789   SURTEES, WILLIAM EDWARD. Recollections of North America in 1849–50–51. [London, 1852]. 2 pts. in 1 vol.   **DLC Uk**

Repr. of articles from *New Monthly Mag.*, XCIV (Jan. 1852), 1–22, (Feb. 1852), 208–235, "with some slight alterations and additions."

790   SYNGE, MILLINGTON HENRY. Great Britain one empire. On the union of the dominions of Great Britain by inter-communication with the Pacific and the East via British North America. With suggestions for the profitable colonization of that wealthy territory. By Capt. Millington Henry Synge. London, 1852. 124 p.   **DLC Uk**

Comment on U.S., passim. See also his *Canada in 1848. Being an examination of the existing resources of British North America. With considerations for their further and more perfect development, as a practical remedy, by means of colonization, for the prevailing distress in the United empire, and for the defense of the colony*, London, [1848].

791   THEOBALD, JOHN. Mormonology; or the blasphemies of the latter-day-saints exposed. Being the substance of the first lecture of a series delivered in various parts of the United Kingdom. London, [1852]. 22 p.   **DLC**

Advertisement on back of cover: "Works ready for the press. By J. Theobald. Mormonism harpooned. Mormon hypocrites unmasked. The Book of Mormon Tested. Joe Smith's Ghost. Mormonism dissected, second edition. Outthrow of infidel Mormonism, second edition. The Soul damning sin, second edition. An address to the British churches on the infernal system. A looking-glass for Christians." None found.

792   TREMENHEERE, HUGH SEYMOUR. Notes on public subjects made during a tour in the United States and in Canada. London, 1852. 320 p.   **DLC Uk**

See R.K. Webb, "A Whig inspector," *J. Mod. Hist.*, XXVII (Dec. 1955), 352–364.

Reviews: *Athenaeum* (1852), 646; *Dublin Rev.*, (Apr., 1852), 442; *Edinb. Rev.*, C, 236; *Nat. Rev.*, II, 433; *Quar. Rev.*, CIX, 1; *Westmin. Rev.* (Am. ed., LIX), 255.

793   THE TROUBLED ASPECT of affairs, etc. [London? 1852]. 23 p.   **Uk**

Priv. pr. pamphlet, no t.p., title or heading. Dated "*Begin*. Nov. 20th, 1852." On the affairs on the U.S. and the West Indies.

794   TYSON, THOMAS. Joseph Smith, the great American impostor; or, Mormonism to be false, by a fair examination of its history and pretensions. London, 1852. 59 p.   **MH Uk**

795   UNCLE TOM'S CABIN ALMANACK; or, Abolitionist memento for 1853. London, [1852]. 70 p.   **DLC Uk**

796   WATKIN, *SIR* EDWARD WILLIAM. A trip to the United States and Canada: in a series of letters. London, 1852. 149 p.   **DLC Uk**

Portions repr. in his later work: *Canada and the states*, [1887], below.

797   WEBB, RICHARD D[AVIS]. The national anti-slavery societies in England and the United States; or, Strictures on "A reply to certain charges brought against the American and foreign anti-slavery society, etc., etc.; by Lewis Tappan of New York, United States: with an introduction, by John Scoble." Dublin, 1852. 56 p.   **DLC**

See the American answer to the Tappan and Scoble pamphlet: Edmund Quincy, *An examination of the charges of Mr. John Scoble & Mr. Lewis Tappan against the American anti-slavery society*, Dublin, 1852, 27 p. See also *American and English oppression, and British and American abolitionists; a letter addressed to R. D. Webb, esq. By an American in his fatherland*, London, 1853; dated London, April, Dec., 1852. For discussion, and 316 pages of the actual correspondence on these issues, see Frank J. Klingberg and Annie H. Klingberg, *A side-light on Anglo-American relations, 1839–58 furnished by the correspondence of Lewis Tappan and others with the British and foreign anti-slavery society*, Lancaster, Pa., 1927.

798   [WELBY-GREGORY, *HON.* VICTORIA ALEXANDRINA MARIA LOUISA (STUART-WORTLEY), *Lady*]. A young traveller's journal of a tour in North and South America during the year 1850. London, 1852. 260 p.   **DLC Uk**

The 12-year-old author was the daughter of Lady Emmeline Stuart-Wortley, whose book on their tour preceded her own, 1851, above. See the account in *Wanderers: episodes from the travels of Lady Emmeline Stuart-Wortley and her daughter Victoria, 1849–1855*, by Mrs. Henry Cust, New York, 1928; Pt. I, "The American journey," pp. 29–188, and the appendix which contains additional letters, etc., relating to the U.S.

799   [WYLD, JAMES]. Notes on the distribution of gold throughout the world, including Australia, California & Russia. With four maps: 1. The world, shewing the gold districts. 2. The gold districts of Australia. 3. The gold district from Bathurst to Sidney. 4. The gold districts of California. London, [1852?]. 44 p.   **DLC Uk**

Inside t.p., at head of text: "Notes on the gold districts of California, New Holland, Russia, Virginia, and America." Dedication signed, James Wyld; text refers to earlier works as if he had written them. 3d ed. carried title, *Gold fields of Australia. Notes on the distribution of gold throughout the world, including Australia, California, and Russia*, London, 1853.

1853

800   [ALLSOP, THOMAS]. California and its gold mines: being a series of recent communications from the mining districts, upon the present condition and future prospects of quartz mining; with an account of the richer deposits, and incidental notices of the climate, scenery, and mode of life in California. Edited by Robert Allsop, of the stock exchange. London, 1853. 149 p.   **DLC Uk**

Communications are signed "A. T." (i.e., Thomas Allsop, father of Robert, to whom letters are addressed). Portions were originally pub. in "a contemporary journal."

801   AN APPEAL ON BEHALF of fugitives from slavery in America. London, 1853.

No locations found; Sabin #81872. Signed by Joseph Crosfield on behalf of the Committee of Friends.

802   [ARMISTEAD, WILSON, *comp.*]. Five hundred thousand strokes for freedom. A series of anti-slavery tracts, of which half a million are now first issued by the friends of the negro. London, 1853. 352 p.   **DLC Uk**

Collection of Leeds Anti-slavery Series, No. 1–82, originally issued separately and varying from 1 to 24 pages. At head of title, "Liberty is the birthright of all." Also printed and issued with the tracts: A *'cloud of witnesses' against slavery and oppression. Containing the acts, opinions, and sentiments of individuals and societies in all ages. Selected from various sources, and for the most part chronologically arranged*, ed. by Wilson Armistead, London, 1853; *A garland of freedom: a collection of poems, chiefly anti-slavery. Selected from various authors by a friend to the Negro*. 3 parts, London, 1853. See also Armistead's

Anthony Benezet: From the original memoir: rev., with additions, London, 1859; his *A tribute for the Negro: being a vindication of the moral, intellectual, and religious capabilities of the coloured portion of mankind; with particular reference to the African race*, Manchester, 1848, esp. pp. 85–98; and his introd. to *Incidents in the life of the Rev. J[eremiah] Asher, pastor of Shiloh (Coloured) Baptist church, Philadelphia, United States*, London, 1850, pp. 1–13.

Review: *Anti-Slavery Advocate*, I, 104.

803   AUSTIN, WILLIAM. On the imminent depreciation of gold and how to avoid loss. London, 1853. 48 p.   **MH-BA Uk**

On use of silver as coinage in U.S. and France, pp. 9–12; on gold and silver supplied to Europe by U.S., pp. 36–42.

804   [BALLENTINE, GEORGE]. Autobiography of an English soldier in the United States' army. Comprising observations and adventures in the States and Mexico. London, 1853. 2 vols.   **DLC**

New York, 1853 ed., 2 vols. in 1. Later ed. pub. under title, *The Mexican war, by an English soldier. Comprising incidents and adventures in the United States and Mexico with the American army*, New York, 1860. Appeared originally under title, "Adventures of an English soldier in Mexico," *Colburn's United Serv. Mag.*, Sept., 1851–Dec., 1852. Ballentine was in America in 1845.

805   BENWELL, J[OHN]. An Englishman's travels in America: his observations of life and manners in the free and slave states. London, [1853]. 231 p.   **DLC Uk**

ICN has original ms., bound, with title *Incidents of travel. Being a narrative of four years in the United States, and territories of America*, Bristol, 1852; changes, as well as change of title, were incorporated in the book.

806   "BREAD UPON THE WATERS," or, Letters, illustrative, moral, and practical, addressed generally to the women of Great Britain and Ireland, on the subject of the "Stafford House Memorial," recently transmitted to the women of the United States, concluding with an appeal to gentlemen connected with the cotton question. By the author of "A word on behalf of the slave"; "The Bible rights of the slave, or Jewish servitude and American slavery compared"; etc., etc. London, 1853.   **Uk**

807   [BRIGHT, HENRY ARTHUR]. Free blacks and slaves. Would immediate abolition be a blessing? A letter to the editor of the Anti-Slavery advocate. By a Cambridge man. London, 1853. 27 p.   **MH TxU Uk**

See answer in the *Anti-Slavery Advocate*, I (July 1853), 77. See also *Happy country this America: the travel diary of Henry Arthur Bright*, ed., with an introd. by Anne Henry Ehrenpreis, Columbus, [Ohio], 1978. Son of a wealthy Unitarian merchant family, Bright visited U.S. at age 22, touring the East Coast south to Virginia, and as far west as St. Louis and Minnesota. Met and later became the "closest English friend" of Nathaniel Hawthorne (introd., p. 14).

Review: *Chr. Reformer* (by Russell Lant Carpenter), IX, n.s. (Aug. 1853), 473; this review pub. separately (see entry for Carpenter, 1853, below).

808   BUNN, ALFRED. Old England and New England, in a series of views taken on the spot. London, 1853. 2 vols.   **DLC Uk**

2d London ed. and Philadelphia ed. (both in 1 vol.) appeared the same year.

809   BURNS, DAWSON. Mormonism, explained and exposed. London, 1853. 56 p.

CU CtY NN Uk

Uk lists author as James Dawson Burns.

810   [CARPENTER, RUSSELL LANT]. Free blacks and slaves. From the Christian reformer for August 1853. London, 1853.   **MH NN**

Repr. of review of Bright, 1853 above, signed "R.L.C.," in the *Chr. Reformer*, IX, n.s., (1853), 473–485. See also series of articles by Carpenter on American slavery: *Chr. Reformer*, VII, n.s., (1851), 483–494, 537–548, 585–597, 650–660, 717–737; IX, n.s., (1853), 551–560, 640–651; XII, n.s., (1856?), 288–295.

811   [CARTER, HARRY LEE]. A descriptive hand-book to "The two lands of gold," or, the Australian and Californian directory for 1853. Profusely illustrated. London, [1853]. 38 p.   **CSmH Uk**

A description of the scenes of a diorama. Pref., written and arranged by Carter and Shirley Brooks, is signed H.L.C. and gives George Catlin and Wm. Kelly as sources; songs written by Henry Russell. Diorama was sketched by Charles S. James.

812   CHESTERTON, GEORGE LAVAL. Peace, war and adventure: an autobiographical memoir of George Laval Chesterton . . . London, 1853. 2 vols.   **DLC Uk**

On War of 1812; Chesterton served with the British in the U.S., 1814–15, I, 111–240.

813   COX, SAMUEL HANSON. Interviews: memorable and useful; from diary and memory reproduced. New York, 1853. 325 p.   **DLC**

Two interviews with Dr. Thomas Chalmers, with an account of his comments on American slavery, etc., pp. 31–143. For other accounts of Chalmers' views see *Memoirs of the life and writings of Thomas Chalmers, DD., Ll.D. By his son-in-law, the Rev. William Hanna*, Edinburgh, 1849–52, 4 vols.; Hanna's *Selections from the correspondence of the late Thomas Chalmers*, Edinburgh, 1853; and, Rev. Thomas Smyth's *The character of the late Thomas Chalmers . . . and the lessons of his life, from personal recollections*, Charleston, S.C., 1848, esp. pp. 14–19 for an account of Chalmers' opposition to the anti-slavery movement.

814   DAVIES, JOHN. The Rev. Edward Mathews, of Wisconsin, Ohio, U.S. America. Is he an accredited anti-slavery agent or is he not? The affirmative proved, in a letter, etc., etc., addressed to John Jayne, of Pantybaili, esq. By John Davies, Llanelly, Breconshire. Crickhowell, 1853. 12 p.   **NN**

815   DENMAN, THOMAS DENMAN, *baron*. Uncle Tom's cabin, Bleak house, slavery and the slave trade. Six articles . . . reprinted from the "Standard," with an article, containing facts connected with slavery, by Sir George Stephen, reprinted from the "Northhampton Mercury." London, 1853. 51 p.   **Uk**

ICN, NN have 2d ed., London, 1853, with title amended to "seven articles," 60 p.

816   EDINBURGH LADIES EMANCIPATION SOCIETY. Mrs. Stowe's letter to the women of England [a reply]. [Edinburgh, 1853?]. 2 p.   **NIC**

817   ELLIOTT, EDWARD BISHOP. The downfall of despotism; or, The last act of the European tragedy: showing, in accordance with the principles recognized by the Rev. E. B. Elliott, author of Horae Apocalyptical, the overthrow of the allied powers of popery and

despotism in Europe—the mission of the Russians—the fall of the Turkish Empire—the invasion of Britain, and the reign of liberty in the new world. London, 1853. 62 p.

NN Uk

Significant comment on U.S. Reviewed in *The Coming struggle again*, Edinburgh, 1853, q.v. under answers to David Pae, 1853, below.

818 EMIGRATION CONSIDERED; or, A general description of the leading countries most adapted to emigration. London, 1853.

No locations found; listed in Sabin #22492.

819 THE FASHIONABLE PHILANTHROPY of the day. Some plain speaking about American slavery. London, 1853.   **UkENL**

820 A FEW PLAIN WORDS about Mormonism. Showing that Latter-day saints are no saints at all, proved by extracts from their writings. By the author of A few plain words about popery and the Pope . . . Bristol, [1853]. 16 p.   **CSmH CtY NN Uk**

Uk gives pub. date [1880?].

821 FINCH, MARIANNE. An Englishwoman's experience in America. London, 1853. 386 p.

DLC Uk

In the U.S., Aug. 1850–June 1851.

822 FISHERIES AND RECIPROCAL TRADE with the United States of America. Joint address of both houses of the legislature of New Brunswick to Her most gracious Majesty. Fredericton, 1853. 8 p.   **CaOOA**

823 FISHWICK, J. F. The false prophet tested; or, Mormonism refuted. London, 1853. 16 p.

NN

824 [GRIFFITHS, JULIA, *ed.*]. Autographs for freedom. Boston, 1853. 263 p.

CLU MB OU Uk

Contains letters from the Earl of Carlisle, pp. 7–11; Joseph Sturge, p. 19; the Bishop of Oxford, p. 28; Wilson Armistead, pp. 55–58.

825 HAYNES, JOHN. The Book of Mormon examined; and its claims to be a revelation from God proved to be false. Brighton, [1853].   **OCIWHi Uk**

Mainly doctrinal, but some comment on the U.S.

826 HISTORY OF THE MORMONS. Edinburgh, 1853. 32 p.   **DLC**

Chambers' Repository of instructive and amusing tracts, vol. VII, no. 53. Sometimes attributed to Robert Chambers.

827 [HOLYOAKE, GEORGE JACOB]. Address from the Democrats of England to the democrats of the United States. London, 1853.

No locations found; cited in William James Linton's *The English republic*. Signed by Holyoake, et al.

828 [HOPE, *pseud.*] A few observations relative to the defences and defenders of Canada. Brighton, 1853. 22 p.   **CaOTU**

829 HUMANITY [*pseud*]. The history of Uncle Tom's countrymen; with a description of their sufferings in the capture, the voyage, and the field. Manchester, 1853. 48 p.   **OCIWHi**

830 HUMPHREYS, EDWARD RUPERT. The dangers and duties of the present time: being the substance of two lectures delivered in the Library and Philosophical institution, Cheltenham, on the 11th and 25th of January, 1853. London, 1853. 64 p.

CtY MB RPB Uk

Contents: "Freedom vs. absolutism; or, The coming struggle"; "Our Anglo-Saxon brothers; or, Union is safety." Humphreys eventually settled in the U.S., and by 1869 described himself as a naturalized citizen of several years standing. During the Civil War he interpreted U.S. events in British publications. See also his *America, past and present. . . . To which are subjoined essays on the higher education of America and England, with an historical sketch of the Queen's colleges in Ireland*, Newport, R.I., 1869.

831 IS MORMONISM TRUE OR NOT? [London, 1853?]. 28 p. **DLC**

Religious Tract Society. Tract No. 600.

832 [JEFFREY, JOHN]. Oregon botanical expedition. [Edinburgh, 1853]. 3 p. **CtY**

Caption title. Leaflet contains statement of the acting committee of the Oregon botanical expedition, dated Edinburgh, 16th April, 1853; gives report on seeds received from John Jeffrey with a letter from him. See also *Names of the plants of which specimens or seeds [were] received from Mr. Jeffrey in boxes, nos. 5 and 6, Oregon botanical association*, [Edinburgh, 1853], 2 p.; caption title; at head of leaflet: "Botanical expedition to Oregon. Preface signed: By order of the Committee. Andrew Murray, Secretary."

833 JERDAN, WILLIAM. Yankee humour, and Uncle Sam's fun. With an introduction by William Jerdan. London, 1853. 115 p. **KEmT**

834 JOHNSON, HENRY T. Mormonism. The claims of the Book of Mormon to be a divine revelation examined, and proved to be false. Brighton, [1853?]. 12 p. **CtY**

835 [LINTON, WILLIAM JAMES]. Holyoake versus Garrison: a defense of earnestness. London, [1853].

No locations found.

836 LONDON TO NIAGARA, and back for £80. By way of Philadelphia, New York, the Hudson river, Albany, Buffalo and Rochester, and returning to New-York by way of Boston, Worcester, New-Haven and Bridgeport, or by steamboat through Long Island Sound, furnishing an opportunity either in going to or returning to inspect the New-York Crystal Palace, for the exhibition of the industry of all nations. New York, 1853. 24 p.

CtY NBuG

837 MACDONALD, *DR*. A. An address to the people of British America, upon subjects relating to the progress of the people and the improvement of the country. [n.p.], 1853. 32 p.

Uk

Pub. by author. Compares Canada and the U.S.

838 MACLAREN, JAMES. The effect of a small fall in the value of gold upon money; the secret progress of a depreciation of the currency; and the power which capitalists have of protecting themselves. London, 1853. 40 p. **CtY ICU PU Uk**

On discovery of gold in California, pp. 15–19; and passim.

839 MACLAREN, JAMES. On the impolicy of providing for a family by life assurance, since the recent discoveries in California and Australia; with a proposal for the establishment of a new office, upon a plan which would secure the assured from the effects of a fall in the value of gold. London, 1853. 81 p. **DLC Uk**

840   MARJORIBANKS, ALEXANDER. Travels in South and North America. London, 1853. 480 p.   **DLC Uk**

841   MATHEWS, *REV.* EDWARD. Uncle Tom's cabin a true picture of slave life. A lecture on American slavery, by Rev. Edward Mathews, of Wisconsin, America. Bristol, [1853]. 12 p.   **IHi OCIWHi**

An abolitionist who returned to England in 1851 after 19 years in the U.S., Mathews served as a representative of the American Baptist free mission society. See *The autobiography of the Rev. E. Mathews. . . .* , 1967, below.

842   MORMONISM. London, [1853?] 24 p.   **CtY NjP UU Uk**

Religious Tract Society, Tract No. 598. NUC catalogs under the Society. Uk gives pub. date as [1880?].

843   MORMONISM AND THE MORMONITES. [London, 1853?]. 8 p.   **CtY NN**

Mostly doctrinal, but some discussion of Joseph Smith.

844   THE MOST COMPLETE authentic exposure ever published of the spiritual courtship and marriages of the Mormons . . . . London, [1853?]. 8 p.   **CtY USIC**

Caption title: The abominations of the Latter-day Saints. Full title continues for more than 250 words: . . . *The gates of the Mormon hell opened, exhibiting the licentious abominations and revellings, etc.*

845   NEWMARCH, WILLIAM. The new supplies of gold: facts, and statements, relative to their actual amount; and their present and probable effects. Revised edition, with five additional chapters. London, 1853. 122 p.   **CSmH CtY NN Uk**

At top of t.p., "From the [London] Morning Chronicle of 28th July 1853. "Revised edition" apparently refers to this pamphlet, a revision of the *Chronicle* article. On California, Australia, etc.

846   [OGDEN, PETER SKENE]. Traits of American-Indian life and character. By a fur trader. London, 1853. 218 p.   **DLC**

Repr. by the Grabhorn Press, San Francisco, 1933, with added illust. See *Peter Skene Ogden's Snake country Journals, 1824–25 and 1825–26*, ed. by E. E. Rich and A. M. Johnson, 283 pp., publications of the Hudson's Bay Record Society, vol. 13. See also the following accounts: Alice B. Maloney, "Peter Skene Ogden's trapping expedition to the Gulf of California, 1829–30," *Calif. Hist. Soc. Quar.*, XIX (Dec. 1940), 308–316; F. W. Howay, "Authorship of Traits of Indian life," *Oregon Hist. Quar.*, XXXV (Mar. 1934), 42–49; Thompson C. Elliott, *Peter Skene Ogden: fur trader*, Portland, 1910 (also appeared in *Oregon Hist. Quar.*, X (1909), 331–365, XI (Sept. 1910), 229–278); "William Kittson's journal covering Peter Skene Ogden's 1824–1825 Snake country expedition," *Utah Hist. Quar.*, XXII (Apr. 1954), 125–142.

847   [PAE, DAVID]. The coming struggle among the nations of the earth; events of the next fifteen years described in accordance with prophecies in Ezekiel, Daniel, and the Apocalypse. Showing also the important position Britain will occupy during, and at the end of, the awful conflict. London, 1853. 32 p.   **CtY ICU NN Uk**

The New York, 1853 ed. was "greatly enlarged" and added "Britain and America" on the t.p.; Sydney ed., 1854, added to Britain "and her Australian colonies."

848   PALLISER, JOHN. Solitary rambles and adventures of a hunter in the prairies. London, 1853. 326 p.   **DLC Uk**

Reissued under title *The solitary hunter; or, Sporting adventures in the prairies*, London, 1856; 1853 ed. repr., with a new introd. by H. A. Dempsey, Rutland, Vt., [1969]. Several vols. of parliamentary reports on Palliser's expedition through the Northwest, 1857–1860, including letters, journals, etc., were also pub.

Reviews: *Athenaeum*, (June 26, 1853), 766; *Dublin Univ. Mag.*, XLII, 47; *Household Words*, VIII, 446; *New Monthly Mag.*, XCVIII, 464.

849   PATTEN, EDMUND. A glimpse at the United States and the northern states of America, with the Canadas, comprising their rivers, lakes, and falls during the autumn of 1852; including some account of an emigrant ship. London, 1853. 109 p.   **DLC**

850   PEYTON, *REV.* ALEXANDER J. The emigrants' friend; or, Hints on emigration to the United States of America, addressed to the people of Ireland. Cork, 1853.

No locations found.

851   [PHILLIPS, GEORGE SPENCER]. Transatlantic tracings; or, Sketches of persons and scenes in America. By the author of "Lions, living and dead," "Pen and ink sketches of authors and authoresses," &c. London, 1853. 337 p.   **DLC**

Usually listed under "John Dix" (*pseud.*); see entry under Phillips, 1845, for discussion of various pen-names used by author. Phillips settled in the U.S., but writes here as an Englishman. See also chaps. 5 and 15 in his *Lions: living and dead; or personal recollections of the "Great & gifted,"* London, 1852; and the few sketches of places included in his *Pulpit portraits, or pen-pictures of distinguished American divines; with sketches of congregations and choirs; and incidental notices of eminent British preachers. By John Ross Dix*, Boston, 1854.

852   THE PROBLEM OF THE AGE; or, The abolition of American slavery considered in a physical and moral aspect. Dedicated to Mrs. Harriet Beecher Stowe. London, 1853. 32 p.   **DLC Uk**

853   REMARKS OCCASIONED BY STRICTURES in the *Courier* and the New York *Enquirer* of December, 1852, upon the Stafford-House address. In a letter to a friend in the United States. By an Englishwoman. London, 1853. 42 p.   **DLC Uk**

854   ROBERTSON, WILLIAM PARISH. A visit to Mexico, by the West India islands, Yucatan and United States, with observations and adventures on the way. London, 1853. 2 vols.   **DLC Uk**

In the U.S. Dec. 1848–Nov. 1849.

855   [ROCHE, ALFRED R.]. Suggestions on the military resources of Canada, and the means of organizing a small provincial army in the event of its being determined by the Imperial authorities to diminish or recall the royal troops so as to render such an organization essential to the defence of the Colony. Reprinted from the letters of the Canada correspondent of the London Morning Post, Sept. 9th, 1853. [n.p., 1853?]. 18 p.   **CaQMBN**

Signed "A. R." Scattered comment on the U.S.

856   ST. GERMAIN, ALFRED H[YACINTHE]. A voyage to California, with an account of the condition of the country, &c., &c., &c. Toronto, 1853. 24 p.   **CtY**

857   SIMPSON, *REV*. WILLIAM SPARROW. Mormonism: its history, doctrines, and practices. London, 1853. 62 p.   **CSmH CU-S NN Uk**

In two lectures.

858   SINCLAIR, JOHN, *Archdeacon of Middlesex*. Great Britain and America; a farewell sermon preached on Sunday, October 15th, 1853, in St. Paul's chapel, New York. New York, 1853. 23 p.   **ICN NN RPB**

Uk has 2d ed., London, 1853. See also Sinclair's *Sketches of old times and distant places*, London, 1875; contains accounts of Washington, D.C. and Niagara in 1853, pp. 215–233, 244–252.

859   SLEIGH, BURROWS WILLCOCKS ARTHUR. Pine forests and hacmatack clearings; or, Travel, life, and adventure, in the British North American provinces. By Lieutenant-Colonel Sleigh. London, 1853. 408 p.   **DLC Uk**

Chap. 13 on the U.S.

860   SPICER, HENRY. Sights and sounds: the mystery of the day: comprising an entire history of the American "spirit" manifestations. London, 1853. 480 p.   **DLC Uk**

861   SPIRIT RAPPING IN ENGLAND and America; its origin and history, including descriptions of the spheres, the spirits and their pursuits, and the various classes of mediums; also records of numerous interviews with spirits and mediums, with full particulars and explanations of the rapping process. London, [1853?]. 272 p.   **DLC Uk**

An enlarged ed. appeared under title, *Spirit rapping in England & America; and table turning & table talking*, London, [1853].

862   STEINTHAL, *REV*. S. ALFRED. American slavery. A sermon, preached at Christ church chapel, Bridgewater, on Sunday, May the first, 1853. Bridgewater, [1853]. 26 p.   **DLC**

863   STEWART, ROBERT, *A.M*. The United States of America: their climate, soil, productions, population, manufactures, religion, arts, government, &c., &c. London, 1853. 399 p.   **CSmH NNC Uk**

One of the *Popular Geographical Library* series.

864   STIRLING, PATRICK JAMES. The Australian and Californian gold discoveries, and their probable consequences; or, An inquiry into the laws which determine the value and distribution of the precious metals: with historical notices of the effects of the American mines on European prices in the sixteenth, seventeenth, and eighteenth centuries. In a series of letters. Edinburgh, 1853. 279 p.   **DLC Uk**

Repr. New York, 1969 with illustrations and bibliographical footnotes.

865   STUART-WORTLEY, *LADY* EMMELINE CHARLOTTE ELIZABETH (MANNERS). &c. London, 1853. 450 p.   **DLC Uk**

Full title is "&c.". From pref.: "My book of American travels was called 'Travels in the United States, &c.' [q.v. 1851, above] and that '&c.' I propose now to take up again."

866   THOMPSON, GEORGE. American slavery. A lecture delivered in the Music hall, Store street, Dec. 13, 1852. London, 1853. 48 p.   **MH Uk**

867   TOWNLEY, *REV*. ADAM. Seven letters on the non-religious common school system of Canada and the United States. Toronto, 1853. 55 p.   **CaOOA**

Townley was "Presbyter of Toronto."

868   TUKE, JAMES HACK. The educational institutions of the United States. A paper read at the annual meeting of the Friends' Educational Society, 1853. York, 1853.   **Uk**

869   THE WAR OF PARTIES and waste of the national resources, with a peep into the policy of European cabinets; or, The history and mystery of increasing taxation, commercial difficulties, pauperism and crime, since the Revolution of 1688, in a series of dialogues between John Bull and Brother Jonathan. London, 1852–53. 4 pts. 64 p.   **MH Uk**

Cataloged under "John Bull". Dialogues illustrate the superiority of the Americans.

870   WICKSTEED, *REV.* CHARLES. The Englishman's duty to the free and enslaved American. A lecture, twice delivered at Leeds, in January, 1853. London, [1853]. 24 p.

    DLC Uk

Leeds anti-slavery series, no. 44. Lists titles of 80 anti-slavery pamphlets, pp. 21f.

Review: *Chr. Reformer*, IX, 394.

871   THE YOUNG EMIGRANTS. London, 1853. 48 p.   **NN Uk**

NN queries date, [185–?].

1854

872   ADAMS, HENRY GARDINER, *ed.* God's image in ebony: being a series of biographical sketches, facts, anecdotes, etc., demonstrative of the mental powers and intellectual capacities of the Negro race. Edited by H. G. Adams; with a brief sketch of the anti-slavery movement in America, by F[rederick] W[illiam] Chesson; and a concluding chapter of additional evidence, communicated by Wilson Armistead, esq. London, 1854. 34, 168 p.

    NN Uk ViU

873   ANSTED, DAVID THOMAS. Scenery, science and art; being extracts from the note-book of a geologist and mining engineer. By Professor D. T. Ansted. London, 1854. 323 p.

    DLC Uk

Four chaps. on the U.S., including one entitled "Slavery as an economical question," pp. 243–311. See also Ansted's "The mountains and valleys of Virginia," in Henry Walter Bates, ed., *Illustrated Travels; a record of discovery, geography and adventure*, London, 1874, VI, pp. 297–300, 368–371.

874   BAINES, *SIR* EDWARD. American slavery. Letter of Edward Baines, esq., editor of the Leeds Mercury. [Reprinted as a tract for the Leeds anti-slavery association by the kind permission of the author.] To the editors of newspapers in Boston, Massachusetts. [Leeds, 1854]. 8 p.   **MH NIC**

No t.p.

875   BLAIKIE, ALEXANDER. The philosophy of sectarianism; or, A classified view of the Christian sects of the United States; with notices of their progress and tendencies, illustrated by historical facts and anecdotes. Boston, 1854. 362 p.   **CLSU NIC PU Uk**

Uk entry reads: London; [printed in U.S.A.], 1854. DLC has 2d ed., Boston, 1856.

876   BOWDEN, JAMES. The history of the Society of Friends in America. London, 1850, 1854. 2 vols.   **CSmH MH NN Uk**

877   BRITISH AND FOREIGN ANTI-SLAVERY SOCIETY, *London*. American slavery and British Christians, a tract containing reprints of the addresses to Christians of all denominations . . . issued by the committee of the British and foreign anti-slavery society in April 1853 and 1854; the speech of the Rev. J[ames] B[arr] Walker of Ohio delivered at Exeter hall . . . in May 1854 shewing the connection of American religious bodies with slavery, and the article entitled "The silent men" from the "Anti-slavery reporter" of July 1853. London, 1854. 24 p.   **CtY MH**

CtY files under title in "Slavery Pamphlets," no. 74.

878   BUCKINGHAM, JAMES SILK. History and progress of the temperance reformation, in Great Britain and other countries of the globe; with statistical and documentary evidence of its beneficial results; and a plea for a Maine law, to enforce the suppression of all traffic in intoxicating drinks. London, 1854.   **DLC Uk**

No. 4, pp. 427–584, part of a larger work published under cover title: *The coming era of practical reform, not "looming in the distance," but "nigh at hand." A new series of tracts for the times, addressed to the public and parliament of 1854. By James Silk Buckingham. No. I –January, 1854*, London, 1853–54. A portion of *History and progress* was pub. separately under the title, *The justice, policy, and safety of a Maine law for England*, Manchester, [1855].

879   CANDLER, JOHN. A friendly mission; John Candler's letters from America, 1853–1854. Indianapolis, 1951. 134 p.   **DLC**

Indiana Hist. Soc. Pubs., vol. 16, no. 1. Letters are to his wife. See also "John Candler's visit to America, 1850," *Bull. Friends Hist. Assn.*, XLVIII (1959), 21–62.

880   CASE, GEORGE. Our "Constitutional rights" vindicated; or, An argument for the legal prescription of the traffic in alcoholic beverages. In six letters to the Hon. F[rances] Hincks. Toronto, 1854. 22 p.   **CaOTP**

881   CASWALL, *REV*. HENRY. The western world revisited. Oxford, 1854. 351 p.   **DLC Uk**

See also *The Californian Crusoe; or, The lost treasure found. A tale of Mormonism*, London, 1854, which has been ascribed to Caswall by Sabin, and also by a ms. notation in the copy in the Coe collection at Yale. This work has generally been accepted as a factual account by Robert Richards, the character who tells the story in the first person; however, it is probably fiction, and no more by Roberts than Robinson Crusoe was by Crusoe.

Review: *Anti-Slavery Advocate*, I, 320.

882   CHAMBERS, WILLIAM. Things as they are in America. London, 1854. 364 p. **DLC Uk**

New York, 1854 ed., adds to title . . . . *With a sketch of the brothers Chambers*; 2d ed., London, 1857, with corrections and additions. Ran serially in *Chambers's J.*, (ser. 3), I, 81, 98, 131, 161, 180, 211, 234, 241, 283, 300, 337, 355, 390; II, 7, 54, 88, 113, 167, 214, 242. Continued as "American jottings," II, 417; III, 42, 70, 101, 141, 185, 228, 267, 319; IV, 24, 188. Chambers visited U.S. in 1853, admired almost everything American, except daily manners and treatment of blacks, and urged British emigration. See also his *American slavery and colour*, London, 1857, below.

Reviews: *Dublin Univ. Mag.*, XLIV, 721; *Natl. Rev.*, II, 433.

883   [CONYBEARE, WILLIAM JOHN]. Mormonism: reprinted from the Edinburgh review, [issue] no. CCII, for April 1854. London, 1854. 112 p.   **CLU MB Uk**

Repr. from *Edinb. Rev.*, XCIX, 319–383; a review of various contemporary works on Mormonism. Also repr. in author's *Essays ecclesiastical and social. Reprinted, with additions, from the Edinburgh review*, London, 1855, pp. 280–376. See also Conybeare's novel, *Perversion: or the causes and consequences of infidelity. A tale for the times*, New York, 1856; a number of chaps. are set in the U.S., esp. among the Mormons.

884   DAY, *REV.* CHARLES. The Latter-day saints, or Mormonites: who and what are they? London, [1854?]. 30 p.   **CSmH CtY NN**

885   DUFF, *REV.* ALEXANDER. An address delivered before the general assembly of the Free church of Scotland, at Edinburgh, on the 26th day of May, 1854, by the Rev. Dr. Duff, upon his return from his visit to the United States: a full and interesting account of the trip is given. Also, Bedini and Dr. Duff, contrasted. By Kirwan. Dedicated to the American people. Washington City, 1854. 32 p.   **DLC Uk**

See also account of author's visit to America in *The life of Alexander Duff, D.D., LL. D.*, by George Smith, New York, [1880?], II, pp. 251–279, 290–291; also in *The life of Alexander Duff*, by Elizabeth Vermilye, New York, 1890, pp. 94–101.

886   DUFF, *REV.* ALEXANDER. Speech of the Rev. Dr. Duff, on foreign missions and America, delivered in the general assembly of the Free Church of Scotland, on the evening of May 29, 1854. Edinburgh, 1854. 47 p.   **CtY NN**

Rev. and corr. from the Glasgow *Guardian* and Edinburgh *Witness*.

887   EMIGRATION, EMIGRANTS, AND KNOW-NOTHINGS. By a foreigner. Philadelphia, 1854. 47 p.   **DLC**

By an English emigrant to the U.S. Compares British and American institutions.

888   FITZGERALD, JOHN, *M.A.* Christian slaveholders disobedient to Christ; or, Ten thousand English Christians invited to protest actively against the sin of the church in the United States; and to cease from purchasing the produce of slave labour. London, 1854. 114 p.   **ICN NIC**

889   FOREIGN LOANS and their consequences considered, in a letter to Benjamin Oliviera . . . by a member of the stock exchange, London. London, 1854. 37 p.   **MBAt PU**
On U.S.

890   FOSTER, VERE [HENRY LEWIS]. Work and wages; or, The penny emigrant's guide to the United States and Canada, for female servants, laborers, mechanics, farmers, etc., containing a short description of those countries, and most suitable places for settlement; rates of wages, board and lodging, house rent, price of land, money matters & c.; together with full information about the preparations necessary for the voyage, instructions on landing, and expenses of travelling in America. With an appendix. London, [1854]. 16 p. **CaOOA**

MB, MH show 5th ed., London, [1851], but internal evidence indicates 1854 as earliest publication. Uk has 5th ed., London, [1855]. This pamphlet sold over 250,000 copies in the first year. Excerpt appeared as *Emigration to America: information about wages of men and women in America; cost of board and lodging; price of land; expenses of voyage and outfit from England; of travelling in America, etc.* [Liverpool, 1854?], 4 p. After 1879, Foster actively promoted emigration of Irish women to the U.S. See also his *Diary of my voyage*, 1851, above; and Mary McNeill, *Vere Foster, 1819–1900: an Irish benefactor*, Belfast, 1971, esp. pp. 60–101, 189–206.

891   FOWLER, REGINALD. Hither and thither; or, Sketches of travels on both sides of the Atlantic. London, 1854. 272 p.   **DLC Uk**

Another London, 1854 ed. titled *Travels, trips and adventures, on both sides of the Atlantic; or, Hither and thither.* Probably in U.S. 1851–1853.

892   FRIENDS, SOCIETY OF. LONDON YEARLY MEETING. Proceedings in relation to the presentation of the address of the Yearly meeting of the religious society of Friends, on the slave-trade and slavery, to sovereigns and those in authority in the nations of Europe, and in other parts of the world, where the Christian religion is professed. London, 1854. 62 p.   **MH NIC OO Uk**

DLC has Cincinatti, 1855, ed. New York ed., 1856, contains "Report on the presentation and circulation of the address in the United States of America," signed by John Forster, John Candler, and William Holmes, pp. 45–61; these men headed the deputation to the U.S.

893   GREAT BRITAIN. COMMISSIONERS APPOINTED TO ATTEND THE EXHIBITION OF INDUSTRY IN THE CITY OF NEW YORK. New York industrial exhibition. General report of the British commissioners. Presented to the House of Commons by command of Her Majesty, in pursuance of their address of February 6, 1854. London, 1854.   **DLC Uk**

Appeared in *House of Commons Sessional Papers,* 1854, XXXVI, 1–7. Followed by a series of Special reports: by George Wallis, pp. 9–102; Joseph Whitworth, pp. 103–148; Charles Lyell, pp. 151–202; Charles Wentworth Dilke, pp. 203–317; and John Wilson, pp. 321–467. Various libraries also catalog separately by some of the authors named. Reports by Wallis and Whitworth also pub. as *The industry of the United States in machinery, manufacturers, and useful and ornamental arts. Compiled from the official reports of Messers. Whitworth and Wallis,* London, 1854; and in Nathan Rosenberg, ed., *The American system of manufactures: the report of the Committee on the machinery of the United States, 1855, and the special reports of George Wallis and Joseph Whitworth,* Edinburgh, 1969 (which includes an extensive general introduction, together with introds. to each report.) Whitworth's report also repr. as an appendix to his *Miscellaneous papers on mechanical subjects,* London, 1858, pp. 85–175.

894   HALL, MARSHALL. The two-fold slavery of the United States; with a project of self-emancipation. London, 1854. 159 p.   **DLC Uk**

CSmH has later ed., with title, *The facts of the two-fold slavery of the United States, carefully collected during a personal tour in the years 1853 and 1854: with a project of self-emancipation and the conversion of the slave into free peasantry; illustrated by shaded maps denoting the degree of slavery, and of unfriendliness to the African race, in the several states,* London, 1856.

895   HAND-BOOK TO CANADA AND THE UNITED STATES, with descent of Niagara and the St. Lawrence. London, 1854.

No locations found; listed in Sabin. Probably earlier issue of Uk copy: *Handbook to the diorama of Canada and the United States. With descent of the rivers Niagara and St. Lawrence,* [London?, 1855?]. The pamphlet is a handbook to a "grand moving diorama" painted by Washington Friend and other members of the New society of painters in water colors. A number of other descriptions of Friend's dioramas were pub. under various titles, e.g.: *Guide book to Mr. Washington Friend's great American tour of five thousand miles in Canada and the United States, including Niagara, and the River St. Lawrence, with the words of the songs & melodies sung by him in his unrivalled entertainment,* Nottingham, [1860?].

896   KENNEDY, JAMES. Probable origin of the American Indians, with particular reference to that of the Caribs. A paper read before the Ethnological society, the 15th March 1854, and printed at their special request. London, 1854. 42 p.   **DLC**

Included as part I in author's *Ethnological and philological essays*, London, 1855; also included in *Essays ethnological and linguistic, by the late James Kennedy*, ed. by C. M. Kennedy, London, 1861, pp. 87–123, which adds material on the American Indians, pp. 124–152. Uk has both above titles.

897   LANDOR, WALTER SAVAGE, *ed.* Letters of an American, mainly on Russia and revolution. London, 1854. 96 p.   **DLC Uk**

Purporting to be written by an American, Jonas Pottinger, this pamphlet indirectly reflects Landor's ideas on America and Americans. Landor wrote several verses on America: "Hymn to America," in the *Examiner*, 1851, repr. in *Last Fruit of an old tree*, London, 1853; "Ode to General Jackson, President of the United States," dated July 3, 1835, in *Pericles and Aspasia*, London, 1836; "To America, on Italy" in *Letters and other unpublished writings of Walter Savage Landor*, ed. by Stephen Wheeler, London, 1897, pp. 208–209; "To friend Jonathan," (1858), in *Complete works*, ed. by Stephen Wheeler, London, 1929, XV, p. 33; George Washington, Franklin and Penn figure in his *Imaginary Conversations*. See also the following items by Landor on America: "The Presidents of France and America," *Examiner*, Oct. 13, 1849, p. 643, and repr. in *Letters*, 1899, pp. 321–324; "Letter to an American," *Examiner*, Aug. 14, 1852, p. 516, repr. in *Letters*, 1899, pp. 337–339; "The American Fishery question," *Examiner*, Aug. 21, 1852, p. 532; and a letter to the London *Daily News*, March 5, 1846. See also Kate Fields, "Last days of W. S. Landor," *Atlantic*, XVII (June 1866), 684–705, for additional comment on American slavery.

898   THE LATTER DAYS. Railways, steam, and emigration, with its consequent rapid peopling of the deserts, also the present going to and fro, and increase of knowledge, foretold by Isaiah, Daniel, and Joel, and indicating the rapid approach of the end of the Latter Days. Dublin, 1854. 24 p.   **CSmH CtY**

899   MACKENZIE, CHARLES. The church in America; or America in connection with Bible truth and missionary exertion. A lecture. London, 1854.   **Uk**

Part II of *Signs of the times. . . . Lectures delivered on behalf of the church of England's Young Men's Society.*

900   MATHEWS, *REV.* EDWARD. Anti-slavery labours in England of the Rev. Edward Mathews, agent of the American Baptist free mission society. Bristol, [1854?]. 12 p.   **Uk**

Uk lists Bristol, 1851 ed., but pamphlet includes summaries of lectures and sermons through June 1854.

901   [MORTIMER, MRS. FAVELL LEE (BEVAN)]. Far off; or, Africa and America described: with anecdotes and numerous illustrations. By the author of "The peep of day," etc. etc. London, 1854. 323 p.   **CU NN Uk**

A sequel, listed as Part II, to *Far off; or, Asia and Australia described: with anecdotes and numerous illustrations*, London, 1852; on U.S. and Canada, pp. 138–225. Many later eds. of both vols.; one, *Far off; or, Australia, Africa, and America described*, London, 1864, combined material from both vols. into one and made additions to the text.

902   NARRATIVE OF THE ILLEGAL SEIZURE of the schooner "Mazeppa," owned by James Reeve, on Lake St. Clair, in British waters; by an American armed gang, June, 1854. Chatham, C.W., 1854. 16 p.   **CaOOA**

903   [PINNOCK, WILLIAM]. Panorama of the Old world and the new. Comprising a view of the present state of the nations of the world, their manners, customs and peculiarities, and their political, moral, social, and industrial condition. Interspersed with historical sketches and anecdotes. Boston, 1854. 616 p.   **MB NNC RPB**

T.p. missing from MB copy. On U.S., pp. 469–471, 487–519.

904   ROUTLEDGE'S AMERICAN HANDBOOK and tourist's guide through the United States. London, 1854. 216 p.   **DLC Uk**

905   THE SECRETS OF MORMONISM DISCLOSED. An authentic exposure of the immorality and licentious abominations of the apostles, prophets, high-priests, and elders of the Latter-day saints, and their spiritual wives; founded on their own quoted writings, doctrines, and official records, and the confessions of male and female members of their church; showing their obscene practices in the temple devoted to public worship, and the profligacy of a Mormon harem, composed of married and single females. Also the adulteries and seductions carried on at the celebration of their spiritual marriages, under the mask of having received divine sanction in visions. Including the horrors of the "Agapemone," or abode of love. London, [1854?]. 12 p.   **CtY MH**

906   STEPHEN, *SIR* GEORGE. Antislavery recollections in a series of letters addressed to Mrs. Beecher Stowe, written at her request. London, 1854. 258 p.   **DLC Uk**

2d ed., with a new introd. by Dr. Howard Temperley, London, 1971.

907   TREMENHEERE, HUGH SEYMOUR. The Constitution of the United States compared with our own. London, 1854. 389 p.   **DLC Uk**

Reviews: *Brit. Quar. Rev.*, XXV, 190; *Natl. Rev.*, II, 433; *Quar. Rev.*, CXI, 239; *Westmin. Rev.*, VII, n.s., 492.

908   TWISLETON, *HON.* EDWARD TURNER BOYD. Evidence as to the religious working of the common schools in the state of Massachusetts; with a preface by the Hon. Edward Twisleton, late chief commissioner of poor laws in Ireland. London, 1854. 98 p.   **NN Uk**

See also letter from Twisleton to William Dwight of Boston dated London, Dec. 7, 1861 in the *Mass. Hist. Soc. Coll.*, (Dec. 1913), 107–109.

909   VINCENT, *REV.* JAMES. American slavery defeated in its attempts through the American board of commissioners for foreign missions, to find a shelter in the British churches. Being a correspondence with the congregational union of England & Wales, on the "American board of missions and slavery," with the discussion which followed at the autumnal meetings of the union at Newcastle, in October, 1854. By James Vincent, minister of the gospel, agent of the American reform tract and book society, Cincinnati. With an introduction by Rev. Professor Scott, Airdale College, Bradford, Yorkshire. London, 1854. 48 p.   **OO Uk**

Vincent was an American, but pamphlet includes much comment by Scott and other British writers.

910   WELTON, THOMAS ABERCROMBIE. Freedom in America; its extent and influence. With some statistical information respecting the population, commerce, industry, education, and natural productions of the United States of America. By T. A. Welton. London, 1854. 24 p.   **CSmH NHi Uk**

See also his *Statistics of the United States of America . . . [Read before the Statistical society, 19th June, 1854.]*, [London, 1854], which is repr. from the *J. Royal Stat. Soc.*, XVII (Dec. 1854), 326–357.

911   WILLIAMSON, JAMES. The inland seas of North America; and the natural and industrial production of Canada, with the real foundation for its future prosperity. Kingston, Ont. 1854. 78 p.   **CtY MH TxU Uk**

Contains two lectures; the first, "The inland seas of North America", 55 p., equally concerned with U.S. and Canada, in their relation to Great Lakes.

1855

912   [ARMISTEAD, WILSON, ed.]. "Guilty or not guilty?" A few facts and feelings regarding the religious bodies of America in the matter of slavery; being a report of an anti-slavery meeting held in Belgrave chapel, Leeds, December 10th, 1855. Containing the addresses of Parker Pillsbury, esq., and the Rev. G. W. Conder. Revised from the columns of the Leeds Mercury. Leeds, 1855. 20 p.   **NHi NIC UkMa**

Pref. and final letter signed "W.A." Pub. by the Leeds Anti-slavery Society. NIC catalogs under the Society.

913   AUCHINLECK, G[ILBERT]. A history of the war between Great Britain and the United States of America. During the years 1812, 1813, and 1814. Toronto, 1855. 408 p.   **DLC**

Originally appeared in Maclean's *Anglo-Am. Mag.*, II–VI (1853–55). Repr., with an introd. by H. C. Campbell, London, 1972.

914   BAXTER, WILLIAM EDWARD. America and the Americans. London, 1855. 244 p.   **DLC Uk**

Lectures delivered at Dundee, Scotland.

Reviews: *Anti-Slavery Advocate*, I, 286; *Chambers's J.*, IV (3d ser.), 24; *Westmin. Rev.*, LXIV, 89.

915   BESTE, JOHN RICHARD DIGBY. The Wabash; or, Adventures of an English gentleman's family in the interior of America. London, 1855. 2 vols.   **DLC Uk**

See esp. vol. II, chap. 11; other comment on U.S., passim.

916   BLACKIE, WALTER GRAHAM. The imperial gazeteer; a general dictionary of geography, physical, political, statistical, and descriptive. Compiled from the latest and best authorities. Edited by W. G. Blackie. . . . With seven hundred illustrations, views, costumes, maps, plans, &c. Glasgow, 1855. 2 vols.   **DLC Uk**

On U.S., II, pp. 1138–1145. See also *A supplement to the imperial gazeteer; a general dictionary of geography, physical, political, statistical, and descriptive. Edited by W. G. Blackie. . . . Illustrated with views and plans of the more remarkable cities, ports, and harbours*, London, 1868; pp. 209–212 on U.S. Glasgow, 1868, ed. included both the gazeteer and supp.: *Imperial gazeteer with supplement.*

917   DAVIS, JOHN E. Mormonism unveiled; or, A peep into the principles & practices of the Latter-day saints, by John E. Davis, (formerly of no. 12, Herbert Street, Cardiff), a deluded brother of the sect, who has had the happiness of recovering from his infatuation by discovering the iniquitous proceedings of the leaders, during nine months' residence among them. Giving an account of his journeyings to Utah, the so-called City of Zion, in the valley of the Salt Lake, in company with upwards of three hundred of the infatuated victims of the deluders. Also his observations on their conduct and practices during his sojourn among them, and his happy escape from the thraldom of the self-interested deceivers, and a safe return to old England. A warning to the credulous. Bristol, 1855. 48 p.   **MH NN**

MH, NN and OClWHi have "second edition, revised and enlarged," which adds to the t.p.: *To which is added a dissertation on 'Polygamy and the Bible' with numerous scripture references and proofs, furnished by a gentleman well versed in such researches,"* Bristol, 1856, 48 p. CtY has 3d ed., Cardiff, 1858, with cover title, "Mormonism imposture exposed."

918   EVEREST, *REV*. ROBERT. A journey through the United States and part of Canada. London, 1855. 178 p.   **DLC Uk**

See also Everest's "On the distribution of the emigrants from Europe over the surface of the United States," *J. Royal Stat. Soc.*, XIX (March, 1856), 49–59.

Reviews: *Chambers's J.*, IV (3d ser.), 24; *Westmin. Rev.*, LXIV, 89.

919   FORBES, EDWARD. Literary papers, by Professor Edward Forbes . . . selected from his writings in the Literary gazette. [Edited with a memoir by L. Reeve.]. London, 1855. 300 p.   **DLC Uk**

Includes "The Salt lake and the Mormonites," pp. 263–277.

920   THE FRIENDLY REMONSTRANCE of the people of Scotland, on the subject of slavery. New York, 1855. 16 p.   **CSmH ICN PHi**

Pub. by the American Anti-slavery society; addressed to Americans.

921   FROTHINGHAM, *REV*. OCTAVIUS BROOKS. Colonization. New York, [1855]. 8 p.
                                                                          DLC

Anti-slavery tracts, No. 3. Pub. by the American anti-slavery society. Includes letter from Thomas Clarkson and a "Protest" (against the Liberian colonization idea) signed by Wm. Wilberforce, Wm. Evans, Samuel Gurney, Thos. Fowell Buxton, James Cropper, Wm. Allen, Daniel O'Connell, and others.

922   HARGRAVES, EDWARD HAMMOND. Australia and its gold fields: a historical sketch of the progress of the Australian colonies, from the earliest times to the present day; with a particular account of the recent gold discoveries, and observations on the present aspect of the land question. To which are added notices on the use and working of gold in ancient and modern times; and an examination of the theories as to the sources of gold. London, 1855. 240 p.   **DLC**

Includes account of author's experiences in Calif. in 1849, pp. 69–97.

923   HOGAN, J[OHN] SHERIDAN. Canada. An essay: to which was awarded the first prize by the Paris exhibition committee of Canada. Montreal, 1855. 86 p.   **DLC Uk**

Comparison of Canada and U.S. Also pub. in *Canada and her resources. Two prize essays, by J. Sheridan Hogan and Alexander Morris . . . the first prize being awarded by the Paris exhibition committee of Canada; and the second by His excellency, Sir Edmund Walker Head, bart.*, London, 1856.

924   HORNBY, *SIR* EDMUND [GRIMALDI]. Opinion pronounced by Mr. Edmund Hornby, the British commissioner, in the case of the Florida bonds, before the mixed commission, under the convention of 1853, for the settlement of claims between Great Britain and the United States. London, 1855. 20 p.   **DLC**

Uk has *Report of the proceedings of the mixed commission on private claims, established under the convention between Great Britain and the United States of America. . . . With the judgments of the commissioners and umpire. Compiled . . . by Edmund Hornby*, London, 1856.

925   [HOWE, JOSEPH]. Recruiting in America. To the editor of the Globe. [London, 1855]. 4 p.   **CaOOA MH**

Letter dated Aug. 31, 1855; Howe's name printed at end. Howe was sent to U.S. clandestinely to interview individuals proposing to furnish American recruits for the Crimean War effort. See also *Joseph Howe*, by James Wilberforce Longley, Toronto, 1904, "Foreign enlistment and the Irish Catholics," pp. 149–172; and J. Bartlett Brebner, "Joseph Howe and the Crimean War enlistment controversy between Great Britain and the United States," *Canadian Hist. Rev.*, XI, n.s. (Dec. 1930), pp. 300–327.

926   HOWE, JOSEPH. Speech of the Hon. Joseph Howe on the union of the North American provinces and on the right of British colonists to representation in the imperial parliament, and to participation in the public employment and distinctions of the empire. London, 1855. 63 p.   **MH Uk**

Much comment on the U.S., passim. Howe pub. this 1854 speech on a visit to England, generating a pamphlet exchange with Sir Francis Hincks. See Hincks' *Reply to the speech of the Hon. Joseph Howe, of Nova Scotia, on the union of the North American provinces. . . . By the Hon. Francis Hincks, member of the Legislative assembly of Canada*, London, 1855, 43 p. (MH, Uk); Howe's *Letter to the Hon. Francis Hincks, being a review of his reply to Mr. Howe's speech, on the organization of the Empire*, London, 1855, 40 p. (CaOOA, MH); and Howe's repr. of the whole exchange, *A speech on the union of the colonies and organization of the empire: delivered in the Nova Scotia legislature, 1854. . . . To which is added a review, by the Honble. Francis Hincks of Canada, together with Mr. Howe's reply. . . .* , Picton, N.S., 1855, 79 p. See also *The speeches and public letters of Joseph Howe*, 1872, below II, pp. 268–295, 310–327, for Howe's speech and his reply to Hincks. For later elaboration of Howe's views, see his *The organization of the empire*, 1866, below.

927   [HOWE, JOSEPH]. To James C. Van Dike, esq., attorney for the United States for the eastern district of Pennsylvania. [n.p., n.d.]. 7 p.   **CaOOA**

Howe's name printed at end of letter written ca. 1855; letter concerns foreign enlistment.

928   [HOWE, JOSEPH]. To the people of the United States. [New York, 1855]. 1 p.
    CaNSHL MH

Dated Apr. 3, 1855, and signed "A British American." Pub. as a broadside, seeking to enlist Americans for service in the Crimean war.

929   HURNARD, JAMES. The true way to abolish slavery. London, [1855]. 8 p.   **CtY ICN Uk**

930   HUSSEY, HENRY. The Australian colonies; together with notes of a voyage from Australia to Panama, in the "Golden Age." Descriptions of Tahiti and other islands in the Pacific and a tour through some of the states of America, in 1854. London, [1855]. 174 p.   **CtY NN Uk**

Tour of the southern states, pp. 112–174.

931   JACKSON, MARY. Rambles in the United States. Liverpool, 1855. 61 p.   **MH**

DLC has microfilm copy.

932   LINDSEY, CHARLES. Prohibitory liquor laws: their practical operation in the United States. The subject discussed as a question of state policy and legislation, with suggestions for the suppression of tippling houses. Toronto, 1855. 32 p.   **CaOTU**

Sabin lists Montreal, 1855 ed., 35 p.

933 MCGEE, THOMAS D'ARCY. The Catholic history of North America. Five discourses. To which are added two discourses on the relations of Ireland and America. Boston, 1855. 239 p. **DLC Uk**

934 MARRYAT, F[RANCIS SAMUEL]. Mountains and molehills; or, Recollections of a burnt journal. By Frank Marryat. London, 1855. 443 p. **NNC Uk**

DLC has New York, 1855 ed., which lacks handsome colored plates of London ed. Later facsimile versions: of London ed., introd. by Robin W. Winks, Philadelphia, [1962]; and of New York ed., introd. and notes by Marguerite Eyer Wilbur, Stanford, [1952]. See also the mimeographed index by Joseph Gaer, ed., Index no. 7, Sera project, California literary research, [n.p., 1935].

Reviews: *Daily Alta California*, VI, 191; *Harper's Mag.*, XI, 18.

935 MERRITT, WILLIAM HAMILTON. Remarks on the extension of reciprocity between Canada and the United States, (now confined to the growth and produce of each) to manufacturers, shipping & coasting, and establishing a commercial system adapted to the geographical position of Canada. St. Catharines, 1855. 12 p. **CaOOA NN**

See also *Report of a committee of the legislative assembly on trade and commerce between Canada and Great Britain, the British North American colonies, the West Indies, the United States, and other foreign parts*, [William Hamilton Merritt, chairman], Quebec, 1855. Also see Donald Campbell Masters, *The reciprocity treaty of 1854; its history, its relation to British colonial and foreign policy and to the development of Canadian fiscal autonomy*, London, [1937].

936 [MOOR, ALLEN PAGE]. Letters from North America, written during the summer of 1853. Canterbury, 1855. 72 p. **DLC**

Priv. pr. Written to the Warden of St. Augustine's by a member of the College.

937 MORMONISM: its blessings and advantages. [London, 1855?]. 8 p. **CtY**

Caption title. Satire on Mormonism, but not factual.

938 MURRAY, ANDREW. Description of new coniferous trees from California. . . . (From the Edinburgh New Philosophical Journal, new series, April 1855.) Edinburgh, 1855. 14 p. **DLC**

Appeared in the *Edinb. New Phil. J.*, I (1855), 284–295. See also his *Notes upon California trees*, 1860, below.

939 MURRAY, HENRY ANTHONY. Lands of the slave and the free; or, Cuba, the United States, and Canada. London, 1855. 2 vols. **DLC Uk**

A captain in the Royal Navy, Murray insisted his observations were "free from political bias," but nevertheless reveals a strong Tory outlook.

940 OLDMIXON, JOHN W. Transatlantic wanderings; or, A last look at the United States. By Capt. Oldmixon, R.N. London, 1855. 189 p. **DLC**

Repr. of 9 articles that had appeared in the *New Monthly Mag.*, (Dec. 1852–Aug. 1853), under the pseudonym of "J.W. Hengiston" [i.e., Cyrus Redding]: XCVI, 459–471; XCVII, 80–94, 223–236, 358–373, 499–516; XCVIII, 109–126, 232–252, 362–378, 485–500. Uk has only in the form of a scrapbook (listed under Hengiston) containing the magazine articles, 24 original watercolor drawings by Oldmixon, and a ms. pref., signed J. W. Oldmixon and dated Sept. 21, 1853, discussing Redding's role in editing and publishing the articles. See also the following articles by Cyrus Redding in the *New Monthly Mag.*, CVI, 409–418; CXXIV, 63–72; 337–347.

941   OLIPHANT, LAURENCE. Minnesota and the far West. Edinburgh, 1855. 306 p. **DLC Uk**

Repr. from *Blackwood's Edinb. Mag.*, where it appeared anonymously, April–Sept. 1855, under title, "Notes on Canada and the north-west states of America." See also Oliphant's *Episodes in a life of adventure; or, Moss from a rolling stone*, 1887, below; and Francis Paul Prucha, "Minnesota 100 years ago as seen by Laurence Oliphant," *Minn. Hist.*, XXXIV (Summer 1954), pp. 45–53.

Reviews: *Athenaeum*, (Nov. 24, 1855), 1363; *Littel's Living Age*, CLXX, 820; *Nation*, VIII, 380; *New Quar. Rev.*, V, 64; *Sat. Rev.* (by A. J. Beresford-Hope), I, 122.

942   PIERCY, FREDERICK HAWKINS. Route from Liverpool to Great Salt Lake Valley, illustrated with steel engravings and wood cuts from sketches made by Frederick Piercy, including views of Nauvoo and the ruins of the temple, with an historical account of the city; views of Carthage jail, and portraits and memoirs of Joseph and Hyrum Smith; their mother, Lucy Smith; Joseph and David Smith, sons of the prophet Joseph; President Brigham Young; Heber C. Kimball; Willard Richards; Jedediah M. Grant; John Taylor; the late chief patriarch, Father John Smith; and the present chief patriarch, John Smith, son of Hyrum. Together with a geographical and historical description of Utah, and a map of the overland routes to that territory from the Missouri river. Also, an authentic history of the Latter-day saints' emigration from Europe from the commencement up to the close of 1855, with statistics. Edited by James Linforth. Liverpool, 1855. 120 p.   **DLC Uk**

Issued in 15 monthly parts, July 1854–Sept. 1855. Outside cover has slightly different title: *Route from Liverpool to Great Salt Lake Valley, illustrated by a series of splendid steel engravings and wood cuts, by Charles Fenn, Edwin Roffe, and Mason Jackson, from sketches made on the spot and from life, expressly for this work by Frederick Piercy, and containing a map of the overland portion of the journey. Edited by James Linforth*, Liverpool. Howes describes as "One of the most elaborately and beautifully illustrated of western books." Linforth's notes are extensive. See also later ed., Cambridge, Mass, 1962, ed. by Fawn M. Brodie.

943   REID, MAYNE. The hunters' feast; or, Conversations around the camp-fire. London, [1855]. 336 p.   **NN Uk**

DLC has New York, [1856] ed. Only a slightly fictionized account of a buffalo hunting trip to the prairies from St. Louis. For accounts of his experiences in the U.S., 1840–48 and 1867–70, see *Mayne Reid; a memoir of his life, by Elizabeth Reid, his widow*, London, 1890; and *Captain Mayne Reid; his life and adventures, by Elizabeth Reid, his widow, assisted by Charles H. Cox, of U.S.A.*, London, 1900. See also Reid's magazine, *Onward* (New York), Jan. 1869–Feb., 1870; esp. his "A dashing dragoon: the Murat of the American army," I (Jan. 1869), 25 (repr. in *Mag. of Hist. with Notes & Queries*, Extra No. (1913), 59–65); and "The Mormon monsters," II (Nov. 1869), 425–426. See also author's "A tour in Texas," *Field*, III (Feb. 1872), 22–24; "Captured by Confeds: an incident of the American rebellion," *London Soc.*, XXI (May 1872), 433–440; "Ghost or grizzly? What I saw in crossing the Rockies," *London Soc.*, XXI (June 1872), 511–518; and "A flying visit to Florida," *Illustrated travels: a record of discovery, geography, and adventure*, ed. by Henry Walter Bates, London, 1872, IV, 1–7, 53–57, 72–78, 98–103, 153–159.

Reid wrote many novels with settings laid in the U.S., and sometimes extensive notes appended; see esp. the following: *The scalp hunters; or, Romantic adventures in Northern Mexico*, London, 1851, 3 vols., Notes, III, pp. 229–299; *The white chief: a legend of Northern Mexico*, London, 1855, 3 vols., Notes, III, pp. 253–307; *Sketches of life in the far west; comprising the adventures of a white chief*, London, [n.d.], Notes, pp. 441–444; *The Quadroon; or, A lover's adventures in Louisiana*, London, 1856, 3 vols., Notes, III, pp.

227–272; *The rifle rangers; or, Adventures of an officer in southern Mexico*, London, 1850, 2 vols.; and *Quadrupeds: what they are and where found: a book of zoology for boys*, London, 1872. See also his *Odd people. Being a description of singular races of man*, London, 1860, pp. 275–297, 318–351. See also Joan Dorothy Steele, "The image of America in the novels of Mayne Reid: A study of a romantic expatriate," unpub. Ph.D. Diss., UCLA, 1970.

944   ROBERTSON, JAMES. A few months in America; containing remarks on some of its industrial and commercial interests. London, [1855]. 230 p.   **DLC Uk**

Reviews: *Brit. Quar. Rev.*, (by Thomas Ballantyne), XXV, 190; XXVI, 416 (review repr. in Ballantyne's *Tracts from the Manchester school*, 1858, below); *Chambers's Jour.*, IV (3d ser.), 24; *Westmin. Rev.*, VIII (n.s.), 170.

945   ROCHE, ALFRED R. A view of Russian America, in connection with the present war. Montreal, 1855. 70 p.   **DLC**

"Read before the Literary and historical society of Quebec, 7th March, 1855, and published in the journal of the society." Considerable comment on relations with U.S. in connection with Northwest territory.

946   ROSS, ALEXANDER. The fur hunters of the far West; a narrative of adventures in the Oregon and Rocky mountains. London, 1855. 2 vols.   **DLC Uk**

Vol. I repr. as one of the Lakeside Classics, ed. by Milo Milton Quaife, Chicago, 1924. A complete edition, ed. by Kenneth A. Spaulding, was issued by the Univ. of Oklahoma Press, Norman, [1956]. Describes Ross's adventures in the Pacific northwest, 1813–25. See also account of this book in George Bird Grinnell, *Beyond the old frontier; adventures of Indian-fighters, hunters, and fur traders*, New York, 1913, pp. 41–123.

Reviews: *Athenaeum*, (November 3, 1855), 1266; *Nation*, IX, 241.

947   RYLE, THOMAS. American liberty and government questioned. London, 1855. 195 p.
    DLC Uk

Review: *Athenaeum* (April 14, 1855), 426.

948   TAYLDER, T. W. P. The Mormon's own book; or, Mormonism tried by its own standards, reason and scripture. . . . Dedicated to the London City mission. London, 1855. 200 p.
    DLC Uk

London, 1857 ed. carried title, *The Mormon's own book; or, Mormonism tried by its own standards, reason and scripture, with an account of its present condition. . . . Also a life of Joseph Smith. New edition.* Scattered comment on the U.S. The following two works by Taylder are mostly doctrinal, but see: *Twenty reasons for rejecting Mormonism. . . . Reprinted from the Christian Cabinet*, London, 1857; *The materialism of the Mormons, or Latter-day saints, examined and exposed*, Woolwich, 1849, 40 p. See also the American response to the last mentioned item in Orson Pratt's *Absurdities of immaterialism; or, A reply to T. W. P. Taylder's pamphlet, entitled, "The materialism of the Mormons or Latter-day saints examined and exposed,"* Liverpool, 1849, 32 p.

949   THOROLD, ALGAR LABOUCHERE. The life of Henry Labouchere. London, 1913. 513 p.   **DLC Uk**

Henry Du Pre Labouchere travelled in the U.S. and was attache at Washington; see account, 1853–55, pp. 35–45; many other references to U.S., passim. See also account in Hesketh Pearson, *Labby*, New York, 1937, pp. 32–39. Labouchere was born in France, but became an English citizen.

950   TO THE RIGHT HON. LORD JOHN RUSSELL, &c, &c, &c. On money, morals, and progress. By Anglo Americana, author of Suggestions for a philosophic currency. London, 1855. 62 p.   **DLC Uk**

Signed, Hastings, July 4, 1855.

951   [TODD, HENRY COOK] Items: (in life of an usher) on travels, anecdote, and popular errors. By one in retirement. Second edition. Quebec, 1855. 306 p.   **DLC Uk**

First ed. not located. Includes notes on the U.S. not appearing in his earlier work, *Notes upon Canada and the United States of America . . .* , 1835, above. See esp. pp. 49–150.

952   WARREN, JOHN COLLINS, *the elder*. The great tree on Boston common. Boston, 1855. 20 p.   **DLC Uk**

Full page engraving of tree.

953   WELD, CHARLES RICHARD. A vacation tour in the United States and Canada. London, 1855. 394 p.   **DLC Uk**

A barrister, publisher and historian of the Royal Society, Weld visited the U.S. in 1850, travelling south to Virginia and west to Chicago. This work dedicated to his half-brother, Isaac Weld, author of the widely-read and -reprinted *Travels through the states of North America, and the provinces of Upper and Lower Canada, during the years 1795, 1796, and 1797*, London, 1799; Charles Weld considered this a continuation of the earlier chronicle.

954   YOUNG, JOHN. Letters to the Hon. Francis Lemieux, chief commissioner public works, on Canadian trade and navigation, and to the citizens of Montreal, on the commerce of the city and the means of its further development. By the Hon. John Young, M.P.P. Montreal, 1855. 32 p.   **DLC Uk**

Discusses Canadian-American trade, etc.

1856

955   AMERICA THE TARSHISH of Holy Scripture. London, 1856. 16 p.   **Uk**

956   AMERICAN SLAVERY. Is Mrs. Stowe wrong in exposing its horrors and iniquities? Leeds, [1856?]. 7 p.   **DHU TNF**

Repr. from the Leeds *Mercury* of Oct. 2, 1856, by the Leeds Anti-slavery Association.

957   BARTLETT, WILLIAM HENRY. The history of the United States of North America; from the discovery of the western world to the present day. By W. H. Bartlett . . . continued by B. B. Woodward. New York, [1855–56]. 3 vols.   **DLC**

The first 3 books of vol. I are by Bartlett, the remainder by Woodward. Uk has later ed., with the title, *History of the United States of America. [By W. H. Bartlett. Continued to the death of President Taylor by B. B. Woodward.] With a continuation, including the presidencies of Pierce and Buchanan, by C. Mackay*, London, 1861–63], 2 vols. See also Bartlett's *The Pilgrim fathers; or, the Founders of New England in the reign of James the First*, London, 1853; and *American scenery; or, Land, lake and river illustrations of transatlantic nature. From drawings by W. H. Bartlett engraved in the first style of the art, by R. Wallis, J. Cousen, Willmore [and others]. The literary department by N[athaniel] P[arker] Willis*, London, 1840. See also Charles Mackay, "President Johnson and the reconstruction of the Union," *Fortnightly Rev.*, IV (Apr. 1, 1866), 477–490.

958   [BISHOP, ISABELLA LUCY (BIRD)] *"Mrs.* John F. Bishop." The Englishwoman in America. London, 1856. 464 p.   **DLC Uk**

Repr. ed., Madison, Wisc., 1969, with forward and notes by Andrew Hill Clark. Later the author of many travel works, Bishop first visited the U.S. in 1854 at age 23. See also her *A lady's life in the Rocky mountains*, 1879, below. For accounts of her travels see: Norreys Jephson O'Conor, "Intrepid lady," *Southwest Rev.*, XXXV (Spring, 1951), 123–129; and Pat Barr, *A curious life for a lady: the story of Isabella Bird*, London, [1970], esp. pp. 60–69 and notes, pp. 341–342.

Reviews: *Athenaeum* (Jan. 19, 1856), 67; *Canadian J.* (by Don Wilson), III, (n.s.), 129; *Fraser's Mag.*, LIII, 522; *Sat. Rev.* (by Mrs. Bennett), I, 282.

959   BOWLBY, RICHARD. Kansas, the seat of war in America. London, 1856. 36 p.   **Uk**

Reviews: *Athenaeum* (Nov. 1, 1856), 1337; *Natl. Rev.* (by James Martineau), IV, 212, (repr. in Martineau's *Essays, reviews, and addresses*, London, 1890–91, I, 495–527).

960   BROTHER JONATHAN, sketched by himself, in the Yankee notions he has of his own importance as a nation. Glasgow, 1856.   **Uk**

961   BROWNE, CHARLES. The United States; their constitution and power. London, 1856. 86 p.   **DLC Uk**

962   CAMERON, JOHN, *comp*. The Canadian tariff as passed by the Provincial legislature, in the session of 1856, and brought into operation on the 5th of July in the same year; also, the American tariff, as imposed by the Act of Congress, July 30, 1846. Arranged by John Cameron. Toronto, 1856. 68 p.   **CaOTP**

963   [CLARENDON, GEORGE WILLIAM FREDERICK VILLIERS, *4th earl of*]. Recruiting in the United States. London, February, 1856. [London, 1856]. 16 p.   **DLC Uk**

Uk catalogs under England—Depts. of State—Army. Extracts from a speech given in Parliament, Jan. 31, 1856 and pub. in the London *Times*, Feb. 1, 1856. For a number of Clarendon's letters on American affairs, see Sir Herbert Maxwell, *The life and letters of George William Frederick, fourth earl of Clarendon*, London, 1913, II, pp. 263–270.

964   DASENT, ARTHUR IRWIN. John Thadeus Delane, editor of "The Times"; his life and correspondence. London, 1908. 2 vols.   **MH NN Or Uk**

DLC has New York, 1908 ed. Visit to the U.S. in 1856, I, pp. 239–247; other comment on American affairs, esp. during the Civil War, passim. See also "Delane's journal of his visit to America [in 1856]," *Notes and Queries* (London), Ser. 12, VI, 285–288, 305–308, 325–328 (ed. by C. W. B.); Arnold Whitridge, "Anglo-American troublemakers: J. G. Bennett and J. T. Delane," *Hist. Today*, VI (Feb. 1956), 88–95; and Raymond William Postgate, *England goes to press; the English people's opinion on foreign affairs as reflected in their newspapers since Waterloo* (1815–1937), New York, 1937, pp. 113–123.

965   EDINBURGH LADIES EMANCIPATION SOCIETY. Appeal on behalf of the sufferers in Kansas. [Edinburgh, 1856?]. 3 p.   **NIC**

966   THE EMIGRANT'S REVERIE and dream: England and America. London, 1856. 186 pp.
                                                                                Uk

Verse. "The emigrant's dream," pp. 53–125, consists of a dialog between a "matron" and her two sons, Britannicus and Americus.

967   FERGUSON, WILLIAM. America by river and rail; or, Notes by the way on the New World and its people. London, 1856. 511 p.   **DLC Uk**

Travelled in the U.S. during 1855. Particularly expressive in his description of mining in the West.

968   GOLOVIN, IVAN [GAVRILOVICH]. Stars and stripes, or American impressions. London, 1856. 312 p.   **DLC Uk**

See Max M. Lasevson, *The American impact on Russia—diplomatic—idealogical—1784–1917*, New York, 1950, pp. 155–161. Russian-born Golovin became a naturalized British citizen in 1843.

Review: *Athenaeum* (Oct. 25, 1856), 1306; see also pp. 1578, 1610f.

969   HALL, EDWARD HEPPLE. Ho! for the West!!! The traveller's and emigrant's handbook to Canada and the Northwest states of America, for general circulation. Containing useful information on all important points, gathered during a residence of eight years in both countries. Compiled from the latest authentic sources, and designed particularly for the use of travellers, emigrants and others. London, 1856. 64 p.   **Uk**

DLC has 3d ed., London, 1858, with variant title. An immigrant who settled in Chicago, Hall describes himself in the pref. as "formerly of Newcastle-on-Tyne, England." His series of annual travel guides resumed with an expanded scope in 1864 under title, *The great West: emigrants', settlers' & travellers' guide and hand-book to the states of California and Oregon, and the territories of Nebraska, Utah, Colorado, Montana, Nevada and Washington. With a full and accurate account of their climate, soil, resources and products*, New York, 1864, 89 p., with subsequent eds. revised and augmented under various sub-titles. By this time, Hall clearly identified himself as American. Also named as author of various eds. of *Appleton's handbook of American travel*; also wrote *The summer tourist's pocket guide to American watering places*, London, 1869.

970   HENNING, THOMAS. Slavery in the churches, religious societies, &c., a review: by Thomas Henning, esq., with prefatory remarks, by J. J. E. Linton, esq., Stratford. Toronto, 1856. 39 p.   **CtY ICN NIC OO**

971   [HOWE, JOSEPH]. For "The Times." Halifax, Nova Scotia, Nov. 24, 1856. To John Arthur Roebuck, esq., M.P. [n.p., n.d.]. 2 p.   **CaOOA**

Letter respecting enlistment in the U.S., for British service; Howe's name printed at end.

972   HOWE, JOSEPH. Letter to the Right Honorable William E. Gladstone, M.P. from the Hon. Joseph Howe, being a review of the debate on the foreign enlistment bill, and our relations with the United States. London, 1856. 71 p.   **CaOOA Uk**

Repr. together with a subsequent brief exchange of letters with Gladstone, in *The Speeches and public letters of Joseph Howe*, 1872, below, II, pp. 329–347.

973   [HUNTLEY, *SIR* HENRY VERE]. California: its gold and its inhabitants. By the author of "Seven years on the slave coast of Africa," "Peregrine Scramble," &c. London, 1856. 2 vols. in 1.   **DLC Uk**

Also pub. under title, *Adventures in California. Its gold fields, and its inhabitants*, [n.p., n.d.], 2 vols. in 1. Sabin lists an unlocated item: *Adventures in California and its gold fields*, London, 1851, 2 vols., which may be by Huntley, although author states in pref. that he was in California in 1852. Name sometimes given "Veel" instead of "Vere"; see Huntley entry, 1850, above. Huntley's *Peregrine Scramble; or, Thirty years' adventures of a blue jacket*, London, 1849, 2 vols., is a fictitious account of happenings in the War of 1812, described by author as "generally founded on fact"; see vol. I, pp. 236–347, and II, pp. 1–95.

Review: *Athenaeum*, (July 12, 1856), 861.

974   KINGSTON, WILLIAM HENRY GILES. Western wanderings; or, A pleasure tour in the Canadas. London, 1856. 2 vols.   **DLC Uk**

Description of New York, Boston, etc., I, pp. 1–67, 281–317; II, 271–324. See also Rev. Maurice Rooke Kingsford, *The life, work and influence of William Henry Giles Kingston,* Toronto, [1947]; discusses Kingston's trip to the U.S., 1853 and 1854, pp. 75–83, 103–121.

975   MARTINEAU, HARRIET. A history of American compromises. Reprinted with additions from the Daily News. London, 1856. 35 p.   **DLC Uk**

Reviews: *Brit. Quar. Rev.,* XXV, 190; XXXIII, 419; *Edinb. Rev.,* CIV, 561; *Natl. Rev.* (by James Martineau), IV, 212 (repr. in his *Essays, reviews and addresses,* London, 1890–91); *Westmin. Rev.,* XII, (n.s.), 137.

976   MURRAY, AMELIA MATILDA. Letters from the United States, Cuba and Canada, by the Hon. Amelia M. Murray. London, 1856. 2 vols.   **DLC Uk**

Travelled along the Atlantic seaboard, and as far south as New Orleans. Pub. of the letters, detailing her conversion to an ardent antislavery position, led to Murray's dismissal as a lady-in-waiting to Queen Victoria. See also Lilla M. Hames, "Amelia M. Murray on slavery—an unpublished letter," *Georgia Hist. Quar.,* XXX (Dec. 1949), 314–317.

Reviews: *Athenaeum* (Jan. 26, 1856), 99, 107; *Canadian J.,* I, 160; *Fraser's Mag.,* LIII, 522; *Nat'l. Quar. Rev.,* I, 350; *Sat. Rev.* (by G. H. Lewes), I, 194, 237; *So. Lit. Mess.,* XXII, 455.

977   NO WAR WITH AMERICA! An address to his countrymen, by an Englishman. London, 1856. 23 p.   **Uk ViU**

978   OUR RELATIONS WITH AMERICA. Correspondence between the English and American governments upon the enlistment question, as presented to the congress of the United States, February 28, 1856. London, 1856.   **Uk**

Uk catalogs under England—Treaties.

979   PLAYFAIR, ROBERT. Recollections of a visit to the United States and British provinces of North America, in the years 1847, 1848, and 1849. Edinburgh, 1856. 266 p.   **DLC Uk**

980   PRATER, HORATIO. Letters to the American people, on Christianity and the Sabbath. London, 1856. 144 p.   **DLC**

981   RODWELL, JAMES. Queen Cora; or, Slavery and its downfall. By James Rodwell, the British Workman. London, 1856.   **MH NHi Uk**

Prose play, but 25 p. introd. discusses slavery in the U.S.

982   RUSSELL, ROBERT. Agricultural notes in Ohio and Michigan. Edinburgh, 1856. 15 p.   **DLC**

Appeared also in the *J. of Agric.* (Edinburgh), Oct. 1856, 451–465. Later formed chap. 6, pp. 90–109 of larger work, *North America, its agriculture and climate; containing observations on the agriculture and climate of Canada, the United States, and the island of Cuba,* 1857, below.

983   SARGANT, WILLIAM LUCAS. The science of social opulence. London, 1856. 509 p.   **DLC Uk**

Comment on U.S., passim.

984 SENIOR, NASSAU WILLIAM. American slavery: a reprint of an article on "Uncle Tom's cabin," of which a portion was inserted in the 206th number of the "Edinburgh Review"; and of Mr. Sumner's speech of the 19th and 20th of May, 1856. With a notice of the events which followed that speech. London, 1856. 164 p. **DLC Uk**

Repr. from *Edinb. Rev.*, CI (Apr. 1855), 293–331, with the addition of passage denouncing slavery which had been cut by the editor of the magazine.

985 SHAW, JOHN. A ramble through the United States, Canada, and the West Indies. London, 1856. 370 p. **DLC Uk**

See also the account of this visit, made in 1845, in author's *Travel and recollections of travel, with a chat upon various subjects*, London, 1857, pp. 83–85, 152–157, 167–197, 207–209.

986 SHAW, PRINGLE. Ramblings in California; containing a description of the country, life at the mines, state of society, &c. Interspersed with characteristic anecdotes, and sketches from life, being the five years' experience of a gold digger. Toronto, [1856?]. 239 p. **DLC**

Authorities differ in the supplied date; some give [1857?].

987 YOUNG, JOHN. Letter of the Hon. John Young, (Member of the Provincial parliament of Canada), on the postal and passenger communication between Great Britain & North America, by the St. Lawrence. London, 1856. 4 p. **DLC**

Inside caption title, "To America by the St. Lawrence, and Canadian trade."

1857

988 ALEXANDER, *SIR* JAMES E[DWARD]. Passages in the life of a soldier; or, Military service in the East and West. By Lieut.-Colonel Sir James E. Alexander, Knt., K.C.L.S., fellow of the Royal geographical and Asiatic societies, &c. London, 1857. 2 vols.

CaOTP Uk

On visit to the U.S., 1853–54, I, pp. 113–160, 197–208, 266–267.

989 THE ATLANTIC TELEGRAPH COMPANY. The Atlantic Telegraph. A history of preliminary experimental proceedings, and a descriptive account of the present state and prospects of the undertaking. Published by order of the directors of the Company. July, 1857. London, 1857. 69 p.

DLC Uk

990 BALLANTYNE, THOMAS. Nett [sic] result of manhood suffrage & the ballot in the United States: letters to R. Cobden. London, [1857]. **UkLL**

991 BORTHWICK, J.D. Three years in California. Edinburgh, 1857. 384 p. **DLC Uk**

In California 1851–1854. New York, 1917 ed. under title, *The gold hunters, By J. D. Borthwick; a first-hand picture of life in California mining camps in the early fifties*, ed. by Horace Kephart. Other eds. under original title: with index and forward by Joseph A. Sullivan, Oakland, Calif., 1948; and selections, ed. by Joseph Arnold Foster, Claremont, 1950, 26 p. See also Joseph Gaer, ed., *Index . . . Three years in California*, [n.p., 1935], Calif. literary research project, index no. 4.

992   BRADSHAW, W[ILLIAM] S. Voyages to India, China, and America, with an account of the Swan River settlement. London, 1857. 230 p.   **DLC Uk**

In U.S., 1851, pp. 144–198.

993   CANADA. PARLIAMENT. SELECT COMMITTEE ON CAUSES OF EMIGRATION. Report of the select committee appointed to enquire into the cause of emigration from Canada to the United States of America and elsewhere. [Toronto, 1857?]. 144 p.

         CaOTU MH

994   CHAMBERS, WILLIAM. American slavery and colour. London, 1857. 216 p.   **DLC Uk**

995   CHANDLESS, WILLIAM. A visit to Salt Lake; being a journey across the plains and a residence in the Mormon settlements at Utah. London, 1857. 346 p.   **DLC Uk**

Records travels July 1855–Feb. 1856; last 60 pp. describe trip to California.

Reviews: *Athenaeum*, (May 23, 1857), 655; *Daily Alta California*, IX, 189; *Sat. Rev.*, III, 505.

996   [COOK, WILLIAM]. The Mormons, the dream and the reality; or, Leaves from the sketch book of experience of one who left England to join the Mormons in the city of Zion and awoke to a consciousness of its heinous wickedness and abominations. Edited by a clergyman [William B. Fowler]. London, 1857. 92 p.   **DLC Uk**

Fowler is sometimes given as the author—also, erroneously, "Flower." The 2d ed., London, 1858, carried the title *The "Fowler's Snare," as craftily laid to catch unwary souls, now fully unmasked and exposed to view, by one who has broken the snare and escaped*. See also arguments against book in the *Western Standard*, June 5th and June 12th, 1857.

Review: *Athenaeum*, (Apr. 18, 1857), 500.

997   CORDNER, *REV.* JOHN. The vision of the Pilgrim fathers. An oration spoken before the New England society of Montreal, in the American Presbyterian church, on 22nd December, 1856 . . . With the proceedings at the dinner. Montreal, 1857. 54 p.   **DLC**

998   THE COTTON CRISIS; and how to avert it. London, 1857. 59 p.   **CSmH CtY Uk**

Review: *Brit. Quar. Rev.* (by Thomas Ballantyne?), XXVI, 416; repr. in Ballantyne's *Tracts for the Manchester School*, 1858, below.

999   COTTON SUPPLY ASSOCIATION, MANCHESTER, ENG. The cultivation of Orleans staple cotton, from the improved Mexican cotton seed, as practiced in the Mississippi cotton growing region. Manchester, 1857. 28 p.   **NhM Uk**

DNAL has 2d ed., Manchester, [1857].

1000   DESCRIPTION OF THE MAMMOTH TREE from California, now erected at the Crystal Palace, Sydenham. [London, 1857]. 24 p.   **DLC**

1001   DUNCAN, JONATHAN. Industry of the United States. No. 2. Political information for the people. London, [1857].   **Uk**

1002   [DYER, JOSEPH CHESSBOROUGH]. Notes on the legalized reclamation of fugitive slaves from the free states of America, according to a recent decision of the Supreme Court. By a native citizen of Connecticut. Manchester, 1857. 24 p.   **UkMa**

Presentation copy, at UkMa, reads "To Samuel Crompton Esq. with J.C. Dyer's best respects."

1003   EVEREST, ROBERT. On the proportion of foreigners to natives, and of foreign and native convicts, in several states of Europe and America. [London, 1857?]. 7 p.   **MB**

Repr. of a paper read before the Statistical society, February 17, 1857; pub. in the *J. Stat. Soc. London*, March 1857. See also his "On the distribution of the emigrants from Europe over the surface of the U.S.," *J. Stat. Soc. London*, XIX (Dec., 1856), 49–59.

1004   [FARRAND, REBECCA]. A sister's memorial; or, A little account of Rebecca Farrand: also, drawn up by her, A brief sketch of an elder sister [Mrs. Eliza (Farrand) Taylor]. London, 1857. 142 p.   **DLC Uk**

Both DLC & Uk list under editor, Sarah Ann Farrand. See account of trip to America, 1855–56, pp. 60–107.

1005   GALTON, *SIR* DOUGLAS STRUTT. Report to the lords of the Committee of privy council for trade and foreign plantations, on the railways of the United States, by Captain Douglas Galton. London, 1857. 40 p.   **DBRE**

See also his *Supplement . . . containing drawings to explain the construction of the rolling stock in use on the American railways*, London, 1858. Presented to both houses of Parliament.

1006   GLADSTONE, THOMAS H. Kansas; or, Squatter life and border warfare in the far West . . . with additions and corrections. London, 1857. 295 p.   **DLC Uk**

Revision of material originally appearing in the London *Times*, 1856. DLC also has the New York, 1857 ed., with title, *The Englishman in Kansas; or, Squatter life and border warfare. With an introd. by Fred. Law Olmstead*, 328 p.

Review: (of New York ed.) *Putnam's Mag.*, IX, 660.

1007   HAWTHORNTHWAITE, [SAMUEL]. Mr. Hawthornthwaite's adventures among the Mormons, as an elder during eight years. Manchester, 1857. 132 p.   **CSmH NN Uk**

Last chap. contains accounts of emigres to Salt Lake City.

1008   [HOWE, JOSEPH]. Letter to the people of Nova Scotia. [Halifax, 1857]. 9 p.
        CaOOA MH

Signed Joseph Howe, Halifax, 2d March, 1857. Contains comment on railway riots and Irish Catholics in the U.S. and Canada.

1009   HOWE, JOSEPH. Speech of the Hon. Joseph Howe, delivered before the Provincial assembly, on 9th February, 1857. [Halifax, 1857]. 8 p.   **MH**

Contains comment on the recruitment controversy.

1010   THE HUDSON'S BAY QUESTION. London, 1857. 28 p.   **DLC**

Articles from "current number" of *Colonial Intelligencer*; pref. dated Nov., 1857. Edited by F.W.C.

1011   HYDE, JOHN, *jun*. Mormonism: its leaders and designs. New York, 1857. 335 p.   **DLC**

Uk has 2d ed., New York, 1857. In Salt Lake, 1853–56.

1012   JOBSON, *REV*. FREDERICK J[AMES]. America, and American Methodism. By the Rev. Frederick J. Jobson. With a prefatory letter by the Rev. John Hannah, D.D. Illustrated from original sketches by the author. London, [1857]. 399 p.   **DLC Uk**

1013   [MACAULAY, THOMAS BABINGTON MACAULAY, *1st baron*]. Macaulay on democracy. Letter from Lord Macaulay on American institutions and prospects. [n.p., n.d.]. 4 p.   **NN**

Letter to Henry S. Randall, dated London, May 23, 1857. Appeared in the *So. Lit. Mess.*, XXX (Mar. 1860), 225–228, and repr. in the New York *Times* and the London *Times*. The letter is also included in Charles A. Betts, "Macaulay's criticism of democracy and Garfield's reply," *Open Court*, XXXII (May 1918), 273–279. Another ed., Pasadena, 1944, *Macaulay on America: from a letter to Henry S. Randall, May 23, 1857*, priv. pr. It also appeared with 3 other letters from Macaulay to Randall (dated Jan. 18, 1857; Jan. 8, 1859; Oct. 9, 1859) in *Harper's Mag.*, LIV (Feb. 1877), 460–462; all 4 letters repr. in the New York, 1878 ed. of Sir George Otto Trevelyan's *The life and letters of Lord Macaulay*, pp. 407–412. Also repr. with the Oct. 9, 1858 letter in *Gunton's Mag.*, I (Sept. 1896), 195–202. A later ed. of the 4 letters with an introd. by Harry Miller Lydenberg carried the title *What did Macaulay say about America? Text of four letters to Henry S. Randall*, [New York], 1925, and was repr. with additions from the *Bull. N.Y. Pub. Lib.*, XXIX (July 1925), 459–481. The Jan. 18, 1857 letter originally appeared in the *So. Lit. Mess.*, XXXI (Aug. 1860), 133–135. See also his speech on the treaty of Washington in his *Miscellanies*, Boston, 1900, 4 vols., I, pp. 347–370; his speech on American slavery, ibid., II, pp. 3–25; and Edwin L. Miller, ed., *Macaulay's speeches on copyright, and Lincoln's address at Cooper's Union*, Boston, [c. 1913]. See also H. H. Clark "The vogue of Macaulay in America," *Trans. Wisc. Acad. of Sciences*, XXXIV (1942), 237–292.

1014   [MARTINEAU, HARRIET]. The 'manifest destiny' of the American union. New York, 1857. 72 p.   **DLC**

Repr. from the *Westmin. Rev.*, XLVIII (July 1857), 137–176. See also the following articles by Martineau: "The slave trade in 1858," *Edinb. Rev.*, CVIII (Oct. 1858), 541–586; "The United States under the presidentship of Mr. Buchanan," *Edinb. Rev.*, CXII (Oct. 1860), 545–582; "The brewing of the American storm," *Macmillans's Mag.*, VI (June 1862), 97–107; and "The Negro race in America," *Edinb. Rev.*, CXIX (Jan. 1864), 203–242. See also her numerous 1858 articles in the *Spectator*: "Where is the mistake?" (May 22), 549–550; "Mischievous masquerading,"(June 5), 599–600; "States rights in America," (June 19), 655; "Lynch law at New York," (Sept. 25), 1011–1012; and "The hour of proof," (Oct. 9), 1067–1068. See also her long series of articles in *Once a Week*: "The Fourth of July, 1861," V (Aug. 3, 1861), 147–151; "American soldiering," (Aug. 24, 1861), 230–234; "New phase of the American strife," (Nov. 30, 1861), 635–639; "Much right and much wrong," VI (Jan. 25, 1862), 118–121; "The slave difficulty in America," (Feb. 1, 1862), 145–148; "Abolition of slavery in the District of Columbia," (May 24, 1862), 599–602; and "A question of democratic ability," (June 21, 1862), 714–718. For her approximately 370 articles on American subjects in the London *Daily News*, 1852–1866, see Robert Kiefer Webb's handlist, deposited in the Library of Congress, and the Boston and New York Public Libraries

1015   MONEY, *REV*. C[HARLES] F[ORBES] S[EPTIMUS]. Mormonism unmasked. London, 1857. 17 p.

No locations found; in Sabin #49969.

1016   MORMONISM CONTRASTED with the Word of God. [London, 1857?]. 16 p.   **CtY**

No t.p.

1017   MURRAY, D. A. B. Information for the use of emigrants. London, 1857.

No locations found.

1018 PAIRPOINT, ALFRED J. Uncle Sam and his country; or, Sketches of America, in 1854–55–56. London, 1857. 346 p.   **CtY MB NN Uk**

Returned to U.S. in 1882; see his *Rambles in America*, 1891, below.

Review: *Athenaeum*, (Nov. 7, 1857), 1389.

1019 PHILLIPPO, JAMES MURSELL. The United States and Cuba. London, 1857. 476 p.
   DLC Uk

One of the best emigrant handbooks of the period, compiled by a missionary to Jamaica. Although relying heavily on secondary sources, author contributed great enthusiasm in urging emigration.

1020 RUSSELL, ROBERT. Extract from journal of a tour in America. By R. Russell, Kilwhiss. The delta of the Mississippi. [Edinburgh, 1857]. 15 p.   **DLC**

Appeared also in the *J. Agric.* (Edinburgh), Jan. 1857, pp. 529–543. Also printed as chap. 14 in Russell's *North America, its agriculture and climate*, 1857, below.

1021 RUSSELL, ROBERT. North America, its agriculture and climate; containing observations on the agriculture and climate of Canada, the United States, and the island of Cuba. Edinburgh, 1857. 390 p.   **DLC Uk**

Chap. 14 had appeared in pamphlet form, under title, *Extracts from journal of a tour in America*, 1857, above.

Reviews: *Athenaeum*, (Jan. 30, 1858), 145; *Westmin. Rev.*, LXVIII, 321.

1022 STAPLETON, AUGUSTUS GRANVILLE. The affair at Grey Town. By Augustus G. Stapleton. London, 1857. 11 p.   **DLC Uk**

On U.S.-British relations, in connection with military action by U.S. naval units.

1023 STIRLING, JAMES. Letters from the slave states. London, 1857. 374 p.   **DLC Uk**

Visited U.S. 1856–57; itinerary also included St. Paul, Chicago and Ohio.

Review: *Brit. Quar. Rev.*, (by Thomas Ballantyne), XXVI, 416; repr. in Ballantyne's *Tracts for the Manchester School*, 1858, below.

1858

1024 ANDERSON, JAMES ROBERTSON. An actor's life, by James R. Anderson, tragedian, with an introduction by William Edwin Adams. London, 1902. 356 p.   **MH Uk**

Repr. from the *Newcastle Weekly Chronicle*; author toured the U.S. several times between 1846 and 1858.

1025 ASHWORTH, HENRY. Recollections of a tour in the United States of America, Canada and Cuba; delivered before the members of the Bolton mechanics' institute. Bolton, [1858?]. 28 p.   **OC**

MH has Bolton, 1859 ed., 46 p. Repr. from the Bolton *Chronicle*. DLC and UK have expanded ed., with title, *A tour in the United States, Cuba, and Canada. . . . A course of lectures delivered before the members of the Bolton mechanics' institution*, London, 1861, 198 p. Tour was in 1857. See also "Mr. Henry Ashworth, in a letter to Mr. Bazley, President of the Manchester chamber of commerce, dated Cincinnati, April 28, 1857," *Brit. Quar. Rev.*, XXVI, 432–434. See also Ashworth's *Cotton, its cultivation, manufacture and uses*, Manchester, 1858; on U.S., passim.

1026 [BACKHOUSE, *MRS.* HANNAH CHAPMAN (GURNEY)]. Extracts from the journal and letters of Hannah Chapman Backhouse. London, 1858. 291 p. **DLC Uk**

In U.S., 1830–35, pp. 78–185.

1027 [BAILLIERE, C. E.?]. Canada and the western states: compiled from the experience and observations of the author, and official documents etc. In two parts. Part I.—Upper and Lower Canada. The western states. Part II.—Emigrants and emigration. Land and agriculture. Illustrated with fifty engravings of the principal cities &c., facsimiles of American coins in circulation, routes of travel, fares, distances, &c., forming a complete handbook for emigrants. London, [1858?]. **UkRCS?**

Catalog of Royal Empire Society lists but could not be located; gives authorship to Bailliere, the publisher. CaQMBN lists London, [1859]; lacks Part II.

1028 BALLANTYNE, THOMAS. The cheap government of the United States: four letters to [Richard] Cobden. [N.p., 1858]. 16 p. **UkLU**

1029 BALLANTYNE, THOMAS. Tracts for the Manchester school. No. I: The cotton dearth. Reprinted from the "British Quarterly Review." London, 1858. 32 p. **Uk**

Appeared in *Brit. Quar. Rev.*, XXVI, (Oct. 1857), 416–448; reviews various books including *The cotton crisis and how to avert it*, 1857, above; *Letters from slave states*, by James Stirling, 1857, above; *A few months in America*, by James Robertson, 1855, above.

1030 BARRY, PATRICK. The theory and practice of the international trade of the United States and England, and of the trade of the United States and Canada; with tables of federal currency, Canadian currency and sterling, exchange formulas, etc. Chicago, 1858. 161 p. **DLC Uk**

1031 BIRD, *REV.* EDWARD. Some account of the great religious awakening now going on in the United States. London, 1858. 16 p. **TxDaM**

Based upon notes supplied by his daughter, Isabella Bird, (later Bishop).

1032 BODICHON, BARBARA LEIGH (SMITH). An American diary, 1857–8. Edited from the manuscript by Joseph W. Reed, Jr. London, 1972. 198 p. **DLC**

A series of letters written during a U.S. tour, Dec. 1857–June 1858. For an account of the visit see Hester Burton, *Barbara Bodichon, 1827–1891*, London, 1949, pp. 115–131.

1033 DOUGLAS, JAMES, *of Cavers*. The American revival. [Edinburgh, 1858]. **Uk**

1034 DRUMMOND, HENRY, *M.P.* A letter to Mr. Bright on his plan for turning the English monarchy into a democracy. London, 1858. 42 p. **CtY MiU**

Uk has 3d ed., London, 1858. References to U.S., accusing Bright of ignoring true conditions in America, particularly racial questions; see pp. 11, 12, 22, 30, 33, 34.

1035 THE ELGIN SETTLEMENT and the coloured population of Canada. [London? 1858?]. 12 p. **CaOTP**

Repr. from *Macphail's Edinb. Eccles. J.* Discusses the underground railroad.

1036   ELLISON, THOMAS. A hand-book of the cotton trade; or, A glance at the past history, present condition, and future prospects of the cotton commerce of the world. By Thomas Ellison. Dedicated, by permission, to the Right Hon. Lord Stanley, M.P., &c., &c. London, 1858. 191 p.   **DLC Uk**

Book II, chap. 1, on the U.S., pp. 14–34; other comment, passim. See also *The cotton trade of Great Britain. Including a history of the Liverpool cotton market and of the Liverpool cotton broker's association. By Thomas Ellison, of Liverpool*, London, 1886; and *Gleanings and reminiscences by Thomas Ellison. With an introduction by Sir Edward Russell*, Liverpool, 1905. Both works include comment on the U.S., passim.

1037   FOLEY, *REV.* DANIEL. The people and institutions of the United States of America: a summer vacation tour. Dublin, 1858. 79 p.   **ICN MoU Uk**

Sabin, 1974 ed., lists London, 1858 ed., (entry #3490), with variation in title: *Account of the people and institutions of the United States, from personal observations during a three months summer tour, in 1857.*

1038   FRANKLIN, JOHN BENJAMIN. The horrors of Mormonism; being a lecture delivered by John Benjamin Franklin, (late manager of the Mormon printing office at the Great Salt Lake City) in several places in England, &c. [n.p., 1858?]. 15 p.   **DLC**

Uk has rev. and augumented ed. under the title *Brigham Young: king of the Utah pandemonium*, London, 1871. Several other eds. also pub. under various titles with additional material, e.g., *A cheap trip to the Great Salt Lake City. An annotated lecture delivered before the President of America and representatives; the mayors of Liverpool & Manchester*, Ipswich, [1864], 32 p.; *One year at the Great Salt Lake City; or, A voice from the Utah pandemonium*, Manchester, [n.d.] 48 p.; *The mysteries and the crimes of Mormonism; or, A voice from the Utah pandemonium*, London, [n.d.].

1039   [GOLOVIN, IVAN GAVRILOVITCH] The refugee: being the life of political exiles in Europe and the United States. By the author of "Stars and stripes." London, 1858.

No locations found; listed in Sabin. See his *Stars and stripes*, 1856, above.

1040   HANNA, *REV.* WILLIAM, *ed.* Essays by ministers of the Free Church of Scotland. Edinburgh, 1858. 358 p.   **PPPrHi Uk**

Includes an essay by John Nelson, "National education in America, with special reference to the settlement of the question in this country," pp. 175–211.

1041   HOW TO ABOLISH SLAVERY in America, and to prevent a cotton famine in England, with remarks upon coolie and African emigration. By a slave-driver. London, 1858. 16 p.   **NHi Uk**

Discussion of slavery in the form of a dialogue between a former American slave-driver, now a British subject raising "free" cotton in Africa, and an Englishman. Pref. says is not "imaginary."

1042   JAMES, JOHN ANGELL. On the revival of religion. [London, 1858]. 12 p.   **TxDaM Uk**

No t.p. Repr. from "The Christian witness." Also pub. under title "The bearing of the American revival on the duties and hopes of British Christians," in Charles Reed, *On religious revivals*, 1858, below, pp. 25–44. Not the same as *Revival of religion*, London, 1859. See his comments on the U.S. in *The life and letters of John Angell James: including an unfinished autobiography. Edited by R[obert] W[illiam] Dale, M.A., his colleague and successor*, London, 1861, esp. pp. 241–272, 338–361, 531–567. See also Henry Clarke Wright, *Christian communion with slave-holders will the alliance sanction it? Letters to Rev. John Angell James, D.D. and Rev. Ralph Wardlaw, D.D., shewing their position in the alliance*, 3d thousand, Rochdale, 1846.

1043   JUKES, HARRIET MARIA. The earnest Christian: memoir, letters, and journals of Harriet Maria, wife of the late Rev. Mark R. Jukes. Compiled and edited by Mrs. H. A. Gilbert. London, 1858.   **Uk**

MiU lists New York, 1859 ed., with variant title. In U.S., Ohio, from 1851–54 (until Rev. Jukes' death); see pp. 256–338.

1044   KELLAND, PHILIP. Transatlantic sketches. By Professor Kelland. Edinburgh, 1858. 77 p.
                                                                                        DLC Uk

1045   [KINGSFORD, WILLIAM]. Impressions of the West and South during a six weeks' holiday. Toronto, 1858. 83 p.   **DLC Uk**

Pref. signed, "W.K." Letters first appeared "in a Toronto newspaper." Author, a Canadian engineer, also wrote *History, structure, and statistics of plank roads, in the United States and Canada*, 1851, above.

1046   MYSTERIES OF MORMONISM. A history of the rise and progress of the notorious Latter day saints, from the time of Joe Smith, the founder of their profligate church, to that of Brigham Young, and his 30 wives. The prophet of Utah, in the Salt Lake valley, with some account of chief elder H. C. Kimball, and his 20 wives, Dr. Richards, and his 11 wives. Elder Benson and Parly P. Pratt. This extraordinary sect number 150,000. Wives, mothers, and daughters, bought and sold by the fiends in human shape. Also the progress of the American government to suppress and exterminate the abominable system. Southwark, [1858?]. 8 p.   **CtY**

Sometimes ascribed to the publisher, H. Wilson.

1047   O'DONOVAN-ROSSA, JEREMIAH. A brief account of the author's interview with his countrymen, and of the parts of the Emerald Isle whence they emigrated, together with a direct reference to their present location in the land of their adoption, during his travels through various states of the Union in 1854 and 1855. London, 1858.

MB, OClWHi list earliest ed. located, Pittsburgh, 1863, 382 p; DLC has Pittsburgh, 1864. An Irish nationalist, manager of the *Irish People*, 1863–65, O'Donovan-Rossa was released in 1871 after 6 years in an English prison, on condition he would migrate to the U.S.

1048   PRESCOTT, HENRY PAUL. Tobacco and its adulterations; with illustrations drawn and etched by Henry P. Prescott, of the inland revenue department. London, 1858. 130 p.
                                                                                        DLC Uk

On U.S., pp. 105–123.

1049   REED, *SIR* CHARLES. On religious revivals. Two papers read by request at the annual meeting of the Congregational union, by Mr. Charles Reed, and the Rev. John Angell James. London, 1858.   **NN Uk**

"On the facts of the religious revival in America," by Charles Reed, pp. 3–24; "The bearing of the American revival on the duties and hopes of British Christians," by the Rev. John Angell James, pp. 25–44. The latter was pub. separately, 1858, above. See also Reed's "England and America," *Leisure Hour*, XXIII, 37–40. For an account of his visits to the U.S. see *Memoir of Sir Charles Reed*, by Charles Edward Baines Reed, London, 1883, pp. 157–165, 173–176. See also Reed's report on education in the U.S. in *Report on the Philadelphia International exhibition of 1876, Great Britain Executive commission, Philadelphia exhibition, 1876*, London, 1877, Vol. I, pp. 299–312.

1050   RELIGIOUS MOVEMENT in the United States. [Edinburgh, 1858]. 16 p.   **Uk**

No t.p. Mainly extracts from letters to the *Chr. Times* by the author of *The Englishwoman in America* (Isabella Bishop), who had just returned from America, and from others; for Bishop work see 1856, above.

1051   [ROBSON, WILLIAM]. Why I have not gone to the South. [New York, 1858]. 4 p. **DLC**

Caption title. Signed, W. Robson. Pub. by the Amer. Anti-Slavery society.

1052   SEYD, ERNEST. California and its resources. A work for the merchant, the capitalist, and the emigrant. London, 1858. 168 p.   **DLC Uk**

1053   SMITH, CHARLES K. Three years in North America; and miscellaneous poems, &c. Glasgow, 1858. 2 parts.   **TxU Uk**

Prose sections on U.S., pp. 1–7, 13–74.

1054   WADDINGTON, ALFRED PENDERILL. The Fraser mines vindicated, or the history of four months. Victoria, [B.C.], 1858. 52 p.   **CSmH CU-BANC**

About the difficulties with Americans, esp. Californians, at the time of gold discoveries in British Columbia. Repr. Vancouver, Canada, 1949, *The Fraser mines vindicated; or, The history of four months, by Alfred Waddington. Here reprinted for the first time exactly as published in 1858, with an introduction by W. Kaye Lamb, Dominican archivist*, 93 p.

1055   [WILSON, LUCY SARAH ATKINS]. The fugitive slaves in Canada. London, 1858. 45 p.   **Uk**

Uk lists this under Canada (Appendix). See also *Sermons [on Rom. xvi 1, 2 and Phil. i 20, 21] preached . . . on the occasion of the death of Mrs. Wilson, etc.*, by Henry Venn, London, 1863.

1056   YOUNG, *HON.* JOHN. Rival routes to the ocean from the west; and docks at Montreal. Considered in a letter to the Harbour commissioners. Montreal, 1858. 66 p.   **NN**

Discusses Canadian-U.S. trade, competition, etc. See also *Rival routes from the west to the ocean, and docks at Montreal: A series of letters by the Honorable John Young, in reply to letters of "A merchant," written by William Workman, esq.*, Montreal, 1859, 49 p. (CSmH)

1859

1057   ANGLO-AMERICAN CHURCH EMIGRANTS' AID SOCIETY. No. 1. Occasional paper of the Anglo-American church emigrants' aid society. [Continued from the "Statement."] . . . February, 1856. London, [1856–59].   **MH Uk**

No. I, Feb. 1856; No. II, Sept. 1857; No. III, Jan. 1859. All signed by secretaries, Rev. Henry Caswall and F. H. Dickinson.

1058   [BARKER, JOSEPH]. John Brown; or, The true and the false philanthropist. [Philadelphia? 1859?]. 28 p.   **DLC**

See also his "Slavery and civil war; or John Brown and the Harper's Ferry insurrection," *Barker's Rev.*, III (Sept., 1862), 1–7.

1059   [BISHOP, ISABELLA LUCY (BIRD). "Mrs. John F. Bishop,]. The aspects of religion in
the United States of America. By the author of "The Englishwoman in America." London,
1859. 189 p.   **MH NN Uk**

First pub. as a series of letters in the *Patriot*. The work is sometimes erroneously ascribed
to Sarah Mytton Maury; Sabin attributes to Miss Catherine Marsh.

1060   [BOLTON, JAMES?]. Brook Farm: the amusing and memorable of American country life.
London, 1859. 183 p.   **CtY Uk**

A description of the author's boyhood in rural New York, with some fictitious names used;
not the Brook Farm in Massachusetts. Sabin credits the London, 1863 ed. to Rev. J. Bolton.

1061   THE BRITISH AMERICAN GUIDE-BOOK: being a condensed gazeteer, directory and
guide, to Canada, the western states, and principal cities on the seaboard. In four parts. Part
I. Upper and Lower Canada. Part II. Scenes and scenery. Part III. The United States. Part
IV. Things as they are in 1859. Illustrated with upwards of one hundred and twenty engravings. First edition. New York, 1859.   **DLC**

Each part has a separate t.p. Another 1859, New York ed. reverses the order of parts I and
III on the t.p. Uk has the London, [1859] ed. with title, *The new world; or, the United States
and Canada, illustrated and described*; this ed. added a 5th part, "Emigration and land and
agriculture," and omitted pp. 79–96 (a list of Canadian towns, with a discussion of each).

1062   BUSK, HANS, *the younger*. The navies of the world; their present state, and future capabilities. London, 1859. 312 p.   **DLC Uk**

On U.S., pp. 104–123.

1063   CAIRD, *SIR* JAMES. Letter on the lands of the Illinois Central Railway Company.
London, 1859. 15 p.   **MH NN**

1064   CAIRD, *SIR* JAMES. Prairie farming in America. With notes by the way on Canada and
the United States. London, 1859. 128 p.   **DLC Uk**

First pub. in part as "Prairie farming in the west" in the Chicago *Press and Tribune*, Mar.
31–Apr. 4, 1859. See also *Caird's slanders on Canada answered & refuted!*, Toronto,
1859; includes a letter from William Hutton and "Personal observations in Illinois" from
the editoral correspondence of "The Leader" communicated by Mr. C. Lindsey. Also see
Ernest S. Osgood, ed., "Minnesota as seen by travellers: an English student of prairie farming," *Minn. Hist.*, IX (June 1928), 135–143.

Reviews: *Athenaeum*, (June 4, 1859), 745; Philadelphia *Daily Evening Bulletin*, Aug. 5,
1859.

1065   COBDEN, RICHARD. American diaries; edited, with an introduction and notes, by
Elizabeth Hoon Cawley. Princeton, 1952. 233 p.   **DLC Uk**

First pub. of Cobden's diaries of visits to the U.S., 1835 and 1859. On the 1835 trip see
John Morley, *The life of Richard Cobden*, Boston, 1881, pp. 20–27. On the 1859 visit see
Walter Harry Green Armytage, "Richard Cobden and Illinois," *J. Illinois State Hist. Soc.*,
XLIII (Autumn, 1950), 187–203.

1066   DYER, JOSEPH CHESSBOROUGH. Democracy: what is it? Let us inquire! Manchester,
1859. 42 p.   **DLC**

1067 [EVANS, ANTHONY WALTON WHITE, *comp*.]. Extracts from English authorities on American locomotives, respectfully addressed to the directors of railways in Chile, and to all who may take any interest in this important subject. Valparaiso, 1859. 33 p. **DLC**

See pp. 9–25; English authorities cited include Passavant, Edward Woods, P. Marshall and T. S. Isaac.

1068 EVANS, DAVID MORIER. The history of the commercial crisis, 1857–58, and the stock exchange panic of 1859. London, 1859. 212 p. **DLC Uk**

Much comment on U.S., passim; see esp. pp. 92–147. See also author's *Speculative notes and notes on speculation, ideal and real*, London, 1864, pp. 44–50 and 118–129.

1069 GOSSE, PHILIP HENRY. Letters from Alabama, (U.S.) chiefly relating to natural history. London, 1859. 306 p. **DLC Uk**

Originally pub. in the *Home Friend*, 1855. See also Gosse's *The romance of natural history*, London, 1860. See also the account of his visit to the U.S., May–Dec. 1838, in *The life of Philip Henry Gosse, F.R.S. By his son, Edmund* [William] *Gosse*, London, 1890; chap. 5 is entitled "Alabama."

1070 GRATTAN, THOMAS COLLEY. Civilized America. London, 1859. 2 vols. **DLC Uk**

2d ed., expanded, London, 1859, 2 vols. in 1. See also New York, 1969 ed., with an introd. by Marvin Fisher.

Review: *Brit. Quar. Rev.*, XXXI, 118.

1071 GREVILLE, CHARLES CAVENDISH FULKE. The Greville diary, including passages hitherto withheld from publication. Edited by Philip Whitwell Wilson. New York, 1927. 2 vols. **DLC Uk**

Vol. II, pp. 536–554, "Word from Uncle Sam." Comments on the period from 1820–1859.

1072 HILL, PHILIP CARTERET. The United States and British provinces, contrasted from personal observation. A lecture delivered before the Halifax Young men's Christian association. Halifax, 1859. 30 p. **CaNSHD**

1073 HORNER, JOSEPH ANDREW. Anti-slavery tactics. A paper read before the members of the Leeds young men's anti-slavery society, on Wednesday evening, March 16th, 1859. . . . William Bilbrough, esq. in the chair. London, [1859]. **MB NIC**

1074 HOWITT, *MRS*. MARY (BOTHAM) "*MRS*. W. HOWITT". A popular history of the United States of America: from the discovery of the American continent, to the present time. London, 1859. 2 vols. **Uk**

DLC has New York, 1860 ed. See esp. the last 3 chaps. See also her *Our cousins in Ohio. . . . From the diary of an American mother*, London, 1849; and *Vignettes of American history*, London, [1868], for additional comment on the U.S. by Mrs. Howitt (DLC and Uk hold both works). Also see Margaret Howitt, ed., *Mary Howitt, an autobiography*, London, 1889.

1075 JAMES, *REV*. JOHN ANGELL. Revival of religion: its principles, necessity, effects. A series of papers. London, 1859. **Uk**

On revival of religion in the U.S. Not same as 1858 item.

1076　KANE, PAUL. Wanderings of an artist among the Indians of North America, from Canada to Vancouver's Island and Oregon, through the Hudson's Bay company's territory and back again. London, 1859. 455 p. **DLC Uk**

A deluxe limited ed. (ed. by Lawrence J. Burpee) pub. by the Radisson Society of Canada, Toronto, 1925. Almost exclusively devoted to Indians, the work includes a little about Wisconsin and Oregon. Reproductions of Kane's drawings and paintings can be found in *Paul Kane, the Columbian wanderer, 1846–7; sketches and paintings of the Indians and his lecture, "The Chinooks,"* ed., with an introd. by Thomas Vaughan, Portland, Or., 1971; and *Paul Kane's frontier; including Wanderings of an artist among the Indians of North America,* ed. with a biographical introd. and a catalog raisonne by J. Russell Harper, Austin, Tx. and Toronto, 1971 (includes 253 plates). Kane also contributed articles on Indians to *Canadian J.,* 1855–57. See also David I. Bushnell, Jr., "Sketches by Paul Kane in the Indian country, 1845–1848," *Smithsonian Misc. Collect.,* XCIX, No. 1, Washington, D.C., 1940.

1077　LONDON EMANCIPATION COMMITTEE. Proceedings of an anti-slavery meeting, held at Spafields chapel, on Friday evening, 14th October 1859. [London, 1859]. 19 p. **CtY MB NIC**

London Emancip. Comm. tract no. 2.

1078　LONDON EMANCIPATION COMMITTEE. Report and proceedings. [London, 1859]. 11 p. **CtY MB**

London Emancip. Comm. tract no. 1. Signed at end by George Thompson, chairman.

1079　LONDON v. NEW YORK. By an English workman. London, 1859. 33 p. **MH N Uk**

Written after three years experiences in the U.S.

1080　LORIMER, JOHN GORDON. The recent and great religious awakening in America, and the lessons which it suggests. Glasgow, 1859.

MiU has on microfilm. Uk has London, 1859 ed.

1081　MACGREGOR, JOHN. Our brothers and cousins: a summer tour in Canada and the States. London, 1859. 156 p. **DLC Uk**

"Letters reprinted from the *Record*".

1082　[MACKAY, CHARLES]. Life and liberty in America; or, Sketches of a tour in the United States and Canada, in 1857–8. London, 1859. 2 vols. **DLC Uk**

For his later accounts of two trips to the U.S., 1857–58, and of experiences as Civil War correspondent for the London *Times,* 1862–65, see *Forty years' recollections of life, literature and public affairs,* London, 1877, 2 vols.; and *Through the long day; or, Memorials of a literary life during half a century,* London, 1887, 2 vols. See also George S. Wykoff, "Charles Mackay: England's forgotten Civil war correspondent," *So. Atlan. Quar.,* XXVI (Jan. 1927), 50.

Reviews: *De Bow's Rev.,* XXVII, 515; *Fraser's Mag.* (by H. A. M.), LXI, 276; *Russell's Mag.,* (by Wm. J. Grayson), VI, 1.

1083　MISSION TO THE FUGITIVE SLAVES IN CANADA. London, 1859. 64 p.

ICN has London, 1860 ed., 80 p.

1084 O'BRIEN, ANDREW LEARY. The journal of Andrew Leary O'Brien; including an account of the origin of Andrew college, Cuthbert, Georgia. Foreword and notes by Annette McDonald Suarez. Athens, Georgia, 1946. 76 p. **DLC**

O'Brien arrived from Ireland in 1837, at the age of 22; journal continues to 1859.

1085 O'BRIEN, WILLIAM SMITH. Lectures on America. Delivered in the Mechanics' institute, Dublin, November, 1859. Dublin, [1859]. **CSmH**

1086 SAGE, WALTER NOBLE. Sir James Douglas and British Columbia. [Toronto], 1930. 398 p. **DLC Uk**

Univ. of Toronto Stud. Hist. & Economics, Vol. VI, no. 1. See account of Douglas' visit to California in 1840–41, pp. 103–112; "San Juan controversy," 1858–59, pp. 235–280; much other comment on U.S., passim. See also "A voyage from the Columbia to California in 1840 from the journal of Sir James Douglas," *Calif. Hist. Soc. Quar.*, VIII (June 1929), 97–115; also see Robert Hamilton Coats and R. E. Gosnell, *Sir James Douglas*, Toronto, 1908.

1087 SIMMONDS, PETER LUND. The curiosities of food; or, The dainties and delicacies of different nations obtained from the animal kingdom. London, 1859. 372 p. **DLC Uk**

References to U.S. throughout. See also the following works by Simmonds which also have many references and comparisons to U.S.: *The animal food resources of different nations, with mention of some of the special dainties of various people derived from the animal kingdom*, London, 1885; *The popular beverages of various countries, natural & artificial, fermented, distilled, aerated & infused, their history, production, and consumption*, London, 1888; *Waste products and undeveloped substances: a synopsis of progress made in their economic utilisation during the last quarter of a century at home and abroad*, London, 1873.

1088 TROLLOPE, ANTHONY. The West Indies and the Spanish Main. London, 1859. 395 p. **CLU ICN MH Uk**

DLC has 1st U.S. ed., New York, 1860. Final chap., pp. 388–395, describes Trollope's first visit to the U.S. on his return from the West Indies in 1859.

1089 [TROTTER, ISABELLA (STRANGE)]. First impressions of the New world on two travellers from the Old, in the autumn of 1858. London, 1859. 308 p. **DLC**

Review: *Fraser's Mag.* (by H. A. M.), LXI, 276.

1090 TURNBULL, JANE M. E., and MARION TURNBULL. American photographs. London, 1859. 2 vols. **DLC Uk**

In the U.S., 1852–57.

1091 VANDENBURGH, O. An inquiry answered. The democratic institutions of America. London, 1859. 48 p. **DLC Uk**

1092 VESSEY, JOHN HENRY. Mr. Vessey of England: being the incidents and reminiscences of travel in a twelve weeks' tour through the United States and Canada in the year 1859. Edited by Brian Waters. New York, [1956]. 184 p. **DLC**

1860

1093   AN ACCURATE AND DETAILED ACCOUNT of the extraordinary revival of religion in America and Ireland. With remarkable incidents in conversions; geographical extent of the work, &c.; as witnessed and narrated by Drs. Cheever, Thompson, General Alexander, Rev. J. Baillie, Mr. Drummond, and others. London, [1860]. 27 p.   **Uk**

1094   AMERICAN SECURITIES. Practical hints on the tests of stability and profit. For the guidance and warning of British investors. By an Anglo-American. London, 1860. 32 p.   **ICN Uk**

    2d ed. "revised," London, 1860, 48 p., 1 map.

1095   AMERICAN SLAVERY. Demonstration in favour of Dr. [George B.] Cheever in Glasgow. Speeches of Revs. Drs. Buchanan, Smyth, and [James] Robertson, and statement of Rev. Dr. Cheever's case by Rev. Henry Batchelor. Reprinted from the Glasgow Examiner. Glasgow, 1860.   **NHi**

    DLC has repr., with extensive additions, titled *American slavery. Demonstrations in favor of Dr. Cheever, in Scotland. Letter of sympathy from distinguished clergymen and other gentlemen. Speeches at meetings in Edinburgh and Glasgow, by Drs. [Robert]Candlish, [Thomas_]Guthrie, [W.]Alexander, Buchanan, and Smyth. And a statement of Dr. Cheever's case, by Rev. H. Batchelor. Letter of Dr. Guthrie to the Presbyterian,* New York, 1860, 77 p.

1096   BARKER, JOSEPH. Slavery and civil war; or, The Harper's Ferry insurrection, with a review of discourses on the subject. [Philadelphia? 1860?]. 24 p.   **DLC**

1097   BARLOW, PETER WILLIAM. Observations on the Niagara railway suspension bridge, made during a recent tour in America. On the practicability of connecting Liverpool and Birkenhead, and New York and Brooklyn, by wire suspension bridges of one span. Containing also some remarks on street railways and the application of the suspension principle to correct the inconveniences of the London street traffic. And a suggestion for a viaduct across the Holborn valley, and across the Mersey at Runcorn. By Peter W. Barlow. London, 1860. 40 p.   **Uk**

    On U.S., pp. 15–37.

1098   BERNARD, MOUNTAGUE. On the principle of non-intervention. A lecture delivered in the hall of All Souls' College. Oxford, 1860. 36 p.   **DLC Uk**

    Uk spells first name, "Montague."

1099   BIRKINSHAW, MARIA LOUISA. The chevaliers; a tale, with a true account of an American revival. London, 1860. 416 p.   **DLC Uk**

1100   BRIDGES, JOHN AFFLECK. A sportsman of limited income; recollections of fifty years. London, 1910. 309 p.   **DLC Uk**

    Contains 3 chaps. on a visit to America, ca. 1857–1860, pp. 52–105; see also the account, "United States of America in 1857," in author's *Victorian recollections*, London, 1919, pp. 135–146.

1101   CORNWALLIS, KINAHAN. Royalty in the New world; or, The Prince of Wales in America. London, 1860. 289 p.   **Uk**

DLC has New York, 1860 ed. Cornwallis emigrated from England in 1860, later became a U.S. citizen. His novel, *Wreck and ruin; or, Modern society*, London, 1859, was about the U.S. For other accounts of the Prince of Wales' visit, listed in this bibliography, see John Gardner Dillman Engleheart, Henry James Morgan (both 1860), Robert Cellem, and Nicholas Augustus Woods (both 1861). For other accounts of the visit, see the following: *The American tour of the Prince of Wales. Biographical sketch of the young man. Account of the tour through the British Provinces and the United States. Programme of reception in Boston. Attractions of Boston and vicinity*, Boston, 1860, 32 p.; Pierre Joseph Olivier Chauveau, *The visit of His Royal Highness the Prince of Wales to America, reprinted from the Lower Canada Journal of education, with an appendix containing poems, addresses, letters, &c.*, Montreal, 1860, 113 p. (1 chap. on U.S. visit); Rafael J. De Cordova, *The Prince's visit: a humorous description of the Tour of His Royal Highness the Prince of Wales, through the United States of America, in 1860*, New York, 1861, 94 p. (in verse); William Everett, *The Prince of Wales at the tomb of Washington*, Cambridge, Mass., 1861, 15 p. (in verse); Edmund Clarence Stedman, *The Prince's ball. A brochure. From "Vanity Fair"*, New York, 1860, 63 p. (satirical poem); and *Visit of His Royal Highness, the Prince of Wales, and suite, to the New York Institute for the instruction of the deaf and dumb, Oct. 12, 1860*, New York, 1860 (from the New York *Herald*, Oct. 12, 1860). See also Lieut. Thomas Banbury Gough, *Boyish reminiscences of His Majesty the King's visit to Canada in 1860*, London, 1910, pp. 162–178; and William J. Baker, "Anglo-American relations in miniature: the Prince of Wales in Portland, Maine, 1860," *New Eng. Quar.*, XLV (Dec. 1972), 559–568.

1102   DAVISON, SIMPSON. The discovery and geognosy of gold deposits in Australia; with comparisons and accounts of the gold regions in California, Russia, India, Brazil, &c. Including a philosophical disquisition on the origin of gold in placer-deposits and in quartz-veins. London, 1860. 484 p.   **DLC Uk**

Account of Davison's visit to California in 1849, pp. 28–64; other discussion of gold in the U.S., pp. 202–230, 285 ff., Appendix A "The gold fields of California," pp. 379–386, and passim.

1103   DYER, JOSEPH CHESSBOROUGH. Notes on the slaveholders' mission to England. [n.p., 1860].

No locations found; listed in *Dictionary of National Biography*. A pamphlet.

1104   EDGE, FREDERICK MILNES. Slavery doomed; or, The contest between free and slave labour in the United States. London, 1860, 244 p.   **DLC Uk**

A later ed. appeared under the title, *America yesterday and today. The United States prior to the rebellion and the prospects of reconstruction of the South*, London, [1869]. See also author's *Whom do English Tories wish elected to the presidency?*, 1864, below; and his *The exploits and triumphs, in Europe, of Paul Morphy, the chess champion; including an historical account of clubs, biographical sketches of famous players, and various information and anecdotes relating to the noble game of chess. By Paul Morphy's late secretary.* [Frederick Milnes Edge], New York, 1859.

Review: *London Rev.*, XV, 111.

1105   ENGLEHEART, *SIR* JOHN GARDNER DILLMAN. Journal of the progress of H.R.H. the Prince of Wales through British North America; and his visit to the United States, 10th July to 15th November, 1860. By Gardner D. Engleheart. [London, 1860?]. 110 p.   **DLC Uk**

Priv. pr.

1106 EURYALUS; tales of the sea, a few leaves from the diary of a midshipman. London, 1860. 332 p. **NN Uk**

   Factual account of visit to California, pp. 186–195, and passim.

1107 FRANKLIN, JANE (GRIFFIN), *Lady*. The life, diaries and correspondence of Jane Lady Franklin 1792–1875, edited by Willingham Franklin Rawnsley. London, [1923]. 242 p. **DLC Uk**

   In U.S., 1860. See esp. section of American letters, 1849–1859, pp. 197–232. See also *Portrait of Jane; a Life of Lady Franklin*, by Frances J. Woodward, London, [1951]; pp. 354–359 describe a trip to the U.S. in 1870.

1108 A FRIENDLY WARNING to the Latter-day saints, or Mormons; in which the character of the Mormon missionaries is plainly set forth by one who was of that community, and a resident in Salt Lake. 61 p. **MH NN**

1109 HAMILTON, PIERCE STEVENS. Letter to His Grace the Duke of Newcastle, upon a union of the colonies of British North America. Halifax, 1860. 18 p. **CaOTP CaOTU**

   Repr. in *Union of the colonies of British North America: being three papers upon this subject, originally published between the years 1854 and 1861*, Montreal, 1864, pp. 81–103. The other two papers, which also make frequent reference to the U.S., are "Observation upon a union of the colonies of British North America," dated 1854–55, pp. 13–55; and "A union of the colonies of British North America, considered nationally," dated 1856, pp. 57–79.

1110 HANCOCK, WILLIAM. An emigrant's five years in the free states of America. London, 1860. 321 p. **DLC Uk**

   Reviews: *Athenaeum*, (Aug. 25, 1860), 252.

1111 HORNER, JOSEPH ANDREW, *ed*. The American board of missions and slavery. A reprint of the correspondence in the "Noncomformist" newspaper; to which is added, an article on the fall of Dr. Pomroy [sic] and his consequent dismissal from office, by Charles K. Whipple, esq., of Boston, U.S. Edited by Joseph A. Horner, honorable secretary to the Wakefield anti-slavery association. Leeds, 1860. 20 p. **DLC**

   No. 1 of *Anti-slavery tracts for the times*. Swan Lyman Pomeroy's name is spelled "Pomroy" throughout the text. Includes letters from Horner, Edward Mathews, William H, Pullen, et al.

1112 LANCE, WILLIAM. Views of Mr. William Lance on American railways, with especial reference to the Atlantic and Great Western railway. [London? 1860]. 15 p. **CtY**

1113 LATHAM, ROBERT GORDON. Opuscula. Essays chiefly philological and ethnographical. London, 1860. 418 p. **DLC Uk**

   "On the languages of the Oregon territory," pp. 249–265, (originally appeared in the *J. Ethnol. Soc. London*, I (1848), 154–166); "Miscellaneous contributions to the ethnography of North America," pp. 275–298; "On the languages of new California," pp. 300–316; "On the languages of northern, western and central America," pp. 326–377.

1114 LILLYWHITE, FRED[ERICK]. The English cricketers' trip to Canada and the United States. London, 1860. 68 p. **DLC Uk**

   Journal, Sept. 7, 1859–Oct. 29, 1859, of the first English cricket team to play in the U.S.

1115   LINDSEY, CHARLES. The prairies of the western states: their advantages and their draw-backs. Toronto, 1860. 100 p.   **CaOOA DLC**

See also Charles Lindsey, "Atlantic fisheries of Canada and the Treaty of 1871," in *Canada: an Encyclopedia of the country*, ed. by J. Castell Hopkins, Toronto, 1898–1900, VI, 119–130.

1116   LONDON EMANCIPATION COMMITTEE. The Rev. John Waddington, D.D. and American slavery. [London, 1860]. 12 p.   **CtY DHU MB**

London Emancip. Comm. tract no. 3.

1117   MACKENZIE, WILLIAM LYON. An Almanac of independence & freedom for the year 1860; containing a plea for the relief of the inhabitants of Canada from a state of colonial vassalage or irresponsible rule; and their early entrance upon a prosperous, happy career, as educated, self-governed freemen; together with considerations with reference to the position in which Upper Canada stands toward the American republic, and a review of the proceedings of the convention which met in Toronto on the ninth of November, 1859. Toronto, [1860?]. 62 columns.   **CaOTP**

Contains Mackenzie's "Appeal to the inhabitants of Upper Canada" and other pro-annexation material.

1118   MAGEE, WILLIAM C[ONNER]. The voluntary system: can it supply the place of the established church? With recent facts and statistics from America. London, 1860. 109 p.   **Uk**

DLC has 3d ed., London, 1861.

1119   MANN, JAMES A. The cotton trade of Great Britain: its rise, progress, & present extent, based upon the most carefully digested statistics, furnished by the several government departments, and most eminent commercial firms. London, 1860. 134 p.   **MH-BA NN Uk**

On U.S., pp. 44–59, 99. See also Mann's *The cotton trade of India. A paper read before the Royal Asiatic society, London, 21st January, 1860*, London, 1860, pp. 2–4, 7–10, 16–22, and passim.

1120   MATHEWS, *REV*. EDWARD. The shame and glory of the American Baptists; or, Slaveholders versus abolitionists. Bristol, [1860]. 23 p.   **CtY Uk**

Lived 19 years in U.S., returning to England in 1851.

1121   MITCHELL, J[OHN], *of London*. The truth about America. The electoral system of the United States: its mechanism and workings. London, 1860. 70 p.   **DLC Uk**

1122   MITCHELL, *REV*. W[ILLIAM] M, *of Toronto*. The under-ground rail-road. [Being an account of the means adopted to aid fugitive slaves, and sketches of slave life. With a preface by W[illiam] H[enry] Bonner.] London, 1860. 172 p.   **ICU NNC NjP Uk**

DLC has 2d ed., London, 1860, *The under-ground rail-road from slavery to freedom*. Includes testimonial letters by George Thompson, F. W. Chesson, Wm. Howard Day, Alex. M. Pollock, et al. Mitchell, an American Negro, became a Canadian citizen. See also W. R. Riddell, "The slave in Upper Canada" and "Notes on Slavery in Canada," *J. Negro Hist.*, IV (Oct. 1919), 372–411.

1123   [MORGAN, HENRY JAMES]. The tour of H.R.H. the Prince of Wales through British America and the United States. By a British Canadian. Montreal, 1860. 271 p.   **DLC Uk**

1124   MURRAY, ANDREW. Notes upon Californian trees. Edinburgh, 1859–60. 2 pts. 31 p.
CSmH

DLC has pt. I, "From the Edinburgh new philosophical journal, new series, for July 1859."
Part II was "From the Edinburgh new philosophical journal, new series, for April 1860."

1125   O'CONNELL, DANIEL. Daniel O'Connell upon American slavery; with other Irish testimonies. New York, 1860. 48 p.   **DLC**

Extracts from O'Connell's speeches, 1829–1845. Also includes comment by John O'Connell; a letter by James Haughton "to Irishmen in America" (with a reply by John O'Connell); and an "Address from the members of the Cuffe-Lane temperance society to their brethren in America, Dublin, 1847, "signed by John Spratt, James Haughton and 881 others."

1126   OLIPHANT, LAURENCE. Patriots and filibusters; or, Incidents of political and exploratory travel. Edinburgh, 1860. 242 p.   **DLC Uk**

Repr. from *Blackwood's Edinb. Mag.*, LXXXII (Jan. 1860), 103–116, with corrections and additions. Includes an account of travels in the Southern states.

1127   PEMBERTON, JOSEPH DESPARD. Facts and figures relating to Vancouver island and British Columbia, showing what to expect and how to get there. With illustrative maps, by J. Despard Pemberton. London, 1860. 171 p.   **DLC Uk**

Much comment on U.S., comparison with Canada, description of transcontinental routes, etc.

1128   PULLEN, WILLIAM H. The blast of a trumpet in Zion, calling upon every son and daughter of Wesley, in Great Britain and Ireland, to aid their brethren in America in purifying their American Zion from slavery. London, 1860. 48 p.   **DLC**

Review: *London Quar. Rev.*, XV, lll.

1129   [RICHARDSON, ANNA H.]. Anti-slavery memoranda. (For private circulation only). To the friends of the slave. [Newcastle-upon-Tyne, 1860?]. 12 p.   **DLC**

No t.p. Signed "Anna H. Richardson" and dated Sept. 22nd, 1860. On U.S.

1130   SINCLAIR, JOHN, *Archdeacon of Middlesex*. On school rates in England and America. A charge delivered to the clergy of the Archdeaconry of Middlesex at the visitation held at St. Paul's Covent gardens on May 30 and 31, 1860. London, 1860. 24 p.   **Uk**

RPB and Uk have 3d ed., corrected and enlarged, London, 1862; added to title: . . . *with a prefatory epistle on the present educational crisis*. 5th ed., London, 1867, titled: *Remarks on school rates.* . . .

1131   THOMPSON, GEORGE. Constitution of the United States. [London, 1860]. 56 p.
CtY MB NIC

London Emancip. Comm. tract no. 5. Two lectures by Thompson, delivered at Glasgow City Hall, Jan. 27 and April 3, 1860. Also includes a lecture by Frederick Douglass, March 26, 1860, at Queen's Rooms, Glasgow.

1132   THOMPSON, GEORGE. Slavery in America: a lecture delivered in the Abbey-close church, Paisley, March 1, 1860. The provost in the chair. [London], 1860. 19 p.   **CtY MB**

London Emancip. Comm. tract no. 4.

1133   VANDENHOFF, GEORGE. Dramatic reminiscences; or, Actors and actresses in England and America . . . Ed., with preface, by Henry Seymour Carleton. London, 1860. 318 p.
DLC Uk

New York ed., 1860, 347 p., carried the title, *Leaves from an actor's note-book; with reminscences and chit-chat of the Green-room and the stage, in England and America.* The reminiscences cover various visits to the U.S. from 1842 to 1858, after which Vandenhoff retired from the stage and settled in America.

1134   [WALLACE, WILLIAM A.]. The Great Eastern's log. Containing her first transatlantic voyage, and all particulars of her American visit. By an executive office. By W. A. W. London, 1860. 91 p.
DLC Uk

1861

1135   [ALEXANDER, W.]. Can we enter into treaty with the new slave trading Confederacy? Leeds, [1861]. 8 p.
MB OClWHi

1136   ALISON, ALEXANDER. Government reform in England and America. Essay No. 4. London, 1861.
DLC Uk

Essay No. 4, pp. 89–128, in a series of 5 essays with separate title pages, which appeared under one binding with index under the title, *The Improvement of society and public opinion*, London, 1862. Essays 2–4 have 1861 imprints.

1137   ANNUAL DEMONSTRATION OF THE LEEDS Young Men's Anti-Slavery Society: Mr. George Thompson and Dr. Cheever on the American crisis. [Leeds, 1861].

No locations found. Repr. from the Leeds *Mercury*, May 30, 1861.

1138   ARTHUR, *REV*. WILLIAM. English opinion on the American rebellion. [Manchester, 1861?]. 4 p.
DLC

No t.p.; under head on p. 1, "(From the 'Watchman.')." Uk, OClWHi have under title *The American question. I.-English opinion on the American rebellion. By the Rev. William Arthur, author of "Italy in transition." II.-Slavery the ground of the Southern secession. Extract from a speech of the Hon. A. H. Stephens, Vice-president of the Southern Confederacy*, London, 1861, 12 p. See also Rev. Georges Fisch, *Nine months in the United States during the crisis; with an introduction by the Hon. Arthur Kinnaird, M.P., and a preface by the Rev. W[illiam] Arthur*, London, 1863.

1139   ATKINS, *REV*. THOMAS. American slavery. Just published: A reply to the letter of Bishop Hopkins, of Vermont, on this important subject. New York, [1861]. 13 p.   **MH Uk**

For an account of the writing of the above pamphlet see author's *Reminiscence of twelve years' residence in Tasmania and New South Wales; Norfolk Island and Moreton Bay; Calcutta, Madras, and Cape Town; the United States of America; and the Canadas*, Malvern, 1869; Atkins visited the U.S. in 1860–61, pp. 251–284.

1140   THE BASTILLE IN AMERICA; or, Democratic absolutism. By an eye-witness. London, 1861. 19 p.
DLC Uk

Includes an account of the imprisonment of a British subject in Fort Lafayette, Maryland.

1141   THE BELOVED CRIME, or the North and the South at issue. A friendly address to the Americans. Also, some remarks on the duty of encouraging free labour produce. By the author of "A word on behalf of the slave," and "Bible rights of the slave." London, [1861]. 40 p.   **DHU ICN**

No t.p.

1142   BERESFORD-HOPE, A[LEXANDER] J[AMES] B[ERESFORD]. A popular view of the American civil war. By A. J. B. Beresford Hope. London, 1861. 28 p.   **DLC Uk**

A defence of the Southern position. Repr. in *The American disruption. 1. A popular view of the American Civil War. 2. England, the North and the South. 3. The results of the American disruption. In three lectures, delivered by request at Kilndown, Hawkhurst, and before the Maidstone literary & mechanics' institution*, London, 1862.

1143   BERKELEY, *HON.* [GEORGE CHARLES] GRANTLEY F[ITZHARDING]. The English sportsman in the western prairies. By the Hon. Grantley F. Berkeley. London, 1861. 431 p.   **DLC Uk**

See author's "A journey to the western prairies of America," *The Field*, XV, 53 to XVI, 5 (Jan.–Aug. 1860). See also author's *My life and recollections*, London, 1865–66, II, pp. 291–299.

1144   BERNARD, MOUNTAGUE. Two lectures on the present American war . . . November, MDCCCLXI. Oxford & London, [1861]. 95 p.   **DLC Uk**

Reviews: *Edinb. Rev.*, CXV, 258; *Quar. Rev.*, CXI, 239; *Westmin. Rev.*, LXXVII, 108 p.

1145   [BLACK, ROBERT]. A memoir of Abraham Lincoln, president elect of the United States of America, his opinion on secession, extracts from the United States Constitution, &c. To which is appended an historical sketch on slavery, reprinted by permission from "The Times." London, 1861. 126 p.   **DLC Uk**

Pref. is signed "R.B." Repr. in the *Mag. of Hist. with Notes & Queries*, Ext. nos. 113–116, XXIX (1925), 5–51.

1146   BOHN, HENRY G[EORGE]. A pictorial hand-book of modern geography, on a popular plan, compiled from the best authorities, English and foreign, and completed to the present time; with numerous tables and a general index. By Henry G. Bohn . . . Illustrated by 150 engravings on wood, and 51 accurate maps engraved on steel. London, 1861. 529 p.   **DLC Uk**

On U.S., pp. 422–433.

1147   BRAMWELL, *REV.* HENRY ROWLAND. The war in America: a sermon preached on Sunday, August 18th, 1861, at St. Peter's church, Congleton. Congleton, 1861. 15 p.   **PHi Uk**

1148   BROMLEY, *MRS.* [CLARA FITZROY (KELLY)]. A woman's wanderings in the western world: a series of letters addressed to Sir Fitzroy Kelly, M.P., by his daughter, Mrs. Bromley. London, 1861. 299 p.   **DLC Uk**

In the U.S. in 1853, pp. 14–52; 67–78.

1149   BURTON, *SIR* RICHARD FRANCIS. The City of the saints, and across the Rocky mountains to California. London, 1861. 707 p.   **DLC Uk**

New York, 1963 ed., with an introd. and notes by Fawn M. Brodie. Burton's observations on sex and marriage customs of American Indians and Utah Mormons repr. in *The erotic traveler*, ed. by Edward Leigh, London, 1966, pp. 111–124. Burton also edited, and furnished notes to, the London, 1863 ed. of Randolph Barnes Marcy, *The prairie traveler. A hand-book for overland expeditions. With illustrations, and itineraries of the principal routes between the Mississippi and the Pacific.* Also see Burton's letter from Salt Lake City, Sept. 7, 1860, in *Proc. Royal Geog. Soc.*, V (Nov. 12, 1860), 112; *Wanderings in three continents*, London, 1901, ed., with a pref. by W. H. Wilkins, pp. 149–195 (a posthumously pub. lecture by Burton on "The city of the Mormons"). For accounts of Burton's trip, see: Francis Hitchman, *Richard F. Burton: his early, private and public life; with an account of his travels and explorations*, London, 1887, II, pp. 49–99; Richard W[alden] Hale, *Sir Richard F. Burton; a footnote to history, being an account of his trip from St. Jo, August 7, 1860, to Salt Lake City, with sartorial particulars of his call on Brigham Young*, Boston, 1930, 11 p.; Fairfax Downey, *Burton. Arabian nights adventurer*, New York, 1931, pp. 165–184; and Fawn M. Brodie, *The devil drives: a life of Sir Richard Burton*, New York, 1967, pp. 79–189.

Reviews: *Athenaeum*, (Nov. 30, 1861), 723; *Daily Alta California*, XIV, no. 4432; Philadelphia *Daily Evening Bulletin*, XIV (April 15); *Edinb. Rev.*, CXV, 185; *Knickerbocker*, LX, 172; *Littel's Living Age*, LXXI, 630; *London Rev.*, XVIII, 351; *No. Am. Rev.*, XCV, 189; *Quar. Rev.*, CXXII, 450.

1150   [BUXTON, CHARLES]. Mr. C. Buxton, M.P., on the settlement of the American dispute. [Darlington, 1861]. 12 p.   **OCIWHi**

No t.p. Lecture delivered at Maidstone, Friday, Dec. 13, 1861.

1151   [CAREY, HENRY CHARLES]. American civil war. Correspondence with Mr. H. C. Carey, of Philadelphia. August–September, 1861. [London, 1861]. 23 p.   **CoDU NN OCIW**

Repr. of letters from the *North American* of Philadelphia and the London *Daily News*. Carey was an American; his unidentified English correspondent signed his letters "D.," Liverpool. See also Carey's *Commerce, Christianity, and civilization, versus British free trade. Letters in reply to the London Times*, Philadelphia, 1876.

1152   CASWALL, *REV.* HENRY. The American church and the American union. London, 1861. 311 p.   **DLC Uk**

Review: *Sat. Rev.*, XII, 284.

1153   CELLEM, ROBERT. Visit of His Royal Highness the Prince of Wales to the British North American provinces and United States in the year 1860. Compiled from the public journals. Toronto, 1861. 438 p.   **CtY ICN**

1154   COBBETT, JAMES PAUL. Causes of the civil war in the United States. London & Manchester, 1861. 16 p.   **DLC Uk**

1155   COLEMAN, BENJAMIN. Spiritualism in America. With fac-similes of spirit drawings and writing. London, 1861. 87 p.   **DLC Uk**

Repr. with additions, from the *Spiritual Mag.* Visited New York and Boston in April, 1861.

1156   THE COMING STRUGGLE IN AMERICA. Laws of nations, privateering and blockades, and the laws of neutral trade. By a lawyer. Ayr, 1861. 42 p.   **MB Uk**

1157   THE COTTON SUPPLY. A letter to John Cheetham, esq., president of the Manchester cotton-supply association. By a fellow of the Royal geographical society. London, 1861. 40 p.   **DLC Uk**

On the U.S. passism.

1158   COWELL, *MRS.* SAM [EMILIE MARGUERITE (EBSWORTH)]. The Cowells in America, being the diary of Mrs. Sam Cowell during her husband's concert tour in the years 1860–1861; ed. by M. Willson Disher. London, 1934. 426 p.   **DLC Uk**

1159   ELLISON, THOMAS. Slavery and secession in America, historical and economical. With coloured map and numerous appendices of state papers, population returns, new and old tariffs, &c., forming a complete handbook of reference on all matters connected with the war. London, [1861]. 371 p.   **DLC Uk**

An enlarged 2d ed. carried the title, *Slavery and secession in America, historical and economical; together with a practical scheme of emancipation . . . With a reply to the fundamental arguments of Mr. James Spence, contained in his work on "the American Union," and remarks on the productions of other writers*, London, 1862.

Reviews: *Edinb. Rev.*, CXIV, 556; *Sat. Rev.*, XII, 303; *Westmin. Rev.*, LXXVI, 263.

1160   EVEREST, *REV.* ROBERT. A comparison between the rate of wages in some of the British colonies and in the United States; with observations thereupon. By the Rev. R. Everest, A.M. London, 1861. 16 p.   **NN Uk**

1161   [FERGUSSON, JAMES]. Notes of a tour in North America in 1861. [Edinburgh, 1861]. 100 p.   **CtY NN**

Printed for priv. circ. See also author's "Some account of both sides of the American war," *Blackwood's Edinb. Mag.*, XC, 768–799; "A report on Civil War America: Sir James Fergusson's five week visit," *Civil War Hist.*, (Dec. 1966), 346–362 (an unpub. letter, ed. by Elizabeth Joan Doyle); and *Rude stone monuments in all countries; their age and uses*, London, 1872, pp. 510–517.

1162   FORWOOD, *SIR* WILLIAM BOWER. Recollections of a busy life, being the reminiscences of a Liverpool merchant 1840–1910. Liverpool, 1910. 269 p.   **CLU Uk**

DLC has Liverpool, 1911 ed. On Civil War, pp. 51–55; on a visit to the U.S. in 1861, pp. 66–71. Visited the U.S. again in 1905. Uk also has a shorter version, *Some recollections of a busy life. . . .* , Liverpool, 1910, and describes *Recollections* as an expanded version.

1163   FRIENDS, SOCIETY OF. *LONDON YEARLY MEETING.* From the yearly meeting, held in London, by adjournments from the 22nd of the fifth month, to the 1st of the sixth month, inclusive, 1861, to Friends in North America. [London? 1861?]. 2 p.   **CSmH PHC**

A broadside signed, "Joseph Thorp, Clerk." MH has New York, 1861 ed., *Address to Friends in North America, from the yearly meeting of Friends held in London in 1861*, 8 p.

1164   [GORDON, GEORGE]. The national crisis. A letter to the Hon. Milton S. Latham, senator from California, in Washington. By Anglo-Californian. From the San Francisco Bulletin, Feb. 4th, 1861. San Francisco, 1861. 21 p.   **CU-BANC**

Not a citizen, although in U.S. "half a generation."

1165   GOULD, ELIZABETH PORTER. The Brownings and America. Boston, 1904. 115 p.   **DLC Uk**

Includes comment on U.S. from letters, etc., of Elizabeth and Robert Browning, through the former's death in 1861. See also *Elizabeth Barrett Browning: letters to her sister, 1846–1859*, ed. by Leonard Huxley, London, 1929, for amusing comment on U.S. and Americans. Also see: *The letters of Elizabeth Barrett Browning*, ed. by Frederic G. Kenyon, London, 1897; Benjamin Brawley, "Elizabeth Barrett Browning and the Negro,"

J. Negro Hist., III (Jan. 1918), 22–28; Hazel Harrod, "Correspondence of Harriet Beecher Stowe and Elizabeth Barrett Browning," *Univ. Texas Stud. in Eng.*, XXVII, 28–34; and *Browning to his American friends: letters between the Brownings, the Storys, and James Russell Lowell, 1841–1890*, ed. by Gertrude Reese Hudson, London, 1965. See also the following poems by Elizabeth Browning: "The runaway slave and Pilgrim's Point," (1848); and "A curse for a nation," (1860).

1166 GOULD, JOHN. A monograph of the *Trochilidae*, or family of humming birds. London, 1852–1861. 5 vols. **DLC**

Uk and NN have 6 vol. ed., London, 1850–87, with a supplement completed after the author's death, by R. Bowdler Sharpe. Pref. and introd. vol. I (360 p.) of original set contain much comment on the U.S.; remaining vols. contain plates of birds.

1167 GRATTAN, THOMAS COLLEY. England and the disrupted states of America. London, 1861. 42 p. **Uk**

DLC has 2d ed., London, 1861. See also author's *Beaten paths; and those who trod them*, London, 1862, vol. II, pp. 241–302, for sketches of several American diplomats in Europe: James M. Bayard, Augustus Davezac, Christopher Hughes, Hugh Legare, Virgil Maxey and William Pitt Preble.

1168 THE GREAT COTTON QUESTION: where are the spoils of the slave? Addressed to the upper and middle classes of Great Britain. By L. Cambridge, England, 1861. 21 p. **DLC Uk**

"L" stands for Greek letter "lambda,' on t.p. Uk catalogs under "L."

1169 HALL, *REV.* [CHRISTOPHER] NEWMAN. No war with America! A lecture on the affair of the Trent. Delivered at Surrey chapel, London, December 9, 1861. London, 1861. 8 p. **NIC OCIWHi**

1170 HOPKINS, JOHN B[AKER]. Peace or war? An unbiased view of the American crisis. London, 1861. 15 p. **CSmH OCIWHi**

Repr. from the *Atlas*, Dec. 7, 1861. See also further comments on the Civil War by Hopkins in his introd. to James Williams' *The South vindicated*, London, [1862], pp. cf. xiii–lx. Also see his "The productiveness of the southern states of America," *Trans. Natl. Assn. for Promotion of Social Science, London meeting, 1862*, London, 1863, pp. 862–866.

1171 HULL, EDWARD. The coal-fields of Great Britain: their history, structure, and duration. With notices of the coal-fields of other parts of the world. With illustrations. London, 1861. 194 p. **DLC Uk**

On U.S., pp. 157–163. Later eds. enlarged, with variant titles.

1172 LEMPRIERE, CHARLES. The American crisis considered. London, 1861. 296 p. **DLC Uk**

Reviews: *Edinb. Rev.*, CXIV, 556; *Sat. Rev.*, XII, 493; *Spectator*, (by J.M. Ludlow), Sept. 14, 1861.

1173 MONTAGU, *LORD* ROBERT. A mirror in America. London, 1861. 108 p. **DLC Uk**

See also his denunciation of U.S. education and politics, "What is education? Comparison between secular and denominational education," in the National Education Union's *Authorised report of the educational congress, held in the town hall, Manchester, on Wednesday and Thursday, Nov. 3rd & 4th, 1869*, London, 1869, pp. 18–40 (on U.S., pp. 33–40).

1174   MORTON, FRANCIS. A manual of geography; being a description of the natural features, climate, and productions of the various regions of the earth. London, [1861].   **Uk**

See pp. 143–146, 153–160. See also the following articles by Morton in *Once a Week*: "An American apple frolic," I (Nov. 5, 1859), 377–381; "Westward Ho.'", III, (Sept. 22, 1860) 341–345; "America Militant," IV (June 22, 1861), 707–712, and V (June 29, 1861), 7–12.

1175   MOSELEY, JOSEPH. What is contraband of war, and what is not. Comprising all the American and English authorities on the subject. London, 1861. 114 p.   **DLC Uk**

1176   THE NORTH ATLANTIC TELEGRAPH, via the Faroe islands, Iceland, and Greenland. Miscellaneous reports, speeches, and papers on the practicability of the proposed North Atlantic telegraph. The results of the surveying expedition of 1859. London, 1861. 76 p.   **C-S CSt**

English and American reports, speeches, etc.

1177   [PHILLIMORE, *SIR* ROBERT JOSEPH]. Case of the seizure of the Southern envoys. Reprinted, with additions, from the "Saturday Review." London, 1861. 26 p.   **DLC UkLFO**

Originally in *Sat. Rev.*, XII (Nov. 30, 1861), 547–548.

1178   PRATT, FREDERIC THOMAS. The law of contraband of war: with the reported cases to the present time, and a selection of unreported cases from the papers of the late Right Hon. Sir George Lee, LL.D., formerly Dean of the Arches, etc. etc., together with the foreign enlistment act and the British and French proclamations respecting the observance of neutrality in the present war in North America. London, 1861. 342 p.   **DLC**

See "The Providence of Boston," pp. 75–85.

1179   [RAMSAY, THOMAS?]. Recent recollections of the Anglo-American church in the United States. By an English layman, five years resident in that republic. London, 1861. 2 vols.   **DLC Uk**

This work has been ascribed to Henry Caswall, but Halkett & Laing note in the *Dictionary of anonymous and pseudonymous English Literature*, Edinburgh, 1926–1962, vol. VI, p. 429: "This could not have been by Henry Caswall, who was not a layman, and had been resident for many more than five years in 1861." They further note that a copy in the library of the General Theological Seminary, New York, was presented by "the author" to the Rev. David A. Bonnar, "upon whose attestation it is there credited to a certain Thomas Ramsay, otherwise unknown."

1180   REID, H[UGO]. Sketches in North America; with some account of Congress and of the slavery question. London, 1861. 320 p.   **DLC Uk**

London, 1862 ed. carried the title, *American crisis; or, Sketches in North America. With some account of Congress and of the slavery question.*

1181   REMY, JULES. A journey to Great-Salt-Lake City. By Jules Remy, and Julius Brenchley, M.A.; with a sketch of the history, religion, and customs of the Mormons, and an introduction on the religious movement in the United States. London, 1861. 2 vols.   **DLC Uk**

1st ed. in French: *Voyage au pays des Mormons. Relation—Geographie—Histoire Naturelle—Histoire—Theologie—Moeurs et costumes*, Paris, 1860, 2 vols. Remy was French, Rev. Julius Lucius Brenchley, English; "Sketch of Mr. Brenchley's journey from the Missouri to the Pacific," in 1850, II, pp. 499–512.

Reviews: *Dublin Univ. Mag.*, LVIII, 411; *Edinb. Rev.* (by Lord Houghton), CV, 185; *London Rev.*, XVIII, 351; *Quar. Rev.*, CXXII, 450; *Westmin. Rev.*, LXXVI, 193.

1182   REPORT OF THE SELECT COMMITTEE, appointed to enquire into the causes which have directed the trade of the west through the United States, by way of the Hudson and port of New York, and the mode of regaining it, together with an appendix to the same. Quebec, 1861. 26 p. **CaOOA**

1183   RHYS, CAPTAIN [CHARLES] HORTON ("MORTON PRICE"). A theatrical trip for a wager! Through Canada and the United States. London, 1861. 140 p. **DLC Uk**

Limited ed., Vancouver, 1966, introd. by Robertson Davies.

1184   RUSSELL, *SIR* WILLIAM HOWARD. The battle of Bull Run. New York, 1861. 30 p. **DLC Uk**

From the London *Times*, Aug. 6, 1861. Also pub. with American editorial comment under title, *Mr. Russell on Bull Run; with a note; from the Rebellion Record*, New York, 1861, 12 p.; 2d ed. changed "a note" to "with notes," New York, 1861, 14 p.

1185   RUSSELL, *SIR* WILLIAM HOWARD. The civil war in America. Boston, 1861. 189 p. **DLC**

Consists of letters to the London *Times*, Mar. 29, to June 19, 1861; same, with exception of the first five letters, carried title, *Pictures of southern life, social, political, and military*, New York, 1861. The series eventually ran from Mar. 29, 1861 to Apr. 3, 1862, pub. as *American letters to the London Times, 1861–62*, [n.p., n.d.]; facsimiles of the actual letters pub. by the Library of Congress as *Letters of William Howard Russell to the London 'Times' on the Civil War in America*, Washington, D.C., 1914. See also passages of letter to the *Times*, May 28, 1861, omitted from publication in book form, in Charles Francis Adams, Jr., "Sectional feeling in 1861," *Proc. Mass. Hist. Soc.*, XLVI (Feb. 1913), pp. 310–315. See also Russell's *My diary North and South*, London, 1863, below, which covers the same period and closely parallels the account in the letters.

1186   SHANKS, *REV.* G. H. The war in America: its origin and object. Together with a letter, addressed to Lord Shaftsbury, by Mrs. Harriet Beecher Stowe. Belfast, 1861. 12 p. **TxU**

1187   SIDDONS, JOACHIM HEYWARD. The Union volunteers' hand-book. Dedicated to the volunteers of New Jersey. Orange, 1861. 32 p. **DLC**

Author was British: see 1864, below his *The emigrant's friend: a true guide to the emigrant proceeding to New York,* and *Yankeeland in big trouble. An Englishman's correspondence during the war.*

1188   SLANEY, R[OBERT] A[GLIONBY]. Short journal of a visit to Canada and the states of America, in 1860. By R. A. Slaney, M.P. London, 1861. 73 p. **DLC Uk**

1189   SMEDLY, JOHN. The cotton question: some remarks, with extracts from pamphlets on the subject; and Mr. Bazley's paper on cotton statistics, read at the meeting of the British association, Manchester, Sept. 6, 1861; also, the Indian finance minister's [i.e., S. Laing's] speech, at Manchester, Sept. 19, 1861; also, extracts from Mr. James Johnstone's pamphlet on the opium trade. London, 1861. **Uk**

"Printed for John Smedley, Lea Mills, Derby, October 18, 1861." See esp. "Remarks and extracts on the cotton question. Printed for John Smedley, Lea Mills, Derby, Sept. 18, 1861," pp. 3–10; "The crisis come, and the fruits of England's hypocritical policy near being realized. A glance at the cotton trade. From papers read at the meeting of the British Association, held at Manchester, September 6, 1861," pp. 11–17 (Mr. Bazley's speech);

"Important meeting of the Manchester chamber of commerce. Conference with Mr. Laing, India finance minister," pp. 25–45 (p. 31, signed John Smedley); much comment on the U.S. and the Civil War, passim.

1190   SMITH, GOLDWIN. The foundation of the American colonies. A lecture delivered before the University of Oxford, June 12, 1860. Oxford, 1861. 32 p.   **DLC Uk**

Repr. in his *Lectures on modern history, delivered in Oxford, 1859–61*, Oxford, 1861, pp. 2–32. See *Remarks on the historical mis-statements and fallacies of Mr. Goldwin Smith . . . in his lecture "On the foundation of the American colonies," and his letter "On the emancipation of the colonies." By a Canadian*, Toronto, 1866. See also Elisabeth Wallace's *Goldwin Smith, Victorian liberal*, [Toronto, 1957], pp. 27–52; and her "Goldwin Smith on England and America," *Am. Hist. Rev.*, LIX (July 1954), 884–894.

1191   SPENCE, JAMES. The American Union; its effect on national character and policy, with an inquiry into secession as a constitutional right, and the causes of the disruption. London, 1861. 366 p.   **DLC Uk**

4th ed., London, 1862, added "notes" in reply to reviewers. See replies by Thomas Ellison, *Slavery and Secession in America*, 1861 above; and Charles Edward Rawlins, *American dis-union*, 1862, below. Spence was an influential champion of the South; he wrote in the London *Times* under the well-known signature, "S."

Reviews: *All the Year Round* (by Henry Morley), VI (Dec. 21 and 28, 1861), 295, 328; *Athenaeum*, (Nov. 23, 1861), 685; *Blackwood's Edinb. Mag.*, XCI, 514; *Edinb. Rev.*, CXVI, 549; *Index*, II, 268; *No. Brit. Rev.*, XXXVI, 122; *Quar. Rev.*, CXI, 239; *Sat. Rev.*, XII, 514; *Westmin. Rev.*, LXXII, 108.

1192   TALLACK, WILLIAM. Friendly sketches in America. London, 1861. 276 p.   **DLC Uk**

In U.S., 1860; visited New York and Pennsylvania, with a special interest in American Quakers. Also traveled overland from California through the Southwest in the same year; see his *Rides out and about; a book of travels and adventures*, 1878, below.

Review: *Athenaeum*, (Mar. 9, 1861), 325.

1193   [VIGIL, *pseud.*]. American difficulties. Letters by Vigil. London, 1861. 44 p.   **DLC Uk**

Letters repr. from the *Torquay Directory*.

1194   WOODS, N[ICHOLAS] A[UGUSTUS]. The Prince of Wales in Canada and the United States. London, 1861. 438 p.   **DLC Uk**

1862

1195   ADDRESSES TO THE WORKING CLASSES, farmers, tradesmen, &c. With the letters of emigrants from Cheltenham to the United States; and tables, containing every useful information for persons disposed to emigrate to Canada. Cheltenham, 1862.   **MB**

T.p. headed: Emigration. Issued first as a series of leaflets, repr. from the Cheltenham *Journal*. Nos. 1–5 read: "An address to the working classes, upon their present condition, and the best means of bettering it: with the letters of William Vines, an emigrant from Stroud, containing an account of his last three years' life in the United States, and other emigrants." Nos. 6–8 contain letters from other emigrants and are headed simply "An address to the working class." Each has separate pagination.

1196 [AINLEY, ———?]. Social wastes and waste lands; flax v. slave grown cotton being a glance at the commercial and social state of the nations; the causes of present commercial depressions; and remedies suggested with observations on the late debates in Parliament upon poor law relief, &c.; and outlines of a plan to render poor law unions self supporting. By Ajax [*pseud*]. London, 1862. 34 p.   **Uk**

Uk lists author as "Ajax, *pseud*. (i.e., Ainley?)." On U.S., pp. 13–19, 22–23, 33.

1197 AINSWORTH, WILLIAM FRANCIS, *ed*. All round the world: an illustrated record of voyages, travels, and adventures in all parts of the globe. London, 1860–62. 4 vols.
CtY MH NB Uk

Contains "From the Atlantic to the Pacific," I, pp. 298–362; "North America," III, pp. 1–64. Vols. I and II repr. under title, *The earth delineated with pen and pencil; or, Voyages, travels, and adventures all round the world*, London, [187–?]; vols. III and IV repr. under title, *Wanderings in every clime; or, Voyages, travels and adventures all round the world . . . A sequel to "The Earth delineated with pen and pencil,"* London, 1872.

1198 ALISON, ALEXANDER. The improvement of society and public opinion. London, 1862. 160 p.   **DLC Uk**

See Essay No. 3, "The political revolutions of 1860 & 1861 in Europe and America," pp. 57–88. Essay No. 4, also on the U.S., pub. separately, under title *Government reform in England and America*, 1861, above.

1199 AMERICAN CIVIL WAR, as seen by an Englishman. [New York? 1862?]. 4 p.   **DLC**

No t.p. Repr. from London *Morning Star* of Aug. 29, 1862?

1200 THE AMERICAN STRUGGLE. An appeal to the people of the North. By Philo-Americanus [*pseud*.]. London, 1862. 32 p.   **MH NN Uk**

The English appeal for peaceable division of the Union.

Review: *Exchange*, II, 57.

1201 ANENT THE UNITED STATES and Confederate States of North America. London, 1862. 7 p.   **DLC Uk**

1202 BALME, *REV*. JOSHUA RHODES. American states, churches and slavery. Edinburgh, 1862. 546 p.   **DLC Uk**

3d ed., enlarged, London, 1865, 776 p.; the added material also separately pub. under title, *Synopsis of the American war*, London, 1865. See also below his *Letters on the American republic . . .* , 1862, and *American war crusade; or, Plain facts for earnest men*, [1863]. An Englishman who emigrated to America in 1852, Balme called himself an "American clergyman." In his writings he is very abusive of the U.S.

1203 BALME, *REV*. JOSHUA RHODES. Letters on the American republic; or, Common fallacies and monstrous errors refuted and exposed. London, 1862. 112 p.   **Uk**

DLC has enlarged ed., London, 1863.

1204 BALSTON, WILLIAM. Cotton supplies from India. A letter to T[homas] Bazley, M.P.P. [n.p.], 1862.   **UkLGl**

1205 BARRETT-LENNARD, C[HARLES] E[DWARD]. Travels in British Columbia, with the narrative of a yacht voyage round Vancouver's Island. By Capt. C. E. Barrett-Lennard. London, 1862. 307 p.   **DLC Uk**

On U.S., pp. 178–204, 218–267, and passim.

1206 BAXTER, WILLIAM EDWARD. The social condition of the southern states of America. A lecture delivered . . . November 5, 1862. 28 p. **MB OClWHi Uk**

1207 BERESFORD-HOPE, ALEXANDER JAMES BERESFORD. England, the North and the South. London, 1862. 40 p. **Uk**

DLC has 3d ed., London, 1862. One of three lectures also repr. in *The American disruption*, London, 1862 (full title given under 1861 entry for Beresford-Hope).

1208 BERESFORD-HOPE, ALEXANDER JAMES BERESFORD. Mr Beresford-Hope's address upon the political questions of the day, at Stoke-upon-Trent town hall, Tuesday, September 9th, 1862. Mr. C. M. Campbell, Chairman. Hanley, 1862. 18 p. **NN Uk**

1209 BERESFORD-HOPE, ALEXANDER JAMES BERESFORD. The results of the American disruption: the substance of a lecture delivered by request before the Maidstone Literary & mechanics institution, in continuation of A Popular view of the American Civil War, and England, the North and the South. London, 1862. 40 p. **CtY ICN Uk**

DLC has 3d ed., London, 1862. One of three lectures also printed in *The American disruption*, London, 1862 (for full title see 1861 entry for Beresford-Hope).

1210 BERNARD, MOUNTAGUE. Notes on some questions suggested by the case of the "Trent." Oxford, [1862]. 39 p. **DLC Uk**

Review: *Quar. Rev.*, CXI, 239.

1211 BOOTY, JAMES HORATIO. Three months in Canada and the United States. London, 1862. 94 p. **DLC Uk**

Priv. pr. diary from May 18–July 23, 1859.

1212 BRIGHT, JOHN. A liberal voice from England. Mr. John Bright's speech at Rochdale, December 4, 1861, on the American crisis. New York, 1862. 13 p. **DLC**

Later appeared in the *Rebellion record: a diary of American events with documents, narratives, illustrative incidents, poetry, etc.*, supp., vol. I, New York, 1864. Includes comment on the speech from the London *Times*, pp. 12–13. See also Bright's *Speeches*, 1865, below, for repr. of this and numerous other speeches on the U.S. See also entries for Richard Cobden, 1862, below.

1213 BRIGHT, JOHN. Speech of Mr. Bright, M.P., in the Town hall, Birmingham, December 18, 1862. Birmingham, [1862?]. 20 p. **DLC Uk**

On the cotton famine and war in the U.S.

1214 BRITISH AND FOREIGN ANTI-SLAVERY SOCIETY, LONDON. The crisis in the United States. London, 1862. 4 p. **DLC Uk**

Tracts on Slavery in America, no. 2. Contains address of the committee of the Society, and a "Letter to President Lincoln," both signed by Thomas Binns, Chairman, and L.A. Chamerovzov, Secretary..

1215 BRITISH AND FOREIGN ANTI-SLAVERY SOCIETY, LONDON. What the South is fighting for. London, [1862]. 8 p. **DLC Uk**

Tracts on Slavery in America, no. 1. See also *British aid to the Confederates*, 1863, below (tract no. 3).

1216 BRITISH OPINION OF THE AMERICAN CONTEST. A letter from England, dated September 24. London, [1862?]. **NN**

A broadside; no t.p.

1217   CAIRNES, J[OHN] E[LLIOTT]. The revolution in America: a lecture by J. E. Cairnes. Delivered before the Dublin Young men's Christian association, in connexion with the United church of England and Ireland, in the Metropolitan hall, October 30th, 1862. [Dublin], 1862. 43 p.   **DLC**

Uk has Dublin, 1863 ed. New York, 1862 ed. carried title, *The American Revolution*, etc. The lecture was repr. in *Lectures delivered before the Dublin Young men's Christian association in connexion with the United church of England and Ireland. Patron: His Grace the Archbishop of Dublin. During the year 1862*, Dublin, 1863, pp. 347–390, and in Cairnes' *Political Essays*, London, 1873, pp. 59–108.

Reviews: *Barker's Rev.*, III, 325; *Edinb. Rev.*, CXVI, 549; *Westmin. Rev.*, LXXIX, 300.

1218   CAIRNES, JOHN ELLIOTT. The slave power: its character, career, and probable designs: being an attempt to explain the real issues involved in the American contest. London, 1862. 304 p.   **DLC Uk**

2d ed., much enlarged London, 1863, 410 p; New York, 1969, ed. by Harold D. Goodman. See also Adelaide Weinberg, *John Elliot Cairnes and the American Civil War: a study in Anglo-American relations*, London, 1970.

Reviews: *Barker's Rev.*, III, 335; *Dublin Rev.*, IV (n.s.), 328; *Dublin Univ. Mag.*, LXI, 604; *Fraser's Mag.*, LXVIII, 419; *No. Am. Rev.* (by J. Q. Bettinger), 467; *No. Brit. Rev.*, XXXVII, 488; *Spectator*, XXXV, 690; *Westmin. Rev.* (by J. S. Mill), XXII (n.s.), 489 (repr. in Mill's *Dissertations and discussions*, III, 264).

1219   THE CASE OF THE TRENT EXAMINED. London, 1862. 24 p.   **DLC**

Uk copy destroyed. See also "The Trent incident" from the London *Times*, Jan. 13, 1862, in Sir James Marchant (ed.), *History through "The Times,"* London, [1937], pp. 196–200; Charles Francis Adams, "The Trent affair, November, 1861," *Proc. Mass. Hist. Soc.*, XLV (Nov. 1911), 35–148; Fred Landon, "Trent affair of 1861," *Canadian Hist. Rev.*, III (1923), 48–57.

1220   THE CIVIL WAR & SLAVERY in the United States. A lecture delivered at Arley chapel, Bristol, June 10, 1862. [London? 1862.] 24 p.

DLC and Uk have 3d ed., London, 1862.

1221   CLARK, CHARLES. The Trent and San Jacinto; being the substance of a paper on this subject, read before the Juridical society on the 16th December 1861. London, 1862. 46 p.   **DLC Uk**

Uk gives pub. date incorrectly as 1861.

1222   [COBDEN, RICHARD and JOHN BRIGHT]. A friendly voice from England on American affairs. New York, 1862. 30 p.   **DLC**

Contains letter from Cobden dated Dec. 2, 1861, and a speech given by John Bright, Dec. 4, 1861 (the latter repr. separately as *A liberal voice . . .* , 1862, above). See Donald Read, *Cobden and Bright: A Victorian political partnership*, London, 1967, chap. 12, "The American Civil War." For more on Cobden's views on the war see entries for 1862 and 1863, below.

1223   COBDEN, RICHARD. Letter from Mr. Cobden, M.P., to Henry Ashworth, esq., president of the Manchester chamber of commerce, upon the present state of international maritime law, as affecting the rights of belligerents and neutrals. Manchester, 1862. 16 p.   **MB NN UkMa**

Letter dated April 10, 1862. Repr. in Cobden's *Political writings*, London, 1867, II, pp. 5–22.

1224   COBDEN, RICHARD. Maritime law and belligerent rights. Speech of Richard Cobden, esq., M.P., advocating a reform of international maritime law; delivered to the Manchester chamber of commerce, on Friday, October 25, 1862. Revised and corrected by the author. Manchester, [1862]. 33 p.   **CtY MH UkMa**

See reply by Edward Lewis Blackman, *Our relations with America*, 1863, below.

1225   COWELL, JOHN WELSFORD. Southern secession. A letter addressed to Captain M. T. Maury, Confederate navy, on his letter to Admiral Fitzroy. London, 1862. 99 p.   **DLC Uk**

An appendix includes other letters originally pub. in the *Examiner*. Cowell lived in the U.S. 1837–39.

1226   D., B. Federals and Confederates: for what do they fight? The true issue of the American Civil War stated. London, 1862. 16 p.   **Uk**

MB, MBAt, and OClWHi have 3d ed., London, 1863.

1227   DALLING AND BULWER, WILLIAM HENRY LYTTON EARLE BULWER, *baron*. A collection of speeches, delivered in America, by the Right Hon. Sir Henry Lytton Bulwer, G.C.B., her Majesty's envoy and Minister plenipotentiary to the United States. Together with the opinions of the American press thereon. Constantinople, 1862. 35 p.   **CSmH**

NcD lists Constantinople, 1862 ed., 128 p., with 5 additional speeches delivered in Constantinople and Alexandria (Egypt), 1859–64, bound in at end. See also author's "Great Britain and the United States," *Edinb. Rev.*, CIV (July 1856), 267–298; and *Speeches of Mr. Webster at Capon Springs, Virginia; together with those of Sir. H. L. Bulwer & Wm. L. Clarke, esq., June 28, 1851*, [Washington, 1851], pp. 14–16. See also the *Cambridge Hist. J.*, III (1931) no. 3: G. F. Hickson, "Palmerston and the Clayton-Bulwer treaty," 295–303; J. D. Ward, "Sir Henry Bulwer and the United States Archives," 304–313.

1228   DAY, SAMUEL PHILLIPS. Down South; or, An Englishman's experience at the seat of the American war. London, 1862. 2 vols.   **DLC Uk**

Day was a special correspondent to the London *Morning Herald*.

Reviews: *Athenaeum*, (March 22, 1862), 393; *Dublin Univ. Mag.*, LXIII, 214; *Nat. Rev.*, XXVII, 492.

1229   DEFENCE OF CANADA. 1st. General character of country—strength of militia—lake district from Lake Superior downwards to the Falls of Niagara. 2nd. The district from Ogdensburg to Montreal, including the country between Lake Champlain and Montreal,— and the American position at Rouse's Point. 4th. The Route from the ocean to Quebec— the means of inland communication by the canals and railways to the West—and the importance of a thoroughly organized system for the defence of the works. 5th. The importance of obtaining command of the upper Lakes—the number of American and British vessels;—and certain practical suggestions. [London?, 1862?]. 7 p.   **CaOTP**

At head of title: "Strictly private and confidential."

1230   THE DESPOTISM AT RICHMOND. The Confederate loan in England. The Slave Power and its supporters. [New York, 1862].   **MH OU**

A broadside; from the London *Daily News*, March 20, 1862.

1231   DUNLOP, HENRY. The cotton trade: its national importance, present difficulties, and future prospects: a lecture delivered in the Queen's rooms, Glasgow, January 8, 1862, by Henry Dunlop, esq., President of the chamber of commerce and manufactures in the city of Glasgow. Published by request of the Glasgow chamber of commerce. Glasgow, 1862. 36 p.   **NNC Uk**

Comment on U.S., passim.

1232   DYER, J[OSEPH] C[HESSBOROUGH]. Letter to the Honorable William H. Seward, Secretary of state, Washington. Manchester, 1862. 14 p.   **DS PHi**

NUC entry for PHi incorrectly gives pub. date as 1868.

1233   DYER, J[OSEPH] C[HESSBOROUGH]. Notes on political mistakes, addressed to the people of England, by J. C. Dyer. Manchester, [1862]. 24 p.   **Uk Vi**

On U.S. Civil War.

1234   EMIGRATION FROM THE BRITISH ISLANDS, considered with regard to its bearing and influence upon the interests and prosperity of Great Britain. London, 1862. 17 p.
IU UkENL

1235   EVANS, THOMAS. Why without cotton? An address. . . . Manchester, [1862?]. 15 p.
PHi

1236   FAIR-PLAY [*pseud.*]. The true state of the American question. Reply to Mr. Thurlow Weed [i.e., to his letter on American affairs]. London, 1862. 28 p.   **DS MH PU Uk**

1237   [FIELD, EDWIN WILKINS]. Correspondence on the present relations between Great Britain and the United States of America. Boston, 1862. 153 p.   **DLC Uk**

Correspondence between Field, an English lawyer, and Charles Greely Loring, an American lawyer.

Review: *Chr. Examiner*, LXXIV, 295.

1238   FORTS VERSUS SHIPS: also Defence of the Canadian lakes and its influence on the general defence of Canada. By an officer. London, 1862. 43 p.   **CaOTU Uk**

On U.S., pp. 18–43.

1239   FOX, FRANKLIN. Glimpses of the life of a sailor. London, 1862.   **Uk**

Semi-fictionized account of visit to the U.S., pp. 96–166; sketches appeared originally in *People's J.*, *Howitt's J.*, and in *Household Words*.

1240   FREE LABOUR COTTON: it can be had. [London, 1862]. 4 p.   **UkENL**

Denounces slave-grown cotton.

1241   GOW, DAN. Civil War in America: a lecture delivered in aid of the Lancashire relief fund, on November 24th, 1862, in Sydenbam chapel, Forest Hill. Manchester, 1862. 34 p.
MH Uk

1242   GREENWOOD, JAMES. Wild sports of the world. A boy's book of natural history and adventure. London, 1862. 426 p.   **CU CtY ICU**

DLC has New York, 1870 ed; Uk has London, 1880 ed. Includes comment on animals in the U.S.; map on p. 97 shows habitats of animals and plants in North America. See also comments on American Indians in his *Curiosities of savage life (Second series)*, London, 1864, which was repr. under various titles: *Savage habits and customs*, London, 1865; *Stirring scenes in savage lands*, London, 1879?; *The wild man at home; or, pictures of life in savage lands*, London, 1879.

1243   HALL, [CHRISTOPHER] NEWMAN. The American war. A lecture to working men, delivered in London, October 20, 1862. London, [1862]. 31 p.   **DLC Uk**

DLC also has New York, 1862 ed, 48 p.

1244   HANNAY, CHARLES JAMES JENKINS. The maritime rights & obligations of belligerents, as between themselves, their allies and neutrals, as recognized by English maritime courts. With the decision of Sir William Scott in the case of the "The Maria." London, 1862. 72 p.   **DLC Uk**

Written to clarify the situation during the Civil War, but not on the U.S. per se.

1245   HAY, *SIR* JOHN [CHARLES] DALRYMPLE. The reward of loyalty. Edinburgh, 1862. 21 p.   **ICU OCIWHi Uk**

On the Civil War.

1246   [HODGE, CHARLES]. England and America. 2d ed. Philadelphia, 1862. 31 p.   **DLC**

No record of a separately pub. 1st ed.; repr. from *Princeton Rev.*, XXXIV, (Jan. 1862), 147–177. Author is American, but describes pro-Confederate English opinion, esp. in the wake of the Trent affair; followed by arguments addressed to English readership, to convince them that slavery is the issue.

1247   KIRKUP, THOMAS. A memoir of Duncan Wallace, being a narrative of his voyages, shipwrecks, travels and battles by sea and by land, during a period of eighty-three years, dictated by himself, and written and collated by Thomas Kirkup, Fatfield. Newcastle-on-Tyne, 1862. 210 p.   **GU ICN Uk**

Includes incidental comment on U.S. and American ships.

1248   LEATHAM, EDWARD ALDAM. Speech of E. A. Leatham, esq., M.P., upon American affairs. Woodhead, 1862. 20 p.   **MoU MsU**

1249   LEWIS, *SIR* GEORGE CORNEWALL. Recognition of the independence of the southern states of the North American Union. London, 1862. 25 p.   **CU MH**

Printed for the confidential use of the Cabinet, Nov. 7, 1862.

1250   LONDON CONFEDERATE STATES AID ASSOCIATION. An address to the British public and all sympathizers in Europe, from the London Confederate states aid association. . . . Established August, 1862. London, 1862. 16 p.   **DLC**

Secretary, Frederick Nurse.

1251   LORD, HENRY WILLIAM. The highway of the seas in times of war. Cambridge, 1862. 56 p.   **DLC Uk**

On maritime disputes between the U.S. and England.

1252   LUCAS, SAMUEL. Secularia, or Surveys on the mainstream of history. London, 1862. 410 p.   **DLC Uk**

"On some preparatives of the American Revolution," pp. 250–267; "Revolutions in progress and prospect, 1862," pp. 384–410. Based in part on author's earlier works: *The causes & consequences of national revolutions among the ancients & moderns compared. A prize essay, read in the Sheldonian theatre, Oxford, June 4th, 1845*, London, 1845; *Characters of the old English colonies in America*, London, 1850.

1253   LUDLOW, JOHN MALCOLM [FORBES]. A sketch of the history of the United States from independence to secession. To which is added, The struggle for Kansas. By Thomas Hughes. Cambridge, 1862. 404 p.   **DLC Uk**

Portion by Hughes from two lectures delivered in 1861.

Review: *Westmin. Rev.*, LXXVIII, 140.

1254   MACQUEEN, JOHN FRASER. Chief points in the laws of war and neutrality, search and blockade; with the changes of 1856, and those now proposed. London, 1862. 108 p.   **DLC Uk**

Chaps. 4–6 on U.S., and passim.

1255   MAGILL, *REV*. D. Lecture on the American conflict. Belfast, 1862. 24 p.   **NN**

1256   MALLET, JOHN WILLIAM. Cotton: the chemical, geological, and meteorological conditions involved in its successful cultivation. With an account of the actual conditions and practice of culture in the southern or cotton states of North America. By Dr. John William Mallet. London, 1862. 183 p.   **DLC Uk**

Author a British national, teaching chemistry at the Univ. of Alabama. This work pub. by his father when the Civil War cut off communications between them.

1257   MARITIME CAPTURE. Shall England uphold the capture of private property at sea? By a lawyer. London, 1862. 41 p.   **DLC Uk**

1258   MARSHALL, T[HOMAS] W[ILLIAM] M. Christian missions: their agents, their method, and their results. London, 1862. 3 vols.   **CLU Uk**

DLC has 2d ed., London, 1863, 2 vols. Chap. 9, pt. 2, "Missions in North America," describes Catholic missions in Texas, California, Oregon, the Rocky Mountains, and other parts of the U.S.

Review: *Dublin Rev.*, VI, n.s., (Jan. 1866), 1.

1259   MASSIE, *REV*. JAMES WILLIAM. The American crisis, in relation to the anti-slavery cause. Facts and suggestions addressed to the friends of freedom in Britain. London, 1862. 11 p.   **ICN MB Uk**

1260   MAYNE, RICHARD CHARLES. Four years in British Columbia and Vancouver Island. An account of their forests, rivers, coasts, gold fields and resources for colonisation. By Commander R. C. Mayne. London, 1862. 468 p.   **DLC Uk**

On San Francisco, pp. 153–163, and some description of California gold mines, passim.

1261   MELLOR, *REV*. ENOCH. War or slavery. [Manchester, 1862?]   **UkLGI**

No t.p.; single page—both sides. The inaugural address at the annual meeting of the Congregational Union held in London. Pub. by the Union and Emancip. Soc., Manchester. Collection of Mellor's tracts on the Civil War, also titled *War or Slavery*, Manchester, [1863?] held by MH and OClWHi.

1262   MILL, JOHN STUART. The contest in America. Boston, 1862. 32 p.   **DLC**

Originally pub. in *Fraser's Mag.*, LXV (Feb. 1862), 258–268. See also Mill's "The Negro question," *Fraser's Mag.*, XLI (Jan. 1850), 23–31; "The slave power," *Westmin. Rev.*, LXXVIII (Oct. 1862), 489–510; and "Mr. Mill on America," *Sat. Rev.*, XV (March 7 1863), 302–303. Also see John O. Waller, "John Stuart Mill and the American Civil War," *Bull. N.Y. Pub. Lib.*, LXVII (Oct. 1962), 505–518.

1263   [MILLER, ———]. Military sketch of the present war in America. [London? 1862?]. 21 p.   **DLC**

Transcript of a lecture.

1264   MITCHELL, DAVID W. Ten years in the United States; being an Englishman's view of men and things in the North and South. London, 1862. 332 p.   **DLC Uk**

In U.S., 1848–58.

Reviews: *Index*, II, 157; *Westmin. Rev.*, LXXIX, 571.

1265   [MORSE, SAMUEL FINLEY BREESE]. The present attempt to dissolve the American Union, a British aristocratic plot. By B. New York, 1862. 42 p.   **DLC Uk**

Although Morse is American, he claims to present British comment, most of it "hearsay evidence."

1266   NICHOLLS, JOHN ASHTON. In memoriam. A selection from the letters of the late John Ashton Nicholls, F.R.A.S. & c. Ed. by his mother [Sarah (Ashton) Nicholls]. Manchester, 1862. 418 p.   **DLC Uk**

Includes a number of letters written during a visit to America shortly before his death.

1267   [RANKEN, GEORGE]. Canada and the Crimea; or, Sketches of a soldier's life. From the journals and correspondence of the late Major Ranken, R.E. Ed. by his brother, W. Bayne Ranken. London, 1862. 319 p.   **DLC Uk**

Includes a description of the U.S. in 1853.

1268   RAWLINS, CHARLES ED[WARD], *jun.* American dis-union: constitutional or unconstitutional. A reply to Mr. James Spence upon the question "Is secession a constitutional right?" discussed in his recent work, "The American Union." London, 1862. 228 p.   **DLC Uk**

A reply, by a fellow Englishman, to Spence's work, 1861, above.

Reviews: *Dublin Rev.*, IV, n.s., 328; *Economist*, XX, 680; *Exchange*, I, 203; *Westmin. Rev.*, LXXVIII, 287.

1269   REID, HUGO. The American question in a nutshell; or, Why we should recognize the Confederates. London, 1862. 31 p.   **DLC Uk**

1270   REID, HUGO. A handbook of the history of the United States; including the discovery and European settlement, the colonial period, the War of Independence, the Constitution, and history to the present time. London, 1862. 208 p.   **NN Uk**

1271   THE RIGHT OF RECOGNITION. A sketch of the present policy of the Confederate States. By a recent tourist. London, 1862. 30 p.   **DLC**

1272   THE RIGHTS OF NEUTRALS and belligerents, from a modern point of view, by a civilian. London, 1862. 41 p.   **DS MH NN**

1273   SELBORNE, ROUNDELL PALMER, [*1st earl of Selborne*]. A speech delivered in the House of Commons, in the debate on the North American blockade, Tuesday, March 7, 1862. London, 1862. 29 p.   **MB OClWHi Uk**

See author's *Memorials. Part I. Family and personal, 1766–1865*, London, 1896, 2 vols.; includes chaps. on The Trent, Alabama, etc., II, pp. 378–452. See also his *Memorials. Part II. Personal and political, 1865–1895*, London, 1898; on the Treaty of Washington and arbitration at Geneva, I, pp. 227–279.

1274   SINCLAIR, PETER. Freedom or slavery in the United States, being facts and testimonies for the consideration of the British people. London, [1862]. 160 p.   **OCIW**

DLC has 2d ed., London, 1862; Uk lists 2d ed., [1863?]. Author lived over four years in U.S.

1275   [SMITH, A.]. The defences of England. Nine letters. By a journeyman shoemaker. Eight letters before the affair of the "Trent." One letter afterwards. London, 1862.   **NN Uk**

Repr. from Nottingham *Weekly Times*.

1276   SMITH, PHILIP ANSTIE. The seizure of the southern commissioners, considered with reference to international law, and to the question of war or peace. London, 1862. 44 p.

DLC Uk

1277   SOMERVILLE, ALEXANDER. Canada, a battle ground; about a Kingdom in America. By Alexander Somerville. "One who has whistled at the plough." Author of works in Britain on political economy, military strategy, and conservative science of nations. Hamilton, Canada West, 1862. 64 p.   **CaOTP MH Uk**

Cover title; at head of title, "First part." Uk lists title as *"Canada, a battle field. . . . "* In pref. to his *Narrative of the Fenian invasion of Canada*, 1866, below, Somerville refers to the above work and quotes from pp. 54–55.

1278   SPENCE, JAMES. On the recognition of the Southern confederation. London, 1862. 48 p.

DLC Uk

Reviews: *Exchange*, II, 54; *Quar. Rev.*, CXII, 535.

1279   STACK, JOHN HERBERT. Historic doubts relative to the American war. London, 1862. 22 p.   **CtY OCIWHi**

Uk has Birmingham, 1862 ed. Portion repr. from "Aris's Birmingham Gazette," Nov. 15, 1862. Modelled on Archbishop Whately's *Historic doubts relative to Napoleon Bonaparte* and also his *Historic certainties respecting the early history of America*, and dedicated to Whately.

1280   STODDARD, ARTHUR FRANCIS. The Civil War in America: an address. Glasgow, May 22nd, 1862. Glasgow, 1862. 31 p.   **CtY MB**

1281   SULLIVAN, ALEXANDER M[ARTIN]. The Phoenix societies in Ireland and America, 1858 and 1862. A letter etc. etc. By Arthur M. Sullivan, editor of "The Nation." Dublin, [1862]. 19 p.   **MH Uk**

Arthur M. Sullivan's letter bound in the same volume. See Alexander Sullivan's *New Ireland*, London, 1877; II, pp. 77–107 contain some comment on the U.S. See also his "The Irish abroad," [18th March, 1861], *Speeches & addresses . . . 1859–1881*, Dublin, 1886, pp. 14–17. Timothy Daniel Sullivan's *A. M. Sullivan. A memoir*, Dublin, 1885, refers to Sullivan's "Lecturing tour in America," (1882), pp. 150–151.

1282   THOMPSON, GEORGE. The American question: a speech delivered in the Music Hall, Leeds, Mar. 25th, 1862, on the anniversary of the Leed's Young Men's Anti-Slavery Society. Leeds, 1862. 16 p.   **MH NIC**

1283   TROLLOPE, ANTHONY. North America. London, 1862. 2 vols.   **DLC Uk**

DLC also has 1 vol. ed., New York, 1863, 623 p. Critical eds.: with an introd., notes and new materials, by Donald Smalley and Bradford Allen Booth, New York, 1951; and ed. by Robert Mason, Harmondsworth, 1968. See also account of visit, 1861–62, in *The letters of Anthony Trollope*, ed. by Bradford Allen Booth, London, 1951, pp. 149–168; and in his

Autobiography, ed. by Bradford Allen Booth, Berkeley, 1947, pp. 136–140. Trollope made five visits to the U.S.: see Willard Thorp, "Trollope's America," in *Two addresses delivered to members of the Grolier club*, New York, 1950, pp. 5–23; Philip David Stryker, "Anthony Trollope in the United States" (unpub. Ph.D. diss., Northwestern Univ., 1947); "Trollope in Boston," *More Books: the Bull. of the Boston Pub. Lib.*, XXI, 6th ser. (1946), 30–31; Lucy Poate Stebbins and Richard Poate Stebbins, *The Trollopes: the chronicle of a writing family*, London, 1947; Ada B. Nisbet, "Trollope's 'North America'," *Nineteenth Cent. Fict.*, VI (March 1952), 286–290; Peter Conrad, *Imagining America*, New York, 1980, pp. 38–48; and Helen Heineman, "Anthony Trollope: the compleat traveller," *Ariel: A Review of Internat. Eng. Lit.*, (Jan. 1982), 33–50. See also Trollope's American story, "The widow's mite," *Good Words* IV, (1863), 33–43; and his novel *The American senator*, Toronto, 1877 (reviewed in the *Canadian Monthly & Natl. Rev.*, XII, 319). See Philip David Stryker, "The significance of Trollope's *The American Senator*," *Nineteenth Cent. Fict.*, V (1950), 141–149; and Robert H. Tayler, "The manuscript of Trollope's *American Senator*," *Bibliog. Soc. Am. Papers*, XLI (1947), 123–129.

Reviews: *Am. Theol. Rev.*, IV, 581; *Athenaeum*, (May 24, 1862), 685; *Blackwood's Edinb. Mag.*, XCII, 372; *Chambers's J.*, XVII, 408; *Dublin Univ. Mag.*, LX, 75; *Fraser's Mag.*, LXVI, 256; the *Friend* (Honolulu), XIX, 93; *Harper's Mag.*, XXV, 262; *Home & For. Rev.*, I, 111; *Index* (London), I, 140; *Ladies Repository*, XX, 509; *London Rev.*, IV, 597; *London Quar. Rev.*, XIX, 234; *No. Am. Rev.* (by J. Cooke), XCV, 416; *No. Brit. Rev.*, XXXVII, 488; *Presb. Quar. Rev.*, II, 173, 177; *Quar. Rev.*, CXII, 535, CXV, 291; *Sat. Rev.*, XIII, 625; *Spectator*, XXXV, 635; London *Times*, June 11, 1862, p. 6; *Westmin. Rev.*, XXII, n.s., 536 or LXXVIII (Amer. ed.), 288.

1284   THE UNITED STATES AND CANADA, as seen by two brothers in 1858 and 1861. London, 1862. 137 p.   **DLC Uk**

Pref. signed "J.C., jun." Chap. 1 gives the itinerary of "J.C., jun." in 1858 and "A.C." in 1861.

1285   URQUHART, DAVID. Analysis of M. Thouvenel's despatch. By David Urquhart, esq. (From the Free press of Jan. 1, 1862.) [London, 1862]. 6 p.   **DLC Uk**

No t.p. Discusses the Trent affair.

1286   URQUHART, DAVID. Answer to Mr. Cobden on the assimilation of war and peace. Also analysis of the correspondence with the United States, showing the Declaration of Paris to have been violated by England and France. London, 1862. 64 p.   **DLC Uk**

Answer to Cobden's letter to Manchester chamber of commerce, 1862, above.

1287   URQUHART, DAVID. The right of search: Two speeches by David Urquhart. (January 20 and 27, 1862). Showing: In what it consists. How the British empire exists by it. That it has been surrendered up. With an introduction on Lord Derby's part therein. London, 1862. 113 p.   **DLC Uk**

1288   THE VOLUNTARY PRINCIPLE in America. By an English clergyman. Cambridge, [1862].   **CLU Uk**

Bound with *Tracts for priests and people*, London, [1860?–1862], vol. II, *Supplementary number to the second series*, pp. 37–53.

1289   WADDINGTON, JOHN. The American crisis in relation to slavery. London, 1862. 32 p.   **MH NN OCIWHi Uk**

1290   THE WAR IN AMERICA: Negro slavery and the Bible. A politico-religious essay. By an old politician. Stirling, 1862. 51 p.   **Uk**

Copy in Uk bound with Political Tracts, 1856–64.

1291   WESTLAKE, JOHN. Commercial blockades, considered with reference to law and policy. London, 1862. 28 p.   **DLC Uk**

On U.S. See Westlake's paper devoted to the question of Irish Fenians claiming American citizenship, "On naturalisation and expatriation or, on change of nationality," *Sessional proc. Natl. Assn. for the Promotion of Social Science (London)*, I, No. 8 (Jan. 30, 1868), pp. 97–130.

1292   WIGHT, ROBERT. Notes on cotton farming, explanatory of the American and East Indian methods, with suggestions for their improvement. Reading [England], 1862. 44 p.

DLC Uk

1293   WILLSON, HUGH BOWLBY. The military defences of Canada, considered in respect to our colonial relations with Great Britain, in a series of letters published in the Quebec "Morning Chronicle." Quebec, 1862. 43 p.   **CaBVaU NN Uk**

1294   WILSON, CHARLES WILLIAM. Mapping the frontier. Charles Wilson's diary of the survey of the 19th parallel, 1858–1862, while secretary of the British Boundary Commission. Ed., with an introd. by George F. G. Stanley. Seattle, 1970. 182 p.   **CLU NRU**

Uk

Survey in concert with American Boundary Commission. Travelled along Columbia River and made brief visits to San Francisco. See esp. pp. 89–97, 142–144, 168–170, 175–176, and passim.

1295   WILSON, *SIR* DANIEL. Prehistoric man: researches into the origin of civilization in the old and new world. Cambridge, 1862. 2 vols.   **DLC Uk**

On U.S., passim. See also H. H. Langton's *Sir Daniel Wilson: a memoir*, Edinburgh, [1929], pp. 53–56.

1296   WOLSELEY, GARNET JOSEPH WOLSELEY, *1st viscount*. The story of a soldier's life, by Field-Marshal Viscount Wolseley. Westminster, 1903. 2 vols.   **DLC Uk**

Chap. 35, "Visit to the Confederate Army, [Sept. 11–Oct. 21], 1862," II, pp. 117–144. See also his anonymous account, "A month's visit to the Confederate headquarters. By an English officer," *Blackwood's Edinb. Mag.*, XCIII (Jan. 1863), 1–29; his "General Lee," *Macmillan's Mag.*, LV (March 1887), 321–333; and his series of articles under the title, "An English view of the civil war," *No. Am. Rev.*, (June–Dec. 1889), CXLVIII, 538–563, CXLIX, 30–43, 164–181, 278–292, 446–459, 594–606, 713–727. All of the articles are repr. in *The American Civil War, an English view*, ed., with an introd. by James A. Rawley, Charlottesville, Va., [1964]. For answers to the series in *No. Am. Rev.*, see General James B. Fry, "Lord Wolseley answered," ibid., CXLIX, 728–740, and Jefferson Davis, "Lord Wolseley's mistakes," ibid., CXLIX, 472–482. See also excerpts from and comment on by Charles Francis Adams, "Wolseley and the Confederate Army," *Proc. Mass. Hist. Soc.*, XLVII (Oct. 1913), 9–24. For further extracts from Wolseley's journal (and for an account by the London *Times* correspondent, Frank Lawley), see Charles Rathbone Low, *General Lord Wolseley (of Cairo) . . . A memoir*, 2d ed., London, 1883, pp. 156–178 (1st ed., *A memoir of Lieutenant-General Sir Garnet J. Wolseley*, London, 1878, 2 vols., has no pagination).

See also the following articles by Wolseley: "General Forrest," *United Service Mag.*, V, n.s. (Apr.–May 1892), 1–14, 113–124; "General Sherman," ibid., III, n.s. (May–July 1891), 97–116, 193–216, 289–309; *General Lee*, Rochester, [New York], 1906, repr. from *Macmillan's Mag.*, LV (Mar. 1887), 321–331; "Military genius," *Fortnightly Rev.*, n.s. (Sept. 1888), 297–312. See also author's letters to General Sir Robert Biddulph in H. Biddulph's "Canada and the American civil war: more Wolseley letters," *J. Soc. for Army Hist. Res.*, XIX (1940), 112–117. For additional comment on the Civil War see *The life of Lord Wolseley*, by Major General Sir Frederick Maurice and Sir George Arthur, with a foreword by General Sir. R. Wingate, Garden City, 1924, pp. 34–53; and *All Sir Garnet. A Life of Field-Marshall Lord Wolseley*, by Joseph H. Lehmann, London, [1964], pp. 114–123.

1863

1297   ADAMS, W[ILLIAM] E[DWIN]. The slaveholders' war: an argument for the North and the Negro. Manchester, 1863. 24 p.   **MH UkLGl**

See author's discussion of the writing of this pamphlet and other reminiscences of the American civil war in his *Memoirs of a social atom*, London, 1903, 2 vols., II, pp. 418–438.

1298   ADDRESS OF THE FRENCH PROTESTANT PASTORS to ministers and pastors of all denominations in Great Britain, on American slavery; and the reply of the British ministers; with a report of the Ministerial anti-slavery conference, held in Manchester, June 3rd, 1863, and the address to ministers & pastors of all Christian denominations throughout the states of America, adopted by the conference. Manchester, 1863. 34 p.   **CtY NIC NN**

Final address signed by Richard Slate, chairman; pub. by the Union and Emancip. Soc., Manchester.

1299   THE "ALABAMA": a statement of facts from official documents, with the sections of the Foreign enlistment act violated by her equipment. London, 1863. 16 p.   **DLC Uk**

See also *The Alabama case . . . Articles and letters relating to the same which have appeared in the London newspapers*, [n.p., 1872?]; and James D. Bulloch, *The secret service of the Confederate States in Europe; or, How the Confederate cruisers were equipped*, New York, 1884, which contains many letters and other contemporary comment from England. Also see the accounts in Brooks Adams, "The seizure of the Laird rams," *Proc. Mass. Hist. Soc.*, XLV (Dec. 1911), 243–333; and by the American consul at Liverpool, Thomas H. Dudley, in the *Penn. Mag. Hist. & Biog.*, XVII (1893), 34–54.

1300   AMERICAN THANKSGIVING DINNER, at St. James' hall, London, Thursday, November 26, 1863. London, 1863. 94 p.   **DLC Uk**

Includes remarks of George Thompson, Capt. [Robert] Mayne Reid, Robert J. Walker, et al.

1301   THE AMERICAN WAR. The whole question explained. [Manchester? 1863?]. 23 p.
    OCIWHi

See also the answer, *Fallacies of freeman and foes of liberty. A reply to "The American war: the whole question explained,"* 1863, below.

1302   BALME, *REV.* JOSHUA RHODES. American war crusade; or, Plain facts for earnest men. London, [1863]. 40 p.   **DLC Uk**

1303   [BARKER, JOSEPH]. The American question. A lecture delivered in the Corn exchange, Manchester, in answer to the speeches delivered by the Hon. and Rev. B[aptist Wriothesley] Noel, Dr. [James William] Massey [sic], and others, in the Free-trade hall, Manchester, on June 3rd. London, 1863. 8 p.   **Uk**

The last of the three speeches on "The American question," repr. from *Barker's Rev.*, III, (June 13, 1863), 533–536.

1304   [BARKER, JOSEPH]. The American question. A speech delivered at a public meeting, Burnley, in reply to Messrs. Dennison and Sinclair. London, 1863. 8 p.   **Uk**

Repr. from *Barker's Rev.*, III (May 30, 1863), 501–503.

1305   BARKER, JOSEPH. The American question. Mediation, intervention, recognition. A lecture by Mr. Barker at Mossley. [London, 1863]. 8 p.   **NHi Uk**

Caption title; no t.p. Repr. from *Barker's Rev.*, III (June 6, 1863), 517–520.

1306   BARKER, THO[MA]S H. Union and emancipation: a reply to the 'Christian News' article on 'Emancipation and war.' . . . (Reprinted from the Christian News of Sept. 5th and 12th, 1863.) [Manchester, 1863]. 23 p.   **MB MH OCIWHi TxU**

1307   BARRY, MICHAEL JOSEPH. Irish emigration considered. Cork, 1863. 20 p.   **UkLRC**

1308   BASS, CHARLES. Lectures on Canada, illustrating its present position, and shewing forth its onward progress and predictive of its future destiny. Hamilton, 1863. 45 p.

CaOTP MH

Discussion of visit to the U.S., the Civil War, etc., pp. 13–20, 37–42, and passim.

1309   BEECHER, HENRY WARD. American rebellion. Speech of the Rev. Henry Ward Beecher, delivered in the Free trade hall, Manchester, 9th October, 1863. With a report of the proceedings of the meeting. Manchester, [1863]. 25 p.   **MH Uk**

American ed.: *England and America: speech of Henry Ward Beecher at the Free-trade hall, Manchester, October 9, 1863*, Boston, 1863. Repr. in his *American rebellion. Report of the speeches of the Rev. Henry Ward Beecher*, etc., Manchester, 1864, below.

1310   [BERESFORD-HOPE, ALEXANDER JAMES BERESFORD]. The American church in the disruption. London, 1863. 32 p.   **MB Uk**

Contains the pastoral of the bishops of the Episcopal Church in the Confederate States. Repr. from the *Chr. Remembrancer* for January, 1863.

1311   BERESFORD-HOPE, A[LEXANDER] J[AMES] B[ERESFORD]. The social and political bearings of the American disruption. London, 1862. 42 p.   **N Uk**

DLC has 3d ed., London, 1863.

1312   BERNARD, MOUNTAGUE. A lecture on alleged violations of neutrality by England in the present war. London, 1863. 45 p.   **DLC Uk**

1313   BLACKMAN, *REV*. E[DWARD] L[EWIS]. Our relations with America. A reply to the arguments of Mr. Cobden, in the House of Commons, as to the supply of ammunition of war to the belligerents; and of "Historicus" in the "Times," as to our interest in maintaining the Federal pretensions of international polity. Manchester, [1863]. 23 p.

MB NNC OCIWHi Uk

Four letters to the Ipswich *Journal*, Apr. 29–June 18, 1863.

1314   BLACKMAN, *REV*. E[DWARD] L[EWIS]. "Shall we recognize the Confederate States?" The question considered in three letters with reference to our national interest and duty, and to slavery as illustrated in the history of our West Indian possessions. Ipswich, 1863. 24 p.   **OCIWHi Uk**

Repr. from the Ipswich *Journal*.

1315   BRICE, A[LEXANDER] C[HARLES]. Indian cotton supply, the only effectual and permanent measure for relief to Lancashire. London, 1863. 88 p.   **ICU NN PPL Uk**

Comment on conditions in U.S., and comparison with India.

1316   A BRIEF REPLY to an important question; being a letter to Professor Goldwin Smith from an implicit believer in Holy Scripture. London, 1863. 24 p.   **NjP OCIWHi Uk**

Answer to Goldwin Smith's pamphlet, *Does the Bible sanction American slavery?*, 1863, below.

1317   BRITISH AND FOREIGN ANTI-SLAVERY SOCIETY, LONDON. British aid to the confederates. Tracts on slavery in America, No. III. [London, 1863]. 8 p.   **DLC**

Listed under title in most libraries. Tracts I and II, 1862, above. Thomas Binns, chairman, and L. A. Chamerovzow, secretary.

1318   BROWN, F[RANCIS] C[ARNAC]. The supply of cotton from India. Letters by F. C. Brown, Esq. of Tellicherry. Author of "Obstructions to trade in India," "Free trade and the cotton question in India," etc. London, 1863. 40 p.   **Uk**

Eds. pref. signed J.M.L. On growing American cotton in India, shortage of cotton caused by Civil War; references to U.S. throughout.

1319   BROWN, GEORGE. The American war and slavery. Speech of the Hon. George Brown delivered at the anniversary meeting of the Anti-slavery society of Canada, held at Toronto, on Wednesday, February 3, 1863. Manchester, 1863. 16 p.   **NNC OCIWHi Uk**

Repr. in *The life and speeches of Hon. George Brown*, by Alex. Mackenzie, Toronto, 1882, pp. 286–298; also included in this vol. are other speeches, letters, comment on the U.S., passim. See also *George Brown*, by John Lewis (The Makers of Canada, vol. XIX), Toronto 1910: "Against American slavery," pp. 11–119; "The reciprocity treaty of 1874," pp. 223–233, and passim. See also [Wharton Barker], *Letter to George Brown, esq., on the commercial relations between Canada and the United States*, Philadelphia, 1880.

1320   [C., T. E.]. Battle-fields of the South, from Bull Run to Fredericksburg; with sketches of Confederate commanders and gossip of the camps. By an English combatant (lieutenant of artillery on the field staff.) London, 1863. 2 vols.   **DLC Uk**

Dedication signed "T.E.C." Includes letters from other correspondents.

Reviews: *Blackwood's Edinb. Mag.* (by E. B. Hamley), XCIV, 750; *Index*, III, 459.

1321   CAIRD, THOMAS. Cotton supply. Speech in the House of Commons, on Friday, 3rd July, 1863. Westminster, 1863. 16 p.   **NN**

1322   CAIRNES, JOHN ELLIOTT. The Southern Confederacy and the African slave trade. The correspondence between Professor Cairnes, A.M., and George M'Henry, esq. [reprinted from the "Daily News"]. With an introduction and notes by the Rev. George B. Wheeler, A.M. Dublin, 1863. 61 p.   **DLC Uk**

1323   CAIRNES, J[OHN] E[LLIOT]. Who are the canters? London, [1863]. 8 p.   **DLC Uk**

Ladies' London Emancip. Soc., tract no. 3.

1324   CANADA AND INVASION. [n.p., 1863?]. 20 p.   **MiD-B**

1325   CASWALL, *REV*. HENRY. The wrongs and claims of Africans. A sermon, preached in the Abbey church at Sherborne, on the 2d February, 1863. (The purification of the Virgin Mary). London, 1863. 11 p.   **NHi Uk**

On the Civil War in the U.S.

1326   CHEADLE, WALTER BUTLER. Cheadle's journal of trip across Canada, 1862–1863, with introduction and notes by A. G. Doughty and Gustave Lanctot. Ottawa, 1931. 311 p.   **DLC Uk**

The Canada series, vol. 1. On U.S., pp. 27–42, 272–290 (on California), and 300–306. First section noted above repr., with some deletions, in *Cheadle's journal; being the account of the first journey across Canada undertaken for pleasure only by Dr. Cheadle and Lord [William Fitzwilliam] Milton, 1862/1863. Edited by John Gellner. Drawings partly from Dr. Cheadle's own sketches, by Jean Redfern.* Toronto, [1966?].

1327   CHESNEY, CHARLES CORNWALLIS. A military view of recent campaigns in Virginia and Maryland. London, 1863. 230 p.   **Uk**

DLC and Uk have rev. and enlarged ed., London, 1863–65, 2 vols.

1328   CIVIS ANGLICUS [*pseud.*]. A voice from the motherland, answering Mrs. H. Beecher Stowe's appeal. London, 1863. 46 p.   **DLC**

1329   COBBE, FRANCES POWER. The red flag in John Bull's eyes. London, 1863. 24 p.   **DLC Uk**

Ladies' London Emancip. Soc., tract no. 1. See also Cobbe's "The American sanitary commission and its lesson," *Fraser's Mag.*, LXXV (Mar. 1867), 401–414.

1330   [COBBE, FRANCIS POWER]. Rejoinder to Mrs. Stowe's reply to the address of the women of England. London, 1863. 11 p.   **MH NNC Uk**

1331   [COBDEN, RICHARD]. Speech of Mr. Cobden, on the "Foreign enlistment act", in the House of Commons, Friday, April 24, 1863. London, 1863. 25 p.   **DLC Uk**

For two other speeches of the same year, see Cobden's speeches on the "American War"—one to the House of Commons, April 24, 1863, and one to his constituents at Rochdale, Nov. 24, 1863, in his *Speeches on Questions of Public Policy* (eds., John Bright and James E. Thorold Rogers), London, 1870, 2 vols. (Many of Cobden's other speeches have much about the U.S. esp. those on education.) For additional letters on the Civil War see John Atkinson Hobson, *Richard Cobden: the international man*, London, 1919, chap. 12, "The Civil War and the Summer letters," pp. 331–381; and John Morley, *The life of Richard Cobden*, London, 1881, chap. 34, "The American War," pp. 558–592.

1332   CORRESPONDENCE RESPECTING THE "ALABAMA;" also respecting the bark "Maury," at New York, during the Crimean war; and the temporary act of Congress passed by the United States at the instance of Great Britain, in 1838, to meet the case of the rebellion in Canada. [London? 1863?]. 56 p.   **DLC**

Correspondence between Charles Francis Adams and Earl John Russell, and between other Englishmen and Americans.

1333   [CORSAN, W. C.]. Two months in the Confederate states; including a visit to New Orleans under the domination of General Butler. By an English merchant. London, 1863. 299 p.   **DLC**

Uk lists in title index under U.S., but entry is missing.

Reviews: *Home and For. Rev.* (by Lord Acton), III, 323; *Reader* (by Thomas Hughes), I, 424; *Spectator*, XXXVI, 2237.

1334 COWELL, JOHN W[ELSFORD]. Lancashire's wrongs and the remedy: two letters addressed to the cotton operatives of Great Britain. By John W. Cowell, esq., factory commissioner in 1833, for the Lancashire district. London, 1863. 35 p.   **PU Uk**

Signed at end, "John W. Cowell. Cannes (Alpes maritimes in France), Maison Delaup, Route de Grasse, January 7, 1863."

1335 CULL, GEORGE SAMUEL. The youthful travels and adventures of George Samuel Cull, a deaf and dumb cripple . . . including a sketch of seventeen years' residence in England, and five years' travelling through Canada and the United States. Written by himself. Toronto, 1863. 105 p.   **CtY**

CtY copy: "contents at end incomplete".

1336 DAWSON, *SIR* J[OHN] W[ILLIAM]. Further observation on the Devonian plants of Maine, Gaspe, and New York. [London, 1863]. 469 p.   **DLC**

From the *Quar. J. Geol. Soc.*, Nov. 1863.

1337 [DENISON, *CAPT.* GEORGE TAYLOR]. A review of the militia policy of the present administration. By Junius Jr. "O Tempora, O Mores." Hamilton, 1863. 15 p.   **N NcD**

See also his *Soldiering in Canada. Recollections and experiences*, London & Toronto, 1900; and *The struggle for imperial unity. Recollections and experiences*, London, 1909. The latter contains extensive comment throughout on Denison's role and views on the continuing issues of commercial and/or political union with the U.S., and U.S.-British relations.

1338 DICEY, *SIR* EDWARD [JAMES STEPHEN]. Labour and slavery. London, [1863]. 16 p.
        DHU MH NIC

Ladies London Emancip. Soc. Tract. no. 4.

1339 DICEY, *SIR* EDWARD [JAMES STEPHEN]. Six months in the Federal states. London, 1863. 2 vols.   **DLC Uk**

Portions first pub. in the London *Daily Telegraph, Macmillan's Mag.* and the *Spectator*, for which Dicey was special correspondent in 1862. Chicago, 1971 ed., under title *Spectator of America*, ed., with an introd. by Herbert Mitgang. See also the following articles on the U.S. by Dicey: "Social life in the United States," *Victoria Mag.*, I (May 1863), 2–14; "A retrospect of the war," ibid., I (Sept. 1863), 462–473; "Lincolniana," *Macmillans's Mag.*, XII (June 1865), 185–192, repr. in *Mag. of Hist. with Notes & Queries*, Ext. no. 185, 16–27; "Religion in America," *Macmillan's Mag.*, XV (March 1867), 440–448; "American feeling towards England," *Fortnightly Rev.*, XI (June 1869), 704–712; "The Republican defeat in the United States," *Fortnightly Rev.*, XVI (Dec. 1874), 824–835; and "The new American imperialism," *Nineteenth Cent.*, XLIV (Sept. 1898), 487–501. See also John O. Waller, "Edward Dicey and the American Negro in 1862: an English working journalist's view," *Bull. N.Y. Pub. Lib.*, LXVI (1962), 31–45; and Esmond Wright "William Howard Russell and Edward Dicey," in *Abroad in America; visitors to the new land, 1776–1914*, ed. by Marc Pachter, Reading, Mass, 1976, pp. 144–156.

Reviews: *Athenaeum* (May 2, 1863), 582; *Home & For. Rev.*, III, 323; *Reader* (by Thomas Hughes), I, 424, 449; *Spectator*, XXXVI, 1956.

1340 DILL, R[ICHARD]. The American conflict; a lecture. Reprinted from the "Northern Whig" of April 22, 1863. Belfast, 1863. 23 p.   **DLC**

1341 EDGE, FREDERICK MILNES. The destruction of the American carrying trade. A letter to Earl Russell, K.G., Her Majesty's personal secretary of state for the foreign department. London, 1863. 27 p.   **DLC Uk**

Letter dated Nov. 21, 1863.

1342 ELLIS, THOMAS T. Leaves from the diary of an army surgeon; or, Incidents of field, camp, and hospital life. New York, 1863. 312 p.   **DLC Uk**

Ellis, a retired English military surgeon, joined the northern forces as a volunteer during the Civil War.

1343 ESTCOURT, J. H. Rebellion and recognition. Slavery, sovereignty, secession, and recognition considered. Manchester, 1863. 28 p.   **DLC Uk**

1344 FAIRBANKS, CHARLES. The American conflict as seen from a European point of view. A lecture delivered at St. Johnsbury, Vt., June 4, 1863. Boston, 1863. 44 p.   **DLC Uk**

An American on English attitudes.

1345 FALLACIES OF FREEMAN and foes of liberty. A reply to "The American war: the whole question explained." Manchester, 1863. 36 p.   **CSmH ICN MH NIC**

Pub. by the Union and Emancip. Soc., Manchester. See *The American war. The whole question explained*, 1863, above.

1346 FERGUSSON, W. F. Letter to Lord Stanley, on the dearth of cotton, and the capability of India to supply the quantity required. London, 1863. 40 p.   **MB TxU Uk WU**

1347 FERRAND, WILLIAM BUSFIELD. The cotton trade, past and present. Speech in the House of Commons on Monday, April 27, 1863. London, 1863.   **NHi**

DLC and Uk have in Hansard's Parliamentary debates, under date listed above. References to U.S. throughout.

1348 FLETCHER, *REV*. JOSEPH. The American war. A lecture delivered in the town hall, Christchurch, at the request of the Committee of the working men's institute . . . on Thursday evening, November 19, 1863. The Mayor of Christchurch in the chair. Manchester, 1863. 16 p.   **NB OCIWHi**

Review: *Westmin. Rev.*, XXVIII (n.s.), 43.

1349 FORSTER, WILLIAM EDWARD. Speech of Mr. W. E. Forster, M.P., on the slaveholders' rebellion; and Professor Goldwin Smith's letter on the morality of the Emancipation proclamation. Manchester, 1863. 15 p.   **DLC Uk**

1350 FREEMAN, EDWARD AUGUSTUS. History of federal government, from the foundation of the Achaian league to the disruption of the United States. London, 1863. 721 p.

DLC Uk

Contains scattered comment on the U.S. Repr. under title, *History of federal government in Greece and Italy*, ed. by John Bagnall Bury, London, 1893.

1351 FREMANTLE, [*SIR* ARTHUR JAMES LYON]. Three months in the southern states, April–June, 1863. By Lieut.-Col. Fremantle. Edinburgh, 1863. 316 p.   **DLC Uk**

Repr. Boston, [1954] and London, [1956], *The Fremantle diary: being the journal of Lieutenant Colonel James Arthur Lyon Fremantle, Coldstream Guards, on his three months in the southern states. Editing and commentary by Walter Lord; introd. by Maurice Ashly*. A portion of the diary appeared in *Blackwoods Edinb. Mag.*, XCIV (Sept. 1863), pp.

365–394, and in an appendix to Edward Albert Pollard's *The Second year of the war*, Richmond, 1863, pp. 326–374, under the title "The battle of Gettysburg and the campaign in Pennsylvania. Extract from the diary of an English officer present with the Confederate Army." Section of the diary from June 20 to July 15, 1863, repr. in *Two views of Gettysburg, by Sir Arthur J.L. Fremantle and Frank Haskell*, ed. by Richard Harwell, Chicago, 1964. See also Fremantle's letter to the *Times* in George W. Egleston, *Reply to a letter of an English Colonel respecting cruelties sustained by Union soldiers at the hands of the South*, New York, 1866, pp. 4–5.

Reviews: *Blackwood's Edinb. Mag.*, (by E. B. Hamley), XCIV, 750; *Dublin Univ. Mag.*, LXIII, 112, 214; *Index*, III, 523; *Quar. Rev.*, CXV, 289; *Spectator.*, XXXVI, 2886.

1352 FRIENDS, SOCIETY OF, LONDON YEARLY MEETING. From the yearly meeting of the religious Society of Friends held in London, fifth month 1863, to Friends in North America. [n.p., 1863?]. 7 p. **PHC**

1353 [FULLAM, GEORGE TOWNLEY]. The cruise of the "Alabama," from her departure from Liverpool until her arrival at the Cape of Good Hope. By an officer on board. Liverpool, 1863. 48 p. **DLC**

Another ed., printed from a supp. to the *So. African Advertiser and Mail*, Cape Town, Sat., Sept. 19, 1863, under title, *Our cruise on the Confederate states' war steamer Alabama*, [London, 1863?]; and in 1864, *The cruise of the "Alabama." Raphael Sommes, Commander, from her departure from Liverpool July 29, 1862. By an officer on board, with gleanings from other sources*, [n.p.]. Extracts also appeared in *Cornhill Mag.*, LXXV (May 1897), 592–603. From the private journal of the boarding-officer of the Alabama, covering the period from July 29, 1862 to Jan. 20, 1864. Work has also been ascribed to P. D. Haywood.

1354 GARRATT, *REV*. SAMUEL. The Bible and slavery, London, 1863. 44 p.
MiU-C NHi UkENL

On U.S. See also Evelyn R. Garratt, *Life and personal recollections of Samuel Garratt*, London, 1908: a paper by Samuel Garratt on "The present crisis and our duty" (on American slavery), pp. 52–64; and his recollections on the Civil War, 254–262, and "Revival" in the U.S., 274–278.

1355 GIBBS, FREDERICK WAYMOUTH. The Foreign enlistment act. London, 1863. 74 p.
DLC UK

On U.S., pp. 1–51, and passim.

1356 GIBBS, FREDERICK WAYMOUTH. Recognition: a chapter from the history of the North American & South American states. London, 1863. 46 p. **DLC Uk**

Review: *Brit. Quar. Rev.*, XXXVIII, 220.

1357 GODDARD, SAMUEL ASPINWALL. Reply to Mr. [John Arthur] Roebuck's speech at Sheffield, on the American question. [Birmingham, 1863]. 9 p. **MH NNC Uk**

No t.p. Roebuck's speech dated Aug. 1862, by the *Edinb. Rev.*, CXVI, 577.

1358 [GRAVES, RICHARD HASTINGS]. Some remarks on slavery as established in the Confederate States of America—privately and respectfully addressed to those journalists who support the United church of England and Ireland. [Mitchelstown, 1863].
ICN OCIWHi

No t.p.; priv. pr. Signed by Graves, D.D., Brigoun, Glebe, Mitchelstown, Dec., 1863.

1359 HAIG, *CAPT*. FELIX THACKERAY. Notes on the river navigations of North America. Madras, 1863. 99 p. **DLC Uk**

1360 HALL, [*REV*. CHRISTOPHER] NEWMAN. The pro-slavery religion of the South. To the editors of "Good Words," "The Evangelical Magazine," and other religious periodicals which have admitted the appeal from the clergy of the Confederate states. [Manchester, 1863]. 2 p. **IU MH**

No t.p.; pub. by the Union and Emancip. Soc., Manchester. Signed by Newman Hall and dated Surrey Chapel, London, Aug. 6, 1863.

1361 [HALL, *REV*. CHRISTOPHER NEWMAN]. A reply to the pro-slavery wail, which issued forth last month. [London? 1863?]. 15 p. **NHi OO**

1362 [HARCOURT, *SIR* WILLIAM GEORGE GRANVILLE VENABLES VERNON]. Belligerent rights of maritime capture. By Historicus [*pseud*.]. Liverpool, 1863. 22 p.
DLC Uk

Originally appeared in the London *Times*; repr. in *Additional letters by Historicus on some questions of international law*, London, 1863.

1363 [HARCOURT, *SIR* WILLIAM GEORGE GRANVILLE VENABLES VERNON]. Letters by Historicus [*pseud*.] on some questions of international law. Reprinted from '*The Times*' with considerable additions. London, 1863. 212 p. **DLC Uk**

For an account of Harcourt's writing of the letters, see Alfred George Gardiner's *The Life of Sir William Harcourt*, London, 1923, pp. 125–207. See also the following replies to the letters: Juridicus [Millard Fillmore], *The recognition of the Confederate states considered in a reply to the letters of "Historicus" in the London Times*, Charleston, S.C., 1863; and Charles Greely Loring, *England's liability for indemnity: remarks on the letter of "Historicus" dated November 4th, 1863; printed in the London "Times", November 7th; and reprinted in the "Boston daily advertiser", November 25th*, Boston, 1864.

1364 THE HISTORY OF A COTTON BALE. London, [1863]. 12 p. **Uk**
On cotton planting along the Mississippi.

1365 HOLE, *REV*. J[OHN] E[LDON] and *REV*. J[OHN] M[ASON] NEALE. "North and South." Letters to "The Guardian," (a church of England paper published in London), by the Revs. J. E. Hole, and J. M. Neale, on the subject of "North and South," with replies by the Rev. of the diocese of C.W. [Canada West], recently a presbyter of the Protestant Episcopal church in the Confederate States of America. [n.p.], 1863. **ICN MdBJ PPL**

1366 HOME, D[ANIEL] D[UNGLAS]. Incidents in my life. London, 1863. 288 p. **DLC Uk**
Lived in U.S. from age 9 to 22; see pp. 17–94, 149–163, and passim. Various eds. appeared; an enlarged ed. appeared New York, 1872, 374 p. Uk indicates holding is Series 1 & 2, London, 1863–72. For additional comment on the U.S., see author's *Lights and shadows of spiritualism*, London, 1877.

1367 [HOPLEY, CATHERINE COOPER]. Life in the South; from the commencement of the war. By a blockaded British subject. Being a social history of those who took part in the battles, from a personal acquaintance with them in their own homes. From the spring of 1860 to August, 1862. London, 1863. 2 vols. **DLC Uk**

Pref. signed, "S. L. J." i.e., Sarah L. Jones, *pseud*.

Review: *Athenaeum*, (April 18, 1863), 521.

1368   [HOPLEY, CATHERINE COOPER]. "Stonewall" Jackson, late general of the Confederate States army. A biographical sketch, and an outline of his Virginian campaigns. By the author of "Life in the South." London, 1863. 178 p.   **DLC Uk**

1369   HOW TO MAKE INDIA TAKE THE PLACE of America as our cotton field. Communicated to the Economist. London, 1863.

No locations found. From the *Economist* XXI (Apr. 11, 1863), 396–397.

1370   HUGHES, THOMAS. The cause of freedom: which is its champion in America, the North or the South? (Being a speech delivered by him at Exeter hall on the 29th of January, 1863). [London, 1863]. 16 p.   **DLC Uk**

See author's "Opinion on American affairs," *Macmillan's Mag.*, IV (Sept. 1861), 414; and "Peace on earth," ibid., XIII (Dec. 1865), 195–201, (also in *Old South Leaflets*, no. 181, Boston, 1907). Hughes was also special London correspondent of the New York *Tribune*, Sept.–Dec. 1866, and wrote numerous articles on America.

1371   HUNT, JAMES. On the negro's place in nature. London, 1863. 60 p.   **MH NN Uk**

DLC has New York, 1864 ed., 27 p. Read before the Anthropological Society of London, Nov. 17, 1863. Also repr. as Anti-abolition tract no. 4, New York, 1866.

1372   INGRAM, JOHN KELLS. Considerations on the state of Ireland: being an address delivered before the Statistical and Social Inquiry Society of Ireland, at the opening of the seventeenth session, on Wednesday, November 18, 1863. Dublin, 1863. 20 p.   **NN**

Uk has 2d ed. to which is added *With an appendix, containing a comparison of the English and Irish poor laws with respect to the conditions of relief*, Dublin, 1864, 35 p. Also appeared in the *J. Stat. & Social Inquiry Soc. of Ireland*, IV (1864–66), 13–26. On emigration to America, etc.

1373   JONES, ERNEST [CHARLES]. The slaveholder's war. A lecture delivered in the Town hall, Ashton-under-Lyne . . . on Monday, November 16th, 1863. Hugh Mason, esq., in the chair. Ashton-under-Lyne, [1863]. 44 p.   **MH Uk**

Another ed., Manchester, 1863.

1374   KEEFER, THO[MA]S C[OLTRIN]. A sketch of the rise and progress of the reciprocity treaty; with an explanation of the services rendered in connection therewith. Toronto, 1863. 34 p.   **CaOTP NNC**

1375   KEMBLE, FRANCIS ANNE (BUTLER). Journal of a residence on a Georgian plantation in 1838–1839. London, 1863. 434 p.   **DLC Uk**

Critical ed., with extensive notes, ed. by John A. Scott, New York, 1961; Chicago, 1969 ed. with foreword by Jean-Louis Brindamour, repr. of New York, 1864 ed. Selections, together with correspondence with her American publisher, issued as *The views of Judge Woodward and Bishop Hopkins on Negro slavery at the South, illustrated from the 'Journal of a residence on a Georgian plantation'*, Philadelphia, 1863; selections also appeared under title *The essence of slavery*, ed. by Isa Craig, London, 1863. The *Journal* was written during 4 months on the island plantation of her American husband, Pierce Butler, but not revised and pub. until long after their divorce. Also see her "A winter's tour to Georgia, U.S.," *Bentley's Misc.*, XII (1842), 1–13, 113–123. Kemble had taken up permanent residence in the U.S. in 1848, remaining about 30 years. She returned to England in 1877, and subsequently pub. three books of recollections and letters: *Records of a girlhood*, London, 1878, based on a series of 21 articles for the *Atlantic*, Aug. 1875–Apr. 1877, under the title "Old woman's gossip"; *Records of later life*, London, 1882, covering the period 1834–1848; and *Further records. 1848–1883*, London, 1890. See also *Fanny the American Kemble: her journals and unpublished letters*, ed. and annot. by Fanny Kemble Wister, Tallahassee, 1972.

See also the following biographies: Una Pope-Hennessy, *Three English women in America*, London, 1921; Dorothy Bobbe, *Fanny Kemble*, New York, 1931; Leota S. Driver, *Fanny Kemble*, Chapel Hill, 1938; Margaret Armstrong, *Fanny Kemble, a passionate Victorian*, New York, 1938; Henry Gibbs, *Affectionately yours, Fanny*, London, 1947; Robert Rushmore, *Fanny Kemble*, New York, 1970; Constance Wright, *Fanny Kemble and the lovely land*, New York, 1972; and Dorothy Marshall, *Fanny Kemble*, London, 1977. See also the following articles: Janet Stevenson, "A woman's place," *Am. Heritage*, XIX (1968), 6–11, 96–102; and Robert Wernick "Glamorous actress found no glamour in slavery," *Smithsonian*, V (1974), 74–81.

Reviews: *Athenaeum* (June 6, 1863), 737; *Atlantic*, XII, 260; *Brit. Quar. Rev.* XXXVII (July 1863), 244; *Harper's Mag.*, XXVII, 416; *London Rev.*, V (June 6, 1863), 608; *No. Am. Rev.*, XCVII, 582; *Sat. Rev.*, XV (June 13, 1863), 768; *Spectator*, LVI (May 30, 1863), 53. See also Mildred E. Lombard, "Contemporary opinions of Mrs. Kemble's *Journal of a residence on a Georgian plantation*," *Georgia Hist. Quar.*, XIV (1930), 335–343. For reviews of the 1961 Scott edition, see *Georgia Hist. Quar.*, XLVI, 208; and *J. Negro Hist.*, XLVI, 261.

1376   KENNEDY, *REV*. JOHN. Hebrew servitude and American slavery: an attempt to prove that the Mosaic law furnishes neither a basis nor an apology for American slavery. London, 1863. 60 p. **DLC Uk**

Review: *Brit. & For. Evang. Rev.*, (By "H."), XII, 801.

1377   [KING, A.]. British sympathy in the American crisis. A letter on the address of the Protestant pastors of France to Christian ministers of all denominations in Great Britain and Ireland. By an Irishman. Dublin, 1863. 15 p. **DLC**

1378   L., E. Notes on American affairs. London, 1863. 30 p. **DLC**

1379   [LAWRENCE, GEORGE ALFRED.]. Border and Bastille. By the author of "Guy Livingstone." London, [1863]. 277 p. **ICU MH PSC TU**

DLC has 2d ed., rev., London, 1863; Uk has 3d ed., London, 1863. Experiences of an Englishman captured while attempting to join the Confederate army.

Review: *Index*, III, 299.

1380   [LEHMANN, AUGUSTUS FREDERICK]. Memories of half a century, a record of friendships; compiled and edited by R[udolph] C[hambers] Lehmann. London, 1908. 362 p. **DLC Uk**

Listed in both DLC and Uk under Rudolph Chambers Lehmann. Augustus Lehmann made frequent visits to the U.S. between 1852 and 1863; Part II, "American Memories," pp. 269–354. See also John Lehmann's *Ancestors and friends*, Spotteswode, 1962, "Frederick in America," pp. 235–266.

1381   LENG, [*SIR*] WILLIAM C[HRISTOPHER]. The American war: the aims, antecedents, and principles of the belligerents. A lecture, delivered on the 10th December, 1862, in Castle street church. Dundee, 1863. 38 p. **DLC Uk**

Leng also wrote leaders for the Dundee *Advertiser*; for a discussion see David C. Carrie, *Dundee and the American civil war, 1861–65*, [Dundee, 1953].

1382   LEWIS, *SIR* GEORGE CORNEWALL, *2d bart*. A dialogue on the best form of government. London, 1863. 117 p. **DLC Uk**

On U.S., pp. 60–117.

Reviews: *Home & For. Rev.*, (by Lord Acton), II, 651; *Quar. Rev.*, CLII, 518.

1383   LINDSAY, WILLIAM SCHAW. Letter to Lord [John] Russell on belligerent rights, with reference to merchant shipping; and the reply thereto. London, [1863]. 6 p.   **RPB Uk**

1384   LUDLOW, J[OHN] M[ALCOM] [FORBES]. The Southern minister and his slave-convert. A dialogue. Manchester, [1863?]. 4 p.   **MH**

Repr. from *Good Words*, (1863), 616–618.

1385   MCGEE, THOMAS D'ARCY. The present American revolution. The internal condition of the American democracy considered, in a letter from the Hon. Thomas D'Arcy M'Gee . . . to the Hon. Charles Gavan Duffy. London, 1863. 19 p.   **DLC**

See also McGee's article, "Some observations on the internal condition of the American democracy," *Nation*, March 22, 1862, p. 473–474.

1386   MAGUIRE, JOHN FRANCIS. Father Mathew: a biography. London, 1863. 55 p.

    DLC Uk

Abridged version ed. by Rosa Mulholland, Dublin, [1890?], 228 p. On Theobald Mathew's tour of the U.S., 1849–51, pp. 460–518; other comment on America, passim. For other discussions of his American visit see Samuel R. Wells, *Father Mathew, the temperance apostle: his character and biography*, New York, [1867]; Henry Wilson, *Father Mathew the temperance apostle. An address before the Monument association of New York, March, 1873*, New York, 1873, pp. 15–19; Frank J. Mathew, *Father Mathew. His life and times*, London, 1890, pp. 169–202; *The Father Mathew Man. May, 1923–January, 1925, Nos. 1 to 20, Inclusive*, New York, [1925?] (a temperance leaflet pub. monthly, containing scattered references to the U.S.); Rev. Patrick Rogers, *Father Theobald Mathew, apostle of temperance. . . . With an introduction by the Right Rev. David Mathew . . . and a foreword by the Very Rev. Father James*, New York, 1945, pp. 120–140; Rev. Father Augustine, *Footprints of Father Theobald Mathew, O.F.M. CAP. Apostle of temperance*, Dublin, 1947, pp. 485–522. See also *Remarks of Hon. H[enry], S[tuart] Foote, of Mississippi, in the senate, December 10, 1849, on the resolution to permit the Rev. Theobald Mathew to sit within the bar of the senate*, [n.p., n.d.], pp. 1–3.

1387   MALET, *REV.* WILLIAM WYNDHAM. An errand to the South in the summer of 1862. London, 1863. 312 p.   **DLC**

Reviews: *Sat. Rev.*, XVI, 28; *Spectator.*, XXXVI, 2237.

1388   MARK, W[ILLIA]M. Cariboo: a true and correct narrative by Wm. Mark. Containing an account of his travel over ten thousand miles, by sea, rivers, lakes and land, to the Cariboo gold diggings, British Columbia. Stockton [Eng.], 1863. 34 p.   **CtY**

Considerable comment on New York, San Francisco, etc.

1389   MASON, GEORGE HOLDITCH. The cotton question and colonisation. Norwich, 1863.

No locations found.

1390   MASSIE, [*REV.*] JAMES W[ILLIAM]. The case stated: the friends and enemies of the American slave. Manchester, 1863. 8 p.   **DLC UkLGI**

Pub. by the Union & Emancip. Soc., Manchester.

1391   MASSIE, *REV.* J[AMES] W[ILLIAM]. International sympathies. Report of the farewell meeting for Rev. J. W. Massie, D. D., of London, at the Broadway Tabernacle church, New York, September 27, 1863. New York, 1863. 31 p.   **DLC**

Speech of Dr. Massie, pp. 16–27; also account of his visit to the U.S. with Rev. J. H. Rylance, of St. Paul's, Westminster, to present the "Address to ministers and pastors. . . ." Signed by 4,000 British ministers.

1392   [MAXSE, FREDERICK AUGUSTUS]. Pro patria: being a letter addressed by Captain Maxse, R.N., to the "Morning Post" upon the subject of our American attitude. London, 1863. 8 p.   **DLC**

1393   [MERCER, CHARLES FENTON]. The weakness and inefficiency of the government of the United States of North America; by a late American statesman. Ed. by a member of the Middle Temple, London. London, 1863. 382 p.   **DLC Uk**

See introd. pp. vii–xii, in which the pro-Confederate British editor states that this work, originally written in 1845?, was suppressed by its American author. It is a repr., however, of the priv. pr. *An exposition of the weakness and inefficiency of the government of the United States of North America*, [n.p.], 1845, 380 p.

1394   MERRITT, W[ILLIAM] H[AMILTON]. Journal of events principally on the Detroit and Niagara frontiers, during the war of 1812. By Capt. W. H. Merritt, of the prov. light dragoons. St. Catharines, C.W., 1863. 82 p.   **DLC**

See also Jedediah Prendergast Merritt, *Biography of the Hon. W. H. Merritt, M.P., of Lincoln, District of Niagara, including an account of the origin, progress and completion of some of the most important public works in Canada. Compiled principally from his original diary and correspondence*, St. Catharines, 1875, 429 p. (held by DLC). For additional material on W. H. Merritt see Hugh G. J. Aitken, *The Welland Canal Company; a study in Canadian enterprise*, Cambridge [Mass.], 1954. For other works by W. H. Merritt see above, 1845, 1847 and 1855.

1395   MIALL, CHARLES S. The proposed slave empire: its antecedents, constitution, and policy. London, 1863. 32 p.   **DLC Uk**

Review: *Brit. Quar. Rev.*, XXXVIII, 220.

1396   MILLER, MARMADUKE. Slavery and the American war; a lecture. Manchester, [1863]. 46 p.   **ICN MH NIC**

Uk has a copy dated Manchester, [1865]. Pub. by the Union & Emancip. Soc., Manchester.

1397   [MONK, HENRY WENTWORTH]. An appeal to the American people and a protest against the American people: together with three letters in reference to the great American question, peace or war. Toronto, 1863. 11 p.   **DLC**

1398   MORNING STAR. Great demonstration of trade's unionists of London to express sympathy with the Northern States of America and in favor of negro emancipation. [London?], 1863.   **UkLSE**

1399   MORTON, E. J. The American war, and the conflict of principles therein involved. Halifax, 1863. 16 p.   **MoU MsU PPL**

1400   THE NEGRO; or, The crimes and the recompence of the North and South. Manchester, 1863. 16 p.   **NHi NNC**

1401   NEWMAN, F[RANCIS] W[ILLIAM]. Character of the southern states of America. Letter to a friend who had joined the Southern independence association . . . . Manchester, 1863. 14 p.   **DLC Uk**

See also author's *Miscellanies; chiefly addresses, academical and historical*, London, 1869–1891, 5 vols.: "Example of American administration" (from the *Westmin. Rev.*, Apr. 1855), III, pp. 1–12; and "Charles Sumner's Alabama speech" (from the London *Morning*

Star, May 11, 1868), III, pp. 195–197. Vol. III has t.p., *Miscellanies, vol. III. Essays, tracts or addresses, political and social*, London, 1889.

Review: *Sat. Rev.* (by J. F. Stephen), XVII, 11.

1402   NEWMAN, F[RANCIS] W[ILLIAM]. The good cause of President Lincoln. A lecture by Professor F. W. Newman. [London, 1863]. 24 p.   **DLC Uk**

Repr. in his *Anglo-Saxon abolition of Negro slavery*, London, 1889, pp. 109–136.

1403   NOEL, *HON*. AND *REV*. WRIOTHESLEY. Freedom and slavery in the United States of America. London, 1863. 242 p.   **CU MH NIC Uk**

1404   NOEL, *HON*. AND *REV*. WRIOTHESLEY. The rebellion in America. London, 1863. 494 p.   **DLC Uk**

Review: *Dublin Univ. Mag.*, LXIII, 112.

1405   ONESIMUS SECUNDUS, *pseud*. The true interpretation of the American civil war, and of England's cotton difficulty; or, Slavery, from a different point of view, shewing the relative responsibilities of America and Great Britain. London, 1863. 47 p.   **DLC Uk**

1406   OZANNE, T. D. The South as it is; or, Twenty-one years' experience in the southern states of America. London, 1863. 306 p.   **DLC Uk**

By an English clergyman who lived in the South from 1841 to 1862, and in Philadelphia for five years before that.

1407   PARKER, *REV*. JOSEPH. American war and American slavery. A speech delivered . . . in the Free trade hall, Manchester, on Wednesday, June 3, 1863. Thomas Bayley Potter, esq., in the chair. Manchester, 1863. 8 p.   **DLC Uk**

Pub. by the Union and Emancip. Soc., Manchester.

1408   POPE, SAMUEL. The American war: secession and slavery. A lecture . . . delivered at Tunstall, Staffordshire. Manchester, 1863. 16 p.   **DLC**

Union and Emancip. Soc., Manchester, tract no. 1; repr. from the Staffordshire *Sentinel* of Jan. 17, 1863.

1409   POPE, SAMUEL. Legal view of the "Alabama" case, and ship building for the Confederates; speech at the public meeting in Free Trade Hall, Manchester, on Monday, April 6, 1863. Manchester, 1863. 8 p.   **MH OCIWHi Uk**

Pub. by the Union and Emancip. Soc., Manchester.

1410   A PROTOCOL for the settlement of the strife in North America, February, 1863. London, [1863]. 4 p.   **Uk**

Uk lists under America, North.

1411   RECOGNITION OF THE SOUTHERN CONFEDERACY, indispensable for resolving the American question. London, 1863.   **NN OCIWHi**

Uk lists in title index to U.S.A., but main entry omitted.

1412   REFUTATION OF FALLACIOUS ARGUMENTS anent the American question. London, 1863. 8 p.   **CSmH DS MB Uk**

1413   REMARKS ON THE POLICY of recognizing the independence of the southern states of North America, and on the struggle in that continent. By Nemo [*pseud*.]. London, 1863. 31 p.   **DLC Uk**

1414   [RUSSELL, JOHN RUSSELL, *1st earl*]. Earl Russell and the slave power. Manchester, 1863. 11 p.   **DLC Uk**

Sabin lists as *Earl Russell and the slave trade*. Issued by the executive of the Union and Emancip. Soc., Manchester. For Russell's remarks on the Treaty of Washington see his *Recollections and suggestions, 1813–1873*, London, 1875, pp. 393–407. For various comments on the U.S. and its affairs see the following: *Selections from speeches of Earl Russell 1817 to 1841, and from despatches, 1859 to 1865*, London, 1870, II, pp. 491–499, a despatch to Adams, Nov. 3, 1865; Spencer Walpole, *The Life of Lord John Russell*, London, 1889, vol. II, pp. 338–367, and passim; Stuart J. Reid, *Lord John Russell*, New York, 1895, pp. 310–319; George Peabody Gooch, ed., *The later correspondence of Lord John Russell, 1840–1878*, London, 1925, II, pp. 317–336, and passim; A. Wyatt Tilby, *Lord John Russell: a study in civil and religious liberty*, London, 1930, pp. 189–225; Paul Knaplund, ed., *Letters from Lord Sydenham, governor-general of Canada, 1839–1841, to Lord John Russell*, London, [1931]. See also Russell's speech before Congress and three letters from him in *Letter from George Bancroft, esq., directed to Hon. E. B. Washburne, chairman, etc., transmitting correspondence with Earl Russell relative to a portion of the memorial address on Abraham Lincoln, delivered before both houses of Congress*, [Washington, D.C., 1866]; and see Thomas Butler King, *Letter to Lord John Russell*, London, 1861 (repr. in *Commercial relations between the confederate states and England*, Mobile, 1862).

1415   [RUSSELL, WILLIAM H. C.?]. Running the blockade. By Lieut. [Robert] Warneford, R.N. [*pseud.*], author of "Tales of the coast guard," "Cruise of the blue jacket," etc. etc. London, 1863. 315 p.   **CtY ICN Uk**

NUC notes that the pseudonym has been attributed to A. C. Gunter and C. P. Morgan, as well as W. H. C. Russell. Work contains semi-fictionalized accounts by various English skippers; violently pro-South.

1416   RUSSELL, *SIR* WILLIAM HOWARD. My diary North and South. London, 1863. 2 vols.
                                                                          DLC Uk

Uk lists as London, 1863–65, 3 vols., including his *Canada; its defences, condition, and resources*, 1865, below, which continued the account. The diary covers the period Mar. 16, 1861–Apr. 1862, and follows closely the letters printed in the London *Times*. Portions had appeared earlier in his *The civil war in America*, 1861, above. For an American retort to "Bull-run Russell," see Andrew Dickson White's *A letter to William Howard Russell, LL.D., on passages in his "Diary North and South,"* London, 1863. See also the American *Train on Russell. The American champion & the English libeller*, [n.p., n.d.]. Also see Russell's *The Atlantic Telegraph*, [1865, below]; and his "Recollections of the Civil War," *No. Am. Rev.*, CLXVI (1898), 234–249, 362–373, 491–502, 618–630, 740–750. For accounts of the 1861 visit to America, see John Black Atkins, *The life of Sir William Howard Russell, C.V.O., LL.D. The first special correspondent*, London, 1911, II, pp. 1–115 (review in New Zealand *Military J.*, by B. W., II (Apr. 1913), 197–209, q.v.); and Esmond Wright, "William Howard Russell and Edward Dicey," in *Abroad in America: visitors to the new nation, 1776–1914*, ed. by Marc Pachter, Reading, Mass., 1976, pp. 144–156.

Reviews: *Atlantic*, (by J. R. Lowell), XI, 391; *Athenaeum*, (Dec. 1862, ii), 798; *Chr. Examiner*, LXXIV, 309; *Index*, II, 140; London *American*, Jan. 28, 1863, p. 4; London *Times*, Feb. 4, 1863, p. 4; *No. Am. Rev.*, XCVI, 578; *Quar. Rev.*, CXIII, 322; *Reader*, I, 11; *Spectator*, XXXV, 1448.

1417   RUSSIA, AMERICA, FRANCE, AND ENGLAND, passing through the fire to Mars, Moloch, and Mammon. By the author of The Great slave show, Black and White, &c. &c. Edinburgh, 1863. **Uk**

Some comment on U.S.

1418   THE SEIZURE OF THE "PETERHOFF"; being a statement of the facts, the reason, the law and the consequences. With the correspondence. London, 1863. 32 p. **DLC Uk**

DLC, Uk both list under Peterhoff. See also *The United States vs. the steamer Peterhoff and her cargo*, New York, 1864.

1419   [SELBORNE, ROUNDELL PALMER, *1st earl*]. Speech of Sir Roundell Palmer delivered in the House of Commons on the "Alabama" question on Friday, March 11, 1863. London, 1863. **CSmH Uk**

See also an American response to Selborne's later speech: George Bemis, *Precedents of American neutrality, in reply to the speech of Sir Roundell Palmer in the British House of Commons, May 13, 1863*, Boston, 1864; and the review of Bemis's views, *Chr. Examiner*, LXXVII, 239.

1420   [SEWELL, *MRS*. MARY (WRIGHT)]. An appeal to Englishwomen. By the author of "Mother's last words." [London, 1863]. 4 p. **Uk**

On slavery in the U.S.

1421   SHANKS, *REV*. G. H. Freedom and slavery: an explanation of the principles & issues involved in the American conflict; and the duty of the people of Britain in relation to that momentous struggle. Belfast, [1863]. 63 p. **NHi NIC**

1422   SIMPSON, JOHN HAWKINS. Horrors of the Virginian slave trade and of the slave-rearing plantations. The true story of Dinah, an escaped Virginian slave, now in London, on whose body are eleven scars left by tortures which were inflicted by her master, her own father. Together with extracts from the laws of Virginia, showing that against these barbarities the law gives not the smallest protection to the slave, but the reverse. London, 1863. 64 p. **DLC Uk**

1423   THE SLAVERY QUARREL; with plans and prospects of reconciliation. By a poor peacemaker. London, 1863. 51 p. **OCIWHi Uk**

Dedicated to Carlyle.

1424   SMITH, GOLDWIN. Does the Bible sanction American slavery? Cambridge, 1863. 107 p. **DLC Uk**

1425   SMITH, SAMUEL. The cotton trade of India, being a series of letters written from Bombay in the Spring of 1863. London, 1863. 67 p. **DLC Uk**

On U.S., pp. 61–67, and passim. See also scattered comments on America in author's *Bimetallic money . . . a paper read before the society for the reform and codification of the law of nations, on the 15th August, 1879*, Liverpool, 1879; repr. with four other pamphlets by Smith, all of which include incidental references to the U.S., in *The bimetallic question*, London, 1887. Some comment also in Smith's *Bimetallism. Speech of Samuel Smith, esq., M.P. in the House of Commons, June 4th, 1889*, Manchester, 1889.

1426   "SOUTHERN RECOGNITION" and "real emancipation". Manchester, 1863. 2 p. **DS MH**

No t.p.; pub. by Union and Emancip. Soc., Manchester. DS lists under the Society.

1427 SPENCE, JAMES. Southern independence: an address delivered at a public meeting, in the city hall, Glasgow, by James Spence, 26th November, 1863. London, 1863. 39 p.
DLC Uk

1428 STOCK, *REV*. JOHN. The duties of British Christians in relation to the struggle in America; being the substance of a discourse delivered in Morice square Baptist chapel, Davenport . . . 7th June, 1863. London, 1863. 28 p. **DLC**
Pub. by request with additional notes.

1429 STODDARD, ARTHUR FRANCIS. Slavery or freedom in America; or, The issue of the war. A lecture delivered in Paisley, January 28, 1863. Glasgow, 1863. 64 p. **DLC Uk**

1430 STRATHEDEN, WILLIAM FREDERICK CAMPBELL, *2d baron*. Speech of Lord Campbell in the House of Lords, on the right of the neutral powers to acknowledge the southern confederacy, March 23, 1863. London, 1863. 28 p. **DLC Uk**

1431 [TENNANT, CHARLES]. The American question, and how to settle it. Canada. North South free trade. London, 1863. 313 p. **DLC Uk**
Review: *Westmin. Rev.*, LXXIX, 302.

1432 THOMAS, *REV*. ALFRED C. Prayerful sympathy invoked for America. A sermon preached at Cross street chapel, Islington, England, on Sunday, December 21st, 1862. Philadelphia, 1863. 32 p. **DLC**

1433 [THOMPSON, HENRY YATES]. An Englishman in the American Civil War; the diaries of Henry Yates Thompson, 1863. Edited by Sir Christopher Chancellor. Preface by W. M. Whitehill. London, 1971. 185 p. **DLC Uk**

1434 TREMLETT, *REV*. F[RANCIS] W[ILLIAM]. Christian brotherhood: its claims and duties, with a special reference to the fratricidal war in America. A sermon preached in St. Peter's church, Belsize park, London, on the 1st November, 1863. London, 1863. 16 p.
OCIWHi Uk

1435 TRIMBLE, ROBERT. The negro, North and South: the status of the coloured population in the northern and southern states of America compared. London, 1863. 34 p. **DLC Uk**

1436 TRIMBLE, ROBERT. Popular fallacies relating to the American question. A lecture, delivered in November, 1863. London, 1863. 36 p. **DLC**

1437 TRIMBLE, ROBERT. Slavery in the United States of North America. A lecture delivered in Liverpool, December, 1861. London, 1863. 31 p. **DLC Uk**

1438 TROLLOPE, ANTHONY. The present condition of the northern states of the American union. London, [1863?]. 32 p.
No holding found for original ed. DLC and Uk have repr. in *Anthony Trollope: Four lectures: The civil service as a profession (1861); The present condition of the northern states of the American union (1862 or 1863); Higher education of women (1868); On English prose fiction as a rational amusement (1870). Printed verbatim from the original texts. Edited with collations, notes, etc., by Morris L. Parish*, London, [1938].

1439 TWELVETREES, HARPER, *Ed*. The story of the life of John Anderson, the fugitive slave. Edited by Harper Twelvetrees, M.A., chairman of the John Anderson committee. London, 1863. 182 p. **DLC Uk**

Uk catalogs under Anderson. See esp. proceedings of meetings during Anderson's visits to Canada (pp. 43–53) and England (pp. 85–124, 147–179); also extensive quotes from Canadian and British press and antislavery activists, passim.

1440   TWISS, *SIR* TRAVERS. The law of nations considered as independent political communities. On the rights and duties of nations in time of war. Oxford, 1861–1863. 2 vols.
DLC Uk

On U.S.: I, pp. 53–56, 166–188; II, a few scattered comments.

Review: *Edinb. Rev.*, CXV, 258.

1441   VIGNE, G[ODFREY] T[HOMAS]. Travels in Mexico, South America, etc. etc. London, 1863. 2 vols.   **DLC Uk**

On U.S., I, pp. 100–176.

1442   WARSHIPS FOR THE SOUTHERN CONFEDERACY: report of public meeting in the Free-trade hall, Manchester; with letter from Professor Goldwin Smith to the "Daily News." Manchester, 1863. 36 p.   **DLC Uk**

Pub. by the Union and Emancip. Soc., Manchester.

1443   WIGHAM, ELIZA. The anti-slavery cause in America and its martyrs. London, 1863. 168 p.   **DLC Uk**

1444   WILKS, WASHINGTON. English criticism on President Lincoln's anti-slavery proclamation & message. [London, 1863]. 8 p.   **DLC**

Uk has London, 1864 ed.

1445   WILLIAMS, MAURICE. The cotton trade of 1861 and 1862. With a glance at the course of events for the first 2 months of 1863, and the future prospects for the year . . . Liverpool, 1863. 36 p.   **CtY Uk**

See also *The cotton trade of Europe. 1866. Maurice Williams & Co. Liverpool, January 1st, 1867*, Liverpool, [1867], 26 p.

1446   WORDEN, JOHN. The plain English of American affairs. London, 1863. 63 p.   **DLC**

1447   THE WORKING MEN OF MANCHESTER and President Lincoln. [Manchester, 1863?]. 4 p.   **DLC**

Tract no. 2 of the Union and Emancip. soc., Manchester; DLC lists under the Society. Repr. from the Manchester *Guardian*, Jan. 1, 1863, of "Address from working men to President Lincoln"; at a public meeting, Dec. 31, 1862, addressed by Thomas Bazley, Thomas B. Potter, Samuel Pope, Dr. John Watts, and six working men. Also includes Lincoln's reply and newspaper comment. Later repr. ed. by F. Hourani, under title, *Manchester and Abraham Lincoln; a side-light on an earlier fight for freedom*, [Manchester, 19—?].

1448   YATES, EDWARD. A letter to the women of England, on slavery in the southern states of America; considered especially in reference to the condition of the female slaves, most of the facts from the observation of the author while travelling in the South. London, 1863. 68 p.   **CSmH MH NN Uk**

DLC has New York, 1863 ed.

1864

1449   ABRAHALL, JOHN HOSKYNS-, *jun*. Western woods and waters: poems and illustrative notes. By John Hoskyns-Abrahall, Jun., M.A. With map and frontispiece. London, 1864. 419 p.   **DLC Uk**

On U.S., passim; appendix is entitled "Authorities," a bibliography of Indian and Great Lakes materials used by author, pp. 402–406.

1450   ANDERSON, WILLIAM JAMES. The gold fields of the world, our knowledge of them, and its application to the gold fields of Canada. Quebec, 1864. 46 p.   **CSmH Uk**

On U.S., pp. 15–22.

1451   ANENT THE NORTH AMERICAN CONTINENT. London, 1864. 15 p.   **DLC Uk**

1452   ARNOLD, *SIR* R[OBERT] ARTHUR. The history of the cotton famine from the fall of Sumter to the passing of the public works act. London, 1864. 570 p.   **NcD Uk**

1453   ASHWORTH, HENRY. International maritime law and its effects upon trade. By Henry Ashworth, esq., president of the Manchester chamber of commerce. Read before the National association for the promotion of social science, at their annual meeting held at York, September, 1864. Manchester, 1864. 13 p.   **DLC UkLGI**

On the "Alabama" and "Georgia" controversy.

1454   BATCHELER, *CAPT*. HORACE [i.e., HORATIO] P[ETTUS]. Jonathan at home; or, A stray shot at the Yankees. London, 1864. 287 p.   **DLC Uk**

Horace on t.p.; DLC lists Horatio.

1455   [BAYMAN, *MRS*. A. PHELPS]. Notes and letters on the American war. By an English lady. London, 1864. 82 p.   **DLC Uk**

Edited by "J. O." to whom the letters are addressed. They were written in answer to articles by A. J. Beresford-Hope in the *Guardian*. Letters dated July 15, 1862–March 2, 1864.

1456   BEECHER, HENRY WARD. American rebellion. Report of the speeches of the Rev. Henry Ward Beecher, delivered at public meetings in Manchester, Glasgow, Edinburgh, Liverpool, and London; and at the farewell breakfasts in London, Manchester, and Liverpool. Manchester, 1864. 175 p.   **DLC Uk**

Pub. by the Union and Emancip. Soc., Manchester; includes speeches and remarks by English speakers, passim. Later pub. as *Speeches of Rev. Henry Ward Beecher on the American rebellion, delivered in Great Britain in 1863. Revised and now first published in America*, New York [1887].

1457   BRIGHT, JOHN. Speech, at Birmingham, Jan. 26, 1864. Reprinted from the "Manchester examiner and times" of Jan. 27, 1864. [Manchester, 1864]. 8 p.   **ICN NN**

Extracts also pub. in John Bright, *Speeches*, 1865, below.

1458   BRITISH AND FOREIGN ANTI-SLAVERY SOCIETY. The first (—twenty-fifth) annual report, etc. London, 1840–64.   **Uk**

OU has microfilm copy. "The 16th–21st Reports were issued as supps. to the *Anti-Slavery Reporter*."

1459   [BROOM, WALTER WILLIAM]. The anti-southern lecturer. [n.p., 1864?].   **OClWHi**

A series of lectures given in England by Broom.

1460   BUCHANAN, ISAAC. The relations of the industry of Canada, with the mother country and the United States, being a speech by Isaac Buchanan, esq., M.P., as delivered at the late demonstration to the parliamentary opposition at Toronto. Together with a series of articles in defence of the national sentiments contained therein, which originally appeared in the columns of the "Hamilton spectator," from the pen of Mr. Buchanan. To which is added a speech delivered by him at the dinner given to the pioneers of Upper Canada, at London, Canada West, 10th December, 1863. Now first published in a complete and collected form, with copious notes and annotations, besides an extended introductory explanation, and an appendix containing various valuable documents. Edited by Henry J. Morgan. Montreal, 1864. 551 p.   **DLC Uk**

1461   CAIRNES, J[OHN], E[LLIOTT]. England's neutrality in the American contest. Reprinted, with additions, from "Macmillan's magazine." London, 1864. 23 p.   **DLC Uk**

    See author's "International law" (from the *Fortnightly Rev.*, Nov. 1865), *Political Essays*, London, 1873, pp. 109–126.

1462   THE CAREER OF THE ALABAMA ('No 290') from July 29, 1862, to June 19, 1864. London, 1864. 43 p.   **Uk**

    DLC has repr. in the *Mag. of Hist. with Notes & Queries*, Ext. no. 2, New York, 1908, pp. 101–139; includes 3 p. addition, "Aboard a Semmes prize," by Capt. Strout. Uk lists under "Alabama."

1463   CAVENDISH, FRANCIS WILLIAM HENRY. Society, politics and diplomacy, 1820–1864; passages from the journal of Francis W. H. Cavendish, with four illustrations. London, [1913]. 416 p.   **DLC Uk**

    On U.S., pp. 360–378.

1464   CLARK, CHARLES. "Principles that ought naturally to govern the conduct of neutrals and belligerents;" a paper read before the Juridical society, 1 February 1864. London, 1864. 42 p.   **DLC**

    Uk lists as "missing." Also appeared in *Papers read before the Juridical society: 1863–1870*, III (1871), 13–37, with corrected title, "Principles that ought mutually to govern the conduct of neutrals and belligerents."

1465   COFFIN, WILLIAM FOSTER. 1812; the war, and its moral: a Canadian chronicle. By William F. Coffin, esquire. Montreal, 1864. 296 p.   **DLC Uk**

    Cover title: "1812. Chronicle of the war."

1466   COLES, COWPER P[HIPPS]. English versus American cupolas. A comparison between Capt. Coles's & Capt. Ericsson's turrets. February the 4th, 1864. Portsea, 1864. 11 p.   **DLC**

    Coles was English; Ericsson, American. A discussion of the new iron-clad warship technology.

1467   COLLINS, DAVID, et al., *defendants*. "The Chesapeake." The case of David Collins, et al., prisoners arrested under the provisions of the imperial act, 6 & 7 Vic., cap. 76, on a charge of piracy, investigated before Humphry T. Gilbert, Esq., Police Magistrate of the City of St. John, and the arguments on the return to the order of Habeas Corpus, before His Honor, Mr. Justice Ritchie, with his decision. Compiled from the original documents. St. John, N.B., 1864. 62 p.   **DLC**

    Uk lists as missing.

1468 COSSHAM, HANDEL. The American war: facts and fallacies. A speech, delivered by Handel Cossham, esq., at the Broadmead rooms, Bristol, on Friday, February 12, 1864. Bristol, [1864]. 24 p.   **CSmH MH OClWHi**

DLC has New York, 1865 ed. See also his "America: past, present, and future," *Pitman's Popular Lecturer & Reader*, VIII, n.s. (Mar. 1863), 65–90.

1469 COSSHAM, HANDEL. The resources of America, a lecture delivered by Handel Cossham, esq., at Stroud. Bristol, [1864?]. 23 p.   **DLC**

1470 COTTON: THE PRESENT and prospective position of supply and demand considered, by an Onlooker. London, 1864. 23 p.   **NN Uk**

1471 THE COTTON QUESTION. Rev. ed. London, [1864?]. 30 p.   **OClWHi PU**

Inside caption title: "The Cotton question. A portion of the following letter appeared in the London *Morning Herald* on January 28, 1864." Item includes a letter from the American George McHenry dated Feb. 12, 1864, followed by extracts from the British press on the question (pp. 11–27).

1472 [DAWSON, SAMUEL EDWARD]. The Northern kingdom, by a colonist. Montreal, [1864?]. 18 p.   **CaOTP N MnU Uk**

Uk gives date 1864 under cross-reference from Dawson, misprinted as 1804 in main entry. NUC entries dated [1866?]. On annexation, etc.

1473 DREW, [ANDREW]. A narrative of the capture and destruction of the steamer "Caroline" and her descent over the falls of Niagara. On the night of the 29th of December, 1837. With a correspondence. By Rear Admiral Drew. London, 1864. 31 p.   **CaOTP Uk**

Priv. circ. See also Robert Stuart Woods, *The cutting out of the Caroline . . . and other reminiscences of 1837–38*, 1885, below.

1474 DUNCAN, *MAJOR* FRANCIS. Our garrisons in the West; or, Sketches in British North America. London, 1864. 319 p.   **DLC Uk**

On U.S., pp. 153–164, 187–191, 223–227, 281–286, 294–306, and passim. Duncan arrived in Canada in the wake of the Trent affair and travelled along the U.S.-Canadian border to join a Great Lakes garrison.

1475 [EDGE, FREDERICK MILNES]. The Alabama and the Kearsarge. An account of the naval engagement in the British channel, on Sunday, June 19th, 1864, from information furnished to the writer by the wounded and paroled prisoners of the Confederate privateer "Alabama," and the officers of the United States sloop-of-war "Kearsarge", and citizens of Cherbourg. London, 1864. 48 p.   **DLC Uk**

A popular account that went into many eds. New York, 1864 ed. carried the title, *An Englishman's view of the battle between the Alabama and the Kearsarge*, etc. Repr. in the *Mag. of Hist. with Notes & Queries*, Ext. no. 2 (pt. 1), New York, 1908.

1476 EDGE, FREDERICK MILNES. England's danger and her safety. A letter to Earl Russell. 31 p.   **DLC Uk**

1477 EDGE, FREDERICK MILNES. President Lincoln's successor. London, 1864. 34 p.   **DLC Uk**

1478 [EDGE, FREDERICK MILNES]. Whom do English Tories wish elected to the Presidency? New York, 1864. 4 p.   **DLC**

Loyal Pub. Soc. pamphlets, No. 69.

1479   EDGE, FREDERICK MILNES. A woman's example: and a nation's work. A tribute to Florence Nightingale. London, 1864. 90 p.   **CSmH NN Uk**

Discusses U.S. sanitary commission.

1480   [ERNE, JOHN HENRY CRICHTON, *4th Earl*]. A tour in British North America and the United States, 1863; a lecture delivered to the Young men's Christian association at Lisnaskea, by Viscount Crichton. Dublin, 1864. 63 p.   **DLC**

1481   FIELD, CYRUS WEST. Europe and America. Report of the proceedings at an inauguration banquet, given by Mr. Cyrus W. Field, of New York, at the Palace hotel, Buckingham gate, on Friday, the 15th April 1864; in commemoration of the renewal by the Atlantic Telegraph Company (after a lapse of six years) of their efforts to unite Ireland and Newfoundland, by means of a submarine electric telegraph cable. London, 1864. 32 p.   **MH NN**

For priv. circ. See also Field, *Europe and America*, 1868, below, for a repr. of these proceedings, together with a report of another banquet on March 10, 1868.

1482   FREE TRADE VERSUS PROTECTION: being a series of papers illustrative of what protection has done for "The United States of America" and for "Russia," and of what free trade has done for "Switzerland." Reprinted from "the Argus." Melbourne, 1864. 21 p.   **DLC**

1483   GALTON, *SIR* FRANCIS, *ed.* Vacation tourists and notes of travel in 1862–3. London, 1864. 524 p.   **DLC Uk**

Vol. 3 in a series, with the same title, for 1860 and 1861, Cambridge, 1861–62. Chap. by Charles Mayo, "The medical service of the Federal army," p. 372–416.

1484   GEIKIE, JOHN CUNNINGHAM. George Stanley: or, Life in the woods. A boy's narrative of the adventures of a settler's family in Canada. Edited by John C. Geikie. With illustrations. London, 1864. 408 p.   **DLC Uk**

London, 1873 ed. carried title, *Life in the woods: a true story of the Canadian bush. By Cunningham Geikie, D.D.*; an unauthorized repr., Philadelphia, [1882], carried title *Adventures in Canada; or, Life in the woods*. For comment on American and Americans see esp. pp. 350–390.

1485   GODDARD, S[AMUEL] A[SPINWELL]. Reply to Mr. Lindsay's speech at Sunderland, August, 1864, on the American question. Birmingham, 1864. 16 p.   **DLC Uk**

William Schaw Lindsay's speech was reported in the London *Morning Star*.

1486   GREEN, J[ACOB] D. Narrative of the life of J. D. Green, a runaway slave from Kentucky; containing an account of his three excapes [sic] in 1839, 1846 and 1848. Huddersfield, 1864.   **InU**

1487   HOLLINGS, GEORGE SEYMOUR. An essay on cotton growers and cotton workers: an account of the culture of the plant and the manner of its manufacture. Prize paper written for the Boy's Own Magazine. London, 1864. 12 p.   **Uk**

Also appeared in *Prize papers written on various subjects for the Boy's own magazine*, London, 1864, pp. 80–92.

1488   THE HUMANITY OF THE CONFEDERATES, or the massacre at Fort Pillow. London, 1864. 31 p.   **MH OCIWHi**

Ladies London Emancip. Soc., tract no. 12.

1489   JONES, ERNEST CHARLES. Oration of Ernest Jones on the American rebellion. Delivered at the public hall, Rochdale, Monday, March 7th, 1864. The Mayor of Rochdale in the chair. Rochdale, [1864]. 16 p.   **NIC OCIWHi**

Repr., with additions, from the Rochdale *Observer*.

1490   KERSHAW, T. BENTLEY. The truth of the American question: being a reply to the prize essay of Mr. [J.C.] Rowan. Manchester, 1864. 32 p.   **Uk Vi**

OCIWHi has same title, London, [n.d.], 43 p. Rowan's essay appeared in the *Bradford Rev.*, Jan. 2, 1864.

1491   LAMONT, JAMES. A lecture on the civil war in America, delivered at the Rothesay mechanics' institute. Glasgow, 1864. 30 p.   **DLC UkLGI**

1492   LANCE, WILLIAM. Letters on American railways. No. 1. The Atlantic and Great Western railway. London, [1864?]. 18 p.   **DBRE**

1493   LAWRENCE, GEORGE GUERARD. Three months in America, in the summer of 1863. Two lectures given in Huddersfield . . . Part I. What I saw. Part II. What I thought. Huddersfield, [1864]. 63 p.   **MB Uk**

DLC has London, 1864 ed.

1494   [LEFROY, CHRISTOPHER EDWARD?]. Secession, slavery, and war. By Peter, the Hermit. Warrington, 1864.   **NHi**

1495   LOTHIAN [WILLIAM SCHOMBERG ROBERT KERR, *8th*], *MARQUESS*. The Confederate secession. By the Marquess of Lothian. Edinburgh, 1864. 226 p.   **DLC Uk**

Reviews: *Dublin Rev.*, IV, n.s., 328; *Index*, IV, 651; *Quar. Rev.*, CXVII, 249; *Westmin. Rev.*, LXXXVIII, 280.

1496   LUDLOW, J[OHN] M[ALCOLM FORBES]. American slavery. London, 1864. 30 p.
                                    MH NIC

Ladies' London Emancip. Soc., tract no. 8. Repr. from *Good Words*, IV, 826.

1497   MCGEE, THOMAS D'ARCY. The crown and the Confederation. Three letters to the Hon. John Alexander McDonald, Attorney General for Upper Canada. By a Backwoodsman. Montreal, 1864. 36 p.   **CaOTP MB MH**

1498   [MARSHALL, JOHN GEORGE]. Remarks upon the proposed Federation of the provinces. By a Nova Scotian. Halifax, 1864. 16 p.   **CaOTP**

Argues against federation for Canadian provinces.

1499   MASSIE, [*REV.*] JAMES WILLIAM. America: the origin of her present conflict; her prospect for the slave, and her claim for anti-slavery sympathy; illustrated by incidents of travel during a tour in the summer of 1863, throughout the United States, from the eastern boundaries of Maine to the Mississippi. London, 1864. 472 p.   **DLC Uk**

Review: *New Englander*, XXIII, 346.

1500   MATHEWS, *REV.* EDWARD. American slavery and the war; lecture delivered in Matlock Green, on the 15th August, 1864. Wirksworth, [1864]. 8 p.   **MH**

1501   MILNER, *REV.* THOMAS. The gallery of geography; a pictorial and descriptive tour of the world. London, [1864]. 950 p.   **DLC Uk**

Uk dates [1863], but pref. indicates 1864. On U.S., pp. 793–805, 823–845.

1502   MITCHEL, JOHN. Jail journal; or, Five years in British prisons. Commenced on board the Shearwater steamer, in Dublin bay, continued at Spike island—on board the Scourge, war steamer—on board the Dromedary hulk, Bermuda—on board the Neptune convict ship—at Pernambuco—at the Cape of Good Hope (during the anti-convict rebellion)—at Van Diemen's land—at Sydney—at Tahiti—at San Francisco—at Greyton—and concluded at no. 3, pier, North river, New York. Dublin, 1864. 204 p.   **DLC**

Uk has New York, 1868 ed; 2d ed., Dublin, 1913, "with a continuation of the journal in New York and Paris, a preface, appendices, and illustrations." This ed. "is repr. from 'The Citizen'—Mitchel's first New York newspaper—in which the 'Jail journal' was originally pub., from Jan. 14th, 1854, to Aug. 19th, 1854." The continuation in New York and Paris, pp. 367–417, was originally pub. in Mitchel's *Irish Citizen*, New York, 1869–70. Mitchel also edited the *Southern Citizen*, Dec. 1858–Aug. 1859, and the Richmond *Enquirer*, 1862–63; see P. A. Sillard, *Life of John Mitchel. With an historical sketch of the '48 movement in Ireland*, 2d ed., Dublin, 1901, pp. 242–260. For a discussion of Mitchel's life in the U.S., 1853–1875, see William Dillon, *Life of John Mitchel*, London, 1888, II, pp. 29–287; and Louis J. Walsh, *John Mitchel*, Dublin, [1934], pp. 85–90.

1503   MORRIS, MAURICE O'CONNOR. Rambles in the Rocky mountains: with a visit to the gold fields of Colorado. London, 1864. 264 p.   **DLC Uk**

Morris was in the U.S. in the 1860's; he mentions going west with Dudley Ryder in his *Memini; or, Reminiscences of Irish Life*, London, 1892, pp. 183–200.

Reviews: *Athenaeum*, (Oct. 8, 1864), 458; *Field*, XXIV, 71; *Sat. Rev.*, XVIII, 216.

1504   MUTER, [ELIZABETH (MCMULLIN)] *MRS*. D. D. Travels and adventures of an officer's wife in India, China, and New Zealand. By Mrs. Muter, wife of Lieut.-Colonel D. D. Muter. London, 1864. 2 vpls.   **DLC Uk**

On visit to U.S., I, pp. 203–211.

1505   NARRATIVE OF THE CRUISE OF THE ALABAMA, and list of her officers and men, by one of the crew. London, 1864. 16 p.   **DLC**

1506   [NEWELL, FREDERICK SAMUEL]. Newell's notes on Abraham Lincoln, President of the United States of America, with extracts from his speeches on slavery, secession, and the war. London, [1864].   **Uk**

Newell's Notes, no. 2.

1507   [NEWELL, FREDERICK SAMUEL]. Newell's notes on tar and feathers, and the atrocities of lynch law in the slave states of America. London, [1864].   **Uk**

Newell's Notes, no. 3; last in a series.

1508   [NEWELL, FREDERICK SAMUEL]. Newell's notes on the cruel and licentious treatment of the American female slaves. London, [1864]. 15 p.   **MH Uk**

Newell's Notes, no. 1; a series of three, then discontinued.

1509   NICHOLS, THOMAS LOW. Forty years of American life. London, 1864. 2 vols.   **DLC Uk**

An American born in 1821, a physician and social reformer, Nichols emigrated to England in 1862, in protest against the Civil War.

Review: *New Eng. Quar.*, L, 802

1510   PAPERS RELATING TO THE CONDEMNATION of the British barque "Springbok" and her cargo, by the District prize court of New York, U.S.; with the opinions of the press thereon. London, 1864. 112 p.   **DLC Uk**

Uk lists under "Springbok." Verso of t.p.: "Extract from 'Correspondence relating to the civil war in the United States of North America.' No. 1 (1863), presented to both houses of Parliament by command of Her Majesty." For additional correspondence on the issue, see *Papers relating to the illegal seizure . . .* , 1868, below.

1511   PARTRIDGE, J. ARTHUR. The false nation and its "bases"; or, Why the south can't stand. London, 1864. 60 p.   **DLC Uk**

1512   PAYTON, *SIR* CHARLES ALFRED. Days of a knight: an octogenarian's medly of memories (life, travel, sport, adventure). London, [1924]. 320 p.   **DLC Uk**

Uk gives 1925 pub. date. Visited the U.S. in 1864; see pp. 42–54.

1513   PHILLIPS, HENRY. Musical and personal recollections during half a century. London, 1864. 2 vols.   **DLC Uk**

Visit to U.S., 1844–45, II, pp. 80–209.

1514   A PLEA FOR THE SOUTH. London, 1864. 8 p.   **Uk**

1515   [PUTNAM, GEORGE PALMER, *ed.*]. Letters from Europe touching the American contest, and acknowledging the receipt, from citizens of New York, of presentation sets of the "Rebellion record," and "Loyal publication society" publications. New York, 1864. 27 p.   **DLC**

Includes letters from John Bright, Richard Cobden, Harriet Martineau and Goldwin Smith.

1516   RAWLINGS, THOMAS. Emigration, with special reference to Minnesota, U.S., and British Columbia. London, [1864]. 24 p.   **CaBVaU NN Uk**

On verso of t.p.: "Gresham House, London, Feb. 20, 1864."

1517   RECEPTION OF GOLDWIN SMITH by the Union league club of New York (the evening before his departure for Europe). With the remarks on the occasion, December 1864. [New York? 1864].

No locations found. Cited in catalog of New York (City) Union league club.

1518   ROCHE, JAMES. Origin and progress of the American republic and the war. A lecture, delivered in Dublin and London, December, 1864. Dublin, [1864]. 35 p.   **DS MH**

NUC incorrectly gives the date as [1874], and identifies the author as James Roche, of Cork. A reply to John Mitchell on the American question.

1519   ROOKER, ALFRED. Does it answer? Slavery in America. A history. London, 1864. 34 p.   **DLC Uk**

1520   ROSS, ALEXANDER M[ILTON]. Canada branch of the U.S. Sanitary commission, its objects and purposes. By Dr. Alexander M. Ross, of the Sanitary commission of the United States army. Montreal, 1864. 7 p.   **MH**

1521   ROSS, ALEXANDER M[ILTON]. Speech of Dr. Alexander M. Ross, delivered on the 21st October, 1864, at the annual meeting of the Society for the abolition of human slavery. Held in Montreal, Canada. Montreal, 1864. 8 p.   **MH**

1522 SEMMES, RAPHAEL. The cruise of the Alabama and the Sumter. From the private journals and other papers of Commander R. Semmes, C.S.N., and other officers. London,
1864. 2 vols. **DLC Uk**

See appendices: "Mr. Laird's speech on the Alabama," II, 334–340; "The Alabama in Table
Bay [From the South African *Cape Argus*]", II, 347–361; "Correspondence respecting the
Tuscaloosa. Rear-admiral Sir B. Walker to the secretary to the Admiralty. August 19,
1863," II, 362–435.

1523 SHIRREFF, EMILY [ANNE ELIZA]. The chivalry of the South. London, 1864. 14 p.
MB NIC Uk

Ladies' London Emancip. Soc. tract, no. 6.

1524 SHIRREFF, EMILY [ANNE ELIZA]. A few more words on the chivalry of the South.
London, 1864. 38 p. **MH NIC**

Ladies' London Emancip. Soc. tract, no. 11.

1525 SIDDONS, J[OACHIM] H[EYWARD]. The emigrant's friend; a true guide to the emigrant proceeding to New York, Boston, Philadelphia or the Canadas. Liverpool, 1864.
35 p. **MH**

1526 [SIDDONS, JOACHIM HEYWARD]. Yankeeland in her trouble. An Englishman's correspondence during the war. [n.p., 1864?]. 12 p. **DLC**

Three letters addressed to John Bright's newspaper, the *Star*, and signed "Muzafir."

1527 SMALL, H[ENRY] BEAUMONT. The animals of North America. [Ser. 1]. Montreal,
1864. 112 p. **DLC Uk**

See also Series II, 1865, below.

1528 SMITH, GOLDWIN. A letter to a Whig member of the Southern independence association. London, 1864. 76 p. **CSmH Uk**

DLC has Boston, 1864 ed., 64 p. Includes address of the Southern Independence Assoc.

Review: *No. Am. Rev.*, XCIX, 523.

1529 SOMMERVILLE, *REV.* WILLIAM. Southern slavery not founded on scripture warrant: a
lecture, by the Rev. William Sommerville, A.M. reformed Presbyterian minister,
Cornwallis, N.S. Saint John, N.B., 1864. 27 p. **MH**

1530 STALEY, [JOHN] EDGCUMBE. An essay on Negro slavery. By Edgcumbe Staley, Como
Terrace, Rochdale, aged 17 years. [London, 1864]. **NHi Uk**

Also appeared in *Prize papers written on various subjects for the Boy's own magazine*,
London, 1864.

1531 STURTEVANT, JULIAN MONSON. Three months in Great Britain. A lecture on the present attitude of England towards the United States, as determined by personal observation.
Chicago, 1864. 43 p. **DLC**

See also author's *English institutions and the American rebellion. Extracts from a lecture
delivered at Chicago, April 28, 1864*, Manchester, 1864, 32 p. Sturtevant, an American,
was president of Illinois College.

1532 TAYLOR, CHRISTOPHER. The probable causes and consequences of the American war.
Liverpool, 1864. 31 p. **MB Uk**

Sympathetic to the Confederacy.

1533 TERRILL, EDWARD C. Canadian sympathies in the American rebellion, and Canadian choice in the American election. An address delivered before the Union club at old Cambridge, Nov. 4, 1864. [Cambridge? 1864]. 20 p. **DLC**

No t.p.; priv. pr.

1534 THOMPSON, GEORGE. Address of George Thompson (M.P.), of England, to the legislature and citizens of Vermont. Delivered in the Representatives' hall, October 22, 1864. Montpelier, 1864. 18 p. **DLC**

1535 THOMPSON, THOMAS PHILLIPS. The future government of Canada: being arguments in favor of a British American independent republic. Comprising a refutation of the position taken by the Hon. T. D'Arcy McGee, in the British American magazine, for a monarchical form of government. St. Catharines, C.W., 1864. 24 p. **CaOTP MH PPL**

See McGee's article, "A plea for British American nationality," *Brit. Am. Mag.*, I (Aug. 1863), 337–345.

1536 TOBITT, JOHN H. What I heard in Europe during the "American excitement"; illustrating the difference between government and people abroad in their hostility and good wishes to the perpetuity of the great republic. New York, 1864. 133 p. **DLC Uk**

DLC gives 1865 date, noting that pref. is dated Jan. 1864, but 1864 on title page of its copy altered to 1865. Records conversations, lectures, etc. by Englishmen. Tobitt, born in England, came to the U.S. as a child.

1537 [TORRANCE, FREDERICK W.?]. The St. Albans raid. Investigation by the police committee, of the City Council of Montreal, into the charges preferred by Councillor B. Devlin, against Guillaume Lamothe, Esq., Chief of Police; and the proceedings of the Council in reference thereto. Montreal, 1864. 75 p. **DLC**

NUC entries under Montreal. City Council. Police committee.

1538 TORRENS, WILLIAM TORRENS MCCULLAGH. Lancashire's lesson; or, The need of a settled policy in times of exceptional distress. A letter addressed to the Right. Hon. Charles Pelham Villiers, M.P., president of the Poor law board. London, 1864. 191 p.
DLC Uk

On U.S., pp. 10–25.

1539 TRIMBLE, ROBERT. A review of the American struggle, in its military and political aspects, from the inauguration of President Lincoln, 4th March, 1861, till his re-election, 8th November, 1864. London, 1864. 48 p. **DLC Uk**

1540 UNION AND EMANCIPATION SOCIETY, MANCHESTER. Address of the Union and emancipation society, Manchester, to his Excellency Abraham Lincoln, on his re-election to the presidency, November 8th, 1864. [Manchester, 1864]. **CSmH**

Signed by Thomas Bayley, Potter, et al.

1541 VIGILANS [*pseud.*]. The foreign enlistment acts of England and America. The "Alexandra" & the rams. London, 1864. 124 p. **DLC Uk**

DLC lists under title. Work reportedly subsidized by Confederacy.

1542 THE WAR UPON AMERICAN COMMERCE; by subjects of Great Britain. Boston, 1864. 20 p. **CtY IU NjP**

NUC enters under Thomas Baring. Collection of speeches by Baring, W. E. Forster, and Richard Cobden.

1543 WELCOME TO GOLDWIN SMITH, regius professor of modern history in the University of Oxford, England, by citizens of New York, at a breakfast given at the rooms of the Union league club, Union square, Saturday, November 12, 1864. New York, 1864. 56 p.

DLC Uk

DLC lists under New York (City) citizens; Uk, under Smith. Includes speech by Smith, pp. 10–13. See account of the meeting by G. W. Curtis in his "Editor's easy chair," *Harper's Mag.*, XXX (Jan. 1865), 263–264. See also Smith's journal, Aug. to Dec. 1864, pub. for the first time in *Goldwin Smith, his life and opinions, by his literary executor [Theodore] Arnold Haultin . . . to which is appended "U.S. notes," being Goldwin Smith's journal during his first visit to America in 1864*, London, [1913], pp. 253–292. See also Smith's *Reminiscences*, ed. by Arnold Haultain, New York, 1910, for accounts of his various visits to the U.S. Also see *A selection from Goldwin Smith's correspondence, comprising letters chiefly to and from his English friends, written between the years 1846 and 1910, collected by his literary executor, Arnold Haultain*, London, 1913?

1544 WHITBY, *REV.* WILLIAM. American slavery; a sketch. London, 1864. 210 p. **DLC**

1545 WRIGHT, JOSEPH. Self reliance, or a plea for the protection of Canadian industry. Dundas [C.W.], 1864. 54 p. **CaOTP CaOTU**

1865

1546 ALISON, ALEXANDER. The independence of Canada. A tract for general circulation. London, 1865. 8 p. **CaOOA Uk**

1547 ANENT THE AMERICAN WAR. London, 1865. 11 p. **DS MH NNC Uk**

1548 ARGYLL, [GEORGE DOUGLAS CAMPBELL, *8th duke*]. National committee of British freed-men's aid societies. Speech of His Grace the Duke of Argyll, at a meeting held at the Westminster palace hotel, May 17, 1865. London, 1865. 32 p. **NHi Uk**

Cataloged under the National committee. Also pub. in National committee . . . *Report of the proceedings held at the Westminster palace hotel, May 17, 1865 . . . containing the speech of His Grace the Duke of Argyll; also, speeches by Lord Houghton [and others]*, London, 1865, 76 p. (DLC has on microfilm.) Contains report of the proceedings and comments by Lord Houghton, Sir Thomas Fowell Buxton, Charles Buxton, Thomas Hughes, Rev. H. M. Storrs, Rev. R. Vaughan, J. M. Ludlow, et al. For Argyll's views on the Civil War, see his "Letters of the Duke and Duchess of Argyll to Charles Sumner," in *Proc. Mass. Hist. Soc.*, XLVII (1913–14), 66–107; and Argyll's *Autobiography and memoirs*, London, 1906, II, pp. 54–65, 169–213, and passim.

1549 THE ASSASSINATION of President Lincoln. From the Northern Whig. Belfast, May 1st, 1865. [Dublin, 1865]. 2 p. **MH**

1550 THE ATTEMPT OF THE NORTH to subdue the Southerners and the attempt of Spain to subdue the Netherlanders. Is there any analogy between them? An offhand inquiry. By the author of "Uncle John's cabin, next door to Uncle Tom's cabin." By a neutral. London, 1865. 16 p. **RPB Uk**

Also author of *A reply to a critique on Uncle John's cabin*, London, 1865, below.

1551   ATTWOOD, R. H. Persecution in Salt lake city. [Aberdar, 1865]. 4 p.   **NN**

Signed "R. H. Attwood." Recto and verso in English and Welsh. Pub. by the Reformed Latter-Day Saints Church.

1552   [AVEBURY], JOHN LUBBOCK, *1st baron*. Pre-historic times as illustrated by ancient remains and the manners and customs of modern savages. By Sir John Lubbock. London, 1865. 512 p.   **DLC Uk**

On U.S., pp. 206–228, 386–421, and see index. See also his "North American Archaeology," *Smithsonian Ann. Rept. 1862*, Washington, 1863, pp. 318–336 (from *Nat. Hist. Rev.*, Jan. 1863). For additional comment on the American Indian see his *The origin of civilization and the primitive condition of man. Mental and social condition of savages*, London, 1870.

1553   BACON, GEORGE WASHINGTON, *comp*. The life and administration of Abraham Lincoln. Presenting his early history, political career, speeches, messages, proclamations, letters, etc., with a general view of his policy as President of the United States . . . Also the European press on his death. London, 1865. 183 p.   **DLC Uk**

Condensed version pub. in the *Mag. of Hist. with Notes & Queries*, Ext. nos. 188, 189, (1933). Sources are largely American, but the appendix contains selections from commentary on Lincoln's death in English journals, pp. 95–109, 113–115.

1554   BARRINGTON, WILLIAM L. The true origin of the American rebellion: being a lecture delivered in the Friends' institute, Molesworth-street, Dublin, November 26th, 1864. Dublin, 1865. 33 p.   **DLC Uk**

1555   BENJAMIN, L. N., *comp*. The St. Albans raid; or, Investigation into the charges against Lieut. Bennett H. Young and command, for their acts at St. Albans, Vt., on the 19th October, 1864. Being a complete and authentic report of all the proceedings on the demand of the United States for their extradition, under the Ashburton treaty. Before Judge Coursol, J.S.P., and the Hon. Mr. Justice Smith, J.S.C. With the arguments of counsel and the opinions of the judges revised by themselves. Montreal, 1865. 480 p.   **DLC Uk**

See account of St. Albans raid in William Weir, *Sixty years in Canada*, Montreal, 1903, pp. 212–224; and [Frederick Torrance], *The St. Albans raid. . . .*, 1864, above.

1556   BORRETT, GEORGE TUTHILL. Letters from Canada and the United States. London, 1865. 294 p.   **DLC**

Priv. pr.; Uk has 2d ed., under the title *Out west: a series of letters from Canada and the United States*, London, 1866. Parts of the book were repr. in "An Englishman in Washington in 1864," the *Mag. of Hist. with Notes & Queries*, Ext. no. 149 (1929), 5–15; and in "Minnesota as seen by travelers; an English visitor of the Civil War period," *Minn. Hist.*, IX (1928), 270–284, 379–383.

1557   BREEZE, J[AMES] T. The assassination of President Lincoln. A poem. Belleville [Ont.], 1865. 8 p.   **RPB**

Later pub. under title, *The martyred president. A poem on the genius and character of Abraham Lincoln*, [Milwaukee?], 1874. Author also listed as J. T. Breese.

1558   [BRIGGS, THOMAS]. Correspondence on the cotton famine [with Lord Edward Howard], showing how it affects the present position and future prospects of the common interests of Britain. Manchester, 1865. 16 p.   **CtY UkLGl**

1559   [BRIGHT, JOHN]. Speeches of John Bright, M.P., on the American question. With an introduction by Frank Moore. Boston, 1865. 278 p.   **DLC Uk**

Repr. 10 speeches and extracts from speeches, Aug. 1, 1861–Mar. 23, 1865. 1) Extract from a speech delivered at a meeting at Rochdale, to promote the election of John Chatham, esq., for the Southern Division of the county of Lancaster, Aug. 1, 1861. 2) Speech at a dinner at Rochdale, December 4, 1861. Delivered during the excitement caused by the seizure of Mason and Slidell on board the "Trent" steamer. (Printed originally as *A liberal voice from England*, 1862, above; also in the *Rebellion Record: a diary of American events with documents, narratives, illustrative incidents, poetry, etc.*, ed. by Frank Moore, supp., vol. I, New York, 1864, 1–13; James E. Thorold Rogers, ed., *Speeches on questions of public policy*, London, 1868; and *John Bright on America: the Trent affair; slavery and secession; the struggle in America, 1861–3*, New York, 1891.) 3) Speech at Birmingham December 18, 1862. (Pub. originally as *Speech of Mr. Bright. . . .*, 1862, above; also in James E. Thorold Rogers, op cit.) 4) Speech on slavery and secession, delivered at Rochdale, at a meeting held for the purpose of passing a resolution of thanks to the American subscribers in aid of the unemployed work-people of Lancashire, February 3, 1863. (Also in *John Bright on America*.) 5) The struggle in America in relation to the working-men of Britain: address at a meeting of the Trade's unions of London in St. James's Hall, March 26, 1863, with the resolutions and address to President Lincoln. (Also in James E. Thorold Rogers, op cit.; *John Bright on America*.) 6) Speech at the London tavern, June 16, 1863, at a meeting held under the auspices of the emancipation society, to hear from Mr. D. Conway, of Eastern Virginia, an address on the war in America. 7) Speech in the House of Commons, on Mr. Roebucks's motion for recognition of the Southern confederacy, June 30, 1863. 8) Conclusion of a speech at a meeting at Rochdale, Nov. 24, 1863, held to enable Mr. Cobden to meet his constituents. 9) Extract from a speech at Town hall, Birmingham, January 26, 1864 (Printed originally as *Speech at Birmingham . . .*, 1864, above.) 10) Speech on the Canadian fortifications, delivered in the House of commons, March 23, 1865. (Repr. in *World's Best Orations*, ed. by David J. Brewer, St. Louis, 1899, II, pp. 620–637.)

See also the following items: "An address to the Birmingham Chamber of Commerce on some incidents in the American war," (Birmingham, Jan. 15, 1863), *Public addresses by John Bright, M.P.*, ed. by James E. Thorold Rogers, London, 1879, pp. 1–14; "America and the Civil War," *The life and speeches of the Right Hon. John Bright, M.P.*, George Barnett Smith, London, 1881, II, pp. 78–116, and other comment passim; many letters on America in *The public letters of the Right Hon. John Bright, M.P.*, ed. by H. J. Leeds, London, 1885; two letters from Bright (Mar. 3, Aug. 8, 1882) in Matthew Mark Trumbull, *The free trade struggle in England*, 2d ed. rev. and enlarged, Chicago, 1892; Whitelaw Reid, *"The Practical side" of American education—John Bright and the Civil War*, (John Bright Memorial School, Llandudno, North Wales. Opening address, September 25, 1907), London, 1907; Lawrence V. Roth, ed., *John Bright and the American civil war*, Boston, 191–?; R. Barry O'Brien, *John Bright*, London, 1910, "The American Civil War," pp. 257–287; "Bright-Sumner letters, 1861–62," *Proc. Mass. Hist. Soc.*, XLV (Nov. 1911), 148–159, XLVI (Oct. 1912), 93–164; George Macaulay Trevelyan, *The life of John Bright*, Boston, 1913, "The American civil War," pp. 296–327; "The friend of the North," *The diaries of John Bright, with a foreword by Philip Bright*, London, 1930, pp. 52–92; Joseph Travis Mills, *John Bright and the Quakers*, London, 1935, II, pp. 221–246; and Keith Robbins, *John Bright*, London, 1979, "The American Civil War, 1863–67," pp. 154–168, and passim.

1560   [BROOM, WALTER WILLIAM]. Abraham Lincoln's character. Sketched by English trav-
        elers. [Brooklyn? 1865]. 4 p.   **DLC**

        Caption title; signed, "W. W. B., Brooklyn, April 30, 1865." See also Sir James Marchant,
        ed., *History through the Times. . . . 1800–1937*, London, [1937], "Abraham Lincoln" (April
        27, 1865), pp. 222–225.

1561   BROOM, WALTER WILLIAM. An Englishman's thoughts on the crimes of the South,
        and the recompence of the North. By W. W. Broom, of Manchester. New York, 1865.
        24 p.   **DLC**

        Also pub. same year, as pamphlet no. 84 by the Loyal Pub. Soc., New York.

1562   [BROOM, WALTER WILLIAM]. Great and grave questions for American politicians.
        With a topic for America's statesmen. By Eboracus [*pseud.*]. New York, 1865. 122 p.
                                                                                    DLC Uk

1563   BUCHANAN, ISAAC. The British American Federation a necessity; its industrial policy
        also a necessity. Hamilton, 1865. 48 p.   **ICU MH OCIWHi**

1564   BUCHANAN, ISAAC. Memorial to the Commercial convention in Detroit. Hamilton,
        1865.

        No locations found. According to Sabin, printed but not distributed.

1565   [BURN, JAMES DAWSON]. Three years among the working classes of the United States
        during the war. By the author of "The autobiography of a beggar-boy." London, 1865.
        309 p.   **DLC Uk**

        Review: *Athenaeum* (Nov. 18, 1865), 681.

1566   [CAMPBELL, JOHN FRANCIS]. Frost and fire. Natural engines, tool marks and chips,
        with sketches taken at home and abroad. By a traveller. Edinburgh, 1865. 2 vols.
                                                                                    DLC Uk

        In the U.S. in 1864; see esp. chap. 43.

        Reviews: *Edinb. Rev.*, CXXII, 422; *No. Brit. Rev.*, XLIII, 105.

1567   [CAMPBELL, JOHN FRANCIS]. A short American tramp in the fall of 1864, by the edi-
        tor of "Life in Normandy." Edinburgh, 1865. 427 p.   **DLC Uk**

        Review: *Athenaeum* (May 28, 1865), 677.

1568   [CANNIFF, WILLIAM]. The future of British America. Independence! How to prepare for
        it. Consolidation is preparation for a new nation; confederation is preparation for annexa-
        tion. . . . The simple question to be determined is: shall the constitution of the United
        Provinces of British America be formed after the model afforded us by the constitution of
        the United Kingdoms or that of the United States? Toronto, 1865. 16 p. **CaOOA MH NN**

        Letters originally pub. in the *Leader* under the pseud. Paul I. Tickle. NUC lists under
        Tickle.

1569   CASSELL'S EMIGRANTS' HANDY GUIDE to California. London, [1865]. 24 p.
                                                                                 CU-BANC Uk

        CU-BANC gives [1855?] pub. date, but p. 5 notes that progress since 1849 includes "cities
        . . . [in] the wilderness of but fifteen years ago." See also *Cassell's emigrants' handy guide
        to North America*, London, [1865], 24 p.; pp. 4–8 on U.S. Both guides part of *Cassell's
        emigrants' handy guides*, London, [1865], 13 pts.

1570 CECIL, *LORD* EUSTACE [BROWNLOW HENRY GASCOYNE.] Impressions of life at home and abroad. By Lieut.-Colonel Lord Eustace Cecil. London, 1865. 277 p. **DLC Uk**

"After dark in New York," pp. 131–154, repr. from *St. James's Medley.*

1571 CHURCH, R[ICHARD] S[TEPHEN] H[AMILTON]. The two rebellions! A few words to his excellency the Hon. C. F. Adams, etc., etc. touching his hereditary relations to rebellion, from one who like himself is the grandson of an American rebel. London, 1865. 16 p. **DLC Uk**

Born in New York, Church became a British subject. He also translated Cornelis Henri de Witt's, *Jefferson and the American democracy*, London, 1862.

1572 [CLOUGH, ARTHUR HUGH]. Letters and remains of Arthur Hugh Clough, sometime fellow of Oriel College, Oxford. London, 1865. 328 p. **CSmH MH NN Uk**

Gives account of his early years in America, 1823–26, and his later visit, 1852–53, including his letters from America, pp. 230–258. See also *The correspondence of Arthur Hugh Clough*, ed. by Frederick L. Mulhauser, Oxford, 1957, II, 321–390, and passim. Also see *Emerson-Clough letters*, ed. by Howard F. Lowry and Ralph Leslie Rusk, Cleveland, 1934. For accounts of Clough's visit to America, see: Katharine Chorley, *Arthur Hugh Clough, the uncommitted mind: a study of his life and poetry*, Oxford, 1962, pp. 267–291; Evelyn Barish Greenberger, *Arthur Hugh Clough: the growth of a poet's mind*, Cambridge, Mass, 1970, pp. 148–167; and David Williams, *Too quick despairer: a life of Arthur Hugh Clough*, London, 1869, pp. 103–121.

1573 COLLINS, ELIZABETH. Memories of the southern states. Taunton, 1865. 116 p. **DLC Uk**

1574 CORDNER, *REV.* JOHN. The American conflict: an address, spoken before the New England society of Montreal, and a public audience, in Wordheimer's hall, Montreal, on Thursday evening, 22nd December, 1864. Montreal, 1865. 48 p. **DLC**

Uk has Manchester, 1865 ed., under title, *Canada and the United States: an address on the American conflict, delivered at Montreal, on Thursday evening, December 22, 1864.*

1575 COSSHAM, HANDEL. Mr. Cossham on America. (From the Stroud journal of Dec. 16.) [Bristol, 1865]. 22 p. **MH**

DLC has in Cossham's *Lectures*, [n.p., n.d.]. No t.p.; the lecture in the Stroud *Journal*, Dec. 16, 1865, was entitled "America: What I saw and heard." For an account of Cossham's writings see *Friends of America in England. Handel Cosham [sic], esq. From the Federal American monthly . . .*, Washington, 1865.

1576 [COSSHAM, HANDEL]. Soiree of the Emancipation society. [Bristol, 1865]. **ICN**

No t.p.; repr. from the Liverpool *Daily Post*, Dec. 1, 1865; a report of a speech by Cossham.

1577 COWELL, JOHN WELSFORD. France and the Confederate States. London, 1865. 37 p. **Uk**

DLC has microfilm copy. NN and Uk have Paris, 1865 ed., *La France et les états Confederes.*

1578 DENISON, *LIEUT. COL.* GEORGE TAYLOR, *Jr.* The petition of George Taylor Denison, jr., to the honorable the House of assembly, praying redress in the matter of the seizure of the steamer "Georgian," together with copies of the petition and affidavits, filed in the county court of the county of Simcoe. Toronto, 1865. 15 p. **CaOTP**

1579   DERBYSHIRE, ALEXANDER. Sufferings of the needy; or, A journey to the west and back again; with its privations and difficulties, as related by Alexander Derbyshire. To which is added a short sketch of the life of John A. Brewer, who died on the coast of South America. A true account from real life, by Maria Gibson. Picton [Canada], 1865. 45 p.

NN

Derbyshire in U.S. in 1850.

1580   THE DOBBS FAMILY IN AMERICA by our own "special" correspondent. London, 1865. 312 p.   **DLC Uk**

Uk lists as London, 1865 [1864]. Semi-fictionized account; an imitation of Lever's works on the Dodd family's travels.

Review: *Athenaeum* (Feb. 4, 1865), 162.

1581   DONALDSON, LAUCHLAN. Letter from Lauchlan Donaldson to John Boyd on commercial and reciprocal trade between the United States and the British provinces, and other subjects. Saint John, N.B., 1865. 8 p.   **CaOOA**

1582   [DONALDSON, *SIR* STUART ALEXANDER]. Mexico thirty years ago, as described in a series of private letters, by a youth . . . London, 1865. 236 p.   **DLC**

Letters from New York and New Orleans, pp. 1–27. Dedication signed, Stuart Alexander Donaldson; "For private circulation only."

1583   DRUMMOND, ROBERT BLACKLEY. President Lincoln and the American war. A funeral address delivered on Sunday, April 30, 1865. Edinburgh, 1865. 12 p.   **DLC Uk**

1584   EDGE, FREDERICK MILNES. Major-General McClellan and the campaign on the Yorktown peninsula. London, 1865. 203 p.   **DLC Uk**

Also pub. as pamphlet no. 81, by the Loyal Pub. Soc.

1585   FISHER, HERBERT W[ILLIAM]. Considerations on the origin of the American war. London, 1865. 97 p.   **DLC Uk**

1586   FORSTER, WILLIAM. Memoirs of William Forster. Edited by Benjamin Seebohm. London, 1865. 2 vols.   **DLC Uk**

First two visits to U.S., 1820–25 and 1845, I, 247–394; II, 1–50; third visit to and death in U.S., 1853–1854, II, 354–400. See also account in biography of his son by T. Wemyss Reid, *Life of William Edward Forster*, London, 1888, 2 vols.

1587   THE FREEDMEN IN AMERICA. Speeches of the Hon. C[harles] C. Leigh, of New York, Fred Tompkins, . . . the Rev. Wm. Arthur . . . , the Rev. W[illiam] B[ennington] Boyce, and Mr. T[homas] B[ywater] Smithies, at a meeting held at the Wesleyan mission house, June 9, 1865. Four million free. London, [1865]. 31 p.   **DLC**

1588   FRIENDS, SOCIETY OF. *Central committee of Great Britain and Ireland for the relief of the emancipated slaves of North America.* Case and claims of the emancipated slaves of the United States; being the address of the Society of Friends in Great Britain and Ireland, to the British public. London, 1865. 15 p.   **NHi**

DLC and Uk have rev. ed., London, 1865, 16 p., with added "P.S." signed by J. H. Address signed by John Hodgkin, "on behalf of the Committee."

1589 GASKELL, *MRS*. ELIZABETH CLEGHORN (STEVENSON). Letters of Mrs. Gaskell and Charles Eliot Norton, 1855–1865, edited with an introduction by Jane Whitehill. London, 1932. 131 p.   **DLC Uk**

Gaskell's side of the correspondence also included in *The Letters of Mrs. Gaskell*, ed. by J. A. V. Chapple and Arthur Pollard, Cambridge, Mass., 1967, 1010 p. Scattered comment on American affairs, 1857–1865. See discussion of these letters in A. B. Hopkins, *Elizabeth Gaskell: her life and work*, London, 1952, pp. 234–244, and passim. See also Mrs. Gaskell's pref. to *Mabel Vaughan* by Maria S. Cummins, London, 1857.

1590 HALL, [CHRISTOPHER] NEWMAN. The assassination of Abraham Lincoln. A lecture by Newman Hall, LL.B., author of "Come to Jesus," etc. etc. London, [1865]. 31 p.
CSmH MB OCIWHi Uk

DLC has Boston, 1865 ed., with title, *A sermon on the assassination of Abraham Lincoln, preached at Surrey Chapel, London, Sunday May 14, 1865*. Repr. in *Mag. of Hist. with Notes & Queries*, Ext. no. 40, (1915).

1591 [HARCOURT, *SIR* WILLIAM GEORGE GRANVILLE VENABLES VERNON]. American neutrality: by Historicus [*pseud*.]. Reprinted from the London Times of December 22d, 1864. New York, 1865. 11 p.   **DLC**

See also "Communication of Historicus to the London Times of March 22d, 1865: the neutrality of England," repr. as appendix, pp. 47–57, to George Bemis, *Hasty recognition of rebel belligerency, and our right to complain of it*, Boston, [1865].

1592 HARCOURT, *SIR* WILLIAM GEORGE GRANVILLE VENABLES VERNON ("HISTORICUS"). Neutrality laws and Alabama claims. With appendices. Prepared for the Foreign office. [n.p., 1865].

No locations found. See also Harcourt, "The rights and duties of neutrals in time of war," *Royal United Serv. Inst. J.*, IX (May 1865), 313–345; and James Phinney Baxter, "Some British opinions as to neutral rights, 1861 to 1865," *Am. J. Internat Law*, XXIII (July 1929), 517–537.

1593 HARVEY, ARTHUR. The reciprocity treaty: its advantages to the United States and to Canada. Quebec, 1865. 29 p.   **DLC**

At head of t.p., "First prize essay." Received first prize from Montreal *Trade Rev.*, 1865.

1594 HOLYOAKE, GEORGE JACOB. Public performances of the dead. A review of American spiritualism. [From the "Newcastle Chronicle," with additions]. London, [1865]. 11 p.
MH Uk

In America in 1879 and 1882; for discussion of these visits see Holyoake's *Among the Americans, and A stranger in America*, 1881, below; "American and Canadian notes," *Nineteenth Cent.*, XIV (Aug. 1883), 292–299 (repr. in *Eclectic Mag.*, CI (Oct. 1883), 494–499); *Travels in search of a settler's guide-book of America and Canada*, 1884, below; and Joseph McCabe's *Life and letters of George Jacob Holyoake*, London, 1908, II, pp. 109–134. See also Holyoake's "The advantages of emigration," Co-operative Wholesale Soc. Ltd., *Annual and diary for the year 1885*, Manchester, [1886?], pp. 245–253; "Emigrant education," *Nineteenth Cent.*, XLIV (Sept. 1898), 427–436; and *The history of co-operation in England: its literature and its advocates*, London, 1875–79, II, pp. 284–299 (rev. ed., New York, 1906). Also see W. J. Linton, "Holyoake *versus* Garrison," the *English Republic*, II, (1853), 257–262.

1595   HOWE, JOSEPH. The reciprocity treaty, its history, general features, and commercial results; a speech delivered by the Honorable Joseph Howe, of Nova Scotia, on the 14th day of July, 1865, at the great International commercial convention held at the city of Detroit. Specially revised for publication by Mr. Howe. Hamilton, 1865. 15 p.   **DLC**

Repr. London, 1865, under title *Speech delivered by the Hon. Joseph Howe at the Detroit convention, on the commercial relations of Great Britain and the United States, August* [*sic*] *14, 1865*, 47 p.; added were a 2 p. introd. and a 3 p. appendix of press commentary on the speech. Also repr. in William Weir's *Sixty years in Canada*, Montreal, 1903, pp. 226–244; and in George Edward Fenety's *Life and times of the Hon. Joseph Howe, (The great Nova Scotian and ex-Lieut. Governor.) With brief references to some of his prominent contemporaries*, St. John, N.B., 1896, pp. 314–335. Fenety's volume includes an open letter by Howe (signed Sydney) to George Bancroft on the occasion of Bancroft's eulogy on Lincoln, pp. 298–313. For earlier speeches and visits to the U.S. see, *The speeches and public letters of the Hon. Joseph Howe*, 1872, below, II, pp. 119–123, 221–230, and passim.

1596   KEAN, MRS. ELLEN [TREE]. Death and funeral of Abraham Lincoln, with some remarks on the state of America at the close of the civil war. A contemporary account contained in two long descriptive letters from Mrs. Ellen Kean, the actress, whilst touring the United States in 1865. With prefatory note by John Drinkwater, author of "Abraham Lincoln," a play. London, 1921. 27 p.   **DLC Uk**

Priv. pr.; 50 copies only. Letter from New York, Apr. 16, 1865, to her daughter Mary; second letter from Baltimore, May 13, 1865, to Miss Sherritt.

1597   [KENNARD, EDWARD]. Transatlantic sketches; or, Sixty days in America. London, 1865. 34 p.   **DLC Uk**

Cataloged under title, but DLC attributes to Kennard. Sketches cover the period Feb. 24–Apr. 25, 1865.

1598   KINNEAR, ALFRED. Across many seas. A story of action from Crimea to coronation. Bristol, 1902. 411 p.   **Uk**

Visit to America during the Civil War, pp. 32–64. (1863–1865?)

1599   KIRBY, WILLIAM. President Lincoln. [n.p., 1865].

No locations found. Repr. from *Macmillan's Mag.*, XI (Feb. 1865).

1600   [LEVER, CHARLES JAMES]. Cornelius O'Dowd [*pseud.*] upon men and women and other things in general. [1st], 2d, and 3d series. Edinburgh, 1864–65. 3 vols.   **DLC Uk**

New ed., London, 1874. Originally pub. in *Blackwood's Edinb. Mag.* See "Of our brothers beyond the border," I, pp. 249–255; "Some pros and cons of life abroad," II, pp. 177–185; "The fight over the way," II, pp. 241–249 (ibid., XCVII (Jan. 1865), 57–59); "The Adams-Russell correspondence," III, pp. 158–163 (ibid., XCVIII (Nov. 1865), 539–540). See also Lever's "America as an ally," ibid., C (Aug. 1866), 240–244, in which he comments on an article with the same title in the *Pall Mall Gazette*, III (June 29, 1866), 1. See also two other articles by him in *Blackwood's*: "American diplomacy," CIV (Dec. 1868), 747–751; "The American 'Revoke'," CXI (Mar. 1872), 364–367. And see his "A nut for 'Tourists'," pp. 153–156, in his *Nuts and nutcrackers*, London, 1845. Also, Lever's novel, *Confessions of Con Cregan, the Irish Gil Blas*, London, 1850, deals with the hero's experiences in America.

1601   LORIMER, JAMES. The rights and duties of belligerents and neutrals with reference to maritime commerce . . . A lecture delivered to the Leith Chamber of commerce on December 29, 1864. Edinburgh, 1865. 28 p.   **DLC Uk**

1602   MACDONALD, DUGALD. A lecture on the American war of secession delivered . . . on the 9th of August, 1864, in the hall of the Mechanics' institute, Montreal. Montreal, 1865.   **CSmH OCIWHi**

1603   MCGEE, THOMAS D'ARCY. Speeches and addresses chiefly on the subject of British-American union. London, 1865. 308 p.   **DLC Uk**

Two speeches repr. in *1825—D'Arcy McGee—1925: a collection of speeches and addresses*, Toronto, 1937: "Canada's interest in the American Civil War," pp. 168–190; and "Emigration and colonization," pp. 191–214.

Review: *Athenaeum*, (July 22, 1865), 112.

1604   MCGEE, THOMAS D'ARCY. Two speeches on the union of provinces. Toronto, 1865. 34 p.   **CtY NRU Uk**

Speeches delivered Dec. 22, 1864 and Feb. 9, 1865; references to U.S. (particularly Civil War), pp. 7, 11, 17, 20. Feb. 9 speech repr. in *1825—D'Arcy McGee—1925*, pp. 215–266.

1605   MACKENZIE, ROBERT. America and her army. London, 1865. 60 p.   **DLC Uk**

1606   MALET, *SIR* EDWARD BALDWIN. Shifting scenes; or, Memories of many men in many lands; by the right Honourable Sir Edward Baldwin Malet. London, 1901. 335 p.   **DLC Uk**

Covers diplomatic career in the U.S., 1862–65.

1607   MILLER, *REV.* MARMADUKE. America: as seen at the close of the war. A lecture delivered . . . in Manchester, Huddersfield, &c. London, [1865?]. 32 p.   **NN**

In U.S., 1865–75.

1608   MILLS, THOMAS. Abraham Lincoln and the American war. A lecture delivered in Leigh by Rev. Thomas Mills. Leigh, 1865. 24 p.   **IHi**

Bound in pamphlet with two other lectures.

1609   NEAVE, JOSEPH JAMES. Leaves from the journal of James Joseph Neave. Edited by Joseph J. Green. London, 1910. 228 p.   **NcD PPFr Uk**

Uk dates 1911. Includes diary of a visit to U.S., 1864–65; a Quaker view of the Civil War.

1610   NEWTON, [THOMAS WODEHOUSE LEGH, *2d baron*]. Lord Lyons. A record of British diplomacy. By Lord Newton. London, 1913. 2 vols.   **DLC Uk**

Lord Lyons was minister to the U.S., 1859–1865; letters from the U.S., etc., I, 12–143. See also British official publications during the Civil War, such as *Despatch from Lord Lyons respecting the obstruction of the Southern harbours*, London, [1862]; *Despatch from Lord Lyons respecting the reciprocity treaty*, London, [1862]; etc.

1611   NORTON, ROBERT. Maple leaves from Canada, for the grave of Abraham Lincoln: being a discourse delivered by Rev. Robert Norton, pastor of the First Presbyterian church, and address by Rev. Robert F. Burns, pastor of the Canada Presbyterian church, at St. Catharines, Canada West, April 23rd, 1865, together with proceedings of public meetings, &c. St. Catharines, 1865. 39 p.   **DLC**

DLC lists under title. Repr. in *Mag. of Hist. with Notes & Queries*, Ext. no. 85 (1922).

1612   ORPEN, [ADELA ELIZABETH RICHARDS] ("MRS. G. H. ORPEN."). Memories of the old emigrant days in Kansas, 1862–1865, also of a visit to Paris in 1867, by Mrs. Orpen. Edinburgh and London, 1926. 324 p.   **DLC Uk**

Recalls experiences 60 years earlier, as a young girl between 7 and 9 years of age.

1613   PARKER, JOSEPH. For peace in America: a report from Mr. Joseph Parker of Manchester, to Sir Henry De Hoghton, Bart., of his mission as bearer of the peace address from the people of Great Britain and Ireland to the people of the United States of America. [n.p., 1865?]. 19 p.   **Uk**

De Hoghton had collected, at his own expense, 360,000 British signatures to an "Address to the people of the United States," which Parker carried to New York in Oct., 1864.

1614   PARROTT, WILLIAM SAUNDERS. The veil uplifted; or, The religious conspirators of the Latter-day exposed. . . . Who are the Mormons? And what are the Latter-day saints about? Bristol, 1865. 63 p.   **ICN MH Uk**

1615   PETO, *SIR* SAMUEL MORTON. Speech by Sir S. Peto, bart., M.P., at Bristol, Monday, November 13th, 1865, on his return from the United States. [London, 1865]. 20 p.   **MB OClWHi**

Speech also fully reported in *Anglo-American Times*, Nov. 17, 1865, pp. 1–3.

1616   PROCEEDINGS OF THE COMMERCIAL CONVENTION, held in Detroit, July 11th, 12th, 13th and 14th, 1865. Detroit, 1865. 276 p.   **CaOTP**

Includes speeches, discussions, etc. by Canadians.

1617   PROOFS OF THE FALSITY OF CONOVER'S testimony before the military court at Washington City. Montreal, 1865. 20 p.   **CSmH IHi**

Testimony of Sandford Conover concerned assassination of President Lincoln; Conover's real name Charles A. Dunham.

1618   RAWLINGS, THOMAS. The confederation of the British North American provinces; their past history and future prospects; including also British Columbia & Hudson's bay territory; with a map, and suggestions in reference to the true and only practicable route from the Atlantic to the Pacific ocean. By Thomas Rawlings, of Gresham House, London, author of "The United States and its future." London, 1865. 244 p.   **DLC Uk**

Part II, pp. 138–203, on the U.S. See also Rawling's letter to the *Anglo-American Times*, Dec. 9, 1865, pp. 2–3.

Review: *Anglo-American Times*. Nov. 24, 1865, p. 2.

1619   A REPLY TO A CRITIQUE on "Uncle John's cabin," which appeared in the "Dundee Advertiser," April 1, 1865. By the author of "The attempt of the North to subdue the southerners," &c. Liverpool, 1865. 45 p.   **MB NHi Uk**

Repr. the Dundee *Advertiser* "critique," pp. 5–10. See also *Uncle John's cabin*, 1865, below.

1620   ROBINSON, *REV.* STUART. Slavery, as recognized in the Mosaic civil law, recognized also, and allowed, in the Abrahamic, Mosaic, and Christian church. Being one of a series of Sabbath evening discourses on the laws of Moses. . . . With notes from orthodox British, and continental biblical critics and commentators. Toronto, 1865. 90 p.   **DLC**

On slavery in the U.S.

1621   ROSS, ALEXANDER MILTON. Address to the people of Canada. [Toronto, 1865]. 3 p.
MH

Dated Toronto, 4th Apr., 1865, and signed by Ross. On the Civil War in the U.S.

1622   ROSS, ALEXANDER MILTON. Human slavery in the southern states. Toronto, 1865. 8 p.
MH

1623   ROSS, ALEXANDER MILTON. Letters on Canadian independence. Toronto, 1865. 8 p.
CaOTP MB MH

On Canadian attitudes toward the U.S. and the Civil War.

1624   ROSS, ALEXANDER MILTON. The slaveholders' rebellion; its internal causes. Toronto, 1865. 8 p.
DLC

1625   ROSS, FITZGERALD. A visit to the cities and camps of the Confederate states. Edinburgh, 1865. 300 p.
DLC Uk

Repr. from *Blackwood's Edinb. Mag.*, XCVI (Dec. 1864), 645–670; XCVII (Jan. 1865), 26–48; (Feb. 1865), 151–175. New ed. under title, *Cities and camps of the Confederate States*, ed. by Richard Barksdale Harwell, Urbana, Ill., 1958.

Reviews: *Athenaeum* (May 13, 1865), 646; *Index*, IV, 778, V, 75; *Sat. Rev.* XIX, 545.

1626   RUSSELL, [SIR] W[ILLIAM] H[OWARD]. The Atlantic telegraph. [Annapolis, Md?], 1865. 117 p.
RP WaT

First pub. in the U.S. by Naval Institute Press. DLC, Uk have [London, 1866] ed.

1627   RUSSELL, *SIR* WILLIAM HOWARD. Canada; its defences, condition, and resources. Being a third and concluding volume of "My diary, North and South." London, 1865. 352 p.
DLC Uk

Boston, 1865 ed. carried title, *Canada: its defences, condition and resources. Being a second and concluding volume of "My diary, north and south."* First 3 chaps. on U.S.; other comment, passim.

1628   SALA, GEORGE AUGUSTUS [HENRY]. My diary in America in the midst of war. London, 1865. 2 vols.
DLC Uk

Parts appeared originally in the London *Daily Telegraph*, for which Sala was American correspondent. For an account of a later visit see his *America revisited*, 1880, below. Also see accounts in his two memoirs: *Things I have seen and people I have known*, London, 1894, 2 vols.; and *The life and adventures of George Augustus Sala, written by himself*, New York, 1895, 2 vols. See his account of the American exhibitions, esp. pp. 372–396, in his *Notes and sketches of the Paris exhibition*, London, 1868. See also his introds. to *Yankee drolleries: The most celebrated works of the best American humorists. Complete editions,* London, 1866; *More Yankee drolleries. A second series of celebrated works by the best American humorists*, London, [1869]; and *A third supply of Yankee drolleries*, London, [1870].

Reviews: *Athenaeum*, (Jan. 28, 1865), 117; *London Quar. Rev.*, XXIV, 147.

1629   THE SANITARY COMMISSION of the United States army. Its organization, purposes and work. By an Englishman. London, 1865. 24 p.
DLC Uk

1630   SEEBOHM, F[REDERIC]. The crisis of emancipation in America; being a review of the history of emancipation, from the beginning of the American war to the assassination of President Lincoln. London, 1865. 40 p.   **DLC Uk**

Printed for the "central committee of the Society of Friends for the relief of the emancipated slaves of North America."

1631   SENIOR, NASSAU WILLIAM. Historical and philosophical essays. London, 1865. 2 vols.   **DLC**

On U.S., I, pp. 18–33 (part of chap., "France, America and Britain," which appeared originally in *Edinb. Rev.*, Apr. 1842); pp. 91–117; and pp. 387–414 (part of longer chap., "Confederacy and union," repr. fron *Edinb. Rev.*, Jan. 1846). Also includes repr. of *The Oregon question*, 1845, above) in II, pp. 3–44.

1632   [SHEEPSHANKS, *REV*. JOHN, *Bishop of Norwich*]. A bishop in the rough; ed. by the Rev. D[avid] Wallace Duthie. With a preface by the Right Rev. the Lord Bishop of Norwich. London, 1909. 386 p.   **DLC Uk**

An account of Sheepshanks' life and travels, compiled from his journal. In U.S., 1859, 1864–65.

1633   SIMMONS, *SIR* JOHN LINTORN ARABIN. Defence of Canada considered as an imperial question with reference to a war with America. By J. L. A. Simmons, C.B. London, 1865. 27 p.   **DLC Uk**

DLC misspells name as Sir John *Linton* Arabin Simmons.

1634   SMALL, H[ENRY] BEAUMONT. The animals of North America. Series II. Fresh-water fish . . . Dedicated by permission to the Montreal fish and game protection club. Montreal, 1865. 72 p.   **CaOTP MH Uk**

See also his *The Animals of North America*, series I, 1864, above.

1635   SMITH, GOLDWIN. England and America. A lecture read before the Boston fraternity, and published in the *Atlantic* for December, 1864. Boston, 1865. 56 p.   **DLC Uk**

Contains prefatory letter, dated Dec. 5, 1864, to Charles G. Loring. The English ed., with an 8 p. introductory letter dated Jan. 16, 1865, carries the title, *England and America: a lecture, delivered by Goldwin Smith before the Boston fraternity, during his recent visit to the United States. Reprinted from "The Atlantic Monthly." With an introduction addressed, by the author, to the president of the Union and emancipation society, Manchester*, Manchester, 1865. Appeared in *Atlantic*., XIV (Dec. 1864), 749–769. See also Smith's "The case of the Alabama," *Macmillan's Mag.*, XIV (Dec. 1865), 162–176; his "Has England an interest in the disruption of the American Union?" ibid., X (May 1864), 49–52 (also in *Littel's Living Age*, LXXXI, 483); and his "The Danger of war with America," ibid., XI (Apr. 1865), 417–425.

Review: *No. Am. Rev.* (by C. E. Norton), C, 331.

1636   [SNOW, WILLIAM PARKER]. Southern generals, who they are, and what they have done. New York, 1865. 473 p.   **DLC**

Uk has later ed., under title, *Southern generals, their lives and campaigns*, New York, 1866; also pub. as *Lee and his generals*, New York, 1867. For incidental references to America, see his *British Columbia, emigration, and our colonies, considered practically, socially, and politically*, London, 1858.

Review: *Athenaeum*, (July 15, 1865), 82.

1637   STEINTHAL, *REV.* S. ALFRED. Address on the assassination of Abraham Lincoln, delivered at Platt chapel in the morning, and in the Ashton town hall in the afternoon of Sunday, the 7th May, 1865. London, 1865. 26 p.   **DLC**

See also author's "The great north-west: the Pacific slope," *J. Manchester Geog. Soc.,* I (Nov., 1885), 241–268; and his "Chicago and the World's fair: notes of a recent visit," ibid., (Apr. 1894), 177–182.

1638   S[TEPHEN], *SIR* L[ESLIE]. The "Times" on the American war: a historical study. London, 1865. 107 p.   **DLC Uk**

Repr. in *Mag. of Hist. with Notes & Queries,* Ext. no. 37, X (1915), 3–104. See also Stephen's articles on the U.S.: "American humor," *Cornhill Mag.,* XIII (Jan. 1866), 28–43; "Thoughts of an outsider: international prejudices," ibid., XXXIV (1876), 45–59 (repr. in S. O. A. Ullman, ed., *Men, books, and mountains,* London, 1956, pp. 145–167); "Some remarks on travelling in America," ibid., XIX (1869), 321–339; "An American protectionist [i.e., Erastus B. Bigelow]," *Macmillan's Mag.,* VII (Dec. 1862), 126–133. For an account of his visits to America in 1862–3 and 1868, see Frederick William Maitland's *The life and letters of Leslie Stephen,* London, 1906, pp. 105–129, 202–210. For American reactions to British periodical views, see [Edward Vernon Childe], *Letters to the London "Times", and New York "Courier and Inquirer". By A "States-" man,* Boston, 1857; Henry B[oynton] Smith's *British sympathy with America. A review of the course of the leading periodicals of Great Britain upon the rebellion in America,* New York, 1862 (Repr. from *Am. Theol. Rev.,* July 1862, 487–552, the pamphlet refers chiefly to "The American republic: resurrection through dissolution," *No. Brit. Rev.,* Feb. 1862, p. 123); William Barrows, "English parties on American affairs," *Boston Rev.,* III (Mar. 1863), 138–153; Rev. Joseph Parrish Thompson, *England during our war,* New Haven, 1862 (From the *New Englander,* XXI (July 1862), 556–586); *Letter from General C[harles] F[rederick] Henningsen in reply to the letter of Victor Hugo on the Harper's Ferry invasion; with an extract from the letter of the Rev. Nathan Lord, D.D., President of Dartmouth College, New Hampshire; and an article from the London "Times" on slavery,* New York, 1860, pp. 29–32. See also *The history of the Times: the tradition established: 1841–1884,* New York, 1939, pp. 359–391; William Beach Taylor, *The story of the Spectator, 1828–1928,* London, 1928, pp. 184–204; and *The Times reports the American Civil war: extracts from The Times, 1860–65,* introd. and ed. by Hugh Brogan, London, 1975.

1639   SULLIVAN, A[LEXANDER] M[ARTIN]. A visit to the valley of Wyoming, with an authentic narrative of the massacre from particulars collected in the valley. Dublin, 1865. 33 p.   **PSt**

Account of visit to Wyoming valley in Pennsylvania, in the summer of 1857; massacre in question was a 1778 Indian attack.

1640   SURBY, RICHARD W. Grierson raids, and Hatch's sixty-four days march, with biographical sketches, also the life and adventures of Chickasaw, the scout. Chicago, 1865. 396 p.   **DLC Uk**

Repr. in author's *Two great raids. Col. Grierson's successful swoop through Mississippi. Morgan's disastrous raid through Indiana and Ohio. Vivid narratives of both these great operations, with extracts, from official records. John Morgan's escape, last raid, and death,* Washington, D.C., 1897. Surby, a Canadian enlistee in the northern forces, recounts his experiences as one of the Grierson raiders.

1641   TINLEY, ROBERT. My life in the army, three years and a half with the Fifth Army corps, Army of the Potomac, 1862–1865. Philadelphia, 1912. 247 p.   **DLC Uk**

1642   TRIMBLE, ROBERT. The present crisis in America. London, 1865. 10 p.   **DLC Uk**

1643   UNCLE JOHN'S CABIN (next door to Uncle Tom's cabin) containing an answer to pro-slavery men, an answer to others, and an impeachment. By a neutral. London, 1865.   **Uk**

Uk lists under Neutral. See also *A reply to a critique on "Uncle John's cabin,"* 1865, above.

1644   WALSH, WILLIAM S[HEPARD], *ed.* Abraham Lincoln and the London Punch; cartoons, comments and poems, published in the London charivari, during the American civil war (1861–1865). New York, 1909. 113 p.   **DLC**

For discussion of *Punch* and Abraham Lincoln see the following: Oscar Maurer, "'Punch' on slavery and civil war in America, 1841–1865," *Victorian Stud.*, I (Sept. 1957), 5–28; Theodore Christian Blegen, *Abraham Lincoln and European opinion*, Minneapolis, 1934; Fred Landon, "Canadian opinion of Abraham Lincoln," *Dalhousie Rev.*, III (Oct. 1922); [Tom Taylor], *Abraham Lincoln foully assassinated April 14, 1865. A poem with an illustration from the London Punch, for May 6, 1865. Republished with an introduction by Andrew Boyd*, Albany, New York, 1868; George Soses Layard, *Shirley Brooks of Punch: his life, letters, and diaries*, London, 1907, which discusses *Punch* and the Civil war and positively identifies Tom Taylor (author of *Our American cousin. A drama in 3 acts*, London, [1858?]) as the author of the above poem, pp. 239–248. See also Matthew Somerville Morgan, *The American War. Cartoons by Matt Morgan and other English Artists*, 1874, below.

1645   WAYMAN, *REV.* JAMES. The passing away of human greatness: a sermon on the death of President Lincoln, preached on a Sunday evening, May 7, 1865, in Newington chapel, Renshaw street. Liverpool, [1865]. 8 p.   **DLC**

1646   [WHEAR, THOMAS TREVARTHEN]. The American war: a tale of two Cornish miners! Or, the humorous adventures of Nicky Polyglase and Willy Pender, in the United States of America. Their interview—as they thought—with old Abe. How he wanted to make them sogers. Their escape from the draft. And their opinion of the Yankees. Camborne, [1865]. 12 p.   **IHi MiU Uk**

Purports to be real adventures of two Cornish miners who emigrated to the U.S., told in their own dialect.

1647   [WHITE, RICHARD GRANT]. Rebel brag and British bluster; a record of unfulfilled prophecies, baffled schemes, and disappointed hopes, with echoes of very insignificant thunder. Very pleasant to read and instructive to all who are capable of learning. By Owls-Glass [*pseud.*]. New York, 1865. 111 p.   **DLC**

DLC lists under Owls-Glass. Written by an American; includes excerpts from British periodicals pub. during the Civil War.

1648   WOOD, *REV.* JOHN. Abraham Lincoln, the martyr president: being two discourses delivered on the day of his funeral obsequies, April 19th, 1865, in Zion church, Brantford, C.W., by the Rev. J. Wood and the Rev. W. Cochrane, M.A. Published by request. Brantford, 1865. 38 p.   **CSmH RPB**

1649   WRAXALL, *SIR* FREDERICK CHARLES LASCELLES, *3rd Bart.* Scraps and sketches gathered together. London, 1865. 2 vols.   **DLC Uk**

On U.S., I, pp. 286–311 (an adaptation from the German of Frederick Gustacker?); II, pp. 34–62, 188–217 (fiction), 232–253, 316–344 (semi-fiction). See also Wraxall's "The federal spy" in his *Historic bye-ways*, London, 1864, II, pp. 339–372; and his *Criminal celebrities: a collection of memorable trials*, London, 1861, pp. 85–97. Wraxell also edited Friedrich Armand Strubberg's *The backwoodsman; or, Life on the Indian frontier*, London, 1864 (a translation of *Amerikanische Jagd-und Reiseabenteur aus meinem Leben in den westlichen Indianergebieten*, Stuttgart, 1858).

1650   [YOUNG, ROBERT]. Abraham Lincoln: a study. Liverpool, 1865. 32 p.   **DLC**

Repr. in *Mag. of Hist. with Notes & Queries*, Ext. no. 49, pt. 2 (1916). Signed "R.Y."

1866

1651   ACTON, JOHN EMERICH EDWARD DALBERG ACTON, *1st Baron*. Historical essays and studies. Ed. by John Neville Figgis and Reginald Vere Laurence. London, 1907. 544 p.   **DLC Uk**

Includes "The Civil war in America: its place in history," a lecture delivered at the Literary and Scientific Institution, Bridgnorth, Jan. 18, 1866. See also "Lord Acton's American diaries," *Fortnightly Rev.*, CX (1921), 727–742, 917–934, CXI (1922), 63–83; records a two-month visit in 1853, largely concerned with conversations with intellectuals in the Boston area. For discussion of Acton's visit and views on Civil War, see Robert Schuettinger, *Lord Acton: historian of liberty*, La Salle, Ill., 1976, pp. 32–40, 120–129; and Gertrude Himmelfarb, *Lord Acton: a study in consciousness and politics*, London, 1952, pp. 77–83 and passim.

1652   ADDRESS OF THE FREE TRADE ASSOCIATION, of London, to the American Free Trade league, New York; being a resume of the financial changes of recent years, and their effect upon revenues and trade. London, 1866. 20 p.   **DLC Uk**

DLC lists under Free Trade Union; Uk under London—Free Trade Association. Signed Richard Moore, chairman, and John Noble, secretary.

1653   THE ATLANTIC TELEGRAPH: its history, from the commencement of the undertaking in 1854 to the sailing of the "Great eastern" in 1866. Accompanied with a familiar explanation of the theory of telegraphy; a chronological summary of the progress of the art; and a tabular list of the submarine cables now in operation; also an account of the leading submarine and land lines in progress and projected. From authentic sources. Illustrated with maps, drawings, portraits, a view of the "Great eastern," etc. London, 1866. 116 p.
        DLC Uk

See esp. pp. 10–22. See also "The Atlantic cable" from London *Times*, July 30, 1866, in Sir James Marchant, ed., *History thru 'The Times*,' London, [1937], pp. 207–211.

1654   BACON, GEORGE WASHINGTON and WILLIAM GEORGE LARKINS. Bacon's descriptive handbook of America. Comprising history, geography, railways, mining, finance, government, politics, public lands, laws, etc. London, [1866]. 392 p.   **DLC Uk**

DLC ascribes authorship only to Bacon. Rev. and enlarged ed., London, 1870, carried title, *Bacon's guide to America and the colonies, for the capitalist, tourist, or emigrant. Embracing climate, soil, agriculture, manufactures, prices of lands, and how to secure them, homestead laws, naturalization, wages, cost of voyage, railway fares and distances, and a mass of other general information.*

Review: *Westmin. Rev.*, LXXXV, 422.

1655 [BALLANTYNE, THOMAS]. Americanization: a letter to J. S. Mill, esq., M.P. By an old Whig. London, 1866. **UkLL**

1656 BARRINGTON, WILLIAM L. Reflections on some of the results of the late American war: being a lecture, delivered in the Friends' institute, Molesworth-street, Dublin, on Thursday, March 29th, 1866. Dublin, 1866. 43 p. **CSmH MH**

1657 BARRY, P[ATRICK]. Over the Atlantic and Great Western railway. London, 1866. 146 p. **DBRE Uk**

Sent to America as special commissioner of the *Money Market Rev.* Includes some correspondence with Richard Cobden about American affairs previous to his mission to the United States.

1658 BIRD, MARK BAKER. The victorious. A small poem on the assassination of President Lincoln. Jamaica, 1866. 57 p. **DLC**

By a British missionary residing in Haiti.

1659 BREEZE, JAMES T. The Fenian raid'. The Queen's own.' Poems on the events of the hour. Napanee, 1866. 6 p. **CaQMBN**

1660 BREEZE, J[AMES] T. The great theme of the age; a poem of the confederation of the British American provinces. Ottawa, 1866. 23 p. **CaOTU CaQMBM**

1661 CLYNE, JOHN. Hints to emigrants on the purchasing and clearing of land in America, with some observation on the manner of living in the United States and Canada. London, [1866]. 31 p. **Uk**

Clyne had lived in Ohio for 30 years.

1662 CROOK, *REV.* WILLIAM, *the Younger.* Ireland and the centenary of American Methodism. Chapters on the Palatines; Philip Embury and Mrs. Heck; and other Irish emigrants, who instrumentally laid the foundation of the Methodist church in the United States of America, Canada, and eastern British America. 2d thousand. London, 1866. 263 p. **DLC Uk**

1663 DAVIDGE, WILLIAM [PLEATER]. Footlight flashes. New York, 1866. 274 p. **DLC Uk**

Memoirs, apparently compiled from material written at different times, by a British actor who arrived in the U.S. in 1850 on contract to a New York theater and remained permanently. See pp. 115–123 for recollections of the voyage to New York.

1664 DENISON, *MAJOR* GEORGE T[AYLOR], *jr.* History of the Fenian raid on Fort Erie; with an account of the battle of Ridgeway. Toronto, 1866. 92 p. **DLC**

3d ed., Toronto, 1866, *The Fenian raid on Fort Erie; with an account of the battle of Ridgeway, June, 1866.* See also comments on U.S. and Canadian affairs in his *Soldiering in Canada: recollections and experiences*, Toronto, 1900; and in his *The struggle for imperial unity: recollections and experiences*, London, 1909. See also his "The burning of the Caroline," *Canadian Month. & Natl. Rev.*, III (Apr. 1873), 289.

1665 DRISCOLL, FREDERICK. The twelve days' campaign. An impartial account of the final campaign of the late war. Montreal, 1866. 103 p. **DLC**

See also his "Memoirs of a Canadian," Montreal *Gazette*, 1860.

1666 EDWARDS, PIERREPONT. A practical guide for British shipmasters to the United States ports. London, 1866. 323 p. **DLC Uk**

1667   THE FENIAN RAID on Fort Erie, June the first and second, 1866. With a map of the Niagara peninsula, showing the route of the troops; and a plan of the Lime Ridge battle ground. Toronto, 1866. 95 p.   **CaOOA MH**

1668   FERGUSON, ROBERT. America during and after the war. London, 1866. 280 p.**DLC Uk**

Visited the U.S. twice: to the North in 1864, to the South in 1865.

Review: *Athenaeum* (Sept. 1, 1866), 268.

1669   FLACK, *CAPTAIN* ("THE RANGER"). A hunter's experiences in the Southern States of America; being an account of the natural history of the various quadrupeds and birds which are the objects of chase in those countries. London, 1866. 359 p.   **DLC Uk**

Author in Texas and the West, 1836–1865. Pref. states he had been writing articles for the *Field* under pseud. "The Ranger." See his "Wild life [in the far west]," *Field*, XXVI (July 8, 1865), 18–19, 77, 110, 168–169, 219–220, 246, 266, 281; "The camp hunt," ibid., XXVIII (Sept. 1, 1866), 169–170, 192–193, 212–213, 243, 261, 280, 297, 323, 388–389; "Deer driving in a Texan forest," *ibid.*, XXIX (1867), 26; "A winter's run in Texas," *ibid.*, XXX (1867), 292–93, 341, 377, 475, 537–538, and XXXI (1868), 92, 179–180, 317, 372, 407.

Reviews: *Athenaeum*, (Dec. 1, 1866), 708; *Sat. Rev.*, XXII, 621.

1670   FLACK, CAPTAIN ("THE RANGER"). The Texan ranger; or, Real life in the backwoods. London, [1866]. 319 p.   **Tx Uk**

Fictionized sketches which originally appeared in the *Field*; see note to his *A hunter's experiences*, 1866, above. See also his novels: *The prairie hunter*, London, [1866], also pub. as *Indian Jake: or, The prairie hunter*, New York, [1869?]; and *The wigwam in the wilderness*, London, [1868].

1671   FLACK, CAPTAIN ("THE RANGER"). The Texan rifle-hunter; or, Field sports on the prairie. London, 1866. 333 p.   **DLC**

Book is autobiographical.

1672   FLETCHER, [HENRY CHARLES]. History of the American war, by Lieut.-Colonel Fletcher. London, 1865–66. 3 vols.   **DLC Uk**

Visited both sides during the Civil War; see his "A run through the southern states. By an English officer," *Cornhill Mag.*, VII (Apr. 1863), 495–515.

Reviews: (of first two volumes) *Athenaeum*, March 11, 1865, 345; *Quar. Rev.*, CXVIII, 106, *Westmin. Rev.*, XXVIII, 43.

1673   [FRASER, *REV.* JAMES]. Report to the commissioners appointed by Her Majesty to inquire into the education given in schools in England not comprised within Her Majesty's two recent commissions, and to the commissioners appointed by Her Majesty to inquire into the schools in Scotland, on the common school system of the United States and of the provinces of Upper and Lower Canada . . . Presented to both houses of Parliament by command of Her Majesty. London, 1866. 435 p.   **DHEW MH**

NUC lists under Great Britain—Schools inquiry commission. Uk has Sydney, 1868 ed., pub. by the New South Wales Legislative Assembly. For other comment on the U.S., see Fraser's *National education. A sermon, preached in the church of St. Edmund, Salisbury, on Sunday, October 25th, 1868*, London, [1868]; and his *The spirit of a public school. A sermon preached at the public opening of the new buildings of Shrewsbury school, on July 28th, 1882*, London, 1885. For comments on Fraser's visit to the U.S. in 1865, see Thomas Hughes' *James Fraser, second bishop of Manchester, a memoir, 1818–1885*, London, 1887, pp. 115–136.

Reviews: *Brit. Quar. Rev.*, XLVIII, 429; *Nation*, V, 205.

1674   [FREER, *REV*. RICHARD LANE, *Archdeacon of Hereford*]. Memoir, extracts of speeches, diary of a journey to America, &c. In memoriam; Hereford, 1866. 294 p.   **DLC Uk**

Priv. pr.; comp. by Mrs. Harriet (Clutton) Freer. "Journal of a voyage to America" (in 1862), pp. 248–283.

1675   GAUUST, DOSCEN. History of the Fenian invasion, of Canada, with numerous illustrations. Hamilton, C.W., [1866?]. 32 p.   **CaOTP**

Satirical account.

1676   GENERAL HINTS TO EMIGRANTS: containing notices of the various fields for emigration, with practical hints on preparation for emigrating, outfit for the voyage, the voyage, landing, obtaining employment, purchase and clearing of land, etc.; together with various directions and recipes useful to the emigrant. With a map of the world. London, 1866. 209 p.   **ICU MB NjP UkENL**

On U.S., pp. 18–22, passim. 2d ed., "carefully revised and corrected," London, 1875.

1677   HAMLEY, *SIR* EDWARD BRUCE. The operations of war explained and illustrated. Edinburgh, 1866. 438 p.   **ICJ MB PPL Uk**

DNW gives pub. date as 1865. Several other eds. slightly altered or revised: 2d ed., 1869; 3d ed., 1872; 4th ed., 1878 (held by DLC); 6th ed., 1907, rev. by L. E. Kiggell. On U.S. Civil War, passim; see esp. pp. 169–178, 200–206, 252–263. See also Alexander Innes Shand, *The life of General Sir Edward Bruce Hamley, K.C.B., K.C.M.G. . . . .With two portraits*, Edinburgh, 1895, I, pp. 135–137, 143–144, 185–191, and passim. Hamley also wrote many articles for *Blackwood's Edinb. Mag.*: the only one positively identified as his was, "Books on the American war," XCIV (Dec. 1863), 750–768; however, he probably also wrote "The battle of Gettysburg and the campaign in Pennsylvania. Extract from the diary of an English officer present with the Confederate army," ibid., XCIV (Sept. 1863), 365–394.

1678   HOBART, VERE HENRY, *Lord*. Political essays. London, 1866. 152 p.   **ICU MU Uk**

Relates to intervention, maritime capture, blockade, etc.; see esp. pp. 59–74. Also see Hobart's "The Alabama claims," *Macmillan's Mag.*, XXIII (Jan. 1871), 224–231, repr. in his *Essays and miscellaneous writings . . . with a biographical sketch; ed. by Mary, Lady Hobart*, London, 1885, II, 222–241.

1679   HOWE, JOSEPH. Confederation considered in relation to the interests of the Empire. London, 1866. 37 p.   **CtY MH Uk**

Compares Canada and the U.S.

1680   HOWE, JOSEPH. The organization of the Empire. London, 1866. 33 p.   **MH Uk**

References to U.S., passim. See also his *Speech of the Hon. Joseph Howe on the Union of the North American provinces and on the right of British colonists to representation in the imperial parliament*, 1855, above.

1681   INTERNATIONAL POLICY. Essays on the foreign relations of England . . . London, 1866. 603 p.   **DLC**

Includes "Note on the United States of America," by Richard Congreve, pp. 44–49; other references, passim. The "Note" also repr. in Congreve's *Essays: political, social, and religious*, London, 1874, pp. 159–164.

1682 KEAN, CHARLES JOHN, and MRS. (ELLEN TREE). Letters of Mr. and Mrs. Charles Kean relating to their American tours, ed., William G. B. Carson. St. Louis, 1945. 181 p.

DLC Uk

Wash. Univ. *Stud. Lang. & Lit.*, n.s., No. 15. Letters in this collection repr., with a few additional ones written from America and a series from Australia, in *Emigrant in motley: the journey of Charles and Ellen Kean in quest of a theatrical fortune in Australia and America, as told in their hitherto unpublished letters*, ed. by J. M. D. Hardwick, with a foreword by Anthony Quayle, London, [1954], 260 p. Some of the American letters, however, are pub. in more complete form in the Carson ed., and a few letters in the latter do not appear in the Hardwick volume. The Keans toured America in 1830–33, 1838–40, 1845–47, 1864–66. See also the account in *The life and theatrical times of Charles Kean, F.S.A.*, by John William Cole, London, 1859, 2 vols.

1683 KELVIN, WILLIAM THOMSON, *1st baron*. Atlantic telegraph cable. Address delivered before the Royal society of Edinburgh, December 18th, 1865, with other documents. London, 1866. 31 p.

NN Uk

See his "The Atlantic telegraph," *Good Words*, Jan. 1867, 43–49. See also "Lord Kelvin's views on Niagara development," *Western Electrician*, XXI (Aug. 21, 1897), 109. For other comment on America, see Andrew Gray, *Lord Kelvinian account of his scientific life and work*, New York, 1908; and Silvanus Phillips Thompson, *The life of William Thomson, baron Kelvin of Largs*, London, 1910.

1684 LOCKE, STEPHEN. English sympathies and opinions regarding the late American civil war. London, 1866. 26 p.

CtY MnU Uk

1685 LORD, JOHN KEAST. The naturalist in Vancouver Island and British Columbia. London, 1866. 2 vols.

DLC Uk

Deals extensively with California, Oregon and Washington in the 1860's. See also his "Game birds of the Rocky mountains. Notes on game birds found on the western slope of the Rocky mountains, & their adaptability to acclimatisation," *Field*, XXIV (Oct. 1864), 255–256, 306. Also see Lord's *At home in the wilderness; being full instructions how to get along, and to surmount all difficulties by the way*, London, 1867, below.

1686 LUDLOW, J[OHN] M[ALCOLM] F[ORBES]. President Lincoln self-pourtrayed [sic]. London, 1866. 239 p.

DLC Uk

Pub. for the benefit of the British and Foreign Freedman's Aid Society. Largely drawn from American sources, but includes author's "The martyred president," from *Good Words*, June 1, 1865. Ludlow also wrote *The war of American independence, 1775–1783*, London, 1876.

1687 MCGEE, THOMAS D'ARCY. The Irish position in British and in republican North America. A letter to the editors of the Irish press, irrespective of party. Montreal, 1866. 36 p.

DLC

Uk has 2d ed., Montreal, 1866, 45 p.

1688 [MACLEOD, MALCOLM]. Practical guide for emigrants to the United States. By a Lancashire artisan. Manchester, 1866.

UkMA has 3d ed., Manchester, 1870, under title: *Practical guide for emigrants to the United States and Canada*; LU has microfilm copy of this ed.

1689   MARX, KARL and FREDERICK ENGELS. The civil war in the United States. (Ed. by Richard Enmale). New York, 1937. 325 p.   **DLC Uk**

Includes seven articles on British public opinion on the Civil War, pub. in the New York *Daily Tribune*, 1861–62, pp. 3–54. Also contains correspondence between Marx and Engels on broader social and political issues in the U.S., 1861–66, pp. 221–277.

1690   MURRAY, ANDREW. The geographical distribution of mammals. London, 1866. 420 p.   **DLC Uk**

Includes much on the mammals of the U.S., passim.

1691   OLIPHANT, LAURENCE. On the present state of political parties in America. Edinburgh, 1866. 30 p.   **DLC Uk**

1692   PARTRIDGE, J. ARTHUR. The making of the American nation; or, The rise and decline of oligarchy in the West. London, 1866. 523 p.   **DLC Uk**

Reviews: *London Quar.*, XXVIII, 239; *No. Am. Rev.* (by C. E. Norton), CIV, 247.

1693   PARTRIDGE, J. ARTHUR. On democracy. London, 1866. 418 p.   **DLC Uk**

Author states that "this work arose out of considerations suggested by" the work published concurrently, *The making of the American nation, or the rise and decline of oligarchy in the west*, 1866, above.

Reviews: *Athenaeum*, (July 14, 1866), 47; *No. Am. Rev.*, (by C. E. Norton), CIV, 247; *Westmin. Rev.*, LXXXVIII, 479.

1694   PETO, *SIR* S[AMUEL] MORTON. The resources and prospects of America, ascertained during a visit to the States in the autumn of 1865. London, 1866. 428 p.   **DLC Uk**

See also author's *Speech by Sir S. Peto . . . on his return from the United States*, 1865, above.

Reviews: *Athenaeum* (1866), 555; *Chambers's J.*, XL, 438; *Fortnightly Rev.* (by A. Trollope), V, 126.

1695   PHILLIPS, JOHN ARTHUR. Report on the property of the California borax company. San Francisco, 1866. 26 p.   **DLC**

1696   RAWLINGS, THOMAS. What shall we do with the Hudson's bay territory? Colonize the "fertile belt," which contains forty millions of acres. By Thomas Rawlings, F.R.G.S., author of "America from the Atlantic to the Pacific." London, 1866. 83 p.   **DLC Uk**

Contains comment on Chicago, St. Louis, Colorado, Utah, etc.

1697   REMARKS ON THE HISTORICAL MIS-STATEMENTS and fallacies of Mr. Goldwin Smith, (late Regius professor of modern history at Oxford University) in his lecture, "On the foundation of the American colonies," and his letters "On the emancipation of the colonies." By a Canadian. Toronto, 1866. 16 p.   **DLC**

1698   SKINNER, J[OHN] E[DWIN] HILARY. After the storm; or, Jonathan and his neighbors in 1865–6. London, 1866. 2 vols.   **DLC Uk**

Review: *Athenaeum*, (Aug. 11, 1866), 173.

1699   SMITH, GOLDWIN. The civil war in America: an address read at the last meeting of the Manchester Union and emancipation society. London, 1866. 96 p.   **DLC Uk**

Report of the final meeting of the Union and Emancip. Soc., Jan. 22, 1866. CtY holds Anthony Trollope's copy, including his marginal notes and manuscripts of his review.

Review: *Fortnightly Rev.* (by A. Trollope), V, 251.

1700   SOMERVILLE, ALEXANDER. Narrative of the Fenian invasion of Canada . . . with a map of the field of combat, at Limestone ridge. Hamilton, C.W., 1866. 128 p.   **DLC Uk**

On U.S.-Canadian relations, passim. See also his 1 p. pamphlet on the Fenian danger, *New militia force.* [*A letter on the militia force of Canada.*] *(From the Hamilton Daily Spectator, March 14, 1868),* [Hamilton, 1868], no t.p. Also see author's comments on American presidents in the 1 p. pamphlet, *Royal Supremacy. (From the Hamilton Spectator, of March 30th, 1868.) Letters to the manhood and youth of Canada. No. 1,* [Hamilton, 1868], no t.p.

1701   STACKE, HENRY. The story of the American war. 1861–1865. London, 1866. 264 p.
DLC Uk

Repr. anonymously as *Heroism and adventure in the nineteenth century: as exemplified in the American civil war,* London, 1867.

1702   STAMER, WILLIAM ('MARK TAPLEY, *junr.*'). Recollections of a life of adventures. London, 1866. 2 vols.   **DLC Uk**

Includes sketches of America: I, pp. 15–27, 169–286; II, 210–300. See also the semi-fictionized article, signed "Mark Tapley," "The wilderness [of New York state]," *Field*, XXV (Jan. 7, 1865), 4–5, 31–32, 39–40, 56–57, 73, 104, 135–136, 144.

1703   URQUHART, DAVID. Sparing private property in war at sea. Two letters to Mr. [Sir William Henry] Gregory on his motion of March 2, 1866. London, 1866. 32 p.   **DLC Uk**

1704   WATTS, JOHN. The facts of the cotton famine. London, 1866. 472 p.   **DLC Uk**

On the war in the U.S., pp. 102–113, and passim.

1705   [YOUNG, JOHN]. On the changed opinions, since 1848, of the Montreal board of trade, respecting a canal to connect Lake Champlain with the St. Lawrence. Montreal, 1866. 25 p.   **CSmH MH NRU**

On trade between Canada and the U.S., etc.

1867

1706   AMBERLEY, JOHN RUSSELL, *Viscount.* The Amberly papers; the letters and diaries of Lord and Lady Amberley, edited by Bertrand and Patricia Russell. London, 1937. 2 vols.
DLC Uk

Repr. London and New York, 1966, under the title: *The Amberley papers; the letters and diaries of Bertrand Russell's parents.* Visited U.S. in 1867, II, pp. 9, 48–112. See also Viscount Amberley's "The Latter-day Saints," *Fortnightly Rev.,* XI (VI, n.s.), Part I (Nov. 1869), 511–535; Part II (Dec. 1869), 665–691.

1707   [ARGYLL, JOHN GEORGE EDWARD HENRY DOUGLAS SUTHERLAND CAMP-BELL, *9th duke*]. A trip to the tropics and home through America. By the Marquis of Lorne. London, 1867. 355 p.   **DLC Uk**

See also his account of a visit to the U.S. in 1866 in his *Passages from the past*, London, 1907, I, pp. 225–235; and the fictionized account of his experiences in California in his *From shadow to sunlight*, London, 1891. See also scattered comments on America in his *The Canadian north-west. Speech delivered at Winnipeg by His Excellency the Marquis of*

Lorne, governor general of Canada, after his tour through Manitoba and the north-west, during the summer of 1881, Ottawa, 1881, 22 p.; and *Memories of Canada and Scotland: speeches and verses by the right honorable the Marquis of Lorne*, Montreal, 1884. The following articles on the U.S. also are by the Duke of Argyll: "First impressions of the new world," *Fraser's Mag.*, C (Dec. 1879), 748–766, CI (Jan. 1880), 40–57, *Littel's Living Age*, CXLIV, 33, 279, and *Eclectic Mag.*, XCIV, 151, 274; "Distrust of popular government," *Forum*, VI (Sept. 1888), 34–44; "Obstacles to annexation," ibid., VI (Feb. 1889), 634–643 (an answer to Goldwin Smith, q.v.); "Canada and the United States," *No. Am. Rev.*, CLII (May 1891), 557–566 (an answer to Erastus Wiman, q.v.); "The Canadian Fisheries Dispute," *Fortnightly Rev.*, XLVII (Mar. 1877), 459–468.

1708   BATTY, JOSEPH. Over the wilds to California; or, Eight years from home . . . Ed. by Rev. John Simpson. Lees, 1867. 64 p.   **DLC**

1709   [BELL, *SIR* GEORGE]. Rough notes by an old soldier, during fifty years' service, from Ensign G.B. to Major-General C.B. London, 1867. 2 vols.   **DLC Uk**

New ed. London, 1956, under title *Soldier's glory, being Rough notes of an old soldier; arranged and edited by his kinsman Brian Stuart*. Bell visited the U.S. in 1838 and 1861.

1710   BENTHAM, GEORGE. Address of George Bentham, esq., F.R.S., president, read at the anniversary meeting of the Linnean society on Friday, May 24, 1867. London, 1867. 24 p.   **DLC**

On the biological sciences in the U.S.

1711   BLACKIE, JOHN STUART. On democracy. A lecture delivered to the Working men's institute, Edinburgh, on the 3d of January, 1867. Edinburgh, 1867. 54 p.   **CtY NN Uk**

Several eds. in 1867; DLC has "2d ed.," Manchester, 1885, *Democracy. A debate between Professor Blackie . . . and the late Ernest Jones. . . . Held at Edinburgh, January, 1867*. Jones' reply also pub. separately, *Democracy vindicated. . . .* , 1867, below.

1712   CARLYLE, THOMAS. Shooting Niagara: and after? (Reprinted from Macmillan's for August 1867, with some additions and corrections.) London, 1867. 55 p.   **DLC**

Repr. from *Macmillan's Mag.*, XVI, 319–336. Discusses the "late American war" and "the Nigger question," pp. 5–8. See also Carlyle's "Ilias (Americana) in nuce. [The American Iliad in a nutshell.]" *Macmmillan's Mag.*, VIII (Aug. 1863), 301. See also Charles Eliot Norton, ed., *The correspondence of Thomas Carlyle and Ralph Waldo Emerson, 1834–1872*, London, 1883; *Supplemental letters*, Boston, 1886; and Edwin W. Marrs, Jr., ed., *The letters of Thomas Carlyle to his brother Alexander, with related family letters*, Cambridge, Mass., 1968, passim. For discussions of Carlyle's views of America and American democracy, see Benjamin Evans Lippincott, *Victorian critics of democracy*, Minneapolis, 1938, pp. 6–53; and Andrew Hook, *Carlyle and America*, Edinburgh, 1970 (Occasional paper no. 3 of the Carlyle Society).

Reviews: *Catholic World*, VI, 86; Chicago *Tribune* (Aug. 21, 1867), 3; *Sat. Rev.*, XXIV, 176, 430; *Westmin. Rev.*, LXXXIX, n.s., 1.

1713   CLARKE, *SIR* EDWARD [GEORGE]. A treatise upon the law of extradition. With the conventions upon the subject existing between England and foreign nations, and the cases decided thereon. London, 1867. 183 p.   **DLC**

Uk lists all eds. as missing. On U.S., pp. 23–49, 122–130.

1714   DENIEFFE, JOSEPH. A personal narrative of the Irish revolutionary brotherhood, giving a faithful report of the principal events from 1855 to 1867; written, at the request of friends . . . to which is added, in corroboration, an appendix containing important letters and papers written by James Stephens, John O'Mahony, John Mitchel, Thomas J. Kelly, and other leaders of the movement. New York, 1906. 293 p.   **DLC**

"Printed serially in the *Gael* . . . New York, 1904." Repr. Shannon [Ireland], 1969, with an introd. by Sean Luing. Foreword to appendix signed, Stephen J. Richardson. Denieffe made two visits to the U.S., described here, and later settled in Chicago.

1715   DIXON, WILLIAM HEPWORTH. New America. London, 1867. 2 vols.   **DLC Uk**

5th ed., rev., London, 1867; many other eds.

Reviews: *All the Year Round*, XVII, 252; *Athenaeum*, (Jan. 19, 1867), 79; *Brit. Quar. Rev.*, XLV, 538; *Chambers's J.*, XLIV, 229; *Chr. Remembrancer*, LIII, 429; *Dublin Rev.*, VIII, n.s., 316; *Dublin Univ. Mag.*, LXIX, 279; *Eclectic Rev.*, XII, n.s., 221; *Fraser's Mag.*, LXXV, 640; *London Quar. Rev.*, XXVIII, 293; *Macmillan's Mag.* (by Edward Dicey), XV, 440; *Nation*, IV, 165; *Quar. Rev.* (by Philip Smith), CXXII, 450; *Sat. Rev.*, XXIII, 144; London *Times*, Jan. 28, 1867, 4; *Westmin. Rev.*, XXXI, n.s., 401.

1716   DODD, GEORGE. Railways, steamers and telegraphs; a glance at their recent progress and present state. London, 1867. 326 p.   **DLC**

Uk has Edinburgh ed., 1867. "Railway peculiarities in America," pp. 96–103; other comment, passim.

1717   ESSAYS ON REFORM. London, 1867. 336 p.   **DLC Uk**

Repr. in *A plea for democracy, an edited selection from the 1867 Essays on reform and Questions for a revised Parliament*, London, 1967. See the essays by James Bryce, "The historical aspect of democracy," pp. 239–278; Goldwin Smith, "The experience of the American commonwealth," pp. 217–238; and Leslie Stephen, "On the choice of representatives by popular constituencies," pp. 85–126.

1718   FORMBY, *REV*. HENRY. The cause of poor Catholic emigrants pleaded before the Catholic congress of Malines, September 5, 1867; being an address before the second section of the congress sitting on questions of Christian charity and social economy. With a general introductory letter, and a copious appendix. London, 1867. 56 p.   **MB Uk**

1719   [FRASER, WILLIAM]. The emigrant's guide; or Sketches of Canada, with some of the northern and western states of America. By a Scotch minister, thirty-six years resident in Canada, from 1831–1867. Glasgow, 1867. 72 p.   **CaOTP ICU MH UkLU-G**

1720   G., A. B. President Johnson and Congress. Audi et alteram partem. What is thought at some of the clubs, and elsewhere in London, of the threatened impeachment. London, 1867. 40 p.   **DLC Uk**

Authorship represented on title page by 3 Greek letters alpha, beta, gamma.

1721   GREGG, GEORGE R., and E. P. RODEN. Trials of the Fenian prisoners at Toronto, who were captured at Fort Erie, C.W., in June, 1866. Toronto, 1867. 222 p.   **CaOTU ICU MH**

Stenographic reports of the trials. See also [Frank Hayward Severance], "The Fenian raid of 1866," *Buffalo Hist. Soc. Pub.*, XXV (1921), 263–285.

1722   HAVELOCK[-ALLAN], *SIR* HENRY [MARSHMAN]. Three main military questions of the day: I. A home reserve army. II. The more economic military tenure of India. III. Cavalry as affected by breechloading arms. By Sir Henry M. Havelock, bart., major unattached. London, 1867. 209 p.   **DLC Uk**

"What mounted riflemen can accomplish in war, illustrated by the operation before and after the fall of Richmond in April 1865, till the surrender of Lee's army," pp. 66–114; other comment, passim.

1723   HIRST, FRANCIS WRIGLEY. Early life & letters of John Morley. London, 1927. 2 vols.   **DLC Uk**

Morley visited the U.S. in 1867; see I, pp. 119–124. See also George Meredith to Morley, "Lines to a friend visiting America," *Fortnightly Rev.*, VIII (n.s. II) (Dec. 1867), 727–731.

1724   [HOBART-HAMPDEN, *HON.* AUGUSTUS CHARLES ("Admiral Hobart Pasha")]. Never caught. Personal adventures connected with twelve successful trips in blockade-running during the American civil war, 1863–4. By Captain Roberts [*pseud.*]. London, 1867. 123 p.   **DLC Uk**

Uk catalogs under A. Roberts. Repr., with minor changes, in his *Sketches from my life. By the late Admiral Hobart Pasha*, London, 1886, pp. 88–185. Also repr. in *Hobart Pasha, by Augustus Charles Hobart-Hampden. Blockade-running, slave-hunting, and war and sport in Turkey*, ed. by Horace Kephart, New York, 1915; and in Ext. no. 3 of the *Mag. of Hist. with Notes & Queries*, I (1908), 143–205.

1725   HOPKINS, JOHN BAKER. The fall of the Confederacy. London, [1867?]. 96 p.   **DLC Uk**

Uk dates London, [1868]; Sabin gives [1867]. See also author's "America v. England," *Gentlemen's Mag.*, VIII, n.s., (Feb. 1872), 185–193; and "John and Jonathan," ibid., (March 1872), 353–366.

1726   HOSMER, JOHN ALLEN. A trip to the states by way of the Yellowstone and Missouri . . . with a table of distances. Virginia City, Montana Terr., 1867. 82 p.   **CtY MtU**

New ed., *A trip to the States in 1865, written and printed by J. Allen Hosmer at Virginia City, Montana, in 1867*, Missoula, [1932], ed. by Edith M. Duncan.

1727   HOWARD, JAMES. A trip to America. Two lectures. Rev. ed. Bedford [Eng.], [1867]. 60 p.   **DLC Uk**

No earlier ed. found; priv. pr. On Chicago and the West.

1728   JAMES, EDWIN [JOHN]. The Bankrupt law of the United States. 1867. With notes, and a collection of American and English decisions upon the principles and practice of the law of bankruptcy. Adapted to the use of the lawyer and the merchant. New York, 1867. 325 p.   **DLC Uk**

By a disbarred British lawyer who, after financial and political difficulties, came to the U.S. in the 1860s, practiced law in New York, and later returned to England.

1729   JEX-BLAKE, SOPHIA. A visit to some American schools and colleges. London, 1867. 250 p.   **DLC Uk**

Made two visits to the U.S., 1864–66 and 1866–68; for an account see Margaret Todd, *The life of Sophia Jex-Blake*, London, 1918, pp. 159–209.

Reviews: *Athenaeum*, (July 20, 1867), 76; *Brit. Quar. Rev.*, XVIII, 429; *Westmin. Rev.*, XXXIII, n.s., 252.

1730 JONES, ERNEST [CHARLES]. Democracy vindicated. A lecture delivered to the Edinburgh working men's institute, on the 4th January 1867, in reply to Professor Blackie's lecture on democracy, delivered on the previous evening. Edinburgh, 1867. 23 p.   **CSmH NN Uk**

See John Stuart Blackie, *On democracy*, 1867, above. See also Jones' contributions to *Notes to the people*: I (May 1851), 1–15 ("Introduction to *The New World: a democratic poem dedicated to the people of the United Kingdom and of the United States*"); and I (Aug. 1851), 276–278 ("The young republic and the rights of labour"); both repr. in John Saville, *Ernest Jones: Chartist. Selections from the writings of Ernest Jones with introduction and notes*, London, 1952, pp. 133–136, 276–278.

Reviews: *Bee-hive*, Jan. 12, 1867; *Blackwood's Edinb. Mag.*, CI, 230; *Reynold's Weekly Newspaper*, Jan. 13, 1867.

1731 KENNAWAY, [*SIR*] JOHN H[ENRY]. On Sherman's track; or, The South after the war. London, 1867. 320 p.   **DLC Uk**

1732 LACROIX, HENRY. The present and future of Canada. Montreal, 1867. 32 p.   **DLC**

Translation of Lacroix's *Opuscule sur le present et l'avenir de Canada, Montreal, 1867.* On U.S., passim., but U.S. influence implicit throughout.

1733 LATHAM, HENRY. Black and white. A journal of a three months' tour in the United States. London, 1867. 304 p.   **DLC Uk**

In U.S., Dec. 1866–Apr. 1867.

Review: *Athenaeum*, (Oct. 26, 1867), 528.

1734 LAWRENCE, *REV*. GEORGE GUERARD. A tour in the southern states of America in the year 1866: a lecture delivered in Huddersfield. London, [1867]. 44 p.   **Uk**

Sabin and UkENL give 1866 as pub. date.

1735 [LORD, JOHN KEAST]. At home in the wilderness; being full of instructions how to get along, and to surmount all difficulties by the way; by "The wanderer." London, 1867. 323 p.   **DLC Uk**

Slight changes in title in later editions; e.g., *At home in the wilderness: what to do there and how to do it. A handbook for travellers and emigrants*, London, 1876. Photograph-frontispiece is signed, "J. K. Lord". Much on hunting, etc. in the U.S., passim.

Reviews: *Athenaeum*, (July 6, 1867), 15; *Sat. Rev.*, XXIII, 763.

1736 [MACINTOSH, L.]. Class despotism, as exemplified during the four years struggle for freedom in the United States of America; and the evils of individual wealth considered, as reflecting the well-being and lives of the mass of a people. London, 1867. 337 p.   **OCl Uk**

Pref. is signed by L. M'Intosh.

1737 MCLENNAN, JOHN. Notes of a winter trip to Cuba and back by way of the Mississippi. Montreal, 1867. 54 p.

No locations found.

1738 MATHEWS, EDWARD. The autobiography of the Rev. E. Mathews, the "Father Dickson," of Mrs. Stowe's "Dred"; also a description of the influence of the slave-party over the American presidents, and the rise and progress of the anti-slavery reform; with a preface by H[andel] Cossham, esq. London, [1867]. 444 p.   **ICU MB NN TU Uk**

Pref. signed and dated Oct. 11, 1866, iii–xii. Mathews spent 19 years, 1832–1851, in America; he is identified as "Father Dickson" in Mrs. Stowe's *Key to Uncle Tom's cabin*.

Review: *Athenaeum*, (Nov. 2, 1867), 568.

1739 [MONKSWELL, ROBERT PORRETT COLLIER, *baron*]. £7 per cent. Confederate cotton loan. Case submitted to Sir. R. P. Collier, and his opinion thereon. Letter from the Committee. London, [1867]. **UkLGI**

1740 NATIONAL FREEDMEN'S AID UNION OF GREAT BRITAIN AND IRELAND. Actual and impending famine, and disastrous destitution in the Southern states of America. [London, 1867?]. 4 p. **NIC**

1741 NATIONAL FREEDMEN'S AID UNION OF GREAT BRITAIN AND IRELAND. The industry of the freedmen in America . . . [Birmingham, 1867]. 23 p. **MiU**

1742 [NORTON], C[HARLES] B[OWYER] ADDERLEY, [*1st baron*]. Europe incapable of American democracy, an outline tracing of the irreversible course of constitutional history. London, 1867. 45 p. **MH Uk**

See also his pref. to the 2d ed. (1st ed., London, 1861, without pref.) of *Letter to the Right Hon. Benjamin Disraeli, M.P., on the present relations of England with the colonies. . . . With a preface on Canadian affairs; and an appendix of extracts from evidence taken before the select comittee on colonial military expenditure*, London, 1862, pp. v–xvi. See also W. S. Childe-Pemberton, *Life of Lord Norton, 1814–1905*, London, 1909, p. 277.

1743 PHILLIPS, JOHN ARTHUR. The mining and metallurgy of gold and silver. London, 1867. 532 p. **DLC Uk**

On U.S., pp. 29–76, 128–202, 287–310, and passim.

1744 THE PROPOSED B.N.A. CONFEDERATION: a reply to Mr. Penny's reasons why it should not be imposed upon the colonies by imperial legislation. From the Montreal "Daily News." Montreal, 1867. 13 p. **CaOOA**

1745 QUESTIONS FOR A REFORMED PARLIAMENT. London, 1867. 328 p. **CU NN Uk**

Includes essays by various contributors; see Frederic Harrison, "Foreign policy," pp. 234–242.

Uk lists in England-Parliament-Appendix.

1746 [RUSSELL, JOHN RUSSELL, *1st earl, ed.*]. The official correspondence on the claims of the United States in respect to the 'Alabama'. London, 1867. 297 p. **MH-L MU N Uk**

NUC lists under title. Preface is signed "R." An appendix contains the correspondence between the U.S. and Portugal on the claims of Portuguese subjects against the U.S., 1816–1851, pp. 235–249.

1747 SEYMOUR, SILAS. Incidents of a trip through the great Platte valley, to the Rocky mountains and Laramie plains, in the fall of 1866, with a synoptical statement of the various Pacific Railroads, and an account of the great Union Pacific railroad excursion to the one hundredth meridian of longitude. 129 p. **DLC Uk**

See also author's *A reminiscence of the Union Pacific railroad. . . .*, 1873, below.

1748 SHAW, *REV*. JAMES. Twelve years in America; being: observations on the country, the people, institutions and religion; with notices of slavery and the late war; and facts and incidents illustrative of ministerial life and labor in Illinois, with notes of travel through the United States and Canada. London, 1867. 440 p. **DLC Uk**

2d 1867 ed. added cover title, *American resources. Life, labor and travels.*

1749   SMITH, SAMUEL. Reflections suggested by a second visit to the United States of America, being a paper read before the Liverpool philomathic society, March 13, 1867. Liverpool, [1867]. 35 p.   **MH**

Repr. in his *Occasional essays*, Edinburgh, 1874, pp. 125–155, together with another paper on his earlier visit of 1860, "American institutions," pp. 38–77. See also author's *America revisited*, 1896, below.

1750   THE STREET RAILWAYS OF AMERICA. A review of a pamphlet recently issued, entitled Facts respecting street railways. Reprinted from the *Morning Post* of Friday, December 21, 1866. Also the correspondence which appeared in the "Daily News," respecting the effect of street railways in increasing trade and improving property in the streets through which they run. London, 1867. 11 p.   **MH-BA Uk**

Uk lists under America.

1751   [WALTER, JOHN, *the younger*]. First impressions of America. London, 1867. 131 p.
DLC Uk

Signed "J. W." Priv. circ. Walter, editor and proprietor of the London *Times*, toured the U.S. for three months in 1866.

1752   WARD, JAMES, *of London*. Workmen and wages at home and abroad; or, The effects of strikes, combinations, and trades' unions. London, 1867. 314 p.   **DL**

DLC and Uk have London, 1868 ed.

1753   WORDSWORTH, CHRISTOPHER, *bishop of Lincoln*. Mormonism and England: a sermon, preached in Westminster Abbey, on Sunday evening, July 28, 1867. By Christopher Wordsworth, Archdeacon of Westminster. London, 1867. 22 p.   **CtY MH Uk**

Sermon based on William Hepworth Dixon's *New America*, 1867, above.

1868

1754   THE ALL-ROUND ROUTE GUIDE. The Hudson River; Trenton falls; Niagara; Toronto; the Thousand islands and the river St. Lawrence; Ottawa; Montreal; Quebec; the lower St. Lawrence and the Saguenay rivers; the White mountains; Boston, New York. Montreal, 1868. 86 p.   **DLC**

Uk has Montreal, 1872 ed., with title: *Chisholm's all-round route and panoramic guide of the St. Lawrence; the Hudson river;* etc. Many subsequent eds., rev. and expanded, have variations on the title; eds. after 1880 add substantial material on the West.

1755   ANGLO-AMERICAN TELEGRAPH COMPANY. Replies to, and correction of, statements made at the general meeting of the shareholders of the Atlantic Telegraph Company on the 24th January, 1868. [London, 1868]. 12 p.   **NN**

No t.p.

1756   ANNEXATION TO THE UNITED STATES: is it desirable? and is it possible? By "One of the people." Halifax, N.S., 1868. 64 p.   **DLC**

1757   [BARNSTON, GEORGE and JOHN SWANSTON]. The Oregon treaty and the Hudson's Bay Company. [n.p., 1868?]. 15 p.   **CSmH CtY ICN**

1758   BLUNDELL, B[EZER]. The contributions of John Lewis Peyton to the history of Virginia and of the civil war in America, 1861–65. Reviewed by B. Blundell. London, 1868. 46 p.   **DLC Uk**

1759   BOWEN, CHARLES SYNGE CHRISTOPHER BOWEN, *baron*. The 'Alabama' claims and arbitration considered from a legal point of view. London, 1868. 77 p.   **DLC Uk**

See also author's "Passing events: breaking the blockade," *Macmillan's Mag.*, V (March 1862), 432–440.

1760   COLLINGS, JESSE. An outline of the American school system; with remarks on the establishment of common schools in England. Birmingham, [1868]. 55 p.   **DLC Uk**

Derived from the report of the Rev. James Fraser, q.v., 1866, who was sent to the U.S. to inquire into the method of education. New ed., issued by the National Education League, London, 1872, carried the title *An outline of the American school system; with remarks on the establishment of common schools in England. To which is added, a reply to the statements of the Manchester education union with respect to the common school system of the United States.* See also Collings' views on the American civil war in *The life of the Right Hon. Jesse Collings. Part I, by the Rt. Hon. Jesse Collings; Part II, by Sir John L. Green.* . . . , London, 1920, pp. 80–84.

Review: *Brit. Quar. Rev.*, XLVIII, 429.

1761   CROMWELL, JOHN G[ABRIEL]. Popular education in America, illustrated by extracts drawn chiefly from the official reports of the United States . . . With an appendix, relating to popular education in England. London, 1868. 44 p.   **Uk**

See also author's speech on U.S. schools in *National education union. Authorized report of the educational congress, held in the Town hall, Manchester, on Wednesday and Thursday, Nov. 3rd & 4th, 1869*, London, 1869, pp. 79–82.

Review: *Brit. Quar. Rev.*, XLVIII, 429.

1762   DAWSON, S[IMON] J[AMES]. Report on the line of route between Lake Superior and the Red River settlement. Ottawa, 1868. 43 p.   **DLC Uk**

1763   DENISON, *LIEUT.-COL.* GEORGE T[AYLOR], *Jr.* Modern cavalry, its organisation, armament, and employment in war. With an appendix containing letters from Generals Fitzhugh Lee, Stephen D. Lee, and T. L. Rosser, of the Confederate States' cavalry, and Col. Jenyns' system of non-pivot drill in use in the 13th hussars. London, 1868. 376 p.

DLC Uk

See also "The American civil war," in author's *A history of cavalry from the earliest times, with lessons for the future*, London, 1877, pp. 436–484.

1764   DILKE, *SIR* CHARLES WENTWORTH. Greater Britain: a record of travel in English-speaking countries during 1866 and 1867. London, 1868. 2 vols.   **NjP PU Uk**

DLC has various 1869 eds.; London, 1885 ed. has added chapters. On U.S., I, pp. 1–222. See Stephen Gwynn, *The life of the Rt. Hon. Sir Charles W. Dilke*, completed and ed. by Gertrude M. Tuckwell, London, 1917, I, pp. 60–66.

Reviews: *Athenaeum* (Nov. 14, 1867), 633; *Blackwood's Edinb. Mag.*, CVII, 220; *Edinb. Rev.*, CXXIX, 455.

1765   DIXON, WILLIAM HEPWORTH. Spiritual wives. London, 1868. 2 vols.
CtY MB NN Uk

DLC has 2d ed., Philadelphia, 1868.

Review: *Westmin. Rev.*, XXXIII (n.s.), 456.

1766   [FIELD, CYRUS WEST]. Europe and America. Reports of proceedings at an inauguration banquet given by Mr. Cyrus W. Field of New York, at the Palace Hotel, Buckingham gate, London, on Friday, the 15th April, 1864, in commemoration of the renewal by the Atlantic telegraph company (after a lapse of six years) of their efforts to unite Ireland and Newfoundland by means of a submarine telegraph cable: and at an anniversary banquet given also by Mr. Cyrus W. Field, at the same hotel, on Tuesday, the 10th March, 1868, in commemoration of the signatures of the agreement for the establishment of a telegraph across the Atlantic, on the 10th of March, 1854. [London, 1868]. 68 p.   **DLC Uk**

The 1864 proceedings also pub. separately, 1864, above. Includes speeches by John Bright, Robert Grimston, Thomas Brassey, Cromwell F. Varley, John Walter, Sir Daniel Gooch, Capt. Mackinnon, Sir Charles T. Bright, Charles Edwards, Samuel Gurney, William H. Russell, Rev. Newman Hall, et al. See the verse satire on the occasion: *Alderman Rooney at the cable banquet: an improvised epic by himself* . . . Edited by D. O'C. T[ownley], New York, 1866. For an account of Field's career, construction of the Transatlantic cable, and activities among the British, see Carter Samuel, III, *Cyrus Field: man of two worlds*, New York, 1968.

1767   [FIELD, CYRUS WEST]. Proceedings at the banquet held in honour of Cyrus W. Field, esq., of New York, in Willis's rooms, London, on Wednesday, 1st July, 1868. Revised by the speakers. London, 1868. 80 p.   **DLC Uk**

Speeches on Anglo-American friendship by Duke of Argyll, Sir John Parkington, Sir Stafford Northcote, John Bright, Viscount Stratford de Redcliffe Earl of Morley, John Horatio Lloyd, Lord William Hay; also comments from the English press on the occasion.

1768   GRANT DUFF, *SIR* MOUNTSTUART E[LPHINSTONE]. A political survey. Edinburgh, 1868. 240 p.   **DLC Uk**

"The United States," pp. 119–151. See also his *Some brief comments on passing events, made between February 4th, 1858 and October 5th, 1881*, Madras, 1884, pp. 108–114.

1769   GUNDRY, HAMILTON D. Chips from a rough log kept on board the good ship Parisian. London, 1868. 146 p.   **DLC Uk**

Visits to Pacific coast, 1866, pp. 96–133.

1770   HALIBURTON, ROBERT GRANT. Intercolonial trade our only safeguard against disunion. Ottawa, 1868. 42 p.   **DLC Uk**

On Canadian-American-British relations. See also his articles in the *Proc. Royal Colonial Inst.*: "Influence of American legislation on the decline of the United States as a maritime power," III (1872), 194–209; "American protection and Canadian reciprocity," VI (1875), 205–227.

1771   HALL, *REV.* [CHRISTOPHER] NEWMAN. Newman Hall in America. Rev. Dr. Hall's lectures on temperance and missions to the masses; also, an oration on Christian liberty; together with his reception by the New York Union league club. Reported by Wm. Anderson. New York, 1868. 137 p.   **DLC Uk**

The oration on Christian liberty, repr. here, pub. under the title, *Christian liberty. A sermon delivered in the House of representatives, Washington, by invitation of the Hon. Mr. Speaker Colfax, on Sunday morning, November 24, 1867*, London, [1867]. See also his "A letter to the clergy and Christian people of America," pp. 9–12, and "Relations of Great Britain and America," pp. 277–282, in his *Sermons. . . . with a history of Surrey Chapel and its institutions*, New York, 1868. Also see his "An address to the American people, *Harper's Mag.*, XXXVII (July 1868), 230–239.

1772   HEAVISIDE, JOHN T. C. American antiquities; or, The New World the old, and the Old World the new. London, 1868. 45 p.   **DLC Uk**

1773   THE INTERESTS of the British empire in North America. [Ottawa], 1868. 16 p.
                                                                                CaOTP MH

On American trade and traffic, passim.

1774   JENNINGS, LOUIS J[OHN]. Eighty years of republican government in the United States. London, 1868. 288 p.   **DLC Uk**

See also his novels on Americans: *The millionaire*, London, 1883, said to depict the life of Jay Gould; and *The Philadelphians*, New York, 1891.

Reviews: *Athenaeum*, (Dec. 7, 1867), 758; London *Times*, (Dec. 26, 1867), 5.

1775   KERR, WILLIAM [WARREN] HASTINGS. The fishery question; or, American rights in Canadian waters. Montreal, 1868. 17 p.   **DLC Uk**

1776   MACKAY, CHARLES. Street tramways for London. . . . With some remarks, on the working of street railways in the United States and Canada. London, 1868. 20 p.   **Uk**

1777   MACMILLAN, ALEXANDER. A night with the Yankees: a lecture delivered in the town hall, Cambridge, on March 30, 1868. [Ayr], 1868. 60 p.   **DLC Uk**
Priv. pr.

1778   MAGUIRE, JOHN FRANCIS. The Irish in America. London, 1868. 653 p.   **DLC Uk**
Pref. dated Nov. 27, 1867.

Reviews: *Edinb. Rev.*, CXXVII, 502; *Fortnightly Rev.*, (by John Morley), IX, 220; James Alexander Mowatt, *Maguire's "Irish in America."* . . . , 1868, below (repr. from the London *Temperance Star*).

1779   MANNING, FREDERICK NORTON. Report on lunatic asylums. Sydney, 1868. 287 p.
                                                                          DNLM MB PPL Uk

An official report for the New South Wales government. Manning visited asylums in Europe and the U.S.; comments on 14 U.S. institutions (list on p. iii), passim.

1780   [MERRYWEATHER, FREDERICK SOMNER?]. From England to California. Life among the Mormons and Indians. Truth really stranger than fiction. The experiences and observations of the author during a period of eight years; giving the most thrilling account of the murders in Utah and the massacres on the overland line by the Indians; together with some very amusing scenes connected with Indian life. Sacramento [1868]. 146 p.
                                                                              CU-BANC ICN

CU-BANC and NUC give author as [F. Merryweather], cataloged separately from Frederick Somner Merryweather; CU-BANC also questions authorship. Semi-fictionized; 1856–62. See also Merryweather's "The far west," *Eliza Cook's J.*, I (Oct. 27, 1849), 401–403.

1781   MITCHELL, A., *jun*. Notes of a tour of America, in August and September, 1865. Glasgow, 1868. 152 p.   **DLC**
Priv. circ.

1782   MONRO, ALEXANDER. Annexation, or union with the United States, is the manifest destiny of British North America. By Alexander Munro [sic]. Saint John, N.B., 1868. 52 p.   **DLC**

1783   MOWATT, JAMES ALEXANDER. Maguire's "Irish in America." Being a review of Mr. Maguire's work, especially in its references to teetotalism and prohibition. By J. A. Mowatt, Dublin. Reprinted from the London "Temperance Star." London, [1868]. 30 p.

NcD Uk

See Maguire's work, 1868, above. See also author's comments on the temperance movement in the U.S. in his fictional *The autobiography of a brewer's son*, London, 1869.

1784   NATIONAL FREEDMEN'S-AID UNION OF GREAT BRITAIN AND IRELAND. The final report of the National freedmen's-aid union of Great Britain and Ireland; with the names of the newly-elected committee of correspondence with American freedmen's-aid associations; and reports of proceedings on the presentation of addresses to their excellencies the Hon. C. F. Adams and the Hon. R. Johnson, the late and present United States ministers to Great Britain. London, 1868. 39 p.   **DHU MB**

DLC shows only fragmentary title for this date: "The final report . . . "; DHU entry in NUC shows 1865, but is corrected in their own catalog. Contains addresses by the president, Sir Thomas Fowell Buxton, and others. The two addresses also pub. separately: *Presentation of an address to his excellency the Honorable Charles Francis Adams, envoy extraordinary and minister plenipotentiary to this country from the United States of America. April 3, 1868*, Birmingham, 1868; *Presentation of an address to . . . Honorable Reverdy Johnson*, London, 1868.

1785   NEWMAN, ALFRED. Ups and downs in America; or, Sketches of every-day life, manners and customs; with incidents of travel and adventure during a seven years' sojourn in America, before and during the war. An autobiography of Alfred Newman. Edited and rearranged by his brother George Newman. London, 1868. 83 p.   **Uk**

1786   PAPERS RELATING TO THE ILLEGAL SEIZURE of the British barque "Springbok", by an American cruiser, and the wrongful condemnation of her cargo, by the Supreme court of the United States. London, 1868. 70 p.   **DLC**

Different from *Papers relating . . .* , 1864, above, which Uk has. Reprint, by the owners of the cargo, of the official parliamentary correspondence. Extract from "Correspondence relating to the civil war in the United States of North America no. 1 (1863) presented to both houses of Parliament by command of her Majesty."

1787   PHILLIPS, GEORGE SEARLE ("JANUARY SEARLE"). Chicago and her churches. Chicago, 1868. 568 p.   **DLC Uk**

Phillips visited the U.S. in 1826–27, then returned permanently in the early 1860s. See also his *Emerson, his life and writings. By January Searle*, London, 1855.

1788   PHILLIPS, JOHN ARTHUR. Notes on the chemical geology of the gold-fields of California. [London? 1868]. 28 p.   **CSmH**

No t.p.; at head of caption-title: "From the Philosophical magazine for November, 1868." The substance of a paper read before the Royal Soc., March 12th, 1868.

1789   PROBYN, JOHN WEBB. Essays on Italy and Ireland, and the United States of America. London, 1868. 336 p.   **DLC Uk**

"The United States Constitution and the secessionists; reprinted from the *Westminster review* of April 1866"; *Westmin. Rev.*, XXIX, n.s., 422–451. This essay includes reviews of American books.

1790   PROCEEDINGS AT THE PUBLIC BREAKFAST held in honour of William Lloyd Garrison, esq., of Boston, Massachusetts, in St. James hall, London, on Saturday, June 29th, 1867. Revised by the speakers; with an introduction by F[rederick] W[illiam] Chesson, and opinions of the press. London, 1868. 96 p.   **DLC Uk**

Chesson's introd., pp. 3–11; speeches by John Bright (chair.), pp. 17–24, Duke of Argyll, pp. 24–29, Goldwin Smith, pp. 29–30, Earl Russell, pp. 31–33, J. S. Mill, pp. 33–35, George Thompson, pp. 46–52, and by Mr. Stanfield, W. Vernon Harcourt and E. Lyulph Stanley; comments of English press, pp. 57–96.

1791   THE REAL EXPERIENCES of an emigrant. London, [1868]. 128 p.   **MnHi Uk**

Uk lists under Emigrant; MnHi gives date [187–?]. On U.S.

1792   ROSE, GEORGE, "ARTHUR SKETCHLEY." The great country; or, Impressions of America. London, 1868. 416 p.   **DLC Uk**

See also his fictionzed sketches *Mrs. Brown in America . . . Reprinted from "Fun." With several unpublished papers*, London, 1868; and *Mrs. Brown on the Alabama claims*, London, [1872?].

Reviews: *Athenaeum*, (Oct. 24, 1868), 525; *Fun* (by T. Hood), (Oct. 24, 1868), 74.

1793   RYERSON, *REV*. [ADOLPHUS EGERTON]. Report on institutions for the deaf and dumb and the blind in Europe and in the United States of America. With appendices and suggestions for their establishment in the province of Ontario. By the Rev. Dr. Ryerson, chief superintendent of education for Ontario. Presented to the Legislative assembly by command of His Excellency. Toronto, 1868. 58 p.   **DHEW Uk**

Cataloged under Ontario Dept. of Educ.

1794   RYERSON, *REV*. [ADOLPHUS] EGERTON. A special report on the systems and state of popular education on the continent of Europe, in the British Isles, and the United States of America, with practical suggestions for the improvement of public instruction in the province of Ontario. . . . Presented to the legislative assembly by command of His Excellency. Toronto, 1868. 198 p.   **CaBVaU DHEW MH Uk**

Cataloged under Ontario Dept. of Educ. "Education in the United States of America," pp. 150–186. For scattered comments on his several visits to the U.S., see Ryerson's *The story of my life*, Toronto, 1883; and C. B. Sissons' *Egerton Ryerson, his life and letters . . . with a foreword by E. W. Wallace*, London, 1937–47.

1795   SHERLOCK, *REV*. WILLIAM. Church organization. The constitution of the church in the United States of America, in Canada, and in New Zealand. &c. With an introduction by the Rev. W. Sherlock, B.A., curate of Bray. Dublin, 1868. 130 p.   **Uk**

MB has 2d ed., rev., Dublin, 1869. The introd., pp. lx–xxxiv, deals largely with the organization of the American church; other comments, passim.

1796   SOME NOTES ON AMERICA to be rewritten: suggested, with respect, to Charles Dickens, esq. Philadelphia, 1868. 20 p.   **DLC Uk**

Uk catalogs under America. Author was Englishman living in U.S.

1797   STEINMETZ, ANDREW. The romance of duelling in all times and countries. London, 1868. 2 vols.   **DLC Uk**

"Duelling in the United States," II, pp. 298–317.

1798   [SUTHERLAND, *MRS*. (REDDING)]. Five years within the Golden Gate. By Isabelle Saxon [*pseud*.]. London, 1868. 315 p.   **DLC Uk**

In California and the West approx. 1861–66. Returned to England for a visit in 1866 and, encouraged to record her experiences, did so upon her return to San Francisco.

1799 THOMAS, DAVID. My American tour: being notes taken during a tour through the United States shortly after the close of the late American war. Bury, 1868. 203 p. **DLC**

1800 VINCENT, HENRY. Henry Vincent's visit to Mt. Lebanon, Columbia county, New York. Albany, 1868. 12 p. **DLC**

Shaker tracts, no. 1. Vincent visited the U.S. in 1866, 1867, 1869, and 1875–76; see account in William Dorling, *Henry Vincent: a biographical sketch . . . With a preface by Mrs. Vincent*, London, 1879, pp. 58–69; also included is a letter from John Bright on U.S., pp. 60–61.

1801 WADDINGTON, ALFRED PENDERILL. Overland route through British North America; or, The shortest and speediest road to the East. With a coloured map. London, 1868. 48 p. **DLC Uk**

On Canada, but much discussion of and comparison with the U.S.

1802 WALLER, W. H. Something about Ireland as it is, and Fenianism: together with some suggestions for the consideration of the Canadian people and government. Ottawa, 1868. 30 p. **CaOTP**

On Fenianism in the U.S., pp. 24–30.

1803 WHYMPER, FREDERICK. Travel and adventure in the territory of Alaska, formerly Russian America—now ceded to the United States—and in various other parts of the north Pacific. London, 1868. 331 p. **DLC Uk**

Last 3 chaps. on California, pp. 269–306. See also author's articles in Henry Walter Bates, ed., *Illustrated travels: a record of discovery, geography, and adventure*, London, [1869–1871]; "California and its prospects," I (1869), 103–110; "From ocean to ocean— the Pacific railroad," II (1870), 1–12, 33–40, 65–71. See also his "Notes on California," *Field*, I (Aug.–Nov. 1870), 243–244, 329–332.

Reviews: *Athenaeum*, (1868), 673; *Sat. Rev.*, XXVI, 834.

1804 WILLIAMS, R[OBERT] H[AMILTON]. With the border ruffians; memories of the Far West, 1852–68. Edited by E. W. Williams. London, 1907. 478 p. **Uk**

DLC has New York, 1907 ed. R. H. Williams had served in the Kansas and Texas Rangers.

1805 ZINCKE, *REV*. F[OSTER] BARHAM. Last winter in the United States; being table talk collected during a tour through the late southern confederation, the far West, the Rocky mountains, &c. London, 1868. 314 p. **DLC Uk**

Reviews: *Athenaeum*, (Dec. 12, 1868), 789; *Nation*, VII, 533.

1869

1806 ATKINS, *REV*. THOMAS. Reminiscences of twelve years' residence in Tasmania and New South Wales; Norfolk Island and Moreton Bay; Calcutta, Madras, and Cape Town; the United States of America; and the Canadas. Malvern, 1869. 292 p. **DLC Uk**

Visited the U.S. in 1861, pp. 251–282. The chapters on the U.S. and Canada were added to a new ed. of *The wanderings of the clerical Eulysses [sic] described in a narrative of ten years' residence in Tasmania and New South Wales; at Norfolk Island and Moreton Bay; in Calcutta, Madras, and Cape Town*, Greenwich, [1859].

1807   BAGEHOT, WALTER. A practical plan for assimilating the English and American money, as a step towards a universal money. London, 1869. 70 p.   **DLC Uk**

Repr. from the *Economist*, with additions and a pref.; 2d ed. London, 1889. See also author's essay, The American constitution at the present crisis," in the *Natl. Rev.* (Oct. 1861); repr. in *Bagehot's historical essays*, ed., with an introd. by Norman St. John-Stevas, London, 1971, pp. 348–380. Bagehot continued this discussion in his *The English constitution*, London, 1867, 348 p.; (repr. from the *Fortnightly Rev.* I–VII, May 15, 1865–Jan. 1, 1867), contrasting English and American systems. See also the long introd. to the 2d ed., London, 1872, pp. 51–66. Also see Alastair Buchan, *The spare chancellor: the life of Walter Bagehot*, London, 1959, pp. 150–158, and passim; and Michael Churchman, "Walter Bagehot and the American Civil War," *Dublin Rev.* (Winter, 1965–66), 377–393.

1808   BARTLETT, WILLIAM and HENRY CHAPMAN. A handy-book for investors; comprising a sketch of the rise, progress, and present character of every species of investment, British, colonial, and foreign; including an estimate of their comparative safety and profit. London, 1869. 484 p.   **NN Uk**

On U.S., pp. 102–104, 238–244, 463–468. See also Bartlett's *The investor's directory to marketable stocks and shares, with a description of their nature, security, etc.; also suggestions how to invest, so as to make the safest and most profitable investments*, London, [1876], pp. 17–20, 41–42, 59.

1809   BAYLEY, *REV.* JOHN. Facts for the people of Great Britain and Ireland, concerning the United States of America. London, 1869. 107 p.   **CtY MH Uk Vi**

1810   BELL, WILLIAM A[BRAHAM]. New tracks in North America. A journal of travel and adventure whilst engaged in the survey for a southern railroad to the Pacific Ocean during 1867–8. [With contributions by General W. J. Palmer, Major A. R. Calhoun, C. C. Parry, and Capt. W. F. Colton]. London, 1869. 2 vols.   **DLC Uk**

Bracketed material not on t.p., but is on t.p. of London, 1870, 2d ed.; this 1 vol. ed. also added Appendix A, pp. 521–533, a list of plants prepared by C. C. Parry of collections made between Kansas and San Francisco. A portion of the book repr. under title, "Redman and buffalo," in *Travels in many lands*, London, 1915, pp. 5–126. See also Bell's "Ten days' journey in southern Arizona," in Henry Walter Bates, ed., *Illustrated travels, a record of discovery, geography, and adventure*, London, [1869–71], I ([1869]), 147–148, and repr. in *Wonderful adventures. A series of personal experiences among the native tribes of America*, London, [1872], pp. 25–59. See also the following articles by Bell: "On the native races of New Mexico," *J. Ethnol. Soc. London*, I, n.s. (Oct. 1869), 222–274; "The Pacific railroads," *Fortnightly Rev.*, XI (May 1, 1869), 562–578; "On the basin of Colorado and the Great basin of North America," *J. Royal Geog. Soc.*, XXXIX (1869, a paper read Mar. 8, 1868), 95–120; a discussion of the paper, "On the physical geography of the Colorado basin and the Great basin region of North America," ibid, XIII (July 20, 1869), 140–144. For an account of Bell's experiences as photographer in William Blackmore's surveying tours in the 1870s, see Herbert O. Brayer, *A case study in the economic development of the west*, Denver, 1949, Vol. II, *William Blackmore: early financing of the Denver & Rio Grande railway and ancillary land companies, 1871–1878*.

Reviews: *Academy* (by H. W. Bates), I, 105; *Field*, XXXV, 50; *Littel's Living Age*, CIV, 245, *Nation*, XI, 371; *Sat. Rev.*, XXVIII, 456.

1811 BLACKMORE, WILLIAM, [*ed.*]. Colorado: its resources, parks, and prospects as a new field for emigration; with an account of the Trenchara and Costilla estates, in the San Luis park. London, 1869. 217 p. **DLC Uk**

Also priv. pr. anonymously the same year. Consists of extracts from various English and American travel accounts. For various comments on the Blackmore work, see the compilation of extracts from London papers entitled *The parks, prospects, and resources of Colorado*, 1869, below. See also Herbert O. Brayer, *A case study in the economic development of the west*, Denver, 1949: Vol. I, *William Blackmore: the Spanish-Mexican land grants of New Mexico and Colorado, 1863–1878*; Vol. II, *William Blackmore: early financing of the Denver & Rio Grande Railway and ancillary land companies, 1871–1878*.

1812 BRAGG, H. "Under which king, Bezonian?" A challenge elicited by the Honorable J. Lorthrop Motley's address on historic progress and American democracy. Inscribed respectfully (but without leave) to Professor Blackie, whose arguments in his celebrated lecture on democracy much of the quoted matter herein goes strongly to support. London, 1869. 56 p. **MB NN Uk**

Portions appeared in the Liverpool *Daily Courier*, July 3 and 5, 1869.

1813 BRIGHT, JOHN. Speeches on the public affairs of the last twenty years. London, 1869. 346 p. **LU PST TU**

Uk, many U.S. libraries have 2d ed. adding *With the speech on the Irish church bill, March 19, 1869*, London, 1869. Contains speech delivered at Rochdale, Dec. 4, 1861, "Seizure of the Southern commissioners," pp. 108–138; speech delivered at Birmingham, Dec. 18, 1862, "The American war and the distress in the cotton districts," pp. 138–167; speech delivered at St. James's hall, March 26, 1863, "America and England," pp. 167–176; speech delivered in the House of Commons, June 30, 1863, "Mr. Roebuck's motion for recognition of the southern confederacy," pp. 176–193; and "Letter from Mr. Bright to Mr. Horace Greeley, Oct. 1864," p. 193. See also an article on Bright's letters in the *Quar. Rev.*, CXVII (April 1865), 249–286.

1814 CANNON, JOHN. History of Grant's campaign for the capture of Richmond (1864–1865), with an outline of the previous course of the American civil war. London, 1869. 470 p. **DLC Uk**

1815 CHESTER, GREVILLE JOHN. Transatlantic sketches in the West Indies, South America, Canada, and the United States. London, 1869. 405 p. **DLC Uk**

About half of the book is on an 1868 visit to the U.S.

1816 CHURCH ESTABLISHMENTS and the effect of their absence in America. London, [1869]. 11 p. **CtY TxDaM Uk**

Uk lists under USA; TxDaM dates [1862], but their copy cites an 1866 work.

1817 CLARK, *SIR* JAMES. A memoir of John Conolly, M.D., D.C.L., comprising a sketch of the treatment of the insane in Europe and America. London, 1869. 298 p. **CLU DNLM IU Uk**

DLC lists same title, also London, 1869, but only 16 p. ("From the American journal of insanity for April 1870"); Uk also has this version.

1818 THE CLERGY OF AMERICA: anecdotes illustrating the life and labour of ministers of religion in the United States. London, [1869?]. 478 p. **CU**

Uk, NN, PPL have Philadelphia, 1869 ed., with title: *The clergy of America: anecdotes illustrative of the character of ministers of religion in the United States*, 480 p.

1819   CORRESPONDENCE RELATING TO THE FENIAN invasion and the rebellion of the
        Southern states. Ottawa, 1869.   **DLC Uk**

        DLC and Uk list under Canada—Dept. of the Secretary of State. Consists of short official
        letters, etc.

1820   DAWSON, *SIR* JOHN WILLIAM. Notes of a visit to scientific schools and museums in
        the United States, by Principal Dawson. [Montreal, 1869]. 13 p.   **DLC**

        Repr. from the *Canadian Naturalist*, IV, n.s.

1821   DEEDES, HENRY. Sketches of the South and West; or, Ten months' residence in the
        United States. Edinburgh, 1869. 170 p.   **DLC Uk**

        Visited the U.S. in 1859 and in 1867–68.

1822   EDGE, FREDERICK MILNES. Great Britain and the United States; a letter to the Right
        Honourable William Ewart Gladstone, M.P., Her Majesty's first lord of the Treasury.
        London, 1869. 38 p.   **MH Uk**

        DLC has on microfilm.

1823   EDWARDS, EDWARD. Free town libraries, their formation, management, and history; in
        Britain, France, Germany, & America. Together with brief notices of book-collectors, and
        of the respective places of deposit of their surviving collections. London & New York,
        1869. 371, 262 p.   **DLC Uk**

        On U.S.: pp. 269–343.

1824   FRITH, JOSEPH. Far and wide. A diary of long and distant travel, 1857–1860. London,
        1869.   **Uk**

        On U.S., pp. 382–391, 405–486.

1825   [GILLMORE, PARKER]. Accessible field sports; the experiences of a sportsman in North
        America. By "Ubique" [*pseud.*]. London, 1869. 336 p.   **DLC Uk**

1826   [GILLMORE, .PARKER]. Gun, rod, and saddle. Personal experiences. By Ubique
        [*pseud.*]. London, 1869. 295 p.   **CSmH MH Uk**

        DLC has New York, 1869 ed.; Uk also has new enlarged ed., London, 1893, 341 p. Articles
        originally pub. in *Land and Water*; much comment on U.S.

1827   [GOODCHILD, *REV*. GEORGE]. Common sense applied to the immigrant question:
        showing why the "California immigrant union" was founded and what it expects to do. By
        C[asper] T[homas] Hopkins. [San Francisco, 1869]. 64 p.   **DLC**

        Includes Goodchild's "Letter on British emigration to California."

1828   [HARVEY, WILLIAM HENRY]. Memoir of W. H. Harvey, M.D., F.R.S., etc., etc., late
        professor of botany, Trinity College, Dublin. With selections from his journal and corre-
        spondence. By a cousin. London, 1869. 372 p.   **DLC Uk**

        Visited the U.S. in 1849, pp. 164–211, and passim. Composed largely of private letters.

1829   HOOK, WALTER FARQUHAR. The disestablished church in the republic of the United
        States of America. A lecture delivered at the church institute, Leeds, on Thursday, February
        4, 1869. London, 1869. 67 p.   **CtY MH Uk**

        See also Hook's pref., pp. i–xxvii, to John McVickar's *The Early life and professional
        years of Bishop Hobart. With a preface containing a history of the church in America, by
        Walter Farquhar Hook, D.D., Vicar of Leeds, prebendary of Lincoln, and chaplain in ordi-
        nary to the Queen*, Oxford, 1838 (held by DLC and Uk).

1830   HUNTINGTON, *HON*. L[UCIUS] S[ETH]. The independence of Canada. The annual
address delivered before the Agricultural society of the country of Missisquoi at Bedford,
Sept. 8, 1869. Montreal, 1869. 14 p.   **DLC**

On U.S., passim.

1831   L[ANCELOT], D. California. . . . By D. L. [London? 1869]. 208 [i.e. 170] p.   **CLU**

No real t.p.; erratic pagination; priv. pr.

1832   LEES, *DR*. FREDERICK RICHARD. Text-book of temperance. Rockland, Me., 1869.
312 p.   **DLC**

Uk has London, 1871 ed. Chap. 8, "The national question and the remedy," pp. 176–266;
repr. separately under title: *National intemperance and the remedy, as illustrated chiefly
from the history of the United States. Addressed to statesmen, politicians, and social
reformers*, Manchester, 1871. See also accounts of his trips to the U.S. in 1853, 1869–70,
and 1875 in Frederick Lees' *Dr. Frederic Richard Lees, a biography*, London, 1904, pp.
71–84, 127–142, 174–177.

1833   [LONGWORTH, MARIA THERESA, VISCOUNTESS AVONMERE; "THERESE
YELVERTON," *pseud*.]. Saint Augustine, Florida. Sketches of its history, objects of interest, and advantages as a resort for health and recreation. By an English visitor. With notes
for northern tourists on St. John's River, etc. New York, 1869. 62 p.   **DLC Uk**

Another New York, 1869 ed., 68 p.

1834   [MCLEOD, MALCOLM]. A letter to The Honourable Charles Sumner, upon his speech
delivered on the Alabama claims convention, from Britannicus [*pseud*.]. Liverpool, 1869.
14 p.   **DLC Uk**

Author not identified by DLC or Uk.

1835   MAGUIRE, JOHN FRANCIS. America, in its relation to Irish emigration: a lecture delivered at Cork and Limerick. Cork, 1869.   **NcD**

1836   MAHAFFY, *SIR* JOHN PENTLAND. Twelve lectures on primitive civilizations, and their
physical conditions. (Delivered at the Alexandra College.) London, 1869. 296 p. **DLC Uk**

On California and the far west, pp. 267–282.

1837   [MANLEY, H. F.]. The other side the herring-pond. (American notes). By May Fly
[*pseud*.]. London, 1869. 97 p.   **MH Uk**

DLC has on microfilm. Authorship ascribed to Manley by DLC and Emanuel Green's
Bibliotheca somersetensis. Uk mistakenly gives authorship to "Wellington Somerset," a
misreading of place of publication; MH ascribes to John Anderson.

1838   MAYNE, J. T. Short notes of tours in America and India. Madras, 1869. 193 p.   **DLC Uk**

In America in 1859.

1839   MILTON, WILLIAM FITZWILLIAM, *Viscount*. A history of the San Juan water boundary question, as affecting the division of territory between Great Britain and the United
States . . . Collected and compiled from official papers and documents printed under the
authority of the governments respectively of Great Britain and Ireland and of the United
States of America, and from other sources. London, 1869. 442 p.   **DLC Uk**

1840   NELSON, JOSEPH. Emigration to North America. A letter to the Right honourable
G[eorge] J[oachim] Goschen, M.P., president of the Poor law board. London, 1869. 19 p.
                                                                                                                              MnHi

1841   [NYE, GIDEON]. Casual papers on the "Alabama" and kindred questions and, incidentally, upon national amenities. (First published in the Hongkong Daily Press 1862–1865). 2d ed. Hong Kong, 1869. 86 p.   **DLC**

Autograph presentation copy to Hamilton Fish from Nye, who is named as "the amateur publisher" of the papers in a manuscript note on p. 2. Nye was an American, but the book contains much British comment.

1842   OLD, R[OBERT] O[RCHARD]. Colorado: United States, America. Its history, geography, and mining. Including a comprehensive catalogue of nearly six hundred samples of ores. London, 1869. 64 p.   **DLC**

London, 1872 ed., with additions, carried title, *Colorado: United States, America, its mineral and other resources. Including a descriptive list of a large number of the principal mines; advantages of soil and climate; railway system; journey from England, &c., &c.*

1843   THE PARKS, PROSPECTS, AND RESOURCES OF COLORADO. Opinions of the press. (Leading article from the "Standard" of August 19, 1869.) [London, 1869]. 48 p.

    DLC

Caption title. A compilation of extracts from London papers, relating to William Blackmore's *Colorado: its resources, parks, and prospects*, 1869, above.

1844   RUSSELL, ALEXANDER JAMIESON. The Red River country, Hudson's Bay, and North-west Territories, considered in relation to Canada, with the last report of S. J. Dawson . . . on the line of route between Lake Superior and the Red River settlement. Ottawa, 1869. 202 p.   **DLC**

Uk has 3d ed., Montreal, 1870, "with the last two reports of S. J. Dawson."

1845   SHERWELL, SAMUEL. Old recollections of an old boy. New York, 1923. 271 p.   **DLC**

In America 1858–69, pp. 34–151; returned to the U.S. in 1871, and remained.

1846   SMITH, GOLDWIN. England and slavery. Lecture by Professor Goldwin Smith at Case hall, Cleveland, Ohio, July 31, 1869. [Cleveland], 1869. 13 p.   **OCIWHi**

Priv. pr.

1847   SMITH, GOLDWIN. The relations between America and England, an address delivered before the citizens of Ithaca . . . May 19, 1869. A reply to the late speech of Mr. Sumner. London, 1869.   **CSmH MH Uk**

DLC has Ithaca, N.Y., [1869] ed. Smith was at Cornell University, 1868–70; see his *The early days of Cornell*, Ithaca, 1904, 23 p. See also his lecture comparing American and English education, "University education," *J. Social Sciences*, I (June 1869), 24–55; and see an undergraduate account of Smith's first lecture at Cornell in *Cornell Era*, I (Nov. 28, 1868).

1848   STEPHENS, WILLIAM W. The settlement of the Alabama question with self-respect to both nations; being a speech on the exemption from seizure of all private property on sea. Delivered before the Edinburgh Chamber of commerce, 6th May, and the joint Chambers of Edinburgh and Leith, 21st May, 1869. Edinburgh, 1869. 27 p.   **MH NHi Uk**

1849   TAYLOR, F. S. Notes on some distinctive features of railway construction in the United States. Calcutta, 1869. 22 p.   **WU**

1850 THORNEYCROFT, T[HOMAS]. A trip to America . . . September 1, 1869. Wolverhampton, 1869. 59 p. **DLC**

Priv. pr.; in verse.

1851 TOWNSHEND, *CAPT.* F[REDERICK] TRENCH. Ten thousand miles of travel, sport, and adventure. London, 1869. 275 p. **DLC Uk**

Hunting in America in Aug. 1868.

Review: *Field*, XXXIV, 250.

1852 WALTER, *MAJOR* JAMES. Notes and sketches during an overland trip from New York to San Francisco, (made on first opening of the Central and Union Pacific Railways, in May 1869). Liverpool, 1869. 88 p. **DLC**

Repr. from articles in the Liverpool *Daily Post* and Liverpool *Albion*.

1870

1853 ARMYTAGE, WALTER HARRY GREEN. A. J. Mundella, 1825–1897; the Liberal background to the Labour movement. London, [1951]. 386 p. **DLC Uk**

Anthony Mundella's visit to the U.S. in 1870, pp. 84–91. See also Armytage's "Mundella in America," *Queen's Quar.*, LV (Spring, 1948), 46–56.

1854 BELL, JOHN H. Western skies, a narrative of American travel in 1868. [n.p.], 1870. 379 p. **DLC**

Priv. circ. Part I, 24 chaps., deals with the U.S. Part II deals with Canada.

1855 BERNARD, MOUNTAGUE. A historical account of the neutrality of Great Britain during the American civil war. London, 1870. 511 p. **DLC Uk**

Review: *No. Brit. Rev.* (by Lord Acton?), LII, 299.

1856 BRITISH AND FOREIGN ANTI-SLAVERY SOCIETY, LONDON. [Circular on Chinese immigration into the United States]. London, 1870. **MB**

A broadside. Resolution of a meeting held on Jan. 4, 1870.

1857 BRITTEN, EMMA (HARDINGE). Modern American spiritualism: a twenty years' record of the communion between earth and the world of spirits. New York, 1870. 565 p. **DLC**

Uk has 4th ed., New York, 1870. New ed., with an introd. by E. J. Dingwall, New Hyde Park [N.Y.], [1970]. A British actress and Spiritualist, Britten repeatedly lived in the U.S. between 1855 and 1881. See her *Autobiography*, ed. by Margaret Wilkinson, Manchester, 1900; most of the book deals with experiences in the U.S.

1858 [BURN, RICHARD, *of Manchester*]. The present and long-continued stagnation of trade: its causes, effects, and cure. Being a sequel to An inquiry into the commercial position of Great Britain, etc. By a Manchester Man. Revised and enlarged edition. Manchester, [1870]. 39 p. **DLC Uk**

No 1st ed. located. DLC gives date as [1869?]. References to U.S. on pp. 9, 13–15, 19, 21, 26, 34.

1859   [CARR, A.]. Illustrated hand-book of California: her climate, trade, exports, &c., &c., agricultural and mineral wealth. London, 1870. 97 p.   **C Uk**

Pub. by the American Emigrant Aid Society. CLU, CtY, Uk have 2d ed., pub. by Samson Low, with same title, but with addition of a map, London, 1870; reissued as *The modern El Dorado; or, The Land of the setting sun*, London, [1871]. Pref. signed "A. Carr."

1860   [CLARKE, PETER DOOYENTATE]. Origin and traditional history of the Wyandotts, and sketches of other Indian tribes of North America. True traditional stories of Tecumseh and his league, in the years 1811 and 1812. Toronto, 1870. 158 p.   **DLC**

Pref. signed: Peter Dooyentate Clarke.

1861   CLEMENS, LOUISA PERINA COURTAULD. Narrative of a pilgrim and sojourner on earth, from 1791 to the present year, 1870. Edinburgh, 1870.

Uk has only part of copy, related "chiefly to Edward Irving."; no complete copy located. Chap. 4: "Residence in America from 1833 to 1857."

1862   CLERK, ALICE M. (FRERE). "MRS. GODFREY CLERK." The antipodes and round the world; or, Travels in Australia, New Zealand, Ceylon, China, Japan, and California. London, 1870. 633 p.   **DLC Uk**

1863   [COBDEN CLUB]. Systems of land tenure in various countries. A series of essays published under the sanction of the Cobden club. London, 1870.   **DLC Uk**

Uk lists under London—Cobden Club. See "Farm land and land laws of the United States," pp. 398–420.

1864   [COFFIN, WILLIAM FOSTER]. Thoughts on defence from a Canadian point of view. By a Canadian. Dedicated, by permission, to the Hon. Sir George E. Cartier, bart., and offered, as a tribute of respect, to those statesmanlike qualities which have made him minister of militia and defence for the dominion of Canada. Montreal, 1870. 55 p.   **MH Uk**

On U.S.-Canadian affairs.

1865   COLLINSON, JOHN, and W[ILLIAM] A[BRAHAM] BELL. The Denver Pacific railway: its present position and future prospects. London, 1870. 11 p.   **DBRE**

1866   COLLINSON, JOHN and W[ILLIAM] A[BRAHAM] BELL. The Maxwell land grant, situated in Colorado and New Mexico, United States of America. London, 1870. 32 p.   **CtY**

CSmH and NN have Dutch ed., Amsterdam, 1870.

1867   CONSTANTINE, I. On the influence of American ideas in the Anglican church in the Diocese of Montreal (with other matter). Montreal, 1870.

CaOOA has an incomplete copy, 16 p.

1868   CRACROFT, SOPHIA. Lady Franklin visits the Pacific Northwest; being extracts from the letters of Miss Sophia Cracroft, Sir John Franklin's niece, February to April 1861 and April to July 1870. Ed., with an introd. and notes by Dorothy Blakely Smith. Victoria (B.C.), 1974. 157 p.   **DLC**

Provincial Archives of British Columbia, memoir no. 11. Cracroft travelled with Lady Jane Franklin. In 1861 visited Oregon and San Francisco, pp. 82–93; in 1870, Alaska, San Francisco and San Juan Island, pp. 94–112, 120–123, 125–143, 145–149. Other comment on Americans, pp. xxiii–xxvii, and passim.

1869   DAWSON, *REV.* AENEAS MACDONELL. Our strength and their strength. The North West Territory, and other papers chiefly relating to the Dominion of Canada. Ottawa, 1870. 326 p.   **DLC Uk**

First paper, "Our strength and their strength," pp. 3–52, answers the pro-American arguments of Goldwin Smith and Robert Lowe.

1870   DEMPSEY, J. MAURICE, *ed.* Our ocean highways: a condensed universal route book, by sea, by land, and by rail. Alphabetical, commercial, consular, monetary, and parliamentary; postal, statistical, telegraphic, and topographical. With tables, showing all the great ocean routes, dates of sailing, fares, etc., and map. London, 1870. 453 p.   **DLC Uk**

Rev. ed., London, 1871, ed. by Dempsey and William Hughes: *Our ocean highways: a condensed universal hand gazetteer and international route book. . . .*

1871   DRAFT STATEMENT proposed to be submitted to an international arbitrator of the differences now existing between the governments of Great Britain and the United States arising out of the late war. London, [1870?]. 22 p.   **DLC**

1872   THE FENIAN RAID OF 1870. By reporters present at the scenes. Montreal, 1870. 79 p.   **CaNSWA**

DLC and Uk have 3d ed., Montreal; DLC dates 1872, Uk gives 1871.

1873   GODDARD, SAMUEL A[SPINWALL]. The American rebellion. Letters on the American rebellion . . . 1860–1865, etc. London, 1870. 583 p.   **DLC Uk**

Letters originally written to the Birmingham *Daily Post* and the London *American* and Birmingham *Daily Gazette*. Portions on Lincoln pub. separately the same year as *Extracts from Letters on the American rebellion*, London, 1870. Letters also repr. in the *Mag. of Hist. with Notes & Queries*, Ext. no. 19 (1912), pp. 7–22.

1874   GRANT, DANIEL. Home politics; or, The growth of trade considered in its relation to labour, pauperism and emigration. London, 1870. 185 p.   **DLC Uk**

1875   HALL, *REV.* [CHRISTOPHER] NEWMAN. From Liverpool to St. Louis. London, 1870. 294 p.   **DLC Uk**

Appeared originally under title, "My impressions of America," in *Broadway*, I (Sept. 1868–Feb. 1869), 64, 130, 298, 330, 486, 577; II (Mar.–Aug. 1869), 151, 214, 361, 452. Hall was in the U.S. in 1867: see "Rev. Newman Hall," *Harper's Weekly*, XI (Nov. 23, 1867), 741–742; and *Newman Hall: an autobiography*, London, 1898, pp. 165–178, and on later visits, pp. 179–199. For Hall's Niagarized sermon, see his *A warning cry from Niagara*, London, [1853].

1876   HICKS-BEACH, *LADY* VICTORIA [ALEXANDRINA]. Life of Sir Michael Hicks-Beach (Earl St. Aldwyn). London, 1932. 2 vols.   **DLC Uk**

In U.S., 1869–70; see I, pp. 27–33. Includes excerpts from Sir Michael's diary.

1877   [JONES, *REV.* HARRY]. Letters from America. [n.p.], 1870. 135 p.   **MH Uk**

DLC has on microfilm. Priv. pr. Signed on last page, "H. J." London, [1878?] ed. carried title, *To San Francisco and back. By a London Parson: published under the direction of the committee of general literature and education, appointed by the Society for promoting Christian knowledge*, 223 p.; on back of t.p., "Reprinted from the People's Magazine." *People's Mag.*, Jan–July 1871, 31–42, 101–114, 161–170, 217–224, 287–296, 352–360.

1878   MACDONALD, JOHN A[LEXANDER]. Troublous times in Canada, a history of the Fenian raids of 1866 and 1870. By Capt. John A. Macdonald (a veteran of 1866 and 1870). Toronto, 1910. 255 p.   **DLC Uk**

On Canadian-American relations, 1867–1891. See Donald Creighton's *John A. Macdonald, the old chieftan*, Boston, 1956. See also *Correspondence of Sir John Macdonald. . . . made by his literary executor, Sir Joseph Pope*, New York, 1921; also, Pope's *Memoirs of the Right Honourable Alexander Macdonald, G.C.B. first prime minister of the Dominion of Canada*, London, 1894.

1879   MACKENZIE, ROBERT. The United States of America: a history. London, 1870. 278 p.   **DLC Uk**

Included, with additions, as Part I, pp. 11–308, in author's *America. A history. I.—The United States. II.—Dominion of Canada. III.—South America, etc.*, London, 1882.

1880   MACRAE, *REV.* DAVID. The Americans at home: pen and ink sketches of American men, manners and institutions. Edinburgh, 1870. 2 vols.   **DLC Uk**

Glasgow, 1871 ed. uder title *Home and abroad, sketchings and gleanings*; rev. eds. appeared in 1874, 1908 and 1952. Sketches appeared originally in various Scottish, Indian and American newspapers. Macrae revisited the U.S. in 1898 and in the early 20th century; both later visits described in *America revisited and men I have met*, Glasgow, 1908.

Review: *Graphic*, II, 131.

1881   MASON, *REV.* FRANCIS. The story of a working man's life: with sketches of travel in Europe, Asia, Africa, and America, as related by himself. . . . With an introduction by William R. Williams. New York, 1870. 462 p.   **DLC Uk**

Came to U.S. in 1818 and remained. On U.S., pp. 85–187.

1882   THE MEMORIAL & PETITION of the people of Rupert's land and North-west territory, British America, to his excellency, U. S. Grant, president of the United States. [Red River? 1870]. 11 p.   **DLC**

Letter is dated Oct. 3, 1870, at Red River.

1883   MILLS, DAVID. Speech of David Mills, M.P., at St. Thomas, on the 12th November, 1869, on the present and future political aspects of Canada, with an appendix, containing the letters of the Rev. St. George Caulfield on the Irish question, with Mr. Mills' replies thereto. London, 1870. 38 p.   **CaOOA**

1884   [MITCHELL, PETER]. Review of President Grant's recent message to the United States' Congress, relative to the Canadian fisheries and the navigation of the St. Lawrence river. [Ottawa, 1870]. 64 p.   **DLC**

Cover title. Dated, Ottawa, 12th December, 1870.

1885   NEWTON, JOSEPH. Emigration to Virginia (east), "or the Old Dominion state." Report from Joseph Newton of London, England. London, 1870. 52 p.

DLC has [3d ed.] London, [1871]. Period covered, 1869–1870.

1886   O'CONNOR, JOHN. Letters of John O'Connor, esq., M.P., on Fenianism. Addressed to His excellency the Right honourable Sir John Young . . . Governor general of Canada, etc., etc., etc. Toronto, 1870. 17 p.   **CaQMBM**

1887   PROBYN, JOHN WEBB. National self-government in Europe and America. By J. W. Probyn, author of "Essays on Italy, Ireland, and the United States." London, 1870. 248 p.   **MB NN Uk**

On U.S., pp. 125–177, and passim.

1888   RAE, W[ILLIAM] F[RASER]. Westward by rail: the new route to the East. London, 1870. 391 p.   **DLC Uk**

Portion first appeared in the London *Daily News*; 2d ed., London, 1871, with new introd. chapter, carried title, *Westward by rail: a journey to San Francisco and back and a visit to the Mormons*. See also the supp. vol., *Columbia and Canada*, 1877 below. See also Rae's "American claims on England," *Westmin. Rev.*, XXXVII, n.s., (Jan. 1870), 211–234; and his *Leaders from the Gloucester journal* [weekly], London, 1860–61, 2 vols. of newspaper clippings, July 21, 1860–Nov. 23, 1861.

Reviews: *Athenaeum*, (July 2, 1870), 9; *Atlantic*, XXVII, 138; *Field*, XXXVI, 556; *Nation*, XII, 184; New York *Herald*, Mar. 6, 1871; *Overland Monthly*, VI, 192; *Sat. Rev.*, XXXII, 403.

1889   RIDGWAY, CHARLES. Through the Golden Gate: a story of remarkable adventures in California and along the west coast of America. Yokohama, 1917. 79 p.   **C**

CLU, NN, OrHi, WHi have Yokohama, 1923 ed. In California in 1870.

1890   [RIVINGTON, ALEXANDER and WILLIAM AUGUSTUS HARRIS]. Reminiscences of America in 1869. By two Englishmen. London, 1870. 332 p.   **MB NNC Uk**

DLC has 2d ed., London, 1870. See also Rivington's *In the track of our emigrants. The new dominion as a home for Englishmen. Illustrated with heliotype maps*, London, 1872.

Review: *Athenaeum*, (July 2, 1870), 9.

1891   SOARES, G[USTAVE] DE M[IRELLES]. Sketches on the wing. London, 1870. 315 p.   **CSmH Uk**

First appeared under Meirelles [sic] in a weekly no. of the Calcutta *Englishman*. Includes 3 chapters on California and 1 on Niagara.

1892   STEINMETZ, ANDREW. The gaming table: its votaries and victims, in all times and countries, especially in England and France. London, 1870. 2 vols.   **DLC Uk**

Chap. 9, "Gambling in the United States," pp. 221–253.

1893   STEVENS, EDWARD THOMAS. Flint chips. A guide to pre-historic archaeology, as illustrated by the collection in the Blackmore museum, Salisbury. London, 1870. 593 p.   **DLC Uk**

Half of book is devoted to describing the remains found by American archaeologists Ephraim G. Squier and Edwin H. Davis in the Mississippi and Ohio valleys. Includes articles on the U.S. by John D. Sherwood and A. H. Church. See also *Some account of the Blackmore Museum, Salisbury. The opening meeting*, London, 1868.

1894   STEWART, W. M. Eleven years' experience in the western states of America . . . With an analysis of the prairie soil, by Dr. Stevenson Macadam, F.R.S.F. . . . London, 1870. 139 p.   **DLC Uk**

1895   WALLETT, WILLIAM FREDERICK. The public life of W. F. Wallett, the queen's jester; an autobiography of forty years' professional experience and travels in the United Kingdom, the United States of America (including California), Canada, South America, Mexico, the West Indies, &c. Ed. by John Luntley. London, 1870. 188 p.   **DLC Uk**

Accounts of visits to the U.S. in the 1850's and 1860's: pp. 95–113, 123–139, 161–171.

1896   WHITCHER, W. F. Report on the fishery articles of treaties between Great Britain and the United States of America, and questions arising out of the same. Ottawa, 1870. 31 p.   **CaOOA**

1897   WHITE, JOHN. Sketches from America. Part I.—Canada. Part II. —A picnic to the Rocky mountains. Part III.—The Irish in America. London, 1870. 373 p.   **DLC Uk**

Review: *No. Am. Rev.* (by C. F. Adams, Jr.), CXIII, 228.

1898   WILSON, EDWARD. A scheme of emigration on a national scale. Read at the Emigration conference at the Society of the arts. London, [1870]. 15 p.   **Uk**

1899   WOOD, *REV*. JOHN GEORGE. The natural history of man; being an account of the manners and customs of the uncivilized races of men. London, 1868–70. 2 vols.   **DLC Uk**

Most subsequent eds. under title: *The uncivilized races of men in all countries of the world; being a comprehensive account of their physical, social, mental, moral and religious characteristics.* On American Indians, II, 640–695.

1871

1900   THE ANGLO-AMERICAN ASSOCIATION. Report on the questions between Great Britain and the United States with respect to the North American fisheries. London, 1871. 35 p.   **DLC Uk**

Uk lists under London—misc. institutions.

1901   AROUND THE WORLD BY STEAM, via Pacific Railway. London, 1871. 30 p.   **DLC Uk**

DLC lists under Union Pacific Railroad Co.; Uk under Union & Pacific.

1902   BRADY, WILLIAM. Glimpses of Texas: its divisions, resources, development and prospects. Houston, 1871. 104 p.   **DLC Uk**

Uk lists 83 p. Contains lecture by the Rev. Father Nugent, of Liverpool, who travelled in Texas in 1870, pp. 8–12. Brady was an American.

1903   A BRIEF ACCOUNT of the Fenian raids on the Missisquoi frontier, in 1866 and 1870. Montreal, 1871. 32 p.   **CaOOA**

1904   BUSS, HENRY. Wanderings in the West, during the year 1870. London, 1871. 196 p.   **DLC**

Priv. circ. Descriptive poems of travel experiences in America.

1905   BUTLER, *SIR* WILLIAM FRANCIS. Report by Lieut. Butler, (69th regt.) of his journey from Fort Garry to Rocky Mountain house and back, during the winter of 1870–71. [Winnipeg? 1871?]. 23 p.   **CaNSWA CtY**

Later included in appendix to author's *The great lone land: a narrative of travel and adventure in the North-west of America*, 1872, below. The report attacks the Montana Indian traders.

1906   CALIFORNIA AS A FIELD FOR EMIGRATION for the farmer, labourer, and mechanic; and paramount advantages over Australia. London, [1871]. 17 p.   **Uk**

Author had recently returned from California

1907   CAMPBELL, *REV*. W. GRAHAM. The new world; or, Recent visit to America. Together with introductory observations for tourists, and four appendices, including all suitable information for emigrants, &c. London, 1871. 208 p.   **DLC Uk**

1908   CATLIN, WILLIAM. Emigration to Canada and the United States. Report of the Cow Cross Canadian emigration society. [London], 1871. 73 p.   **CaNSWA**

1909   THE CONVENTION OF WASHINGTON contrived for the destruction not the reconciliation of Great Britain and the United States. London, 1871. 8 p.   **DLC Uk**

A petition to the Queen signed by John Hindle, et al. Uk catalog lists under *England.*

1910   COWANS, DAVID. Anecdotes of a life on the ocean, being a portion of the experiences of twenty-seven years' service in many parts of the world. Montreal, 1871. 198 p.   **DLC**

Trip to Lake Superior, from Cleveland and Detroit, pp. 174–182.

1911   CROPPER, JAMES. Life in America as it concerns working men in England. A lecture, October 30, 1871. Kendal [Eng.], 1871. 31 p.   **CSmH NN**

1912   EAST TENNESSEE LAND PROPRIETORS, LONDON. Description and price of improved farms in the state of Tennessee, United States of America, for sale by the East Tennessee land proprietors. . . . describing the . . . land . . . farm buildings, mills, and water power; with the mining, manufacturing, and other advantages of each locality. London, [1871?]. 157 p.   **DLC**

Title almost identical to work by J. Gray Smith, *Description of improved farms. . . .* , 58 p., 1843, above. Date of the later work is questioned. DLC gives [1842?]. However, Thomas D. Clark, *Travels in the new South, a bibliography*, Norman, 1962, I, no. 303, gives 1871 and quotes from the DLC copy: "In 1871 a company of Englishmen believed they would make their fortunes from the industrial development of east Tennessee." DLC copy is bound with Thomas A. Anderson, *The Ocoee district, south east Tennessee. . . .* , London, 1842, which may explain confusion of dates.

1913   EASTON, GEORGE. Travels in America. With special reference to the province of Ontario as a home for working men. Glasgow, 1871. 183 p.   **DLC Uk**

Includes New England.

1914   EMIGRATION! The emigrants' guide to the British colonies & America. London, [1871]. 16 p.   **Uk**

Listed in Uk under England—Colonies, etc.

1915   EXTENSION OF PEACE; proposal for the amalgamation of Great Britain and the United States. London, 1871. 16 p.   **MH UkLSE**

DLC has microfilm of MH copy; last page missing from both.

1916   GILLMORE, PARKER ("UBIQUE"). All round the world. Adventures in Europe, Asia, Africa, and America. London, 1871. 270 p.   **DLC Uk**

Last 5 chaps. on the U.S. Later eds. appeared under variant titles, e.g., *Adventures in many lands*, London, 1871.

1917   GILLMORE, PARKER ("UBIQUE"). A hunter's adventures in the great West. London, 1871. 336 p.   **DLC Uk**

Reviews: *Athenaeum*, (Dec. 10, 1870), 752; *Chambers's J.*, XLVIII, 98; *Field*, XXXVI, 505.

1918   [HAMER, P. W.?]. From ocean to ocean, being a diary of a three months' expedition from Liverpool to California and back, from the Atlantic to the Pacific by the overland route. [London], 1871. 108 p.   **DLC**

DLC presentation copy inscribed by Hamer. Also ascribed to R. W. Flowers. DLC catalogs under title.

1919   HARGRAVE, JOSEPH JAMES. Red river. Montreal, 1871. 506 p.   **DLC Uk**

Travel in U.S., pp. 33–57; other comment on border difficulties, etc., passim.

1920   HOWE, JOSEPH. Address delivered by the Hon. Joseph Howe, secretary of state for the provinces, at the Howe festival, Framingham, Massachusetts, August 31, 1871. Boston, 1871. 21 p.   **MH**

On U.S.

1921   JOHN B____ AND JONATHAN. An instructive story. Founded on fact. Exeter, 1871. 12 p.   **MB Uk**

Uk lists under Jonathan. A satire on English neutrality during the Civil War, and on post-war Reconstruction.

1922   MACAULAY, JAMES. Across the ferry: first impressions of America and its people. London, 1871. 424 p.   **DLC Uk**

Repr. from the *Leisure Hour*, of which Macaulay was editor. 3d ed., London, 1884, has new introd.

1923   MCCARTHY, JUSTIN. The settlement of the Alabama question. The banquet given at New York to Her Britannic Majesty's high commissioners, by Mrs. Cyrus W. Field. A report, ed., with a short introd., by Justin McCarthy. London, 1871. 721 p.   **DLC Uk**

Speeches by Earl de Grey, Sir Stafford Northcote, Lord Tenterden, et al.

1924   MARKHAM, PAULINE. [PAULINE MARGARET HALL]. Life of Pauline Markham. Written by herself. New York, 1871. 31 p.   **DLC**

Authorship sometimes ascribed on doubtful authority to Richard Grant White. Markham's first visit to New York, pp. 16–31. Several subsequent trips to America, 1868–1888.

1925   MARSHALL, CHARLES. The Canadian dominion. London, 1871. 331 p.   **DLC Uk**

Discussion of the political relations of the U.S. and Canada, pp. 239–269. See also author's "Salt Lake City and the valley settlements," *Fraser's Mag.*, IV, n.s., (July 1871), 97–108; and his "Characteristics of Mormonism. By a recent visitor to Utah," ibid., III, n.s., (June 1871), 692–702, repr. in *Transatlantic Mag.*, IV (May–Aug. 1871), 166.

1926   NOTON, THOMAS. Two lectures on America: being a few jottings made during a tour in the United States of America. London, 1871. 32 p.   **IHi OClWHi**

1927   OLLIVANT, J[OSEPH] E[ARLE]. A breeze from the Great Salt Lake; or, New Zealand to New York by the new mail route. London, 1871. 176 p.   **DLC Uk**

1928   [POWELL, *COL.* WALKER]. A few words on Canada. By a Canadian. Ottawa, 1871. 72 p.   **CaOTU CSmH CtY MH**

Mainly devoted to discussion of Canadian-American affairs.

1929   ROBERTSON, WILLIAM and W. F. ROBERTSON. Our American tour: being a run of ten thousand miles from the Atlantic to the Golden gate, in the autumn of 1869. Edinburgh, 1871. 148 p.   **DLC**

1930   ROSSER, W[ILLIAM] H[ENRY]. The Bijou gazetteer of the world: briefly describing, as regards position, area, and population, every country and state, their subdivisions, provinces, counties, principal towns, villages, mountains, rivers, lakes, capes, etc. London, [1871]. 636 p.   **MH Uk**

Pref. dated Jan. 1871. New ed., with revisions by William John Gordon, London, 1883. On U.S., passim.

1931   SELBORNE, ROUNDELL PALMER, *1st earl*. The treaty of Washington. A speech delivered in the House of commons on Friday, August 4, 1871. London, 1871. 34 p.

CaBVaU Uk

For an American response, see Reverdy Johnson, *A reply to a recent speech of Sir Roundell Palmer on the Washington treaty, and the Alabama claims*, Baltimore, 1871, 50 p. (held by DLC).

1932   SEYD, ERNEST. Suggestions in reference to the metallic currency of the United States of America. London, 1871. 253 p.   **DLC UkLU-G**

Priv. pr. See also author's *The United States of America and the question of silver and its coinage in 1880*, London, 1880, below.

1933   [SMILES, SAMUEL, *Jr.*]. A boy's voyage round the world; including a residence in Victoria, and a journey, by rail, across North America. Edited by Samuel Smiles. London, 1871. 304 p.   **DLC Uk**

New York, 1872 ed., *Round the world; including a residence in Victoria, and a journey by rail across North America. By a boy. Edited by Samuel Smiles*. Written by Samuel Smiles' 16-yr. old son; last 6 chaps. describe cross-country tour of the U.S.

1934   SOMERS, ROBERT. The southern states since the war, 1870–1. London, 1871. 286 p.

DLC Uk

Repr. University, [Alabama, 1965], with introd. and index by Malcolm C. McMillan. Review: *Edinb. Rev.*, CXXXVI, 148.

1935   SPENCE, THOMAS. Manitoba and the North-west of the Dominion, its resources and advantages to the emigrant and the capitalist, as compared with the western states of America; its climate, soil, agricultural and manufacturing facilities; its unparalleled salubrity, growth and productiveness; and the elements of its future greatness and prosperity; land growth and land policy, latest information, cheapest and best way to get to Red river, and what is required. Toronto, 1871. 46 p.   **DLC**

2d ed., rev. and enlarged, Ottawa, 1874; Uk has French translation of 2d ed., 1874.

1936   TALLACK, WILLIAM. Humanity and humanitarianism. With special reference to the prison systems of Great Britain and the United States, the question of criminal lunacy, and capital punishment. London, 1871. 32 p.   **DLC Uk**

1937   TUCKER, LOUIS. Sketches of travels in America. From the Atlantic to the Pacific. Lahore, 1871. 74 p.   **CtY**

1938   URTICA [*pseud.*]. The story of John and Jonathan. [Ottawa]?, 1871. 28 p.

No location found.

1939   WILDMAN, RICHARD. The president of the United States and the Alabama. London, 1871.   **UkLGI**

Uk copy destroyed. See also author's *Institutes of international law*, London, 1849–50, 2 vols. (held by DLC and Uk).

1872

1940   THE AMERICAN COMMISSIONERS and the statement of Sir Stafford Northcote at Exeter, in relation to an alleged promise of exclusion of the indirect claims of the United States. Washington, [D.C.], 1872. 20 p.   **DLC**

Contains speeches and letters of Sir Stafford Northcote and the Marquis of Ripon [George Frederick Samuel Robinson, 1st marquis], and extracts from the London *Times*. For Northcote's diaries covering the visit to the U.S., see 1890 entry under Lang.

1941   BARKER (afterwards BROOME), MARY ANN, *Lady*. Travelling about over new and old ground. London, 1872. 353 p.   **DLC Uk**

Not her own travels, but a review of other accounts. See "North America," pp. 79–143.

1942   BELL, WILLIAM MORRISON. Other countries. London, 1872. 2 vols.   **DLC Uk**

Vol. II, chaps. 9–25, describe a cross-country tour of the U.S.

1943   [BLACKER, MURRAY M.]. From England to Virginia. London, [1872?].   **CSmH**

Letter originally pub. in the *Field*.

1944   BONWICK, JAMES. The Mormons and the silver mines. London, 1872. 425 p.   **MH Uk**

See author's account of this visit in his *An octogenarian's reminiscences*, London, 1902, pp. 280–289.

1945   BRASSEY, THOMAS BRASSEY, *1st earl*. Work and wages practically illustrated. London, 1872. 296 p.   **MB Uk**

DLC has New York, 1872 ed., and *On work and wages. By Thomas Brassey, M.P. Third edition*, London, 1872. Brassey's work was later continued by Sir Sydney John Chapman, *Work and wages in continuation of Lord Brassy's "Work and wages" and "Foreign work and English wages,"* introd. by Lord Brassey, London, 1904–14, 3 vols. Original work dedicated to Thomas Hughes; chap. 10, "Influence of American wages on the English labour market," pp. 200–224; also pp. 132–139, and passim. See also author's "Agriculture in England and the United States: inaugural address as President of the Statistical society, delivered on Tuesday, November 18, 1879," in *Papers and addresses by Lord Brassey, K.C.B., D.C.L. Work and wages, edited by J. Potter with an introduction by George Howell, M.P.*, London, 1894, pp. 272–290. See also extensive discussion of conditions in the U.S. in author's *Foreign work and English wages, considered with reference to the depression of trade*, London, 1879.

Review: *Fortnightly Rev.* (by Frederick Harrison), LXIX, 268.

1946   BUTLER, *MAJOR* [*SIR*] W[ILLIAM] F[RANCIS]. The great lone land: a narrative of travel and adventure in the North-west of America. London, 1872. 388 p.

     CU MH TxU Uk

DLC has 7th ed., London, 1875. See also Robert Larmour, *Canada's opportunity: a review of Butler's "Great lone land" in its relation to present day conditions and future prospects*, Toronto, 1907, 32 p. For further observations on the U.S., see *Sir William Butler: an autobiography*, London, 1911.

1947   CARLISLE, A[RTHUR] D[RUMMOND]. Round the world in 1870: an account of a brief tour made through India, China, Japan, California, and South America. London, 1872. 408 p.   **DLC Uk**

On California, pp. 230–273.

1948 COCKBURN, *SIR* ALEXANDER JAMES EDMUND. Reasons of Sir Alexander Cockburn for dissenting from the award of the tribunal of arbitration at Geneva. London, 1872. 252 p. **MnU NcD OO**

Dated Sept. 14, 1872. On the U.S.

1949 THE COTTON FAMINE OF 1862–63, with some sketches of the proceedings of the Lisburn relief committee. Second edition. Belfast, 1872. 135 p. **ICJ UkLU-G**

No 1st ed. located. Pref. signed by "H."; on flyleaf of UkLU-G copy: "The author . . . may have been Hugh McCall." Considerable comment on U.S. New ed., Belfast, 1881, . . . *to which is added a brief notice of the late Mr. A. T. Stewart*, 220 p., (held by IU).

1950 CROPPER, JAMES. Working men in America, a lecture to workingmen in England. London, [1872?]. 48 p. **IU NNC Uk**

1951 DISRAELI, BENJAMIN, *1st earl of Beaconsfield*. Speech of the Right Hon. B. Disraeli, M.P., at the Free trade hall, Manchester, April 3, 1872. [London, 1872]. 27 p. **MH NN Uk**

Pub. No. XIV of the National Union of Conservative and Constitutional Associations. Repr. as "Lord Beaconsfield. On the principles of the conservative party. Delivered at Manchester, April 3, 1872," in Charles Kendall Adams' *Representative British orations with introductions and explanatory notes*, New York, 1884, III, pp. 216–276. An extract appeared as "Conservative principles," in *Tory democrat; two famous speeches, edited by Sir Edward Boyle. Foreword by Walter Elliot*, [London, 1950], pp. 35–37; includes extract from Disraeli's speech at Aylesbury, 1859, on necessity of Anglo-American accord. The Manchester speech also included in *Selected speeches of the late Right Honourable the Earl of Beaconsfield*, arranged and ed. with introd. and explanatory notes by T. E. Kebbel, London, 1882, II, pp. 490–522. See also Wilbur Devereux Jones, "The British conservatives and the American civil war," *Am. Hist. Rev.*, LVIII (Apr. 1953), 527–543; includes letters to Disraeli from Russell, Stanley, Cecil, Derby, Clarendon, Malmesbury, Lennox, et al., 1861–65.

1952 [DOYLE, RICHARD?]. The American tour of Messers. Brown, Jones and Robinson, being the history of what they saw and did in the United States, Canada and Cuba. By Toby [*pseud.*]. New York, 1872. 74 leaves. **DLC**

Authorship unclear; many libraries attribute to Doyle. A collection of caricatures, satirizing conventional sightseers.

1953 ELGIN, JAMES BRUCE, *Earl*. Letters and journals of James, eighth earl of Elgin. Edited by Theodore Walrond, C.B. With a preface by Arthur Penrhyn Stanley, D.D. London, 1872. 467 p. **DLC Uk**

Governor of Canada 1845–54. Comment on U.S., chap. 5 (pp. 158–164); also chaps. 3, 4, and 6, passim.

1954 EMIGRANTS' GUIDE to the United States and the Dominion of Canada, with the provinces of Ontario, Quebec, Nova Scotia, New Brunswick, Manitoba, British Columbia, and the North-west territory. Chiefly compiled from information prepared by the American social science association, and the United States and Canadian government authorities. London, [1872?]. 32 p. **NN Uk**

Uk lists under U.S.A.—Appendix.

1955 ENDERBY, CHARLES. A proposition from England to America: how to arrange, settle, and avoid disputes between the two nations. London, [1872]. **Uk**

1956   FIELD, CYRUS WEST. Proceedings at the banquet given by Mr. Cyrus W. Field at the Palace hotel, Buckingham Gate, London, on Thursday, the 28th November, 1872, the day appointed by the President of the United States for the annual Thanksgiving. London, 1872. 45 p.   **DLC**

Contains speeches by Gladstone and British officers of the Anglo-American Telegraph Company, and repr. articles on the occasion from the London *Times*, London *Daily News*, London *Daily Telegraph*, and *Anglo-American Times*.

1957   FITZMAURICE, EDMOND GEORGE PETTY-FITZMAURICE, *1st baron*. The life of Granville George Leveson Gower, second Earl Granville, K.G., 1815–1891. By Lord Edmond Fitzmaurice. London, 1905. 2 vols.   **CSmH Uk**

DLC has 2d ed., London, 1905. "The Geneva arbitration," II, pp. 81–118; see also I, pp. 400–402, 440–444.

1958   GIFFEN, *SIR* ROBERT. American railways as investments. London, 1872. 71 p.   **DLC**

Uk has 2d ed., London, 1873. At head of t.p., "Cracroft's investment tracts." Introd. by Bernard Cracroft. See General William Mahone's *Memorandum on Mr. Griffen's pamphlet, "American railways as investments;" being an examination into the financial position of the railways of Virginia, U.S.A.*, London, 1873. See also Giffen's "The foreign trade of the United States," in his *Essays in finance*, 2d ser., London, 1886, pp. 116–131; his *The progress of the working classes in the last half century . . . with note on American wages*, New York, 1885, pp. 40–43 (1st ed., London, 1884, did not contain the "note on American wages."); and his "The American silver bubble," *Nineteenth Cent.*, XXVIII (Aug. 1890), 309–324, (repr. in his *The Case against bimetalism*, London, 1892, pp. 163–192).

1959   GILLMORE, PARKER ("UBIQUE"). Prairie farms and prairie folk. London, 1872. 2 vols.
                                                                                  DLC Uk

A narrative of author's experiences in Indiana and Illinois during the Civil War.

1960   GRAY, JOHN HAMILTON. Confederation; or, The political and parliamentary history of Canada, from the conference at Quebec, in October, 1864, to the admission of British Columbia, in July, 1871. Toronto, 1872. Vol. I.   **DLC Uk**

A projected Vol. II was never published. Much comment on the U.S., passim.

1961   HOPLEY, CATHERINE COOPER. Rambles and adventures in the wilds of the West. London, 1872. 126 p.   **CSt NHi TxU Uk**

A true account written for children. See also Hopley's "Among the Shakers, by the author of 'Life in the South' [Signed S. L. J., i.e. Sarah L. Jones, *pseud.*], *Leisure Hour*, XX (Dec. 16, 1871), 790–792; "The Shakers," *St. James's Mag.*, XXX (1872), 329–337; and her "A reminiscence of the West," ibid., XXXI ("Xmas Box"), 148–155. See also her *Life in the South*, 1863, above; and her *Stories of the red men from early American history*, London, [1880].

1962   HOWE, JOSEPH. The speeches and public letters of Joseph Howe. (Based upon Mr. Annand's edition of 1858). New and complete edition. Revised and edited by Joseph Andrew Chisholm. Halifax, 1909. 2 vols.   **DLC Uk**

Adds considerable pre-1858 material not included in William Annand's ed., and comment on the U.S. through 1872. Discusses Canadian-American affairs, passim; see esp. II, pp. 349–355, 438–463, 619–630.

1963   IRONS, L. C. The Alabama controversy: its past history and present phase. London, 1872. 80 p.   **DLC Uk**

1964   JAMES, EDWIN [JOHN]. The political institutions of America and England. London, 1872. 42 p.   **MB Uk**

1965   JOHN BULL AND UNCLE SAM; or, The Alabama fever. Its origin, progress, and method of treatment. London, [1872]. 30 p.   **NN T Uk**

NUC lists under Bull, John; queries date. Satire on the Alabama dispute.

1966   JOHNSON, R[ICHARD] BYRON. Very far west indeed: a few rough experiences on the north-west Pacific coast. London, 1872. 280 p.   **CU NN Uk WaU**

Includes chap. on San Francisco.

Reviews: *Athenaeum*, (July 6, 1872), 8; Philadelphia *Daily Evening Bulletin*, Jan. 25, 1873; *Sat. Rev.*, XXX, 668.

1967   JONATHAN'S BUNKUM. London, 1872.   **Uk**

Dialogue between John Bull and Jonathan; a satire on the Alabama question.

1968   KNOWLES, RICHARD BRINSLEY. Life of James Sheridan Knowles. By his son. London, 1872. 177 p.   **DLC Uk**

Priv. pr.; rev. and ed. by Francis Harvey. Describes a 9-month tour in the U.S. in 1834, pp. 118–123.

1969   LEGARD, A[LLAYNE] B[EAUMONT]. Colorado. London, 1872. 170 p.   **DLC Uk**
Priv. pr.

1970   MACCARTHY, JUSTIN. Prohibitory legislation in the United States . . . Republished from the "Fortnightly review." London, 1872. 60 p.   **MH NjP Uk**

From the *Fortnightly Rev.*, XVI (1871), 166.

1971   MACDONALD, *SIR* JOHN ALEXANDER. Speech of Sir John. A. Macdonald, on intro-ducing the bill to give effect to the Treaty of Washington as regards Canada, delivered in the House of Commons of Canada, on Friday the 3rd May, 1872. [Ottawa, 1872]. 27 p.
CtY MH

See Sir Joseph Pope's *Memoirs of the Right Honourable Sir John Alexander Macdonald, G.C.B., first Prime minister of the Dominion of Canada*, London, 1894, II, pp. 80–140, on the Treaty of Washington; see also Pope's (ed.), *Correspondence of Sir John Alexander Macdonald*, New York, 1921. See also George R. Parkin, *Life of Sir John Alexander Macdonald*, Toronto, 1910: "The Washington treaty, 1871," pp. 165–192; and "The last election, commercial union, unrestricted reciprocity, 1891," pp. 291–317.

1972   MAW, WILLIAM HENRY and JAMES DREDGE. Modern examples of road and railway bridges; illustrating the most recent practice of leading engineers in Europe and America. London, 1872. 180 p.   **DSI MB NN Uk**

1973   MR. BULL AND HIS FAMILY TROUBLES, especially in relation to "the case" Jonathan *versus* Bull. London, 1872. 29 p.   **Uk**

On the Alabama controversy.

1974   MRS. BULL'S LITTLE BULL, an allegory, in six parts. London, 1872. 36 p.   **NjP Uk**
Uk lists under Bull, Mrs.; a satire on the Alabama claims.

1975   ODGER, GEORGE. Odger's monthly pamphlets on current events, etc. No. 1. Republicanism versus monarchy. London, [1872]. 16 p.   **Uk**

Uk lists under Periodicals—London. On U.S., pp. 4, 10–16.

1976   OTTLEY, HENRY. On the errors and mischiefs of modern diplomacy, as based upon the assumed prerogative of the crown in matters of peace and war; with particular reference to the treaty of Washington of 1871 and the negociations [sic] connected with it, down to the adjournment of the Tribunal of arbitration on the 28th June. London, 1872. 188 p.

DLC Uk

Part II, pp. 78–185, on the U.S. and the Treaty of Washington.

1977   PATTERSON, HENRY. "Songs in travel." Montreal, 1872. 186 p.   **NN RPB**

1978   [PHILLIPS, JOHN SEARLE RAGLAND]. The Alabah [i.e., Alabama] claims, and how the Ya-kees "fixed" the Yn-Gheesh. Being a fragment of some lately discovered annals of monkeydom. London, 1872. 32 p.   **NN Uk**

NN lists under title; Uk spells middle name "Searles."

1979   PLAYER-FROWD, J. G. Six months in California; sketches of San Francisco, mines and mining, beet sugar and olive culture; the zoology and flora of California. London, 1872. 164 p.   **DLC Uk**

Review: *Athenaeum*, (July 20, 1872), 74.

1980   PUBLIC POLICY, PERSONAL FEELING, and the treaty of Washington. London, 1872. 14 p.   **Uk**

Uk lists under England—Treaties—Victoria. See James Phinney Baxter, "The British high commissioners at Washington in 1871," *Proc. Mass. Hist. Soc. for 1932–36*, LXV (1940), 334–357.

1981   REED, EDWARD. America as it is. A hand book for emigrants, and all others, desiring official information respecting the United States; giving an account of every state and territory, the rates of wages paid in each, cost of subsistence; railway fares to all parts of the country, from ports of landing, and much useful additional information compiled from official sources. London, [1872]. 130 p.   **Uk ViU**

DLC has Dutch ed., 1873.

1982   REED, EDWARD. A lecture on emigration to the United States. [London, 1872].   **Uk**

1983   REPUBLICANISM AND MONARCHY contrasted, in a friendly argument between a republican and a monarchist. London, 1872. 16 p.   **ICN**

The U.S. used as an example.

1984   ST. HELIER, SUSAN MARY ELIZABETH (STEWART-MACKENZIE) JEUNE, *Baroness*. Memories of fifty years, by Lady St. Helier (Mary Jeune). London, 1909. 358 p.   **DLC Uk**

Account of a visit to the U.S. in 1872, pp. 127–148.

1985   [SELBORNE, ROUNDELL PALMER, *1st earl*]. Argument of Her Britannic Majesty's counsel on the points mentioned in the resolution of the arbitrators of July 25, 1872. Geneva, 1872. 70 p.   **DLC**

On the Alabama claims. Repr. in *The argument at Geneva. A complete collection of the forensic discussions on the part of the United States and of Great Britain, before the Tribunal of Arbitration under the Treaty of Washington*, New York, 1873, pp. 385–441.

1986   [SELBORNE, ROUNDELL PALMER, *1st earl*]. Argument of Her Britannic Majesty's counsel on the question of the recruitment of men for the Shenandoah at Melbourne, pursuant to the liberty given by the resolution of the Tribunal of August 19, 1872. London, 1872. 9 p.   **DLC**

Repr. in *The argument at Geneva*, pp. 520–530 (see note above).

1987   [SELBORNE, ROUNDELL PALMER, *1st earl*]. Argument of Her Britannic Majesty's counsell [sic] (presented in accordance with the resolution of the arbitrators of August 21, 1872) on the special question as to the legal effect of the entrance of the Florida into the port of Mobile on the responsibility, if any, of Great Britain for that ship. Geneva, 1872. 6 p.   **DLC**

Repr. in *The argument at Geneva*, pp. 541–545 (see note above).

1988   [SELBORNE, ROUNDELL PALMER, *1st earl*]. Argument on the claim of the United States for interest by way of damages. (Pursuant to the resolution of the tribunal of Aug. 30, 1872.) London, 1872. 14 p.   **MH**

DLC has French version., Geneva, 1872. Repr. in *The argument at Geneva,* pp. 550–567 (see note above).

1989   STENHOUSE, MRS. T[HOMAS] B. H. (FANNY). Expose of polygamy in Utah. A lady's life among the Mormons. A record of personal experience as one of the wives of a Mormon elder during a period of more than twenty years. New York, 1872. 221 p.   **DLC Uk**

Later eds. (New York, 1872; London, 1873) carried title, *A lady's life*, etc. See also her sequel, *Tell it all*, 1874, below.

Reviews: *Athenaeum*, (April 26, 1873), 527; Philadelphia *Daily Evening Bulletin*, Mar. 1, 1873; *Harper's Mag.*, XLVII, 299; New York *Herald*, Mar. 10, 1873.

1990   TAYLOR, WILLIAM CLARE. Jottings on Australia: with remarks on the California route to New York and Liverpool. London, 1872. 267 p.   **CSmH**

See pp. 200–258, on trip from San Francisco to New York.

1991   VIGIL [*pseud.*]. America. Letters by Vigil. Reprinted from the "Torquay directory." London, 1872. 30 p.   **DLC**

1992   WATSON, JOHN. Souvenir of a tour in the United States of America and Canada. In the autumn of 1872. Glasgow, 1872. 91 p.   **DLC Uk**

Priv. circ. DLC identifies as John Watson of Glasgow; Uk as John Watson of Nielsland.

1993   WHAT I SAW IN TEXAS. London, [1872]. 92 p.   **UkLRC**

1994   YEATS, JOHN. A manual of recent and existing commerce, from the year 1789 to 1872. Showing the development of industry at home and abroad during the Continental system, the Protection policy, and the era of Free Trade. By John Yeats . . . assisted by several gentlemen. London, 1872. 420 p.   **DLC Uk**

On U.S., pp. 236–246, 261–268, 279–281, and passim.

1995   YOUNG, JOHN. Letters, &c., first published in the "Northern Journal," during 1871, by the Hon. John Young on various questions of public interest. Montreal, 1872. 37 p.

    CSmH MH NN

Canadian-American economic relations, passim.

1873

1996   ALBEMARLE, WILLIAM COUTTS KEPPEL, *7th earl*. Balance sheet of the Washington treaty of 1872, [i.e. 1871] in account with the people of Great Britain and her colonies. By the Right Hon. Viscount Bury. London, 1873. 27 p.   **DLC Uk**

1997   ASHLEY, ANTHONY EVELYN MELBOURNE. A monarchy and a republic: a lecture delivered in the Mechanics' institute, at Bradford, January, 1873. London, 1873. 22 p.   **Uk**

Compares political conditions in England and the U.S.

1998   BLISS, WILLIAM. Glimpses of American life and scenery, sketched in letters and diary of a tour in the United States and Canada, during the summer and autumn of 1872. [London, 1873]. 46 p.   **DLC**

Priv. pr.

1999   BRASSEY, ANNIE (ALLNUTT), *Baroness*. A cruise in the "Eothen." 1872. London, 1873. 166 p.   **DLC**

Priv. circ. U.S. tour of 3 months in 1872, pp. 73–143.

2000   CHARLTON, [*REV.*] WILLIAM HENRY. Four months in North America. Hexham, [1873]. 55 p.   **MH Uk**

DLC has microfilm. First appeared as 5 letters in Hexham *Courant*, (1872 or 1873?). Author in the U.S. Sept. 1872–Feb. 26, 1873.

2001   COBDEN CLUB. Free trade and free enterprise. Report of the proceedings at the dinner of the Cobden Club, June 28, 1873. The Right Hon. T. Milner Gibson in the chair. Speech of the Hon. David A. Wells. Being a retrospect of the results of protection in the United States of America. With preface by Sir Louis Mallet, C.B., and list of members. London, 1873. 132 p.   **DLC Uk**

Uk lists under London—Cobden Club. Mallet's pref. on U.S., pp. 5–20.

2002   COOK, THOMAS. Letters from the sea and from foreign lands, descriptive of a tour round the world . . . with an 1873 appendix . . . Concluding with a description of the Yosemite valley, by Dr. Jabez Burns. London, [1873]. 124 p.   **DLC**

Letters repr. from the London *Times*; first 2 letters on the U.S., pp. 9–23; article on the Yosemite Valley, California, by Burns, pp. 119–124. See "Our American relations: showing how certain dreams come true," in Cook's *Single journey tickets to all parts of the United States & Canada, available by any line of steamers, from Liverpool or Glasgow*, London, 1874, pp. 20–27; also his many pamphlets describing tours in America: e.g., Colorado, New Mexico and California—all pub. in the U.S. although probably not written by Cook. See also John Pudney, *The Thomas Cook story*, London, 1953, for comment on Cook's visit to America in 1865, pp. 141–149.

2003   CROASDAILE, HENRY E. Scenes on Pacific shores; with a trip across South America. London, 1873. 173 p.   **DLC**

2004   CROPPER, JAMES. A month in California. London, 1873. 44 p.   **Uk**

Pub. by the Society for Promoting Christian Knowledge.

2005 DALLAS, A[LEXANDER] G[RANT]. San Juan, Alaska, and the North-west boundary. By A. G. Dallas, late Governor of Rupert's land. London, 1873. 11 p. **CtY Uk**

2006 DAVIN, NICHOLAS FLOOD. British versus American civilization. A lecture delivered in Shaftesbury hall, Toronto, 19th April, 1873. (Rev. Dr. McCaul, President of University college, in the chair.) Toronto, 1873. 45 p. **DLC**

2007 DRUMMOND, A[NDREW] T[HOMAS]. A Canadian national spirit. A lecture delivered before the Young men's association of St. Andrew's church, Montreal, on December 8th, 1873. [n.p., n.d.]. 13 p. **CaBVaU**

2008 EARDLEY-WILMOT, *SIR* S[YDNEY MAROW], *ed.* Our journal in the Pacific. By the officers of H.M.S. Zealous. Arranged and edited by Lieutenant S. Eardley-Wilmot. London, 1873. 333 p. **DLC Uk**

Includes account of 3 visits to California, 1870–71.

2009 FERGUSON, RICHARD SAUL. Moss gathered by a rolling stone; or, Reminiscences of travel. Part I.—Eastward ho [Egypt & up the Nile]. Part II.—Guide book to Thebes and its ruins. Part III.—Round the world. Carlisle, 1873. **UkCU**

On U.S., pp. 43–105.

2010 FITZGERALD, R[OBERT] A[LLAN]. Wickets in the West; or, The twelve in America. London, 1873. 335 p. **DLC Uk**

Includes 3 chaps. on the U.S.

2011 GADSBY, JOHN. A visit to Canada and the United States of America. Also a second visit to Spain. London, 1873. 104 p. **MoU TxFTC Uk**

2012 GARDINER, DAVID. Canada vs. Nebraska. A refutation of attacks made on Canada, by C. R. Shaller, commissioner of the Missouri railroad company, in the "People's journal", of Dundee, Scotland. Ottawa, 1873. 25 p. **DLC**

2013 GILLMORE, PARKER ("UBIQUE"). Adventures afloat and ashore. London, 1873. 2 vols. **DLC Uk**

Largely concerned with life and sport on Chesapeake Bay.

2014 [HAMMERSLEY, *MRS.* SARAH]. An account of a visit to the United States and Canada, 1872–3. [Alsager? 1906]. 20 p. **CaOTP**

Author given on cover title. First article, "Life in North Carolina," appeared in the London *Daily News*, Aug. 1874. The second compares life in North Carolina and Canada.

2015 [LAWRENCE, GEORGE ALFRED]. Silverland. By the author of "Guy Livingston," &c. London, 1873. 259 p. **DLC Uk**

Description and travel in California and the western states.

Review: *Athenaeum*, (April 5, 1873), 436.

2016 LEIFCHILD, JOHN R. On coal at home and abroad with relation to consumption, cost, demand, and supply and other inquiries of present interest; being three articles contributed to the Edinburgh Review, with an appendix. London, 1873. 141 p. **DLC Uk**

"On the coal mines of North America and Great Britain," pp. 49–87; originally a review of an American work by Henry Darwin Rogers, *Essays on the coal formation and its fossils, and a description of the coal fields of North America and Great Britain*, Edinburgh, 1858, 3 vols.

2017　[LIGHT, BIANCA]. Our American cousins at home. By "Vera" [*pseud.*] . . . Illustrated with pen-and-ink sketches by the author, and photographs. London, 1873. 268 p.　　**DLC Uk**

2018　MACDONALD, GREVILLE. George Macdonald and his wife . . . with an introduction by G. K. Chesterton. London, [1924]. 575 p.　　**DLC Uk**

　　　Author accompanied his father, George Macdonald, on visit to U.S., 1872–73; see pp. 409–461, for an account of the elder Macdonald's trip, including many of his letters. See also author's account of his own experiences on the trip, in *Reminiscences of a specialist*, London, [1932], pp. 47–52.

2019　MEDLEY, JULIUS GEORGE. An autumn tour in the United States and Canada. London, 1873. 180 p.　　**DLC Uk**

　　　In U.S., Sept.–Nov. 1872.

2020　MONCK, [*MRS.*] FRANCES ELIZABETH OWEN (COLE). My Canadian leaves. Dorchester, 1873. 166 p.　　**OKentU**

　　　Only 10 copies priv. pr. and circ. DLC and Uk have London, 1891 ed., 367 p., described by Canadian Library Service as "expurgated." In original version, in U.S., pp. 7–11, 25–27, 70–75; considerable comment on Americans throughout. In 1891 ed., on U.S., pp. 10–23, 159–170. Facsim. repr. of original ed., Toronto, 1963, includes marginal ms. notes.

2021　MURPHY, JOHN MORTIMER, *comp.* The Oregon hand-book and emigrants' guide. Portland, Oregon, 1873. 136 p.　　**DLC**

　　　Repr., with additions, as *Oregon business directory and state gazetteer*, Portland, Oregon, 1873. For a brief description of his experiences in America, see "An old Portland journalist. A brief sketch of John Mortimer Murphy, once connected here with the press," *Morning Oregonian*, July 1, 1889, p. 3.

2022　NOTES ON THE GEOGRAPHY of North America, physical and political. Intended to serve as a text-book for the use of elementary classes, and as a handbook to the wall-map prepared under the direction of the Society for promoting Christian knowledge and the National society for promoting the education of the poor. London, 1873. 52 p.　　**Uk**

　　　Uk lists under North America.

2023　O'DOWD, JAMES. The law and facts of the case of the "Alabama," with reference to the Geneva arbitration. London, 1873.　　**C-S IU PU-L Uk**

　　　Also ascribed to Sir James Cornelius O'Dowd and James Klyne O'Dowd.

2024　PAFFARD, S[AMUEL] T[HOMAS]. The true history of the Emma Mine. London, [1873]. 60 p.　　**CtY Uk**

2025　PUNSHON, *REV.* W[ILLIAM] MORLEY. Lectures and sermons. New York, 1873. 378 p.　　**DLC**

　　　Includes the lecture, "A pilgrimage to two American shrines," pp. 295–305. Uk has separate titles, *Sermons* and *Lectures*, both London, 1882, but neither list the above lecture. For a diary account of author's visit to Canada and the U.S., 1868–73, see *The life of William Morley Punshon*, ed. by Frederick W. Macdonald, London, 1887.

2026　REDESDALE, ALGERNON BERTRAM FREEMAN-MITFORD, *baron.* Memories. London, 1915. 2 vols.　　**DLC Uk**

　　　On Lord Lyons in America, 1861, I, pp. 131–149; on crossing the U.S., 1873, II, pp. 586–639.

2027   RIGG, JAMES HARRISON. National education in its social conditions and aspects, and public elementary school education, English and foreign. London, 1873. 517 p.   **DLC Uk**

Chap. 3 covers education in the U.S., pp. 91–142.

2028   [ROSEBERY, *LORD* ARCHIBALD PHILIP PRIMROSE]. Lord Rosebery's North American journal—1873. Edited by Antony R. C. Grant and Caroline Combe. London, 1967. 191 p.   **DLC Uk**

For an account of this visit, and subsequent trips to the U.S. in 1874, 1876 and 1883, see Robert Offley Ashburton Crewe-Milnes Crewe, *Lord Rosebery*, London, 1931, I, pp. 66–83; other comment, passim.

2029   SEEBOHM, B[ENJAMIN] and E[STHER]. Private memoirs of B. and E. Seebohm. Edited by their sons. London, 1873. 443 p.   **DLC Uk**

Correspondence during his residence in the U.S., 1846–1851, pp. 171–342.

2030   SEYMOUR, SILAS. A reminiscence of the Union Pacific railroad, containing some account of the discovery of the eastern base of the Rocky mountains; and of the great Indian battle of July 11, 1867. By Silas Seymour consulting engineer. With illustrations by I. P. Pranishnikoff, civil engineer. (Our special artist on the spot.) Quebec, 1873. 74 p.   **DBRE**

2031   SMITH, WILLIAM, *banker*. Notes of a short American tour, by Wm. Smith, banker, Moniaive. Dumfries, 1873. 82 p.   **DLC**

Pub. originally in the Dumfries and Galloway *Courier*.

2032   SPROAT, GILBERT MALCOLM. Canada and the empire: a speech. London, 1873. 35 p.   **MH Uk**

2033   STANNARD, M. Memoirs of a professional lady nurse. London, 1873. 239 p.   **CaBVaU Uk WaS**

In U.S. 1864–65, and on later occasions, pp. 132–149; 211–222.

2034   STENHOUSE, THOMAS B. H. The Rocky mountain saints: a full and complete history of the Mormons, from the first vision of Joseph Smith to the last courtship of Brigham Young. New York, 1873. 761 p.   **DLC Uk**

See also *Broadside announcing four lectures by Elder Stenhouse in June 1849*, Southampton, 1849; and *Broadside announcing a public discussion between Elder Stenhouse and Reverend Enos Couch*, Southampton, 1850. See also accounts by Mrs. Stenhouse, 1872, above, and 1874, below.

Review: *Harper's Mag.*, XLVII, 299.

2035   THORNBURY, [GEORGE] WALTER. Criss-cross journeys. London, 1873. 2 vols.   **DLC Uk**

Comments on the American scene in the 1860's, repr. from *All the Year Round* and other periodicals.

2036   [TYNDALL, JOHN]. Proceedings at the farewell banquet to Professor Tyndall. Given at Delmonico's, New York, February 4, 1873. New York, 1873. 90 p.   **DLC**

See "Address of Professor Tyndall at the farewell banquet given in his honor at New York, February 4, 1873," in author's *Lectures on light. Delivered in the United States in 1872–73 . . . With an appendix*, New York, 1873, pp. 184–194. See also his article "Niagara," a discourse delivered before the Royal Institution, Apr. 4, 1873, in *Macmillan's Mag.*, XXVIII (May 1873), 49–62. For comment on his American visit, 1872–73, see chap. 14 in Arthur Stewart Eve and Clarence Hamilton Creasey, *Life and work of John Tyndall*, London, 1945. Also see "Professor Tyndall in America," *Nature*, VII, (June 23, 1873), 224.

1874

2037 [BECK, JOSEPH]. Rambling rhymes on western travel. London, 1874. 61 p. **DLC Uk**
Priv. pr.

2038 BELL, WILLIAM ABRAHAM. The colonies of Colorado in their relation to English enterprise and settlement. London, [1874]. 16 p. **NcD Uk**

Pioneer Papers, no. 7. NcD and Uk also have this work bound with William Jackson Palmer's *The westward current of population in the United States*, London, 1874.

2039 BERNARD, WILLIAM BAYLE. The life of Samuel Lover, R.H.A., artistic, literary, and musical, with selections from his unpublished papers and correspondence. London, 1874. 2 vols. **DLC Uk**

Describes a visit to the U.S., 1846–47, I, pp. 249–318; Lover's previously unpub. "American sketches," II, pp. 65–101.

2040 BODDAM-WHETHAM, J[OHN] W[HETHAM]. Western wanderings; a record of travel in the evening land. London, 1874. 364 p. **DLC Uk**
On the American West.

2041 CAMERON, WILLIAM. A month in the United States and Canada in the autumn of 1873. Greenock, 1874. 295 p. **DLC**

2042 CAMPBELL, *HON*. DUDLEY. Mixed education of boys and girls in England and America. London, 1874. 19 p. **DLC Uk**

Repr. from *Contemp. Rev.*, XX (July 1873), 257–265. Author visited colleges and universities in the U.S.

2043 CHESNEY, CHARLES CORNWALLIS. Essays in military biography . . . Reprinted chiefly from the 'Edinburgh Review'. London, 1874. 414 p. **DLC Uk**

Uk entry reads: *Essays on military biography.* . . . First four essays on American Civil War figures; a defence of Americans as soldiers and as a people.

2044 COFFIN, *LIEUT.-COLONEL* WILLIAM FOSTER. Quirks of diplomacy. Read before the Literary and scientific society of Ottawa, January 22, 1874. Montreal, 1874. 31 p. **DLC**

For further comment by the author on Canadian-American-British relations, see "How treaty making unmade Canada," *Canadian Monthly & Natl. Rev.*, IX (May 1876), 349–359.

2045 FLETCHER, HENRY CHARLES. Report on the military academy at West Point, U.S. [Ottawa? 1874]. 26 p. **MH Uk**

See also author's *Memorandum on the militia system of Canada*, Ottawa, 1873, pp. 6–7, 12–13.

2046 FONBLANQUE, ALBANY WILLIAM. The life and labours of Albany Fonblanque, edited by his nephew Edward Barrington de Fonblanque. London, 1874. 546 p. **DLC Uk**

Selection of writings from the *Examiner* includes "The new world way to pay old debts [on American repudiation]," pp. 384–387 (1843), and "The triumphs of Metaphor," (on the American eagle), pp. 480–482.

2047   G[ASCOYNE], A[NNIE] M. Sunbeams from a western hemisphere. Dublin, 1874. 117 p.
DLC Uk

2048   GILLMORE, PARKER ("UBIQUE"). Prairie and forest: a description of the game of North America, with personal adventures in their pursuit. London, 1874. 383 p. **DLC Uk**

Review: New York *Herald*, Nov. 16, 1874.

2049   GREG, WILLIAM RATHBONE. Rocks ahead; or, The warnings of Cassandra. London, 1874. 233 p.
CtY MH Uk

DLC has 2d ed., Boston, 1875, with added pref., "Reply to critics and objectors." See esp. Appendix C: "Three men and three eras: Washington, Jackson, Buchanan," pp. 177–218; "United States in recent years," pp. 218–233.

2050   HALL, WILLIAM EDWARD. The rights and duties of neutrals. London, 1874. 210 p.
DLC Uk

See also commentary on the U.S. in author's *A treatise on international law*, London, 1880, passim.

2051   THE HISTORY OF THE LAKE SUPERIOR RING. An account of the rise and progress of the Yankee combination, headed by the Hon. Alexander Mackenzie, Premier of Canada, and the Browns, for the purpose of selling their interest and political power to enrich Jay Cooke & Co. and other American speculators. . . . Toronto, 1874. 14 p.   **CaOOA**

2052   HORETZKY, CHARLES. Canada on the Pacific: being an account of a journey from Edmonton to the Pacific by the Peace River Valley; and of a winter voyage along the western coast of the Dominion; with remarks on the physical features of the Pacific railway route and notices of the Indian tribes of British Columbia. Montreal, 1874. 244 p.
DLC Uk

Chap. 13, "Nanaimo to San Francisco," pp. 184–193. See also his *Some startling facts relating to the Canadian Pacific railway and the north-west lands, also a brief discussion regarding the route, the western terminus, and the lands available for settlement*, Ottawa, 1880, for scattered comment on U.S. interests in Canadian railroad routes.

2053   HOWARD ASSOCIATION, LONDON. The magistracy in England and America. [London, 1874?]. 4 p.
DLC

Caption title. Letter from the secretary of the Association, Mr. William Tallack . . . in a London newspaper.

2054   JAMES, H. J. STANLEY. Virginia, U.S.A.: its resources, adaptability for settlement, rates of wages, etc. London, 1874. 10 p.
Uk ViU

Pioneer Papers, no. 3.

2055   KINGSLEY, CHARLES. American notes: letters from a lecture tour, 1874. Edited by Robert Bernard Martin. Princeton, 1958. 62 p.   **CLU CtY NN Uk**

See S. P. Culthrop, "Cambridge and Kingsley on American affairs," *Chr. Examiner*, LXXV (Nov. 1863), 421–434; Arthur A. Adrian, "Charles Kingsley visits Boston," *Huntington Lib. Quar.* (Nov. 1956), 94–97; R. B. Martin, *The dust of combat: a life of Charles Kingsley*, London, [1959], esp. pp. 257–261, 281–290; and Susan Chitty, *The beast and the monk: a life of Charles Kingsley*, London, 1974, "The American lecture tour, 1874–1875," pp. 283–298. For Kingsley's ideas on Negro slavery see his novel, *Two years ago*, esp. the prologue; see also his letters to the London *Times* on "North and South," Nov. 18, 22, 1862.

2056   KINGSLEY, ROSE GEORGINA. South by West; or, Winter in the Rocky mountains and spring in Mexico. Ed., with preface by Rev. Charles Kingsley. London, 1874. 411 p.

DLC Uk

Uk lists under Rev. Charles Kingsley.

2057   KINGSTON, WILLIAM HENRY GILES. The western world. Picturesque sketches of nature and natural history in North and South America. London, 1874. 736 p.   **DLC Uk**

Pp. 1–235 on the U.S. See also author's fictionized accounts of the U.S. in *In the Rocky mountains, a tale of adventure*, London, 1878; *In the wilds of Florida. A tale of warfare and hunting*, London, 1880; and, *Among the red-skins; or, Over the Rocky mountains*, London, [1880].

2058   [LONGWORTH, MARIA THERESA]. Teresina peregrina; or, Fifty thousand miles of travel round the world. By Therese Yelverton (viscountess Avonmore). London, 1874. 2 vols.   **DLC**

I, pp. 1–60 on the U.S. See interesting account of author and her *Zanita; a tale of the Yosemite*, London, 1872, in Francis P. Farquhar's *Yosemite, the big trees, and the high Sierra: a selective bibliography*, Berkeley, 1948, p. 45f, 45, 46. See also Mary Viola Lawrence, "Summer with a countess," *Overland Monthly*, VII (Nov. 1871), 473–479; and Duncan Crow, *Theresa: the Yelverton case*, London, 1966, esp. pp. 253–273 on her trip to the U.S. Review: *Chambers's J.*, (by W. C.), XI, 285.

2059   MEMORANDUM ON THE COMMERCIAL RELATIONS, past and present, of the British North American provinces and the United States of America. [n.p., 1874]. 32 p.

DLC

Signed, Wash., D.C., 27 April 1874, Edward Thornton and George Brown. Appendix contains the full text of the old Reciprocity Treaty of 1854, and the full text of the proposed Reciprocity Treaty.

2060   MEREWETHER, HENRY ALWORTH, *the younger*. By sea and by land; being a trip through Egypt, India, Ceylon, Australia, New Zealand, and America, all round the world. London, 1874. 343 p.   **DLC Uk**

Pp. 244–315 on the U.S.; travelled in 1872.

2061   MORGAN, MATTHEW SOMERVILLE. The American war. Cartoons by Matt Morgan and other English artists. With illustrative notes. London, 1874. 224 p.   **DLC Uk**

Ed. by Henry Llewellyn Williams, Jr., an American. Pro-Confederacy cartoons. See also the cartoons on the Civil War in Sir John Tenniel's *Cartoons from Punch*, London, [1862], and in *Punch*, XL–XLIX (1861–65). See also William S[hepard] Walsh, ed., *Abraham Lincoln and the London Punch*, 1865, above.

2062   MORRIS, WILLIAM [*of Swindon, Eng.*]. Letters sent home. Out and home again by way of Canada and the United States; or, What a summer's trip told me of the people and the country of the great West. Swindon, [1874?]. 477 p.   **CSmH CtY Uk**

DLC has 2d ed., New York, [1875]. Originally in Swindon *Advertiser*, weekly nos. through 1874. On U.S., pp. 238–442.

2063   [MULLEN, W.]. Rambles after sport; or, Travels and adventures in the Americas and at home. By "Oliver North" [*pseud.*]. London, 1874. 268 p.   **DLC Uk**

Uk lists under North. Articles repr. from the *Field*; e.g., "Bear shooting in California," XLI (Apr. 19, 1873), 379–380. Mullen was in the U.S. in 1860.

2064   PIERCE, WALTER. America: a lecture. . . . Delivered at the Young men's temperance hall, General Fairchild, United States consul in the chair. Liverpool, 1874. 74 p.   **Uk WHi**

2065   REMARKS ON RECIPROCITY and the [Sir Edward] Thornton-Brown memorandum. By a Quebec liberal. Montreal, 1874.   **CaOOA**

2066   REMINISCENCES OF A STONEMASON, by a working man. London, 1908. 260 p.   **DLC Uk**

Uk lists under Working Man. Account of life in U.S., 1872–74, pp. 124–178.

2067   ST. AUBYN, ROBERT J. Middle-class emigration: its present position and prospects. With a short account of all the various fields of settlement. By Commander St. Aubyn, R.N. London, 1874.   **Uk**

The Pioneer Papers, no. 1, Introductory (Uk has complete set of Pioneer Papers). On the U.S. pp. 14–18.

2068   SIMPSON, WILLIAM. Meeting the sun: a journey all round the world, through Egypt, China, Japan, and California, including an account of the marriage ceremonies of the emperor of China. 2 pts. London, 1874. 413 p.   **C DN NIC Uk**

DLC has microfilm. On the U.S., pp. 347–413. See also *Picturesque people: being groups from all quarters of the globe. By William Simpson, F.R.G.S. special artist to the "Illustrated London News." With an introduction and descriptive letterpress. By the artist himself*, London, 1876.

2069   STAMER, W[ILLIAM]. The gentleman emigrant: his daily life, sports, and pastimes in Canada, Australia, and the United States. London, 1874. 2 vols.   **DLC Uk**

On the U.S., II, pp. 38–141.

Reviews: *Canadian Monthly & Natl. Rev.*, VI, 515; *Chambers's J.*, LI (Oct. 10, 1874), 650.

2070   STENHOUSE, *MRS*. T. B. H. (FANNY). "Tell It All": the story of a life's experience in Mormonism. An autobiography: by Mrs. T[homas] B. H. Stenhouse of Salt Lake City, for more than twenty years the wife of a Mormon missionary and elder. With introductory preface by Mrs. Harriet Beecher Stowe. Hartford, Conn., 1874. 623 p.   **CU CtY NN Uk**

Numerous later eds. Hartford, 1879 ed. added to the title, . . . *including a full account of the Mountain meadows massacre, and of the life, confession, and execution of Bishop John D. Lee*. London, 1880 ed. carried the title, *An English woman in Utah: the story of a life's experience in Mormonism. An autobiography*, etc. DLC has London, 1888 ed. under title, *The tyranny of Mormonism; or, An Englishwoman in Utah*, etc. See also her *Expose of polygamy*, 1872, above.

Reviews: *Academy*, XX, 47; *Athenaeum*, (May 8, 1880), 593; Philadephia *Daily Evening Bulletin*, Apr. 22, 1882.

2071   TAYLOR, WILLIAM CLARE. A trip to South Carolina, in 1873, in search of a missing brother. London, 1874. 71 p.   **NHi NN**

2072   TEXAS, U.S.A. Contents: What is Texas? What is its extent and population? Is the country healthy? Stockraising. What minerals are found there? What can land be got for? What railways are in operation? What are the prices of stock and provisions, etc.? Who should not go to Texas? Who should go to Texas? Which is the way to Texas? London, 1874. 13 p.   **Uk**

The Pioneer Papers, no. 2.

2073 TOWNSHEND, R[ICHARD] B[AXTER]. A tenderfoot in Colorado. London, 1923. 282 p. **CSmH CtY MH NN Uk**

DLC has New York, 1923 ed. New ed., Norman [Ok.], [1968], introd. by Jay Monaghan. Semi-fictionized account of life in Colorado, 1869–74. See sequel, *The tenderfoot in New Mexico*, 1885, below.

2074 A WARNING VOICE from America to Victoria. Melbourne, 1874. 11 p. **Uk**

A repr. of a review from the *Record*, May 1, 1874, commenting upon Rev. E. M. Rate's review of *A nation's right to worship God*, by Rev. Charles Hodge of Princeton University.

2075 WILSON, [WILLIAM] WRIGHT. The life of George Dawson, M.A., Glasgow, being an account of his parentage and his career as a preacher, lecturer, municipal and social reformer, politician and journalist. Birmingham, 1905. 215 p. **DLC Uk**

Wilson's visit to America in 1874, pp. 130–145.

1875

2076 ADAMS, FRANCIS, *of Birmingham*. The free school system of the United States. London, 1875. 309 p. **DLC Uk**

Discussed in "The free school system of the United States," *Westmin. Rev.*, XLIX (Jan. and Apr. 1876), 239–254.

2077 [BASS, *REV.* JAMES CRAIG]. Glimpses in America; or, The new world as we saw it. With notices of the Evangelical alliance, the Pacific railway, and California. London, 1875.

CL

2078 BECK, MARY E[LIZABETH]. East and west. London, [1875]. 220 p. **DLC**

On the U.S., pp. 139–220; first 138 pp. appeared originally under title *Through Egypt to Palestine*, London, 1873.

2079 BELL, *SIR* I[SAAC] LOWTHIAN, *1st bart*. Notes of a visit to coal and iron mines and ironworks in the United States. By I. Lowthian Bell. Newcastle-on-Tyne, 1875. 66 p.

CSt MHBA

Repr. from *J. Iron & Steel Inst.*, IX (1875), 80–150. See also author's "Report on the iron manufacture of the United States of America and a comparison of it with that of Great Britain," in Great Britain Executive Commission, Philadelphia exhibition, 1876, Education department, *Reports on the Philadelphia International exhibition of 1876*, London, 1877, I, 3–40; and his *The iron trade of the United Kingdom compared with that of the other chief iron-making nations*, London, 1886, pp. 60, 125–146.

2080 BELT, THOMAS. Niagara. Glacial and post-glacial phenomena. [London, 1875]. 22 p.

DLC

No t.p. Repr. from *Quar. J. Science*, XII (Apr. 1875), 135–156.

2081 BINNEY, FRED[ERIC]K A. Californian homes for educated Englishmen. A practical suggestion for a model colony. London, 1875. 73 p. **DLC Uk**

2082 BRADLAUGH, CHARLES. American politics. [London, 1875?]. 12 p. **DLC**

See also his *Cromwell and Washington. A contrast*, London, [1877].

2083   BRADY, *SIR* ANTONIO. America in its relation to foreign trade and commerce, being an address to the Glasgow conservative association, on 16th February 1875. . . . The Lord Dean of Guild, James King, esq., Yr. of Levernholm, in the chair. Glasgow, 1875. 40 p.

DLC

2084   BRERETON, ROBERT MAITLAND. Propositions for English upper class colonies in California, or in any of the English colonies. Westminister, 1875. 11 p.   **NjP NN**

CLSU, CtY, Uk have London, 1876 ed., 37 p. Maitland was involved in California irrigation projects, 1871–76, and eventually settled in the U.S. See his *Reminiscences of an old English civil engineer, 1858–1908*, Portland, Or., 1908, esp. pp. 18–31, 38–43.

2085   BROOKS, SHIRLEY [CHARLES WILLIAM]. Wit and humour: poems from Punch. London, 1875. 328 p.   **DLC Uk**

Poems on US: pp. 54–59, 102, 163, 187, 197, 198.

2086   BURNS, *REV.* JABEZ. A retrospect of forty-five years' Christian ministry. Public work in other spheres of benevolent labour, and tours in various lands with papers on theological and other subjects in prose and verse. London, 1875. 444 p.   **MH-AH Uk**

In the U.S. in 1847 and 1872; see earlier account of 1847 visit in his *Notes of a tour*, etc., 1848, above.

2087   CALMAN, A[NDREW] L. Life and labours of John Ashworth, author of "Strange tales," etc. . . . ***The profits to be devoted to the Chapel for the destitute. Manchester, 1875. 363 p.   **Uk**

DLC has "Sixteen thousand," Manchester, [187–?]. Ashworth visited the U.S. in 1873, pp. 221–288.

2088   CANNIFF, WILLIAM. Canadian nationality: its growth and development. Toronto, 1875. 20 p.   **CaOOA CtY Uk**

Discusses annexation of Canada to the U.S., pp. 16–20.

2089   CHAPMAN, CHARLES. The ocean waves: travels by land and sea. London, 1875. 323 p.

CSmH CU Uk

NjP lists 295 p.

2090   CHESSON, FREDERICK WILLIAM. The Atlantic cables. A review of recent telegraphic legislation in Canada. London, 1875. 83 pp.   **DLC Uk**

On Canadian-U.S. relations.

2091   CLAY, JOHN, *Jr.* New world notes: being an account of journeyings and sojournings in America and Canada. Kelso [Scotland], 1875. 200 p.   **DLC**

Repr. from the *No. Brit. Agriculturist* and the Kelso *Chronicle*. The author later settled in America. For an interesting account of the early Scotch and English cattle business in the west, see author's *My life on the range*, Chicago, 1924; repr. with index and introd. by Donald R. Ornduff, Norman, [Okla.], 1962.

2092   COBDEN CLUB. Free trade and the European treaties of commerce; being 1. Report of proceedings at the dinner of the Cobden club, July 17, 1875. 2. Correspondence on the prospects of free trade in Germany, Austria, Italy, the United States, Australia, etc. 3. Discussion on the treaties of commerce. . . . London, 1875. 175 p.   **DLC Uk**

2093 CRUMP, F[REDERICK] OCTAVIUS. The principles of the law relating to marine insurance and general average in England and America, alphabetically arranged: with occasional references to French and German law. London, 1875. 340 p. **DLC Uk**

2094 CUNLIFFE, MARY. Letters from abroad. London, [1875?]. 201 p. **Uk**
Priv. pr. Visited U.S. in 1872; see pp. 74–143.

2095 CURLEY, EDWIN A. Nebraska, its advantages, resources and drawbacks. Illustrated. London, 1875. 433 p. **Uk**
DLC has New York, 1875 ed. Author is described on t.p. as "Special commissioner from 'The Field' to the emigrant fields of North America." Weekly letters signed, "E. A. C." appeared in *Field* between XLI (Jan. 4, 1873), 5 and XLV (June 19, 1875), 624, under the title "Emmigrant fields of North America." Also see the answer to Curley, "Emigration to North America," by John H. Charnock, *Field*, XLI (Jan. 25, 1873), 78; and 4 English letters in reply to Charnock under the same title in *Field*, XLI (Feb. 1, 1873), 107.

2096 DAWSON, GEORGE MERCER. British North American boundary commission. Report on the geology and resources of the region in the vicinity of the forty-ninth parallel, from the Lake of the woods to the Rocky mountains. With lists of plants and animals collected, and notes on the fossils. Montreal, 1875. 387 p. **DLC Uk**
DLC lists under British North American Boundary Commission. See also author's *Preliminary note on the geology of the Bow and Belly river districts, North west territory, with special reference to the coal deposits*, Montreal, 1882; *Report on the tertiary lignite formation in the vicinity of the forty-ninth parallel . . . addressed to Capt. D.R. Cameron*, Montreal, 1874; *On the superficial geology of the central region of North America*, [n.p.], 1875 (from the *Quar. J. Geol. Soc.* for Nov. 1875, pp. 603–623; *On the Canadian Rocky mountains, with special reference to that part of the range between the forty-ninth parallel and the head-waters of the Red Deer river*, [Montreal? 1886]; and, "Travelling notes on the surface geology of the Pacific slope," *Canadian Naturalist*, VIII, n.s. (1878), 389–399. For additional comment on the U.S. see *The life of George Mercer Dawson* [compiled from the journals, letters, newspaper clippings, etc., by his niece, Lois Winslow-Spragge, Ontario? 1962], passim.

2097 FLETCHER, *COL.* HENRY CHARLES. A lecture delivered at the Literary and scientific institute, Ottawa, . . . February, 1875. Ottawa, [1875]. 19 p. **CaOTP**
Inside caption title: "The defence of Canada."

2098 FRASER, HUGH, *botanist*. Handy book of ornamental conifers and of rhododendrons and other American flowering shrubs suitable for the climate and soils of Britain. Edinburgh, 1875. 292 p. **DLC Uk**

2099 FROST, THOMAS. Circus life and circus celebrities. London, 1875. 328 p. **DLC Uk**
On American circuses, pp. 194–224; other comment on the U.S., passim.

2100 GALT, *SIR* A[LEXANDER] T[ILLOCH]. The political situation. A letter to the honorable James Ferrier, Senator. Montreal, 1875. **CaBViP CaOTU**
On U.S., pp. 5, 7–8.

2101 GUILLEMARD, ARTHUR G. Over land and sea. A log of travel round the world in 1873–1874. London, 1875. 355 p. **DLC Uk**
10 chaps. on the U.S.

2102   HALF HOURS IN THE WIDE WEST over mountains, rivers, and prairies. London, 1875. 345 p.   **Uk**

DLC has microfilm; Uk doesn't list title but has as part of the Half hour library of travel, nature and science for young readers. On the U.S., pp. 77–315.

2103   HALF HOURS IN WOODS AND WILDS. Adventures of sport and travel. London, 1875. 308 p.   **Uk**

Uk has as part of the Half hour library of travel, nature and science for young readers. ICJ has 1897 London ed. On California, pp. 3–23; on Maine, pp. 279–296.

2104   HARTLEY, *SIR* CHARLES AUGUSTUS. Letter on jetties at the passes of the Mississippi. Washington, D.C., 1875. 20 p.   **DLC**

2105   HARTLEY, *SIR* CHARLES AUGUSTUS. Notes on public works in the United States and in Canada, including a description of the St. Lawrence and the Mississippi rivers and their main tributaries. Excerpt minutes of proceedings of the Institution of civil engineers, Vol. XL, session 1874–75, Part II. London, 1875. 81 p.   **DLC UkLSE**

2106   HASTINGS, FREDERICK. Sundays spent about the world. Bristol, [1875].   **Uk**

MB dates Bristol, [1876]. Reissued [London, 1897] as *Sundays round the world*. On U.S., pp. 7–24.

2107   HOLT, *MISS* [C. E.]. An autobiographical sketch of a teacher's life, including a residence in the northern and southern states, California, Cuba and Peru. Quebec, 1875. 104 p. **DLC**

Pref. signed, "C. E. H." Miss Holt was in U.S., 1852–1870; see pp. 7–23, 43–62.

2108   HOW I SPENT MY TWO YEARS' LEAVE; or, My impressions of the mother country, the continent of Europe, United States of America, and Canada. By an Indian officer. London, 1875. 336 p.   **CU NN**

NUC lists under Cumberland, R. B.; 3 chaps. on U.S.

2109   JENKINS, [JOHN] EDWARD. The great dominion. An address, delivered at the request of the members of the Manchester Reform club. Montreal, 1875. 39 p.   **Uk**

CSmH and CaOOA have Montreal, 1875 ed., 30 p. References to U.S., pp. 15, 17–20, 22–24, 28, 32–35. See also his *State emigration: an essay*, London, 1869, esp. pp. 6–13; and *Canadian emigration in 1875*, 1876, below.

2110   LEECH, ARTHUR BLENNERHASSET. Irish riflemen in America. London, 1875. 216 p.   **DLC Uk**

Detailed account of the trip of the Irish rifle team to America in 1874.

2111   [LONGWORTH, MARIA THERESA]. Teresina in America. By Therese Yelverton (viscountess Avonmore). London, 1875. 2 vols.   **DLC Uk**

2112   MCDOUGALL, JOHN. On western trails in the early seventies; frontier life in the Canadian North-west. Toronto, 1911. 279 p.   **DLC Uk**

On U.S., pp. 70–78, 143–146, 253–271. See also his *Forest, lake and prairie. Twenty years of frontier life in western Canada—1842–62*, Toronto, 1895, pp. 57–60.

2113   [MACKEAN, WILLIAM]. Letters home, during a trip in America, 1869. Paisley [Scotland], 1875. 240 p.   **NIC**

Priv. pr.

2114   [MCLEOD, MALCOLM]. BRITANNICUS [*pseud*.]. The Pacific railway. Britannicus' letters from the Ottawa Citizen. Ottawa, 1875. 42 p.   **DBRE**

14 letters written in opposition to the "Mackenzie plan," called a plan which favors American over Canadian interests.

2115   [MACREADY, WILLIAM CHARLES]. Macready's reminiscences, and selections from his diaries and letters. Ed., Sir Frederick Pollock. London, 1875. 2 vols.   **DLC Uk**

London, 1912 ed., 2 vols., ed. by William Toynbee and enlarged by inclusion of many suppressed passages, under title, *The diaries of William Charles Macready*. See *The journal of William Charles Macready*, abridged and ed. by J. C. Trewin, London, 1967, pp. 203–219. See also various biographical accounts, esp. William Thompson Price's (New York, 1894) which deals with Macready's American experiences. See also account of American visits (1843–44, 1848–49) in J. C. Trewin, *Mr. Macready: a nineteenth-century tragedian and his theatre*, London, 1955, pp. 200–206, 217–226; Charles H. Shattuck, *Bulwer and Macready: a chronicle of the early Victorian theatre*, Urbana, Ill., 1958, pp. 220–225, 235–239; Phillip Leonard Pfeiffer, "The American tours of William Charles Macready," unpub. M.A. thesis, Univ. of Calif., Los Angeles, 1960; and Alan S. Downer, *The eminent tragedian, William Charles Macready*, Cambridge [Mass.], 1966, pp. 106–110, 257–270, 290–310. See also W. C. Miller, "The Macready riot in New York. By an eye-witness," *Longman's Mag.*, III (Apr. 1884), 636–643; and *A rejoinder to "The replies from England, etc. to certain statements circulated in this country respecting Mr. Macready." Together with an impartial history and reviews of the lamentable occurrences at the Astor palace opera house, on the 10th of May, 1849. By an American citizen* [Edward Stranahan], New York, 1849.

Reviews: *Edinb. Rev.*, CXLI, 416; *Quar. Rev.* CXXXVIII, 305; *Nation* (by Henry James, Jr.) XX, 297; *Westmin. Rev.*, CIV, 41.

2116   NORTH CAROLINA: its resources and progress; its beauty, healthfulness and fertility; and its attractions and advantages as a home for immigrants. Compiled by the Board of immigration, statistics and agriculture. Raleigh, 1876. 99 p.   **DLC**

DLC has Raleigh, 1876 ed. Both cataloged under North Carolina. Bureau of immigration. Contains series of letters by Duncan Stewart, "Glimpses of the southern states of America," first pub. in the Hamilton (Scotland) *Advertiser*; also letters by an English lady who lived in Ashville, 1862–74, originally printed in the London *Daily News*.

2117   REID, *SIR* GEORGE HOUSTOUN. Five free trade essays. Melbourne, 1875. 75 p.
                                                                    CSt NN Uk

"Production in the U.S.," pp. 21–36.

2118   ROSS, ALEXANDER MILTON. Recollections and experiences of an abolitionist; from 1855 to 1865. Toronto, 1875. 224 p.   **DLC Uk**

On U.S., passim. See also Frederick Landon, "A daring Canadian abolitionist," *Mich. Hist. Mag.*, V (Oct. 1921), 364–373; and T. E. Champion, "The Underground railway and one of its operators," *Canadian Mag.*, V (May 1891), 9–16.

2119   ROUGH NOTES of journeys made in the years 1868, '69, '70, '71, '72, & '73, in Syria, down the Tigris, India, Kashmir, Ceylon, Japan, Mongolia, Siberia, the United States, the Sandwich Islands, and Australasia. London, 1875. 605 p.   **DLC**

On U.S., pp. 171–202.

2120   [SMITH, T.]. Rambling recollections of a trip to America. Edinburgh, 1875. 55 p.

DLC Uk

Priv. pr. Principally on New York City, Toronto.

2121   SOLLY, SAMUEL EDWIN. Manitou, Colorado, U.S.A., its mineral waters and climate. Saint Louis, 1875. 39 p.   **DLC Uk**

Emigrated to the U.S. in 1875. See also his *Colorado for Invalids,* 1880, below.

2122   TOWNSHEND, F[REDERICK] TRENCH. Wild life in Florida, with a visit to Cuba. London, 1875. 319 p.   **DLC Uk**

Review: *Field*, XLV, 65.

2123   [TROLLOPE, ANTHONY]. A letter from Anthony Trollope describing a visit to California in 1875. San Francisco, 1946. 32 p.   **DLC**

No. 5 of the Colt Press series of California classics, repr. from "Trollope in California," ed. by Bradford Allen Booth, *Huntington Lib. Quar.,* III (Oct. 1939), 119–124. The last of a series of signed letters which appeared originally in the Liverpool *Mercury,* July 3, 1875–Nov. 13, 1875; the letter has also been repr. in Bradford A. Booth, ed., *The tireless traveler: twenty letters to the Liverpool Mercury by Anthony Trollope, 1875,* Berkeley, 1941, pp. 212–221; and in *North America,* ed. by Donald Smalley and Bradford A. Booth, New York, 1951, pp. 541–547.

1876

2124   [ADAMS, WILLIAM HENRY DAVENPORT]. Animal life throughout the globe. An illustrated book of natural history. London, 1876. 704 p.   **CtY NjP Uk**

Pref. signed W. H. D. A. Semi-fictionized. Book First, pp. 16–118, contains scattered refs. to the U.S.; Book Third, pp. 498–564, on the U.S. See also author's *Celebrated women travellers of the nineteenth century,* London, 1883, passim.; his *Washington and other great military commanders: a series of biographical sketches,* London, [n.d.], pp. 271–323 on Washington and pp. 325–356 on Grant; his *Wrecked lives; or, Men who have failed,* 2d ser., London, 1880, on E. A. Poe; and his *Dewey: and other great naval commanders, a series of biographies,* London, [1899?].

2125   BARCLAY, ROBERT. The inner life of the religious societies of the commonwealth: considered principally with reference to the influence of church organization on the spread of Christianity. London, 1876. 700 p.   **DLC Uk**

On U.S., pp. 119–125, 557–570, and appendix to chap. 28.

2126   BELL, JOHN. The United States of America proved to be the messianic world-kingdom. With a diagram exhibiting the fulfilment of the apocalypse. London, 1876. 72 p.   **Uk**

See pp. 57–72.

2127   BELT, THOMAS. Report on the coal and iron deposits of the southern Colorado coal and iron company. London, 1876.   **CoD**

2128 BROWN, ROBERT. The races of mankind: being a popular description of the characteristics, manners and customs of the principal varieties of the human family. London, [1873–76]. 4 vols. **DLC Uk**

Enlarged ed. with title, *The peoples of the world*, London, 1881–86, 6 vols. On American Indians, I, pp. 2–230; this section repr. in Edwin Hodder, ed., *The world: its cities and peoples*, London, [1889], IV, pp. 14–209. See also Brown's "A journey across the Cascade mountains into eastern Oregon and a description of Idaho territory," *Proc. Royal Geog. Soc.*, XI, Feb. 11, 1867, 84–97.

2129 BUCKNILL, *SIR* JOHN CHARLES. Notes on asylums for the insane in America. London, 1876. 88 p. **CtY-M DNLM Uk**

2130 CAMPBELL, J[OHN] F[RANCIS]. My circular notes. Extracts from journals, letters sent home, geological and other notes, written while travelling westwards round the world, from July 6, 1874, to July 6, 1875. London, 1876. 2 vols. **DLC Uk**

New York, 1876 ed., 2 vols. in 1. On U.S., pp. 1–150.

2131 CORRESPONDENCE RELATING TO the proposed joint purse arrangement between the Direct U.S. cable co. and the Anglo-American telegraph company. [London, 1876?]. 16 p. **MB NN**

See also *Anglo-American telegraph company. Replies to, and correction of, statements at the general meeting of the shareholders of the Atlantic telegraph company, on the 24th January, 1868*, [London, 1868?].

2132 CURLEY, EDWIN A. Glittering gold. The true story of the Black Hills. Illustrated with accurate colored maps and engravings. Chicago, 1876. 128 p. **DLC**

2d ed., rev. and enlarged, under title *Guide to the Black Hills, comprising the travels of the author and his special artist*, Chicago, 1877, 136 p.; facsim. repr. of 2d ed., with introd. by James D. McLaird and Lesta V. Turchen, Mitchell, S.D., 1973. Curley may have become a U.S. citizen later in life.

2133 DAVENPORT, MONTAGUE. Under the gridiron. A summer in the United States and the far west, including a run through Canada. London, 1876. 143 p. **DLC Uk**

Review: *Field*, XLVII, 658.

2134 DIXON, WILLIAM HEPWORTH. White conquest. London, 1876. 2 vols. **DLC Uk**

Uk dates 1876 [1875]. Describes travels in the Indian Territory, Texas and Louisiana.

Reviews: *Athenaeum*, (Oct. 30, 1875), 567; *Chambers's J.*, LII, 4th ser., 769; New York *Herald*, Dec. 8, 1875; *Westmin. Rev.*, CV, 42.

2135 DUNRAVEN, WINDHAM THOMAS WYNDHAM-QUIN, *4th earl*. The great divide: travels in the upper Yellowstone in the summer of 1874, by the Earl of Dunraven. London, 1876. 347 p. **DLC Uk**

New York, 1917 ed., by Horace Kephart, ed. carried the title *Hunting in the Yellowstone.* . . . For Dunraven's account of various visits to the U.S. between 1869 and 1896, see *Past times and pastimes*, London, 1922, 2 vols. See also his *Canadian nights, being sketches and reminiscences of life and sport in the Rockies, the prairies, and the Canadian woods*, New York, 1914, pp. 20–100, repr. with slight changes 3 articles from *Nineteenth Cent.*: "A Colorado sketch," VIII (Sept. 1880), 445–457; "Wapiti-running on the plains," VIII (Oct. 1880), 593–611; and "Sheep hunting in the mountains," X (Nov. 1881), 683–700. See also Dunraven's "The America cup," *Field*, LXXXVI (Nov. 9, 1895), 772–773; the pamphlet answer, *Report of the special committee of the New York yacht club relative to certain charges made by the Earl of Dunraven concerning the recent match for the America's cup*, New York, 1896; and A. T. Quiller-Couch, "Lord Dunraven and the cup," *Contemp. Rev.*, LXVIII (Dec. 1895), 797–804. See also Norreys Jephson O'Conor, "An Irish sportsman in the far west," *Arizona Quar.*, V (Summer 1949), 108–118.

Review: *Field*, XLVII, 191.

2136   FALDING, F[REDERICK] J. Notes of a journey round the world: made in 1875, by Thomas Coote, esq., jun., and Dr. Falding. Sheffield, 1876. 208 p.   **NN Uk**

Cross-country tour of U.S., pp. 125–208; Coote was an American, Falding an Englishman.

2137   FEATHERSTONHAUGH, ALBANY. Narrative of the operations of the British North American boundary commission, 1872–76. . . . From the "Professional papers" of the Corps of Royal Engineers, vol. XXIII, n.s. Wolwich, 1876. 72 p.   **DLC**

Uk has the *Professional papers*.

2138   FISHER, WALTER M[ULREA]. The Californians. London, 1876. 236 p.   **DLC Uk**

Also a San Francisco, 1876 ed.

Reviews: *Academy*, (by W. B. Cheadle), XI, 337; *Atlantic*, XXXIX, 371; Philadelphia *Daily Evening Bulletin*, Jan. 6, 1877; *Nation*, XXIV, 47; *Scribner's Monthly*, XIV, 860.

2139   FLEMING, *SIR* SANDFORD. The Intercolonial. A historical sketch of the inception, location, construction and completion of the line of railway uniting the inland and Atlantic provinces of the Dominion. . . . Montreal, 1876. 268 p.   **DLC Uk**

On Canadian-U.S. relations, passim.

2140   HARRIS, FRANK. On the trail; my reminiscences as a cowboy. London, [1930]. 247 p.   **DLC Uk**

New York, 1930 ed., *My reminiscences as a cowboy*, has added chap., and introd. by H. M. Kallen. Describes life in the west in the 1870's. The rev. and abridged version of his *My life and loves*, Paris, 1922–27, 4 vols., with an introd. by Grant Richards and entitled *Frank Harris, his life and adventures; an autobiography*, London, 1947 (new ed., reset, 1952), describes his life in the U.S. as a boy in his teens, 1870–76, pp. 48–143. Born in Ireland, Harris came to America when he was 14 and became a naturalized citizen. See also the accounts in Samuel Roth, *The private life of Frank Harris*, New York, 1931, pp. 35–123; A. I. Tobin and Elmer Gertz, *Frank Harris: a study in black and white*, Chicago, 1931, pp. 38–74; Edward Merrill Root, *Frank Harris*, New York, 1947, pp. 17–40; Robert B. Pearsall, *Frank Harris*, New York, 1970, chaps. 1–2; Linda Morgan Bain, *Evergreen adventurer: the real Frank Harris*, London, 1975, pp. 22–54; and Philippa Pullar, *Frank Harris*, London, 1975, pp. 300–318.

2141   HINCHLIFF, THOMAS WOODBINE. Over the sea and far away, being a narrative of wanderings round the world. London, 1876. 416 p.   **DLC Uk**

On California, pp. 196–316.

2142   HOME INDUSTRIES. Canada's national policy. Protection to native products. Development of field and factory. Speeches by leading members of Parliament. Free trade theories versus national prosperity . . . [Ottawa], 1876. 70 p.   **CaOTU**

References to the U.S. throughout.

2143   HOPKINS, LIVINGSTON. A comic history of the United States. New York, 1876. 223 p.
                                                                        DLC Uk

New York, 1880 ed. has subtitle, *Copiously illustrated by the author from sketches taken at a safe distance.*

2144   HOUGHTON, RICHARD MONCKTON MILNES, [*1st baron*]. Social relations of England and America. London, 1876. 40 p.   **NjP NN**

Originally pub. in the *Quar. Rev.*, CXLII (July 1876), 251–289, and repr. in *Littel's Living Age*, CXXX (Sept. 16, 1876), 707. For accounts of visit to the U.S. in 1875, and for other references to America, see Thomas Wemyss Reid, *The life, letters, and friendships of Richard Monckton Milnes, first lord Houghton*, London, 1890; and James Pope-Hennessy, *Monckton Milnes: the flight of youth, 1851–1885*, London, 1951, pp. 239–245, and passim.

2145   JENKINS, [JOHN] EDWARD. Canadian immigration in 1875. Report by Edward Jenkins . . . agent general of Canada, to . . . the Minister of agriculture, upon the position and prospects of immigration, and with comparative statements of emigration from Great Britain during the past four years. Montreal, 1876. 44 p.   **ICU Uk**

2146   [KENNEDY, DAVID]. Kennedy's colonial travel; a narrative of a four years' tour through Australia, New Zealand, Canada, &c. By David Kennedy, jun. Edinburgh, 1876. 440 p.
                                                                        NN Uk

Appeared originally, 1873–76, in the Edinburgh newspapers *Daily Review* and *North British Advertiser and Ladies Journal*; repr. here "with some alterations and many additions". Chaps. 25 and 26, pp. 328–360, devoted to U.S. DLC has, rev. and condensed, with two other vols., in *David Kennedy, the Scottish singer: reminiscences of his life and work, by Marjory Kennedy [Mrs. Fraser], and Singing round the world, a narrative of his colonial and Indian tours, by David Kennedy, jun.*, Paisley, 1887. See also Marjory Kennedy-Fraser, *A life of song*, London, 1929.

2147   KENNEDY, *SIR* W[ILLIAM] R[OBERT]. Sporting adventures in the Pacific, whilst in command of the "Reindeer." London, 1876. 303 p.   **DLC Uk**

Includes account of San Francisco, pp. 207–209, and of cross-country trip from San Francisco to New York, pp. 288–303.

2148   LEWIS, [*SIR*] CHARLES E[DWARD]. Two lectures on a short visit to America. London, 1876. 106 p.   **DLC Uk**

Priv. circ. In U.S. Nov. 1875–Jan. 1876.

2149   LINDSAY, WILLIAM SCHAW. History of merchant shipping and ancient commerce. London, 1874–1876. 4 vols.   **DLC Uk**

Comment on U.S. throughout; see esp. vols. II, pp. 320–407, III, pp. 1–26, 161–190, and IV, pp. 121–220. For other brief references to America, see author's *Our navigation and mercantile marine laws considered with a view to their general revision and consolidation; also, an enquiry into the principal maritime institutions*, London, 1852; *Our merchant shipping: its present state considered*, London, 1860; and his *Manning the Royal navy and mercantile marine; also belligerent and neutral rights in the event of war. A review of the past and present methods of manning, with suggestions for its improvement; and, the formation of more reliable and permanent reserves; also an inquiry into the operation of the Declaration of Paris of 1856, and proposals for obviating its injurious effects on British maritime commerce*, London, 1877, pp. 103–133.

2150   LITTLE, JAMES. The timber supply question, of the Dominion of Canada and the United States of America. Montreal, 1876. 23 p.   **DLC**

2d ed., with additions, Montreal, 1876, 26 p.

2151   LOFTUS, CHARLES. My youth by sea and land from 1809 to 1816. London, 1876. 2 vols.   **DLC Uk**

On U.S., I, pp. 236–325, II, pp. 1–45.

2152   MACDOUGALL, ALEXANDER W. Emma Mine. Further notes by Mr. Macdougall on the preparation of the prospectus. [London, 1876]. 29 p.   **CtY**

2153   MACGREGOR, WILLIAM LAIRD. San Francisco, California, in 1876. Edinburgh, 1876. 71 p.   **CSmH**

Priv. circ.

2154   MACRAE, *REV.* DAVID. Amongst the darkies, and other papers. Glasgow, 1876. 128 p.   **MoKU TNF Uk**

DLC has Glasgow, 1880 ed.

2155   MANNING, *REV.* SAMUEL. American pictures drawn with pen and pencil. [London, 1876]. 224 p.   **DLC Uk**

2156   O'LEARY, PETER. Working-class emigration. London, 1876.   **Uk**

Pioneer papers, no. 14; Uk has the series.

2157   PARKER, *MRS.* M[ARGARET] E. Six happy weeks among the Americans . . . With an introduction by the Rev. Professor [John] Kirk. [Glasgow, 1876]. 128 p.   **DLC**

2158   PATTERSON, WILLIAM J. Another trade letter. What is the commercial outlook? Can there be an enlargement of our trade relations with the West Indies and South America? Montreal, 1876. 46 p.   **CaOOA CaOTP**

Comparisons with U.S. trade throughout.

2159   REID, [SIR THOMAS] WEMYSS. William Black, novelist: a biography. New York, 1902. 400 p.   **DLC Uk**

Black's visit to the U.S. in 1876, pp. 146–158. Black also recorded his observations in his novel, *Green pastures and Piccadilly . . . in conjunction with an American writer*, London, 1877; the novel also ran serially in *Canadian Monthly & Natl. Rev.*, XI–XIII (Apr. 1877–Jan. 1878), and in *Littel's Living Age*, CXXXII–CXXXV.

2160   ROSS, *REV.* W[ILLIAM] W[ILSON]. 10,000 miles by land and sea. Toronto, 1876. 284 p.   **DLC Uk**

2161   SALA, GEORGE AUGUSTUS HENRY. Elkingtons and electro: an essay (Elkington & Co. International exhibition of 1876, Philadelphia. Descriptive essay by George Augustus Sala). London, [1876?]. 35 p.   **MH MWA NN**

No real t.p.

2162   [SHEARMAN, H. F.]. Martin county, and the other border counties of southern Minnesota, and upper Iowa. London, [1876]. 47 p.   **DLC**

Mainly compiled from U.S. government reports, but contains introd. remarks by the editor-publisher, H. F. Shearman, as well as letters from English settlers, etc.

2163   [SILLARD, ROBERT M.]. Barry Sullivan and his contemporaries; a histrionic record. London, 1901. 2 vols.   **DLC Uk**

Sullivan toured U.S. in 1858–60 and 1875–76: vol. II, pp. 1–30, 143–180.

2164   SMITH, C. HAROLD. The bridge of life. . . . Illustrated by Ferdinand E. Warren. New York, 1929. 271 p.   **DLC Uk**

U.S. travels, from San Francisco to New York, in 1876, 28–44.

2165   [SMITH, JOHN, *Professor of chemistry*]. Wayfaring notes. Second series. A holiday tour round the world. Reprinted, from the "Sydney Morning Herald," for private distribution. Aberdeen, 1876. 405 p.   **ICN Uk**

Pref. signed J.S. On U.S. in 1871, pp. 25–58, 264–405, passim.

2166   SOCIAL RELATIONS of England and America. [London, 1876?]. 40 p.   **ICJ NN**

"Reprinted from the 'Quarterly review' for July, 1876."

2167   TURNER, JOHN. Pioneers of the West; a true narrative. Cincinnati, [1903]. 404 p.   **DLC**

Experiences, 1871–76, of an English family in Boone County, Nebraska.

2168   YULE, JAMES COLTON. Records of a vanished life: lectures, addresses, etc. . . . A memoir by his wife, a funeral sermon, by R. A. Fyre, and some additional papers. Toronto, 1876. 174 p.   **CaNBFU ICU RPB TxU**

1877

2169   AMERICA AND ITS PEOPLE. London, 1877.

No locations found.

2170   BARCLAY, JAMES W[ILLIAM]. The Denver & Rio Grande railway of Colorado. London, [1877?]. 28 p.   **DLC**

CoD gives [1876]. See also author's "Colorado," *Fortnightly Rev.*, XXXII, n.s., (Jan. 1, 1880), 119–129; repr. in *Library Mag.*, III (1880), 262–272.

2171   [BECKETT, RICHARD]. Ten thousand miles in fifty days: being an account of a flying visit to the Dominion of Canada and the northern and southern states of America.   **NHi**

Reprinted from the Bolten Weekly Journal. Bolten, 1877. 127 p.

2172   BLACKMORE, WILLIAM. A brief account of the North American Indians, and particularly of the hostile tribes of the Plains; principal Indian events since 1862; causes of Indian wars; Indian atrocities and western reprisals; and war of extermination now being waged between the white and red men, being an introduction to Col. R[ichard] I[rving] Dodge's 'Hunting grounds of the great west.' London, 1877. 45 p.   **CtY Uk**

Priv. circ. repr. of Blackmore's introd. to Dodge's *The hunting grounds of the great West; a description of the plains, games and Indians of the great North American desert*, London, 1876; New York, 1877 ed. carried title *The plains of the great West*. (Both in DLC).

2173   CANNIFF, [WILLIAM]. Fragments of the war of 1812. The Rev. George Ryerson and his family. By Dr. Canniff. [n.p., 1877]. 10 p.   **DLC**

Caption title.

2174 CASTLETOWN, BERNARD EDWARD BARNABY FITZPATRICK, *2d baron*. "Ego". Random records of sport, service, and travel in many lands, by Lord Castletown. London, 1923. 245 p. **DLC Uk**

In Far West in 1877, pp. 38–41, 90–118.

2175 CORRESPONDENCE BETWEEN THE DIRECT United States Cable company, and Dominion Telegraph co. of Canada, in relation to the proposed joint purse arrangement with the Anglo-American Telegraph co. and the liquidation of the Direct U.S. Cable co. [n.p., 1877]. **CaOTP**

Correspondence among Laurence Oliphant, (then of New York), John Pender (London), Thomas Swinyard (Toronto), et al. See Oliphant's satire on his experiences with the Direct United States Cable Company in "Anatomy of a joint stock company," *Blackwood's Edinb. Mag.* (May 1878).

2176 FALK, ALFRED. Trans-Pacific sketches; a tour through the United States and Canada. Melbourne, 1877. 313 p. **DLC**

On U.S., pp. 13–85, 117–313.

2177 GEORGE, ALFRED. Holidays at home and abroad. London, 1877. 199 p. **DLC**

Priv. pr. Includes "First journey to America" (1872), "Second journey to America," (1876), etc.

2178 [GISSING, GEORGE ROBERT]. Letters of George Gissing to members of his family, collected and arranged by Algernon and Ellen Gissing; with a preface by his son. . . . London, 1927. 414 p. **DLC Uk**

Visit to the U.S., 1876–77, pp. 12–21. Gissing described his adventures in America in his novel *New grub street*, Leipzig, 1891. See Michael Collie, *George Gissing: a biography*, Folkestone, 1977, pp. 32–35.

2179 HARRISON, *SIR* RICHARD, *G. C. B*. The officer's memorandum book for peace and war. London, 1877. **Uk**

See also Harrison's *Recollections of a life in the British army during the latter half of the 19th century*, London, 1908; in U.S. 1863–64, pp. 106–115.

2180 HARTLEY, JOHN. Grimes's trip to America. Ten letters from Sammywell to John Jones Smith. Wakefield, [1877]. 121 p. **CLU Uk**

Dedication signed and dated "Sammywell Grimes. Bradford, 1877." Fictional and written in Yorkshire dialect.

2181 HIND, HENRY YOULE. The effect of the fishery clauses of the Treaty of Washington [May 8, 1871] on the fisheries and fishermen of British North America. Halifax, 1877. 2 pts. **DLC Uk**

2182 HODGINS, J[OHN] GEORGE. Special report to the Honourable the Minister of education, on the Ontario educational exhibit, and the educational features of the International exhibition, at Philadelphia, 1876. Toronto, 1877. 306 p. **CaOTU DHEW MH NN**

NUC catalogs under Ontario Education Dept.

2183 HUXLEY, THOMAS H[ENRY]. American addresses, with a lecture on the study of biology. New York, 1877. 164 p. **DLC Uk**

See esp. the "Address on the occasion of the opening of the Johns Hopkins University" (Sept. 12, 1876), pp. 97–127. See also "Prof. Huxley in America," New York *Tribune*, Ext.

No. 36, Sept. 23, 1876, for a series of addresses by Huxley. For accounts of the visit by Huxley see Leonard Huxley, *Life and letters of Thomas Henry Huxley*, New York, 1900, I, pp. 493–502; and William P. Randel, "Huxley in America," *Proc. Am. Phil. Soc.*, CXIV (April 1970), 73–99. For earlier views see *Professor Huxley on the Negro question*, comp. by Mrs. Peter Alfred Taylor, London, 1864 (Ladies' London Emancip. Soc. Tract, no. 10).

2184   KINGSBURY, W[ILLIAM] G[ILLIAM]. A description of south-western and middle Texas (United States). The soil, climate, and productions; together with prospective sources of wealth. Also the great inducements offered all classes of European emigrants, etc. London, 1877. 48 p.   **NN**

DLC has 5th ed., London, 1883. Written by an American land agent with offices in England, but contains many excerpts from letters of English settlers. See also author's *Why go to Texas?* London, 1878, which contains "A Swansea emigrant's letter from Texas"; his *Emigration. An interesting lecture on Texas & California*, London, 1883; and his *A tour through Texas and California in 1884*, London, [n.d.]. For amusing comments on Kingsbury, see Alex. Sweet and J. Asmoy Knox, *On a Mexican mustang through Texas, from the Gulf to the Rio Grande*, Hartford, Conn., 1883, pp. 193–202.

2185   LENG, [*SIR*] JOHN. America in 1876. Pencillings during a tour in the centennial year: with a chapter on the aspects of American life. Dundee, 1877. 346 p.   **DLC**

Repr. newspaper letters which appeared in the Dundee *Advertiser*, of which Leng was editor, under title "Across the Atlantic." See remarks on Leng in David C. Carrie, *Dundee and the American civil war, 1861–65* (Abertay Hist. Soc. Pubs., No. 1, 1953).

2186   [LEVESON, HENRY ASTBURY]. Sport in many lands: Europe, Asia, Africa and America. By H. A. L., "The old Shekarry." London, 1877. 2 vols.   **CU ICRL NN Uk**

On U.S., II, pp. 196–295. DLC has London, 1890 ed., 587 p.

2187   MACDONALD, ALEXANDER, *M.P.* Report by A. Macdonald to the members of the Miners' national union on the conditions and prospects of labour in the United States. [London? 1877?]. 12 p.   **CU-BANC**

President of the Miners' National Union, and the first working class member of Parliament; made 3 visits to the U.S.

2188   MACFARLANE, THOMAS. To the Andes; being a sketch of a trip to South America; with observations by the way on the family, the church and the state. Toronto, 1877. 174 p.

DLC

"Across the Continent", pp. 1–33, on the U.S.

2189   MACGREGOR, WILLIAM LAIRD. Hotels and hotel life, at San Francisco, California, in 1876. San Francisco, [1877]. 45 p.   **DLC**

2190   MACKAY, ANGUS. Report upon sugar plantations. Brisbane, [1877]. 9 p.

No locations found. Report on Mackay's tour of the U.S. and West Indies. Also printed in Queensland, *Votes and proceedings of the Legislative Assembly during the session of 1877*, vol. III, pp. 1129–1137. See also his "Cane fields of the United States and West Indies," *Sugar Cane*, IX (Apr. 7, 1877–June 1, 1877), pp. 174–187, 255–262, 293–300.

2191   [MARTIN, JOHN BIDDULPH]. The default of the United States government; being the case of the bond-holders of the Confederate cotton loan of 1863, as submitted to the Committee of the Stock exchange. London, 1876. 27 p.   **Uk**

Uk lists in U.S.A.-Appendix, under title.

2192   MORRIS, AUGUSTUS. Observations on railroads in the United States. Sydney, 1877. 26 p.   **CSmH NN UkLSE**

Official report to the Colonial Secretary of Australia by the Executive Commission to the Philadelphia International Exhibition of 1876.

2193   NOURSE, BENJAMIN F. The silver question. Papers read before the American Social science association, at Saratoga, September 5, 1877. By B. F. Nourse, of Boston, U.S.A., and Prof. W. Stanley Jevons, of London, Eng. Boston, 1877. 32 p.   **DLC Uk**

Uk lists under Boston, Mass.—American Assn. for the Promotion of Social Sciences. Paper by Jevons, pp. 26–32, "The silver question," also appeared in *Banker's Mag.*, XXXVII (Dec. 1877), 989–996; and in *J. Social Science* (Boston), No. IX (Jan. 1878), 14–20. See also William Stanley Jevons' *Letters & journal of W. Stanley Jevons*, ed. by his wife, London, 1886, pp. 141–146, for an account of his visit to the U.S. in 1859.

2194   O'LEARY, PETER. Travels and experiences in Canada, the Red river territory, and the United States. London, [1877]. 226 p.   **DLC Uk**

Travels in the U.S., pp. 163–192, 206–219.

2195   OLLIER, EDMUND. Cassell's history of the United States. London, [1874–1877]. 3 vols.   **DLC Uk**

History of the U.S., 1826–77, but vol. III also includes contemporary opinion on 19th century Anglo-American relations.

2196   THE PICTURESQUE TOURIST: a handy guide round the world; for the use of all travelers between Europe, America, Australia, New Zealand, India, China, and Japan, across the American continent. London, 1877.   **Uk**

Uk has "ninth thousand"; UU has 2d ed., London, 1877. On U.S., pp. 7–134.

2197   PRICE, *SIR* ROSE LAMBART. The two Americas; an account of sport and travel. With notes on men and manners in North and South America. London, 1877. 368 p.
                                                                                         NIC NjP Uk ViU

DLC has 1877 Philadelphia ed., and 2d London ed. (also 1877). Includes 4 chaps. on western U.S. Returned to America in 1897; see his *A Summer in the Rockies*, 1898, below.

Review: *Field*, XLIX, 65.

2198   RAE, W[ILLIAM] FRASER. Columbia and Canada: notes on the Great Republic and the New Dominion. A supplement to "Westward by rail." London, 1877. 217 p.   **NN Uk**

DLC has 2d ed., New York, 1879; chaps. 1–12 on U.S. See Rae's *Westward by rail*, 1870, above. Also see his novel about a tour in the U.S., *An American duchess*, London, 1890–91.

2199   REPORT OF THE CANADIAN COMMISSION at the International exhibition of Philadelphia, 1876. Ottawa, 1877. [122 p.].   **CU-BANC MB**

Various paging. Signed by C. P. Pelletier, E. G. Penny and D. McDougall. CU-BANC lists under Canada. Commission at the International Exhibition. . . .

2200   [ROBSON, WALTER]. An English view of American Quakerism: the journal of Walter Robson (1842–1929) written during the fall of 1877, while travelling among American Friends. Edited by Edward B. Bronner. Philadelphia, 1970. 162 p.   **CLU CtY NIC Uk**

2201 RUTHERFORD, JOHN. The secret history of the Fenian conspiracy: its origin, objects, & ramifications. London, 1877. 2 vols. **DLC Uk**

On the U.S., I, pp. 89–100, 206–258, II, pp. 1–30, 210–232, 241–267, 287–315.

2202 ST. JOHN, MOLYNEUX. The sea of mountains: an account of Lord Dufferin's tour through British Columbia in 1876. London, 1877. 2 vols. **DLC Uk**

In U.S., I, pp. 1–129, II, pp. 241–274.

2203 SEYMOUR W[ILLIAM] D[EANE]. Journal of a voyage round the world. Cork, 1877. 169 p. **MnHi**

Chaps. 1–3 on the U.S.

2204 SMITH, GOLDWIN. The political destiny of Canada . . . with a reply, by Sir Francis Hincks. Toronto, 1877. 32 p. **DLC Uk**

The Smith paper, pp. 3–21, repr. from *Fortnightly Rev.*, XXI, n.s. (Apr. 1, 1877), 431–459. See also Toronto, 1878 ed. which added "and some remarks on that reply." Essay also included in Edward Livermore Burlingame, ed., *Current discussion; a collection from the chief English essays on questions of the time*, New York, 1878, vol. I. For remarks on the Trent affair, see Smith's *The empire, A series of letters published in "The Daily News," 1862, 1863*, Oxford, 1863, pp. 1–40.

2205 SPENCE, THOMAS. The Saskatchewan country, of the Northwest of the Dominion of Canada, presented to the world as a new and inviting field of enterprise for the emigrant and capitalist, its comparison as such with the western states and territories of America; its climate, soil, agriculture, etc. Montreal, 1877. 60 p. **CtY MnHi**

2206 THE SUGAR QUESTION in Europe and America. [Manchester?] 1877. 8 p. **DLC**

Caption title; repr. from the *Sugar Cane*, IX (August 1877), 385–392.

2207 TO THE FREEHOLDERS OF CANADA. Political facts for consideration; with a short treatise on free trade and protection. [n.p., 1877?]. 29 p. **CaOOA**

Papers are signed, "A Freeholder." The second paper, the "treatise on free trade," deals with Great Britain and the U.S., pp. 25–29.

2208 TOLMIE, W[ILLIAM] FRASER. Canadian Pacific railway routes. The Bute Inlet and Esquimalt route no. 6, and the Fraser Valley and Burrard Inlet route no. 2, compared to the advantages afforded by each to the Dominion and to the Empire. By Wm. Fraser Tolmie. Victoria, 1877. 16 p. **DBRE WaS**

2209 TUBAC MINING AND MILLING CO. LTD. Memorandum and articles of Association. London, 1877. 52 p.

No locations found; Merril's Pamphlets, no. 708.

2210 TURLAND, EPHRAIM. Notes of a visit to America: eleven lectures. Manchester, 1877. 190 p. **DLC Uk**

2211 TWISS, *SIR* TRAVERS. The doctrine of continuous voyages, as applied to contraband of war and blockade, contrasted with the declaration of Paris of 1856 . . . read before the Association for the reform and codification of the law of nations, at the Antwerp conference, 1877. London, 1877. 36 p. **DLC Uk**

On England and the U.S.

2212 VICTORIA, AUSTRALIA. COMMISSION, PHILADELPHIA EXHIBITION, 1876. International exhibition at Philadelphia, 1876. Report of the commissioners for Victoria to His Excellency the Governor. Melbourne, 1877. 279 p. **DLC Uk**

Uk lists under Philadelphia (International Exhibition).

2213 WRIGHT, JOSEPH. A centennial tour in the United States and Canada. Macclesfield, 1877. 159 p. **CSmH CtY ICU NN Uk**

Spent 3 months in the U.S., Autumn, 1876.

1878

2214 ACKRILL, ROBERT. A scamper from Yorkshire to the United States, with a glance at Canada. Harrogate, 1878. 179 p. **DLC**

Editor of the Harrogate *Herald*, where material first appeared as letters to friends.

2215 B., R. H. Three weeks in America. 1877. [Aberdeen?], 1878. 19 p. **DLC Uk**

First appeared in the form of letters in an Aberdeen newspaper.

2216 BELT, THOMAS. Discovery of stone implements in glacial drift in North America . . . Reprinted from the Quarterly journal of science, January, 1878. London, 1878. 22 p. **DLC**

Quar. J. of Science, XV (Jan. 1878), 55–74.

2217 [BORLASE, WILLIAM COPELAND]. Sunways: a record of rambles in many lands. Plymouth, 1878. 484 p. **NjP NNEC Uk UU**

On U.S., pp. 1–226.

2218 BRADLAUGH, CHARLES. Hints to emigrants to the United States of America. London, [1878]. 62 p. **MH NN Uk**

An account of labor conditions in the U.S., portions of which had appeared in the weekly letters Bradlaugh wrote for the *Natl. Reformer* during his lecture tours in the U.S. in 1873, 1874 and 1875. See also accounts of these tours in *Charles Bradlaugh; a record of his life and work by his daughter*, Hypatia Bradlaugh Bonner, London, 1895, I, chap. 38, II, chap. 1; and in Charles R. Mackay, *Life of Charles Bradlaugh, M.P.*, London, 1888, pp. 406–417.

2219 BRAITHWAITE, R[OBERT]. The *sphagnaceae* or peat-mosses of Europe and North America. London, 1878. 91 p. **DNAL**

Uk has 1880 London ed.

2220 BRASSEY, THOMAS BRASSEY, *1st earl*. Lectures on the labour question, by Thomas Brassey, M.P. London, 1878. 267 p. **CU IaU Uk**

DLC has 2d and 3d London eds., both also 1878. Lecture 4, "Public elementary education in the United States," pp. 81–101; Lecture 9, "On Canada and the United States," pp. 212–224; other comment on U.S. passim. Also much comment on the U.S. in author's *Foreign work and English wages considered with reference to the depression of trade*, London, 1879; see also chap. 6, "A flying visit to the United States in 1886," pp. 222–247, in *Voyages and travels of Lord Brassey . . . from 1862 to 1894. Arranged and ed. by Captain S. Eardley-Wilmot*, London, 1895, 2 vols.

2221 [BROWN, JOHN]. Life of John Eadie, D.D., LL.D. London, 1878. 409 p.   **DLC Uk**

"Visit to America" in 1873, pp. 300–335.

2222 BUCKNILL, JOHN CHARLES. Habitual drunkenness and insane drunkards. London, 1878. 103 p.   **DLC Uk**

Written after making a tour of the U.S., to study methods of treating alcoholism. Bucknill, a "mental physician" and member of Parliament, visited American asylums and institutions. His report was presented to the House of Commons.

2223 CAMPION, JOHN S. On the frontier. Reminiscences of wild sports, personal adventures, and strange scenes. London, 1878. 372 p.   **Uk**

DLC has 2d ed., London, 1878.

2224 COLBY, CHARLES CARROLL. Tariff re-adjustment. Canada's national policy. Mr. C. C. Colby's great speech on tariff revision, House of Commons: March, 1878. To which is added an open letter from Mr. Colby and the amendment moved by Sir John Macdonald on a re-adjustment of the Dominion tariff, with the division thereon. [Ottawa? 1878]. 47 p.   **CaBViP CaOTU MH**

Much discussion of Canadian-U.S. relations. According to MH, ed. by C. H. Mackintosh.

2225 CUNNINGHAM, DAVID. Conditions of social well-being; or, Inquiries into the material and moral position of the populations of Europe and America, with particular reference to those of Great Britain and Ireland. London, 1878. 357 p.   **DLC Uk**

2226 DALE, R[OBERT] W[ILLIAM]. Impressions of America. New York, 1878. 163 p.   **DLC Uk**

Appleton's New Handy-Volume series, vol. X. Repr. of a series of articles from *Nineteenth Cent.*, III (March–June 1878), 457, 757, 949, and IV (July–Oct. 1878), 98, 713; from *Eclectic Mag.*, XC, 665; and *Pop. Science Supp.*, III (June–Aug. 1878), 138, 206, 339. See also his "American Education," the *Scholastic Register*, I (June 1878), 43, (Aug. 1878), 80–81.

Review: *Nation* (by W. C. Brownell), XXIX, 181.

2227 DEBY, JULIEN MARC. Report on the progress of the iron and steel industries in foreign countries. II.–1877. Newcastle-upon-Tyne, 1878.   **DLC Uk**

Pub. by the Iron and Steel Institute; DLC catalogs under the Institute. Pp. 5–108 on the U.S. Bound 2 vols. in 1 with the Institute's *Journal* for 1877, with reports for 1871–76 by David Forbes, and for 1876 by Deby, pp. 213–304, of which pp. 253–295 are on the U.S.

2228 FAWCETT, HENRY. Free trade and protection. An inquiry into the causes which have retarded the general adoption of free trade since its introduction into England. London, 1878. 173 p.   **DLC Uk**

On U.S., passim. See also *Essays and lectures on social and political subjects*, by Henry Fawcett and Millicent Garrett Fawcett, London, 1872, which contains "An American on representation. M. G. F.," pp. 318–335 (from *Fraser's Mag.*, Feb. 1872), and comments on American education of women, pp. 197–199. See also Henry Fawcett's "The recent development of socialism in Germany and the United States," *Fortnightly Rev.*, XXIV, n.s. (Nov. 1, 1878), 605–615.

2229 FERGUSON, FERGUS. From Glasgow to Missouri and back. Glasgow, 1878. 370 p.   **DLC**

Considerable comment on Illinois, Chicago; only brief description of St. Louis.

2230   FREE TRADE for the people. Protection for the favored few. Toronto, 1878. 15 p.

        CaOTP MH

        On protectionism in the U.S.

2231   GREAT BRITAIN. EXECUTIVE COMMISSION. PHILADELPHIA EXHIBITION, 1876. Reports on the Philadelphia international exhibition of 1876. Presented to both houses of Parliament by command of Her Majesty. London, 1877–78. 3 vols.   **DLC**

        At head of title, "Education department." Vol. I is devoted to a comparison of British and American productions and manufactures; includes articles by Lowthian Bell, Sir Douglas Galton, William Henry Barlow, Sir Charles Reed, R. H. Soden Smith, John Anderson, Frederick Arthur Paget, Isaac Watts, Henry Mitchell, and others. The Canadian commissioner's report in vol. II also compares Canadian-American economic relations, pp. 69–86. For other comment on the U.S., see *Official catalogue of the British section. Part 1,* London, 1876; and *The international exhibition of 1876, Philadelphia, Exhibitor's commercial guide, containing, among other papers, the United States tariff of import duties upon articles of produce and manufactures, in English currency; together with an epitome of the American laws relating to patents and trade marks. Compiled, and arranged with introductory notes, for the guidance of exhibitors and manufacturers by the secretary of the British commission,* London, 1876.

2232   HAMILTON, FREDERICK J. The new declaration. A record of the reception of the Sixth fusiliers, of Montreal, by the citizens of St. Albans, Vermont, July 4th, 1878. Montreal, 1878. 53 p.   **CaOOA Uk**

2233   HISLOP, HERBERT ROBERT. An Englishman's Arizona; the ranching letters of Herbert R. Hislop, 1876–78. Introduction by Bernard L. Fontana. Tucson, 1965. 74 p.   **DLC**

2234   LYNCH, J[OHN] J[OSEPH], *Archbishop.* Recent converts to the Catholic church in England, with an introduction by His Grace the most Reverend J. J. Lynch, Archbishop of Toronto; and an appendix on the progress of the church in America. Toronto, 1878. 23 p.   **CaOTP**

        See p. 23, on church in U.S.

2235   MACDONALD, JAMES. Food from the far West; or, American agriculture, with special reference to beef production and importation of dead meat from America to Great Britain. London, 1878. 331 p.   **DLC Uk**

        First appeared as a series of letters in the Edinburgh *Scotsman.*

        Review: *Sat. Rev.,* XLV, 538.

2236   MACLEAN, JOHN, *comp.* The tariff hand-book, shewing the Canadian customs' tariff, with the various changes made during the last thirty years; also the British and American tariffs, in full; and the more important portions of the tariffs of France, Germany, Holland, Belgium, Italy and Switzerland; all taken from the best authorities. Toronto, 1878. 160 p.   **DLC**

        "United States tariff," pp. 45–96, includes duty schedules, etc.; also, 2 letters from Yorkshire manufacturers. "Reciprocity. The Draft treaty of 1874," includes, besides the draft of the treaty pp. 97–116, the speech of Hon. George Brown before the Canadian senate on Feb. 22, 1875, pp. 116–133.

2237   MANIGAULT, GABRIEL. The United States unmasked. A search into the causes of the rise and progress of these states, and an exposure of their present material and moral condition. London, [Ont.], 1878. 178 p.   **OCIWHi**

        CSmH, IU, NN, Uk have London, [Eng.], 1879 ed. Uk ascribes incorrectly to Gabriel Edward Manigault. Author was born in South Carolina, moved to Canada after the Civil War.

2238   MASON, STEPHEN. America. Glasgow, 1878.   **MB**

2239   MOSELEY, H[ENRY] N[OTTIDGE]. Oregon: its resources, climate, people, and produc-
        tions. London, 1878. 125 p.   **DLC Uk**

2240   NASH, WALLIS. Oregon: there and back in 1877. London, 1878. 285 p.   **DLC Uk**

        Repr., Corvallis [Ore.], 1976, with foreword and notes by J. Kenneth Munford. See sequel
        Two years in Oregon, 1882, below. See also *A lawyer's life on two continents*, Boston,
        [1919]. Nash returned to America in 1879 and remained.

        Reviews: *Academy*, XIII, 577; *Athenaeum*, (June 15, 1878), 756; Philadelphia *Daily
        Evening Bulletin*, Oct. 19, 1878; *Sat. Rev.*, XLV, 802.

2241   [NORMAN, *SIR* HENRY WYLIE]. Calcutta to Liverpool, by China, Japan, and America,
        in 1877. By H. W. N. Calcutta, 1878. 85 p.   **NSyU Uk**

        On U.S., pp. 39–61, 69–85.

2242   PHIPPS, R[AMSAY] W[ESTON]. Free trade and protection. Considered with relation to
        Canadian interests. Toronto, 1878. 20 p.   **CaOTU MH NNC Uk**

        Example of U.S. cited throughout.

2243   [PRICE, WILLIAM EDWIN]. America after sixty years; the travel diaries of two generations
        of Englishmen. By M[organ] Philips Price. London, [1936]. 235 p.   **DLC Uk**

        DLC and Uk list under Morgan Philips Price. Accounts of visits to America by Captain
        (later Major) William Price in 1869 and 1878; and of his son, Morgan Price, in 1934–35.

2244   RAINS, FANNY L. By land and ocean; or, The journal and letters of a young girl who went
        to South Australia with a lady friend, then alone to Victoria, New Zealand, Sydney, Singapore,
        China, Japan, and across the continent of America to home. London, 1878. 250 p.   **DLC Uk**

        Last 2 chaps. on the U.S.

2245   RIDES OUT AND ABOUT. A book of travels and adventures. London, [1878]. 150 p.
                                                                         CSmH ICN Uk

        Includes William Tallack's "The Californian overland express; or, The longest stage-ride
        in the world," pp. 91–153, which first appeared in *Leisure Hour*, XIV (Jan. 1865), 11–64.
        Tallack's article has been repr. in the following: *The Californian overland express, the
        longest stage-ride in the world . . . With an introduction by Carl I. Wheat, and a check list
        of published material on the Butterfield overland mail by J. Gregg Layne*, Los Angeles,
        1935 (Hist. Soc. of So. Calif. Spec. Pub. No. I); *Hist. Soc. So. Calif. Quar.*, introd. by Carl
        Wheat, XVII, No. II (June 1935), 35–43, 45–78, (Sept. 1935), 83–95; and Walter B. Lang,
        ed., *The first overland mail, Butterfield trail, St. Louis to San Francisco, 1858–1861*, [East
        Aurora, N.Y., 1940], priv. pr., pp. 129–163.

2246   ROGERS, *MRS.* CLARA KATHLEEN (BARNETT). Memories of a musical career. By
        Clara Kathleen Rogers (Clara Doria). London, 1919. 503 p.

        DLC has Boston, 1919 ed.; Uk has Norwood, 1932. Tour of the U.S., 1871–1878, pp.
        387–474. See accounts of later visits to the U.S., 1878–1918, in her *The story of two lives:
        home, friends, and travels. Sequence to "Memories of a musical career"*, London, 1932.
        Mrs. Rogers crossed the Atlantic 41 times.

2247   SPENCER, HERBERT, *ed.* Descriptive sociology; or, Groups of sociological facts, classi-
        fied and arranged by Herbert Spencer. Compiled and abstracted by David Duncan . . .

Richard Scheppig . . . and James Collier. No. 6. Division 1. Part 4-A. American races. Compiled and abstracted by Prof. David Duncan. London, 1878.   **DLC UK**

Vol. 6 of *Descriptive sociology.*

2248   SWANSEA, HENRY HUSSEY VIVIAN, *1st baron.* Notes of a tour in America. From August 7th to November 17th, 1877. London, 1878. 260 p.   **DLC Uk**

Repr. from the Swansea *Cambrian.*

Review: *Sat. Rev.,* XLVI, 564.

2249   TAIT, J. L. A six months exploration of the state of Texas; giving an account of its climate, soil, productions, and mineral resources. London, 1878.   **CtY NjP Tx**

On spine: "A trip to Texas." Author, also identified as "A Scotchman," described as "Geologist and Mineralogist, London." States he was invited to visit Texas by officials of the Galveston, Harrisburg, and San Antonio Railroad; had previously travelled extensively in the U.S. east of the Mississippi.

2250   TUNSTALL, JOHN HENRY. The life and death of John Henry Tunstall; the letters, diaries and adventures of an itinerant Englishman supplemented with other documents and annotations. Compiled and edited by Frederick W. Nolan. Albuquerque, 1965. 408 p.   **DLC**

The young Englishman visited the U.S. in 1872 (pp. 23–45), then returned as a rancher in New Mexico from 1876 to his murder in 1878 during the "Lincoln County War," (pp. 94–282).

Reviews: *Am. Hist. Rev.* (by B. Noggle), LXXII, 319; *J. Am. Hist.* (by G. M. Gressky), LIII, 374; *Times Literary Supp.* (Mar. 31, 1966), 260.

2251   WHITEING, RICHARD. My harvest. London, 1915. 339 p.   **Uk**

DLC has New York, 1915 ed. Discusses visits to the U.S. in 1876 and 1878, pp. 206–220; interview with Gladstone on America, pp. 99–107. Also see author's "British opinion of America," *Scribner's Mag.,* XIX (Mar. 1896), 371–377.

2252   WILSON, ALEXANDER JOHNSTONE. The resources of modern countries; essays towards an estimate of the economic position of nations, and British trade prospects. . . . Reprinted, with emendations and additions, from Fraser's Magazine. London, 1878. 2 vols.   **DLC Uk**

On U.S., I, pp. 140–211; II, pp. 358–359.

1879

2253   ACLAND, *SIR* HENRY WENTWORTH [DYKE]. Medical education. A letter adressed to the authorities of the Johns Hopkins Hospital and the Johns Hopkins university. [Baltimore, 1879]. 14 p.   **DNLM MH**

2254   BARRY, WILLIAM JACKSON. Up and down; or, Fifty years' colonial experiences in Australia, California, New Zealand, India, China, and the South Pacific; being the life history of Capt. W. J. Barry, written by himself, 1878. London, 1879. 307 p.   **DLC Uk**

In California during the gold rush, pp. 97–141.

Reviews: *Athenaeum,* (Jan. 31, 1880), 148; *Sat. Rev.,* XLIX, 609.

2255   BISHOP, *MRS.* ISABELLA LUCY (BIRD). A lady's life in the Rocky mountains. London, 1879. 296 p.   **DLC Uk**

Repr. from *Leisure Hour*. "Letters from the Rocky Mountains," XXVII (1878), 24, 61, 72, 110, 136, 215, 280, 360, 471, 501, 615, 634, 669, 693, 740, 781, 795. Norman [Ok.], 1960 ed., introd. by Daniel J. Boorstin. See also Robert Cochrame, *Recent travel and adventure*, London, 1886, pp. 119–135; William Henry Davenport Adams, *Celebrated women travellers of the nineteenth century*, New York, 1903, pp. 418–437; Constance Williams, *The adventures of a lady traveller. The story of Isabella Bird Bishop*, London, 1909; Reginald Horsley, *Isabella Bird, the famous traveller*, London, 1912; and Norreys Jephson O'Conor "Intrepid lady," *Southwest Rev.*, XXXV (Spring 1951), 123–129.

Reviews: *Academy*, XVII, 211; *Athenaeum*, (Dec. 27, 1879), 845; *Atlantic.*, XLVI, 266; *Chambers's J.*, LVII, 129; *Critic*, VII, 41; Philadelia *Daily Evening Bulletin*, Apr. 3, 1880; *Eclectic Mag.*, XCIV, 379; *Nation*, XXX, 15; New York *Herald*, Dec. 8, 1879; *Sat. Rev.*, XLVIII, 577.

2256   BULLOCK-WEBSTER, H[ARRY]. Memories of sport and travel fifty years ago, from the Hudson's bay company to New Zealand. Ludlow, Shropshire, 1938. 235 p.   **NN Uk**

"Edited by Mrs. Armel O'Connor (Violet Bullock-Webster)." In North America, 1874–79; on the U.S., pp. 54–70.

2257   CAMPBELL, *SIR* GEORGE. White and black; the outcome of a visit to the United States. London, 1879. 441 p.   **DLC Uk**

New York, 1889 ed., under title, *The American people; or, The relations between the white and the black; an outcome of a visit to the United States*. From a series of addresses and from articles, "Black and white in southern states," *Fortnightly Rev.*, XXV, n.s. (Mar. 1879), 449–468; (Apr. 1879), 588–607. In U.S. in 1878.

Reviews: *Athenaeum*, (June 28, 1879), 815; *Nation* (by W. C. Brownell), XXIX, 181.

2258   CARPENTER, J[OSEPH] ESTLIN. The life and work of Mary Carpenter. London, 1879. 495 p.   **DLC Uk**

London, 1881 ed., repr. with index added, Montclair, N.J., 1974. Visit to U.S. in 1873, pp. 407–423; many other comments on America, esp. slavery in America, pp. 89–97, 119–131, and passim.

2259   DODMAN, G. SUTHERLAND. A voyage round the world in 500 days, with details compiled and arranged by G. Sutherland Dodman. Giving an account of the principal parts to be visited, with a brief description of the scenery and all particulars connected with the undertaking. London, 1879. 173 p.   **CLU Uk**

DLC has 3d ed., London, 1880.

2260   DREDGE, JAMES. The Pennsylvania railroad: its organization, construction, and management. London, 1879. 274 p.   **DBRE Uk**

"Chiefly reproduced from 'Engineering'."

2261   FINLAYSON, ARCHIBALD W. A trip to America: a lecture delivered by Archibald W. Finlayson, Johnstone, near Glasgow in the public hall of the Johnstone working men's institute, 18th March, 1879. Glasgow, 1879. 54 p.   **DLC**

2262   FORD, PAUL [*pseud.*]. The annexationist agitation; or, The sayings and doings of the Public notoriety club, as witnessed by a Canadian spectator. Edited by "Paul Ford." Montreal, [1879]. 16 p.   **CaOTU**

2263   GLADSTONE, WILLIAM EWART. Gleanings of past years, 1843–78. London, [1879]. 7 vols.   **DN MH Uk**

DLC has New York, 1879 ed., also 7 vol. "Kin beyond the sea," I, pp. 203–248, repr. from *No. Am. Rev.*, CXXVII (Sept. 1878), 179–212; also in *Old South Leaflets*, Gen. Ser., VIII, no. 190, Boston, 1907. See also the review of this article, "American facts and Gladstone fallacies," *Pop. Science Supp.* (Dec. 1878), 181; and an interview with Gladstone on this article in Richard Whiteing, *My Harvest*, London, 1915, pp. 99–107. See also "Letter of Mr. Gladstone to General Schenck, minister of the United States at the court of London, respecting certain passages in the American case laid before the arbitrators at Geneva," *Harper's Mag.*, LIV (Dec. 1876: letter dated 28th Nov., 1872), 105–111; and the pamphlet answer, which also contains a brief note from Gladstone dated June 23, 1877, *Correspondence in reference to the unexpended balance of the Geneva award on the Alabama claims, between Charles Ewart and the Hon. William Ewart Gladstone*, Coatesville, Pa., 1877; and *Correspondence in reference to the Alabama claims, between Charles Ewart and her Britannic Majesty's government*, Coatesville, Pa., [1872?], which includes very brief notes from Sir Stafford H. Northcote and W. B. Gordon and J. A. Godley answering for Gladstone.

For additional comment on the American Civil War and other affairs, see Gladstone's speech "On domestic and foreign affairs, delivered at West Calder, November 27, 1879," *Representative British orations*, ed. by Charles Kendall Adams, New York, 1884, III, pp. 287–345; John Morley's *The life of William Ewart Gladstone*, New York, 1903, II, pp. 69–86, 393–473; Philip Guedalla, ed., *The Palmerston papers: Gladstone and Palmerston, being the correspondence of Lord Palmerston with Mr. Gladstone*, 1851–1865, New York, 1928; C. Collyer, "Gladstone and the American civil war," *Proc. Leeds Phil. Soc.*, VI (1951), 583–594; *The political correspondence of William Gladstone and Lord Granville, 1868–1876*, ed. for the Royal Hist. Soc. by Agatha Ramm, London, 1952, 2 vols.; and Robert L. Reid, "William E. Gladstone's 'Insincere neutrality' during the Civil war," *Civil War Hist.*, XV (1969), 293–307.

2264   [HAROLD, JOHN]. Chapters on Erie and Atlantic & great western. [London, 1879?]. 112 p.   **DLC**

Introd. chap. signed by John Harold.

2265   HOOKER, *SIR* JOSEPH DALTON. The distribution of North American flora. London, 1879. 13 p.   **MH-A**

Repr. from *Proc. Royal Inst. Great. Brit.*, 1879, VIII, 568–580; also ran in *Gardener's Chron.*, X (1878), 140–142, 216–217. See description of his visit to the U.S., 1877, in Leonard Huxley's *Life and letters of Sir Joseph Dalton Hooker, based on materials collected and arranged by Lady Hooker*, New York, 1918, 2 vols., II, pp. 205–221; also much comment on U.S., esp. in letters to Asa Gray, passim. See also Hooker's "Notes on the Botany of the Rocky mountains," *Nature*, XVI (Oct. 1877), 539–540; *Am. J. Science*, XIV (1877), 505–509; *Archives des Sciences Physiques et Naturelles*, LXIII (1878), 240–247; "Presidential address to the Royal Society, November 1877," *Proc. Royal Soc. 1877*, XXVI (1878), 427–446 (also pub. separately under title, *The scientific work of the year*, London, 1877); "The vegetation of the Rocky mountain region and a comparison with that of other parts of the world" (in collaboration with Asa Gray), *Bull. U.S. Geol. & Geog. Survey of the Territories*, VI (1882), 1–62; and "The botany of the Rocky mountain region; a review," *Nature*, XXXIII (1886), 433–435.

2266   HORN, HENRY HARCOURT. An English colony in Iowa. Boston, [1931?]. 91 p. **DLC**

An account of an English family's early experiences as settlers in Iowa, 1868–79.

2267 INDEPENDENT ORDER OF ODD-FELLOWS, M[ANCHESTER] U[NITY]. Tour of the grand master, Henry Outram, esq., in Canada and United States with an account of his reception at Montreal, &c. . . . Durham [Eng.], 1879. 40 p. **CaOOA**

2268 KINGSLEY, GEORGE HENRY. Notes on sport and travel . . . With a memoir by his daughter, Mary H. Kingsley. London, 1900. 544 p. **MH Uk**

"Hunting in the U.S.," pp. 123–189. Letters, ed. by Mary Kingsley. Wrote for *Field* under signature "Doctor." In U.S. on various occasions, 1874–79.

2269 LESLIE, THOMAS EDWARD CLIFFE. Essays in political and moral philosophy. Dublin, 1879. 483 p. **DLC Uk**

"The wealth of nations and the slave power," pp. 51–61, repr. from *Macmillan's Mag.*, Feb. 1863. Also, a "new edition modified in certain respects" under the title, "*Essays in political economy*, 2d ed., Dublin, 1888, adds a new chap. on the U.S., "Political economy in the United States," pp. 126–154, repr. from *Fortnightly Rev.*, XXXIV (Oct. 1, 1880), 488–509.

2270 LOUDON, JOHN BAIRD. A tour through Canada and the United States of America, containing much valuable information to intending emigrants and others. Coventry [Eng.], 1879. 132 p. **CtY IU NNC Uk**

2271 [MATHEWS, CHARLES JAMES]. The life of Charles James Mathews, chiefly autobiographical, with selections from his correspondence and speeches; ed. by Charles Dickens [jr.]. London, 1879. 2 vols. **DLC Uk**

In U.S. in 1838, 1857–58, 1870–72. For an account of the 1838 trip, see James H. Butler, "The ill-fated American theatrical tour of Charles James Mathews and his wife, Madame Vestris," *Theatre Research*, VIII (1966), 23–36.

2272 MONRO, ALEXANDER. The United States and the Dominion of Canada: their future. St. John, N.B., 1879. 192 p. **DLC**

2273 MURPHY, JOHN MORTIMER. Rambles in north-western America, from the Pacific ocean to the Rocky mountains. Being a description of the physical geography, climate, soil, productions, industrial and commercial resources, scenery, population, educational institutions, arboreal botany, and game animals of Oregon, Washington territory, Idaho, Montana, Utah, and Wyoming. London, 1879. 364 p. **DLC Uk**

See also his "Ramblings in Oregon," *Field*, LII, 462, 682, 788; LIII, 102–103, 219–220.

Reviews: *Academy*, XVI, 96; *Field*, LIII, 502, *Sat. Rev.*, XLVII, 531.

2274 MURPHY, JOHN MORTIMER. Sporting adventures in the far West. London, 1879. 404 p. **NN Uk**

DLC has New York, 1880 ed.

Reviews: *Academy*, XVI, 334; *Athenaeum*, (Nov. 1, 1879), 558; *Field*, LV, 373; *Sat. Rev.*, XLVIII, 577.

2275 PALMER, GEORGE. The migration from Shinar; or, The earliest links between the old and new continents. London, 1879. 251 p. **DLC Uk**

Contains accounts of anthropological explorations in North and South America.

2276   PULLAR, ROBERT. Notes of an American trip: being the substance of an address delivered in Free St. Leonard's church hall, Perth . . . on the evening of Saturday, November 22, 1879. Reprinted from the "Perthshire Advertiser". [Perth, 1879].   **ICHi**

2277   PULLER, ARTHUR GILES. Notes on a journey to the United States of America. Being a lecture delivered in the Memorial school at High Cross, on Wednesday, January 15th, 1879. Ware, 1879. 72 p.   **CSmH CtY NNC**

2278   SAMUELSON, JAMES. Useful information for intending emigrants to the western prairies of the United States. With two maps, showing the chief railways, nature of soil, temperature, rainfall, &c. London, 1879. 32 p.   **NN Uk**

2279   SAUNDERS, WILLIAM. Through the light continent; or, The United States in 1877–8. London, 1879. 407 p.   **DLC Uk**

Reviews: *Athenaeum* (June 28, 1879), 815; *Nation* (by W. C. Brownell), XXIX, 181.

2280   SOLLY, SAMUEL EDWIN. The influence of the climate of Colorado upon the nervous system . . . (Reprinted from the Transactions of the Colorado Medical Society.) Colorado Springs, Colo., 1879. 12 p.   **CSmH**

Emigrated from England in 1874; continued to write on climate and health.

2281   SPENCE, THOMAS. The prairie lands of Canada; presented to the world as a new and inviting field of enterprise for the capitalist, and new superior attractions and advantages as a home for immigrants as compared with the western prairies of the United States. The elements of our future greatness and prosperity. Montreal, 1879. 56 p.   **DLC Uk**

2282   STANLEY, ARTHUR PENRHYN. Addresses and sermons, delivered during a visit to the United States and Canada in 1878. London, 1879.

MH, NN have New York, 1879 ed., 255 p.; Uk has London, 1883 ed. Many of the addresses contain comment on the U.S. For a description of his visit, see *The life and correspondence of Arthur Penrhyn Stanley, D.D., late Dean of Westminster. By Rowland E. Prothero . . . with the co-operation and sanction of . . . Very Reverend G. G. Bradley, D. D., Dean of Westminster*, London, 1893, II, pp. 510–533. See also Rowland E. Prothero, ed., *Letters and verses of Arthur Penrhyn Stanley, D.D. Between the years 1829 and 1881*, London, 1895, pp. 419–432.

2283   STRANGE, T[HOMAS] B[LAND]. The military aspect of Canada. By Lieut.-Colonel T. B. Strange, R.A., Dominion inspector of artillery. A lecture delivered at the Royal united service institution. [London, 1879]. 66 p.   **CaNSWA**

Priv. circ. Lecture dated Fri., May 2, 1870. Also printed in *Royal United Serv. Inst. J.*, XXIII, No. 102 (1879), 738–764. Discusses military aspects of the Canadian-U.S. boundary line. See also brief comments on the U.S. in author's *Gunner Jingo's jubilee; an autobiography*, London, 1893.

2284   THE TOUR OF THE AUSTRALIAN ELEVEN through England, America, and colonies, with Conway's Australian cricketers' annual for 1877–78. Melbourne, 1879. 399 p.   **CSt**

On U.S., pp. 282–285.

2285   TOWNSHEND, S[AMUEL] NUGENT. Colorado: its agriculture, stockfeeding, scenery and shooting. By S. Nugent Townshend, J.P. ("St. Kames"). London, 1879. 122 p. **NN Uk**

Ran originally in the *Field*, 1877–78, under pseud. of "St. Kames."

2286   VIVIAN, *SIR* ARTHUR PENDARVES. Wanderings in the western land. . . . With illustrations from original sketches by Mr. Albert Bierstadt and the author. London, 1879. 426 p. **DLC Uk**

Account of author's hunting trip in the Rocky Mountains.

Reviews: *Academy* (by Robert Brown), XVI, 260; *Athenaeum*, Sept. 20, 1879), 360; *Field*, LIV, 532, *Sat. Rev.*, XLVIII, 452.

2287   WILDE, JANE FRANCESCA [ELGEE]. The American Irish. Dublin, [1879?]. 47 p. **DLC**

See also Wilde's *Social studies*, 1893, below, for chap. on American women.

2288   WISE, B[ERNHARD] R[INGROSE]. Facts and fallacies of modern protection, being the Oxford Cobden prize essay for 1878. London, 1879. 119 p. **DLC Uk**

See chap. 4, "History of the American iron trade," pp. 79–116, and passim. See also author's *Industrial Freedom*, London, 1892.

2289   WOLVERHAMPTON CHAMBER OF COMMERCE. European and United States tariffs . . . with . . . percentage of duties . . . also tables shewing total value of British exports to various foreign countries from . . . 1840 to 1878, etc. Wolverhampton, 1879. 51 p.

        CtY Uk

2290   WOOD, JOSEPH. The failure of protection in the United States: a paper read at the Hightown Liberal Club, Manchester, February 1st, 1878. Manchester, 1879. 15 p. **NNC**

2291   WYLIE, A[LEXANDER] H[ENRY]. Chatty letters from the East and West. London, 1879. 224 p.   **CSmH MH NN Uk**

Letters from U.S., 1877–78, pp. 181–219. Also the anon. author of *American corn and British manufactures*, 1845, above.

1880

2292   [ALLAN-OLNEY, MARY]. The new Virginians, by the author of 'Junia' [etc.] . . . Edinburgh, 1880. 2 v. **DLC Uk**

Commentary on Virginia, 1876–1879.

Review: *Field*, LVII, 174.

2293   BADEN-POWELL, *SIR* GEORGE SMYTH. Protection in the United States and its lessons. London, 1880.

No locations found. A report of the British Association for the Advancement of Science. See also Baden-Powell's *State aid and state interference, illustrated by results in commerce and industry*, 1882, below.

2294   BARKER, JOSEPH. Life of Joseph Barker. Written by himself. Edited by his nephew, John Thomas Barker. London, 1880. 385 p. **MH Uk**

Repr., with a continuation, of his *The history and confessions of a man, as put forth by himself*, Wortley, 1846. Contains accounts of visits to the U.S. in 1847, 1851–60, and 1868–75. See also the *Natl. Reformer*, ed. by Barker from Apr. 14, 1860–Aug. 31, 1861, from which he resigned "in disgust" to found *Barker's Rev.* I–III, Sept. 7, 1861–Aug. 1, 1863. These publications contained his "American reminiscences" and many other articles on American affairs, slavery and the Civil War. Barker also edited the Chartist periodical *The People*, which includes much comment on the U.S.

2295 BENNOCH, FRANCIS. Report by Mr. Francis Bennoch on Virginia. September, 1880. London, 1880. 8 p. **DLC Uk**

2296 BERRY, C. B. The other side, how it struck us. London, 1880. 296 p. **DLC Uk**

Travelled in the U.S., 1879–80, south to Virginia and as far west as Chicago.

2297 BEVAN, GEORGE PHILLIPS. Primer of the industrial geography of the United States. London, 1880. 100 p. **Uk**

2298 [BOND, JESSIE]. Life and reminiscences of Jessie Bond the old Savoyard, as told by herself to Ethel Macgeorge. London, 1930. 243 p. **DLC Uk**

In America, 1879–80.

2299 BRITISH AND FOREIGN ANTI-SLAVERY SOCIETY, London. Exodus of colored freedmen from the southern states into Kansas. [London? 1880?]. 7 p. **DLC**

Repr. of correspondence from the London *Times.*

2300 BROWN, WILLIAM, *of Montreal.* Silver in its relation to industry and trade: the danger of demonetizing it. The United States monetary commission of 1876: review of Professor Francis Bowen's minority report. Montreal, 1880. 132 p. **DLC Uk**

See also scattered comment on the U.S. in author's *The labour question. Thoughts on paper currency and lending on interest: as affecting the prosperity of labour, commerce, and manufacturers*, London, 1872, 240 p.

2301 BUTLER, [*SIR*] WILLIAM FRANCIS. Far out: rovings retold. By Lieut.-Col. W. F. Butler. London, 1880. 386 p. **DLC Uk**

Repr. from various magazine articles. Includes several chaps. on California.

Review: *Sat. Rev.,* L, 810.

2302 CARPENTER, PHILIP PEARSALL. Memoirs of the life and work of Philip Pearsall Carpenter; B.A. London, Ph.D. New York. Chiefly derived from his letters. Edited by his brother, Russell Lant Carpenter, B.A. London, 1880. 360 p. **DLC Uk**

In U.S., 1858–60, pp. 170–279. See the short biographical pamphlet *Remarks of Robert E. C. Stearns on the late Doctor Philip P. Carpenter, before the California academy of sciences, July 2d, 1877,* [San Francisco? 1877]. See Philip Carpenter's *Report on the present state of our knowledge with regard to the Mollusca of the west coast of North America. . . . [From the Report of the British association for the advancement of science for 1856.*], London, 1857; and the *Supplementary report on the present state of our knowledge with regard to the Mollusca of the west coast of North America*, London, 1864, pp. 517–686, repr. in Smithsonian Misc. Collection, X (1873), *The mollusks of western North America. . . . Embracing the second report made to the British association on this subject, with other papers; reprinted by permission, with a general index,* Washington, 1873, pp. 1–172. The latter vol. also repr. Carpenter's "Diagnosis of new forms of mollusca, from the west coast of North America, first collected by Col. E. Jewett," pp. 277–289; "Diagnoses des Mollusques nouveaux prevenant de Californie," pp. 295–317; "On the Pleistocene fossils collected by Col. E. Jewett at Santa Barbara, California; with descriptions of new species," pp. 319–325.

See also articles by Carpenter in the *Proc. Zool. Soc.*: Part xxiii (1855), "Descriptions of (supposed) new species and varieties of shells, from the Californian and west Mexican coasts, principally in the collection of H. Cuming, esq.," pp. 228–235; part xxiv (1856), "Description of shells from the Gulf of California, and the Pacific coasts of Mexico and California. Part II," by A. A. Gould, M.D., and Philip P. Carpenter, pp. 198–208; "Monograph of the shells collected by T. Nuttall, esq., on the Californian coast in the years 1834–5," pp. 209–229. See also author's *Lectures on Mollusca; or, "Shell-fish" and their allies. Prepared for the Smithsonian institution*, Washington, 1861.

2303   CLOSE, W[ILLIA]M B[ROOKS]. Farming in north-western Iowa, United States of America. A pamphlet for emigrants and a guide to north-western Iowa. By Wm. B. Close, B.A., Trin. Coll., of Close Brothers & Co. Manchester, 1880. 32 p.

ICJ and MH have later printings, both Manchester, 1880.

2304   COLLINS, [WILLIAM] WILKIE. Considerations on the copyright question addressed to an American friend. London, 1880. 12 p.   **MH Uk**

Repr. from *Internat. Rev.*, VIII (June 1880), 609–618. See accounts of his visit to America, 1873–74, in Wybert Reeve, "Recollections of Wilkie Collins," *Chambers's J.*, IX (June 1906), 458–461; Clyde K. Hyder, "Wilkie Collins in America," *Humanistic Stud.* (Univ. of Kansas), VI (1940), 50–58, also repr. separately under the same title, Lawrence, [1940?]; and in Kenneth Robinson, *Wilkie Collins: a biography*, London, 1951, pp. 264–274. See also Robert Ashley, "Wilkie Collins and a Vermont murder trial," *New Eng. Quar.*, XXI (Sept. 1948), 368–373.

2305   COLOMB, *SIR* JOHN CHARLES READY. The defense of Great and Greater Britain. Sketches of its naval, military, and political aspects, annotated with extracts from the discussions they have called forth in the press of Greater Britain. London, 1880. 264 p.   **DLC Uk**

Scattered references throughout to U.S. naval forces. See also, *The protection of our commerce and distribution of our naval forces considered.* London, 1867; and Imperial strategy, London, 1871.

2306   COMBES, EDWARD. Report on the lighting, heating, and ventilation of school buildings in Great Britain, the continent of Europe, and America, with remarks on school discipline, normal colleges, and the "Kindergarten" system; also on the technical educational institutions of the above countries . . . Ordered by the Legislative assembly to be printed, 18 May, 1880. Sydney, 1880. 264 p.   **DLC**

At head of title: "1878–80. Legislative assembly. New South Wales," Scattered comment on the U.S.; see esp. pp. 90–98.

2307   CURETON, STEPHEN. Perseverance wins: the career of a travelling correspondent. . . . England, Canada, United States, Hawaiian Islands, New Zealand, Australia, Egypt, Italy. Toronto, 1880. 269 p.   **CaOONL**

Fiction, based on author's own travels. On U.S., pp. 179–181, 193–205.

2308   DAWSON, [*SIR*] J[OHN] W[ILLIAM]. Fossil men and their modern representatives. An attempt to illustrate the characters and condition of prehistoric men in Europe, by those of the American races. London, 1880. 348 p.   **DLC Uk**

Portions which appeared originally in *Leisure Hour*, under title, "The New world and the old," did not mention U.S.

2309   DAY, SAMUEL PHILLIPS. Life and society in America. London, 1880. 2 vols. **DLC Uk**

2310   DENISON, E. Sketches of America; from the Yorkshire Post. [Leeds, c1880]. 77 p.   **ICN**

Bound vol. of newspaper cuttings.

2311   DUDLEY, THOMAS HAINES. Protection or free trade for the United States of America? Discussed in two letters between the Hon. Thos. H. Dudley, ex-United States consul to Liverpool, and Charles Edward Rawlins, an ex-president of the Chamber of Commerce, Liverpool. Liverpool, 1880. 29 p.   **UkLRC**

CtY, NN have 2d ed., Liverpool, 1880.

2312　EVANS, ANTHONY WALTON WHITE. A commentary on criticisims [sic] concerning American v. English locomotives, with testimony by English engineers. New York, 1880. 55 p.　**MiU NN**

See also Evans' *American v. English locomotives. Correspondence, criticism and commentary respecting their relative merits*, New York, 1880; and *American engines and Fairlie engines compared*, [n.p., 1877?] (both held by DLC).

2313　FARRAR, [J.] MAURICE. Five years in Minnesota. Sketches of life in a western state. London, 1880. 269 p.　**DLC Uk**

Review: *Athenaeum*, (April 24, 1880), 533.

2314　FITZGIBBON, MARY AGNES. A trip to Manitoba. London, 1880. 248 p.　**DLC Uk**

Toronto, 1880 ed., 267 p., carried title, *A trip to Manitoba; or, Roughing it on the line*. In U.S., pp. 17–38, 235–248.

2315　HARDWICKE, HERBERT JUNIUS. Medical education and practice in all parts of the world. London, 1880. 209 p.　**DHEW Uk**

On U.S., pp. 135–190 (Survey by state).

2316　HAROLD, JOHN. Farming and railroad interests in America. London, [1880]. 71 p.　**DBRE MdBJ Uk**

2317　HIND, HENRY YOULE. Falsified departmental reports. A letter to his excellency, the Marquis of Lorne, governor general of Canada. Windsor, N.S., 1880. 48 p.　**DLC**

NcD gives 58 p. On statistics of U.S.-Canadian fishery trade.

2318　[KINGSLEY, HENRY]. Adventures round the world with numerous illustrations. London, [1880]. 280 p.　**Uk**

Semi-fictionized account of author's experiences in San Francisco in 1851 and 1852, pp. 29–44, 67–74.

2319　[LEATHES, EDMUND JOHN]. An actor abroad; or, Gossip dramatic, narrative and descriptive, from the recollections of an actor in Australia, New Zealand, the Sandwich islands, California, Nevada, Central America, and New York. London, 1880. 317 p.　**DLC Uk**

Author's real name, Edmund John Donaldson.

2320　MITCHELL, PETER. The West and North-west. Notes of a holiday trip. Reliable information for immigrants, with maps, &c. Montreal, 1880. 64 p.　**DLC Uk**

2321　MONGREDIEN, AUGUSTUS. The western farmer of America. London, 1880. 30 p.　**DLC Uk**

Pub. by the Cobden Club and included in its *Free trade tracts: a series of essays published under the sanction of the Cobden Club in 1881–2*, London, [1882]. See American replies: *An argument for a protective tarriff. The farmer's question: being a reply to the Cobden club tract entitled "The western farmer of America,"* by Jonathan B. Wise, [i.e., John Lord Hayes], Cambridge [Mass.], 1880; Thomas Haines Dudley, *Reply to Augustus Mongredien's appeal to the western farmer of America. Showing the prosperity of America under protection and the decline of England under her so-called free-trade system*, Philadelphia, 1880; and Dudley's *Protection to home industry. Shall England interfere in our election and make our tarrif laws for her benefit? Reply to Augustus Mongredien's appeal to the western farmer of America*, [Philadelphia, 1880]. Also, on Mongredian in part and anti-Cobden Club in general, see Dudley's *The Cobden club of England and protection in the United States. A speech made at a Republican meeting, held at Astoria, New York, October 23rd, 1884*, [n.p., n.d.].

2322 NEWMARCH, W[ILLIA]M THOMAS. Letters written home in the years 1864–5 describing residence in Canada, and journeys to New York, Washington and the Pennsylvanian oil region, and a visit to the Army of the Potomac; to which are added letters written home in 1865, from the iron region of Styria, and from Austria and Hungary. [London], 1880. 202 p.   **DLC Uk**
Priv. circ.

2323 POTTS, *REV.* JOHN FAULKNER. Letters from America. London, 1880. 303 p.   **ICN Uk**
Repr. from the *Morning Light*.

2324 PRACTICAL SUGGESTIONS AS TO INSTRUCTION in farming in the United States & Canada. A self-supporting occupation and opening in life for gentlemen's sons, and a prudent way of starting for any who desire to engage in agriculture in America. London, [1880?].
CaOONL has 5th ed., London, 1881, earliest located; Uk has 7th ed., London, 1882 (and several later eds.); DLC has 10th (London, [1883]), 16th and 17th eds., all listed under William Wilbraham Ford. Other eds. give credit to Ford, Rathbone and Walter as joint authors. Sometimes cataloged under American Colonization Company. Probably written originally by the publisher, H.F. Shearman. A very popular work that went into many eds. with variant titles.

2325 SALA, GEORGE AUGUSTUS HENRY. America revisited. New York, 1880. 224 p.**DLC**
Paper-covered Standard Series of Travels, no. 45. Uk has enlarged ed., London, 1882, 2 vols., entitled *America revisited: from the bay of New York to the Gulf of Mexico, and from lake Michigan to the Pacific*. Originally pub. as a series of letters in the London *Daily Telegraph*. Describes visit of 1879–80, as does his "Now and then in America," *No. Am. Rev.*, CXXX (Feb. 1880), 147–162. See also his accounts of this and other visits to the U.S. in *Things I have seen and people I have known*, London, 1894, 2 vols.; and, *The life and adventures of George Augustus Sala*, London, 1895, 2 vols.

2326 SENIOR, NASSAU WILLIAM. Conversations with distinguished persons during the second empire, from 1860 to 1863. Edited by his daughter M. C. M. Simpson. London, 1880. 2 vols.   **DLC Uk**
Conversations with or including Americans: I, pp. 284–286, II, pp. 2–11, 76–81, 124, 130–147, 306–311.

2327 SEYD, ERNEST. The United States of America and the question of silver and its coinage in 1880. The views of Mr. Ernest Seyd, F.S.S., of London, as to the attitude and legislation to be adopted by the Union at the present time. [n.p., 1880?]. 16 p.   **MH**
See also *Letter from Ernest Seyd to Samuel Hooper on the subject of coinage*, Washington, D.C., 1893.

2328 SOLLY, SAMUEL EDWIN. Colorado for invalids. . . . Reprinted from "New Colorado and the Santa Fe Trail," by permission of Harper Bros.). Colorado Springs, Colo., 1880. 28 p.   **DLC**
Repr. of chap. entitled "The health seeker" in Augustus Allen Hayes, *New Colorado and the Santa Fe Trail*, New York, 1880, pp. 180–196; repr. from *Harpers Mag.* and *the Internat. Rev.*

2329   SOMERSET, EDWARD ADOLPHUS SEYMOUR, *12th duke*. Monarchy and democracy, phases of modern politics. London, 1880. 192 p.   **DLC**

"The great republic," pp. 65–84, and other comment on U.S., passim. For Somerset's 1862 visit to the U.S., see *Letters of Lord St. Maur and Lord Edward St. Maur* [*i.e., Somerset*], *1846 to 1869*, London, 1888, pp. 244–263; and "Ten days in Richmond," *Blackwood's Edinb. Mag.*, XCII (Oct. 1882), 391–402.

Review: *Quar. Rev.*, CXLIX, 230.

2330   TANGYE [*SIR*] RICHARD. Reminiscences of travel, and other papers written, in leisure hours, on board the good ship "Parramatta," when voyaging from Plymouth to Sydney, in the autumn of 1879. Birmingham, 1880. 48 p.   **CSmH CtY**

Repr. from the *Factory Herald*. Includes description of 1876 voyage from Honolulu to San Francisco, and overland travel from California across the U.S.: pp. 11–37. Repr., with additions, in *Reminiscences of travel in Australia, America, and Egypt*, Birmingham, 1883, pp. 127–178. See also his *English notes for American circulation. (With apologies to Charles Dickens)*, Birmingham, 1895: imaginary account by an American visiting his long-lost English relatives.

2331   THOMAS, CYRUS. The frontier schoolmaster: the autobiography of a teacher, an account not only of experiences in the schoolroom but in agricultural, political, and military life, together with an essay on the management of our public schools. Montreal, 1880. 465 p.   **CLU NN**

In Union army during the Civil War, pp. 357–395; other visits to the U.S., teaching, etc., passim.

2332   TOWNSHEND, S[AMUEL] NUGENT. Our Indian summer in the far West. An autumn tour of fifteen thousand miles in Kansas, Texas, New Mexico, Colorado, and the Indian territory. London, 1880. 123 p.   **DLC**

Under *pseud*. of "St. Kames," see author's "Notes from America," in *Field* during the years 1876–1880.

2333   WALSINGHAM, THOMAS DE GREY, *6th baron*. Pterophoridae of California and Oregon. London, 1880. 66 p.   **CLU Uk**

In U.S., 1871–72. See his "North American coleophorae," *Trans. Entomol. Soc. London*, XVII (1882), 429–442; "North American tortricidae," ibid., (1884), 121–147; "Description of a new tortricid from California," *Insect Life*, III (1891), 465.

2334   WARING, CHARLES. Some things in America set forth in thirteen letters. London, 1880. 78 p.   **DLC Uk**

Repr. from *Vanity Fair*.

2335   WILLIAMSON, ANDREW. Sport and photography in the Rocky mountains. Edinburgh, 1880. 55 p.   **DLC Uk**

Reviews: *Nation*, XXXI, 347; *Sat. Rev.*, L, 587.

2336   WILSON, ALEXANDER JOHNSTONE. Reciprocity, bi-metallism and land tenure reform. London, 1880. 256 p.   **DLC Uk**

On U.S., pp. 153–192. Appeared originally in *Macmillan's Mag.*, XXXIX, (Feb–Apr. 1879), 357–368, 466–480, 573–584.

2337 WOOD, JOHN, [*Writer on Finance*]. American protection *versus* Canadian free trade. A plea for British agriculture. London, 1880. 46 p. **ICU NN Uk**

2338 ZIGZAG, ZELOTES [*Pseud.*]. "Astonished at America." Being cursory deductions elucidated from genuine hearsay, intelligent judges, keen landowners, many nondescripts, official people, queer republicans, sundry travellers, undoubtedly veritable, without exaggeration, yet zealously admiring America. London, 1880. 107 p. **NNC PPL TxU Uk**

1881

2339 [AMERICAN RAILWAY SYSTEMS]. American and Canadian railway systems. No. 2. The grand trunk of Canada revisited . . . Reprinted from "the Railway News." London, 1881. 27 p. **Uk**

Cities served include Milwaukee, Chicago, Detroit.

2340 BARTON, HARRY SCOTT. What I did in "The long." Journals home during a tour through the United States and Canada, in the long vacation of 1881. [London, 1881?]. 91 p. **DLC Uk**

Priv. pr.

2341 BROWN, ROBERT. The countries of the world: being a popular description of the various continents, islands, rivers, seas, and peoples of the globe. London, [1876–81]. 6 vols. **DLC Uk**

On U.S., I, pp. 251–320; II, 1–234. See also author's *Our earth and its story: a popular treatise on physical geography*, London, [1887–89], 3 vols.

2342 CAMPBELL, JOHN. Asiatic tribes in North America. [Toronto, 1881]. 38 p. **DLC**

From the *Proc. Canadian Inst.*, I, 171–206.

2343 CASHMAN, D. B. The life of Michael Davitt. With a history of the rise and development of the Irish national land league. Boston, 1881. 256 p. **DLC**

UkLSE has Glasgow, [n.d.] ed., 256 p., with title: *The life of Michael Davitt, founder of the National land league. To which is added, the secret history of the Land league*. Davitt visited America in 1878–79, pp. 67–132, and in 1880, pp. 222–235.

2344 [DAY, JAMES E.]. [Letter to the St. George's society, dated Toronto, December 17th, 1881, and signed Jas. E. Day and Alfred Piddington. Toronto, 1881]. 3 p. **CaOTP**

In defense of Goldwin Smith against objections that he favored annexation and "dismemberment of the empire." See also the 3 p. broadside *Two letters of resignation*, [Toronto, 1896], signed "Academicus": on the resignation of Mr. Justice Falconbridge from the senate of the Univ. of Toronto because of a resolution to confer an honorary degree on Goldwin Smith.

2345 DEATH OF PRESIDENT GARFIELD. Meeting of Americans in London at Exeter Hall, 24 September 1881; to which is added by permission the address of His Grace the Archbishop of Canterbury, delivered at the Church of St. Martin's-in-the-Fields, 26 September, 1881. London, 1881. 60 p. **DLC Uk**

2346   DUN, FINLAY. American farming and food. London, 1881. 477 p.   **DLC Uk**

2347   EURYDICE, AHOY! A short account of a yacht cruise on Lake Champlain, in the summer of 1880. By the author of "One more unfortunate." Montreal, 1881. 66 p.   **CaOTU NRU**

2348   FAGAN, JAMES O[CTAVIUS]. The autobiography of an individualist. Boston, 1912. 290 p.   **DLC Uk**

Narrative of a Scottish emmigrant to New England in 1881. See author's *Labor and the railroads*, Boston, 1909.

2349   FIELDEN, JOHN C. Free trade v. reciprocity. An address by John C. Fielden. Dedicated by permission to the right honorable W. E. Gladstone, M.P. Second edition. Manchester, 1881, 36 p.   **Uk**

No 1st ed. found. On U.S., pp. 5–8, 10, 21–29, 32–33. See also his *Speech on foreign competition in the cotton trade, &c., delivered by John C. Fielden . . . (in reply to Colonel Jackson . . . and others) at a meeting held in Manchester, on Sat., Nov. 30th, 1878*, Blackburn, 1879, passim. (held by UkLGl); and *The cotton trade and the silver question*, London, 1893.

2350   FRANCIS, F[RANCIS], *the younger*. War, waves, and wanderings. A cruise in the "Lancashire Witch." London, 1881. 2 vols.   **DLC Uk**

Vol. II includes a visit to San Francisco and Alaska, pp. 168–190, 206–308. See also his novels, *Mosquito: a tale of the Mexican frontier*, London, 1889; and *Wild rose: a tale of the Mexican frontier*, London, 1895.

2351   GILLMORE, PARKER ("UBIQUE"). Encounters with wild beasts. London, 1881. 305 p.   **Uk**

CtY has 2d ed., NN has 3d ed., both London, 1881. Includes 4 chaps. on hunting in the U.S.

2352   GLASS, CHESTER. The world: round it and over it. . . . Being letters written by the author from England, Ireland, Scotland, Belgium, Holland, Denmark, Germany, Switzerland, France, Spain, Monaco, Italy, Austria, Greece, Turkey, Turkey-in-Asia, the Holy Land, Egypt, India, Singapore, China, Japan, California, Nevada, Utah and New York. Toronto, 1881. 528 p.   **MH MnHi**

Uk has 2d ed., Toronto, 1881. On U.S., pp. 12–16, 501–528.

2353   GLOVER, ELIZABETH ROSETTA (SCOTT), *Lady*. Memories of four continents; recollections grave and gay of events in social and diplomatic life. London, 1923. 317 p.   **DLC Uk**

"Reminiscences of New York" (in 1891), pp. 87–95.

2354   HARDY, MARY [ANNE] (MCDOWELL) DUFFUS, *Lady*. Through cities and prairie lands. Sketches of an American tour. London, 1881. 320 p.   **CtY NN Uk**

DLC has New York, 1881 ed.

Reviews: *Nation*, XXXIII, 519; New York *Herald*, November 21, 1881.

2355   HATTON, JOSEPH. To-day in America. Studies for the old world and the New. London, 1881. 2 vols.   **DLC Uk**

Articles repr. from the New York *Times*, *Tinsley's Mag.*, *Belgravia*, *Theatre*, *New Monthly Mag.*, etc. Hatton was a correspondent for the London *Standard*; travelling with Sir Henry Irving, he made 3 trips to the U.S. in 1876, 1878 and 1880.

2356   HECTOR, JOHN. National and international currency. The deadlock: its premonitory signs; its influence on land, commerce and credit, and its remedy. [London, 1881]. 55 p.
CtY Uk

"The United States," pp. 21–26, and passim. See also author's discussion of relations between English and American currency in his *National and international currency. Continuation of the deadlock*, London, 1881.

2357   HOLYOAKE, GEORGE JACOB. Among the Americans, and A stranger in America. Chicago, 1881. 246 p.
DLC Uk

"Among the Americans," repr. from Manchester *Co-operative News*; "A stranger in America," from *Nineteenth Cent.*, VIII (July 1880), 67–87. Holyoake spent 4 months in the U.S. in 1880. For this and a second visit, see Lee E. Grugel, *George Jacob Holyoake: a study in the evolution of a Victorian radical*, Philadelphia, 1976, pp. 143–151.

2358   HUGHES, THOMAS. Rugby Tennessee; being some account of the settlement founded on the Cumberland plateau by the Board of aid to land ownership, limited; a company incorporated in England and authorised to hold and deal in land by act of the legislature of the state of Tennessee . . . With a report on the soils of the plateau, by the Hon. F. W. Killebrew, A.M., Ph.D., commissioner of agriculture for the state. London, 1881. 168 p. **CtY CU Uk**

DLC has New York, 1881 ed. Repr. Philadelphia, 1975, with a new introd. by W. H. G. Armytage. See also "The new Rugby," *Harper's Weekly*, XXIV (Oct.–Dec. 1880), 665–666, 709–710, 739, 807; "Rugby, Tennessee," *Macmillan's Mag.*, XLIII (Feb. 1881), 310–315; "Thomas Hughes in Rugby, Tennessee," *Eclectic Mag.*, XCV (Dec. 1880), 759–760; E. L. Godkin, "Will Wimbles," *Reflections and comments, 1865–1895*, New York, 1895, pp. 322–328; and Hughes' "Rugby, Tennessee," *The co-operative wholesale society, limited. Annual and diary for the year 1885*, Manchester, [1886?], pp. 254–258. See also Marguerite B. Hamer's accounts in the *No. Carolina Hist. Rev.*: "Thomas Hughes and his American Rugby," V (Oct. 1928), 390–412; and "The correspondence of Thomas Hughes concerning his Tennessee Rugby," XXI, (July 1944), 203–214. See other accounts in Helen H. Turner, "Thomas Hughes' American library," *Wilson Lib. Bull.*, VI (Jan. 1932), 354–357; Grace Stone, "Tennessee: social and economic laboratory," Part III "The new agrarianism in Tennessee: Thomas Hughes," *Sewanee Rev.*, XLVI (Apr.–June 1938), 160–166; and Walter Harry Green Armytage, "New light on the English background of Thomas Hughes' Rugby colony in Tennessee," *E. Tenn. Hist. Soc. Pubs.*, no. 21 (1949), pp. 69–84.

Reviews: *Critic*, I, 173; *Dial* (by N. C. Perkins), II, 78; *Nation* (by E. L. Godkin), XXXI-II, 288; *St. James Mag.* (by Francis Watt), XLIX, 469.

2359   LENG, *SIR* JOHN. American competition and the future of British agriculture. An address delivered at Laurence-kirk, February 16th, 1881. Dundee, 1881. 37 p.
ICU NN

2360   [LOWE, JOHN]. Report on the alleged exodus to western United States. Ottawa, 1881. 11 p.
CaOOA

MnHi has Ottawa, 1883 ed., 16 p. Cataloged under Canada. Dept. of agriculture.

2361   MARSHALL, WALTER GORE. Through America; or, Nine months in the United States. London, 1881. 424 p.
DLC Uk

"New and cheaper edition," with supplement of press opinions at back, London, 1882, 412 p.

Reviews: *Athenaeum*, (Aug. 13, 1881), 200; New York *Herald*, Jan. 14, 1881; *Sat. Rev.*, LI, 600.

2362   MELLERSH, T.G. The English colony in Iowa : with a list of vacancies for boarders and pupils on some of the best farms. Cheltenham, 1881. 12 p.   **IaHi**

See Henry Harcourt Horn, *An English colony in Iowa*, Boston, [c1931].

2363   MONKSWELL, MARY JOSEPHINE (HARDCASTLE) COLLIER, *baroness*. A Victorian diarist; extracts from the journals of Mary, lady Monkswell, 1873–1895, edited by the Hon. E. C. F. Collier. London, [1944–46]. 2 vols.   **DLC Uk**

Daily journal of a tour in the U.S. in 1881, I, pp. 58–96.

2364   NORMAN, *SIR* HENRY. The preservation of Niagara Falls. Letters to the Boston Daily Advertiser, the New York Evening Post, Herald, and Tribune, in August and September, 1881. New York, 1881. 39 p.   **MH Uk**

2365   PARRY, S[YDNEY] H[ENRY] JONES-. My journey round the world . . . via Ceylon, New Zealand, Australia, Torres Straits, China, Japan, and the United States. London, 1881. 2 vols.   **DLC Uk**

Last 8 chaps. on the U.S.

2366   ROGERS, ROBERT VASHON. Drinks, drinkers and drinking; or, The law and history of intoxicating liquors. Albany, 1881. 241 p.   **DLC**

Much on U.S., passim.

2367   SHEPPARD, GEORGE. New homes in Minnesota, North Dakota, Montana. Liverpool, 1881. 36 p.

No locations found; listed in Howes. CtY has microfiche. Authorship also attributed to Northern Pacific Railroad Company. See James J. Talman, "George Sheppard, Journalist, 1819–1912," *Proc. & Trans. Royal Soc. Canada*, 1950, Sect. II, pp. 119–134.

2368   SMITH, GOLDWIN. Economical questions and events in America. An address delivered before the economy and trade section of the Social science association at the Dublin congress, October 7, 1881. London, 1881. 25 p.   **Uk**

See Smith's "Why send more Irish to America?" *Nineteenth Cent.*, XIII (June 1883), 913–919; and the reply by A. M. Sullivan, "Why send more Irish out of Ireland?" ibid., XIV (July 1883), 131–144. See also Smith's "Naseby and Yorktown," *Contemp. Rev.*, XL (Nov. 1881), 683–696.

2369   SMITH, SAMUEL. Free trade versus reciprocity. Liverpool, 1881. 30 p.
    NN UkLSE UkLUC

On U.S.

2370   SPENCE, THOMAS. Useful and practical hints for the settler on Canadian prairie lands and for the guidance of intending British emigrants to Manitoba and the North-west of Canada. With facts regarding to soil, climate, products, etc. And the superior attractions and advantages possessed, in comparison with the western prairie states of America. Montreal, 1881. 40 p.   **CaOOA NN**

MH has 2d ed., rev. and corrected, St. Boniface, 1882.

2371   SUTHERLAND, *REV*. ALEXANDER. A summer in prairie-land. Notes of a tour through the northwest territory. Toronto, 1881. 198 p.   **DLC**

On the U.S., pp. 1–38.

2372   TOWNSHEND, SAMUEL NUGENT. The new southern route from San Francisco, through southern California, Arizona, New Mexico, Colorado and Kansas to New York and the Atlantic seaboard, through St. Louis, Chicago or Canada. Written specially for Australian and New Zealand travel. Chicago, 1881. 43 p.   **MH Uk**

Rev. selections from a long series in *Field*, 1876–81, under pseud. "St. Kames."

2373   WILKINSON, THOMAS READ. Holiday rambles. Manchester, 1881. 127 p.   **DLC Uk**

"A month in America" in 1880, pp. 1–67.

1882

2374   ABBOTT, CHARLES E. Diary of a tour through Canada and the United States. London, 1882. 75 p.   **WHi**

2375   ABBOTT, ETHEL B. A diary of a tour through Canada and the United States. London, 1882. 63 p.   **DLC**

2376   [AITKEN, JAMES]. From the Clyde to California, with jottings by the way. Greenock, 1882. 152 p.   **DLC Uk**

Repr. from the Greenock (Scotland) *Herald*. See his supp. vol., 1894, below.

2377   APPLETON, LEWIS. The gradual progress of international arbitration. London, 1882. 31 p.   **MH RPB Uk**

Pub. by the International Arbitration and Peace Assoc., and bound with J. B. Angell's *Progress of international law*, 1876. References to U.S. throughout. See also author's *Maritime international law*, London, [n.d.], pp. 9–10, 14–18. Both pamphlets repr. in his *Fifty years of foreign policy*, London, [1889–92].

2378   ARCHIBALD, *MRS*. EDITH JESSIE (ARCHIBALD). Life and letters of Sir Edward Mortimer Archibald, K.C.M.G., C.B. A memoir of fifty years of service by his daughter, Edith J. Archibald; with a foreword by the Rt. Hon. Sir Robert Laird Borden, G. C. M. G. Toronto, 1924. 266 p.   **DLC Uk**

British consul in New York, 1857–1882; see pp. 99–226.

2379   ASHBEE, HENRY SPENCER. A Sunday at Coney Island. London, 1882. 7 p.   **Uk**

Repr. from the *Temple Bar*.

2380   BADEN-POWELL, *SIR* GEORGE SMYTH. State aid and state interference. Illustrated by results in commerce and industry. London, 1882. 284 p.   **DLC Uk**

"The failure of protection in the United States," pp. 30–72; see also pp. 182–207, and passim. See also author's "The truth about American competition," *Fraser's Mag.*, XXIII, n.s. (Mar. 1881), 310–324.

2381   BAGENAL, PHILIP HENRY DUDLEY. The American Irish and their influence on Irish politics. London, 1882. 252 p.   **DLC Uk**

Includes 2 letters on Irish colonization, printed originally in the London *Times*, Oct. 1881, during his tour in Minnesota.

2382   BAILLIE-GROHMAN, WILLIAM A[DOLPH]. Camps in the Rockies. Being a narrative of life on the frontier, and sport in the Rocky mountains, with an account of the cattle ranches of the West. London, 1882. 438 p.   **CU MB NN Uk**

DLC has New York ed., 1882; several later eds. Portions appeared originally under pseud. "Stalker", in *Field*, *Fortnightly Rev.*, and *Time*. See critical reactions in *Field*, LV, 90, 116, 152, and 168. See also Norreys Jephson O'Conor, "A British hunter in frontier days," *Arizona Quar.*, V (Autumn, 1949), 242–251; and G. A. Henty's novel inspired by and based on Baillie-Grohman, *In the heart of the Rockies*, London, 1895.

Reviews: *Academy* (by Robert Brown), XXII, 95; *Dial* (by George C. Noyes), III, 75; *Nation*, XXXV, 140.

2383   BEVAN, GEORGE PHILLIPS. A handbook to the industries of the British Isles and the United States. London, 1882. 220 p.   **DLC Uk**

DLC incorrectly gives title as *A handbook of. . . .*

2384   BROWN, ADAM. Notes of a trip to the Northwest territories. Hamilton, 1882. 19 p.   **CaOKQ**

Travel in U.S., pp. 3–5, 15.

2385   BROWN, WILLIAM, *of Montreal*. Proposals for an American bimetallic union. Montreal, [1882]. 23 p.   **DLC Uk**

No t.p.

2386   BROWN, WILLIAM TOWERS. Notes of travel: extracts from home letters written during a two years' tour round the world, 1879–1881. London, 1882. 372 p.   **CSmH ICN NN Uk**

Priv. circ. Cross-country railway tour from Chicago to San Francisco, pp. 13–27.

2387   CHISHOLM, GEORGE GOUDIE. The two hemispheres: a popular account of the countries and peoples of the world. London, 1882. 992 p.   **DLC Uk**

London, 1884 ed. carried title, *The world as it is: a popular account of the countries and peoples of the earth*, 2 vols. On the U.S., pp. 731–780.

2388   CLEAVER, CHARLES. Early Chicago reminiscences . . . [Revised from the Chicago Tribune]. Chicago, 1882. 52 p.   **DLC Uk**

Cleaver emigrated from England to Chicago in 1833, and remained. These "early reminiscences" reflect his British perspective. See also his *History of Chicago from 1833 to 1892. Describing the difficulties of the route from New York to Chicago, and the hardships of the first winter . . .* , Chicago, 1892; and Mabel McIlvaine, comp., *Reminiscences of Chicago during the forties and fifties . . .* , Chicago, 1913, which includes extracts from Cleaver's Jan. 23, 1876 lecture, "What I remember of early Chicago."

2389   CRAIG, JOHN R[ODERICK]. Ranching with lords and commons; or, Twenty years on the range, being a record of actual facts and conditions relating to the cattle industry of the North-west territories of Canada; and comprising the extraordinary story of the formation and career of a great cattle company. Toronto, [1903]. 293 p.   **DLC Uk**

Frequent references to the U.S., esp. Montana, in the 1880's. Also many quotes from Alexander Staveley Hill's *From home to home*, 1885, below.

2390   [CURWEN, JOHN]. Memorials of John Curwen. Compiled by his son, John Spencer Curwen . . . London, 1882. 315 p.   **DLC Uk**

DLC and Uk catalog under John Spencer Curwen. Uk gives 320 p. Includes a letter to Mrs. Curwen from Charles Sumner, agreeing to become an associate member of the London Freedman's Aid Society, written in 1863; and two letters from George F. Root, written to Curwen in 1862.

2391   DAWSON, FRANCIS W[ARRINGTON]. Reminiscences of Confederate service, 1861–65. Charleston, S.C., 1882. 180 p.   **DLC Uk**

Priv. pr., 100 copies. By an English volunteer who remained in the U.S. after the Civil War.

2392   DUFF, *REV.* ROBERT S. Notes of a visit to America during the Pan-Presbyterian council, 1880. Kilmarnock, 1882. 51 p.   **DLC**

Duff was "representative of Tasmania."

2393   EDGAR, *SIR* J[AMES] D[AVID]. "Loyalty," "Independence," and "Veiled treason," defined. Speech delivered . . . at Yorkville, January 13th, 1882, on Canada's right to make her own commercial treaties. Toronto, 1882. 8 p.   **CaOTP**

2394   THE EMIGRANT'S GUIDE for 1883. London 1882. 88 p.   **Uk**

Uk catalogs under Ephemerides.

2395   FARRER, THOMAS HENRY FARRER. Free trade versus fair trade. London, 1882. 189 p.   **DLC Uk**

On U.S., pp. 52–55, 106–108, and passim. 2d ed., rev. and enlarged, London, & New York, 1885, has added chap. on U.S., pp. 144–155.

2396   FLEMING, *SIR* SANDFORD. Standard time. Letter to the President of the American society for the advancement of science, on the subject of standard time for the United States of America, Canada and Mexico . . . Presented at the Montreal conference, August, 1882. Ottawa, 1882. 8 p.   **CaOOA**

See also: *Standard time. Replies to questions submitted by special committee American society civil engineers, 1882*, Ottawa, 1882 (123 p.; also held by CaOOA).

2397   THE GALLYNIPPER in Yankeeland. By himself. London, 1882. 192 p.   **DLC Uk**

Uk lists as 122 p.

2398   GEIKIE, *SIR* ARCHIBALD. Geological sketches at home and abroad. London, 1882. 382 p.   **CLU MH Uk**

DLC has two New York, 1882 eds. On visit from New York to Wyoming and Utah, pp. 205–273. See also Geikie's *A long life's work, an autobiography*, London, 1924, for his U.S. visits in 1879 (pp. 177–187) and 1897 (pp. 284–291).

2399   HENSHAW, GEORGE H., *C. E.* A plan for the improvement of navigation and the prevention of floods in the Mississippi River. Montreal, 1882. 15 p.   **CaOOA**

2400   HUDSON, T. S. A scamper through America; or, Fifteen thousand miles of ocean and continent in sixty days. London, 1882. 289 p.   **DLC Uk**

Review: *Academy*, XXIII, 24 (brief).

2401 HURLBERT, J[ESSE] BEAUFORT. Protection and free trade, with special reference to Canada and newly settled countries: history of tariffs and what they teach. Ottawa, 1882. 208 p. **DLC UkLL**

On U.S., pp. 14–31, and passim.

2402 KER, *REV.* JOHN. America, and the Irish in America, from the Atlantic to the Pacific. Lecture. Londonderry, [1882]. 65 p. **CSmH NN**

2403 KER, *REV.* JOHN. Ireland and America; or, Letters concerning the country I saw, the cities I visited, the churches I preached in, and the people I mingled with on my way from the Atlantic to the Pacific. San Francisco, 1882. 45 p. **CSmH MH**

2404 LINTON, WILLIAM JAMES. The history of wood-engraving in America. Boston, 1882. 71 p. **DLC Uk**

100 copies. All but last chap. first pub. in the *Am. Art Rev.*, (1880), nos. 5–12. An active member of the British Chartist Movement, Linton came to the U.S. in 1866 and remained for 27 years; see accounts in *Threescore and ten years, 1820 to 1890; recollections*, London, 1894 (also pub. as *Memories*, London, 1895). See also his volumes of verse, satire and parody: *England to America, 1876, a New-Year's greeting*, Cambridge, Mass., [1876]; *Ireland for the Irish; rhymes and reasons against landlordism, with a preface on Fenianism and republicanism*, New York, 1867 (written 1849 and pub. mainly in the *Irish Nation*, 1850); *Pot-pourri* [by Abel Reid, *pseud.*], [New York, 1875] (parodies of Poe); *The American Odyssey: adventures of Ulysses (so much as may interest the present time) exposed, in modest Hudibrastic measure. By Abel Reid and A. N. Broome [pseuds.] . . . To which is appended an allegory of King Augeas*, Washington, 1876, 24 p. (satire on Ulysses S. Grant); *This is the house that Tweed built; dedicated to every true reformer— Republican or Democrat—[Cambridge, Mass., 1871]*, 23 p. (attack on Tweed and Tammany machine); *Broadway ballads, collected for the centennial commemoration of the Republic, 1876. By Abel Reid, Deacon, I. P. [pseud.], [New Haven, Conn., 1876]*, 126 p.; and, *A church and a republic, [Brentwood, Coniston, Windemere, n.d.]* (Republican Tract, no. 18, repr. from the *English Republic*, ed. by Linton, 1851–55).

2405 MELLERSH, T. G. The English colony in Iowa and Minnesota, U.S.A. Cheltenham, [1882?]. No locations found.

2406 MURPHY, JOHN MORTIMER. American game bird shooting. New York, 1882. 347 p. **DLC Uk**

2407 NASH, WALLIS. Two years in Oregon. New York, 1882. 311 p. **DLC Uk**

See author's *Oregon: there and back in 1877*, 1878, above.

Reviews: *Academy*, XXI, 173.

2408 NEELE, GEORGE P. Atlantic and American notes . . . A paper read at Euston station, London, on Monday, March 13, 1882, embodying some account of the recent visit of the directors of the London and north western railway to Canada and the United States. London, 1882. 70 p. **DBRE**

2409 NEWMAN, HENRY STANLEY. The young man of God: memories of Stanley Pumphrey. London, [1882]. 298 p. **PSC Uk**

New York, 1883 ed. shortened title to *Memories of Stanley Pumphrey*. In U.S., 1875–79, pp. 102–295.

2410   NICHOL, JOHN. American literature, an historical sketch, 1620–1880. Edinburgh, 1882.
472 p.   **DLC Uk**

Much more than a history of literature; includes notes taken by his father on a visit to the
U.S. in 1848. Articles on Lowell and Emerson appeared in the *No. Brit. Rev.* Author visited America in 1865; see account in William A. Knight, *Memoir of John Nichol, Professor
of English literature in the University of Glasgow*, Glasgow, 1896, pp. 271–277.

2411   NORMAN, *SIR* HENRY. An account of the Harvard Greek play. Boston, 1882. 129 p.
DLC Uk

See also author's "America revisited in war time," *McClure's Mag.*, XI (July 1898),
297–302.

2412   PATTERSON, ROBERT HOGARTH. The new golden age and influence of the precious
metals upon the world. Edinburgh, 1882. 2 vols.   **DLC Uk**

"The golden age in California," I, pp. 98–164; other comment on the U.S., I, 239–270, II,
122–126, 387f. See also author's "California," *Fortnightly Rev.*, XXVIII, n.s. (Sept. 1,
1880), 325–346.

2413   PIDGEON, DANIEL. An engineer's holiday; or, Notes of a round trip from long. 0° to 0°.
London, 1882. 2 vols.   **ICJ Uk**

DLC has 2d ed., London, 1883, 456 p. The whole of vol. I is devoted to an account of a
visit to the U.S.

Review: *Spectator*, LV, 1163, 1227.

2414   PIGOTT, RICHARD. Personal recollections of an Irish national journalist. Dublin, 1882.
447 p.   **DLC Uk**

Includes accounts of Fenians in America.

2415   POTTER, G. Emigrant's guide: where, when & how to emigrate. [London], 1882. 29 p.
UkRCS

2416   RUSSELL, *SIR* WILLIAM HOWARD. Hesperothen: notes from the West; being a record
of a ramble in the United States and Canada in the spring and summer of 1881. London,
1882. 2 vols.   **DLC Uk**

See comment on this trip in John Black Atkins, *The life of Sir William Howard Russell*,
London, 1911, II, pp. 313–314.

Reviews: *Academy* (R. Brown), XXI, 172; *Athenaeum*, (March 4, 1882), 276.

2417   SPICE, R[OBERT] P[AULTON]. The wanderings of the hermit of Westminster between
New York and San Francisco in the autumn of 1881. [London, 1882]. 84 p.   **DLC Uk**
Priv. circ.

2418   SUTTER, ARCHIBALD. American notes, 1881. Edinburgh, 1882. 118 p.   **DLC Uk**
Letters repr. from the Edinburgh *Courant*.

2419   WALPOLE, *SIR* SPENCER. Foreign relations. London, 1882. 162 p.   **DLC Uk**

"The foreign policy of England towards America," pp. 70–82. See also Walpole's *The history of twenty-five years: 1856–1880*, London, 1904–08; considerable comment on U.S.,
passim.

2420   YOUNGMAN, *REV.* WILLIAM ERNEST. Gleanings from western prairies. Cambridge,
1882. 214 p.   **DLC Uk**
Review: *Sat. Rev.*, LIV, 775.

1883

2421 ADAMS, W[ILLIAM] E[DWIN]. Our American cousins: being personal impressions of the people and institutions of the United States. London, 1883. 357 p. **DLC**

Main portion appeared originally in the Newcastle *Weekly Chronicle*. See also Adams' *Memoirs of a social atom*, London, 1903, II, pp. 418–438, 581–590.

Reviews: *Knowledge* (by Richard A. Proctor), IV, 190; *Nation*, XXXVIII, 263.

2422 ASPDIN, JAMES. Emigration. Who should emigrate. How to emigrate. Where to emigrate. Sheffield, 1883. 50 p. **CSmH**

Uk has "Second edition, revised and enlarged," Sheffield, 1884, 58 p. On U.S., pp. 43–50.

2423 BAGGAGE & BOOTS; or, Smith's first peep at America. An instructive tale of travel and adventure. London, 1883. 397 p. **CtY MH Uk**

DLC has microfilm. Pref. signed "A.B." A semifictionized account.

2424 BARTON, BETRAM HUGH. "Far from the old folks at home." My journal letters home during a twenty-one month's tour round the world. London, 1883. 468 p. **NHi NNU**

NNU questions publishing information as [Ireland? 1883?]. On U.S., pp. 5–27, 58–91, 105–158.

2425 BRIDGES, *MRS*. F. D. The journal of a lady's travels round the world: including visits to Japan, Thibet, Yarkand, Kasmir, Java, the Straits of Malacca, Vancouver's island, &c. London, 1883. 413 p. **DLC Uk**
Several chaps. on U.S.

2426 BUXTON, SYDNEY CHARLES, *EARL* BUXTON. Emigration from Ireland; being the second report of the committee of "Mr. Tuke's fund." Together with statements by Mr. Tuke, Mr. Sydney Buxton, Major Gaskell, and Capt. Ruttledge-Fair. London, 1883. 38 p. **Uk**

Uk catalogs under Mr. Tuke's fund.

2427 CANADA. DEPARTMENT OF AGRICULTURE. Canadian North-West. Climate and productions. A misrepresentation exposed. Published by the Department of agriculture of the government of Canada. Ottawa, 1883. 32 p. **CaOTP CSmH CtY MnHi**

Answers "misstatements" of an American guide book. References to U.S., passim.

2428 CENTENNIUS, RALPH [*pseud.*?]. The Dominion in 1983. [Peterborough, Ont.], 1883. 30 p. **CaOTP NN Uk**

Predictions include conditions of U.S. in 1983, comparison of Canada and U.S. in 1880's, and a description of assassination of the President of the U.S. in 1887.

2429 CROKER, JOHN WILSON. The Croker papers. The correspondence and diaries of the late Right Honourable John Wilson Croker. . . . Ed. by Louis J. Jennings. London, 1883. 3 vols. **DLC Uk**

II, pp. 391–401, on boundary dispute, Ashburton treaty, etc.

2430 DANSON, JOHN TOWNE. Underwriting in England, France and America during the last three years. Paris, 1883. **Uk**

2431   DUNCAN, *REV.* GEORGE. Mormon murders! an expose. [London, 1883?]. 8 p.
        CSmH USI

Pub. James Shaile, Penny pamphlets; no t.p.

2432   EDGE-PARTINGTON, JAMES. Random rot; a journal of three years' wanderings about the world. Altrincham, 1883. 606 p.   **NN Uk**

From San Francisco to New York, Dec. 1881 to Jan. 1882, pp. 575–606.

2433   FREEMAN, EDWARD A[UGUSTUS]. Some impressions of the United States. London, 1883. 289 p.   **DLC Uk**

Portions appeared originally in *Fortnightly Rev.*, XXXVIII (Aug. 1882), 133–155, (Sept. 1882) 323–346, and in *Longman's Mag.*, I (Nov. 1882), 80–98, (Jan. 1883) 314–334; repr. in *Littel's Living Age*, CLIV, 600, CLV, 3, CLVI, 213, and in *Eclectic Mag.*, XCIX, 433, 623, CI, 136. See reactions based on individual articles: J. G. Rosengarten, "Views of Americans," *American*, V, 233; L. D., "On American speech," *Lippincott's Mag.*, XXXI (Apr 1883), 378–385. For an account of his visit to the U.S., 1881–82, see W. R. W. Stephens, *Life and letters of Edward A. Freeman*, London, 1895, II, pp. 177–184, 233–257. See also Herbert B. Adams, "Mr. Freeman's visit to Baltimore—1881," followed by Freeman's "An introduction to American institutional history," in *Johns Hopkins Univ. Stud.*, ser. 1, no. 1 (1882), pp. 5–39. Also see Freeman's *Lectures to American audiences . . . I. The English people in its three homes. II. The practical bearings of general European history*, London, [1882]; "Debt of the old world to the new," *Forum*, IV (Jan. 1888), 451–459; and "Imperial federation," *Macmillan's Mag.*, LI (Apr. 1885), 430–445.

Reviews: *Dial* [Chicago] (by Simeon Gilbert), IV, 35; *Nation*, XXXVI, 494; *Spectator* (by Frank Harris?), LVI, 867.

2434   FREWEN, MORETON. "Free grazing." A report to the shareholders of the Powder river cattle Co. limited. [London, 1883]. 20 p.   **Uk**

InU has a later version, London, 1885, 24 p. For accounts of various visits to the U.S., esp. for 1878–85, and Frewen's life on a Wyoming cattle ranch, see his *Molton Mowbray and other memories*, London, 1924, pp. 122–145, 155–252, and passim. See also his "The transatlantic cattle trade," *Fortnightly Rev.*, LV (May 1891), 713–724. For discussions of Frewen, see Anita Leslie, *Mr. Frewen of England: a Victorian adventurer*, London, 1966, pp. 33–42; "Moreton Freewen" in Shane Leslie's *Studies in sublime failures*, London, [1932], pp. 247–295; Herbert O. Brayer, "Moreton Frewen cattleman," the *Westerners Brand Book* (Denver), V (July 1949), 1–21; "Moreton Frewen, British cattleman,' *Western Livestock*, (Oct. 1949), 12ff; and W. Turrentine Jackson, "British interest in the range cattle industry," part 2 of *When grass was king*, by Maurice Frank, et al., Boulder, 1956, pp. 135–330 (includes bibliography). See also Lewis Lovatt Ashford Wise, "Diary of Major Wise, an Englishman, recites details of hunting trip in Powder river country in 1880," Howard B. Lott, ed., *Annals of Wyoming*, XII (Apr. 1940), 85–118; Wise was with Frewen in Wyoming.

2435   GOWER, *LORD* RONALD [CHARLES SUTHERLAND LEVESON]. My reminiscences. London, 1883. 2 vols.   **DLC Uk**

Includes visit to the U.S. in 1878.

2436   GREENWOOD, THOMAS. A tour in the states and Canada. Out and home in six weeks. London, 1883. 170 p.   **DLC Uk**

Pref. dated April 1883; Uk copy cataloged as [1885].

2437 HARDY, MARY [ANNE] (MCDOWELL) DUFFUS, *Lady*. Down South, by Lady Duffus Hardy. London, 1883. 276 p. **DLC Uk**

2438 HARRINGTON, BERNARD JAMES. Life of Sir William E. Logan . . . first director of the Geological survey of Canada. Chiefly compiled from his letters, journals and reports. London, 1883. 432 p. **DLC Uk**

Visit to U.S. in 1841, pp. 101–113.

2439 HIND, HENRY YOULE. An exposition of the Fisheries commission frauds: showing how the frauds were concealed, by the use of the number 666, and the masking numbers 42, 10, 7, 2 taken from the 13th chapter of Revelation. Embodied in lettres [sic], addressed to the President of the United States, and the Right Hon. W. E. Gladstone, with an appeal for official publication. Windsor, N.S., 1883. 36 p. **NN**

2440 THE INFLUENCE ON ENGLISH TRADE & American protection by the development of India. Calcutta, 1883. 44 p. **IaAS Uk**

Uk lists under English Trade.

2441 KEATING, E. H. Preliminary report on the proposed Halifax dry dock, and report on American stone and wooden docks. Halifax, 1883. 28 p. **CaNSWA CaOOA N**

2442 KIRKHAM, GAWIN. A holiday tour in America in 1883. A personal narrative. London, [1883?]. 57 p. **MnHi**

2443 LEACH, ETHEL. Notes of a three months' tour in America. Great Yarmouth, 1883. 66 p. **MH**

2444 LEIGH, *MRS*. FRANCES (BUTLER). Ten years on a Georgia plantation since the war, by Frances Butler Leigh. London, 1883. 347 p. **DLC Uk**

An American, Mrs. Leigh was British on her mother's side and by marriage. This volume is in the nature of a sequel to her mother's more famous book, Francis Anne Kemble's *Journal of a residence on a Georgian plantation in 1838–1839*, 1863, above. The appendix contains letters home from Mrs. Leigh's husband, James Wentworth Leigh, Dean of Hereford. Mrs. Leigh took over the management of her father's plantation in 1866.

2445 LESPINASSE, R., *ed.*. Notes on Niagara. Chicago, 1883. 184 p. **DLC**

Anthology on Niagara Falls, including comments by many foreign travellers.

2446 MATHIESON, KENNETH. How we saw the United States of America. Edinburgh, 1883. 80 p. **MB NN Uk**

Priv. pr. Mr. and Mrs. Kenneth Mathieson were members of a group of 11 invited to visit the U.S. by Andrew Carnegie.

2447 PROCTOR, RICHARD ANTHONY. Light science for leisure hours. A series of familiar essays on scientific subjects, natural phenomena, &c. &c. London, 1871–1883. 3 series. **DLC Uk**

1st ser., "American alms for British science," pp. 90–96 (repr. from London *Daily News*, Nov. 5, 1870); 3rd ser., "The American tariff," pp. 241–251 (from *Echo*, 1877). See author's articles in *Knowledge*: "American manners in travelling," IV (Sept. 7, 1883), 154 (from Newcastle *Weekly Chronicle*); "Paradoxists in America," VI (Aug. 22, 1884), 148;" "Political life in the United States," VI (Dec. 19, 1884), 499; "The gambling spirit in America," VI (Dec. 26, 1884), 519; "Manners and customs in the United States," VII (Jan.

23, 1885), 66–67; "Varieties of American life," XI (Mar. 1, 1888), 103–104; "English and American traits," XI, 268–270; "American politics," XI, 270–271. See also his "Capital and culture in America," *Fortnightly Rev.*, L (Aug. 1, 1888), 260–278.

2448   ROBERTSON, JAMES BARR. Great Britain, the United States, and the Irish question. A contribution to current politics in the Westminster review of October, 1883. London, 1883. 348 p.   **DLC**

From *Westmin. Rev.*, LXIV, n.s. (Oct. 1883), 315–348.

2449   [ROBINSON, LILIAS NAPIER ROSE]. Our trip to the Yo-semite valley and Sierra Nevada range. By L. N. R. R. [London], 1883. 37 p.   **CSmH**

2450   ROBINSON, PHIL[IP STEWART]. Sinners and saints. A tour across the states, and round them; with three months among the Mormons. London, 1883. 370 p.   **MH UU Uk**

DLC has Boston, 1883 ed.

Reviews: *Academy* (by Robert Brown), XXIII, 415; Philadelphia *Daily Evening Bulletin*, June 30, 1883; *Nation*, XXXVI, 556.

2451   ROGERS, JAMES E[DWIN] THOROLD. Ensilage in America: its prospects in English agriculture. London, 1883. 163 p.   **DLC Uk**

Reviews: *Chambers's J.*, XX, ser. 4, 273; *Nature* (by John Wrightson), XXVII, 479.

2452   RUSSELL, CHARLES RUSSELL, *baron*. Diary of a visit to the United States of America in the year 1883, by Charles Lord Russell, of Killowen . . . with an introduction by the Rev. Matthew Russell, S.J., and an appendix by Thomas Francis Meehan, A.M., edited by Charles George Herbermann. New York, 1910. 235 p.   **DLC Uk**

Travel diary (Aug. 14–Oct. 13, 1883) of Russell, later (1894) Lord Chief Justice of England. See also accounts of this visit and one in 1896 in *The life of Lord Russell of Killowen*, by R. Barry O'Brien, London, 1902, pp. 159–177 and 283–290.

2453   STEVENSON, ROBERT LOUIS. The Silverado squatters. London, 1883. 254 p.**DLC Uk**

Originally pub., with omissions, in *Century Mag.*, XXVII (Nov.–Dec. 1883), 27–39, 183–193; 10 or 12 paperbound copies were pub. in Oct. 1883 for copyright purposes, and were composed of the first installment only. Repr. with woodcuts by John Henry Nash in a limited. ed. of 380 copies, pub. by Scribner's, New York, 1923. The journal was also repr. in John E. Jordan, *Silverado journal*, San Francisco, 1954, and in several other eds.—e.g., Grabhorn Press, San Francisco, 1952; Ashland, Or., 1972, with an introd. by Oscar Lewis; and in James D. Hart, ed., *From Scotland to Silverado: the amateur emigrant, from the Clyde to Sandy Hook, Across the plains, the Silverado squatters and four essays on California*, Cambridge, Mass., 1966. Selections from the book also have been printed: *The sea fogs . . . with an introduction by Thomas Rutherford Bacon*, San Francisco, [1907]; *The sea fogs: a chapter from the Silverado squatters*, [San Francisco, 1942]; Katharine D. Osbourne, *Robert Louis Stevenson in California*, Chicago, 1911; and *Napa wine. With an introduction by M. F. K. Fisher*, St. Helena, Calif., 1965.

Also see various books and articles on Stevenson and Silverado: Anne Roller Issler, *Stevenson at Silverado*, Caldwell, Idaho, 1939, and *Our mountain hermitage. Silverado and RLS*, Stanford, [1950]; J. Edgar Ross, "Silverado to-day," *Overland Monthly*, LIII (Mar. 1909), 193–199; Harold Franch, "Silverado—Scene of RLS's honeymoon. How the home of RLS was saved," ibid., XLVIII (Sept., 1906), 129–137; James Beebee Carrington, "A visit to Stevenson's Silverado," *Lamp*, XXIX (Aug. 1904), 7–18, and "Christmas at

Silverado—A memory of the retreat where Stevenson spent his honeymoon," *Mentor*, XVI (Dec. 1928), 39–40; and the fictionized account of Stevenson in California by Anne B. Fisher, *No more a stranger*, Stanford, Calif., 1946. See also various biographies, volumes of letters, bibliographies, etc.

Reviews: *Critic*, IV, 52; *Dial*, IV, 261; *Lit. News*, V, 55; *Lit. World* (Boston), XV, 51; *Nation*, XXXVIII, 149; *Sat. Rev.*, LVII, 520; *Spectator*, LVII, 188.

2454   TURNER, J[OHN] FOX. There and back; or, Three weeks in America, with facsimile letter from the Right Hon. Bright, M.P. London, 1883. 82 p.   **DLC Uk**

Repr. with variations and additions, from the Manchester *Examiner and Times*.

2455   [WEBB, MATTHEW]. The adventurous life and daring exploits in England and America of Capt. Matthew Webb the swimming champion of the world. His boyhood—rescues— crossing the Channel— natatorial feats—and terrible death in the whirlpool of Niagara. Compiled from authentic sources, by Henry Llewellyn Williams. London, [1883]. 8 p. **Uk**

2456   WILDE, OSCAR. Impressions of America. Edited, with an introduction, by Stuart Mason [*pseud.*]. Sunderland, 1906. 40 p.   **DLC Uk**

1st pub. of Wilde's 1883 lecture about his 1882 and 1883 American tours, together with a 13 p. introd. by Mason describing the visits; lecture also included in *The writings of Oscar Wilde*, London, 1907, III, pp. 231–252. See also Wilde's articles in *Court and Soc. News*, "The American invasion," IV (Mar. 23, 1887), 270–271, and "The American man," IV (Apr. 13, 1887), 341–343. For other accounts see Alexander Gardiner, "Oscar in Buncoland, U.S.A.," *Colophon*, XII (1932), 1–8; Lloyd Lewis and Henry Justin Smith, *Oscar Wilde discovers America (1882)*, New York, 1936; Forbes Parkhill, *The wildest of the West*, New York, 1951, pp. 33–39; and Peter Conrad, *Imagining America*, New York, 1980, pp. 61–74. See also the parody by John Wilson Bengough, *Bunthorne abroad. Comic opera*, Toronto, 1883.

2457   WILKINSON, HUGH. Sunny lands and seas. A voyage in the S.S. 'Ceylon.' Notes made in a five months' tour in India—the Straits Settlements—Manila—China—Japan—The Sandwich Islands—and California. London, 1883. 324 p.   **DLC Uk**

Reviews: *Field*, LXI, 385; *Sat. Rev.*, LV, 312.

2458   [YOUMANS, EDWARD LIVINGSTON]. Herbert Spencer on the Americans and the Americans on Herbert Spencer. Being a full report of his interview, and of the proceedings at the farewell banquet of Nov. 9, 1882. New York, 1883. 96 p.   **DLC Uk**

Pref. signed, E. L. Y. Portions by Spencer, pp. 9–20, 28–35. Two other eds. of the same year give date of banquet, Nov. 11, 1882. Repr. with some changes, as "The Americans: a conversation and a speech, with an addition," in *Contemp. Rev.*, XLIII (Jan. 1883), 1–15; in *Littel's Living Age* (Boston), CLVI (Feb. 10, 1883) 323–332; and in *Eclectic Mag.*, C (Mar. 1883), 289–299. Also printed in Spencer's *Essays: scientific, political, and speculative*, New York, 1891, III, pp. 471–492. See "A visit to America," in his *An Autobiography*, New York, 1904, II, pp. 457–481; his "Letter on the feeling in England about the time of the outbreak of the Civil War in the United States," New York *Tribune*, June 28, 1880, p. 1; and the account of his visit in David Duncan, *Life and letters of Herbert Spencer*, New York, 1908, I, pp. 271–306, and passim.

See also Spencer's "On American sins," *Critic*, II (Nov. 4, 1882), 298; "Impressions of America," *Knowledge*, III (Jan. 19, 1883), 41; and "Anglo-American arbitration," in his *Various fragments*, London, 1897. For other discussions of the interview and banquet, see

R. E. Thompson, *America*, V (Oct. 28, 1882), 37; Minot J. Savage, "Herbert Spencer in America," *Knowledge*, III (Feb. 16, 1883), 97; E. L. Godkin and A. G. Sedgwick, "On American civilization," *Nation*, XXXV (Oct. 26, 1882), 348, and *Sat. Rev.*, LIV (Oct. 28, 1882), 557; "Ideas on America," *Spectator*, LV (Nov. 4, 1882), 1405; and an article referring to the banquet in *Pop. Science* XXII (Jan. 1883), 410. See also George Miller Beard, *Herbert Spencer on American nervousness. A scientific coincidence*, New York, 1883 (reviewed by E. S. in *J. of Science*, XX (May 1883), 266); and George William Curtis, "Herbert Spencer on the Yankee," *From the easy chair*, 3d ser., New York, 1894, pp. 56–64.

Review: *Dial* (by Kate B. Martin), III, 205.

2459   ZINCKE, *REV.* FOSTER BARHAM. The plough and the dollar, or the Englishry of a century hence. London, 1883. 48 p.   **DNAL MH NN Uk**

1884

2460   ALDRIDGE, REGINALD. Ranch notes in Kansas, Colorado, the Indian territory and northern Texas. London, 1884. 227 p.   **DLC Uk**

New York, 1884 ed. carried title, *Life on a ranch*, etc.

Reviews: *Academy* (by Robert Brown), XXV, 396; *Argonaut*, XV, 10; *Athenaeum*, (June 21, 1884), 790; the *Book Buyer*, I, 178; Philadelphia *Daily Evening Bulletin*, Dec. 6, 1884; *Eclectic Mag.*, XL, n.s., 567; *Nation*, XXXIX, 293; *Sat. Rev.*, LVII, 695.

2461   [ALGER, W. H.]. Some notes on America. [Plymouth, Eng., 1884?]. 101 p.   **DLC**

Repr. from Plymouth *Western Morning News*, of a series beginning Oct. 22, 1884.

2462   THE AMERICAN EXHIBITION (London, 1886) . . . Public opinion in Great Britain and the United States. London, 1884. 27 p.   **DLC**

DLC lists under "London American Exhibition." British comment, pp. 3–16. See also *The American exhibition (London, 1886). Public opinion in Europe and the United States*, London, [1884?], with cover title dated Dec. 20, 1884: 106 pp. of British comment; a repr. dated Dec. 24, 1884, 112 p., states at end of pamphlet that "This list of extracts from the Press will remain open." See also *American exhibition London. May 2d to Oct. 31st '87. Official catalogue*, New York, 1887, pp. 31–105.

2463   [AUSTIN, LOUIS FREDERIC]. Henry Irving in England and America 1838–84, by Frederic Daly [*pseud.*]. London, 1884. 300 p.   **DLC Uk**

For other accounts of Irving's first trip to America, 1883–84, see Joseph Hatton's *Henry Irving's impressions of America, narrated in a series of sketches, chronicles and conversations*, London, 1884, below.

Review: *Spectator*, LVII, 955.

2464   BALLANTINE, WILLIAM. The Old world and the New. By Mr. Serjeant Ballantine, being a continuation of his 'Experiences.' London, 1884. 259 p.   **DLC Uk**

Title on spine: *From the old world to the new: being some experiences of a recent visit to America, including a trip to the Mormon country*, London, 1884. Ballantine was in America in 1882.

Reviews: *Spectator*, LVII, 1740.

2465   BARCLAY, JAMES W[ILLIAM]. Mormonism exposed. The other side. An English view of the case. [n.p.], 1884. 30 p.   **NN WHi**

Tract no. 1; See also tract no. 3, by Hugh Weightman, *Mormonism exposed . . . From a legal standpoint*, 1884, below.

2466   BARNEBY, WILLIAM HENRY. Life and labour in the far, far West: being notes of a tour in the western states, British Columbia, Manitoba, and the North-west territory. London, 1884. 432 p.   **DLC Uk**

Portions had appeared in Barneby's *Notes from a journal in North America in 1883*, Hereford, [1884?], below.

Reviews: *Athenaeum*, (June 21, 1884), 790; *Dial*, V, 140; *Eclectic Mag.*, XL, n.s., 567; *Field*, LXIV, 149; *Nation*, XXXIX, 385; *New Englander*, XLIII, 855; *Sat. Rev.*, LVIII, 124; *Spectator*, LVII, 1147.

2467   BARNEBY, W[ILLIAM] HENRY. Notes from a journal in North America in 1883. Hereford, [1884]. 91 p.   **DLC**

Repr. from the Hereford *Times*. A portion was incorporated in author's *Life and labour in the far, far West*, 1884, above.

2468   BENHAM, *REV.* WILLIAM. A short history of the Episcopal church in the United States. London, 1884. 148 p.   **DLC Uk**

2469   BURGE, CHARLES ORMSBY. The adventures of a civil engineer; fifty years on five continents. London, 1909. 319 p.   **MdBE NN Uk**

In U.S. in 1884, pp. 225–245.

2470   BUSK, CHARLES WESTLY. Notes of a journey from Toronto to British Columbia, via the Northern Pacific railway (June to July 1884): being letters to his sister and mother from Charles Westly Busk. London, 1884. 48 p.   **DLC**

Priv. circ.

2471   CARPENTER, EDWARD. Days with Walt Whitman, with some notes on his life and work. London, 1906. 186 p.   **DLC Uk**

Chaps. on visits to Whitman in 1877 and 1884, pp. 1–70, originally pub. in the *Progressive Rev.*, Feb. and April 1897.

2472   COLERIDGE, ERNEST HARTLEY. Life and correspondence of John Duke lord Coleridge, lord chief justice of England. Written and edited by Ernest Hartley Coleridge. London, 1904. 2 vols.   **DLC Uk**

"Letters to American friends before the war [1854–50]", I, chap. 12; "Letters to American friends during the war [1861–66]," II, chap. 1; and "Visit to America [1883–84]," II, chap. 11. See also "History of Lord Coleridge's tour," *N. Y. State Bar Assoc. Reports*, VII (1884), 53–166; the text of Coleridge's speech, Oct. 11, 1883, delivered before the New York Bar Assoc. in the *Am. Law Rev.*, XVIII (Jan.–Feb. 1884), 117. See also two articles: "Lord Coleridge in America" and "Lord Coleridge interviewed" in the *Sat. Rev.*, LVI (Sept. 1, 1883), 263–264, (Sept. 8, 1883), 298–299. For much comment on America and American affairs, see *Forty years of friendship, as recorded in the correspondence of John Duke, lord Coleridge, and Ellis Yarnall, during the years 1856 to 1895*, ed. by Charlton Yarnall, London, 1911.

2473 DOW, JOHN LAMONT. The Australian in America: being the letters of J. L. Dow, M.P., the special correspondent of the "Leader," upon American irrigation enterprises; improved railway management; luxurious travelling; hotel system; social characteristics; system of government; displays of wealth; life among Mormons; labour-saving harvest machinery; trotting sport; Vermont sheep; agricultural bureau system; cheap grain handling and railway freights; cattle raising, fattening, and transportation; silver mining; vine and fruit growing; fruit canning; land system, and progress of settlement; patent flour milling; sugar, tobacco, and hop culture; the bee industry; dairy factories; grasses and herbage; farmers' fish ponds; street railroads and cable cars. Melbourne, 1884. 176 p.   **AuSM NN**

2474 DOW, T[HOMAS] K[IRKLAND]. A tour in America. By T. K. Dow, special commissioner of "The Australasian." . . . Farms, vineyards, orchards. San Francisco to New York. Irrigating and railways. The Mormons. Over the Rockies to Niagara. The southern route. Melbourne, 1884. 207 p.   **CU**

First appeared in the *Australasian*.

2475 ESOR [*pseud.*]. Eighty-eight days in America. London, 1884. 129 p.   **DLC**

2476 FAITHFULL, EMILY. Three visits to America. Edinburgh, 1884. 377 p.   **DLC Uk**

Repr. from *Victoria Mag.* (Dec. 1872–Nov. 1873), XX, 117, 209, 343, 445, 538, XXI, 28, 116, 159, XXII, 27; and from *Lady's Pictorial* and *Pall Mall Gazette*. A leading feminist, author visited U.S. in 1872–73, 1882–83, 1883–84.

Reviews: *Athenaeum* (Feb. 7, 1885), 181; *Eclectic Mag.*, XL, n.s., 858; *Nation*, XXXIX, 404; *Spectator*, LVII, 1740; London *Times* (May 30, 1885), 5.

2477 [FITZGERALD, WILLIAM FOSTER VESEY]. Democracy in the Old world and the New; by the author of "The Suez canal; the Eastern question and Abyssinia", "Egypt, India, and the colonies", etc. London, 1884. 143 p.   **DLC Uk**

References to U.S. throughout.

2478 FORWOOD, *SIR* WILLIAM BOWER. The effects of protection in America. [London, 1884]. 2 p.   **CaOOA**

Cobden Club Leaflet, no. 17; CaOOA misspells author's name as Forward.

2479 [GORDON, *MRS*. MARY (WILSON)]. A rapid run to the wild West, by an Edinburgh lady. Edinburgh, 1884. 35 p.   **NN**

Priv. pr.

2480 GORDON-CUMMING, C[ONSTANCE] F[REDERICA]. Granite crags. Edinburgh, 1884. 384 p.   **DLC Uk**

Edinburgh, 1886 ed. carried title, *Granite crags of California*; describes travels in California in 1878. See also various articles by author: "May day in the California Alps," *Gentleman's Mag.*, CCLIV (May 1883), 503–512; "In the Yo-Semite Valley, California," *Tinsley's Mag.*, XXXIII (Nov. 1883), 413–419; "Granite crags," *Temple Bar*, LXIX (Oct. 1883), 244–261; "The Yosemite," *Sat. Rev.*, LV (June 16, 1883), 758–759; "The destruction of the American bison," *Good Words*, XXV (June 1884), 388–391; "Locusts and farmers of America," *Nineteenth Cent.*, XVII (Jan. 1885), 133–153; "Earth's boiling fountains," *Atalanta*, I (Feb. 1888), 261–264, II (Mar. 1888), 310–315; "The world's wonderlands in Wyoming and New Zealand," *Overland Monthly*, V, ser. 2 (Jan. 1885), 1–13. See also interesting account of *Granite Crags* and its author in Francis P. Farquhar, *Yosemite. . . . a selective bibliography*, Berkeley, 1948, pp. 69–71.

Reviews: *Field*, LXIII, 193; *London Quar.*, LVIII, 258; *Spectator*, LVII, 825.

2481 GRIDLEY, CHARLES OSCAR. Notes on America. A paper read on the 2nd of October, 1884. [London? 1884?]. 24 p. **ICN**

Priv. pr. At head of title: Carlyle Society. A paper read before the Carlyle Society.

2482 GRIFFIN, *SIR* LEPEL HENRY. The great republic. London, 1884. 189 p. **DLC Uk**

From articles which appeared originally in the *Fortnightly Rev.* and were repr. in *Eclectic Mag.*

Reviews: *Argonaut*, XV, 12; *Murray's Mag.* (by Theodore Roosevelt), IV, 289; *Spectator*, LVII, 1640.

2483 GRIFFIN, WATSON. The provinces and the states. Why Canada does not want annexation. Toronto, 1884. 85 p. **DLC**

See also his "A Canadian-American liaison," *Mag. of Am. Hist.*, XXI (Feb. 1889), 122–138.

2484 HALL, *MRS.* CECIL [(MARY GEORGINA CAROLYN)]. A lady's life on a farm in Manitoba. London, 1884. 171 p. **DLC Uk**

On U.S., pp. 1–25, 127–167.

2485 HARDMAN, *SIR* WILLIAM. A trip to America. London, 1884. 210 p. **DLC**

See also passim. comment in the series ed. by S. M. Ellis: *A mid-victorian Pepys; the letters and memoirs of Sir William Hardman*, London, [1923]; *The letters and memoirs of Sir William Hardman. . . . Second series: 1863–1865*, London, [1925]; and, *The Hardman papers: a further selection (1865–1868)*, London, 1930, esp. pp. 12–21, on the assassination of Lincoln.

Reviews: *Athenaeum*, (June 21, 1844), 790; *Sat. Rev.*, LVIII, 125.

2486 HARDY, IZA DUFFUS. Between two oceans; or, Sketches of American travel. London, 1884. 355 p. **DLC Uk**

Includes her "In the city of the saints," which first appeared in *Gentleman's Mag.*, CCXLIX (Aug. 1880), 233–241. See also her novels on American life: *Love in idleness: the story of a winter in Florida*, London, 1887, 3 vols.; *The love that he passed by: a tale of Santana city*, London, 1884, 3 vols.

Reviews: *Athenaeum* (June 21, 1884), 790; *Spectator*, LVII, 1410.

2487 HATTON, JOSEPH. Henry Irving's impressions of America, narrated in a series of sketches, chronicles and conversations. London, 1884. 2 vols. **Uk**

DLC has Boston, 1884, 1 vol. ed. For other accounts of Irving's first trip to the U.S., 1883–84, see [Louis Frederic Austin], *Henry Irving in England and America 1838–84, by Frederic Daly [pseud.]*, 1884, above; and William Winter, *Henry Irving*, New York, 1885, a repr. of articles from the New York *Tribune*. Irving made 8 trips to the U.S., the last in 1903–04. For accounts of these visits see the various biographies, esp. *Personal reminiscences of Henry Irving*, by Bram Stoker, London, 1906, 2 vols.; and *Henry Irving: the actor and his world. By his grandson, Laurence Irving*, New York, 1952. See also Irving's article, "The American audience," which appeared in *Fortnightly Rev.*, XLIII (Feb. 1885), 197–201, in *Littel's Living Age*, CLXIV (Mar. 21, 1885), 730–733, and in the *Eclectic Mag.*, CIV (Apr. 1885), 475–479.

Reviews: *Argonaut*, XV, 12; *Spectator*, LVII, 955.

2488   HIND, HENRY YOULE. Fraudulent official records of government. Correspondence with the late Lord Frederick Cavendish, M.P., published with the consent of the Right Hon. the Marquis of Hartington. [n.p., 1884]. 25 p.   **DLC**

Further charges regarding Canadian statistics presented in 1877 to the arbitrators appointed under the Treaty of Washington. Hind subsequently pub. two supps. to the correspondence: *Fraudulent official records of government. First supplement to the correspondence with the late Lord Cavendish*, [n.p., n.d.], 32 p. (held by DLC); and *Fraudulent official records of government . . . An exposition of the principles and methods employed in the fabrication of certain United States and Canadian annual trade tables, from 1867 to 1885, together with the mathematical formulae on which the fabrication is based; as derived from James Bernoulli's Ars conjectandi, published at Basle in 1713*, [n.p., 1886?], 42 p. (held by NNC).

2489   A HOLIDAY SKIP to the far west. By one who has skipped it. London, 1884. 111p.
                                                                       MoKU NHi UkOxU

2490   HOLYOAKE, GEORGE JACOB. Travels in search of a settler's guide-book of America and Canada. London, 1884. 148 p.   **DLC Uk**

Repr. "Hundred days among the Canadians and Americans in 1883" from the Manchester *Co-operative News* and the Boston *Index*. See also his "American and Canadian Notes," *Nineteenth Cent.*, XIV (Aug. 1883), 292–299.

2491   [HOPE, EVA]. New world heroes: Lincoln and Garfield; the life-story of two self-made men, whom the people made Presidents. London, 1884. 363 p.   **NIC**

DLC lists London, n.d., as well as 1885, 1888 and 1893 eds. Uk has London, 1893 ed.

2492   HUGHES, THOMAS, *ed.* G. T. T. Gone to Texas; letters from our boys. London, 1884. 228 p.   **CSmH Uk**

DLC has New York ed., 1884. Letters written home from Texas (1878–1883) by Hughes' nephews William, Gerard, Timothy, their sister Madge, and their uncle Dr. Henry Hughes.

Reviews: *Academy*, XXV, 386; *Critic* V, 16, 33.

2493   IMPERIAL FEDERATION CONFERENCE, London, 1884. Report of the Conference held July 29th, 1884, at the Westminster Palace Hotel, the Rt. Hon. W. E. Forster, M.P. in the chair. London, 1884. 110 p.

No locations found.

2494   JARMAN, WILLIAM. U.S.A., Uncle Sam's abscess; or, Hell upon earth for U.S., Uncle Sam, by W. Jarman, who suffered twelve years in the Mormon hell on earth. Exeter, 1884. 194 p.   **CLU ICU NN Uk**

See also author's *Hell upon earth*, 1887, below, for a discussion between Jarman and Mormon missionaries.

2495   JONCAS, L[OUIS] Z[EPHERIN]. The fisheries of Canada. New York, [1884]. 34 p.
                                                                                CaOTP

At top: "A paper read before the British association for the advancement of science. Montreal meeting, 1884. Commercial union document no. 6." Abstracted in *Bull. U.S. Fish Commission*, Washington, 1884, IV, 457–463. First few pages emphasize the desirability of annexation.

2496   L'ESTRANGE, W. D. Under fourteen flags: being the life and adventures of Brigadier-General [Henry Ronald] MacIver, a soldier of fortune. By Captain W. D. L'Estrange. London, 1884. 2 vols.   **ICN MH Uk**

MacIver's experiences in the Civil War, pp. 105–203. See also the account of his service in the Confederate Army in John W. McDonald, *A soldier of fortune. The life and adventures of General Henry Ronald MacIver, being a history of his brilliant achievements under many flags*, New York, 1888, pp. 63–122.

2497   MALMESBURY, JAMES HOWARD HARRIS, *3d earl*. Memoirs of an ex-minister; an autobiography, by the Right Hon. the Earl of Malmesbury, G. C. B. London, 1884. 2 vols.   **Uk**

DLC has 3d ed., London, 1884, and London, 1885 ed. in 1 vols. On U.S., II, pp. 251–363, passim.

2498   MARTIN, JOHN BIDDULPH. The future of the United States . . . Read before the American association for the advancement of science, Philadelphia, September 5th, 1884. London, 1884. 27 p.   **CU ICN Uk**

Priv. circ.

2499   MATHER, *SIR* WILLIAM. Report on technical education in the United States of America and Canada. London, 1884. 84 p.   **DLC Uk**

Report of the Royal commission on technical instruction. See *The Right honourable Sir William Mather . . . , 1838–1920 . . . Edited by his son, Louis Emerson Mather*, London, [1925] on visits to the U. S. in 1883 and 1887, pp. 166–202.

Review: *Contemp. Rev.* (by James H. Rigg), XLVI, 208.

2500   MAUDE, CYRIL. Behind the scenes with Cyril Maude, by himself. London, [1927]. 331 p.   **DLC Uk**

New York, [1928] ed. carried title, *Lest I forget, being the reminiscences of social & dramatic life in England & America*. Maude was in America, 1883–84.

2501   [MILLAR, J. S.]. Canadian Pacific railway. Correspondence and papers shewing the efforts the company has made to secure Portland for its winter port. [Montreal? 1884?]. 30 p.   **CaOOA DBRE**

Signed, J.S. Millar.

2502   PEEBLES, D. BRUCE. From Edinburgh to Vancouver's island. Some notes of a trip on the occasion of the driving of the last spike in the Northern Pacific railroad. Read before the Royal Scottish society of arts, Edinburgh . . . Reprinted from the transactions of the society, Session 1883–84. Edinburgh, 1884. 114 p.   **CaOTP**

Trans. Royal Soc. of Arts, XI, 75–114; DLC and Uk both have vol. XI. Describes a transcontinental trip across the U.S.

2503   PEGLER, ALFRED. A visit to Canada and the United States, in connection with the meetings of the British association, held at Montreal, in 1884. Southhampton, 1884. 86 p.   **DLC**

Repr. from the Hampshire *Independent*.

2504 PHILLIPPS-WOLLEY, [*SIR*] CLIVE. Trottings of a tenderfoot; or, A visit to the Columbian fiords. London, 1884. 252 p. **DLC**

On U.S. pp. 1–50, 179–252. DLC and Uk have another London, 1884 ed., under the title, *The trottings of a tenderfoot: a visit to the Columbian fiords and Spitzbergen*, 350 p. See also author's "Big game of North America," in *Big game shooting*, London, 1884, I, pp. 346–427, (reviewed in *Nature*, L, 298). See criticism of Phillipps-Wolley by General Richard Dashwood in *Land and Water*, Mar. 24, 1894.

Review: *Academy*, XXVII, 309.

2505 PIDGEON, DANIEL. Old-world questions and New-world answers. London, 1884. 369 p. **DLC Uk**

2506 PRANCE, COURTENAY C. Notes on America. Being two lectures delivered before the Evesham institute, in December, 1884. Evesham [Eng.], 1884. 44 p. **DLC Uk**

2507 RATHBONE, WILLIAM, *the younger*. Protection and communism; a consideration of the effects of the American tariff upon wages. New York, 1884. 42 p. **DLC Uk**
No. XV of "Questions of the day."

2508 RICHARD, HENRY. The recent progress of international arbitration. Two papers read by Mr. Henry Richard, M.P., at the conferences of the Association for the reform and codification of the law of nations, at Cologne, August 19, 1881, and at Milan, September 12, 1883. Sir Travers Twiss, president. London, 1884. 32 p. **Uk**

On U.S., pp. 6, 7, 11, 13, 24–29. DLC has larger compilation of Richard's papers, under title, *Papers on the reasonableness of international arbitration, its recent progress, and the codification of the law of nations. Read at conferences of the Association for the Reform and codification of the law of nations, held at the Hague, Cologne, Milan, Liverpool, and London*, London, [1887].

2509 ROBERTSON, J[AMES] BARR. The Confederate debt and private southern debts. London, 1884. 38 p. **DLC**

2510 R[OBINSON], L[ILIAS] N[APIER] R[OSE]. A short account of our trip to the Sierra Nevada mountains. [London, 1884]. 49 p. **CSmH CtY**

2511 SHEHYN, JOSEPH. Railways versus water-courses. The influence of railways on continental and inland traffic and their bearing upon the natural and artificial water-courses of the United States and the Dominion of Canada, including the question of canal enlargement and the further deepening of the channel between Quebec and Montreal for the purpose of attracting the western trade to the St. Lawrence route. A paper read before the Quebec board of trade by the president, Jos. Shehyn, esq., M.P.P., on the 20th November, 1883. Quebec, 1884. 126 p. **CaOOA DBRE**

2512 SHEPHERD, *MAJOR* WILLIAM. Prairie experiences in handling cattle and sheep . . . London, 1884. 266 p. **DLC UK**

Author travelled in the American West, 1882–83.

2513 SHUTTLEWORTH, T. M. A tour in Canada and the United States of America, from the diary of T. M. Shuttleworth. Preston, 1884. 128 p. **MH**
DLC has microfilm.

2514 SOUTH, COLON. Out west; or, From London to Salt Lake City and back. London, 1884. 269 p. **DLC Uk**

2515 STABLES, [WILLIAM] GORDON. O'er many lands, on many seas. London, [1884]. 176 p. **ICU NN Uk**

On U.S., pp. 164–176; fictionized account. See also his novel for boys, *Wild adventures in wild places*, London, [1881], pp. 161–173.

2516 TAIT, JAMES SELWIN. The cattle-fields of the far West: their present and future. Edinburgh, 1884. 71 p. **DLC Uk**

2517 TRENCH, FREDERIC CHENEVIX. Cavalry in modern war, by Colonel F. Chenevix Trench, military attache at St. Petersburg. Being the sixth volume of military handbooks for officers and non-commissioned officers. Edited by Colonel C. B. Brackenbury, R. A., late superintending officer of garrison instruction. London, 1884. 288 p. **DLC Uk**

On U.S. Civil War, pp. 53, 165–166, 179–180, 188–190, 193–214.

2518 [TUCKER, H. B.]. Letters from abroad; or, Scraps from New Zealand, Australia, and America. By H. B. T. Glasgow, 1884. **AuSM**

On U.S., pp. 132–184.

2519 TWISS, *SIR* TRAVERS. Belligerent right on the high seas, since the declaration of Paris (1856). London, 1884. 32 p. **DLC Uk**

On U.S., pp. 10–32.

2520 [WEDDERBURN, *SIR* DAVID]. Life of Sir David Wedderburn, bart., M.P. Comp. from his journals and writings, by his sister, Mrs. E[dward] H[ope] Percival. London, 1884. 439 p. **DLC Uk**

Toured U.S. in 1866, pp. 74–92 (included is the text of his speech, "The American republic," delivered at Gloucester and Edinburgh in 1867–68); in 1875, pp. 226–232; and 1877, pp. 317–321. See also his "Mormonism from a Mormon point of view," *Fortnightly Rev.,* XX, n.s. (Oct. 1876), 462–478.

2521 WEIGHTMAN, HUGH. Mormonism exposed. The other side. From a legal standpoint. [Salt Lake City?], 1884. [45]–66 p. **DLC**

N.p. At head of title, "No. 3"; pagination continued from first two tracts. See also James Barclay, *Mormonism exposed*, 1884, above.

2522 [WORDSWORTH, CHARLES, *bp. of Saint Andrews, etc.*]. An address, written for the opening of the Seabury commemoration. By the Bishop of Saint Andrews. Edinburgh, 1884. 32 p. **Uk**

On the church in America.

2523 [YATES, EDMUND HODGSON]. Edmund Yates: his recollections and experiences. London, 1884. 2 vols. **DLC Uk**

New York, 1884 ed., 2 pts. in 1 vol., and New York, 1885 ed. carried the title, *Fifty years of London life. Memoirs of a man of the world*. Visit to America, 1872–73, is described in "Under the stars and stripes," II, pp. 376–404.

1885

2524   BRIERLEY, BEN[JAMIN]. Ab-o'-th'-Yate in Yankeeland. The results of two trips to America. Manchester, 1885. 324 p.   **DLC Uk**

Written largely in Lancashire dialect. One of the series, *Ben Brierley's tales and sketches*, 1881–86.

2525   BRIGGS, THOMAS. Correspondence between Thomas Briggs and Sir J. Caird on the question of the relative cost of emigration v. immigration. London [1885].

UkLGl copy discarded. No other locations found.

2526   CARR, RUSSELL. The travel diary of a young New Zealand girl. London, [1926?]. 85 p.   **DLC Uk**

Miss Carr's diary of a tour made in 1884–86; in the U.S., Nov. 6, 1884–Mar. 17, 1885, pp. 1–50.

2527   [COHEN, ALFRED J.]. Jonathan's home, by Alan Dale [*pseud.*]. Bristol, 1885. 160 p.   **DLC Uk**

Arrowsmith's Bristol Library, vol. VII.

2528   DENCHFIELD, *REV.* L. J. Mormonism. A sermon . . . delivered at the Baptist chapel, Rangoon, 12th October 1884, on the origin, history and teaching of Mormonism. Reprinted from the Anglo-Burman Advocate. January 1885. Rangoon, [1885]. 8 p.   **CtY**

2529   DENT, JOHN CHARLES. The story of the Upper Canadian rebellion; largely derived from original sources and documents. Toronto, 1885. 2 vols.   **DLC Uk**

Much comment on William Lyon Mackenzie, the Navy Island and *Caroline* incidents; see esp. II, pp. 140–300, and passim. See [John King], *The other side of the "Story," being some reviews of Mr. J. C. Dent's first volume of "The story of the upper Canadian rebellion," and the letters in the Mackenzie-Rolph controversy. Also, a critique, hitherto unpublished, on "The new story*," Toronto, 1886. For other comment on American affairs, see Dent's *The last forty years: Canada since the Union of 1841*, Toronto, [c 1881], 2 vols.; see esp. I, pp. 163–178, 194–217, II, 41–63.

2530   DOLBY, GEORGE. Charles Dickens as I knew him. The story of the reading tours in Great Britain and America (1866–70). London, 1885. 466 p.   **DLC Uk**

For other accounts of Dickens' second visit to the U.S. in 1867–68, see William Glyde Wilkins, *Charles Dickens in America*, London, 1911, pp. 258–302; Edward F. Payne, *Dickens days in Boston*, Boston, 1927, pp. 137–262; "Dickens in America," *Putnam's Mag.*, I (Jan. 1868), 112–113; "Dickens's readings," ibid., 135; "Dickens dinner," ibid., 774–775. See also the retaliatory works: *An epistle to "Boz" alias Charles Dickens*, by Zedekiah Comitatus, M.P.E.C., Skaggaddahunk [New York?], 1867; and *Some notes on America to be rewritten: suggested with respect to Charles Dickens, Esq.*, Philadelphia, 1868.

2531   FARRAR, REGINALD. The life of Frederic William Farrar . . . , sometime dean of Canterbury, by his son. London, 1904. 351 p.   **DLC Uk**

Describes Farrar's visit to the U.S. in 1885, pp. 284–301.

2532   [FIELD, CYRUS WEST]. Celebration of the Fourth of July in London. Mr. Cyrus W. Field's banquet to His Excellency the Hon. Edward J. Phelps, the American minister, at the Buckingham palace hotel, on July 4th, 1885. Authorized report. London, 1885. 36 p. **DLC**

Priv. pr. Contains speeches by the Duke of Argyll and John Bright, and excerpts from the English press.

2533   FORBES, ARCHIBALD. Souvenirs of some continents. London, 1885. 332 p.   **DLC Uk**

See "Macgahan, the American war correspondent," pp. 47–70; "The American gentleman with the moist eye," pp. 183–198; and "Some society aspects of America," pp. 225–269. See also "Lecturing in two hemispheres," *Century Mag.*, XXIV (n.s., II), 127–134.

2534   FOSTER, ERNEST. Abraham Lincoln. London, 1885. 128 p.   **DLC Uk**

"The World's workers"

2535   FREWEN, MORETON. American competition. London, 1885. 72 p.   **UkLGl**

NcD, Uk have 2d ed., London, 1885. Includes under one cover: "American competition," a paper read before Newcastle Farmer's Club, Apr. 11, 1885; "Progress to poverty," repr. from *Fortnightly Rev.*, XLII (Dec. 1884), 798–810; "A black cloud with a silver lining," repr. interview from the *Pall Mall Gazette*, Apr. 10, 1885.

2536   [HAY, JAMES, *of Southsea*]. Notes of a trip from Chicago to Victoria, Vancouver's Island, and return. 1884. Chicago, 1885. 77 p.   **DLC**

Repr. from the Newcastle *Weekly Chronicle*.

2537   HEWITSON, A[NTHONY?]. "Westward Ho!" Sights on sea and land, rail and river; being an account (Reprinted from the Preston Chronicle") of a recent trip to America. Preston, 1885. 231 p.

No locations found.

2538   HILL, ALEXANDER STAVELEY. From home to home: autumn wandering in the Northwest, in the years 1881, 1882, 1883, 1884. New York, 1885. 432 p.   **DLC**

Uk has 2d ed., London, 1885.

2539   HINCKS, *SIR* FRANCIS. The boundaries formerly in dispute between Great Britain and the United States, a lecture . . . 9th June, 1885. Montreal, 1885. 29 p.   **CSmH NN Uk**

See his "Relations of Canada with the United States," *No. Am. Rev.*, CXXX (Apr. 1880), 338–355, and Goldwin Smith's reply "Canada and the United States," ibid., CXXXI (July 1880), 14–25; see "Canada and Mr. Goldwin Smith," *Contemp. Rev.*, XL (Nov. 1881), 825–840, an answer to Smith's "The Canadian tariff," ibid., XL (Sept. 1881), 378–398. See also Hinck's "Commercial union from a Canadian point of view," *Fortnightly Rev.*, XXXV (May 1, 1881), 618–633; his *Reminiscences of his public life*, Montreal, 1884, pp. 422–436, which includes both a letter to the London *Daily News* dated May 31, 1869 and an anonymous article on the Alabama question from the *Financial Reformer*; and Ronald Stewart Longley's *Sir Francis Hincks: a study of Canadian politics, railways, and finance in the 19th century*, Toronto, 1943, pp. 242–274, 383–406, and passim.

2540   [INGLIS, JAMES]. Notes of a visit to the United States and Canada. Belfast, [1885]. 64 p.   **NN**

Pref. signed J. I.

2541 JOHNSON, JOSEPH. The great Mormon fraud; or, The church of Latter-day saints proved to have had a falsehood for its origin; a record of crime for its history; and for doctrines: cruelty, absurdity, and infamy. The detestable and immoral system of polygamy exposed, and the horrible Mormon doctrine of "Blood atonement" explained. Manchester, 1885. 31 p.   **DLC**

2542 LUCY, [*SIR*] HENRY W[ILLIAM]. East by west. A journey in the recess. London, 1885. 2 vols.   **DLC Uk**

On the U.S., I, pp. 1–162.

Review: *Nation*, XL, 287.

2543 MACKAY, CHARLES. The founders of the American republic; a history and biography, with a supplementary chapter on ultra-democracy. Edinburgh, 1885. 434 p.   **DLC Uk**

See also Mackay's "President Johnson and the reconstruction of the Union," *Fortnightly Rev.*, IV (Apr. 1, 1866), 477–490; and his "England; the United States and Canada," *St. James's Mag.*, XXXI (1872–3), 723–730.

Review: London *Times,* Sept. 15, 1886, p. 3.

2544 MAINE, *SIR* HENRY JAMES SUMNER. Popular government; four essays. London, 1885. 261 p.   **DLC Uk**

Indianapolis, 1886 repr., with an introd. by George W. Carey. "The constitution of the United States," pp. 196–254. For a discussion of this work see John Morley's *Oracles on man and government*, London, 1923, pp. 75–114; and Benjamin Evans Lippincott's *Victorian critics of democracy*, Minneapolis, 1938, pp. 167–206. See also the following articles by Maine: "Our relations with the United States," *Sat. Rev.*, I (Nov. 3, 1855), 2–3; "The war policy of the American government," ibid., (Nov. 24, 1855), 58–59; "American parties," ibid., (Dec. 22, 1855), 133–134; "Progress of the slavery question in America," ibid., III (Feb. 21, 1857), 168–169; "The American senate," ibid., (Feb. 28, 1857), 192–193.

Reviews: *Nineteenth Cent.* (by E. L. Godkin), XIX, 177; see Maine's answer in ibid., XIX (Mar. 1886), 366; ibid. (by Goldwin Smith), XX, 305; *Quar. Rev.*, CLXII, 518.

2545 MARK, JOHN. Diary of my trip to America and Havana. [Manchester, 1885]. 105 p.
                                                                               DLC

Priv. circ. Uk has 2d ed., Manchester, [1885].

2546 O'BRIEN, JAMES BRONTERRE. The rise, progress, and phases of human slavery: how it came into the world, and how it shall be made to go out. London, 1885. 148 p.
                                                                          DL OCIWHi Uk

Pref. signed "Spartacus". On American slavery, pp. 45–53, 104–108, and passim.

2547 P., J. A chat about America. October and November, 1884. (Chiefly extracted from letters written home). Manchester, 1885. 76 p.   **DLC**

DLC catalogs under title. Priv. pr.

2548 PFEIFFER, EMILY JANE (DAVIS). Flying leaves from east and west. London, 1885. 302 p.   **DLC Uk**

2549 RAMSAY, R[OBERT] A. Treaties affecting the boundaries and the fisheries of Canada: a lecture. [Montreal, 1885]. 15 p.   **DLC Uk**

Repr. from the *Legal News*, Montreal.

2550 RAWSON, *SIR* RAWSON W[ILLIAM]. International statistics, illustrated by vital statistics of Europe and of some of the United States of America; being the opening address of Sir Rawson W. Rawson..session 1885–86. Delivered 17th November, 1885. London, 1885. 88 p. **DLC**

2551 ROWBOTHAM, FRANCES JAMESON. A trip to prairie-land; being a glance at the shady side of emigration. . . . In two parts: Part 1.–The life on the prairie. Part 2.–The farming prospects of northern Dakota. London, 1885. 243 p. **DLC Uk**

2552 SHALL WE EMIGRATE? A tour through the states of America to the Pacific coast of Canada. By a family man. Dublin, 1885. 32 p. **CtY Uk**

2553 SMYTH, PATRICK JAMES. The priest in politics. Dublin, 1885. 15 p. **MB Uk**

Escaped to U.S. in 1848; continued to write for Irish journals. See also Caroline Margaret Douglas, *Ireland's Future*, Brideshead, 1886.

2554 [SPICE, ROBERT PAULTON.]. The hermit of Westminster on the tramp among the western states of North America, in the autumn of 1885. New York, 1885. **DLC**

DLC has apparently incomplete copy; contains only chap. 1, an account of the voyage from Liverpool to New York. No other location found.

2555 TAIT, JAMES SELWIN. Emigration by colony for the middle classes. Edinburgh, 1885. 64 p. **MH Uk**

On emigration to Florida, pp. 22–48.

2556 TAYLOR, PERCY S. Go west. London, 1885. 106 p. **Uk**

By an Englishman who settled in Illinois. See his "Notes from the western states," *Field*, XLII (Aug. 30, 1873), 232–233.

2557 TOWNSHEND, RICHARD BAXTER. The tenderfoot in New Mexico. London, 1924. 257 p. **Uk**

DLC has New York, 1924 ed. Semi-fictionized. In Colorado, 1869–74 (see *A tenderfoot in Colorado*, New York, 1923); in New Mexico, 1874 to mid-eighties.

2558 TUCKER, GEORGE A. Lunacy in many lands. Being an introduction to the reports on the lunatic asylums of various countries, visited in 1882–5, by G. A. Tucker, and presented by him to the government of New South Wales, Australia. [Birmingham? 1855]. 136 p. **CSt ICU**

Uk copy destroyed. Contains in Appendix B specimen reports of asylums in Utah, Illinois, and Maine, pp. 91–116. DLC and Uk have Sydney, 1887 ed., 1564 p., which contains Tucker's descriptions of insane asylums in all 38 states, pp. 33–589.

2559 TUKE, *DR*. DANIEL HACK. The insane in the United States and Canada. London, 1885. 259 p. **DLC Uk**

See his "On the past and present provision for the insane in the United States," *J. Mental Science*, XXII (1876–77), 42–58.

2560 [TURNER, W. S.]. Notes by a wanderer from Demerara, in the United States. Demerara, 1885. 126 p. **MB Uk**

2561 T[WEEDIE], R. W. Notes on a tour in America, by R. W. T. [London, 1885?]. 30 p. **MH Uk**

DLC has microfilm. MH dates [1882?].

2562 VERNEY, F[RANCES] P[ARTHENOPE (NIGHTINGALE)], *lady*. Peasant properties and other selected essays. London, 1885. 2 vols. **CtY MH NN Uk**

Includes "The Americans, painted by themselves," II, pp. 237–258, repr. from *Contemp. Rev.*, XLVI (Oct. 1884), 543–555; also appeared in *Eclectic Mag.*, XL (Dec. 1884), 733–741.

2563 VINCENT, [ETHEL GWENDOLINE (MOFFATT), *lady*], *MRS.* HOWARD. Forty thousand miles over land and water; the journal of a tour through the British empire and America. London, 1885. 2 vols. **DLC**

DLC incorrectly catalogs as 1888; Uk has 2d ed., London, 1886. On the U.S., I, pp. 1–25, 40–130. See also her *Newfoundland to Cochin China by the golden wave, New Nippon, and the forbidden city. . . . With reports on British trade and interests in Canada, Japan, and China, by Col. Howard Vincent*, London, 1892, pp. 325–336; and *The life of Sir Howard Vincent*, by S. H. Jeyes, concluded by F. D. How, London, 1912, pp. 151–155.

2564 WILSON, *REV.* JOHN SKINNER, *ed.* Centenary of the consecration of the Right Reverend Samuel Seabury, D.D., first bishop of Connecticut. Authorized report of proceedings in Scotland and elsewhere, October and November, 1884. Aberdeen, 1885. 214 p. **CBGTU MnHi NcD Uk**

Contains addresses, speeches and sermons on the church in America by English clergymen and others.

2565 [WOODS, ROBERT STUART]. The cutting out of the Caroline and other reminiscences of 1837–38. [Chatham, Ont., 1885]. 8 p. **MH CaOTU NBuHi**

Chatham, 1896 ed. carried title, *The burning of the Caroline and other reminiscences of 1837–38, by Rear Admiral Drew, commander of the expedition, and Judge Woods*. First appeared in the Chatham *Planet*. See also George Coventry, "A contemporary account of the Navy Island episode, 1837," ed. by Wm. Renwick Riddell, *Proc. & Trans. Royal Soc. of Canada*, XIII, 3d ser., Section II, (May 1919), 57–76.

1886

2566 BENGOUGH, J[OHN] W[ILSON]. A caricature history of Canadian politics. Events from the union of 1841, as illustrated by cartoons from "Grip," and various other sources. . . . with an introduction by Rev. Principal Grant, D.D., of Queen's University, Kingston. Toronto, 1886. 2 vols . **DLC Uk**

Toronto, 1974 ed., selected and with a new introd. by Doug Fetherling. See numerous cartoons on U.S. See also *The decline and Fall of Keewatin; or, The Free trade redskins. A satire*, Toronto, 1876, illustrated by Bengough; the U.S. is referred to as the "Land of the spread eagle."

2567 BORTHWICK, *REV.* JOHN DOUGLAS. History of the Montreal prison, from A.D. 1784 to A.D. 1886, containing a complete record of the troubles of 1837–1838. Burning of the Parliament buildings, in 1849. The St. Alban's raiders, 1864. The two Fenian raids of 1866 and 1870. And a chronological digest of all the principal events for the past hundred years. Valuable statistical tables from the Police and Recorder's courts. Curious proclamation, warrants and other documents never before printed, relating to the patriots of '37, and the administration of justice from the commencement of the courts in 1874. With descriptions of branding on the hand, standing on the pillory, the stocks, whipping, &c. Montreal, 1886. 269 p. **DLC Uk**

On Canadian-U.S. affairs, pp. 184–223, and passim. See also author's *The battles of the world; or Cyclopaedia of battles, sieges, and important military events. The origin and institution of military titles, etc., etc., alphabetically arranged, with an appendix, containing a chronological table, from the creation to the present day*, Montreal, 1866.

2568 BRADSHAW, B. B. Bradshaw's ABC dictionary to the United States, Canada, & Mexico, showing the most important towns and points of interest. With maps, routes, &c., also large general skeleton map showing the various steamship routes to various ports. London, 1886. 304 p. **Uk**

NN, OCl have 2d ed., London, 1887. On U.S., pp. 7–191.

2569 BUCKLEY, *REV.* M[ICHAEL] B[ERNARD]. Diary of a tour in America . . . by Rev. M. B. Buckley, of Cork, Ireland. A special missionary in North America and Canada in 1870 and 1871. Edited by his sister Kate Buckley. Dedicated to the Irish people at home and abroad. Published for the Editress in Great Britain, Ireland, America and Canada. Dublin, 1886. 384 p. **CU IU MnHi NN**

DLC has London, 1889 ed.; Uk has Dublin, 1889 ed.

2570 BUSH, *REV.* JOSEPH, *ed.* W[illiam] O[verend] Simpson, Methodist minister and missionary. Early life, and life in the home work, by the Rev. Samuel Wray. Mission life, by the Rev. Robert Stephenson, B.S. London, [1886]. 520 p. **DLC Uk**

"Visit to America," made by Simpson in 1879, pp. 446–458.

2571 CAMPBELL, *REV.* JOHN KERR. Through the United States of America and Canada, being a record of holiday rambles and experiences. London, [1886]. 260 p.
CtY MnHi MH NN

2572 COLBY, CHARLES CARROLL. Parliamentary government in Canada. Montreal, 1886. 57 p. **DLC**

A lecture read before the law school of Bishop's College, Sherbrooke, by Charles Carroll Colby, M.P.

2573 DAUNT, ACHILLES. With pack and rifle in the far south-west. Adventures in New Mexico, Arizona, and central America. London, 1886. 389 p. **CtY NN**

2574 EBBUTT, PERCY G. Emigrant life in Kansas. London, 1886. 237 p. **DLC Uk**

In the U.S. for 6 years in the 1870's, age 12–18.

Reviews: *Academy* (by Robert Brown), XXX, 5; *Nation*, XLIII, 337; *Sat. Rev.*, LXII, 492; *Spectator* (by Thomas Hughes), LIX, 935; *Time*, IV (n.s.), 116.

2575 FARRAR, FREDERIC WILLIAM, [*Dean*]. Sermons and addresses delivered in America . . . With an introduction by Phillips Brooks, D.D. New York, 1886. 364 p. **DLC Uk**

Pref. dated Nov. 20, 1885. See "Farewell thoughts on America," pp. 328–364; repr. with 4 of the addresses in his *Lectures and addresses*, New York, 1886, pp. 67–98. See also "A group of eminent Americans," in *Men I have known*, New York, [1897], pp. 154–177; and "Visit to America," in *The life of Frederick William Farrar . . . By his son Reginald Farrar*, New York, 1904, pp. 284–301.

2576 FORREST, JAMES, *ed*. Railway construction and working. Comprising the following papers: I. The construction and operation of railways in countries where small returns are expected. By Robert Gordon, M. Inst. C. E. II. The laying-out, construction and equipment of railways in newly-developed countries. By James Robert Mosse, M. Inst. C. E. III. The Rocky mountain division of the Canadian Pacific Railway. By Granville Carlyle Cuningham, M. Inst. C. E. with an abstract of the discussion upon the papers. London, 1886. 65 p.   **CaOOA**

First 2 papers compare U.S. and Canadian railways, including personal accounts.

2577 FREWEN, MORETON. The free coinage of silver in the United States. [N.p.], 1886. 8 p.   **Uk**

Repr. from the *Financial News*, May 29, 1886.

2578 FROUDE, JAMES ANTHONY. Oceana; or, England and her colonies. London, 1886. 396 p.   **Uk**

DLC has New York, 1886 ed. Includes extensive comment on America. See his "Romanism and the Irish race in the United States," *No. Am. Rev.*, CXXIX (Dec. 1879), 519–536; CXXX (Jan. 1880), 31–50. See also account of his trip to the U.S. in 1872 in Herbert Paul, *The life of Froude*, London, 1905, pp. 201–228.

Reviews: *Academy* (by William Wickham), XXIX, 68; *Athenaeum*, (Jan. 30, 1886), 159; *Blackwood's Edinb. Mag.*, CXXXIX, 218; *Quar. Rev.*, CLXII, 443.

2579 GREEN, FRANK W[ILLIAM]. Notes on New York, San Francisco, and old Mexico. Wakefield, 1886. 173 p.   **DLC**

Letters repr. from the Wakefield *Herald*.

2580 GURNEY, [*REV.*] ALFRED. A ramble through the United States; a lecture delivered (in part) in S. Barnabas' school, February 3, 1886. [London, 1886?]. 63 p.   **DLC Uk**

Priv. pr.

2581 HARDY, IZA DUFFUS. Oranges and alligators: sketches of south Florida life. London, 1886. 240 p.   **DLC Uk**

2582 HARLEY, *REV.* TIMOTHY. Southward ho! Notes of a tour to and through the state of Georgia in the winter of 1885–6. London, 1886. 198 p.   **DLC Uk**

2583 [HENDERSON, *LIEUT-COL.* GEORGE FRANCIS ROBERT]. The campaign of Fredericksburg, Nov.–Dec. 1862; a study for officers of volunteers, by a line officer. London, 1886. 145 p.   **DLC Uk**

Uk lists 1st ed. under Fredericksburg. "An amplification of the chapter on Fredericksburg in Colonel [Charles Cornwallis] Chesney's 'Campaigns in Virginia'." Repr. in Jay Luvaas, ed., *The Civil War: a soldier's view*, Chicago, 1958, chap. 2.

2584 [HERTSLET, *MRS.* EVELYN M.?] Ranch life in California, extracted from the home correspondence of E. M. H. London, 1886. 171 p.   **MdBE Uk**

2585 HYNDMAN, HENRY MAYERS. The Chicago riots and the class war in the United States. A reprint from "Time". London, 1886. 16 p.   **CLU NN**

Visited the U.S. several times, 1874–80; see his *The record of an adventurous life*, New York, 1911, pp. 166–221. For comments on socialism in America, see his *Further Reminiscences*, London, 1912, pp. 312–348. See also his anonymous letter to the *Pall Mall*

Gazette. (1880), enlarged in the *Fortnightly Rev.*, XXXV (Mar. 1881), 340–357, and repr. in the New York *Tribune.* See also the interesting account of the Hyndman-Henry George debates of the 1880's in Elwood P. Laurence, "Uneasy alliance: the reception of Henry George by British socialists in the eighties," *Am. J. of Econ. & Sociol.*, XI (Oct. 1951), 61–74.

2586   JACKSON, MOSES. To America and back: a holiday run. London, 1886. 246 p.

MdBE Uk

2587   [LEAN, FLORENCE (MARRYAT) CHURCH]. Tom Tiddler's ground. By Florence Marryat. London, 1886. 212 p.   **DLC Uk**

Travel account of the U.S. and Canada. See also her *Life and letters of Captain Marryat*, London, 1872; II, pp. 1–73, describes his 1837–39 visit to America.

2588   LINDSEY, ROBERT and SARAH. Travels of Robert and Sarah Lindsey. . . . Edited by one of their daughters ["E. L. G."]. London, 1886. 189 p.   **CSmH NN Uk**

Contains extracts from their journals covering visits to America in 1846–51 and 1859–60. See Sheldon Jackson, ed., "English Quakers tour Kansas in 1858. From the journal of Sarah Lindsey," *Kansas Hist. Quar.*, XIII, no. 1 (Feb. 1944), 36–52.

2589   [MARSTON, EDWARD]. Frank's ranche; or, My holiday in the Rockies. Being a contribution to the inquiry into what we are to do with our boys. By the author of "An amateur angler's days in Dovedale." London, 1886. 214 p.   **CU**

DLC has Boston, 1886 ed.; Uk has 3d ed., London, 1886, cataloged under E. M. (initials after pref.). See also Marston's *Copyright, national and international, from the point of view of a publisher*, London, 1876; pp. 36–41, "International copyright with America."

2590   MONEY, EDWARD. The truth about America. London, 1886. 234 p.   **DLC Uk**

In U.S., mid-1880s; after disappointing land purchases in California and Colorado, returned to England in 1885.

2591   PITT, GEORGE. The collected remarkable travels of George Pitt, (accompanied by his wife), round and over the world. Being a rapid survey of continual facts, with lively geographical and historical sketches of each country, by an original and unconventional writer, in a familiar and interesting style, in which his marvels of economy are illustrated. Originally published in "The British Friend," at occasional intervals. Glasgow, 1886. 320 p.   **CU NN Uk**

On California and across continent, pp. 295–304.

2592   THE QUEEN'S ENEMIES in America. Assembled in convention at Chicago. London, 1886. 77 p.   **ICJ IreDNL Uk**

Uk lists under U.S.A., Misc. institutions, "Irish National League of America."

2593   RICKMAN, THOMAS M. Notes of a short visit to Canada and the States, in August and September, 1885. [London], 1886. 54 p.   **DLC Uk**

Priv. pr.

2594   ROBERTS, *SIR* JOHN HERBERT. A world tour: being a year's diary, written 1884–'85. Liverpool, 1886. 612 p.   **CSmH**

Priv. circ. On U.S., pp. 9–78.

2595   ROBERTSON, JOHN MACKINNON. Equality; a discourse. London, [1886]. 56 p.

NjP Uk

No t.p. Signed and dated Oct. 31, 1886. Compares England and U.S. Pub. by South Place Religious Soc., no. 13. See also author's *Over-population. A lecture delivered for the Sunday lecture society, London, on October 27th, 1889, under the title: "The law of population, its meaning and menace*, London, 1890, 24 p; and his *Walt Whitman, poet and democrat*, Edinburgh, 1884, Round Table Series IV, 52 p.

2596   [SIM, WILLIAM]. The log of the "Old un," from Liverpool to San Francisco. [Exeter, 1886]. 30 p.   **NNC**

Author accompanied an English cricket team on tour in the U.S.

2597   [STANTON, A. J.]. Three months in the United States and Canada. By the editor of the "Western gazette." Yeovil, [1886?]. 162 p.   **DLC**

A series of papers which appeared originally in the *Western Gazette* and *Pulman's Weekly News* between Nov. 1883 and Sept. 1885.

2598   STEVENSON, ROBERT LOUIS. An unpublished letter written by Robert Louis Stevenson on early Californian photography. With greetings of the season from Marjory and Francis Farquhar. San Francisco, 1938. [5] p.   **DLC**

Letter to Mrs. Virgil Williams written in 1886.

2599   STOKER, BRAM. A glimpse of America. A lecture given at the London institution, 28th December, 1885. London, 1886. 48 p.   **ICN NN Uk**

For accounts of his visits to the U.S. with Henry Irving, see Stoker's *Personal reminiscences of Henry Irving*, London, 1906: I, pp. 285–303; (1883–4) II, pp. 229–237, 258–265 (1889, 1893, 1899).

2600   TUPPER, MARTIN FARQUHAR. My life as an author. London, 1886. 431 p.   **DLC Uk**

Uk gives title: *Martin Tupper's autobiography. My life as an author*. The famous author of *Proverbial Philosophy* visited the U.S. in 1851 and 1876; for another account of these visits, see Derek Hudson's *Martin Tupper: his rise and fall*, London, [1949], pp. 107–134, 279–298, and passim. See also Tupper's *Washington: a drama in five acts*, London, 1876; *American Ballads*, London, 1849?; and "Ode America," *U. S. Mag. & Democratic Rev.*, XXIV, 448.

2601   WIGHAM, HANNAH MARIA. A Christian philanthropist of Dublin. A memoir of Richard Allen. . . . with portrait, and illustrations by J. Finnemore. London, 1886. 256 p.

MH NN PPFr Uk

Includes account of visit to the U.S., 1883–84, pp. 212–231; see also pp. 59–68.

2602   WILLSON, [HENRY] BECKLES. The life of Lord Strathcona and Mount Royal [Donald Alexander Smith, 1st baron], G.C.M.G., G.C.V.O. (1820–1914). Boston, 1915. 2 vols.

DLC

Uk has London, 1915 ed., 631 p. Much comment on U.S.-Canadian affairs in 1860's and '70's, passim; see esp. chaps. 9, 10, 12, 13 and 17. The earlier Willson volume, *Lord Strathcona, the story of his life*, London, 1902, 288 p., contains very little comment on the U.S. Brief comments on the U.S. are also to be found in John Macnaughton's *Lord Strathcona*, New York, 1926.

2603   WOTHERSPOON, GEORGE. Mormonism. London, 1886. 27 p.   **CtY Uk**

1887

2604 [ANDERSON, *SIR* ROBERT]. Parnellism and crime. Behind the scenes in America. London, 1887. 42 p.   **IreDNL MH**

Repr. from the London *Times*. Entirely on the U.S. Other vols., not eds. of this work, bearing the same series title, *Parnellism and crime*, contain various material from the *Times*, much of which is repeated; all spring from Anderson's attack on Charles Stewart Parnell, pub. in the *Times*, June 7, 1887. See esp. the 3d and rev. ed., London, 1887 (held by NNU and Uk), which contains *Times* article of March 10, 1887, "A retrospect: America", pp. 20–35. For accounts of Parnell's visit to the U.S. in 1860, see Kenneth Colton, "Parnell's mission in Iowa," *Annals of Iowa*, XXII (Apr. 1940), 312–327; Joan Haslip, *Parnell: a biography*, New York, 1937, pp. 103–114; R. Barry O'Brien, *The life of Charles Stewart Parnell*, New York, 1898, I, 197–207; John Howard Parnell, *Charles Stewart Parnell: a memoir*, New York, 1914, pp. 156–164, 268–276; and Robert M. Post, "Charles Stewart Parnell before Congress," *Quar. J. Speech*, LI (1965), 419–426 (includes Parnell's actual speech before Congress on the Irish National Land League). See also Margaret Leamy, *Parnell's faithful few. . .* , New York, 1936, pp. 43–52, and passim.; appendix repr. Tim Harrington's American diary, pp. 216–235, which also recalls Parnell's visit.

2605 ARNOLD, MATTHEW. General Grant: an estimate. Boston, 1887. 66 p.   **DLC**

Repr. from *Murray's Mag.*, Jan. and Feb. 1887; included also in his *Civilization in the United States*, 1888, below. Also repr. in John Y. Simon, ed., *General Grant. By Matthew Arnold, with a rejoinder by Mark Twain*, Carbondale, 1966.

2606 AVELING, EDWARD [BIBBINS]. An American journey. New York, [1887]. 243 p. **DLC**

No. 1066 of Lovell's Library. Sketches appeared originally in New York *World*, Boston *Herald*, *Court & Soc. Rev.*, *Pall Mall Gazette*, *J. of Educ.*, etc.

2607 BANNATYNE, DUGALD J. Handbook of republican institutions in the United States of America, based upon federal and state laws, and other reliable sources of information. Edinburgh, 1887. 624 p.   **DLC Uk**

2608 BATES, E[MILY KATHERINE]. A year in the great republic. By E. Catherine Bates. London, 1887. 2 vols.   **DLC Uk**

See also author's *Seen and unseen*, New York, 1907: chap. 2, "Investigations in America, 1885–1886," chap. 4, "Hong Kong, Alaska, and New York,' and chap. 10, "Further experiences in America" [in 1897].

Reviews: *Academy* (by Robert Brown), XXXII, 403; *Spectator*, LXI, 633.

2609 [BEADLE, CHARLES]. A trip to the United States in 1887. [London, 1887]. 210 p.
   DLC Uk

Priv. pr.

2610 BERNARD, JOHN. Retrospections of America, 1797–1811 . . . Edited from the manuscript by Mrs. Bayle Bernard, with an introduction, notes, and index by Laurence Hutton and Brander Matthews. New York, 1887. 380 p.   **DLC Uk**

2611 [BROWN, HUGH STOWELL]. Hugh Stowell Brown; his autobiography, his commonplace book and extracts from his sermons and addresses. A memorial volume, ed. by his son-in-law, W. S. Caine, M.P. 2d ed. London, 1887. 548 p.   **DLC Uk**

No record found of 1st ed. Visit to U.S. in 1873, pp. 100–121.

2612   BRYCE, JAMES BRYCE, *Viscount*. The predictions of Hamilton and De Tocqueville. Baltimore, 1887. 57 p.   **DLC Uk**

Johns Hopkins University Studies in Historical and Political Science, 5th ser., IX. Rev. and enlarged in his *Studies in history and jurisprudence*, London, 1901, pp. 301–358.

2613   CALIFORNIA: ITS CLIMATE and prospects for emigrants. In and around Los Angeles, California. [London? 1887]. 8 p.   **Uk**

N.p., n.d. Contains extracts from reports of consuls, Edinburgh newspapers, etc.

2614   COLEMAN, ANN RANEY (THOMAS). Victorian lady on the Texas frontier. The journal of Ann Raney Coleman. Ed. by C. Richard King, Norman, 1971. 206 p.   **DLC UK**

Came to Texas with her family in 1832; final entry in 1887. See esp. 1st section, pp. 3–45, for her arrival and first 5 years.

2615   CONDON, EDWARD O'MEAGHER. The Irish race in America. New York, 1887. 316 p.   **DLC Uk**

Ford's National Library, no. 7.

2616   D., J. E. Imperial Federation on a commercial basis: free trade versus fair trade. A contribution to the Jubilee literature of 1887, from the Antipodes. Hobart, 1887. 14 p.   **Uk**

2617   [DECON, THOMAS WILLIAM]. The experiences of an Englishman in Philadelphia society. As related by himself, and set down by Raconteur [*pseud.*]. [Philadelphia], 1887. 32 p.   **DLC**

2618   ELLIOTT, CHARLES. A trip to Canada and the far North-west. London, [1887?]. 93 p.   **DLC**

Includes account of New York, etc.

2619   FRANCIS, FRANCIS, *Jun*. Saddle and moccasin. London, 1887. 322 p.   **DLC Uk**

Uk incorrectly gives 822 p. Sketches of travel in the U.S.; some repr. from *Nineteenth Cent*.

Review: *Academy* (by Robert Brown), XXXII, 20.

2620   [FYFE, LAWRENCE R.]. The tour of the West Indian cricketeers. August & September, 1886. Demerara, 1887. 92 p.   **PHC PHi**

2621   GIBSON, JOHN. Great waterfalls, cataracts, and geysers, described and illustrated. London, 1887. 288 p.   **PPAN Uk**

Includes description of Niagara, pp. 16–51.

2622   GILCHRIST, ANNE [BURROWS]. Anne Gilchrist, her life and writings. Edited by Herbert Harlakenden Gilchrist. With a prefatory notice by William Michael Rossetti. London, 1887. 368 p.   **DLC Uk**

Includes repr. of "A woman's estimate of Walt Whitman. From late letters by an English lady to W. M. Rossetti," pp. 287–301; appeared originally in the *Radical*, VII (1870), 345–359. See also *The letters of Anne Gilchrist and Walt Whitman*, ed., with an introd. by Thomas B. Harned, Garden City, 1918.

2623   GREATER AMERICA; hits and hints by a foreign resident. New York, 1887. 157 p.   **CU NN**

Review: *Critic*, XI, 202.

2624 GREG, PERCY. History of the United States from the foundation of Virginia to the reconstruction of the Union. London, 1887. 2 vols. **DLC Uk**

Greg was a paid writer for a Confederate publication, the *Index*; after the Civil War he wrote a number of articles for the London *Standard* and other periodicals: see Manchester *Guardian* for Dec. 30, 1889. See also article about Greg by W. E. A. A., *Academy*, XXXVII, 45.

2625 HORT, DORA (*MRS.* ALFRED). Via Nicaragua; a sketch of travel. London, 1887. 267 p. **DLC Uk**

Includes an account of California.

2626 [HUTCHINSON, ELLIOTT ST. MAURICE]. Two years a cow boy, and life on the prairie, among the Indians, and backwoods of America. By Bunny [*pseud.*]. London, 1887. 128 p. **CtY-Mus Uk**

Describes life in California and Colorado in 1884–86.

2627 JACKS, LAWRENCE PEARSALL. The confession of an octogenarian. London, [1942]. 272 p. **DLC Uk**

In U.S., 1886–87, pp. 108–128. See also his *My American friends*, London, 1933, pp. 12–18, 27–47.

2628 [JARMAN, WILLIAM]. Hell upon earth; the doctrines & practices of the "Latter-day saints" in Utah. Discussion between W. Jarman, ex-Mormon priest, from Salt lake city, and Mormon missionaries, from Utah, held at Hoyland common, Yorkshire, June 15th, 16th, and 17th, 1887. [n.p., 1887?]. 15 p. **MH**

2629 KIRKWOOD, *REV.* JOHN. An autumn holiday in the United States and Canada. Edinburgh, 1887. 272 p. **MH NN Uk**

2630 LITTLE, JAMES STANLEY. The United States of Britain, an address on England and her colonies. Being the substance of a lecture delivered at Haslemere on the 19th May, 1886, and at the theatre of the Royal aquarium, Westminster, on the 18th June, 1886, with additions and revision, and a dedication to the Right Hon. Lord Tennyson, D.C.L., president of the Haslemere branch of the Imperial federation league. Guildford, 1887. 32 p. **ICU Uk**

References to U.S. throughout.

2631 MCGOUN, ARCHIBALD. On commercial union with the United States with a word on imperial reciprocity. A paper read . . . before the Montreal branch of the Imperial federation league in Canada, June, 1887. [Montreal, 1887]. 31 p. **MH**

See his "Commercial union with the United States," *Canadian Monthly & Natl. Rev.*, (July 1880), 1–11.

2632 MACNAUGHT, *MRS.* Through distant lands. Diary of a tour round the world in 1886–7. [London?, 1887?]. 224 p. **CtY**

On U.S., pp. 22–92.

2633 OLIPHANT, LAURENCE. Episodes in a life of adventure; or, Moss from a rolling stone. Edinburgh, 1887. 420 p. **DLC Uk**

Oliphant visited the U.S. many times from 1854–81; this work discusses the first trip, pp. 44–59, other recollections, pp. 108–112. For accounts of many later trips to the Harris community at Brockton, Mass., see Herbert W. Schneider and George Lawton, *A prophet and pilgrim. Being the incredible history of Thomas Lake Harris and Laurence Oliphant; their sexual mysticisms and utopian communities. Amply documented to confound the skeptic*, New York, 1942; Richard MacCully, *The Brotherhood of the new life and Thomas Lake Harris*, 1893, below; and Anne Taylor, *Laurence Oliphant, 1829–1888*, Oxford, 1982, pp. 113–145. See also Philip Henderson, *The life of Laurence Oliphant: traveller, diplomat and mystic*, London, 1956, pp. 43–49, 147–162, 192–201, 217–221; and Margaret Oliphant, *Memoir of Laurence Oliphant and of Alice Oliphant, his wife*, New York, 1891, I, pp. 108–134, II, pp. 1–69, 130–168. For additional comment by Laurence Oliphant, see his *Traits and travesties; social and political*, Edinburgh, 1882, pp. 162–231.

2634   [ORD, LEWIS REDMAN]. Reminiscences of a bungle. By one of the bunglers. Toronto, 1887. 66 p.   **N**

2635   O'SULLIVAN, D[ENNIS] A[MBROSE]. Government in Canada. The principles and institutions of our federal and provincial constitutions. The B.N.A. act, 1867, compared with the United States constitution, with a sketch of the constitutional history of Canada. Second edition, enlarged and improved. Toronto, 1887. 344 p.   **DLC**

1st ed., Toronto, 1879, has very little on U.S. 2d ed. "entirely rewritten" and enlarged to "twice its original size"; on U.S., passim.

2636   POWELL, T. P. From Montreal to San Francisco across Canadian territory. Montreal, 1887.   **CaOTP**

On California, pp. 18–30.

2637   [RANDALL, *MRS.* ISABELLE]. A lady's ranche life in Montana; by I. R. London, 1887. 170 p.   **DLC Uk**

2638   ROBERTS, MORLEY. The western Avernus; or, Toil and travel in further North America. London, 1887. 307 p.   **DLC Uk**

Later eds. carried variant titles. In the U.S., 1884–87. See also his 1912 novel *The private life of Henry Maitland; a record dictated by J. H.*

2639   ROBERTSON, EDMUND. American home rule: a sketch of the political system in the United States. Edinburgh, 1887. 131 p.   **Uk**

2640   ROWLEY, CHARLES. A workshop paradise and other papers. London, 1905. 280 p.
                                                                                                            CSt MiD WU

"American notes," [in 1887], pp. 195–246. Also some comment on this visit in his *Fifty years of work without wages*, London, [1911].

2641   RUSKIN, JOHN. Letters of John Ruskin to Charles Eliot Norton. Boston, 1904. 2 vols.
                                                                                                            DLC

Uk has Boston, 1905 ed. Letters, 1855–1887, contain comment on the U.S., passim. See also Benjamin Evans Lippincott, *Victorian critics of Democracy*, Minneapolis, 1938, pp. 55–92. See also many references to America in the index to Ruskin's complete works.

2642   SELF-HELP EMIGRATION SOCIETY. The old country and the new . . . An account of the work of the . . . society. London, 1887. 19 p.   **Uk**

Uk lists under London-Misc. institutions.

2643   SHAW, THOMAS. Plain talks on commercial union between Canada and the United States. Hamilton, [Ont.], 1887. 68 p.   **CaOOA CSmH MH**

At top of t.p., Commercial Union Document, no. 5.

2644   [SMITH, GOLDWIN]. British and Canadian citizens in the United States. [Chicago? 1887]. 4 p.   **DLC**

Repr. from the *Canadian-American*, V (Sept. 23, 1887), 3. See also Smith's "The decline of party government," *Macmillan's Mag.*, XXXVI (Aug. 1877), 298–306.

2645   SMITH, GOLDWIN. The schism in the Anglo-Saxon race . . . An address delivered before the Canadian club of New York. New York, 1887. 43 p.   **CU MH NIC Uk**

Also in *Canadian leaves . . . A series of new papers read before the Canadian club of New York . . . Edited by George Moore Fairchild, Jr., etc.*, New York, 1887, pp. 19–57. See also Smith's "The capital of the United States," *Macmillan's Mag.*, LIV (July 1886), 161–170.

2646   SMITH, R[OBERT] PEARSALL. Anglo-American copyright . . . With comments by Mr. Gladstone, Lord Tennyson, The Duke of Argyll, Archdeacon Farrar, Mr. Rider Haggard, Mr. Lewis Morris, Mr. Justin McCarthy, Sir Thomas Farrer, Mr. Walter Besant, Mr. Matthew Arnold, Professor Huxley, Messers Kegan Paul, Trench, & Co. Philadelphia, 1887. 24 p.   **DLC**

At head of title: "Extracted from the Nineteenth Century . . . No. 129 November 1887, (XXII, pp. 601–624). Smith was an American. See also his *International copyright . . . Protected copyright with free-trade competition, by an American*, [London, 1886].

2647   SUTTER, ARCHIBALD. Per mare, per terras, being a visit to New Zealand by Australia, for the examination of certain lands there during 1883–84 & America in 1885. London, 1887. 281 p.   **DLC Uk**

8 chaps. on the U.S.

2648   [TOD, JOHN]. Bits about America. By John Strathesk [*pseud.*]. Edinburgh, 1887. 192 p.   **CU Uk**

DLC has microfilm. Repr. of a series of articles, "Bits from the Scrap-book of a Scot visiting America," from the Edinburgh *Scotsman*.

2649   WALLACE, ALFRED RUSSEL. My life: a record of events and opinions. London, 1905. 2 vols.   **CU DNLM NN Uk**

DLC has New York, 1905 ed.; abridged ed., 1 vol., London, 1908. Describes a lecture tour in the U.S., 1886–87, II, pp. 107–199.

2650   WATKIN, *SIR* E[DWARD] W[ILLIAM]. Canada and the States; recollections, 1851 to 1886. London, [1887]. 524 p.   **DLC Uk**

Includes portions of an earlier book, *A trip to the United States and Canada*, London, 1852. Watkin was in America in 1851, 1861, and on many later occasions.

Review: *Westmin. Rev.*, CXXIX, 133.

2651   WATSON, WILLIAM, [*of Skelmorlie, Scotland*]. Life in the Confederate army, being the observations and experiences of an alien in the South during the American civil war. London, 1887. 456 p.   **DLC Uk**

Account of experiences in April 1861–Summer 1863. See his *The adventures of a blockade runner*, 1892, below.

2652   WILSON, JOHN. Memories of a labour leader; the autobiography of John Wilson, J.P., M.P. With an introduction by the Dean of Durham and an appreciation by the Bishop of Durham. London, 1910. 319 p.   **DLC Uk**

Uk lists 300 p. In U.S., 1864–67, pp. 148–198, and in 1887, pp. 287–297.

2653   WIMAN, ERASTUS. Commercial union between the United States and Canada. Speech . . . at Lake Dufferin, Ontario, July 1, 1887. Toronto, [1887?] 18 p.   **MH MnU NRU**

DLC and Uk have an expanded ed., with letters, papers, and speeches by Wiman and others, New York, [1887], 35 p.; DLC lists under title. Canadian-born Wiman lived 26 years in New York, but always wrote as a Canadian until he received U.S. citzenship late in life. See also his "Can we coerce Canada?", *No. Am. Rev.*, CLII, (Jan. 1891), 91–102; "The struggle in Canada," ibid., (March 1891) 339–348; and "Canada and the States," *Canadian Rev.* (Apr. 1891), 620–624.

2654   WIMAN, ERASTUS. Does annexation follow? Commercial union and British connection. An open letter . . . to Mr. J. R. Dougall, etc. [New York, 1887?].   **Uk**

Also appeared in the expanded ed. of his *Commercial union between the United States and Canada*, 1887, above.

1888

2655   ABERCROMBY, RALPH. Seas and skies in many latitudes; or, Wanderings in search of weather. London, 1888. 447 p.   **DLC Uk**

2 chaps. on the U.S.

2656   ADAM, GRAEME MERCER, *ed.* Handbook of commercial union: a collection of papers read before the commercial union club, Toronto, with speeches, letters and other documents in favour of unrestricted reciprocity with the United States. Preceded by an introduction by Mr. Goldwin Smith. Toronto, 1888. 296 p.   **DLC**

Pub. by Commercial Union Club of Toronto. Includes 4 letters written by Goldwin Smith to the Toronto *Mail*, a series of articles from the Toronto *Mail* by its editor, Edward Farrer, and various speeches and addresses by other Canadians.

2657   ARNOLD, MATTHEW. Civilisation in the United States; first and last impressions of America. Boston, 1888. 192 p.   **DLC**

Uk has 4th ed., Boston, 1888. Includes 5 essays by Arnold, who visited the U.S. in 1883–84 and 1886. Two essays on Ulysses S. Grant, pp. 1–66, previously also repr. as a pamphlet; see his *General Grant; an estimate,* 1887, above; also repr. with extensive notes in R.H. Super's edition of Arnold's *The last word*, Ann Arbor, 1977, pp. 144–179. The other essays: "A word about America, pp. 69–108, originally pub. in *Nineteenth Cent.*, XI (May 1882), 680–696; repr. in his *Five uncollected essays*, ed. by Kenneth Allott, Liverpool, 1953, pp. 1–23; and repr. with extensive notes in R.H. Super's edition of Arnold's *Philistinism in England and America*, Ann Arbor, 1974, pp. 1–23. "A word more about America," pp. 111–153; orig. pub. in *Nineteenth Cent.*, XVII (Feb. 1885), 219–238; repr. in *Five uncollected essays,* pp. 23–45, and in *Philistinism in England and America*, pp. 194–217. And the title essay, "Civilisation in the United States," orig. pub. in *Nineteenth Cent.*, XXIII (Apr. 1888), 157–192; repr. in *Five uncollected essays*, pp. 46–65, and in *The last word*, pp. 350–359.

See also Arnold's *Discourses in America*, London, 1885, for three lectures delivered during the first American tour; esp. see the lecture on Emerson, pp. 138–207, for some comment on the U.S. For discussion of Arnold's lecture tours in the U.S., and of his views on America, see the following: Henry A. Beers, "Matthew Arnold in America," *Century Mag.*, XXVII (Nov. 1883), 155–157; James Dow McCallum, "The apostle of culture meets America,"

New Eng. Quar., II (July 1929), 357–381; J. B. Orrick, "Matthew Arnold in America," *London Mercury*, XX (Aug. 1929), 389–397; E. P. Lawrence, "An apostle's progress; Matthew Arnold in America," *Philolog. Quar.*, X (Jan. 1931), 62–79; Chilson Hathaway Leonard, "Arnold in America: a study of Matthew Arnold's literary relations with America and of his visits to this country in 1883 and 1886," unpub. Ph.D. dissertation, Yale Univ., 1932; William T. Beauchamp, "Plato on the prairies (Matthew Arnold at Galesburg)," *Educational Forum*, V (March 1941), 285–295; Howard Mumford Jones, "Arnold, aristocracy and America," *Am. Hist. Rev.*, XLIX (Apr. 1944), 393–409; R. L. Lowe, "A note on Arnold in America," *Am. Lit.* XXII (May 1951), 250–252; John P. Long, "Matthew Arnold visits Chicago," *Univ. of Toronto Quar.*, XXIV (Oct. 1954), 34–45; John Henry Raleigh, *Matthew Arnold and American culture*, Berkeley, 1957; Roger L. Brooks, "A Matthew Arnold letter to James Russell Lowell: the reason for the American tour," *Am. Lit.*, XXXI (Nov. 1959), 336–338; David J. De Laura, "Matthew Arnold and the American literary class; unpub. correspondence and some further reasons," *Bull. N.Y. Pub. Lib.*, LXX (1966), 229–250; John Y. Simon, ed., *General Grant. By Matthew Arnold, with a rejoinder by Mark Twain*, Carbondale, 1966 (esp. the introd.); Sidney Coulling, *Matthew Arnold and his critics: a study of Arnold's controversies*, Athens, Ohio, 1974, esp. pp. 137–181, 269–297; and A. L. Rowse, *Matthew Arnold: poet and prophet*, London, 1976, pp. 136–162, 182–204.

2658 AUBERTIN, JOHN JAMES. A fight with distances; the States, the Hawaiian islands, Canada, British Columbia, Cuba, the Bahamas. . . . London, 1888. 352 p.   **DLC Uk**

9 chaps. on U.S.; spent 10 months, 1886–87.

2659 [AVELING, EDWARD BIBBINS and ELEANOR MARX AVELING]. The Chicago anarchists. A statement of facts. Reprinted from "To–day," November, 1887. London, [1888]. 8 p.   **NN Uk**

2660 AVELING, EDWARD [BIBBINS], and ELEANOR MARX [AVELING]. The working-class movement in America. London, 1888. 212 p.   **ICU Uk**

DLC has 2d ed., enlarged, London, 1891.

2661 BARTON, SAMUEL. The battle of the Swash and the capture of Canada. Montreal, [1888?]. 137 p.   **DLC**

Uk has New York, 1889 ed.

2662 BEAR, WILLIAM E. The British farmer and his competitors. London, [1888]. 168 p.   **DLC Uk**

Uk lists under London-Cobden Club. Repr. from the *Quar. Rev.* On U.S., pp. 37–51, 71–87, and passim.

2663 [BEERS, WILLIAM GEORGE]. Young Canada's reply to "Annexation." Montreal, [1888]. 7 p.   **DLC**

Cover title; caption title, Patriotic speech by Dr. W. George Beers. Reply to a toast: "Professional annexation," opposing it. Address delivered at the banquet of the 5th, 6th, 7th, and 8th District Dental Societies of the State of New York in Syracuse, 25 October, 1888.

2664 BLAKE, J[OHN] N. The true commercial policy for Greater Britain. An address, delivered by J. N. Blake . . . before the Commercial Union Club at Assocation hall, Toronto, April 5th, 1888 . . . Toronto, 1888. 46 p.   **DLC**

2665 BRASSEY, THOMAS ALLNUTT, *2d earl*. Diary of a hunting trip 1888. Battle, 1888. 30 p.

No locations found. Subtitle (not on t.p.) "Six weeks in the United States."

2666 BRASSEY, THOMAS ALLNUTT, *2d earl*. Sixteen months' travel, 1886–87. London, 1888. 265 p. **CtY NBuG**

"A month in the Rockies," (1886), pp. 1–22.

2667 [BRIDGE, JAMES HOWARD]. Uncle Sam at home, by Harold Brydges [*pseud.*]. New York, 1888. 244 p. **DLC Uk**

Review: *Nation*, XLVI, 247.

2668 BRITISH COMMENTS on the President's message. Philadelphia, 1888. **OCIWHi**

"Tariff Tract No. 8." Comments on President Cleveland's message. See also Tract No. 13, *Mr. Cleveland to the Mills bill population in England*, Philadelphia, 1888.

2669 BRYCE, JAMES BRYCE, *Viscount*. The American Commonwealth. London, 1888. 3 vols. **MH MN Uk**

DLC has 2 vol. London, 1888 ed. Many subsequent printings, editions, translations and abridgements. Condensed and revised as vol. II of Bryce's *Modern democracies*, London, 1921. New ed., "completely revised throughout with additional chapters," New York, 1922–23. Selections pub. as *Reflections on American institutions*, with an introd. by Henry Steele Commager, Greenwich, Conn., 1961. Bryce was familiar with the U.S. in great detail, visiting in 1870, 1883–84, and 1887. See also H. A. L. Fisher, *James Bryce (Viscount Bryce of Dechmont, O.M.)*, New York, 1927, for Bryce's letters, many of which reveal more of his personal views of the U.S. than do his books; and his *American correspondence*, 1871–1922, introd. by D. S. Porter [East Ardsley, Eng.], 1974 (on microfilm, from originals in the Bodleian library).

See also the following articles by Bryce: "American experience in the relief of the poor," *Macmillan's Mag.*, XXV (Nov. 1871), 54–65; "The legal profession in America," ibid. (Jan. 1872), 206–217; "American judges," ibid. (March 1872), 422–432; "On some peculiarities of society in America," *Cornhill Mag.*, (Dec. 1872), 704–716; "The Mayoralty election in New York," *Contemp. Rev.*, LXXII (Nov. 1897), 750–760; and "America revisited; the changes of a quarter century," the *Outlook*, LXXIX (March 25, 1905), 733–740, (April 1, 1905), 846–855. See also Edmund Ions, *James Bryce and American democracy, 1870–1922*, London, 1968; Ion's chapter in *Abroad in America: visitors to the new nation, 1776–1914*, ed. by Marc Pachter, Reading, Mass., 1976; and Owen Philip Stearns, *James Bryce and American democracy, 1870–1922*, Rochester, 1965 (unpub. Ph.D. dissertation, Univ. of Rochester).

Reviews: (of various editions) *Academy*, XXXV, 49; *Am. Catholic Quar.*, XIV, 183; *Andover Rev.*, II, 481; *Atlantic*, LXIII, 418; *Baptist Rev.* (by P. S. Moxon), II, 153; *Blackwood's Edinb. Mag.*, CXLVI, 276; *Century Mag.* (by E. Eggleston), XV, 789; *Church Quar.*, XXIX, 98; *Cosmopolitan*, VII, 101; *Critic*, XXVI (June 1, 1895), 396; *Dial* (by A. C. McLaughlin), IX, 255, XIV, 310; *Edinb. Rev.*, CLXIX, 481; *Eng. Hist. Rev.* (by Lord Acton), IV, 388, XXVI, 430; *J. Pol. Econ.*, XIX, 359; *Littel's Living Age*, CLXXX, 469; *Macmillan's Mag.*, (by Goldwin Smith), LIX, 241; *Nation* (New York) (by J. D. Cox), XLVIII, 13; *New Englander* (by D. H. Chamberlain), L, 396; *Nineteenth Cent.* (by F. Harrison), XXV, 140; *Outlook*, LI, 829; *Pol. Science Quar.* (by W. Wilson), IV, 153; *Quar. Rev.*, CLXIX, 253; *Rev. of Revs.*, XI, 60; *Sewanee Rev.*, III, 437; *Spectator*, LXI, 1814; *Unitarian Rev.*, XXXI, 212; *Westmin. Rev.*, CXXXI, 383.

2670 CARTWRIGHT, *SIR* RICHARD [JOHN]. Speech on reciprocity with the United States. Delivered in the House of commons, 14th March, 1888. [n.p., 1888?]. 36 p. **NN**

2671 CHARLTON, JOHN. Speech . . . on unrestricted reciprocity with the United States. Delivered in the House of commons, Friday, March 16th, 1888. [London, 1888?]. 34 p. **DLC**

Headed: From the official debates.

2672 [COOK, JOEL]. A visit to the States. A reprint of letters from the special correspondent of the Times. First and second series. London, 1887–88. 2 vols. **DLC Uk**

Often listed as by an English author; Cook was an American. The only comment by a British author is a repr. of the leading article from the London *Times*, Jan. 14, 1888, commenting on the series, II, pp. 278–284.

2673 CRAWFORD, ROBERT. Reminiscences of foreign travel. London, 1888. 308 p. **DLC Uk**

On U.S., pp. 2–19, 25.

2674 CURRAN, J[OHN] J[OSEPH?]. The lessons of history. Speech . . . delivered in the House of commons, Wednesday, March 21st, 1888. London, 1888. 15 p. **CaOTP**

Discusses the evils of reciprocity.

2675 DE RICCI, JAMES HERMAN. The fisheries dispute, and annexation of Canada. London, 1888. 310 p. **DLC Uk**

2676 EDMUNDS, WILFRED. Across the Atlantic: scenes and impressions. [Chesterfield, 1888]. 41 p. **CSmH Uk**

Edmunds was editor of the Derbyshire *Times*, in which the letters appeared originally. On U.S., pp. 26–36, 41; see also appendix: "A Canadian tour," pp. 19–24, 30–36.

2677 FARMER, JOHN STEPHEN. Americanisms—old and new. A dictionary of words, phrases and colloquialisms peculiar to the United States, British America, the West Indies, etc., etc., their derivation, meaning, and applications, together with numerous anecdotal, historical, explanatory, and folk-lore notes. Compiled and edited by John S. Farmer. London, 1888. 564 p. **Uk**

DLC has London, 1889 ed. See also Farmer's *Twixt two worlds: a narrative of the life and works of William Eglinton*, London, 1886; on Eglinton's 1881 visit to the U.S., pp. 85–88.

2678 [FIRTH, JOSIAH CLIFTON]. Our kin across the sea . . . With a preface by J[ames] A[nthony] Froude. London, 1888. 252 p. **DLC Uk**

See Mona Gordon, *The golden age of Josiah Clifton Firth*, Christchurch, N.Z., 1963; "American journey," pp. 218–224.

2679 GRANT, WILLIAM LAWSON and FREDERICK HAMILTON. Principal Grant. Toronto, 1904. 531 p. **CtY-D Uk**

DLC has Edinburgh, 1905 ed., under title, *George Monro Grant*. On G. M. Grant's 1888 visit to the U.S., pp. 395–403.

2680 HOWE, J. B[URDETT]. A cosmopolitan actor. His adventures all over the world. London, 1888. 242 p. **NN**

Repr. from *Tinsley's Mag.*, XL (Jan.–May 1887), 44–435. Contains accounts of several visits to America.

2681 LANGTRY, LILLIE [EMILY CHARLOTTE (LE BRETON)], *Lady de Bathe*. The days I knew. London, [1925]. 319 p. **DLC Uk**

In America, 1882–84 and 1886–88, pp. 187–221.

2682 LEDYARD, T[HOMAS] D. Canadian mines and reciprocity: being a paper read before the Commercial union club. Toronto, 1888. 16 p. **CaOTP**

DLC has bound with John H. Blake's *The true commercial policy for Greater Britain*, 1888, above.

2683 LEES, J[AMES] A[RTHUR], and W[ALTER] J. CLUTTERBUCK. B.C. 1887. A ramble in British Columbia . . . With map and 75 illustrations from sketches and photographs by the authors. London, 1888. 387 p. **DLC Uk**

On U.S., pp. 322–376.

2684 [LIBERAL-CONSERVATIVE PARTY OF CANADA]. Reciprocity negotiations. The position of Canada and of the Liberal-Conservative government. [n.p., 1888]. 8 p. **CaNSWA CSmH**

Information for the Electors, no. 1. On U.S.-Canadian affairs.

2685 MCHUTCHESON, WILLIAM. The New Zealander abroad in England, America and the Highlands of Scotland, in Maderia [sic], Capetown and the Sandwich islands; being notes of a six months holiday tour round the world. Glasgow, 1888. 302 p. **AuCNL CSbC NzWTu**

On U.S., pp. 75–157.

2686 MCMICKEN, GILBERT. The abortive Fenian raid on Manitoba. Account by one who knew its secret history. A paper read before the society, May 11, 1888. Winnipeg, 1888. 11 p. **DLC Uk**

Cover title; at head: The Historical and scientific society of Manitoba. Transaction No. 32—Season 1887-8.

2687 MAPLESON, JAMES HENRY. The Mapleson memoirs, 1848–1888. London, 1888. 2 vols. **TxU Uk**

DLC has New York, 1888 ed. and 2d London ed., 1888. New ed., annotated by Harold Rosenthal, New York, 1966, under title: *The Mapleson memoirs; the career of an operatic impresario, 1858–1888*. Mapleson visited the U.S. in 1875, and annually 1877–87. Extensive comment.

2688 MAYCOCK, *SIR* WILLOUGHBY [ROBERT DOTTIN]. With Mr. [Joseph] Chamberlain in the United States and Canada, 1887–88. London, 1914. 278 p. **DLC Uk**

Chamberlain and Maycock were in the U.S. to arrange for the settlement of the fisheries question. For other accounts of this visit, see N. Murrell Marris' *The Right honourable Joseph Chamberlain: the man and the statesman*, New York, 1900, pp. 278–285; *Mr. Chamberlain's speeches. Edited by Charles W. Boyd with an introduction by the Right honourable Austen Chamberlain, M.P.*, London, 1914, I, pp. 318–324, with other comment on the U.S. passim; James Louis Garvin's *Life of Joseph Chamberlain*, London, 1932–33, II, pp. 322–341, also other comment on the U.S., III, pp. 159–168, 296–306. See also the following Chamberlain articles: "The caucus," *Fortnightly. Rev.*, XXIV, n.s. (Nov. 1, 1878), 721–741; "Shall we Americanize our institutions?" *Nineteenth Cent.*, XXVIII (Dec. 1890), 861–875, and the reply by Henry Cabot Lodge, ibid., XXIX (Mar. 1891), 423–428; "Municipal institutions in America and England," *Forum*, XIV (Nov. 1892), 267–281; and "Recent developments of policy in the United States and their relation to Anglo-American alliance," *Scribner's Mag.*, XXIV (Dec. 1898), 674–682.

2689 MITFORD, *MAJOR-GENERAL* R[EGINALD] C[OLVILLE] W[ILLIAM] REVELEY. Orient and Occident: a journey east from Lahore to Liverpool. London, 1888. 359 p.

DLC Uk

Last 7 chaps. on U.S.

2690 MONTAGUE, FRANCIS CHARLES. Local administration in the United States and in the United Kingdom. London, 1888. 32 p. **CtY MB OO Uk**

Cobden Club pamphlet.

2691 [NORMAN, *SIR* HENRY]. Commercial union as photographed by an intelligent English visitor to Canada. Imperial interview, number ten, in the Pall Mall Gazette. New York, [1888?]. 10 p. **CaOTP MB**

Commercial Union Document No. 10.

2692 OLIPHANT, *MRS*. MARGARET OLIPHANT (WILSON). A memoir of the life of John Tulloch, D. D., LL.D. Edinburgh, 1888. 502 p. **DLC Uk**

In U.S., 1874, pp. 287–303. See also Tulloch's "America and the Americans," *Good Words*, XVI (1875), 641–648, 705–711, 773–776, 817–824.

2693 PENDER, [MARY] ROSE [LADY GREGGE-HOPWOOD]. A lady's experiences in the wild West in 1883. London, [1883]. 80 p. **CoD MH MoU**

2694 [RELPH, HARRY. ("LITTLE TICH")]. Little Tich: a Book of Travels (and wanderings). By Little Tich. London, 1911. 135 p. **IaU MH Uk**

"I visit America," pp. 51–75. Performed in *Crystal Slipper* in New York and Chicago, 1887–88.

2695 ROBERTSON, W[ILLIAM] J[OHN]. A brief historical sketch of Canadian banking and currency, the laws relating thereto since confederation, and a comparison with British and American systems . . . A paper read before the Historical and political science association of the University of Toronto, Feb. 4th, 1888. Toronto, 1888. 32 p. **CaOOA IU MH**

2696 SCHOLFIELD, A[MOS]. Temperance legislation in America. Notes on Canada and the United States of America. Swansea, 1888. 54 p. **NN**

Series of articles repr. from the Cambria *Daily Leader*.

2697 SMITH, GOLDWIN. Speech of Mr. Goldwin Smith at the banquet of the Chamber of commerce of the state of New-York, November 20, 1888. New York, 1888. 9 p. **ICN**

Discusses Canadian-U.S. relations.

2698 [STEVENSON, *MRS*. MARGARET ISABELLA (BALFOUR)]. From Saranac to the Marquesas and beyond; being letters written by Mrs. M. I. Stevenson, during 1887–88, to her sister, Jane Whyte Balfour, with a short introduction by George W. Balfour . . . Edited and arranged by Marie Clothilde Balfour. London, 1903. 313 p. **DLC Uk**

On U.S., pp. 10–62.

2699 TUPPER, *SIR* CHARLES. Recollections of sixty years. London, 1914. 414 p. **DLC Uk**

Contains "Report of the speech of Hon. Sir Charles Tupper, G.C.M.G., C.B., Minister of Finance, and one of Her Majesty's plenipotentiaries at the Washington fishery conference, on the Fishery treaty, delivered in the House of commons of Canada, April 10th, 1888," pp. 335–441; much comment on U.S. affairs, passim. See also the *Political reminiscences of the Right honourable Sir Charles Tupper, bart . . . Transcribed and edited by the late W. A. Harkin. With a biographical sketch and an appendix*, London, 1914, pp. 189–198; also see the account in James Wilberforce Longley, *Sir Charles Tupper* (The Makers of Canada, n.s., vol. I), Toronto, 1916, pp. 193–207, other comment passim. Scattered comment on the fisheries question is also to be found in E. M. Saunders, ed., *The life and letters of the Rt. Hon. Sir Charles Tupper*, London, 1916, 2 vols.

2700   TUPPER, *SIR* CHA[RLE]S H[IBBERT]. Unrestricted reciprocity. Speech by Mr. Chas. H. Tupper, M.P., delivered in the House of commons, on Monday, March 19th, 1888. 22 p. Ottawa, 1888. **CaAEU MeU MH**

On Canadian-U.S. relations. Repr. as a supp. to the *Colonial Standard*. See also his "History of the Behring sea question," in *Canada: an encyclopedia of the country*, ed. by J. Castell Hopkins, Toronto, 1898–1900, VI, pp. 131–145.

2701   TURNER-TURNER, J. Three years' hunting and trapping in America and the great Northwest. London, 1888. 182 p. **DLC**

2702   WEBSTER, W. A. A Canadian farmer's report. Minnesota and Dakota compared with Manitoba and Canadian North-west. The facts as personally seen by a Canadian farmer. By W. A. Webster, a farmer, in the township of Lansdowne, County of Leeds, Ontario. Ottawa, 1888. 16 p. **CtY MH MnHi**

1889

2703   APPLETON, LEWIS. Memoirs of Henry Richard, the apostle of peace. London, 1889. 212 p. **DLC Uk**

On American Civil War, pp. 55–71, and the Alabama controversy, pp. 115–119.

2704   B., H. Three months in America. [n.p.], 1889. 112 p. **DLC**

Priv. pr. A series of letters describing a visit to the U.S., purporting to be written by two Scotchmen, Harry Nesbit and Johnny Sucker; both names are fictitious.

2705   BAINES, THOMAS F. O'MALLEY. My life in two hemispheres: what was suffered for love of country. 3d ed. San Francisco, 1889. 180 p. **CLU ICRL ViU**

No record found of earlier eds. Life in California, 1872–1880, pp. 25–85.

2706   BARNEBY, WILLIAM HENRY. The new Far West and the old Far East, being notes of a tour in North America, Japan, China, Ceylon, etc. London, 1889. 316 p. **DLC Uk**

Chap. on California, pp. 134–149; also repr. a leading article from the London *Times* of Mar. 7, 1889, "The United States and Japan," pp. 294–298.

2707   BRADLEY, ARTHUR GRANVILLE. Emigration of gentlemen's sons to the United States and Canada. London, [1889]. 24 p. **UkRCS**

See also his "Trouting in England and America," *Macmillan's Mag.*, XLVII (Sept. 1883), 368–377; "The Southern view of the election of Cleveland," ibid., LI (Apr. 1885), 372–374; and "Game preserving in the United States," ibid., LVIII (Sept. 1888), 364–370.

2708 BRICE, ARTHUR JOHN HALLAM MONTEFIORE. Florida and the English. London, 1889. 28 p.   **Uk**

Repr. from the *J. Manchester Geog. Soc.*, V (May 1889), 129–150.

2709 CALVERT, [ADELAIDE HELEN (BIDDLES)] *MRS.* CHARLES. Sixty-eight years on the stage. London, [1911]. 273 p.   **DLC Uk**

Toured the U.S. 7 times between 1855 and 1889.

2710 CARBUTT, [MARY (RHODES) *LADY,*] *MRS.* E[DWARD] H[AMER]. Five months' fine weather in Canada, western U.S., and Mexico. London, 1889. 243 p.   **DLC Uk**

Review: *Sat. Rev.*, LXX, 211.

2711 COBBE, FRANCES POWER and BENJAMIN BRYAN. Vivisection in America. I.–How it is taught. II.–How it is practised. London, 1889. 32 p.   **DNLM NN Uk**

DLC has 4th ed., London, 1890.

2712 COCKBURN, [JAMES]. Speech of Mr. Cockburn, M.P., on unrestricted reciprocity, delivered in the House of commons, Ottawa, on Tuesday, March 19th, 1889. Ottawa, 1889. 14 p.   **CaOOA**

2713 COMMERCIAL UNION, a study. By a Quebec Liberal. [Quebec?, 1889?]. 15 p.   **ICN NN NcD**

On Canadian-U.S. relations.

2714 DARLING, HENRY W. Address at the banquet of the Union League of Chicago . . . Toronto, 1889. 14 p.   **NN**

2715 DIGBY, MARGARET. Horace Plunkett; an Anglo-American Irishman. Oxford, 1949. 314 p.   **DLC Uk**

Describes Plunkett's ranch experiences in Wyoming, 1879–89, pp. 21–41. See also Plunkett's "The working of woman suffrage in Wyoming", *Fortnightly Rev.*, LIII (May 1890), 656–669.

2716 DILKES, CHARLES E. The United States of America, as they are: a description of the situation, surface, soil, climate, agricultural, mining, and manufacturing industries; population, history, government, etc., of each state and territory in the Union; compiled from the last national census and the latest official authorities. Liverpool, 1889. 144 p.   **PPWa Uk**

Statistical handbook.

2717 DUFFIELD, A[LEXANDER] J[AMES]. Recollections of travels abroad. With a map showing the author's ocean routes. London, 1889. 327 p.   **CSt CtY Uk**

On U.S., pp. 211–231.

2718 EDWARDS, *SIR* HENRY. A two months' tour in Canada and the United States, in the autumn of 1889. London, 1889. 62 p.   **MdBE**

2719 FACKTZ, P. N. Canada and the United States compared, with practical notes on commercial unions, unrestricted reciprocity, and annexation. Toronto, 1889. 54 p.   **CaOTP**

2720 FREDERICKSON, AUGUSTUS DANIEL. Ad orientem. With illustrations from the author's sketchbook. London, 1890 [1889]. 388 p.   **DLC Uk**

In U.S., pp. 359–380.

2721 GLENNY, H[ENRY]. Jottings and sketches, at home and abroad. By "The Australian Silverpen." Belfast, 1889. 288 p. **CSt**

2722 HAGUE, JOHN. Canada for Canadians. A royalist "Roland," for the annexationist "Oliver" . . . A paper read before the Toronto Branch of the Imperial Federation League, in Association Hall, Toronto, the 23rd of January, 1889. Toronto, [1889]. 40 p. **NN**

2723 HARKER, JOSEPH [CUNNINGHAM]. Studio and stage . . . with an introduction by Sir Johnston Forbes-Robertson. London, [1924]. 283 p. **DLC Uk**

Describes several visits to the U.S. in the 1880s.

2724 HOGAN, JAMES FRANCIS. The Australian in London and America. London, 1889. 280 p. **NN NjP Uk**

Portions repr. from *Chambers's J.*, the *Globe*, and the Melbourne *Argus*. On U.S., pp. 35–133, and passim.

2725 INCIPIENT IRISH REVOLUTION, an expose of Fenianism of to-day in the United Kingdom and America, with the secret code of laws in force in London . . . and containing a map showing spheres of Fenian influence in the United Kingdom in 1889. London, 1889. 46 p. **NN Uk**

Uk lists under "Fenianism and Irish revolution."

2726 JOHNSON, GEORGE. The Dominion Statistician on Mr. Wiman's panacea. A few facts and significant ones too, by George Johnson, Dominion Statistician. [n.p.], 1889. 3 p.

No locations found.

2727 JOHNSON, GEORGE. Progress of Canada. [Ottawa, 1889?].

No locations found. Broadside. Letter to the *Citizen*, dated Ottawa, May 11, 1889.

2728 LETT, WILLIAM PITTMAN. Annexation and British connection. Address to Brother Jonathan. Ottawa, 1889. 20 p. **CaOOA**

2729 LIBERAL-CONSERVATIVE PARTY OF CANADA. The liberals and the trade policy. N.p., 1889?. 11 p. **CaNSWA CSmH**

Information for the Electors, no. 2. U.S.-Canada relations.

2730 [MACINNES, DONALD?]. Notes of our trip across British Columbia; from Golden, on the Canadian Pacific Railway, to Kootenai, in Idaho, on the Northern Pacific Railway, and of our visit to the American national park, "The Yellowstone," in Wyoming, thence home via St. Paul and the new Soo Line. Hamilton, 1889. 34 p. **MnHi NN**

2731 MULHALL, MICHAEL G[EORGE]. The United States and the future of the Anglo-Saxon race, by Rev. Josiah Strong; and The growth of American industries and wealth, by Michael Mulhall. London, 1889. 70 p. **CU ICJ MH**

Papers read before the British Association. Strong was American. See also Mulhall's "Progress of the United States," *No. Am. Rev.*, CLXIV (May 1897), 566–575, CLXV (Nov. 1897), 572–581.

2732 [NELSON, JOHN YOUNG]. Fifty years on the trail, a true story of western life [edited] by Harrington O'Reilly. London, 1889. 381 p. **DLC Uk**

Uk lists under O'Reilly. London, 1891 ed. under title *Life among the American Indians; fifty years on the trail.* . . . Later ed., Norman, Ok., [1963], has subtitle: *The adventures of John Young Nelson as described to Harrington O'Reilly*, with a foreword by Donald E. Worcester.

2733   NEWMAN, F[RANCIS] W[ILLIAM]. Anglo-Saxon abolition of Negro slavery. London, 1889. 136 p.   **DLC Uk**

Parts I and II repr. from *Fraser's Mag.*, XIX, (Jan. and Feb. 1879), pp. 88–106, 170–182; Pt. IV, "The good cause of President Lincoln," repr. of a pamphlet issued in 1863, by the Emancipation Society, q.v.

2734   OSBORN, HENRY J. Does prohibition prohibit? Notes of personal enquiries in the United States and Canada by Henry J. Osborn, (one of the London superintendants of the United Kingdom alliance). With an introduction by Sir Wilfrid Lawson, Bart., M.P. London, 1889. 32 p.   **NN Uk**

2735   PEMBERTON, T[HOMAS] EDGAR. A memoir of Edward Askew Sothern. London, 1889. 314 p.   **DLC Uk**

Sothern was in U.S. on several occasions between 1852–1880. See the account ascribed to Mrs. J. R. Vincent, *Birds of a feather flock together; or, Talks with Sothern*, ed. by Felix Gregory De Fontaine, New York, 1878; see also the account by his son, Edward H. Sothern, *My remembrances. The melancholy tale of "Me"*, New York, 1916.

2736   PETTIFER, H. J. John Bull and Jonathan; or, Free trade versus protection. London, 1889. 16 p.   **IU Uk**

2737   POLLOCK, J[AMES] M[ATTHER]. The unvarnished west: ranching as I found it. London, [1911]. 252 p.   **DLC Uk**

Life in Texas in the 1880's.

2738   [PRIOR, A. G.]. Southern scenes and deeds in "The valley of Virginia." A poem . . . By an Englishman. [Baltimore], 1889. 16 p.   **DLC**

Pref. discusses English attitudes toward the South during the Civil War.

2739   [ROCKLEY, EVELYN CECIL, *baron*]. Notes on my journey round the world; by Evelyn Cecil, B.A. London, 1889. 207 p.   **DLC Uk**

On U.S., pp. 1–52.

2740   SETON-KARR, HEYWOOD W[ALTER]. Ten years' wild sports in foreign lands; or, Travels in the eighties. London, 1889. 333 p.   **CU CtY MH Uk**

2d ed., with additions, with title *Ten years travel and sport in foreign lands; or, Travels in the eighties*, London, 1890. On U.S., pp. 109–139.

2741   SMITH, GOLDWIN. Prohibition in Canada and the United States. London, 1889. 14 p.   **CSmH MB Uk**

Originally in *Macmillan's Mag.*, LIX, (Mar. 1889), 338–349. Repr. in *Essays on questions of the day. Political and social*, New York, 1893 (1894 ed. rev.), pp. 309–333, along with "Communism in the United States—The Oneida community and American socialism," pp. 337–360, repr. from the *Canadian Monthly & Natl. Rev.*, VI (Nov. 1874), 425–437.

2742   STOREY, SAMUEL. To the golden land; sketches of a trip to southern California. London, 1889. 101 p.   **MdBE NN**

Appeared originally in the Newcastle *Daily Chronicle*, Sunderland *Daily Echo*, and other English newspapers.

2743   TALLACK, WILLIAM. Penological and preventive principles, with special reference to Europe and America; and to the diminution of crime, pauperism, and intemperance; to prisons and their substitutes, habitual offenders, sentences, neglected youth, education, police, statistics, etc. London, 1889. 414 p. **DLC Uk**

Enlarged 2d ed., London, 1896. See also author's *The practical results of the total or partial abolition of capital punishment in various countries.* [*Prepared as a summary of the most recent and authentic information on the subject, and inclusive of statistics and reports forwarded to the Royal commission on capital punishment.*] . . . (*Read in the Jurisprudence department of the social science congress, held at Sheffield, October, 1865*), London, 1866, pp. 17–21.

2744   [TOOLE, JOHN LAWRENCE]. Reminiscences of J. L. Toole; related by himself, and chronicled by Joseph Hatton. London, 1889. 2 vols. **DLC Uk**

Abridged ed., London, 1892, 281 p. In America, 1874–75, II, pp. 40–70, 117–124, and 142–144.

2745   TRAVERS, W[ILLIAM] T[HOMAS] LOCKE. From New Zealand to Lake Michigan. Wellington, N.Z., 1889. 274 p. **NN**

DLC has microfilm. On U.S., pp. 24–274.

2746   VAN HORNE, WILLIAM CORNELIUS. Canadian Pacific railway aggressions upon American commerce. A letter addressed to Mr. Joseph Nimmo, jr., by Wm. C. Van Horne, president of the Canadian Pacific railway, and Mr. Nimmo's reply. Washington, D.C., 1889. 15 p. **DBRE**

2747   VISGER, *MRS*. JEAN ALLEN (PINDER) OWEN. After shipwreck. London, [1889]. 216 p. **PPT Uk**

From San Francisco to New York on the newly completed transcontinental railroad, 1869, pp. 59–84; in 1872, from Panama to California, pp. 93–116, and to Hawaii, pp. 119–146.

2748   WINNINGTON-INGRAM, HERBERT FREDERICK. Hearts of oak. London, 1889. 234 p. **DLC Uk**

Includes 2 letters from San Francisco (1849), pp. 129–133.

1890

2749   ASPDIN, JAMES. "Our boys": what shall we do with them? or, Emigration, the real solution of the problem. Showing how youths and young men can be put into the way of obtaining a profitable living for the present and a competence for the future. Manchester, [1890]. 2d ed. 32 p. **Uk**

No 1st ed. found. Emphasis on Canada, but some discussion of U.S.

2750   AUBREY, WILLIAM HICKMAN SMITH. In Memoriam: W. H. S. Aubrey, LL.D. some lectures and extracts from his writings. Compiled by his daughter, [Alice K. S. Aubrey]. London, 1916. 175 p. **CCSC OKenTU Uk**

Letters appeared originally in 1890 in the *Illus. London News, Leisure Hour,* and *Sunday at Home.* On U.S., pp. 142–165. See also Aubrey's "Social problems in America," *Fortnightly Rev.,* XLIII, n.s. (June 1888), 843–861; "Some peculiarities of American life," *Universal Rev.,* VII (Aug. 15, 1890), 565–581; and two additional articles in *Leisure Hour*: "The immediate future of the North-American Indians," (May 1890), 449–452; and "Higher education of girls in America," (Sept. 1890), 757–759.

2751 BAKER, *SIR* SAMUEL WHITE. Wild Beasts and their ways; reminiscences of Europe, Asia, Africa and America. London, 1890. 2 vols. **DNLM Uk**

DLC has London, 1890 ed., 455 p. On expeditions in the U.S., I, chap. 10, II, chaps. 15, 24.

2752 BETTANY, G[EORGE] T[HOMAS]. The red, brown, and black men of America and Australia, and their white supplanters. London, 1890. 289 p. **DLC Uk**

On U.S., pp. 47–83. See also Bettany's "Europe versus the United States: Darwinian forecast," *Contemp. Rev.*, LIII (March 1888), 395–405.

2753 BLAIKIE, *REV.* W[ILLIAM] G[ARDEN]. Summer suns in the far West; a holiday trip to the Pacific slope. London, 1890. 160 p. **MdBE**

Letters appeared originally in various periodicals. See his "Impressions of America and the Americans," *Sunday Mag.*, Oct. 1870–Sept. 1871; "Thoughts in prospect of the Philadelphia Council," *Catholic Presbyterian*, IV (July 1880), 1–8; "Transatlantic notes," ibid., (Oct. 1880), 304–309; "Concluding notes on America," ibid., V (Apr. 1881), 291–299. Blaikie visited the U.S. 5 times between 1870 and 1882. See accounts in Norman L. Walker, ed., *An autobiography, "Recollections of a busy life,"* London, 1901, pp. 214–239. See also Blaikie's "Southern California: past and present," *Scottish Geog. Mag.*, VI (Apr. 1890), 187–202.

2754 BODLEY, JOHN EDWARD COURTENAY. Roman Catholicism in America. Baltimore, 1890. 77 p. **MiU Uk**

Repr. from *Nineteenth Cent.*, XXVI (Nov. 1889), 801–824. Bodley was in the U.S., 1888–89; see account in Shane Leslie, *Memoir of John Edward Courtenay Bodley*, London, [1930], pp. 204–220.

2755 BOURINOT, *SIR* JOHN GEORGE. Canadian studies in comparative politics . . . I. The English character of Canadian institutions. II. Comparison between the political systems of Canada and the United States. III. Federal government in Switzerland compared with that of Canada. Montreal, 1890. 92 p. **DLC Uk**

Repr. from *Proc. & Trans. Roy. Soc. Canada*, VIII (1890), ser II, 37–66; also appeared in *Annals Am. Acad. Pol. & Social Science*, I (July 1890), 1–25. See author's "Canadian studies in comparative policies: parliamentary compared with congressional government," *Proc. & Trans. Roy. Soc. Canada*, XI (1893), ser. II, 77–108; and his "Canada and the United States: an historical retrospect," *Am. Hist. Assoc. Papers*, V (July 1891), pt. 3, 87–147. Most of Bourinot's works on Canada contain frequent references to the U.S.; see esp. *Canada as a home . . . Reprinted from the Westminster Review for July 1882*, London, 1882; *Canada as a nation* (caption title), [.p., 1885?]; *Our intellectual strength and weakness. A short historical and critical review of literature, art and education in Canada*, Montreal, 1893; *The fishery question: its imperial importance . . . (Reprinted from the Westminster Review for April 1886.)*, Ottawa, 1886; *Federal government in Canada*, Baltimore, 1889 (the *Johns Hopkins Univ. Stud.*, 7th ser., X–XII (Oct.–Dec. 1889)).

2756 THE BRITISH COLONIST in North America: a guide for intending emigrants. London, 1890. 320 p. **DLC Uk**

7 chaps. on the U.S.; introd. compares Canada and the U.S. as fields of emigration.

2757 CARTWRIGHT, *SIR* RICHARD [JOHN]. United States and Canada. Speech . . . at the annual banquet of the Board of trade and transportation of New York, Delmonico's, February 21, 1890. New York, [1890]. 13 p. **CaOTP**

At top of t.p., "So near and yet so far."

2758   DILKE, *SIR* CHARLES WENTWORTH. Problems of Greater Britain. London, 1890.
2 vols.   **DLC Uk**

On U.S., I, pp. 89–107, 149–180; II, passim. See also author's "An Anglo-American alliance, *Pall Mall Mag.*, XVI (Sept. 1898), 37–38; and his "The future relations of Great Britain and the United States," *Forum*, XXVI (Jan. 1899), 521–528.

Reviews. *No. Am. Rev.* (by Lorne), CL, 724; *Quar. Rev.*, CLXX, 527.

2759   DUCKWORTH, JAMES. A trip round the world. Rochdale, 1890. 166 p.   **DLC Uk**
On U.S., pp. 141–167.

2760   FITCH, *SIR* JOSHUA GIRLING. Notes on American schools and training colleges. Reprinted from the report of the English education department for 1888–89 with the permission of the controller of H. M. Stationery office. London, 1890. 133 p.   **DHEW Uk**

See also Lecture VIII, "Teachers' institutes and conventions in America," in *Educational aims and methods; lectures and address*, New York, 1900, (An address at the annual meeting of the Teachers' Guild, June 1889), pp. 249–271.

2761   FOSTER, WILLIAM ALEXANDER. Canada first: a memorial of the late William Foster, Q.C. With introduction by Goldwin Smith, D.C.L. Toronto, 1890. 221 p. **CSmH CSt NN**

Prefatory note signed, M. B. F. Repr. of various speeches and magazine articles, most of which deal with Canadian-U.S. relations; see esp. "The Canadian confederacy," pp. 93–138 (repr. from *Westmin. Rev.*, April 1865, pp. 533–560); and "The Canadian confederation and the reciprocity treaty," pp. 139–168 (from *Westmin. Rev.*, Oct. 1866, pp. 394–412).

2762   GORMAN, THOMAS P. Why not have reciprocity? An easy, wise, and practicable method of settling the outstanding disputes between Canada and the United States. Toronto, 1890.
15 p.   **CaOOA**

2763   GRANT, GEORGE MONRO. "Imperial federation." A lecture delivered in Victoria Hall, Winnipeg, on September 13th, 1889, by Rev. G. M. Grant, D.D., Principal of Queen's University, Kingston. Winnipeg, 1890. 15 p.   **CaOOA MH**

Another ed., London, [1891?], under title: *The case for Canada; an address delivered at Winnipeg*.

2764   HARDWICKE, HERBERT JUNIUS. Rambles abroad: in France, Germany, Switzerland, Italy, Spain, Portugal, Morocco, United States and Canada. Sheffield, 1890. 416 p.   **Uk**
On U.S. and Canada, pp. 285–408.

2765   INFORMATION GIVEN regarding annexation and other matters. [Ottawa, 1890]. 4 p.
                                                                           CaOTP

Letters to the *Citizen*, by George Johnson, et al.

2766   JEANS, JAMES STEPHEN. Waterways and water transport in different countries: with a description of the Panama, Suez, Manchester, Nicaraguan, and other canals. London, 1890.
507 p.   **DLC Uk**

On U.S. waterways, pp. 191–215. See author's "American railways and British farmers," *Nineteenth Cent.*, XXVIII (Sept. 1890), 392–409; and for other references to American railways, see his *An inquiry into the economic conditions of railway working in different countries*, London, 1887. Jeans went to the U.S. for the British Iron Trade Assoc. in 1893;

see his "The Columbian exposition from an European standpoint" ("An English view of the world's fair"), *The Engineering Mag.*, VI, no. 3 (Dec. 1893), 265–275; he also edited *American industrial conditions and competition: reports of the commissioners appointed by the British trade association to enquire into the iron, steel, and allied industries of the United States*, London, 1902. See also his *Conciliation and arbitration in labour disputes; a historical sketch and brief statement of the present position of the question at home and abroad*, London, 1894, pp. 131–141.

2767   JESSOPP, AUGUSTUS. The trials of a country parson. London, 1890. 295 p.   **NIC Uk**

DLC has New York, 1890 ed. Includes "Why I wish to visit America," pp. 270–295, repr. from the *No. Am. Rev.*, CXXXIX (Oct. 1884), 310–323.

2768   [JOHNSON, GEORGE]. Our farmers. Their condition and that of the farmers of the United States. The two positions compared. [Ottawa, 1890?]. 3 p.   **CaOTP**

Letter to the *Citizen*, signed George Johnson.

2769   JOHNSON, MATTHEW. America, pictorially described. London, [1890?]. 144 p.   **MH N**

2770   JOHNSTON, J[OHN]. Notes of a visit to Walt Whitman, etc., in July, 1890. Bolton, 1890. 46 p.   **DLC Uk**

Priv. circ. Enlarged ed., Manchester, 1898 under title, *Diary notes of a visit to Walt Whitman and some of his friends in 1890*; a 2d enlarged ed., London, [1917], with title *Visits to Walt Whitman in 1890–1891, by two Lancashire friends*, J. Johnston, M.D., and J. W. Wallace, reviewed by Virginia Woolf in the *Times Literary Supp.*, Jan. 3, 1918 and repr. in *Granite and Rainbow*, London, 1958, pp. 229–231. For accounts of visits to Whitman in 1877 and 1884, see Edward Carpenter's *Days with Walt Whitman. With some notes on his life and work*, London, 1906 (repr. from the *Progressive Rev.*, Feb. & Apr. 1897, and *Reformer*, Feb. 1902); and his *My days and dreams, being autobiographical notes*, London, [1916]. See also Whitman's "Our eminent visitors, (past, present and future)" *Critic*, III (Nov. 17, 1883), 459–460.

2771   KROUPA, B. An artist's tour; gleanings and impression of travels in North and Central America and the Sandwich Islands. London, 1890. 339 p.   **DLC Uk**

Review: *Academy* (by Robert Brown), XXXVII, 280.

2772   LANG, ANDREW. Life, letters, and diaries of Sir Stafford Northcote, first earl of Iddesleigh. Edinburgh, 1890. 2 vols.   **DLC Uk**

"The Alabama claims and the treaty of Washington," II, pp. 1–51, and passim. For a more complete version of the diaries, see *Diaries 1869, 1870, 1871, 1875, 1882, of the first earl of Iddesleigh*, priv. pr., [London, 1907], pp. 154–165, 181–240, and verse dealing with American experiences, pp. 275–280. See also Northcote's verse, "Farewell to a lady in America," in *Scraps, odds and ends*, [London], 1888, p. 425. See also Lang's "International girlishness," *Murray's Mag.*, IV (Oct. 1888), 433–441, also in *Eclectic Mag.*, CXI (Dec. 1888), 739–744; an answer to Theodore Roosevelt, "Some recent criticism of America," *Murray's Mag.*, IV (Sept. 1888), 289–310.

2773   LEE, J[OSEPH W.]. The Indian mutiny; events at Cawnpore . . . also, A narrative of his visit to England & America in 1883. And the manner he was received by his relatives, with some amusing letters from them after the lapse of forty years in India. Cawnpore, 1890. 2 pts. [95 p.].   **DLC**

Uk has Cawnpore, [1893] ed., with title *The Indian mutiny, and in particular, a narrative of events at Cawnpore, June & July, 1857. . . . supplemented by the narrator's travels and visit to England and America in 1883, together with the manner in which he was received by his relatives in different places, with some amusing letters from them after the lapse of forty years in India*; the portion of the book dealing with the Indian mutiny had been pub. separately, Cawnpore, 1884.

2774   [LIBERAL-CONSERVATIVE PARTY OF CANADA]. The changes which time has brought. [n.p., 1890?]. 8 p.   **CaNSWA CSmH**

Information for the Electors, no. 13. U.S.-Canadian relations.

2775   [LIBERAL-CONSERVATIVE PARTY OF CANADA]. The effect of unrestricted reciprocity. [n.p., 1890?]. 12 p.   **CaNSWA CSmH**

2776   [LIBERAL-CONSERVATIVE PARTY OF CANADA]. Facts for the electors. Dissolution of Parliment. [n.p., 1890?]. 30 p.   **CSmH MH**

2777   LOWTHER, *SIR* H[ENRY] C[ECIL]. From pillar to post. By Lieut. Colonel H. C. Lowther. London, 1911. 307 p.   **DLC Uk**

In Montana (c. 1890), pp. 1–19.

2778   MARSHALL, ALFRED. Some aspects of competition. Presidential address delivered to the Economic science and statistics section of the British association at Leeds, 1890. [London, 1890]. 35 p.   **CtY MH-BA UkLU-G**

Uk has repr. in A. C. Pigou, ed., *Memorials of Alfred Marshall*, London, 1925. Compares U.S. and England in respect to the issues of protection versus competition and free trade.

2779   MCCARTHY, EDWARD THOMAS. Incidents in the life of a mining engineer. London, [1918]. 384 p.   **DLC Uk**

NUC lists an [18__?] ed. held by NN, but that is an error; no other evidence of earlier publication. In U.S. in 1870's and 1880's, pp. 6–55, 129–132, 149–161, 166–181.

2780   MCGIBBON, R[OBERT] D[AVIDSON]. Copies of correspondence relative to the libel on H. R. H. Prince George of Wales. Between R. D. McGibbon, Q.C., of Montreal, Canada, and A. Curtis Bond, American manager Dunlap's cable co., foreign connection Dalziel's news co., of New York. [Montreal? 1890]. 18 p.   **CaOOA**

2781   M'QUEEN, JAMES. Notes on a trip to America, 1889. Castle-Douglas, [Scotland], [1890]. 72 p.   **CSmH WHi**

Signed and dated by author: Crofts, Dalbealtie [Scotland], N.B., Jan. 1890.

2782   MESSITER, CHARLES ALSTON. Sport and adventures among the North-American Indians. London, 1890. 368 p.   **DLC Uk**

In the U.S. at various times from 1862 to 1878.

2783   [MORTIMER, C. WHITE]. Southern California. Vice-consul Mortimer's report, with press comments . . . Reprinted from the British foreign office edition no. 718. [n.p.], 1890. 24 p.   **CU-BANC**

CU-BANC lists under Great Britain Foreign office. Caption title: Seventh annual report of Vice-consul Mortimer, on the trade and commerce of Los Angeles and Wilmington, California.

2784   O'CONNOR, THOMAS POWER. Memoirs of an old parliamentarian. [London, 1929]. 2 vols. **DLC Uk**

Visit to the U.S. in 1890, II, pp. 187–197. For accounts of this visit and one in 1881–82, see Hamilton Fyfe's *T. P. O'Connor*, London, 1934, pp. 94–99, 159–160.

2785   [O'HANLON, JOHN]. Life and scenery in Missouri [1843–53]. Reminiscenses of a missionary priest. Dublin, 1890. 292 p. **DLC Uk**

Uk lists under Missouri. See also O'Hanlon's *Irish emigrant's guide*, 1851, above; and his *Irish-American history of the United States*, Dublin, 1903.

2786   PIPKIN, SAMUEL J. A run round the world. Through Canada, New Zealand, Australia, and India. London, [1890?]. 208 p. **CSmH TxU**

On U.S., pp. 16–28, 61–74.

2787   PLAYFAIR, LYON PLAYFAIR, *1st baron*. The tariffs of the United States in relation to free trade. By the Right Hon. Sir Lyon Playfair . . . Speech delivered in Leeds, 13th Nov., 1890. London, 1890. 31 p. **DLC Uk**

Cobden club leaflet. See also his "A foreigner's opinion of American fish-culture," in *Bull. U.S. Fish Commission for 1885*, Washington, 1885, V, 367–369, repr. from the *Angler's Note-book*, no. VI (1884), 91–92. Playfair made annual visits to the U.S. from 1877; see Thomas Wemyss Reid, *Memoirs and correspondence of Lyon Playfair, 1st Lord Playfair of St. Andrews*, London, 1899.

2788   PLIMSOLL, [SAMUEL]. Cattle ships: being the fifth chapter of Mr. Plimsoll's second appeal for our seamen. [Published separately and out of its turn on account of its pressing urgency. Not published before, lest the case should be deemed incomplete.] London, 1890. 150 p. **DLC Uk**

English-American comparison. See also brief references to the U.S. in author's *Our seamen: speeches and facts,* [London, 1878].

2789   PORTEOUS, ARCHIBALD. A scamper through some cities of America; being a record of a three months' tour in the United States and Canada. Glasgow, 1890. 116 p. **DLC Uk**

2790   SAXBY, [*MRS.*] JESSIE M[ARGARET] E[DMONSTON]. West-nor' west. London, 1890. 154 p. **MnHi Uk**

On annexation of Canada, pp. 120–128.

2791   SMITH, GOLDWIN. The political relations of Canada to Great Britain and the United States. An address, delivered to the Nineteenth century club, New York, on the 31st January, 1890. Toronto, 1890. 25 p. **NcD**

See author's "The machinery of elective government," *Nineteenth Cent.*, XI (Jan. 1882), 126–148; "The hatred of England," *No. Am. Rev.*, CL (May 1890), 547–562, and the answer by T. W. Higginson, Andrew Carnegie, Murat Halstead, Horace Porter, Robert Collyer, James H. Wilson, "Do Americans hate England?" ibid., (June 1890), 749–778; "Canada and the United States," *Forum*, VI (Nov. 1888), 241–256. See also George Monro Grant, "Canada and the Empire," *Natl. Rev.*, XXVII (July 1896), 673–685; Smith's "A reply," *Canadian Mag.*, VII (Oct. 1896), 540–544; and Grant's answer "Canada and the Empire. A rejoinder to Dr. Goldwin Smith," ibid., VIII (Nov. 1897), 73–78.

2792   [SOMERSET, SUSAN MARGARET (MCKINNON)] ST. MAUR, *duchess of.*
Impressions of a tenderfoot during a journey in search of sport in the far West. By Mrs.
Algernon St. Maur. London, 1890. 279 p.   **DLC Uk**

On U.S., pp. 100–132, 275–279.

Review: *Sat. Rev.*, LXXI, 173.

2793   STANYON, WILLIAM. Holiday trip to America. London, [1890?]. 156 p.
                                                        CLU-C OKentU Uk

Repr. of letters contributed to the Leicester *Free Press*; letters are dated weekly from Apr.
20 to June 1, 1889.

2794   TAYLOR, H[ERBERT] COUPLAND. Wanderings in search of health; or, Medical and
meteorological notes on various foreign health resorts . . . with illustrations. London, 1890.
259 p.   **DNLM NIC Uk**

Colorado, pp. 232–237; California, pp. 237–239.

2795   THOMAS, W[ILLIAM] HERBERT. Mormon saints. London, 1890. 200 p.
                                                        CU-B MH NN Uk

DLC has microfilm.

2796   WALSH, TOWNSEND. The career of Dion Boucicault. New York, 1915. 224 p. **DLC Uk**
Dionysius Lardner Boucicault lived in the U.S. from 1853–60 (see pp. 47–78), and from
1876 to his death in 1890. See Nils Erik Enkvist, "The *Octoroon* and English opinions of
slavery," *Am. Quar.*, VIII (Summer, 1956), 166–170; and Richard Fawkes, *Dion
Boucicault: a biography*, London, 1979, esp. pp. 78–121 for the visits in the 1850s, before
emigrating, and pp. 186–243 for the later period.

2797   YOUNG, EGERTON RYERSON. By canoe and dog-train among the Cree and Salteaux
Indians. With an introduction by Mark Guy Pearse. Toronto, [1890]. 267 p.   **DLC Uk**
In U.S., pp. 33–40.

1891

2798   ACWORTH, *SIR* WILLIAM MITCHELL. The railways and the traders; a sketch of the
railway rates question in theory and practice. London, 1891. 378 p.   **DLC Uk**
Chap. 9, "American rates," pp. 204–248; extensive references to U.S., passim.

2799   ARNOLD, *SIR* EDWIN. Seas and lands. Reprinted by permission of the proprietors of the
"Daily Telegraph" from letters published under the title "By sea and land" in that journal.
London, 1891. 535 p.   **Uk**

DLC has New York, 1891 ed. On U.S., pp. 41–141. See his *Wandering words. Reprinted,
by permission, from papers published in the "Daily Telegraph" and foreign journals and
magazines*, London, 1894; chap. 2 describes a visit to the Lick observatory in California.
See also "Sir Edward Arnold at Harvard," *New Eng. Mag.*, I, n.s. (Nov. 1889), 315–317.

2800   BLACKWOOD'S EDINBURGH MAGAZINE. Travel, adventure, and sport from
Blackwood's magazine. [Edinburgh, 1889–91]. 6 vols.   **DLC Uk**
Includes "A visit to the big trees," by Dr. Cheadle, IV, pp. 296–305 (from Feb. 1866); and
"A fall hunt in the Rockies," by J. P. Maud, V., pp. 360–380 (from Aug. 1887).

2801   BOND, J. T. A fortnight in America. Notes of a visit by the Mayor of Plymouth, Mr. J. T. Bond, to Canada, and the United States, in June and July, 1891. Plymouth, 1891. 48 p.

CaOTP ICN

Priv. pr.

2802   CANADA'S FUTURE! Political union with the United States desirable. A plain argument for the consideration of thoughtful Canadians. [n.p., 1891?] 4 p.   **CaOOA**

2803   CHAMBERLAIN, ALEXANDER FRANCIS. Modern languages and classics in America and Europe since 1880; ten years' progress of the new learning. Toronto, 1891. 60 p.

CtY NN

On U.S., pp. 5–14. See also his "Africa and America; the contact of Negro and Indian . . . Paper read before the Canadian institute, Toronto, January 24, 1891," *Science*, XVII, No. 419 (Feb. 13, 1891); and "The relationship of the American languages," *Proc. Royal Canadian Inst.*, V, ser. 3 (1887), 57–76.

2804   CHAPLEAU, *SIR* J[OSEPH] A[DOLPHE]. Canada as it is: an address delivered Nov. 28, 1891, before the Commercial club of Providence, R.I.. Providence, 1891. 22 p.   **RPB**

Caption title: Hon. J. A. Chapleau . . . , on the commercial relations between Canada and the United States.

2805   CLOWES, [*SIR*] W[ILLIAM] LAIRD. Black America: a study of the ex-slave and his late master . . . Reprinted with large additions, from "The Times." London, 1891. 240 p.

DLC Uk

Portions repr., London, 1893, under the title *The great peril and how it was averted*. See also author's "American expansion and the inheritance of the race," *Fortnightly Rev.*, LXX (Dec. 1898), 884–892.

2806   COMBES, EDWARD. Report on technical education and manual training at the Paris universal exposition of 1889, and in Great Britain, France, and the United States of America . . . Presented to Parliament by command. Sydney, 1891. 315 p.   **IEN NN**

Visited U.S. after the close of the Paris exhibition of 1878, pp. 53–145; other comment, passim.

2807   [COPE, CHARLES WEST]. Reminiscences of Charles West Cope, R.A. By his son, Charles Henry Cope, M.A. London, 1891. 396 p.   **DLC Uk**

Visited U.S. in 1876, pp. 279–331.

2808   [DEVEREUX, HYACINTHE DALY]. Roughing it after gold. By Rux [*pseud.*]. London, 1891. 152 p.   **MdBE Uk**

On U.S. in 1874–75, pp. 4–109.

2809   DOWSETT, C[HARLES] F[INCH]. A start in life. A journey across America. Fruit farming in California. London, [1891?]. 112 p.   **DLC**

2810   DUFFERIN AND AVA, HARIOT GEORGINA HAMILTON-TEMPLE-BLACKWOOD, *marchioness of*. My Canadian journal, 1872–'78; extracts from my letters home, written while Lord Dufferin was governor-general; by the Marchioness of Dufferin and Ava. London, 1891. 417 p.   **Uk**

DLC has New York, 1891, ed.; Uk lists under Blackwood. Don Mills, Ont., 1969 ed., annotated by Gladys Chantler Walker. Includes accounts of visits, pp. 188–198, 217–226, 257–271, 309–323, 338–343, 422–426.

Review: *Sat. Rev.*, LXXII, 730.

2811   ECLIPSE [*pseud.*]. Ups and downs of an old tar's life. London, [1891]. 211 p.   **PPL Uk**
On U.S. visit of 1854, pp. 152–173, 177–180.

2812   FERGUSON, JOHN. From Ceylon to England by way of China, Japan & the United States; with other contributions to the English & Ceylon press; and a lecture (revised and enlarged) on from California, via Canada, to Florida in the cars. Colombo [Ceylon], 1891. 111 p.   **Uk**
On U.S., pp. 31–36, 73–111.

2813   FITZPATRICK, T[HOMAS]. A transatlantic holiday; or, Notes of a visit to the Eastern States of America. London, 1891. 210 p.   **DLC Uk**

2814   FORBES-ROBERTSON, *SIR* JOHNSTON. A player under three reigns. London, 1925. 291 p.   **DLC Uk**
Includes accounts of tours in the U.S. in 1885–86 and 1891.

2815   GIBSON, GEORGE ALEXANDER. Life of Sir William Tennant Gairdner, K.C.B., M.D., LL.D., F.R.S., Regius professor of practice of medicine in the University of Glasgow . . . With a selection of papers on general and medical subjects. Glasgow, 1912. 817 p.**NN Uk**
Gairdner visited the U.S. in 1891, pp. 277–315; on p. 277 mentions his "Impressions about America for my children," but there is no evidence it was ever published. See also his "Letter addressed to the British Medical Journal, November, 1894" on Oliver Wendell Holmes, pp. 486–491.

2816   GRANT, GEORGE MONRO. Advantages of Imperial federation. A lecture delivered by the Rev. Principal Grant, of Queen's College, Kingston, at a public meeting held in Toronto on January 30th, 1891, under the auspices of the Toronto Branch of the Imperial federation league. Toronto, 1891. 19 p.   **CaOOA NN NRU**

2817   GRATWICKE, *CAPT*. G. F. A trip west and back. Exeter, 1891. 80 p.
No locations found. Letters describing a tour of the Eastern states.

2818   HAGGARD, *SIR* HENRY RIDER. The days of my life, an autobiography . . . edited by C. J. Longman. London, 1926. 2 vols.   **DLC Uk**
In U.S. in 1891, II, pp. 48–51, 70. See also his letters on American copyrights in the London *Times* for Oct. 11, 1887 and June 5, 1890.

2819   HAYNES, T[HOMAS] H[ENRY]. International fishery disputes. London, [1891]. 24 p.   **MH Uk**
On disputes with the U.S.

2820   HOPKINS, J[OHN] CASTELL. The maple-leaf and the union Jack: a brief study of British connection. Toronto, 1891. 15 p.   **CaOTP**
On the annexation question. See also his "Canadian hostility to annexation," *Forum*, XVI (Nov. 1893), 325–335.

2821   HOWLAND, OLIVER AIKEN. The new empire. Reflections upon its origin and constitution and its relation to the great republic. Toronto, 1891. 608 p.   **CLU NN**
DLC has New York, 1891 ed.; Uk has London and New York, 1891 eds. See also his "Canada and international arbitration," in *Canada: an encyclopedia of the country . . .* , ed. by J. Castell Hopkins, Toronto, 1898–1900, VI, 110–118.

2822   KENT, C[LEMENT] B[OULTON] ROYLANCE. Essays in politics, wherein some of the political questions of the day are reviewed from a constitutional and historical standpoint. London, 1891. 190 p.   **CU ICU MB Uk**

Considerable comment on U.S., esp. pp. 129–139 (in Essay V, "Socialistic legislation in Anglo-Saxon communities"); passim., in essays on sovereignty and federal government.

2823   KIPLING, RUDYARD. American notes. . . . and the Bottle imp. By Robert Louis Stevenson. New York, 1891. 160 p.   **DLC Uk**

Kipling's letters during an 1889 trip from India to the U.S. appeared originally in the *Pioneer*, Allahabad, from which this 1st ed. in book form was pirated. Fully repr. in Kipling's *From sea to sea: letters of travel*, New York, 1899, 2 vols.; later eds. included several letters on U.S. written in early 20th century. Partly repr. in *Rudyard Kipling in San Francisco; being an excerpt from his "Anecdotes" as originally published in the "Pioneer" of Allahabad, India, in 1889*, San Francisco, 1926 (priv. pr.). See also "Rudyard Kipling defends 'The beauty for which Brattleboro is so greatly famous': an unpub. letter written in 1895," *Vermont Hist.*, XXXVII (1969), 94–95; D. H. Hill, "Kipling in Vermont," *Nineteenth Cent. Fict.*, VII (1952), 153–170; Earl of Berkenhead "Kipling and the Vermont feud," *Trans. Royal Soc. of Lit. of the United Kingdom*, XXX, n.s. (1960), 85–100; and Peter Conrad, *Imagining America*, Oxford, 1980, pp. 92–107, 114–129.

Reviews: (of *From sea to sea*) *Dial*, (by Hiram M. Stanley), XXVII, 16; *Nation*, LXIX, 194; New York *Times,* June 10, 1899.

2824   LEFROY, AUGUSTUS HENRY FRAZER. The British versus the American system of national government . . . Being a paper read before the Toronto branch of the Imperial federation league on Thursday, December 18th, 1890. Toronto, 1891. 42 p.   **DLC**

2825   LIBERAL-CONSERVATIVE PARTY OF CANADA. The government proposals. [N. p., 1891?]. 3 p.   **CaNSWA CSmH**

Information for the Electors, no. 15. U.S.-Canadian relations.

2826   LONGSTAFF, GEORGE BLUNDELL. Studies in statistics, social, political, and medical . . . With maps and diagrams. London, 1891. 455 p.   **DLC Uk**

On U.S., pp. 43–112.

2827   LOVETT, RICHARD. United States pictures drawn with pen and pencil. With a map and one hundred and fifty-seven engravings. [London, 1891]. 223 p.   **DLC Uk**

Spent 10 years of his boyhood in the U.S., including the Civil War period.

2828   MAGUIRE, THOMAS MILLER. The campaigns in Virginia, 1861–62. . . . Reprinted from the "Illustrated Naval and Military Magazine." London, 1891. 70 p.   **DLC Uk**

See also author's later vols.: *The campaign in Virginia, May and June, 1864*, London, 1908; *Jackson's campaigns in Virginia, 1861–2*, London, 1913.

2829   THE MODERN ODYSSEY; or, Ulysses up to date. With thirty-one illustrations in Collotype. London, 1891. 454 p.   **DLC**

Includes articles repr. from the St. James *Gazette* and the *Illust. Sporting & Dramatic News*. A tour around the world; on U.S., pp. 19–82, 98–113.

2830   NATIONAL CLUB OF TORONTO. Maple leaves; being the papers read before the National club of Toronto, at the "national evenings," during the winter 1890–1891. Toronto, [1891]. 136 p.   **NN**

2831 NORTON, GEORGE PEPLER. The new world: being a story of ten thousand miles travel on the North American continent, in the summer of 1890 . . . Reprinted from the "Watchword." Huddersfield, [1891?]. 59 p.

No locations found. Priv. pr. On U.S., pp. 1–45.

2832 PAIRPOINT, ALFRED J. Rambles in America, past and present . . . With illustrations by Miss N. M. Pairpoint. Boston, 1891. 251 p. **DLC**

See also author's *Uncle Sam and his country; or, Sketches of America in 1854–55–56, 1857*, above. Pairpoint returned to the U.S. from 1882–91.

2833 PAYEN, JAMES THOMAS. A tangled yarn: Captain James Payen's life log. Edited by T[homas] Durley. London, 1891. 222 p. **Uk**

In the U.S., 1840s, pp. 113–118.

2834 PERKINS, JAMES. A tour round the globe. Letters to the "City Press." London, 1891. 76 p. **CSmH NN**

On the U.S., pp. 31–65, 71–76.

2835 PRICE, JAMES P. Seven years of prairie life. Hereford, 1891. 88 p. **DLC**

On a Kansas farm.

2836 QUICKFALL, BOB GRANTHAM, [*pseud.?*]. Western life, and how I became a bronco buster. Founded on facts. London, [1891]. 96 p. **ICN Uk**

2837 REEVE, WYBERT. From life. (Recollections and jottings). London, 1891. 248 p. **ICU**

Uk and MB have London, 1892 eds. Repr. from the *Australasian* and other journals. In U.S., pp. 210–217.

2838 REPORT OF COMPULSORY EDUCATION in Canada, Great Britain, Germany and the United States. Toronto, 1891.

No locations found.

2839 ROBERTS, CECIL. Adrift in America; or, Work and adventure in the States . . . With an appendix by Morley Roberts. London, 1891. 254 p. **DLC Uk**

Reviews: *Sat. Rev.*, LXXIII, 455; *Spectator*, LXVIII, 754.

2840 SLADEN, DOUGLAS BROOKE WHEELTON. Twenty years of my life. New York, [1913]. 365 p. **DLC**

Uk has London, 1915 ed. In U.S., 1888–89, pp. 26–31, 46–56. For another account of this visit and one in 1890–91, see author's *My long life: anecdotes and adventures. With an introduction by Sir Philip Gibbs, K.B.E. With 32 illustrations*, London, [1939], pp. 82–105, 123–128. Sladen also edited an anthology, *Younger American poets, 1830–1890*, London, 1891.

2841 SMITH, GOLDWIN. Canada and the Canadian question. London, 1891. 325 p. **DLC Uk**

Toronto, 1971 ed., with an introd. by Carl Berger. Last 100 pp. discuss advantages of union with the U.S. See also discussion of Canadian-U.S. relations in George R. Parkin, *Imperial federation, the problems of national unity*, London, 1892, pp. 163–191.

Reviews: *Quar. Rev.*, CLXXII, 517; *Sat. Rev.* (by F. Harrison?), LXXI, 474; *Spectator*, LXVI, 479; *Week* (by G. M. Grant), May 1 & 15, 1891.

2842   SMITH, GOLDWIN. Loyalty, Aristocracy and Jingoism. Three lectures delivered before the Young men's liberal club, Toronto. Toronto, 1891. 96 p.   **DLC Uk**

On union with the U.S.

2843   STUART, [HENRY WINDSOR] VILLIERS. Adventures amidst the equatorial forests and rivers of South America; also in the West Indies and the wilds of Florida. To which is added "Jamaica revisited." London, 1891. 268 p.   **DLC Uk**

On U.S., pp. 106–151.

2844   [THOMAS, SIDNEY GILCHRIST]. Memoir and letters of Sidney Gilchrist Thomas, edited by R[obert] W[illiam] Burnie. London, 1891. 314 p.   **DLC Uk**

In U.S., Mar.–July, 1881, pp. 146–158.

2845   WIMAN, ERASTUS. Can Canada be coerced? [New York? 1891?]. 101 p.   **DLC**

Repr. from *No. Am. Rev.*, CLII (Jan. 1891), 91–102. See Sir Charles Tupper's reply, "The Wiman conspiracy unmasked," *No. Am. Rev.*, CLII (May 1891), 548–556. See also Wiman's *The greater half of the continent. Reprinted from the North American Review, January, 1888 [i.e., 1889]*, Toronto, 1889; compares U.S. with Canada, passim.

1892

2846   AUBERTIN, J[OHN] J[AMES]. Wanderings & wonderings. India, Burma, Kashmir, Ceylon, Singapore, Java, Siam, Japan, Manila, Formosa, Korea, China, Cambodia, Australia, New Zealand, Alaska, the States. London, 1892. 448 p.   **DLC Uk**

Last chap. on San Francisco

Review: *Athenaeum*, C, 810.

2847   BADEN-POWELL, BADEN FLETCHER SMYTH. In savage isles and settled lands: Malaysia, Australasia and Polynesia, 1888–1891. London, 1892. 438 p.   **DLC Uk**

"Home thru the States," pp. 392–429.

2848   BAILLIE-GROHMAN, W[ILLIAM] A[DOLPH]. Fifteen years' sport and life in the hunting grounds of western America and British Columbia . . . With a chapter by Mrs. Baillie-Grohman . . . London, 1900. 403 p.   **DLC Uk**

Covers approximately 1877–92; some portions taken from earlier work, *Camps in the Rockies*, 1882, above. See account in Norreys Jephson O'Conor, "A British hunter in frontier days," *Arizona Quar.*, V (Autumn, 1949), 242–251.

2849   [BEACH, THOMAS MILLER]. Twenty-five years in the secret service; the recollections of a spy. By Major Henri Le Caron [pseud.]. London, 1892. 311 p.   **MB**

DLC has 5th ed., Uk has 6th ed., both London, 1892. Uk and other British libraries catalog under Le Caron. Worked as a spy against Irish nationalists in the U.S., 1862–88.

2850   BRODIE, MACLEAN. Round the world with a loop thrown in. Glasgow, 1892. 140 p.   **CSmH NNC**

Priv. circ. "America," pp. 105–124.

2851 BUXTON, EDWARD NORTH. Short stalks; or, Hunting camps, north, south, east, and west. London, 1892. 405 p. **DLC Uk**

"The Rocky Mountains," pp. 73–121.

2852 COLQUHOUN, ARCHIBALD ROSS. Dan to Beersheba; work and travel in four continents. London, 1908. 348 p. **NN Uk**

In U.S. in 1892, pp. 296–319.

2853 CRAIB, ALEXANDER. America and the Americans; a narrative of a tour in the United States and Canada, with chapters on American home life. Paisley, 1892. 325 p. **DLC Uk**

2854 CRANE, WALTER. An artist's reminiscences . . . with one hundred and twenty-three illustrations by the author, and others from photographs. London, 1907. 520 p. **NN Uk**

DLC has New York, 1907 ed. In America, 1891–92, pp. 360–409. See also author's "Some impressions of America," *New Rev.*, X (Jan. & Feb. 1894), 41–54, 150–163.

2855 [DEVEREUX, HYACINTHE DALY]. Through the mill; or, Rambles in Texas. By Rux [*pseud.*]. London, 1892. 136 p. **MdBE Uk**

2856 DEWAR, JAMES CUMMING. Voyage of the Nyanza, R.N.Y.C., being the record of a three years' cruise in a schooner yacht in the Atlantic and Pacific, and her subsequent shipwreck. Edinburgh, 1892. 446 p. **DLC Uk**

On California, pp. 282–309.

Review: *Athenaeum*, CI, 82.

2857 DREDGE, JAMES. Chicago and her exposition of 1893. A stereopticon lecture recently delivered before the London Polytechnic institute . . . with a preface by the author. Chicago, 1892. 59 p. **DLC**

Uk has in *A scamper through the states: being an illustrated guide to the World's Fair of 1893. To which is added an account of the Columbian exposition, by James Dredge, etc.*, London, [1892], pp. 45–87. Cover title of original ed. reads: *The world's Columbian exposition and the city of Chicago viewed from an English standpoint, etc.* See also his later and fuller lecture, "The world's Columbian exposition of 1893," *J. Royal Soc. of Arts*, XLI (Dec. 9, 1892), 58–85; and his "Chicago and the exhibition. Extracts from paper read before the Society of arts on December 9, 1891," in [James Dredge], *Royal Commission for the Chicago exhibition, 1893. Handbook of regulations and general information. May, 1893*, London, 1893, pp. 120–133. Also see his "The Columbian Exposition of 1893," *J. Royal Soc. of Arts*, XL (Dec. 11, 1891) 65–109; "Report of a visit made in September, 1891," co-authored with Sir Henry Trueman Wood, ibid., XXXIX (Oct. 23, 1891), 887–892, and various appendices, etc., dealing with the coming fair of 1893, pp. 892–902); and his "Chicago exhibition, 1893. British section. Report of the Royal commission for the Chicago exhibition," ibid., XLII (May 18, 1894), 548–613.

2858 DREDGE, JAMES. Dedication of the Holley memorial, New York, October, 1890, with the memorial address by James Dredge. New York, 1892. 41 p. **MH NN**

2859 EARDLEY-WILMOT, [SIR] SIDNEY MAROW. The development of navies during the last half-century. London, 1892. 295 p. **NN Uk**

DLC has New York, 1892 ed. On development of U.S. Navy, pp. 270–284. Rev. ed., London, 1900, under title, *Our fleet to-day, and its development during the last half century*; omits earlier material on U.S., but discusses development of American navy in 1890s, pp. 289–308.

2860 ELMHIRST, EDWARD PENNELL ("BROOKSBY"). Fox-hound, forest, prairie. London, 1892. 584 p. **NBuG NN Uk**

On U.S., pp. 325–349, 414–422. See his comments on hunting in the U.S. in 1892, 1894, and 1895 in *The best of the fun, 1891–1897*, London, 1903, pp. 120–153, 275–280, 360–377, 420–424. See also his semi-fictionized "Hunting a Christmas dinner" [in Montana, 1884], *Fores's Sporting Notes*, III (1886–87), 229–237.

2861 ENGLISH VIEWS of American investments. American railways. [Boston? 1892?]. 38 p.
DBRE

Correspondence on U.S. railroad investments repr. from the London *Truth* and the London *Statist*.

2862 FREWEN, MORETON. Address of Moreton Frewen, of England, at the second National silver convention, held at Washington, May 26, 27 and 28, 1892. [Washington? 1892]. 8 p. **DLC**

2863 GORDON, H[ARRY] PANMURE. The land of the almighty dollar. London, [1892]. 216 p. **DLC Uk**

Reviews: *Critic*, XXI, 146; *Dial*, XIII, 190.

2864 GREY, HENRY GEORGE GREY, *3d earl*. The commercial policy of the British colonies and the McKinley tariff. By Earl Grey. London, 1892. 79 p. **DLC Uk**

2865 HICKS, *SIR* [EDWARD] SEYMOUR. Seymour Hicks: twenty-four years of an actor's life, by himself. London, 1910. 321 p. **DLC Uk**

In the U.S., 1889–92? Repr. in *Between ourselves*, London, [1930]; and in *Me and my missus*, London, [1939].

2866 HOWELL, HENRY SPENCER. An island paradise, and reminiscences of travel. Toronto, 1892. 296 p. **DLC Uk**

On U.S., pp. 108–137.

2867 IRON AND STEEL INSTITUTE. The Iron and Steel institute in America in 1890. Special volume of "Proceedings." London, [1892]. 508 p. **DLC Uk**

Uk lists under England—Iron and steel institute. Pref. signed by James Kitson, President of the Institute; contains articles by Sir Isaac Lowthian Bell, William Colquhoun, et al. Bell's article, "On the American iron trade and its progress during sixteen years," repr. Edinburgh, [1892], under title *The Iron and steel institute in America in 1890*, 208 p. (held by IEN). See also Isaac Lowthian Bell, "The iron and steel trade," *Fortnightly Rev.*, XLVII (Jan. 1, 1887), 88–104; James Kitson, "The iron and steel industries of America," *Contemp. Rev.*, LIX (May 1891), 625–641; Sir Robert Hadfield, "Notes on the Chicago exhibition," *J. Iron & Steel Inst.*, XLIV (1893), 182–192; Hilary Bauerman, "Iron and steel at the Chicago exhibition," ibid., 21–44.

2868 JENKYNS, CATHERINE CARLYON, *comp.* Hard life in the colonies, and other experiences by sea and land, now first printed. Comp. from private letters [of Arthur Carter and Gilbert Chilcott Jenkins, and Haln Killagrew Dunbar]. London, 1892. 365 p. **DLC Uk**

Chaps. on San Francisco by G. C. Jenkins and H. K. Dunbar, pp. 311–365. Half-title: The adventure series [no. 11].

2869 LAWDER, ROBERT H. Commerce between the United States & Canada; observations on reciprocity and the McKinley tariff, addressed to D. M. Irwin, esq., President of the Board of trade, Oswego, New York. [Toronto, 1892]. 22 p. **CaOTP NcD**

2870 LAWRENCE, WILLIAM JOHN. The life of Gustavus Vaughan Brooke, tragedian. Belfast, 1892. 283 p. **DLC Uk**

Brooke visited the U.S. 1851–53, pp. 118–128.

2871 [LINTON, WILLIAM JAMES]. The religion of organisation: an essay read to friends in Boston, Jan. 27, 1869. Reprinted from the Boston Radical. [New Haven, 1892]. 39 p.

DLC

Uk dates [1869]. Discussion of American democracy. Linton emigrated to U.S. in 1867; at time essay appeared he was still identified as English.

2872 LOWE, CHARLES. Four national exhibitions in London and their organiser. London, 1892. 548 p. **CSt NN Uk**

Chap. 2, "The American Exhibition, 1887," pp. 31–120; see also pp. 401–448.

2873 MCCORMICK, ROBERT S[ANDERSON], *comp*. The future trade relations between Great Britain and the United States, and the World's Columbian exposition to be held at Chicago in 1893. London, 1892. 48 p. **DLC Uk**

A compilation of magazine and newspaper articles by McCormick, Sir Henry Trueman Wood, James Dredge, et al.

2874 MACDONALD, E[DWARD] A[UGUSTUS]. Address by Ex-Ald. E. A. Macdonald, of Toronto, Ont., delivered in Fanueil Hall, Boston, Mass. Under the auspices of the No. Am. Union League, on Friday, Sept. 23rd, 1892. Toronto, 1892. 15 pp. **CaOOA**

2875 M'DOUGAL, JAMES A. My trip to America. June till August, 1891. [Paisley], 1892. 95 p. **NN**

Priv. circ. Repr. from the Paisley and Renfrewshire *Gazette*.

2876 MACGREGOR, JOHN. Toil and travel, being a true story of roving and ranging when on a voyage homeward bound round the world. London, 1892. 335 p. **DLC Uk**

Visit to U.S. while returning from work as a physician in the Bombay Army, ca. 1881, pp. 262–321.

2877 [MCLEOD, MALCOLM]. Oregon indemnity. Claim of chief factors and chief traders of the Hudson's Bay company, thereto, as partners, under treaty of 1846. [Ottawa], 1892. 57 p. **DLC**

2878 MAGUIRE, THOMAS MILLER. Synopsis of lecture on the importance of the American war of 1861–65 as a strategical study . . . on Tuesday, November 1, 1892, in the Prince Consort's and Military Society's library. London, [1892]. 6 p. **CSmH DNW**

Aldershot Military Soc. Pub. No. XL. Pages numbered 68–74.

2879 MATTERS, CHARLES HARDING. From golden gate to golden horn, and many other world wide wanderings; or 50,000 miles of travel over sea and land. Adelaide, 1892. 237 p. **AuCNL UkLRCS**

2880 [MEATH, MARY JANE (MAITLAND) BRABAZON, *countess*]. The diaries of Mary, Countess of Meath; edited by her husband [Reginald Brabazon, 12th earl of Meath]. London, [1928–29]. 2 vols. **MiU NN Uk**

Uk lists under Brabazon. Visit to U.S. in 1892, I, pp. 169–187. See *Social Aims. By the Right Hon. the Earl & the Countess of Meath*, London, [1893]; contains "Anglo-Saxon unity," [repr. from *Fortnightly Rev.*, LV (Apr. 1891), 615–622], pp. 220–237; also mentions trips to the U.S. in 1864, 1885 and 1892. See also Earl of Meath's *Memories of the nineteenth century*, London, 1923, pp. 83–87, 327; his "A glimpse of America," *Time*, XV (Aug. 1886), 148–154; and his "A Britisher's impressions of America and Australia," *Nineteenth Cent.*, XXXIII (Mar. 1893), 493–514.

2881 MENZIES, WILLIAM JOHN. America as a field for investment. A lecture delivered to the Chartered accountants students' society, February 18, 1892. Edinburgh, 1892. 24 p.
DLC Uk

2882 MORRIS, FELIX. Reminiscences. New York, [1892?]. 176 p. **DLC**

Describes theatrical experiences in the U.S., over 14 years.

2883 NORTH, MARIANNE. Recollections of a happy life; being the autobiography of Marianne North. Edited by her sister, Mrs. John Addington Symonds. London, 1892. 2 vols. **CLU NN Uk**

Describes visits to the U.S. in 1871 and 1875, I, pp. 39–79, 200–212. Abridged version under title *A vision of Eden: the life and work of Marianne North*, New York, 1980, with pref. by J. P. M. Brenan, foreword by Anthony Huxley, and biographical note by Brenda E. Moon.

Review: *Spectator*, LXVIII, 306.

2884 [SAIL, C. R.]. Farthest east, and south and west; notes of a journey home through Japan, Australasia and America by an Anglo-Indian globe-trotter. London, 1892. 343 p.
DLC Uk

Last 2 chaps. on the U.S.

Review: *Athenaeum*, XCIX, 468.

2885 SANTLEY, *SIR* CHARLES. Student and singer; the reminiscences of Charles Santley. London, 1892. 327 p. **CSt MH Uk**

DLC has New York, 1892 ed., 358 p. Visited the U.S. several times, 1871 onward. See also account in author's *Reminiscences of my life*, London, 1909.

2886 SMITH, GOLDWIN. The moral crusader, William Lloyd Garrison; a biographical essay founded on "The story of Garrison's life told by his children." New York, 1892. 200 p.
DLC Uk

See also Smith's review of the first 2 vols. of *William Lloyd Garrison [1805–1849]: the story of his life told by his children*, New York, 1885–89, in *Macmillan's Mag.* LIII (Mar. 1886), 321–331.

2887 SMITH, WILLIAM, *F.S.A.S.* A Yorkshireman's trip to the United States and Canada. London, 1892. 317 p. **DLC Uk**

2888 STEVENSON, JAMES, [*of Quebec*]. The war of 1812 in connection with the army bill act. [Montreal, 1892?]. 79 p. **DLC**

Pref. dated Aug. 10, 1892. Continues the discussion begun in his 1876 volume, *The currency of Canada after the capitulation.*

2889   STEVENSON, ROBERT LOUIS. Across the plains with other memories and essays. London, 1892. 317 p.   **DLC Uk**

Tokyo, 1925 ed., with introd. and notes by Walter Sherard Vinis and Eishire Hori; Hillsboro, Calif., 1950 ill. ed. with an introd. note by Oscar Lewis; also in Cambridge, Mass., 1966 ed., *From Scotland to Silverado: comprising the Amateur emigrant: "From the Clyde to Sandy Hook" and "Across the Plains," The Silverado squatters, & Four essays on California*, ed. by James D. Hart. A portion repr. under the title, *Robert Louis Stevenson's story of Monterey. The old Pacific capital*, San Francisco, [1944]. Contains repr. of the essays: "Across the plains. Leaves from the notebook of an emigrant between New York and San Francisco," *Longman's Mag.*, II (July & Aug. 1883), 285–304, 372–386; "The old Pacific capital, the woods and the Pacific," *Fraser's Mag.*, XXII (Nov. 1880), 647–657, also in *Library Mag.*, VI (1880), 179–190. See the following other articles by Stevenson: "San Carlos day. An article in a California newspaper. By Robert Louis Stevenson. With an introduction by George R. Stewart, Jr.," *Scribner's Mag.*, LXVIII (Aug. 1920), 209–211 (originally printed in the Monterey *Californian* of Nov. 11, 1879); "A modern cosmopolis," *Mag. of Art*, VI (May 1883), 272–276 (repr. in *Works*, Edinburgh, 1895 under title "The new Pacific capital: San Francisco"); "American rights and wrongs," (letter dated Mar. 15, 1886), *Academy*, XXIX (Mar. 20, 1886), 203.

See also the following on Stevenson and America: Arthur S. Acton, "Robert Louis Stevenson and Jules Simoneau—A California friendship," *Mich. Alumni Quar. Rev.*, LVII (May 26, 1951), 221–225; David Anderson, *The enchanted galleon*, [San Francisco], 1930, story of the erection in San Francisco in 1897 of the first Stevenson memorial; Henry Meade Bland, *Stevenson's California*, San Jose, Calif., [1924]; Cornelius Beach Bradley, "Stevenson and California," *Univ. of Calif. Chronicle*, XI (Apr. 1909), 114–121 (repr. as pamphlet, [Berkeley, 1909]); Josephine Mildred Blanch, *The story of a friendship. Robert Louis Stevenson and Jules Simoneau: A Californian reminiscence of Robert Louis Stevenson*, [n.p., 1921]; A. A. Brown, *A friendship: Robert Louis Stevenson—Jules Simoneau*, [San Francisco, 1911]; Dr. Lawrason Brown, "Stevenson and Saranac," *First editions of the works of Robert Louis Stevenson*, New York, 1915, pp. xi–xxiii (repr. as pamphlet, [n.p., n.d.]; Stephen Chalmers, *The Penny piper of Saranac: an episode in Stevenson's life*, Boston, 1916, an essay written in collaboration with Edward Livingston Trudeau and first pub. in *Outlook*, LII (Oct. 1912), 314–320.

See also Joseph Smeaton Chase, "Stevenson and Monterey thirty years after," *Chambers's J.*, 7th ser. II, pt. 16 (March 16, 1912), 241–243; Will M. Clemens, "Stevenson at the Golden gate," *Natl. Mag.*, XII (July 1900), 296–299; Ada Hilton Davies, "Poet's tree . . . which keeps faithful vigil over the 'Old Robert Louis Stevenson house'," *Sunset*, LX (Feb. 1928), 37, 79; William Henry Duncan, Jr., "Stevenson's second visit to America," *Bookman*, X (Jan. 1900), 454–464; Charlotte Eaton, *A last memory of Robert Louis Stevenson*, New York, 1916, and *Stevenson at Manasquan*, Chicago, 1921; Charlton Lawrence Edholm, "In the shadow of the Stevenson monument," *Overland Monthly*, XLVI (Oct. 1905), 291–297; Betty Harcourt, "The unveiling of the Robert Louis Stevenson memorial," ibid., XLV (Mar. 1905), 235–239; Brother Henry, "California in Robert Louis Stevenson," *Moraga Quar.*, St. Mary's College, San Francisco, Fall, 1931, pp. 51–62; Haywood H. Hunt, *The San Francisco of Robert Louis Stevenson, with an introductory on the new city of enchantment showing how the phoenix of romantic past hatched an American eagle from her burned nest*, San Francisco, 1923, priv. pr., (includes excerpt from Stevenson and introd. by Perry Epsten); Anne Roller Issler, *Happier for his presence; San Francisco and Robert Louis Stevenson*, Stanford, Calif., [1949]; George Wharton

James, "Robert Louis Stevenson in California," *Natl. Mag.*, XXXIV (Dec. 1911), 389–405; Robin Lampson, "A casual stroll on Telegraph Hill: Robert Louis Stevenson's first visit to San Francisco in the winter of 1879–80 . . . ," *Natl. Motorist* (San Francisco), Jan. 1939, 5–6, 28.

See also Allan Nevins, "RLS at the Golden gate," *Sat. Rev. Lit.*, XXXII (Sept. 17, 1949), 18; Mrs. Katherine Durham Osbourne, *Robert Louis Stevenson in California*, Chicago, 1911, and "Robert Louis Stevenson in San Francisco," *Out West*, VI, n.s. (July–Aug. 1913), 3–15; The Rambler, [*pseud.*], (Notes concerning the Stevenson monument in San Francisco), *Book Buyer* XV (Jan. 1898), 643–646; " Robert Louis Stevenson and Saranac," *Bookman*, XLII (Oct. 1915), 116; Mrs. Nellie Van de Grift Sanchey, "In California with Robert Louis Stevenson," *Scribner's Mag.*, LX (Oct. 1916), 467–481; H. Scheffauer, "Stevenson and Simoneau," *Cornhill Mag.*, XXXVII, n.s. (Oct. 1909), 459–465; "Stevenson in California," *Bookman*, XXXV (Mar. 1912), 14–16; "Stevenson's Trudeau," ibid., XLII (Feb. 1916), 632–635; Charles Warren Stoddard, "Stevenson's Monterey," *Natl. Mag.*, XXIII (Dec. 1905), 246–259; Thomas Russell Sullivan, "Robert Louis Stevenson at Saranac," *Scribner's Mag.*, LXII (Aug. 1917), 242–246; *To remember R.L.S. November 13th, 1932*, Clare Shield, Camino de Lago Press, 10 copies pr.; Edward Livingstone Trudeau, *An autobiography*, New York, 1916, pp. 225–230; Julia Scott Vrooman, "Stevenson in San Francisco," *Arena*, XXXVIII (Nov. 1907), 526–529, and "The strange case of Robert Louis Stevenson and Jules Simoneau," *Century Mag.*, L, n.s. (July 1906), 343–350; L.E.W., "San Francisco letter. The Stevenson foundation," *Lit. World*, XXVIII (Dec. 11, 1897), 458; Rufus Rockwell Wilson, "Foreign authors in America. Part V," *Bookman,* XIII (June 1901), 368–378.

Reviews: *Academy* (by R. LeGallienne), XLI, 462 (repr. in his *Retrospective reviews: a literary log*, London, 1896); *Argonaut*, XXX, 8; *Athenaeum* (Apr. 23, 1892), 533; *Book Buyer*, IX, 53; *Critic*, XX, 312; *Dial*, XIII, 83; *Gentleman's Mag.*, CCLXII, 638; *Lit. World*, XLV (n.s.), 356; *Nation* (N.Y.), LV, 145; *Natl. Observer*, VII (n.s.), 590; *Overland Monthly*, (by J. W. Tate), XXII (n.s.), 300; *Speaker*, V, 657; *Spectator*, LXIX, 99; *Sat. Rev.*, LXXIII, 630. For brief quotes from reviews, and citations for additional comment on *Across the plains*, see Frederick John Bethke, *Three Victorian travel writers: an annotated bibliography of criticism on Mrs. Frances Milton Trollope, Samuel Butler, and Robert Louis Stevenson*, Boston, 1977, pp. 110–113.

2890   SYNGE, GEORGINA M. A ride through Wonderland. London, 1892. 166 p.   **DLC Uk**

Describes a visit to Yellowstone.

Review: *Sat. Rev.*, LXXIV, 490.

2891   WATSON, WILLIAM, *of Skelmorlie*. The adventures of a blockade runner; or, Trade in time of war. London, 1892. 324 p.   **DLC Uk**

Describes adventures during the Civil War.

Review: *Sat. Rev.*, LXXIV, 147.

2892   WETMORE, C. W. Burning Canadian questions. Inter-provincial communication, Atlantic ports, development of natural resources, labor and capital, immigration, and prohibition. St. John, 1892.   **CaOTP**

CaOTP copy incomplete. On U.S.-Canada trade, annexation, comparisons between U.S. and Canada, passim.

2893   WILKINS, WILLIAM HENRY. The alien invasion . . . with an introductory note by the Right Reverend the Bishop of Bedford. London, 1892. 192 p.   **DLC Uk**

One of a series, *Social questions of today*, ed. by H. de B. Gibbons, M.A. Describes the immigration problems of the U.S., pp. 127–135 [repr. of an article from *Nineteenth Cent.,* XXX (Oct. 1891), 583–595].

2894   WILLIAMSON, ANDREW, *of Edinburgh*. Free trade versus protection in the United States. Edinburgh, 1892. 35 p.   **Uk**

2895   WIMAN, ERASTUS. Closest trade relations between the United States and Canada: points made in a maritime province tour. Toronto, 1892. 40 p.   **DLC**

1893

2896   ALL THE WORLD AT THE FAIR; being representatives of thiry-seven nationalities in gala costume. London, [1893].

Uk copy destroyed; no other locations found.

2897   ARTISAN EXPEDITION TO THE WORLD'S FAIR, Chicago, organised by the Dundee Courier and the Dundee Weekly News. A tour of observation, to get "Information regarding the conditions of the American wage-earners, how they live, what kind of houses they have, what hours they work, what leisure they enjoy, what kind of food they get, &c."— (Mr. D. C. Thomson's letter, 27th April). Trip to the Pacific, etc. Dundee, 1893. 168 p.

    CSmH ICJ

Cover title, "British artisan expedition to America." Repr. of articles from the Dundee *Courier* and the Dundee *Weekly News*. See also "Chicago," *Quar. Rev.*, CLXXVII (Oct. 1893), 297–328.

2898   BAUMANN, ARTHUR ANTHONY. Betterment: being the law of special assessment for benefits in America, with some observations on its adoption by the London county council. London, 1893. 110 p.   **ICU NIC Uk**

See also author's "Note on betterment in America," in his *Betterment, worsement, and recoupment*, London, 1894, pp. 104–116.

2899   BERESFORD, WALTER S. From wealth and happiness to misery and the penitentiary. Kramer, Ga., 1893. 338 p.   **DLC**

Visited the U.S. 3 times, pp. 102–107, 185–186, 204–330; jailed for illegal financial transactions in Georgia.

2900   BESANT, [*SIR*] WALTER. As we are and as we may be. London, 1903. 314 p.   **DLC Uk**

In U.S. in 1893, pp. 203–245. Other accounts of his visit in his *Autobiography . . . With a prefatory note by S. Squire Sprigge*, New York, 1902, pp. 265–272; and in his "Notes from America," *Cosmopolitan Mag.*, XVI (Nov. & Dec. 1893), 64–72, 233–240. See also his "First impressions of Chicago World fair," ibid., XV (Sept. 1893), 528–539; and J[ulian] Hawthorne's "Foreign folk at the Chicago world fair," ibid., 567–576. Also see Besant's satire of American life in his novel (with James Rice), *The golden butterfly*, London, 1876.

2901 BOLITHO, [HENRY] HECTOR. Marie Tempest [by] Hector Bolitho. London, [1936]. 345 p. **DLC Uk**

Dame Mary Susan Gordon Lennox, afterwards Broume, calling herself Marie Tempest, toured the U.S. 1890–93; many references, passim, and verbatim quotes, especially chaps. 2–4.

2902 BURDETT, *SIR* HENRY CHARLES. Hospitals and asylums of the world: their origin, history, construction, administration, management, and legislation; with plans of the chief medical institutions accurately drawn to a uniform scale, in addition to those of all the hospitals of London in the jubilee year of Queen Victoria's reign. London, 1891–93. 4 vols. **DLC Uk**

On U.S., I, pp. 109–110, 123–126, 523–542, 620–622; III, 257–262, 707–720, 750–758, 841–843; IV, 28–30. 66–72; see indexes for descriptions of individual American hospitals.

2903 BURGESS, *REV*. EDWIN H. For Canada and the old flag . . . with a letter of introduction by Sir Charles Tupper . . . High commissioner for Canada. Halifax, 1893. 46 p. **CaOTP**

Attacks annexationists.

2904 CALIFORNIA: ITS LIFE and climate, with an account of the prospects of fruit-growing; being a guide to the seeker after health and fortune. By an Englishman. London, [1893]. 51 p. **Uk**

2905 CAMPBELL, JAMES B. For Canada; transportation the problem. By a grain dealer. Montreal, 1893. 98 p. **MH NN**

Comparison of Canada with the U.S.

2906 CARR, LASCELLES. Yankee land and the Yankees, being notes of a journey to and from the World's fair. Cardiff, 1893. 116 p. **NN**

2907 CATLING, THOMAS. My life's pilgrimage. London, 1911. 384 p. **DLC Uk**

In U.S., 1893, pp. 212–224.

2908 CHARLTON, JOHN. Speech on Canada's tariff. Trade relations with the United States, 22nd February, 1893. [Ottawa, 1893]. 23 p. **MH**

2909 [COMMITTEE OF THE COUNTY OF LEEDS]. A very fair comparison of the relative condition of farmers in New York state and the province of Ontario, made by an influential and impartial committee of the county of Leeds. [Ontario? 1893]. 15 p. **CaOTP NN**

CaOTP gives [Toronto? 1892?], lists under title.

2910 CONTINENTAL UNION ASSOCIATION OF ONTARIO. Continental Union: a short study of its economic side . . . Issued by the Continental Union Association of Ontario, May, 1893. Toronto, 1893. 52 p. **DLC**

2911 COOK, THOMAS *and son*. The world's fair, at Chicago, 1893. Information for travellers. London, [1893]. 90 p. **DLC**

2912 CROSS, J[OHN] W[ALTER]. Impressions of Dante and of the New world, with a few words on bimetallism. Edinburgh, 1893. 314 p. **DLC Uk**

Includes the following repr. articles: "The new world," *Nineteenth Cent.*, XXIX (March 1891), 468–476; "On the extension of railways in America," *Fraser's Mag.*, VII, n.s. (June 1873), 702–712; "The future of agricultural labourers' emigration," ibid., IX, n.s. (Jan. 1874), 100–111; "American rediviva," *Macmillan's Mag.*, XXXIX (Jan. 1879), 220–231; "Social New York," ibid., XXVI (June 1872), 117–125; and "The Future of food," *Contemp. Rev.*, LIV (Dec. 1888), 870.

2913   CROWE, EYRE. With Thackeray in America. London, 1893. 179 p.   **ICRL Uk**

Accompanied Thackeray during his 6-month tour in 1852–53; includes 117 drawings. See also *Thackeray's letters to an American family*, New York, 1904, ed. by Lucy W. Baxter and including drawings by Thackery, with many of the letters written during the American tour, pp. 17–54. See also James Grant Wilson, *Thackeray in the United States, 1852–3, 1855–6*, New York, 1905; and "Dickens and Thackeray in America," *N.Y. State Hist. Soc. Quar.*, LXII (July 1978), 219–237.

2914   THE CUNARD ROYAL MAIL twin-screw steamers, "Campania" and "Lucania," and The world's Columbian Exposition, 1893. London, [1893]. 134 p.   **ICJ NNC Uk**

"The world's Columbian exposition" repr. from *Engineering*, LV, (April 21, 1893), 463–596 (portion on Exposition, pp. 503–596). The 1893 vols. of *Engineering* (LV and LVI) are filled with various accounts of the Exposition; see the index for LVI and the 26 items entitled "Notes from the United States."

2915   DAVID, MICHAEL. Father Ignatius [Joseph Leycester Lyne] in America. By Father Michael, O.S.B., with a preface by Ernest A. Farnol. London, 1893. 373 p.   **DLC Uk**

Uk lists under Michael. Introd. signed: Michael David, O.S.B. Father Ignatius toured the U.S. and Canada, 1890–91.

2916   DE STACPOOLE, [GEORGE STACPOOLE], *Duke*. Irish and other memories. London, 1922. 275 p.   **DLC Uk**

In U.S., 1893, pp. 106–116.

2917   DOUGLAS, JAMES. Facts and reflections bearing on annexation, independence, and imperial federation, by James Douglas, a Canadian residing in the United States. [Ottawa, 1893?]. 72 p.   **DLC**

Uk has New York, 1894 "amplification": *Canadian independence, annexation and British imperial federation*, 114 p. See the following articles by Douglas, who was long resident in the U.S. although he never became a citizen: "The centennial exhibition," *Canadian Monthly & Natl. Rev.*, IX (June 1876), 535–543; "The Philadelphia exhibition; the Australian colonies," ibid., X (Sept. 1876), 239–247; "The copper resources of the United States," *J. Royal Soc. of Arts*, XLI (Dec. 2, 1892), 39–54. See also the account of Douglas in Arizona in H. H. Langton, *James Douglas: a memoir*, Toronto, 1940, pp. 53–57.

2918   DOWLING, EDWARD. Australia and America in 1892: a contrast. Sydney, 1893. 172 p.
            DLC Uk

At head of title: Published by authority of the New South Wales commissioners for the World's Columbian exposition, Chicago, 1893.

2919   F., T. B. Reminiscences of a stampede through the U.S. to the World's Fair and Canada. London, 1893.   **IreDNL MnHi**

Priv. circ.; variant paging. Possibly written by Thomas Buxton Foreman.

2920   FANSHAWE, EVELYN LEIGHTON. Liquor legislation in the United States and Canada. Report of a non-partisan inquiry on the spot into the laws and their operation, undertaken at the request of W. Rathbone, M.P. London, [1893]. 432 p.   **DLC Uk**

2921   FREWEN, MORETON. Silver in the Fifty-third Congress. London, 1893. 24 p.
            DLC UkLU-C

Repr. from the *Natl. Rev.*, XXII (Dec. 1893), pp. 542–557. See also author's *The appreciation of gold and depreciation of silver. An address. . . . before the members of the Bristol incorporated Chamber of commerce and shipping, April, 1887*, Bristol, [1887]; and his "The American elections of 1896," *Natl. Rev.*, XXVIII (Nov. 1896), 400–405.

2922 FRUIT VALE IRRIGATION COLONY, Rio Puerco Valley, New Mexico, U.S.A. Head office:—34, Victoria Street, Westminster, London, S.W. [London, 1893]. 32 p.   **Uk**

Prospectus issued by the London Land Co.

2923 GILLMORE, PARKER ("UBIQUE"). Leaves from a sportsman's diary. London, 1893. 341 p.   **NN Uk**

DLC has microfilm. Contains several chaps. on U.S.: pp. 58–61, 92–137, 156–161, 168–171, 208–212, 299–301, 313–317, 328–330.

2924 HARVEY, *SIR* JOHN MARTIN-. The autobiography of Sir John Martin-Harvey. London, [1933]. 563 p.   **DLC Uk**

2925 HENDERSON, *LIEUT. COL.* GEORGE FRANCIS ROBERT. The battle of Gettysburg, July 1st, 2nd, 3rd, 1863. London, 1893. 20 p.   **CSmH WHi**

Repr. in Neill Malcolm, ed., *The science of war*, London, 1905, pp. 280–306, and Jay Luvaas, ed., *The Civil War: a soldier's view; a collection of Civil War writings by Col. G.F.R. Henderson*, Chicago, 1958, pp. 225–253. The following lectures also printed in both collections: "First lecture on the American civil war, 1861–65. The composition, organization, system, and tactics of the federal and confederate armies," delivered Feb. 9, 1892 (Malcolm, pp. 230–252; Luvaas, pp. 174–197); "Second lecture on the American civil war—a resume of some of the principal events of the war, illustrative of the strategy and tactics of the belligerents," delivered Feb. 16, 1892 (Malcolm, pp. 252–279; Luvaas, pp. 197–224); and "The campaign in the wilderness of Virginia, 1894," delivered Jan. 24, 1894 (Malcolm, pp. 307–357; Luvaas, pp. 254–283; also pub. separately, London, 1908).

2926 HENDERSON, J. GRAHAM. A Scotsman at the World's fair. Hawick, [1893]. 32 p.   **Uk**

2927 HOLE, JAMES. National railways: an argument for state purchase. London, 1893. 385 p.   **CLU DL NN Uk**

DLC has 2d ed., with appendix, London, 1895, 408 p. Chap. 2, "American experience," pp. 12–56; other comment, passim.

2928 LEIGH, J[AMES] W[ENTWORTH, *Dean of Hereford*]. Other days . . . With a preface by Owen Wister. London, [1921]. 255 p.   **CU NN Uk**

Contains accounts of several visits to the U.S., 1869–93, pp. 89–118, 126–191, 221. Leigh was Fanny Kemble's son-in-law.

2929 MACCULLY, RICHARD. The Brotherhood of the new life and Thomas Lake Harris; a history and exposition based upon their printed works and upon other public documents. Glasgow, 1893. 192 p.   **NNC NNUT UkCU**

2930 MACDONELL, JOHN ALEXANDER. Sketches illustrating the early settlement and history of Glengarry in Canada, relating principally to the revolutionary war of 1775–83, the war of 1812–14 and the rebellion of 1837–8, and the services of the King's royal regiment of New York, the 84th or Royal Highland emigrant regiment, the Royal Canadian volunteer regiment or foot, the Glengarry fencible or British Highland regiment, the Glengary light infantry regiment, and the Glengarry militia. Montreal, 1893. 337 p.   **DLC**

On Canadian-U.S. difficulties of 1837–38, pp. 275–321.

2931 MOORE, DAVID RICHARD. Currents and counter-currents in Canadian politics! Or, a brief enquiry into certain factors which to day dominate political life in Canada. Fredericton, N.B., 1893. 21 p.   **CaOTU**

Includes discussion of relations with the U.S., Catholic schools in the U.S., etc.

2932   [MUNRO, FRANK]. Under which flag? The great question for Canada. Also a brief consideration of imperial federation, and a view of naturalization as an immorality. By a Canadian in "the States." Providence, R.I., 1893. 31 p.   **DLC Uk**

Uk lists by title under Canada-Appendix.

2933   NAYLOR, ROBERT ANDERTON. Across the Atlantic. Westminster [London, 1893]. 305 p.   **DLC**

Uk has London, [1896] ed. Pub. by the Roxburghe Press; pref. dated 1893. Records a visit of members of the Arts Society to Chicago for the 1893 world's fair.

2934   PEARSON, CHARLES HENRY. National life and character, a forecast. London, 1893. 357 p.   **DLC Uk**

Appendix B: "Comparative growths of white and black population in the United States."

2935   RHODES, THOMAS. To the other side. London, 1893. 106 p.   **DLC**

2936   ROSS, ALEXANDER MILTON. Memoirs of a reformer. (1832–1892). Toronto, 1893. 271 p.   **DLC**

Almost entirely on U.S. experiences as an ardent abolitionist. See also Judson Newman Smith, *A brief sketch of the life and labours of Alexander Milton Ross, philanthropist and scientist*, Toronto, 1892.

2937   SCOTTISH-AMERICAN SOLDIER'S MONUMENT COMMITTEE. The Lincoln monument, in memory of Scottish-American soldiers, unveiled in Edinburgh, Aug. 21, 1893. Edinburgh, 1893. 48 p.   **DLC**

DLC has also expanded 97 p. ed., Edinburgh, 1893.

2938   SENIOR, WILLIAM ("RED SPINNER"). Lines in pleasant places, being the aftermath of an old angler. London, [1920]. 276 p.   **DLC Uk**

Describes fishing experiences in the U.S., in 1893, pp. 251–267. See also his articles written under the name of "Red Spinner" in the *Field*: LXXXI (May 1893), "The angler at the world's fair," 652, "The angler in America," 692, "The angler at Chicago," 730, "Fishery notes from Chicago," 770; LXXXII (July–Aug. 1893), "Angling notes from Chicago," 62, "Further notes from Chicago," 264.

2939   S[HEPPARD], J[OHN] F[REDERICK]. A trip across the Atlantic, a tour in the States, and a visit to the World's fair. Southampton, 1893. 123 p.   **DLC Uk**

2940   SHONFIELD, PETER, *Comp.* The Columbian exposition and World's fair. Chicago, 1893. Origin, history and progress of Chicago; guide book to the exhibition; illustrations of the principal buildings; advantages to Canada. [Montreal, 1893].   **MH**

2941   SMITH, GOLDWIN. The United States; an outline of political history, 1492–1871. London, 1893. 312 p.   **DLC Uk**

See attack by John Cussons, *United States "history" as the Yankee makes and takes it, by a Confederate soldier*, 3d ed., Glen Allen, Va., 1900; also printed as 1st chap. in his *A glance at current American history*, Glen Allen, Va., 1897. See Woodrow Wilson's "Mr. Goldwin Smith's 'Views' on our political history," *Forum*, XVI (Dec. 1893), 489–499. See also Smith's "The situation at Washington," *Nineteenth Cent.*, XXXIV (July, 1893), 131–144; and his "Imperialism in the United States," *Contemp. Rev.*, LXXV (May 1899), 620–628. Also see R. Craig Brown, "Goldwin Smith and anti-imperialism," *Canadian Hist. Rev.*, XL (1962), 93–105, on Smith's relations with anti-imperialists in the U.S., Canada and Great Britain during the Spanish-American and South African wars.

Review: *Critic*, XX, n.s., 191.

2942   STEWART, GEORGE. Essays from reviews. Quebec, 1892–93. 2 vols.   **MH**

Uk has only "second series", vol. II, 1893. Various libraries hold either vol. In vol. I see: "James Russell Lowell," pp. 69–107 (from *Arena* [Boston], 1891); "John Greenleaf Whittier," pp. 139–171 *(Arena*, Dec. 1891). In vol II, see: "Emerson the thinker," pp. 43–92 *(Scottish. Rev.*, Apr. 1888); "Adirondack Murray," pp. 93–122 *(Belford's Monthly*, March 1891).

2943   SWINGLEHURST, HENRY. Silver mines and incidents of travel. Letters and notes on sea and land. Kendal, 1893. 314 p.   **CLU CtY MH**

On U.S., pp. 97–105, 304–308.

2944   THOMPSON, [*MRS.*] JANE SMEAL [(HENDERSON)] and HELEN G. THOMPSON. Silvanus Phillips Thompson, his life and letters. London, [1920]. 372 p.   **DLC Uk**

Silvanus Thompson in U.S., 1884, and 1893, pp. 118–123. See also his "Practical electrical problems at Chicago," *J. Royal Soc. of Arts*, XLI (May 5, 1893), 620–626; "Utilizing Niagara," *Sat. Rev.*, LX (Aug. 3, 1895), 134–135.

2945   THOMPSON, *SIR* JOHN. Public affairs. Sir John Thompson's Toronto address. The policy of the administration on trade, the tariff, reciprocity, and provincial rights. Mr. Foster's views on the growth of our trade, the soundness of our finance, and the dealing of our country. [Toronto, 1893?]. 16 p.   **CaOOA**

On U.S., passim.

2946   TRUMBULL, M[ATTHEW] M[ARK]. Earl Grey on reciprocity and civil service reform. With comments by Gen. M. M. Trumbull. Chicago, 1893. 27 p.   **MH Uk**

Contains 2 letters from Grey to Trumbull (an American) on the 1892 U.S. presidential election.

2947   USEFUL NOTICES FOR VISITORS to the Chicago Columbian exposition. London, [1893]. 32 p.

Uk copy missing; no other locations found.

2948   [VAUGHAN-HUGHES, JAMES]. Seventy years of life in the Victorian era; embracing a travelling record in Australia, New Zealand, and America, &c. By a physician. London, 1893. 283 p.   **DLC Uk**

DLC lists under title, Uk under Physician; CSmH gives authorship. 10 chaps. are devoted to an account of a transcontinental tour from San Francisco to New York, pp. 222–283.

2949   WILDE, JANE FRANCESCA ELGEE. Social studies. London, 1893. 344 p.   **DLC Uk**

On American women, pp. 123–153.

2950   WIMAN, ERASTUS. Chances of success: episodes and observations in the life of a busy man. New York, 1893. 359 p.   **DLC**

On U.S.

2951   WISHART, ANDREW. The Behring sea question: the arbitration treaty and the award. With a map. Edinburgh, [1893]. 54 p.   **DLC Uk**

2952   WORLD'S FAIR, Chicago, 1893: souvenir. London, 1893. 23 p.   **UkENL**

Colored illustrations and short accounts of principal halls and exhibits.

2953 YOUMANS, *MRS*. LETITIA (CREIGHTON). Campaign echoes. The autobiography of Mrs. Letitia Youmans, the pioneer of the white ribbon movement in Canada. Written by request of the Provincial woman's Christian temperance union of Ontario. Introduction by Miss Frances E. Willard. Endorsed by Lady Henry Somerset. Toronto, [1893]. 311 p.

MiU MnHi OCl

DLC has 2d ed., also Toronto, [1893]. Visited the U.S. in 1874, pp. 96–104, 141–144; in 1878, 212–219; in 1879, 227–246; in 1886, 279–284, 301–309.

1894

2954 AITKEN, JAMES. A run through the States: supplementary to From the Clyde to California. Greenock, [1894]. 74 p. **CSmH**

CSmH describes as a "rare supplement," bound together with Aitken's *From the Clyde to California*, 1882, above. Pref. dated Dec. 1894. Described a visit to the U.S. in 1892.

2955 BARNES, JOHN H. Forty years on the stage; others (principally) and myself. London, 1914. 320 p. **DLC Uk**

Includes accounts of many visits to the U.S., 1874–1894.

2956 BEGG, ALEXANDER. History of British Columbia from its earliest discovery to the present time. Toronto, 1894. 568 p. **DLC Uk**

Comment on Canadian-American relations, passim.

2957 BRAMWELL, A[MY] B[LANCHE] and H. MILLICENT HUGHES. The training of teachers in the United States of America. London, 1894. 198 p. **DLC Uk**

Review: *J. Educ.*, XXVI, 683.

2958 BRINE, LINDESAY. Travels amongst American Indians, their ancient earth works and temples; including a journey in Guatemala, Mexico, and Yucatan, and a visit to the ruins of Patinamit, Utatlan, Palenque and Uxmal. London, 1894. 429 p. **DLC Uk**

On U.S., pp. 1–193.

2959 BURSTALL, SARA ANNIE. The education of girls in the United States. London, 1894. 204 p. **CU ICJ MB NN Uk**

Review: *J. Educ.*, XXVII, 103.

2960 DALE, JOHN. Round the world by doctors' orders. Being a narrative of a year's travel in Japan, Ceylon, Australia, China, New Zealand, Canada, the United States, etc. etc. London, 1894. 350 p. **DLC Uk**

"California," pp. 249–270.

Review: *Athenaeum*, CIII, 210.

2961 DERBY, EDWARD HENRY STANLEY, *15th earl*. Speeches and addresses . . . selected and edited by Sir T. H. Sanderson and E. S. Roscoe. With a prefatory memoir by W. E. H. Lecky. London, 1894. 2 vols. **DLC Uk**

Vol. II, pp. 103–112: "Free trade—Protection in the colonies— Protection in the United States—Commercial treaties—The policy of Cobden."

2962 DEWAR, THOMAS ROBERT, *1st baron.* A ramble round the globe. London, 1894. 316 p. **DLC Uk**

Tour across U.S., pp. 1–110.

2963 DOYLE, *SIR* ARTHUR CONAN. Memories and adventures. London, 1924. 410 p. **DLC Uk**

In U.S. in 1894, pp. 116–119; see accounts of this visit in: Hesketh Pearson, *Conan Doyle, his life and art*, London, [1943], pp. 109–112; John Dickson Carr, *The life of Sir Arthur Conan Doyle*, London, [1949]; and Charles Higham, *The adventures of Conan Doyle: the life of the creator of Sherlock Holmes*, New York, 1976, pp. 133–138, 240–243, 276–290, 296–299, and passim. For Doyle's accounts of later visits, see his *Our American adventure*, London, 1923, and *Our second American adventure*, Boston, 1923.

2964 DREDGE, JAMES. A record of the transportation exhibits at the World's Columbian Exposition of 1893. London, 1894. 779 p. **DLC Uk**

Partly repr. from *Engineering.*

Review: *Casier's Engineering Monthly* (By W. H. Wiley), I, 284.

2965 DUNN, [SARA H.] *MRS.* ARCHIBALD. The world's highway, with some first impressions whilst journeying along it. London, 1894. 376 p. **DLC Uk**

In U.S. and Canada in 1893, pp. 259–376.

Review: *Sat. Rev.*, LXXVIII, 217.

2966 EDGAR, [*SIR*] J[AMES] D[AVID]. Speech on arbitration between Great Britain and the United States. Ottawa, 21st May, 1894. [Ottawa, 1894]. 5 p. **MH**

2967 [EGERTON, ALICE ANNE (GRAHAM-MONTGOMERY) EGERTON, *countess*]. Glimpses of four continents: letters written during a tour of Australia, New Zealand, & North America, in 1893. By the Duchess of Buckingham & Chandos. London, 1894. 291 p. **DLC Uk**

Uk lists under Grenville, Alice Anne Temple-Nugent-Brydges Chandos. Last 2 letters on the U.S.

2968 FITZ GIBBON, MARY AGNES. A veteran of 1812: the life of James Fitz Gibbon. London, 1894. 347 p. **NcD Uk**

DLC has Toronto, 1894 ed. Account of Fitz Gibbon's activities in the War of 1812, 1837–38, etc. He lived in Canada 1801–46, then moved to England.

2969 THE GEOGRAPHY OF NORTH AMERICA: a brief hand book for students. London, 1894 [1893]. 38 p. **Uk**

2970 G[RATWICKE], G. F. Atlantic and American notes, by G. F. G. [Exeter? 1894?]. **DLC**

DLC has microfilm. Repr. from the Devon and Exeter *Daily Gazette*, Nov. 1894.

2971 [GREGORY, *SIR* WILLIAM HENRY]. Sir William Gregory, K.C.M.G., formerly member of Parliament and sometime Governor of Ceylon. An autobiography. Ed. by Lady [Isabella Augusta] Gregory. London, 1894. 407 p. **DLC Uk**

On his visit to the U.S. in 1859, pp. 180–205, as well as comments on the Civil War, etc., passim. See also his "The civil war in America," *Brit. Quar. Rev.*, XXXIV (1861), 203–218.

2972   GRIFFITHS, ARTHUR [GEORGE FREDERICK]. Secrets of the prison-house; or, Gaol studies and sketches. London, 1894. 2 vols.   **DLC Uk**

    "Prisons of United States," I, pp. 429–480; other comment, passim.—see the index. See also his *Mysteries of police and crime. A general survey of wrongdoing and its pursuit*, 2d "Special edition" London, 1901, 3 vols. (1st ed. London, 1898, 2 vols.), "Modern-police-New York," pp. 268–288; other comment passim.

2973   HAMILTON, JAMES CLELAND. John Brown in Canada. A monograph. From Canadian magazine, Dec., 1894. [Toronto? 1894?]. 21 p.   **DLC Uk**

2974   HEDLEY, JAMES [ALEXANDER], *ed.* Canada and her commerce, from the time of the first settler to that of the representative men of to-day, who have shaped the destiny of our country . . . Compiled by H. W. Wadsworth. Montreal, 1894. 179 p.   **DLC**

    References to trade with the U.S., passim.

2975   IIILL, GEORGE BIRKBECK [NORMAN]. Harvard college, by an Oxonian. New York, 1894. 329 p.   **DLC Uk**

    Hill visited the U.S. in 1893 and 1896; for an account of his visit of 1893 see *Letters of George Birbeck Hill, D.C.L., LL.D., Hon.-Fellow of Pembroke college, Oxford. Arranged by his daughter, Lucy Crump*, London, 1906, pp. 216–226.

    Reviews: *Atlantic*, LXXV, 703; *Critic*, XXVI (n.s., XXIII), 45; *Dial* (by B. A. Hinsdale), XVIII, 294; *J. Educ.*, XXVII, 170; *Nation* (by W. R. Thayer?), LX, 14; *Outlook*, LI, 150; *Overland Monthly* (by Arthur Inkersley) XXVI, 221; *Spectator*, LXXIV, 237.

2976   HIND, HENRY YOULE. A history of the year of 1894, with especial reference to Canadian affairs. Toronto, 1894. 210 p.   **CaOKQ**

2977   THE IRON INDUSTRY: what it is to Great Britain and the United States; what it may be to Ontario. Toronto, 1894. 131 p.   **N**

    Campaign literature of the Progressive-Conservative party of Ontario.

2978   JAQUES, MARY J. Texan ranch life; with three months through Mexico in a "Prairie Schooner." London, 1894. 363 p.   **DLC Uk**

    Review: *Sat. Rev.*, LXXVIII, 162.

2979   [JEBB, *MRS.* JOHN BEVERIDGE GLADWYN]. A strange career: life and adventure of John Gladwyn Jebb, by his widow; with an introduction by H. Rider Haggard. Edinburgh, 1894. 335 p.   **DLC Uk**

    Uk lists under Bertha Jebb. Contains 7 chaps. on his life in western U.S., 1867–81.

    Reviews: *Academy* (by J. Stanley Little), XLVI, 488; *Athenaeum*, CIV, 883; *Blackwood's Edinb. Mag.*, CLVI, 862; *Chatauquaun*, XXI, 774; *Critic*, XXVII, 41; *Dial*, XVIII, 245; *Sat. Rev.*, LXXVIII, 636.

2980   JOHNSTONE, CATHERINE LAURA. Winter and summer excursions in Canada. London, [1894]. 213 p.   **DLC Uk**

    Includes comparison of Canadian-U.S. conditions.

2981   MACMASTER, *SIR* DONALD, *bart.* The seal arbitration, 1893. Montreal, 1894. 65 p.   **MH NN**

2982   NOTTAGE, CHARLES G[EORGE]. In search of a climate. London, 1894. 351 p.   **DLC Uk**

    On the U.S., esp. California, pp. 224–336.

2983 PAGE, MARY H. Graded schools in the United States of America. London, 1894. 71 p.

CU CtY Uk

Review: *J. Educ.*, XXVII, 103.

2984 PENNINGTON, MYLES. Railways and other ways: being reminiscences of canal and railway life during a period of sixty-seven years; with characteristic sketches of canal and railway men, early tram roads and trailways, steamboats and ocean steamships, the electric telegraph and Atlantic cable, Canada and its railways, trade and commerce, with numerous incidents and anecdotes, humorous and otherwise, of canal, coach, and rail. Toronto, 1894. 407 p.

DLC

Uk has Toronto, 1896 ed. Accounts of visits to the U.S. in 1851, 1861 and 1893, pp. 260–268, 343–348, 382–388; account of the Atlantic cable, pp. 328–337; other comment, passim.

2985 [POMEROY, *REV.* FRANK T., *ed.*]. Picturesque Brattleboro [Vt.]. Northampton, Mass., [1894]. 96 p.

DLC

Name on verso of t.p. Contains first appearance in book form of Rudyard Kipling's "In sight of Mount Monadnock," pp. 81–86. Only about half of the original article, pub. in the New York *Times and Sun*, Apr. 1892, and later in the Springfield *Republican*, appears here. This portion was repr. in the *Vermonter*, Apr. 1899, and had two separate private printings under the title: *In sight of Mount Monadnock*, [Boston], 1904; and another, [n.p.], falsely dated 1894 on t.p. (actually 1918 or 1919). This sketch was later repr. with additional uncollected sketches on America by Kipling, in *Letters of travel (1892–1913)*, London, 1920.

2986 [RENWICK, *SIR* ARTHUR]. Report of the executive commissioner for New South Wales to the World's Columbian exposition, Chicago, 1893. Presented to Parliament by command. Sydney, 1894. 493 p.

DLC Uk

Cataloged under New South Wales. Commissioners for the World's Columbian exposition. 1893. Another ed., Sydney, 1894, 671 p.

2987 SINCLAIR, JAMES, *ed.* Live stock handbooks. No. II. Light horses. Breeds and management by W[illiam] C[harles] A[rlington] Blew, M.A.; William Scarth Dixon; Dr. George Fleming, C.B., F.R.C.V.S.; Vero Shaw, B.A., etc. London, 1894. 226 p.

N PU Uk

NUC listings under Blew. See "The American trotting horse," pp. 94–104. See also the last handbook in the series, *No. V. Pigs, Breeds and management by Sanders Spencer. With a chapter on the pig by Professor J. Wortley Axe, and a chapter on bacon and ham curing by L. M. Douglas. Illustrated*, London, 1897, pp. 6–11, 36–37 (DNAL lists under Spencer).

2988 [SMITH, N.], *A Birmingham workingman*. A tour through the land of the west, and a visit to the Columbian exposition. London, 1894. 90 p.

Uk

Pref. signed: N. Smith.

2989 STEAD, W[ILLIAM] T[HOMAS]. Chicago to-day; or, The labour war in America. London, 1894. 287 p.

DLC UkLSE

Includes repr. of "Incidents of labour war in America," *Contemp. Rev.*, LXVI (July 1894), 65–76; "My first visit to America," *Rev. of Revs.*, IX (Apr. 1894), 410–417; and "The two Babylons: London and Chicago," *New Rev.*, X (May 1894), 560–570. See also Stead's "Coxeyism and its commonwealers," *Rev. of Revs.*, IX (June 1894), 565–579; "Jingoism in America," *Contemp. Rev.*, LXVIII (Sept. 1895), 334–347; *From the old world to the new; or, A Christmas story of the World's fair [Chicago], being the Christmas number of* the *"Review of Reviews"*, London, 1892, reviewed in *Rev. of Revs.*, VI (Dec. 1892), 615 and (Jan. 1893), 750; and his novel about New York, *Satan's invisible world displayed*, 1898, below. See also articles by his brother, Rev. Francis Herbert Stead: "An Englishman's impressions at the fair," *Rev. of Revs.*, VIII (July 1893), 30–34; and "The civic life of Chicago: an impression left on a guest after a visit of a dozen days," ibid., (Aug. 1893), 178–182. See account of Stead's visit to Chicago in Frederic Whyte, *The life of W. T. Stead*, London, 1925, II, pp. 39–53; and Joseph O. Baylen, "A Victorian's crusade in Chicago, 1893–94," *J. Am. Hist.*, LI (Dec. 1964), 418–434.

2990   STEPHENS, ALFRED GEORGE. A Queenslander's travel-notes. Sydney, 1894. 197 p.
CLU MH Uk

In U.S. in 1893, pp. 19–110.

2991   STEVENS, CHARLES ELLIS. Sources of the Constitution of the United States considered in relation to colonial and English history. New York, 1894. 277 p.   **DLC Uk**

DLC also has 2d ed., rev. and enlarged, New York, 1894, 313 p.

2992   THWAITE, BENJAMIN HOWARTH. The cultivation of the inventive faculty; a lesson from the United States of America. [N.p.], 1894. 16 p.   **Uk**

See also his later book, *The American invasion; or, England's commercial danger and the triumphal progress of the United States with remedies to enable England to preserve her industrial position*, London, 1902.

2993   TISCH, GUSTAV. Tour round the world, by a New Zealander: being a record for circulation amongst friends. Auckland, 1894.   **NzDOt UkRCS**

Visited Chicago exhibition, pp. 102–134.

2994   VINCENT, W[ILLIAM] T[HOMAS]. Recollections of Fred Leslie. By W. T. Vincent. With an introduction by Clement Scott. London, 1894. 2 vols.   **DLC Uk**

Leslie (also known as Frederick Hobson) performed in U.S. in 1881, 1883 and 1888–89. See I, pp. 85–95, 153–162, II, 77–95; includes correspondence from Leslie.

2995   WILLIAMSON, ANDREW, *of Edinburgh*. British industries and foreign competition. London, 1894. 311 p.   **CLU ICU NN UK**

On U.S., pp. 206–209, 226–239, and passim.

2996   ZIMMERN, ALICE. Methods of education in the United States. London, 1894. 178 p.
DHEW Uk

Review: *J. Educ.*, XXVII, 35.

1895

2997   BLACKWELL, ELIZABETH. Pioneer work in opening the medical profession to women; autobiographical sketches. London, 1895. 265 p.   **DLC Uk**

PPFr and PPULC date 1st ed. 1893, other sources agree on 1895. Repr. New York, 1977, with a new introd. by Mary Roth Walsh. Chaps. 1–3 on early life and education in America, 1832–49; chaps. 5–6 on return to U.S., 1851–69.

2998 CAINE, *SIR* [THOMAS HENRY] HALL. My story. London, 1908. 398 p.　　**NN Uk**

DLC has New York, 1909 ed. "My first visits to America," in 1895, pp. 358–373.

2999 CHAPMAN, JOHN. Reflections from sunny memories of a tour through Canada, British Columbia, and the United States of America . . . Reprinted from "The Devon County Standard," "The Isle of Wight Advertiser," and "The Hastings and S. Leonard's News." Edited by Henry Tuckett. Torquay, 1895. 43 p.　　**DLC**

On U.S., pp. 13–17, 26–43. See also his *The cotton and commerce of India, considered in relation to the interests of Great Britain; with remarks on railway communication in the Bombay presidency*, London, 1851, pp. 60–88.

3000 CONTINENTAL UNION ASSOCIATION OF ONTARIO. Our best policy. By constitutional means, involving the consent of the Mother Country, to bring about the union, on fair and honorable terms, of Canada and the United States. Platform of the Association. Issued by the Continental union association of Ontario, August, 1895. Toronto, 1895. 27 p.　**DLC**

3001 CONWAY, ALAN, *ed.* The Welsh in America. Letters from the immigrants. Cardiff, 1961. 341 p.　　**DLC Uk**

Most letters translated from Welsh; many originally appeared in Welsh newspapers and journals. Arranged by subject, letters span period 1816–95.

3002 [COOK, CHARLES HENRY]. Sea fishing, by John Bickerdyke [*pseud.*], with contributions on 'Antipodean and foreign fish' by W[illiam] Senior, 'Tarpon' by A[lfred] C[harles William] Harmsworth, 'Whaling' by Sir H[enry] W[illiam] Gore-Booth, bart. London, 1895. 562 p.　　**CU Uk**

DLC has London, 1895 ed., 513 p. Badminton library of sports and pastimes.

Review: *Academy,* XLIII, 242.

3003 [CRAIGIE, PATRICK GEORGE]. Great Britain. Board of agriculture. Report on the agricultural experiment stations and agricultural colleges of the United States of America. Presented to both houses of Parliament by command of Her Majesty. London, 1895. 80 p.　　**DLC**

3004 CUNINGHAM, GRANVILLE CARLYLE. A scheme for imperial federation; a senate for the empire: Three articles reprinted with additions from the Westminster Review of April, July, and October, 1879 . . . with an introduction by Sir Frederick Young. London and New York, 1895. 116 p.　　**DLC Uk**

See also his article "Federation, Annexation, or Independence" in *Canadian Monthly & Natl. Rev.,* IV (March 1880), 242–252.

3005 DE WINDT, HARRY. My restless life. London, 1909. 366 p.　　**DLC Uk**

In U.S. in 1895, pp. 245–249, 262–268.

3006 ELWES, HENRY JOHN. Memoirs of travel, sport, and natural history . . . edited by Edward G. Hawke . . . with an introduction by the Right Hon. Sir Herbert Maxwell . . . and a chapter on gardening by E. A. Bowles. London, 1930. 317 p.　　**DLC Uk**

Diary accounts of trips to U.S. in 1888 and 1895.

3007 THE FRUIT INDUSTRY OF CALIFORNIA. Containing an official (approximate) statement in respect to the growth, cost, profit, &c., of the principal fruits grown commercially, and other valuable information; being a practical guide for those with limited capital desirous of engaging in this profitable and congenial industry. Also for the sons of gentlemen seeking experience on fruit farms, either with a view to their securing remunerative and permanent positions, or to enable them to eventually start fruit growing on their own account. By an Englishman. (Revised by a practical California fruit-grower of thirty years' standing). London, [1895]. 41 p.   **Uk**

Uk lists under Englishman.

3008   GUEST, *LADY* THEODORA [GROSVENOR]. A round trip in North America. London, 1895. 270 p.   **DLC Uk**

Uk lists under Grosvenor.

Reviews: *Sat. Rev.*, LXXIX, 295; *Spectator*, LXXIV, 881.

3009   HALL, JOHN E. and R. O. MACCULLOCH Sixty years of Canadian cricket in Canada. A complete record of all the great international and interprovincial matches with names and scores. Also excellent papers by cricketing celebrities. Toronto, 1895. 572 p. **MB NN**

Refers throughout to games with U.S. teams.

3010   HISTORY OF THE WELSH IN MINNESOTA, Foreston and Lime Springs, Ia. Gathered by the old settlers. Edited by Revs. Thos. E. Hughes and David Edwards, and Messrs. Hugh G. Roberts and Thomas Hughes. Illustrated. [Mankato], 1895. 306 p.   **DLC Uk**

Title listed in Welsh, with English translation beneath. Part I of text is in Welsh: a collection of accounts by original settlers; part II in English includes brief biographical sketches and a chronological account.

3011   HOLE, *VERY REV.* S[AMUEL] REYNOLDS, *Dean of Rochester.* A little tour in America. London, 1895. 381 p.   **DLC Uk**

See his *More memories: being thoughts about England spoken in America*, London, 1894. See also *The letters of Samuel Reynolds Hole, Dean of Rochester*, London, 1907, pp. 161–166; and the interview "Dean Hole on America," *Critic*, XXVI (Mar. 2, 1895), 171.

Reviews: *Academy* (by Charles J. Robinson), XLIX, 71; *Spectator*, LXXVI, 91.

3012   HOLLINGSHEAD, JOHN. My lifetime. London, 1895. 2 vols.   **DLC Uk**

In America, 1887, II, pp. 218–223.

3013   HUGHES, THOMAS. Vacation rambles. London, 1895. 405 p.   **DLC Uk**

A series of letters with additions and omissions, from the *Spectator*, (1880–1886), LIII, 1153—LIX, 1414, under the signature "Vacuus Viator"; also includes "John to Jonathan; an address delivered in the Music hall, Boston, on the 11th of October, 1870," *Grand Army J.*, I, Oct. 22, 1870 (also in *Macmillan's Mag.*, XXIII [Dec. 1870], 81–91). On U.S., pp. 105–260. See the following articles by Hughes: "Trades' unions, strikes, and co-operation," *Macmillan's Mag.*, XIII (Nov. 1865), 75–80, (Dec. 1865), 176; "The youngest Anglo-Saxon university [Cornell]," *Macmillan's Mag.*, XXII (July 1870), 161–169; "Recollections of American universities: [Harvard and Cornell]," *Every Sat.*, ser. 2, II (Mar. 25, 1871), 286, (Apr. 22, 1871), 370, III (May 20, 1871; with W. D. Rawlins), 466–467; "A week in the west: from a vagabond's notebook," *Macmillan's Mag.*, XXIV (Aug. 1871), 241–248, XXV (Mar. 1872), 376–384; "Rugby Tennessee," ibid., XLIII (Feb. 1881), 310–315; "American humor," *Brit. Quar. Rev.*, LII (Oct. 1, 1870), 324–351; "Letter to a young American," *Critic*, XXV, n.s. (Apr. 11, 1896), 258. See also Walter Harry Green Armytage and Edward C. Mack, *Thomas Hughes, the life of the author of Tom Brown's Schooldays*, London, [1952], pp. 131–143, 174–195, 227–250.

Reviews: *Critic*, XXVIII, 122; *Dial*, XX, 138; *Give & Take* (by Herbert Vivian), I, 8; *Nation*, LXII, 259.

3014 INGRAM, JOHN KELLS. A history of slavery and serfdom. London, 1895. 285 p.

DLC Uk

Abolition of slavery in the U.S., pp. 181–202, 281–285.

3015 [KENDAL, *MRS*. MARGARET SHAFTO (ROBERTSON) GRIMSTON]. Dame Madge Kendal, by herself. London, [1933]. 313 p. **DLC Uk**

Five trips to the U.S., 1889–1895. See also *The Kendals*, by T. Edgar Pemberton, London, 1900.

3016 LUNN, *SIR* HENRY SIMPSON. Chapters from my life, with special reference to reunion. London, 1918. 422 p. **DLC Uk**

In U.S. for the first time in 1895, pp. 185–209.

3017 [MCCREA, DANIEL FRANCIS]. Columbian sketches. By Rudyard Home [*pseud.*]. Dublin, 1895. 370 p. **MH Uk**

First pub. serially in the Belfast *Irish News*.

3018 MACEWEN, ALEXANDER R[OBERTSON]. Life and letters of John Cairns . . . London, 1895. 799 p. **Uk**

DLC has 2d ed., London, 1895. Visit to America in 1880, pp. 684–705.

3019 M'GLADE, *REV*. J[AMES] J. Illustrated story of five years' tour in America. Dublin, [1906]. 199 p. **CtY IreDNL MnU**

In U.S., 1890–95.

3020 ROPER, CHARLOTTE. Zigzag travels. London, 1895. 3 vols. **Uk**

In U.S., I, pp. 55–63, 93–112, 168–229; II, 3–31.

3021 [SACKVILLE, LIONEL SACKVILLE SACKVILLE-WEST, *baron*]. My mission to the United States, 1881–1889. [London, 1895]. 52 p. **CSmH N Uk**

Uk lists under West. Priv. pr. Signed "Sackville, Knole, March, 1895." See the account in Victoria Sackville-West, *Pepita*, New York, 1937, pp. 167–185. See also Paul Knaplund and Carolyn M. Clewes, "Private letters from the British embassy in Washington to the Foreign secretary, Lord Granville, 1880–1885," *Am. Hist. Assn. Ann. Rep.*, I (1941), 73–189; letters from Sackville-West, Dec. 1881–Mar. 1885, pp. 155–183; other letters from Sir Edward Thornton and Victor Drummond.

3022 SINCLAIR, JAMES M. Report on the sugar-beet industry and tobacco culture of the United States. Melbourne, 1895. 47 p. **DLC Uk**

At head of title: Department of agriculture, Victoria.

3023 SINCLAIR, JAMES M. Report . . . on wheat production in the United States, Canada and the Argentine Republic; also the handling and shipment of grain in the United States. Melbourne, 1895. 94 p. **DLC Uk**

At head of title: Department of agriculture, Victoria.

3024 SPRING RICE, *SIR* CECIL [ARTHUR]. The letters and friendships of Sir Cecil Spring Rice, a record; edited by Stephen Gwynn. London, [1929]. 2 vols. **DLC Uk**

In U.S. with the British legation at Washington, 1887–92 and 1894–95, pp. 51–120, 153–177.

3025   STANLEY, *SIR* HENRY MORTON. My early travels and adventures in America and Asia. London, 1895. 2 vols.   **CLU ICN Uk**

DLC has New York, 1895 ed. Vol. I describes incidents during two Indian campaigns of 1867, written originally for the *Missouri Democrat* of St. Louis. See also his *Autobiography*, ed. by Dorothy Stanley, London, 1909, for an account of the years 1859–68 spent in America and later visits in 1872 and 1890–91: pp. 81–215, 220–227, 291, 425–428.

Reviews: *Argonaut*, XXXVI, 9; *Athenaeum*, XCV, 636; *Critic*, XXVII, 56; *Outlook*, LII, 224; *Sat. Rev.*, LXXX, 446; *Spectator*, LXXV, 50.

3026   STEVENSON, ROBERT LOUIS. The amateur emigrant; from the Clyde to Sandy Hook. Chicago, 1895. 180 p.   **DLC**

Last chap. on New York; written in 1879 with first authorized pub. in the collected *Works*, London, 1895; *Across the plains, London*, 1892, above, originaly intended as sequel. Repr. in *Travels and essays of Robert Louis Stevenson*, New York, 1897, and in his *Essays of Travel*, London, 1905, pp. 3–92; in James D. Hart, ed., *From Scotland to Silverado, comprising The amateur emigrant: "from the Clyde to Sandy Hook" and "Across the Plains"* . . . , Cambridge, Mass., 1966; and as *The amateur emigrant, with some first impressions of America*, ed. by Roger G. Swearingen, Ashland, Ore., 1976. See *The essay on Walt Whitman by Robert Louis Stevenson. With a little journey to the home of Whitman by Elbert Hubbard*, [East Aurora, N.Y.], 1900 (repr. from *New Quar. Mag.*, X, (Oct. 1878), 461–481 and repr. in *Familiar studies of men and books*, London, 1882, pp. 91–128). See also Stevenson's essay on Thoreau in *Cornhill Mag.*, XLI (June 1880), 665–682 (repr. in *Familiar Studies*, pp. 129–171). See the *Letters of Robert Louis Stevenson, ed. by Sidney Colvin. A new edition rearranged in four volumes with 150 new letters*, New York, 1911, I, pp. 278–340; III, pp. 3–71; also see letters from U.S. in *Henry James and Robert Louis Stevenson; a record of friendship and criticism*, London, 1948, passim.

See also the following on Stevenson in America: Louis Evan Shipman, "Stevenson's first landing in New York," *Book Buyer*, XIII (Feb. 1896), 13–15; John Alexander Hammerton, *Stevensoniana*, Edinburgh, 1907, pp. 40–52, 83–91; Hailey Millard, "How Stevenson discovered America," *Bookman*, XXXIX (July 1914), 539–544; Clayton Hamilton, *On the trail of Stevenson* . . . New York, 1915, pp. 127–151; and the *Bookman* extra no. on Stevenson by E. B. Simpson, *Robert Louis Stevenson originals*, London, 1913. See also the following biographies for accounts of Stevenson's two visits to the U.S., and his stop in Hawaii: Richard Aldington, *Portrait of a rebel: the life and work of Robert Louis Stevenson*, London, 1957, pp. 108–125, 181–197; Jenni Calder, *Robert Louis Stevenson: a life study*, New York, 1980, pp. 123–149, 229–244, 263–274; Elsie Noble Caldwell, *Last witness for Robert Louis Stevenson*, Norman, Okla., [1960], pp. 25–37, 100–113; Sidney Dark, *Robert Louis Stevenson*, 1931, pp. 112–124, 180–198; Malcolm Elwin, *The strange case of Robert Louis Stevenson*, London, [1950], pp. 138–149; Joseph Chamberlain Furnas, *Voyage to windward: the life of Robert Louis Stevenson*, New York, [1951], pp. 151–179, 266–281; James Pope Hennessy, *Robert Louis Stevenson*, London, 1974, pp. 125–143, 187–202, 210–214; and Sister Martha Mary McGaw, *Stevenson in Hawaii*, Honolulu, 1950. Also see the notes under Stevenson's *Across the plains* . . . , 1892, above, for other accounts of the later visit.

Reviews: *Book Buyer*, XII, 151, 181; *Bookman* (London), VIII, 21; *Bookman* (N.Y.), I, 46; *Dial*, XVIII, 182; *Edinb. Rev.*, CLXXXII, 106; *Lit. World*, XXVI, 90; *Spectator*, LXXIV, 165.

3027 STEWART, WILLIAM. J. Keir Hardie, a biography. With an introduction by Ramsay Macdonald. London, 1921. 387 p. **DL**

1st ed. pub. by National Labour Press. DLC and Uk have another ed., London, [1921]. In U.S. in 1895, pp. 110–123; later trips, pp. 287, 335. Hardie was accompanied by Frank Smith, who wrote a weekly account of their 1895 tour for the *Labour Leader* (edited by Hardie), Sept. 7–Dec. 28, 1895. For accounts of this trip see David Lowe, *From pit to parliament: the story of the early life of James Keir Hardie*, London, 1923, pp. 86–89.

3028 TALLACK, WILLIAM. European and American progress in penal reform. A paper prepared, at the request of the committee of the New York prison association, for its fiftieth anniversary meeting, February 28, 1895. [London, 1895]. 4 p. **DLC**

3029 THOMPSON, GEO[RGE] S. Up to date; or, The life of a lumberman. Illustrated by Captain Geo. S. Thompson. [n.p., 1895]. 126 p. **NN Uk**

On U.S., pp. 38, 39, 99–102.

3030 TUCKWELL, *REV*. JOHN. Letters from around the world, together with memorials of the Tuckwell family and brief biography of the author. London, [1895]. 76 p. **CU-BANC Uk**

Includes letters from San Francisco, Salt Lake, Colorado Springs, Denver, Philadelphia, pp. 29–35.

3031 WARD, MARTINDALE. A trip to Chicago; what I saw, what I heard, what I thought. Glasgow, 1895. 124 p. **ICHi**

1896

3032 ASHTON, JOHN. The devil in Britain and America. London, 1896. 363 p. **DLC Uk**

On witchcraft cases in U.S. (colonial period): pp. 310–336.

3033 BAKER, ARTHUR. Shakers and Shakerism. London, 1896. 30 p. **DLC**

"New Moral World" Series, No. 2.

3034 BANTOCK, *SIR* GRANVILLE and F[REDERICK] G[EORGE] AFLALO. Round the world with "A Gaiety girl." London, 1896. 172 p. **DLC Uk**

U.S. tour, pp. 19–85.

3035 BODDY, *REV*. ALEXANDER ALFRED. By ocean, prairie and peak. Some gleanings from an emigrant chaplain's log, on journey to British Columbia, Manitoba, and Eastern Canada. London, 1896. 204 p. **MB MiD WaU**

Uk copy destroyed. Visited Washington state, pp. 178–182; other comment, passim.

3036 BOOTH, HARE. Glimpses of our American kith and kin. London, [1896]. 178 p. **MB MnU**

3037 BRAKE, HEZEKIAH. On two continents. A long life's experience. Topeka, Kansas, 1896. 240 p. **DLC Uk**

On U.S., passim. Author emigrated to Canada in 1847 and went to U.S. in 1848; early comments reveal attitudes of newly arrived Englishmen.

3038   CALIFORNIA: A HANDBOOK of useful and reliable information. London, [1896?].
No locations found.

3039   [DE WESSELOW], C[HARLES] H[ARE] SIMPKINSON. The life and work of Bishop
Thorold, Rochester 1877–91, Winchester 1891–95. Prelate of the most noble Order of the
garter. By C. H. Simpkinson. London, 1896. 414 p.   **DLC Uk**

Uk lists under Simpkinson. Includes accounts of visits to the U.S. in 1882, 1883 and 1884.
See "To Niagara and back," *Good Words*, XVI (1875), 63–69, 125–131.

3040   DICKSON, FREDERICK S[TOEVER]. "Blackwood's" history of the United States.
Philadelphia, 1896. 27 p.   **DLC**

An American review of Blackwood's comments on the American Civil War, 1860–66.
Repr. in the *Mag. of Hist. with Notes & Queries*, XXVII (1925), no. 1.

3041   DODD, ROBERT, *comp*. Essays on colonizing and changes in the past, present and future
of the world. London, 1896. 101 p.   **DLC Uk**

On U.S., pp. 41–92.

3042   FREWEN, MORETON. The free coinage of silver in the United States. [n.p., 1896?]. 8 p.
LNT

3043   GOODWIN, DANIEL. Thomas Hughes of England, and his visits to Chicago in 1870 and
1880. Chicago, 1896. 58 p.   **DLC Uk**

3044   HAMMERTON, *SIR* JOHN ALEXANDER. Barrie, the story of a genius. London, 1929.
491 p.   **CtY LU Uk**

DLC has New York, 1929 ed. James M. Barrie was in the U.S. in 1896, pp. 266–281;
excerpt from speech by Barrie in 1896 on higher education for women in the U.S., p. 296.
See also Janet Dunbar, *J. M. Barrie: the man behind the image*, Boston, 1970, Chap. 9,
"America," pp. 125–135.

3045   HARRIS, THOMAS L[E GRAND]. The Trent affair, including a review of English and
American relations at the beginning of the civil war. With an introduction by James A.
Woodburn. Indianapolis, 1896. 288 p.   **DLC Uk**

Author American; includes survey of comment by Lord John Russell, Lord Lyons, and
others.

3046   HAWEIS, *REV*. HUGH REGINALD. Travel and talk, 1885–93–95. My hundred thousand
miles of travel through America, Australia, Tasmania, Canada, New Zealand, Ceylon, and
the paradises of the Pacific. London, 1896. 2 vols.   **DLC Uk**

Vol. I and part of vol. II on the U.S. See his "A visit to Walt Whitman," *Pall Mall Gazette*,
XLIII (Jan. 13, 1886), 1–2 (repr. in the *Critic*, V (Feb. 27, 1886), 109); and his "In the
United States, 1885," *Gentleman's Mag.*, XXXVI, n.s. (May 1886), 463. See also his
American humorists, London, 1882.

3047   HOUGHTON, ARTHUR BOYD. Arthur Boyd Houghton; a selection from his work in
black and white, printed for the most part from the original wood-blocks. With an introductory essay by Laurence Housman. London, 1896. 32 p.   **DLC Uk**

Includes illustrated articles on America which appeared originally in the *Graphic*,
(1870–71). See also Sinclair Hamilton, "Arthur Boyd Houghton & his American drawings," *Colophon*, New Graphic Series, No. 2 (New York, 1939).

3048 JEFFERS, J[AMES] FRITH and J[AMES] L[AWRENCE] NICHOLS. Safe citizenship; or, Canadian and American citizenship, an historical parallel of all great events in Canada and the United States: bimetallism, gold and silver coinage, tariffs, etc., fully explained, different systems of government compared and expounded. Toronto, [1896]. 585 p.

DLC Uk

3049 JOHNSON, *REV*. R. CRAWFORD. Impressions of American Methodism, being the address delivered to the Irish conference, 24th June. By fraternal delegate of the Irish conference to the General conference of the Methodist Episcopal Church of America, held at Cleveland, Ohio, in May, 1896. [n.p., 1896?]. 8 p. **DLC**

Repr. from the *Chr. Advocate*, Sept. 1896.

3050 [KENDALL, JOHN]. American memories: recollections of a hurried run through the United States during the late spring of 1896. [Nottingham, 1896?]. 292 p. **MH NN NcD**

3051 KIRBY, WILLIAM. Annals of Niagara. Welland, Ont., 1896. 269 p. **DLC Uk**

Toronto, 1927 ed., with introd. and notes by Lorne Pierce.

3052 LECKY, WILLIAM EDWARD HARTPOLE. Democracy and liberty. London, 1896. 2 vols. **CSmH Uk**

DLC has New York, 1896 ed. Rev. ed., London, 1899 added a new introd. See Lecky's "The relation between the United States and other powers," *Independent*, L (2d half, July 1898), 15–17. For a discussion of Lecky on American democracy see Benjamin Evans Lippincott, *Victorian critics of democracy*, Minneapolis, 1938, pp. 207–243.

Reviews: *Academy* (by J. A. Hamilton), XLIX, 357; *Am. Hist. Rev.* (by A. L. Lowell), II, 153; *Church Quar.*, XLIII, 132; *Dial* (by C. R. Henderson), XXI, 143; *Edinb. Rev.*, CLXXXIII, 516; *Eng. Hist. Rev.* (by W. G. Pogson Smith), XI, 531; *Nation* (by C. G. Sedgwick), LXII, 380; *Nineteenth Cent.* (by John Morley), XXXIX, 697 (repr. in *Littel's Living Age*, CCIX, 643, in *Eclectic Mag.*, n.s., CXXVII, 40, in Morley's *Critical miscellanies*, New York, 1908, IV, pp. 173–219, and in his *Oracles on man and government*, London, 1923, pp. 29–74); *Sat. Rev.*, LXXXI, 400.

3053 LLOYD, FREDERIC. Jottings from a journal of journeys. Comprising glimpses of Australia, Northern Europe and Iceland, America and Greece. Manchester, [1896]. 270 p. **Uk**

"Canada and the States," pp. 159–190.

3054 [LYALL, WALTER TSCHUDI]. Republics: north and south. With an appendix. By one who does not believe in them. Gravesend, 1896. 265 p. **Uk**

DLC has London, 1897 ed., 359 p., under author's name; Uk lists only under title.

3055 MELBA, NELLIE. Melodies and memories. London, [1925]. 335 p. **DLC Uk**

Uk lists under Dame Helen Porter Armstrong. In U.S., 1893–96, pp. 121–167. See John Aikman Hetherington, *Melba: a biography*, London, 1967, for scattered comment on her experiences in New York and Chicago; and Joseph Wechsberg, *Red plush and black velvet; the story of Melba and her times*, Boston, 1961, pp. 238–255.

3056 MOLTENO, PERCY ALPORT. A federal South Africa; a comparison of the critical period of American history with the present position of the colonies and states of South Africa, and a consideration of the advantages of a federal union. London, 1896. 260 p. **DLC Uk**

3057 O'LEARY, JOHN. Recollections of Fenians and Fenianism. London, 1896. 2 vols.
DLC Uk

In U.S. in 1859, I, pp. 80–243, and passim.

3058 PAWLE, F. DALE. A flying visit to the American continent, with notes by the way. London, 1896. 146 p. **MnHi PSC Uk**

3059 POCOCK, ROGER S. Rottenness: a study of America and England. London, 1896. 208 p.
DLC Uk

3060 PORTS OF THE PACIFIC by a peripatetic parson. London, 1896. 388 p. **DLC Uk**

DLC lists under Peripatetic; Uk under Pacific Ocean. On Hawaii, pp. 287–380; U.S. Pacific coast, pp. 381–388.

3061 ROZENRAAD, CORNELIS. The financial and monetary situation in the United States. London, 1896. 32 p. **CtY IEN MH Uk**

3062 [ST. LAURENT, CHARLES F., *pseud.*]. Germanization and Americanization compared. Montreal, 1896. 20 p. **DLC**

3063 [SMITH, RODNEY ("GIPSY")]. Gipsy Smith; his life and work, by himself; introductions by G. Campbell Morgan and Alexander McLaren, D.D. London, 1901. 365 p.
OCl Uk WaU

DLC has New York, 1902 ed., 330 p.; rev. ed, London, 1924. In U.S., 1889, 1891–92, 1892–93, 1896: pp. 160–182, 193–205, 228–249, 296–307. See also accounts in *Forty years an evangelist*, New York, [1923]; *My life story*, New York, [1892]; and *From gipsy tent to pulpit: the story of my life*, London, [1901], 8 p.

3064 SMITH, SAMUEL. America revisited. Liverpool, 1896. 23 p. **CSmH NN**

First visited U.S. in 1860; for accounts of various visits see his *My life-work*, London, 1902, pp. 22–30, 76–85, 361–376, and 428–436; this vol. also includes repr. of articles on America written for the press. See also his *Occasional essays*, London, 1874; and *The bimetallic question*, London, 1887.

3065 TAYLOR, THOMAS E. Running the blockade: a personal narrative of adventures, risks, and escapes during the American civil war . . . With an introduction by Julian Corbett, maps and illustrations. London, 1896. 180 p. **CtY Uk**

DLC has New York, 1896 ed.

3066 TEMPLE, *SIR* RICHARD, *1st bart.* The story of my life. London, 1896. 2 vols. **DLC Uk**

Describes visits to the U.S. in 1882 and 1884, II, pp. 160–180, 181–215. See also "American characteristics," in his *Cosmopolitan essays*, London, 1886, pp. 439–486; and his "An Anglo-American *versus* A European combination," *No. Am. Rev.*, CLXVII (Sept. 1898), 306–317.

3067 THOMSON, *SIR* JOSEPH JOHN. Recollections and reflections. London, 1936. 451 p.
DLC Uk

In U.S., 1896, pp. 164–181.

3068 VENNING, ROBERT NORRIS. The Behring sea question, embracing the fur sealing industry of the north Pacific ocean and the international agreement between Russia and Great Britain. Ottawa, 1896. 50 p. **CSmH**

CaBVaU, CaBViPA have Ottawa, 1897 ed. At head of title: "From report of the Dept. of marine and fisheries, 1895."

3069 [WARBURTON, J. W.]. Report on the distress caused to British emigrants in California by fraudulent land syndicates and emigration agencies. Presented to both Houses of Parliament by command of Her Majesty, September, 1896. London, 1896. 17 p.

CLU CSmH

DLC lists the series noted at head of title: "Great Britain Foreign office. Diplomatic and consular reports. Miscellaneous series, No. 404. Report on subjects of general and commercial interest. United States."

3070 WHITE, RICHARD DUNNING. The narrative of a journey from Quebec to Niagara. Through the states of New York, New England, to Halifax, Nova Scotia, "fifty-six years ago." Exeter, 1896. 36 p. **DLC**

A journal written in 1839.

3071 WHITTLE, JAMES LOWRY. Grover Cleveland. London, 1896. 240 p. **DLC Uk**

See also his article, "A glimpse of the United States," *Cornhill Mag.*, XLVI (Oct. 1882), 427–439.

1897

3072 ABERDEEN AND TEMAIR, ISHBEL MARIA (MARJORIBANKS) GORDON, *Lady*. The Canadian journal of Lady Aberdeen, 1893–98, edited by John T. Saywell. Toronto, 1960. 517 p. **NIC NN Uk**

Uk catalogs under Gordon. Wife of John Hamilton Gordon, 7th Earl of Aberdeen; visited U.S. in 1897, pp. 383–392.

3073 BATTLES OF THE NINETEENTH CENTURY, described by Archibald Forbes, G[eorge] A[lfred] Henty, Arthur Griffiths, and other well-known writers; with a chronological list of the more important battles of the century. London, 1896–97. 2 vols. **DLC**

Uk has under Forbes, 7 vols. "special edition" with plates and illustrations, London, [1901]. Chaps. on U.S. (in 1st ed.) by Forbes, I, pp. 692–703, II, 1–11, 710–719; and by Griffiths, I, 380–387, II, 720–729.

3074 BRADLEY, ARTHUR GRANVILLE. Sketches from old Virginia. London, 1897. 284 p.

DLC Uk

Repr. with additions and omissions in *Other days. Recollections of rural England and old Virginia, 1860–1880*, London, 1913. Sketches appeared originally in *Macmillan's Mag.*, *Blackwood's Edinb. Mag.*, *Badminton Mag.*, and *Fortnightly Rev.*

3075 CHADWICK, EDWARD MARION. The people of the Long house. Toronto, 1897. 166 p.

DLC Uk

History and discussion of the Iroquois.

3076 COOK, *SIR* THEODORE ANDREA. The sunlit hours. A record of sport and life. London, [1925]. 330 p. **DLC Uk**

In U.S., 1895–97, pp. 97–153.

3077 CROFTON, FRANCIS BLAKE. For closer union: some slight offerings to a great cause. (Articles reprinted from periodicals, advocating the federation). Halifax, 1897. 57 p.

DLC Uk

Refers to U.S. throughout.

3078   DURAND, CHARLES. Reminiscences of Charles Durand of Toronto, barrister. Toronto, 1897. 534 p.   **CSmH Uk**

DLC has 2d ed., 2 vols. in 1, Toronto, 1897[–99]. Account of life in Chicago, 1839–44, pp. 372–403. Also, chaps. 10–13 on the Canadian rebellion.

3079   EDWARDS, *DR.* WILLIAM ALOYSIUS and BEATRICE HARRADEN. Two health-seekers in Southern California. Philadelphia, 1897. 114 p.   **DLC Uk**

Edwards an American. Chaps. 1 and 4 by Harraden; see also her "Some impressions of Southern California," *Blackwood's Edinb. Mag.*, CLXI (Feb. 1897), 172–180.

3080   GOLDIE, JOHN. Diary of a journey through Upper Canada and some of the New England states. 1819. Toronto, 1897. 56 p.   **CaOKQ CSmH NN**

On Niagara, pp. 23–29; on travels in U.S., pp. 34–56.

3081   [HOWARD, ESME WILLIAM HOWARD, *baron*]. Theatre of life. By Lord Howard of Penrith. London, [1935–36]. 2 vols.   **DLC Uk**

In U.S., 1897, I, pp. 228–231. Also extensive comment on later experiences as a diplomat in the U.S., 1907–1909.

3082   HOWARD, WINIFRED MARY (DE LISLE) HOWARD, *baroness of Glossop*. Journal of a tour in the United States, Canada, and Mexico, by Winefred [sic], lady Howard of Glossop. London, 1897. 355 p.   **DLC Uk**

In U.S., 1894–95, for a 4 months' tour.

3083   MADDEN, JOHN. The wilderness and its tenants: a series of geographical and other essays illustrative of life in a wild country, together with experiences and observations culled from the great book of nature in many lands. London, 1897. 3 vols.   **DLC Uk**

Includes much comment on the U.S., passim.

3084   MASEFIELD, JOHN. In the mill. London, 1941. 160 p.   **DLC Uk**

Memories of two years [c. 1895–97] in the author's boyhood, during which he was employed in a carpet mill at Yonkers, New York.

3085   MONSON, *SIR* EDMUND [JOHN]. Washington and the mother country; an address by the British ambassador to France. Paris, [1897]. 16 p.   **DLC Uk**

Delivered before the American university dinner club, at Paris, February 22, 1897.

3086   MORRIS, MARTIN [HENRY FITZPATRICK]. Transatlantic traits. London, 1897. 122 p.   **MB MH OCl PPL**

Appeared originally in *New Review*, XIII (Sept. & Oct. 1895), 296, 434; repr. in *Eclectic Mag.*, CXXVI (Jan. 1896), 40–44.

3087   PATER PATRONUCUS [*pseud.*]. The coming struggle in the United States and Canada and its origin. [Toronto, 1897]. 16 p.   **CaOTU**

Caption title.

3088   PETERS, GEORGE HENRY. Impressions of a journey round the world including India, Burmah and Japan. London, 1897. 373 p.   **MH Uk**

On U.S., pp. 294–358.

3089   POMEROY, ELSIE M. Sir Charles G. D. Roberts; a biography . . . Introductions by Lorne Pierce. Toronto, 1943. 371 p.   **DLC Uk**

In U.S., 1897, pp. 147–153.

3090   SAINT-PIERRE, T[ELESPHORE], *comp.* The Americans and Canada in 1837–38; authentic documents. Montreal, 1897. 58 p.   **DLC**

3091   SELOUS, PERCY. Travel and big game . . . with two chapters by H[enry] A[nderson] Bryden. London, 1897. 195 p.   **DLC Uk**

Selous on hunting in the American Rockies: pp. 65–93, 153–165.

Review: *Nation*, LXIV, 366.

3092   SHARP, ELIZABETH A. William Sharp (Fiona Macleod): a memoir compiled by his wife. London, 1910. 433 p.   **PHC Uk**

DLC has New York, 1912 ed. In U.S. in 1889, pp. 149–157; in 1892, pp. 193–195; and in 1897, pp. 273–275. See also William Sharp's "The art treasures of America," *Nineteenth Cent.* XLIV (Sept. 1898), 359–372; (Oct. 1898), 601–617.

3093   SIM, EDWARD COYSGARNE. Our travels round the world. 1892–94. London, 1897. 140 p.   **CU NIC Uk**

Cross-country tour of the U.S., pp. 132–139.

3094   SOLDENE, EMILY. My theatrical and musical recollections. London, 1897. 315 p.   **DLC Uk**

Made several American tours between 1874 and 1891.

3095   STEAD, W[ILLIAM] T[HOMAS]. Satan's invisible world displayed; or, Despairing democracy. A study of greater New York. New York, [1897]. 300 p.   **DLC**

Uk has only London ed., as the *Review of Reviews annual*, 1898. See also author's *Mr. Carnegie's conundrum. £40,000,000, what shall I do with it?* London, 1900 (on cover: "Review of reviews" annual, 1900).

3096   STEEVENS, GEORGE WARRINGTON. The land of the dollar. London, 1897. 316 p.   **DLC Uk**

Pub. originally in the London *Daily Mail*; Steevens assigned to cover U.S. presidential election of 1896.

3097   TREVOR, JOHN. My quest for God. London, 1897. 274 p.   **DLC Uk**

In U.S., 1878–79, pp. 120–147.

3098   VANBRUGH, VIOLET. Dare to be wise. London, [1925]. 160 p.   **DLC Uk**

Toured with the Kendals in America, 1889–91, 1896–97, pp. 43–55, 76–80.

3099   WHITELAW, DAVID. A bonfire of leaves. London, 1937. 276 p.   **DLC Uk**

In U.S., 1896–97, pp. 27–72.

3100   WILLISON, *SIR* JOHN STEPHEN. The railway question in Canada, with an examination of the railway law of Iowa. [Toronto, 1897]. 73 p.   **DLC**

1898

3101   ACWORTH, *SIR* WILLIAM MITCHELL. American and English railways compared; being four letters . . . published in the London Times. Chicago, 1898. 24 p.   **N**

3102   ANGELL, *SIR* [RALPH] NORMAN. After all; the autobiography of Norman Angell. London, 1951. 370 p.   **DLC Uk**

Contains account of his 7 years as a young man in California, 1891–98, pp. 32–91.

3103   ARCH, JOSEPH. Joseph Arch. The story of his life told by himself; and edited with a preface by the Countess of Warwick [Frances Evelyn (Maynard) Greville]. London, 1898. 412 p.   **DLC Uk**

Visit to Canada and the U.S. in 1873, pp. 174–197. As leader of the Agricultural Labourers Union, Arch was in America looking for new fields of emigration for impoverished English farmers; see account in the Cincinnati *Daily Gazette*, Sept. 13, 1873. See also Arthur Clayden, *The revolt of the field: a sketch of the rise and progress of the movement among the agricultural labourers, known as the "National agricultural labourers' union;" with a reprint of the correspondence to the Daily News during a tour through Canada with Mr. Arch*, London, 1874, pp. 231–234.

3104   BELL, C. LOWTHIAN. Notes on a visit to the United States, September, 1897. Middlesborough, 1898. 92 p.   **DLC Uk**

3105   BOWYER, *MRS.* EDITH M. (NICHOLL). Observations of a ranchwoman in New Mexico. London, 1898. 271 p.   **DLC Uk**

Uk lists under Nicholl; lived 20 years in the U.S.

3106   CAMPBELL, FRANCIS WAYLAND. The Fenian invasions of Canada of 1866 and 1870 and the operations of the Montreal militia brigade in connection therewith. A lecture delivered before the Montreal military institute, April 23rd, 1898 . . . Montreal, 1904. 55 p.   **DLC Uk**

3107   CHEVALIER, ALBERT. Before I forget—. The autobiography of a chevalier d'industrie. London, 1901. 258 p.   **MH Uk**

DLC has London, 1902 ed. A comedian who toured America several times, 1896–98.

3108   CONANT, THOMAS. Upper Canada sketches. Toronto, 1898. 243 p.   **DLC Uk**

On U.S., pp. 137–180.

3109   CROIL, JAMES. Steam navigation, and its relation to the commerce of Canada and the United States. Toronto, 1898. 381 p.   **DLC Uk**

For accounts of visits to the U.S. in 1841, 1845, 1876 and 1899, see *Life of James Croil, Montreal; an autobiography, 1821–1916*, Montreal, 1918, pp. 57–59, 65–66, 85–88, 146–150, 160–166.

3110   CROSWELLER, WILLIAM THOMAS. Our visit to Toronto, the Niagara Falls and the United States of America; being a short account of a tour in connection with the meeting of the British association for the advancement of science, held at Toronto, Canada, August 18 to 25, 1897. [n.p.], 1898. 136 p.   **DLC**

Priv. pr. On U.S., pp. 94–120.

3111   DICEY, ALBERT VENN. Memorials of Albert Venn Dicey, being chiefly letters and diaries, edited by Robert S. Rait. London, 1925. 304 p.   **DLC Uk**

Accounts of his 1870 and 1898 visits to the U.S., pp. 55–75, 145–174. For an account of the 1870 visit see Richard D. Cosgrove, *The rule of the law: Albert Venn Dicey, Victorian jurist*, Chapel Hill, 1980, pp. 34–38. See also Dicey's articles: "Americomania in English politics," *Nation* (N.Y.), XLII (Jan. 21, 1886), 52–53; "A common citizenship for the English race," *Contemp. Rev.*, LXXI (April 1897), 457–476; "The new American imperialism," *Nineteenth Cent.*, XLIV (Sept. 1898), 487–501; "England and America," *Atlantic*, LXXXII (Oct. 1898), 441–445; and "The teaching of English law at Harvard," *Contemp. Rev.*, LXXVI (Nov. 1899), 742–758.

3112   GARNETT, RICHARD. To America; after reading some ungenerous criticisms. Jamaica, N.Y., 1898.   **DLC Uk**

Single sheet; a sonnet written by the keeper of printed books, British Museum.

3113   GILES, ARTHUR. Across western waves and home in a royal capital: America for modern Athenians; modern Athens for Americans, a personal narrative in tour and time. London, [1898]. 376 p.   **DLC**

Uk has London, [1899] ed. Chaps. 1–5 on the U.S.

3114   [GLEN, FRANCIS WAYLAND]. Letter favoring the political union of the United States and British America, addressed to the Honorable John C. M'Guire . . . by an ex-member of the Canadian Parliament. New York, August 1st, 1898. [New York? 1898]. 4 p.   **DLC**

Caption title; signed by Glen. See also the American replies, ed. by Glen, *Letters relating to continental union; or, The creation of a greater United States*, [New York? 1898?], 4 p. See also author's "The political reunion of the United States and Canada. By an ex-member of the Canadian Parliament," *Am. J. Politics*, Dec. 1893, pp. 561–578.

3115   GRAHAM, [*SIR*] FREDERICK ULRIC. Notes of a sporting expedition in the far west of Canada, 1847. (Explanatory notes by Jane Hermione Graham). London, 1898. 120 p.   **CtY**

Priv. pr. On U.S., passim.

3116   GROSSMITH, GEORGE. "G.G." London, [1933]. 288 p.   **DLC Uk**

An autobiography; visited the U.S. 1895–96, pp. 36–44, 1898, pp. 62–69.

3117   [HAWKINS, *SIR* ANTHONY HOPE]. Memories and notes. By Anthony Hope [*pseud.*]. London, [1927]. 256 p.   **DLC Uk**

In U.S. 1897–98, pp. 199–216. See also account in Sir Charles Mallet, *Anthony Hope and his books*, London, [1935], pp. 118–125; and James Burton Pond, *Eccentricities of genius: memories of famous men and women of the platform and stage*, London, 1901, pp. 477–489.

3118   HENDERSON, *LIEUT.-COL.* GEORGE FRANCIS ROBERT. Stonewall Jackson and the American Civil War. London, 1898. 2 vols.   **DLC Uk**

2d ed., New York and London, 1899, introd. by Viscount Wolseley; many subsequent editions and printings.

3119   LAUGHTON, *SIR* JOHN KNOX. Memoirs of the life and correspondence of Henry Reeve. London, 1898. 2 vols.   **CLU MB NN UK**

See vol. I, passim., for discussion of Reeve's relations with Tocqueville, as translator of *Democracy in America*. Also see pp. 393–401 specifically for account of reactions to 3 articles by Reeves in the *Brit. & For. Rev.* (c. 1835–37), and to his Oct. 1858 article in *Edinb. Rev.* on the slave trade and the U.S., "The slave trade in 1858," CVIII, 541–586.

3120　LYDEKKER, RICHARD. The deer of all lands: a history of the family Cervidae living and extinct. London, 1898. 329 p.　　**DLC Uk**

"The American deer" (portions on North America), pp. 243–280. See also chap. on "American bison" in author's *Wild oxen, sheep & goats of all lands, living and extinct*, London, 1898, pp. 79–91.

3121　MEIKLEJOHN, MAX JOHN CHRISTIAN. The United States, their geography, resources, commerce and history, with chapters on the tides and chief ocean currents. London, [1898]. 93 p.　　**DLC Uk**

A geography text and guide book.

3122　MILLAR, JOHN [*of Toronto*]. The school system of the state of New York (as viewed by a Canadian). Prepared under the authority of the honorable the Minister of education, as an appendix to his annual report. Toronto, 1898. 204 p.　　**DHEW**

3123　MORGAN, T. R. Californian sketches. Towyn, 1898. 100 p.　　**C CtY**

3124　MUIRHEAD, JAMES FULLARTON. The land of contrasts; a Briton's view of his American kin. Boston, 1898. 282 p.　　**DLC Uk**

London, 1902 ed. carried the title, *America, the land of contrasts*, etc.; the 4th ed., London, 1911, carried the title *America, land of contrasts*. Portions repr. from the *Arena*. Muirhead also compiled the Karl Baedeker handbook, *The United States, with an excursion into Mexico*, Leipzig, 1893. In America in 1888 and 1890–1893.

3125　MURRAY, DAVID CHRISTIE. The Cockney Columbus. London, 1898. 292 p. **DLC Uk**

Partly repr. from New York *Herald* and the *Contemp. Rev.* On U.S., pp. 1–146. Murray gave a lecture tour in America in 1895–96; see the American letter "Advice on going to America," in his *Recollections*, London, 1908, p. 291.

3126　OUR KIN ACROSS THE SEA; one hundred and ninety-two American views including, among others, some places of interest in connection with the Spanish-American war and the gold-fields of Alaska. London, 1898. 196 p.　　**DLC**

Photographs with running commentary.

3127　PRICE, *SIR* ROSE LAMBART. A summer on the Rockies. London, 1898. 279 p.

DLC Uk

3128　REDDAWAY, WILLIAM FIDDIAN. The Monroe doctrine. Cambridge, [Eng.], 1898. 162 p.　　**DLC Uk**

3129　REYNOLDS, J[AMES] H. Report of a visit to technical colleges, institutions, schools, libraries, museums, and works in the United States and Canada, April and May, 1898. [Manchester? 1898?]. 67 p.　　**NN**

Caption title.

3130　[RITCHIE, JAMES EWING]. Christopher Crayon's recollections: the life and times of James Ewing Ritchie, as told by himself. London, 1898. 268 p.　　**Uk**

Two sketches on American experiences: "How I was made a fool of," pp. 241–249; and "Interviewing the President," pp. 253–258. See also author's article "Iowa as a field for emigration," *Christian World*, London, 1857. [Repr. in the Iowa *State Register* (Des Moines), Feb. 1, 1871].

3131 SELOUS, FREDERICK COURTENEY. Sport and travel east and west. London, 1900. 311 p. **DLC Uk**

In American Rockies, 1897 and 1898, pp. 144–311. See account in J. G. Millais, *Life of Frederick Courtenay Selous, D.S.O., Capt. 25th Royal Fusiliers*, London, 1918, pp. 228–233.

Review: *Quar. Rev.*, CXCVII, 172.

3132 SHEEHY-SKEFFINGTON, F[RANCIS]. Michael Davitt, revolutionary, agitator and labour leader . . . with an introduction by Justin McCarthy. London, 1908. 291 p. **DLC Uk**

Contains accounts of Davitt's visits to the U.S. in 1878, 1880, 1882, 1886 and 1898.

3133 SMITH, *SIR* GEORGE ADAM. The life of Henry Drummond. New York, 1898. 541 p. **DLC**

Uk has London, 1899 ed. Includes diary accounts of visits to America in 1879, pp. 136–138, 165–189; in 1887, pp. 368–385; and in 1893, pp. 450–457. See also Drummond's *Stones rolled away and other addresses to young men delivered in America*, London, 1900; C. K. Ober, "Professor Drummond in the American colleges," *Our Day*, I (Apr. 1888), 306–312.

3134 SMYTHE, ARTHUR J. The life of William Terriss, an actor . . . with an introduction by Clement Scott. Westminster, 1898. 212 p. **DLC Uk**

In the U.S. at various times from 1871 on.

3135 STOCKTON, ALFRED AUGUSTUS. The Monroe doctrine and other addresses. St. John, N.B., 1898. 191 p. **DLC Uk**

"The Monroe Doctrine," pp. 1–75.

3136 [TREVELYAN, *SIR* CHARLES PHILIPS]. Letters from North America and the Pacific, with a foreword by Leonard Woolf. London, 1969. 238 p. **DLC Uk**

Review: *Spectator* (by Oliver Warner), CCXXIII, 906.

3137 WARD, ROWLAND. The English angler in Florida; with some descriptive notes of the game animals and birds. London, 1898. 125 p. **DLC Uk**

3138 WEBB, BEATRICE. Beatrice Webb's American diary: 1898. Edited by David A. Shannon. Madison, Wisc., 1963. 181 p. **DLC UkLSE**

See also her *My apprenticeship*, New York & London, 1926, pp. 63–70, for excerpts from diary of her 1873 U.S. visit; and Norman Mackenzie, ed., *The letters of Sidney and Beatrice Webb*, Cambridge, 1978, I, pp. 8–10 (1873 letter from Beatrice Webb in San Francisco), II, pp. 60–75 (from her 1898 visit). See also Kitty Muggeridge and Ruth Adam, *Beatrice Webb: a life, 1858–1943*, London, 1967, pp. 47–50 (1873 visit), 157–159 (1898).

3139 WEIR, ARTHUR. A Canuck down south. Montreal, 1898. 182 p. **DLC**

Experiences in California.

3140 WEIR, WILLIAM. Sixty years in Canada. . . . secretary of the Tariff reform association of 1858 and government agent for the exportation of American silver coin in 1870. Montreal, 1903. 268 p. **DLC Uk**

Includes letters and addresses of author and of others concerned with Canadian-U.S. affairs, 1842–98.

1899

3141 THE AMERICAN-SPANISH WAR; a history by the war leaders, illustrated with numerous original engravings, maps, and diagrams. Norwich, Connecticut, 1899. 607 p.

DLC Uk

"What England Feels," by Hon. Justin McCarthy, pp. 487–508.

3142 AMERICAN ENGINEERING COMPETITION; being a series of articles resulting from an investigation made by "The Times", London. New York, 1901. 139 p. **DLC Uk**

Writer visited the U.S. in 1899; articles appeared in the London *Times*, Apr. 20, 1900–June 11, 1900.

3143 ARCHER, WILLIAM. America to-day; observations and reflections. New York, 1899. 260 p. **DLC**

Uk has London, 1900 ed. Letters and essays repr. from the *Pall Mall Gazette*, *Pall Mall Mag.*, and New York *Times*. In U.S. in 1877 and 1899; see accounts in Charles Archer's *William Archer, life, work and friendships*, New Haven, 1931, pp. 54–62, 233–236. See also the account of the 1877 visit in "San Francisco thirty years after," London *Daily News & Leader*, May 11, 1912. See also author's "America and the English language," *Pall Mall Mag.*, XVI (Oct. 1898), 231–235; XIX (Oct. 1899), 188–196.

3144 ATKINS, JOHN BLACK. The war in Cuba; the experiences of an Englishman with the United States Army. London, 1899. 291 p. **DLC Uk**

Originally appeared as letters in the Manchester *Guardian*, Apr.–Oct. 1898. See also account in author's *Incidents and reflections*, Toronto, 1947, pp. 98–118.

3145 BERESFORD, CHARLES WILLIAM DE LA POER BERESFORD, *1st Baron*. The memoirs of Admiral Lord Charles Beresford, written by himself. London, 1914. 2 vols.

DN NN PU

DLC, Uk have 2d ed., London, 1914. In U.S. in 1866 and 1899, pp. 69, 458–460 (chap. 46, "Traffic and discoveries: III. The United States.")

3146 BEVAN, LOUISA JANE, *comp*. The life and reminiscences of Llewelyn David Bevan, L.L.B., D.D. Melbourne, 1920. 317 p. **CtY Uk**

London ed., 1921. Describes visits to the U.S. in 1874, 1876–81, and 1899, pp. 131–162, 236–242.

3147 BLACKWOOD, ALGERNON. Episodes before thirty. London, 1923. 311 p. **DLC Uk**

Virtually all on U.S. In New York in 1890's; left for Ireland in 1899.

3148 BOYD, [*MRS.*] MARY STUART. Our stolen summer, the record of a roundabout tour, with 170 sketches by A. S. Boyd. Edinburgh, 1900. 392 p. **DLC Uk**

In U.S. in 1899, pp. 333–381. Portions had appeared in *Blackwood's Edinb. Mag.*, the London *Morning Post*, and the *Graphic*.

3149 [BRITANNICUS, *pseud*.] Our duty towards our working millions. Britain and America, the two great manufacturing countries, the natural protectors and reformers of China. London, 1899. 24 p. **DLC Uk**

Signed "Britannicus."

3150 BROOKFIELD, CHARLES H[ALLAM] E[LTON]. Random reminiscences. London, 1902. 305 p. **DLC Uk**

On U.S., pp. 288–298. Date of visit not given; between 1886 and 1902.

3151 [CAFFYN, WILLIAM]. Seventy-one not out. The reminiscences of William Caffyn, member of the all England and united elevens, of the Surrey County eleven, of the Anglo-American team of 1859, and of the Anglo-Australian teams of 1861 and 1863. Edited by Mid-on. Edinburgh, 1899. 265 p. **PPL Uk**

2d ed., rev., Edinburgh, 1900. A professional cricketer who toured the U.S. several times, 1852–1863.

3152 CAMPBELL, FRANCIS WAYLAND. The war of 1812–13–14 between Great Britain and the United States. A lecture delivered at the Montreal military institute and before the Numismatic and antiquarian society of Montreal in February 1899. Montreal, 1899. 47 p. **DLC**

3153 CARSON, THOMAS. Ranching, sport and travel. London, 1911. 319 p. **CU NN Uk**

NN also lists New York, [1910?]; DLC has New York, [1912] ed. A cattle rancher in Arizona, New Mexico and Texas, 1881–1899, pp. 42–233.

3154 CAVE-BROWNE-CAVE, *SIR* GENILLE, *bart*. From cowboy to pulpit. London, 1926. 312 p. **DLC Uk**

In U.S. in 1890's, pp. 88–89, 96–117. See also account of life in western U.S. in author's *Why I preach*, London, 1919.

3155 CHAPMAN, *SIR* SYDNEY JOHN. The history of trade between the United Kingdom and the United States, with special reference to the effect of tariffs. London, 1899. 118 p. **DLC Uk**

3156 CLARKE, WILLIAM. William Clark: a collection of his writings, with a biographical sketch. London, 1908. 420 p. **DLC Uk**

Repr. his answer to George Anderson's "The future of the Canadian dominion," in the *Contemp. Rev.*, XXXVIII, pt. 1 (Sept. 1880), 396–411; Clarke's answer carried identical title, "The future of the Canadian Dominion," ibid., pt. 2, (Nov. 1880), 805–826. Also repr. articles on U.S. from the *Spectator* for May 29, 1897, June 4, 1898, and Dec. 16, 1899; from *Prophets of the Century*, 1898; and from *The Young Man*, July 1900. (See pp. 129–158, 175–208, 259–268, 312–323, 332–341.) See also Clarke's comments on American democracy in his "The 'Spoils' system in American politics," *Contemp. Rev.*, XL (Oct. 1881), 633–650; "Industrial," *Fabian essays in Socialism*, ed. by G. Bernard Shaw, London, 1889, pp. 62–101; and Chaps. 2 and 4 in his *Walt Whitman*, London, 1892.

3157 COCHRAN, *SIR* CHARLES BLAKE. The secrets of a showman. London, 1925. 436 p. **DLC Uk**

In U.S. 1890–1902, pp. 7–61, 68–77. See also his account of American experiences through 1899 in *I had almost forgotten . . . with a preface by A. P. Herbert*, London, [1932], pp. 35–39, 187–196. See also Charles Graves, *The Cochran story; a biography of Sir Charles Blake Cochran*, London, [1951], pp. 6–15, 21–23.

3158 CROOKES, *SIR* WILLIAM. The wheat problem; based on remarks made in the presidential address to the British association at Bristol in 1898, revised, with an answer to various critics. With two chapters on the future wheat supply of the United States by Mr. C. Wood Davis and the Hon. John Hyde. London, 1899. 207 p. **DLC Uk**

Extensive comment by Crookes on U.S. wheat production.

3159   DAVIES, W[ILLIAM] H[ENRY]. The autobiography of a super-tramp, with preface by
        Bernard Shaw. New York, 1907. 345 p.   **RPB**

        DLC, Uk have London, 1908 ed. Describes experiences in U.S., 1894–99. See also
        accounts in the later volumes: *The true traveller*, London, 1912, and *The adventures of
        Johnny Walker, tramp*, London, [1926]. See also accounts by Lawrence William Hockey,
        W. H. Davies, Cardiff, 1971, pp. 14–19; and Richard James Stonesifer, *W. H. Davies, a crit-
        ical biography*, Middletown, Ct., [1965], pp. 26–36.

3160   [DEVOY, JOHN]. Devoy's post bag, 1871–1928. Edited by William O'Brien and
        Desmond Ryan. Introduction by P. S. O'Hegarty. Dublin, 1948–1953. 2 vols.
                                                                        CSmH MH UkLSE

        I, 1871–1880; II, 1880–1928. In America, the entire period. See accounts in Devoy's
        *Recollections of an Irish rebel. The Fenian movement . . . personalities of the organization,
        the Clan-na-gael and the rising of Easter week, 1916. A personal narrative*, [New York,
        1929], pp. 17–25, and passim; and in Desmond Ryan, *The phoenix flames. A study of
        Fenianism and John Devoy*, London, 1937.

3161   DOBSON, GEO[RGE] H. Modern transportation and Atlantic express tracks. Halifax,
        1899. 50 p.   **CaNSWA**

        Reference and comparisons to U.S. throughout. See also his *Ocean routes and modern
        transportation. Canada's splendid opportunity*, Halifax, 1898, pp. 3–5 and passim.

3162   DREW, LOUISA (LANE). Autobiographical sketch of Mrs. John Drew. With an introduc-
        tion by her son John Drew; with biographical notes by Douglas Taylor. New York, 1899.
        199 p.   **DLC Uk**

        Most of the book on the actress's many U.S. experiences, from 1827–1896.

3163   DUGMORE, ARTHUR RADCLYFFE. Bird homes. The nests, eggs and breeding habits
        of the land birds breeding in the eastern United States; with hints on the rearing and pho-
        tographing of young birds. New York, 1900. 183 p.   **DLC Uk**

        Dugmore travelled through the Eastern U.S. 1889 to 1892 and then settled in the vicinity
        of New York City. See his *The autobiography of a wanderer*, London, 1930, pp. 73–108,
        for experiences in the U.S. through 1899. See also Lowell Thomas, *Rolling stone; the life
        and adventures of Arthur Radclyffe Dugmore*, Garden City, N.Y., 1931, pp. 124–150.

3164   FAIRBROTHER, SYDNEY. Through an old stage door. London, [1939]. 256 p. **DLC Uk**

        In U.S. on several tours with the Kendals, 1890–99.

3165   FELL, *REV*. JAMES. British merchant seamen in San Francisco, 1892–1898. London,
        1899. 206 p.   **DLC Uk**

3166   FOUNTAIN, PAUL. The great deserts and forests of North America . . . With a preface by
        W. H. Hudson. London, 1901. 295 p.   **DLC Uk**

        Covers hunting experiences 1865 to end of century. See sequel, *The great Northwest and
        the great lake region of North America*, London, 1904 (Review in the *Dial*, by H. E.
        Coblentz, XXXVI, 362); and his *The eleven eaglets of the west*, London, 1906 (on exten-
        sive travels in the West in the 1860s and 1870s; reviews: *Athenaeum* (Apr. 7, 1906), 419;
        Book Rev. Digest, II, 108).

        Reviews: *Athenaeum* (Jan. 4, 1902), 9; *Nation*, LXXIV, 20.

3167   FRASER, [*SIR*] JOHN FOSTER, S. EDWARD LUNN, and F. H. LOWE. Round the world on a wheel; being the narrative of a bicycle ride of nineteen thousand two hundred and thirty-seven miles through seventeen countries and across three continents. London, 1899. 532 p.   **DLC Uk**

Repr. from *Travel*, IV (Aug.–Dec. 1899), 149–341. In U.S., pp. 463–529. See also Fraser's *America at work*, London, 1903; his "Impressions of a world wanderer," *Contemp. Rev.*, LXXV (Jan. 1899), 73–83; and his "Mankind as seen by an English cyclist," *Rev. of Revs.*, XIX (Feb. 1899), 233.

3168   FRENCH, *HON*. WILLIAM [JOHN]. Some recollections of a western ranchman; New Mexico, 1883–1899. London, 1927. 283 p.   **MH NN Uk WHi**

DLC has New York, [1928] ed.

3169   GANTHONY, ROBERT. Random recollections. London, [1899]. 244 p.   **DLC Uk**

In U.S., pp. 31–55.

3170   GRESWELL, *REV*. WILLIAM HENRY PARR. The United States and their industries. London, 1899. 91 p.   **MiU PU Uk**

3171   GREY, FREDERICK WILLIAM. Seeking fortune in America. London, 1912. 307 p.   **DLC Uk**

In U.S., 1893–1904. See also his "The theory and practice of American popular government," *Westmin. Rev.*, CXL (Aug. 1893), 175–186.

3172   HARBORD, M[AURICE] A[SSHETON]. Froth and bubble. London, 1915. 335 p.   **DLC Uk**

In U.S., 1895–99, pp. 10–99; remained until 1915.

3173   HODGINS, THOMAS. British and American diplomacy affecting Canada. 1782–1899. A chapter of Canadian history. Toronto, 1900. 102 p.   **DLC Uk**

Originally appeared in *Canadian Mag.*, X (Mar. 1898), 379–389. Also appeared in *Canada: an encyclopedia of the country*, ed. by J. Castell Hopkins, Toronto, 1898–1900, VI, 88–109.

3174   HOLLOWELL, JAMES HIRST. The school system of the United States: features worthy of English imitation. A paper read at Newcastle-on-Tyne, England, at a conference called by the Congregational church aid and home missionary society (during the autumnal meeting of the Congregational union of England and Wales) on Tuesday, Oct. 16th, 1900. Castlemore, Rochdale, England, 1900. 16 p.   **DHEW**

Visited Massachusetts schools in 1899. See also his "Modern tendencies in education," *Education*, XX (Nov. 1899), 143–151, apparently a lecture given in the U.S.

3175   [HOLMES, OLIVER WENDELL and *SIR* FREDERICK POLLOCK]. Holmes-Pollock letters; the correspondence of Mr. Justice Holmes and Sir Frederick Pollock, 1874–1932, edited by Mark De Wolfe Howe . . . with an introduction by John Gorham Palfrey. Cambridge, Mass., 1941. 2 vols.   **DLC**

Uk has Cambridge, Eng., 1942 ed., *Pollock-Holmes letters* . . . For letters through 1899, see vol. I, pp. 3–98. Pollock was in U.S. in 1895; see his account in *For my grandson; remembrances of an ancient Victorian*, London, 1933, pp. 192–199.

3176   KELLY, ETHEL KNIGHT. Twelve milestones: being the peregrinations of Ethel Knight Kelly. London, 1929. 240 p.   **IaU NN Uk**

In U.S., pp. 27–88.

3177   KENNEDY, BART. A man adrift: being leaves from a nomad's portfolio. London, 1899. 342 p.   **Uk**

NN, WaU have New York, 1900 ed. About U.S. experiences, but no dates given. See also incidental comment in *Footlights*, London, 1928.

3178   KERR, FRED [i.e., FREDERICK GRINHAM KEEN]. Recollections of a defective memory. London, 1930. 285 p.   **DLC Uk**

Describes various tours in America in the 1880's and 1890's.

3179   LAWRENCE, ARTHUR. Sir Arthur Sullivan: life-story, letters, and reminiscences . . . With critique by B. W. Findon, and bibliography by Wilfrid Bendall. London, 1899. 360 p.   **DLC Uk**

Accounts of visits to the U.S. in 1878–80 and 1885, pp. 126–153, 172–173. See also Herbert Sullivan and Newman Flower, *Sir Arthur Sullivan, his life, letters & diaries*, New York, 1927 (new ed., 1950), pp. 131–143, 194–201.

3180   LIPTON, *SIR* THOMAS J[OHNSTONE], *bart.* Leaves from the Lipton logs. London, [1931]. 278 p.   **DLC Uk**

New York, [1932] ed. carried title *Lipton's autobiography; with twenty-four illustrations.* In the U.S., pp. 61–82, 142–161, 181–193, 235–248, and passim. See also the account of the 1899 race in Charles T. Bateman, *Lipton and the American cup*, Edinburgh, 1901, pp. 51–73.

3181   LONGLEY, JAMES WILBERFORCE. Sir Wilfrid Laurier at Washington. From February number of National Review. [Halifax? 1899].   **CSmH**

Priv. pr. See Ulric Barthe, comp., *1871–1890. Wilfrid Laurier on the platform: collection of the principal speeches made in Parliament or before the people by the Honorable Wilfrid Laurier, P.C., Q.C., M.P., member for Quebec-East in the Commons, since his entry into active politics in 1871 . . . illustrated with a portrait of Mr. Laurier and prefaced with a sketch of his career and work*, Quebec, 1890, pp. 41–50, 389–438, 463–492. See also comments on U.S. in Oscar Douglas Skelton, *Life and letters of Sir Wilfrid Laurier*, New York, 1922, II, pp. 119–133, and passim; and in Sir John Willson, *Sir Wilfrid Laurier*, New York, 1926, pp. 187–200.

3182   LOW, *SIR* ALFRED MAURICE. America at home. London, 1908. 231 p.   **DLC Uk**

In U.S., 1880–1900. See also his *The American people. A study in national psychology*, Boston, 1909–1911, 2 vols.; "Some light on the Canadian enigma," *Forum*, XXVII (June 1899), 479–490; and the series "The month in America," *Natl. Rev.*, (Apr. 1897–Jan. 1900), XXVIII, 228–XXXIV, 714.

3183   LUBBOCK, A[LFRED] BASIL. Round the horn before the mast. London, 1902. 375 p.   **NN Uk**

DLC has London, 1903 ed.; many later eds. In San Francisco in 1899, pp. 1–75.

3184   LUSK, HUGH H[ART]. Our foes at home. London, 1899. 297 p.   **Uk**

DLC has New York, 1899 ed. Entire book on U.S.

Review: *Dial* (by M. West), XXIX, 178.

3185 MCCARTHY, JUSTIN. Reminiscences. London, 1899. 2 vols.   **DLC**

In U.S., 1868–71 and 1886–87, I, pp. 190–307; II, pp. 1–23, 61–88, 369–373. See other accounts of his U.S. experiences in his "American men and Englishmen," *Galaxy*, IX (June 1870), 758–770; "American women and English women," ibid., X (July 1870), 25–36; *The story of an Irishman*, London, 1904, pp. 138–180; and letters to Mrs. Campbell-Praed in *Our book of memories*, London, 1912. See also Campbell-Praed's "Some American impressions," *Temple Bar*, LXXX (July 1887), 315–326, (Aug. 1887), 482–491, LXXXI (Sept. 1887), 61–75. See also McCarthy's and Sir John R. Robinson's *"Daily News" jubilee: a political and social retrospect of fifty years of the Queen's reign*, London, 1896, pp. 44–48, 69–77; and McCarthy's "What England feels," in *The American-Spanish war; a history by the war leaders. . . .*, Norwich, Conn., 1899, pp. 487–508.

3186 MASON, ARTHUR. Ocean echoes: an autobiography. With an introduction by William McFee. New York, 1922. 287 p.   **DLC Uk**

London, 1923 ed. under title: *Wide seas and missing lands*. Account of adventures in California in the 1890s; came to U.S. in 1893 and became a citizen in 1899, pp. 89–179.

3187 MEDLEY, GEORGE WEBB. Pamphlets and addresses. London, 1899. 413 p.
    CSt NjP Uk

DLC has New York, 1899 ed. Uk lists under London-Cobden Club. Contains extensive comment on trade relations, passim., in a series of essays written between 1881–1899, most of which had appeared earlier in pamphlet form. See esp. "England under free trade. An address delivered to the Sheffield Junior liberal association, 8th November, 1881," (London, 1881), pp. 43–83; "The trade depression: its causes and its remedies," (London, 1885), pp. 115–166; "Fair trade unmasked; or, Notes on the minority report of the Royal commission on the depression of trade and industry," (London, [1887] pp. 167–279; and, "The triumph of free trade. An address delivered at the annual general meeting of the Cobden club, 1890," (London, 1890), pp. 285–307.

3188 MILLAR, JOHN, [*of Toronto*]. Technical education. Report of a visit to the schools of Massachusetts, and opinions on the subject of technical education. Toronto, 1899. 12 p.
    CaOTU DHEW

3189 MILLS, DAVID. The Canadian view of the Alaskan boundary dispute as stated by Hon. David Mills, Minister of justice, in an interview with the correspondent of the Chicago Tribune on the 14th August, 1899. Ottawa, 1899. 23 p.   **DLC**

See also author's "The new Monroe doctrine of Messrs. Cleveland and Olney," *Canadian Mag.*, VI (Feb. 1896), 365–380.

3190 MILLWARD, JESSIE. Myself and others. (In collaboration with J[ohn] B[ennion] Booth). London, 1923. 318 p.   **DLC Uk**

In U.S. several times, 1883–1899.

3191 MORGAN, WILMA, "MRS. R. C. MORGAN." Glimpses of four continents being an account of the travels of Richard Cope Morgan. London, 1911. 388 p.   **DLC Uk**

In U.S., 1897–98 and 1899, pp. 61–94. See also Morgan's and Mrs. Morgan's accounts of these visits in his "American Notes," the *Christian*, (1897), Dec. 16, p. 13; Dec. 23, p. 14; Dec. 30, p. 16; (1898), Jan. 27, p. 20; Feb. 10, p. 20; Feb. 17, p. 14; Mar. 3, p. 18; Mar. 10, p. 14; Mar. 24, p. 12; Mar. 31, p. 13; Apr. 14, p. 13; Apr. 21, p. 13; May 12, p. 12; May 26, p. 15; June 9, p. 13; June 16, p. 12; (1899), Mar. 9, p. 21; Mar. 16, p. 15; Mar. 23, p. 12; Mar. 30, p. 12; Apr. 6, p. 19; Apr. 13, p. 18; Apr. 20, p. 19; Apr. 27, p. 12; May 4, p. 12; May 11, p. 13; May 25, p. 14; June 1, p. 13; June 8, p. 21. See also account of the earlier visit of 1876 in George E. Morgan, *"A veteran in revival." R. C. Morgan: his life and times*, London, 1909, pp. 177–182.

3192   MOSCHELES, FELIX. Fragments of an autobiography. London, 1899. 364 p.   **DLC Uk**

In U.S. 1883–85: "A trip to America in 1883," pp. 208–233; "Grover Cleveland 'viewed'," pp. 234–244.

3193   MOWAT, ROBERT BALMAIN. The life of Lord Pauncefote, first ambassador to the United States. London, [1929]. 306 p.   **DLC Uk**

In U.S., 1889–1902; last 15 chaps. deal with years of his ministry.

3194   MUSGRAVE, GEORGE CLARKE. Under three flags in Cuba: a personal account of the Cuban insurrection and Spanish-American war. London, 1899. 365 p.   **Uk**

DLC has Boston, 1899 ed.

3195   OSLER, *SIR* WILLIAM. An Alabama student, and other biographical essays. Oxford, 1908. 334 p.   **MB NN Uk**

DLC has New York, 1908 ed. Contains several essays and addresses of the 1890's on various American figures, pp. 1–18, 55–67, 108–158, 211–231. Title essay is repr. from the *Johns Hopkins Hosp. Bull.*, No. 58, (Jan. 1896), pp. 6–11, as is "Influence of Louis on American Medicine," ibid., (Aug.–Sept. 1897), 161–167. For an extended account of his years (1884–1905) as Professor of Medicine at the University of Pennsylvania and at Johns Hopkins University, see Harvey [Williams] Cushing's *The life of Sir William Osler*, Oxford, 1925, I, pp. 233–685. See also Bull. No. IX of the Intern. Assoc. of Medical Museums and Jour. of Technical Methods: *Sir William Osler, Memorial number. Appreciation and reminiscences*, Montreal, 1926, pp. 52–58, 205–345, 439–441; Howard L. Holley, *A continual remembrance: letters from Sir William Osler to his friend Ned Milburn, 1865–1919*, Springfield, Ill., [1968], pp. 55–79; and William Sydney Thayer, *Osler and other papers*, Freeport, N.Y., [1969], pp. 18–41.

3196   PORTER, T[HOMAS] C[UNNINGHAM]. Impressions of America. . . . Illustrated with diagrams and stereoscopic views. London, 1899. 241 p.   **DLC Uk**

Priv. pr.

3197   ROWNTREE, JOSEPH and ARTHUR SHERWELL. The temperence problem and social reform. London, 1899. 626 p.

No 1st ed. located. CoDI, PGC, NSbSU have 2 ed., London, 1899; DLC, UK have 5th ed., London, 1899. 7th ed., rev. and enlarged, New York, 1900. On U.S., passim. One of the authors in the U.S. in 1899.

3198   SALMON, DAVID. Some impressions of American education: a lecture delivered on Monday, July 3rd, 1899, at the Swansea training college, by the principal, David Salmon. Swansea, [1899?]. 32 p.   **CtY DHEW**

Also pub. in *Educational Rev.* (N.Y.), XVIII (Dec. 1899), 437–450; XIX (Jan. 1900), 36–48.

3199   SETON, ERNEST THOMPSON. Trail of an artist-naturalist: the autobiography of Ernest Thompson Seton. With illustrations by the author. New York, 1940. 412 p.   **DLC**

Uk has London, 1941 ed. In U.S., 1882, pp. 156–161; in 1883, pp. 211–213, 239–249; in 1885, pp. 279–281; in 1892–94, pp. 304–339; 1896–1940, pp. 343–387. Changed name from Seton-Thompson to Seton, p. 392. See also his chronicles of life in New Mexico in *Wild animals I have known*, London, 1898, pp. 17–54, 229–270.

3200 SIMPSON, ALEXANDER G. The life of a miner in both hemispheres. New York, [1903]. 300 p. **CLU IHi MH NN**

Describes visits to America in 1871 and 1880; following the second visit he settled in U.S. See pp. 149–179, 222–292.

3201 SMITH, EDWARD. England and America after independence; a short examination of their international intercourse, 1783–1872. Westminster, 1900. 297 p. **DLC Uk**

Pref. dated Aug. 1899.

3202 SMITH, THOMAS WATSON. The slave in Canada. Halifax, 1899. 161 p. **CU CtY ICJ MB**

Nova Scotia Hist. Soc. Collections, 1896–98, vol. 10.

3203 STEAD, W[ILLIAM] T[HOMAS]. The United States of Europe on the eve of the parliament of peace. London, 1899. 215 p. **DLC Uk**

DLC also has New York, 1899 eds. Describes impact on European attitudes of U.S. war with Spain. See also Stead's *The Americanization of the World; or, The trend of the twentieth century*, New York, 1901, for the British journalist's celebration of an American century.

3204 SYKES, GODFREY GLENTON. A westerly trend, being a veracious chronicle of more than sixty years of joyous wanderings, mainly in search of space and sunshine. Tucson, 1944. 325 p. **DLC**

Came to U.S. as a young man in 1879; returned to England during World War I, and returned to U.S. again in 1938.

3205 TERRY, *DAME* ELLEN (ALICE). The story of my life. London, 1908. 381 p. **DLC Uk**

New York, 1908 ed. carried title, *The story of my life; recollections and reflections*. A later ed., with biographical additions, ed. by Edith Craig and Christopher St. John, was entitled *Ellen Terry's memoirs*, London, 1932. The actress toured America 8 times, 1883–1907.

3206 VACHELL, HORACE ANNESLEY. Life and sport on the Pacific slope. London, 1900. 312 p. **CSmH InU MH UK**

DLC has New York, 1901 ed. London, 1908 ed. had title: *Sport and life on the Pacific slope*. In California, 1882–99. See author's *Distant fields, a writer's autobiography*, London, 1937; and his *Fellow-travellers*, London, 1923. See also the account in Norreys Jephson O'Conor, "Magnificent adventurer," *Arizona Quar.*, VII (Autumn 1951), 241–252. See also Vachell's novels, many of which depict life in California.

Reviews: *Bookman*, XX, 58; *Field*, XCVI, 913.

3207 [WALSTON, *SIR* CHARLES]. The expansion of western ideals and the world's peace. By Charles Waldstein. New York, 1899. 194 p. **DLC Uk**

Waldstein later known as Walston. Repr. a lecture from the *No. Am. Rev.* for Aug. 1898; also contains the lecture "The English-speaking brotherhood," delivered at the Imperial Institute, July 7, 1898. See Lord Rosebery's response to the 2d lecture in his *Appreciations and addresses*, London, 1899, pp. 261–269.

3208 WALTERS, FREDERICK RUFENACHT. Sanatoria for consumptives in various parts of the world. London, 1899. 374 p. **DLC Uk**

On U.S., pp. 83–119.

3209   WARNER, PELHAM FRANCIS. Cricket in many climes. London, 1900. 271 p.

MB OCI PPL Uk

On cricket tours to the U.S., 1887, pp. 81–115, 1899, pp. 145–169. See also his *My cricketing life*, London, [1921?].

3210   WEBLING, PEGGY. Peggy; the story of one score years and ten. London, [1924]. 303 p.

ICU NN Uk

Toured the eastern U.S. in 1891–92, pp. 171–186; and in the western states in 1899, pp. 263–274.

3211   YOUNGHUSBAND, *SIR* GEORGE JOHN. The Philippines and round about, by Major G. J. Younghusband. New York, 1899. 230 p.   **DLC Uk**

Describes American activities during the Spanish-American War, including a chapter on "The American soldier."

Author Index

References are by year and entry numbers (e.g., 32-24 refers to 1832, entry 24). Boldface indicates author of main entry. Others indicate authors of secondary works or reviews, or editors of subsequent versions of the main entries.

Abbott, Charles E., **82-2374**

Abbott, Ethel B., **82-2375**

Abbott, Rev. Joseph, **42-324**

Abdy, Edward Strutt, **35-91, 42-325**

Abercromby, Ralph, **88-2655**

Aberdeen, George Hamilton Gordon (4th Earl), 46-507

Aberdeen and Temair, Ishbel Maria (Marjoribanks) Gordon, Lady, **97-3072**

Abrahall, John Hoskyns-, Jun., **64-1449**

Ackrill, Robert, **78-2214**

Acland, Sir Henry Wentworth Dyke, **79-2253**

Acton, Arthur S., 92-2889

Acton, Lord John Emerich Edward Dalberg, 63-1333, 63-1382

Acworth, Sir William Mitchell, **91-2798, 98-3101**

Adam, Graeme Mercer, **88-2656**

Adam, Ruth, 98-3138

Adam, William Patrick, **52-737**

Adams, Brooks, 63-1299

Adams, Charles Francis, 62-1219, 62-1296, 63-1332

Adams, Charles Francis, Jr., 42-349, 61-1185, 70-1897

Adams, Charles Kendall, 72-1951, 79-2263

Adams, Ephraim Douglass, 42-351, 43-363, 46-478

Adams, Francis (of Birmingham), **75-2076**

Adams, George J., **41-281**

Adams, Henry Gardiner, **54-872**

Adams, Herbert B., 83-2433

Adams, William Edwin, 58-1024, **63-1297, 83-2421**

Adams, William Henry Davenport, 47-555, **76-2124,** 79-2255

Adamson, John, **47-531**

Adrian, Arthur A., 42-339, 74-2055

Aflalo, Frederick George, **96-3034**

Aiken, Peter Freedland, **42-326**

Ainley, ———?, **62-1196**

Ainsworth, William Francis, **62-1197**

Aitken, Hugh G. J., 63-1394

Aitken, James, **82-2376, 94-2954**

Aitken, W., **45-431**

Ajax, **62-1196**

Albemarle, William Coutts Keppel (7th Earl), **73-1996**

Aldington, Richard, 95-3026

Aldridge, Reginald, **84-3460**

Alexander, George William, **42-327**

Alexander, Sir James Edward, **33-31, 49-593, 57-988**

Alexander, W., 60-1095, **61-1135**

Alger, W. H., **84-3461**

Alison, Alexander, **61-1136, 62-1198, 65-1546**

Allan-Olney, Mary, **80-2292**

Allardice, Robert Barclay, **42-328**

Allen, Richard, **41-304**

Allott, Kenneth, 88-2657

Allsop, Thomas, **53-800**

Altman, Gail Platt, 42-339

Amberley, John Russell (Viscount), **67-1706**

Title Index

This index includes both the main entry titles (and significant variations) and other books by the main authors selected for significant comments on the United States. References are by year and entry numbers (e.g., 32-24 refers to 1832, entry 24). Boldface refers to the main entry.

The adventures, sufferings and observations of James Wood, containing amongst other things, a description of various places lying between the Gulfs of Darien and St. Lawrence, with an account of the manners of the inhabitants of the places described, **40-280**

The adventurous life and daring exploits in England and America of Capt. Matthew Webb the swimming champion of the world, **83-2455**

Advice and guide to emigrants, going to the United States of America, **34-83**

Advice to emigrants; or, An impartial guide to the Canadas, New Brunswick, Nova Scotia, the United States, **32-8**

Advice to emigrants, who intend to settle in the United States of America, **32-1**

The affair at Grey Town, **57-1022**

After all; the autobiography of Norman Angell, **98-3102**

After shipwreck, **89-2747**

After the storm; or, Jonathan and his neighbors in 1865–66, **66-1698**

Agricultural notes in Ohio and Michigan, **56-982**

Agricultural tour in the United States and upper Canada, with miscellaneous notices, **42-328**

The Alabah [i.e., Alabama] claims, and how the Ya-kees "fixed" the Yn-Gheesh. Being a fragment of some lately discovered annals of monkeydom, **72-1978**

The Alabama and the Kearsarge. An account of the naval engagement in the British channel, on Sunday, June 19th, 1864, **64-1475**

The 'Alabama' claims and arbitration considered from a legal point of view, **68-1759**

The Alabama controversy: its past history and present phase, **72-1963**

An Alabama student, and other biographical essays, **99-3195**

"The Alabama": a statement of facts from official documents, with the sections of the Foreign enlistment act violated by her equipment, **63-1299**

The alien invasion, **92-2893**

The all-round route guide. The Hudson River; Trenton falls; Niagara; Toronto; the Thousand islands and the river St. Lawrence; Ottawa; Montreal; Quebec; the lower St. Lawrence and the Saguenay rivers; the White mountains; Boston, New York, **68-1754**

All round the world. Adventures in Europe, Asia, Africa, and America, **71-1916**

All round the world: an illustrated record of voyages, travels, and adventures in all parts of the globe, **62-1197**

All the world at the fair; being representatives of thiry-seven nationalities in gala costume, **93-2896**

An Almanac of independence & freedom for the year 1860; containing a plea for the relief of the inhabitants of Canada from a state of colonial vassalage or irresponsible rule . . . . together with considerations with reference to the position in which Upper Canada stands toward the American republic, **60-1117**

Altowan; or, Incidents of life and adventure in the Rocky mountains, **46-518**

The amateur emigrant; from the Clyde to Sandy Hook, **95-3026**

The Amberly papers; the letters and diaries of Lord and Lady Amberley, **67-1706**

America, **78-2238**

America: a four years' residence in the United States and Canada; giving a full and fair description of the country, as it really is, with the manners, customs, & character of the inhabitants, **49-598**

America: a lecture. . . . Delivered at the Young men's temperance hall, **74-2064**

America after sixty years; the travel diaries of two generations of Englishmen, **78-2243**

America, and American Methodism, **57-1012**

America and England contrasted, in a series of letters, from settlers in the United States & Canada, **32-2**

America and her army, **65-1605**

American civil war. Correspondence with Mr. H. C. Carey, of Philadelphia.
August–September, 1861, **61-1151**

The American colonization scheme further unravelled, **33-60**

The American commissioners and the statement of Sir Stafford Northcote at Exeter,
in relation to an alleged promise of exclusion of the indirect claims of the
United States, **72-1940**

The American commonwealth, **88-2669**

American competition, **85-2535**

American competition and the future of British agriculture, **81-2359**

American confessions of a layman, as connected with the workings of democracy in the
United States; with their application to the present condition of Europe, **48-569**

The American conflict; a lecture, **63-1340**

The American conflict: an address, spoken before the New England society of Montreal,
65-1574

The American conflict as seen from a European point of view, **63-1344**

American corn and British manufactures, **45-462**

The American crisis considered, **61-1172**

The American crisis in relation to slavery, **62-1289**

The American crisis, in relation to the anti-slavery cause, **62-1259**

American diaries, **59-1065**

An American diary, 1857–58, **58-1032**

American difficulties. Letters by Vigil, **61-1193**

American dis-union: constitutional or unconstitutional, **62-1268**

An American duchess, 77-2198

American engineering competition; being a series of articles resulting from an investigation
made by "The Times", **99-3142**

American factories and their female operatives; with an appeal on behalf of the British
factory population, **45-456**

American farming and food, **81-2346**

American game bird shooting, **82-2406**

American home rule: a sketch of the political system in the United States, **87-2639**

American humorists, 96-3046

The American invasion; or, England's commercial danger and the triumphal progress of the
United States, 94-2992

The American Irish, **79-2287**

The American Irish and their influence on Irish politics, **82-2381**

An American journey, **87-2606**

American liberty and government questioned, **55-947**

American literature, an historical sketch, 1620–1880, **82-2410**

American memoranda, by a mercantile man, during a short tour in the summer of 1843,
44-420

American memories: recollections of a hurried run through the United States during the late
spring of 1896, **96-3050**

American neutrality, **65-1591**

American notes, **91-2823**

American notes, 1881, **82-2418**

American notes for general circulation, **42-339**

American notes: letters from a lecture tour, 1874, **74-2055**

The American people. A study in national psychology, 99-3182

American photographs, **59-1090**

The autobiography of Sir John Martin-Harvey, **93-2924**

The autobiography of the Rev. E. Mathews, the "Father Dickson," of Mrs. Stowe's "Dred"; also a description of the influence of the slave-party over the American presidents, and the rise and progress of the anti-slavery reform, **67-1738**

Autographs for freedom, **53-824**

An autumn holiday in the United States and Canada, **87-2629**

An autumn tour in the United States and Canada, **73-2019**

B. C. 1887. A ramble in British Columbia, **88-2683**

Bacon's descriptive handbook of America. Comprising history, geography, railways, mining, finance, government, politics, public lands, laws, etc., **66-1654**

Baggage & boots; or, Smith's first peep at America, **83-2423**

Balance sheet of the Washington treaty of 1872, [i.e. 1871] in account with the people of Great Britain and her colonies, **73-1996**

The Bankrupt law of the United States. 1867, **67-1728**

The Baptists in America; a narrative of the deputation from the Baptist Union in England, to the United States and Canada, **36-127**

Baring Brothers and Co. Statement of their transactions with S. Jaudon, agent of the Bank of the United States, **40-245**

The Barnabys in America; or adventures of the widow wedded, 32-28

Barrie, the story of a genius, **96-3044**

Barry Sullivan and his contemporaries; a histrionic record, **76-2163**

The Bastille in America; or, Democratic absolutism, **61-1140**

The battle of Bull Run, **61-1184**

The battle of Gettysburg, July 1st, 2nd, 3rd, 1863, **93-2925**

The battle of the Swash and the capture of Canada, **88-2661**

Battle-fields of the South, from Bull Run to Fredericksburg; with sketches of Confederate commanders and gossip of the camps, **63-1320**

Battles of the nineteenth century, **97-3073**

Beaten paths; and those who trod them, 61-1167

Beatrice Webb's American diary: 1898, **98-3138**

The beauties of America, **36-132**

Before I forget—The autobiography of a chevalier d'industrie, **98-3107**

Behind the scenes with Cyril Maude, **84-2500**

The Behring sea question, **96-3068**

The Behring sea question: the arbitration treaty and the award, **93-2951**

Belligerent right on the high seas, since the declaration of Paris (1856), **84-2519**

Belligerent rights of maritime capture, **63-1362**

The beloved crime, or the North and the South at issue, **61-1141**

Betterment: being the law of special assessment for benefits in America, **93-2898**

Between two oceans; or, Sketches of American travel, **84-2486**

The Bible and slavery, **63-1354**

The Bijou gazetteer of the world: briefly describing, as regards position, area, and population, every country and state, **71-1930**

Bird homes. The nests, eggs and breeding habits of the land birds breeding in the eastern United States, **99-3163**

A bishop in the rough, **65-1632**

Bits about America, **87-2648**

Black America: a study of the ex-slave and his late master, **91-2805**

Black and white. A journal of a three months' tour in the United States, **67-1733**

A brief reply to an important question; being a letter to Professor Goldwin Smith from an implicit believer in Holy Scripture, **63-1316**

A brief review of the revenue, resources, and expenditures of Canada compared with those of the neighboring state of New-York, **45-451**

A brief view of the operations and principles of temperance societies; with a sketch of their origin and progress in America, **33-33**

Britain and America united in the cause of universal freedom: being the third annual report of the Glasgow emancipation society, **37-163**

Britain redeemed and Canada preserved, **50-685**

British aid to the confederates. Tracts on slavery in America, No. III, **63-1317**

The British American Federation a necessity; its industrial policy also a necessity, **65-1563**

The British American guide-book: being a condensed gazeteer, directory and guide, to Canada, the western states, and principal cities on the seaboard, **59-1061**

British and American diplomacy affecting Canada. 1782–1899, **99-3173**

British and Canadian citizens in the United States, **87-2644**

A British army, as it was, is, and ought to be: illustrated by examples during the Peninsular war: with observations upon India, the United States of America, Canada, the boundary line, the navy, steam warfare, & c., **40-248**

The British colonist in North America: a guide for intending emigrants, **90-2756**

British Columbia, emigration, and our colonies, considered practically, socially, and politically, 65-1636

British comments on the President's message, **88-2668**

British diplomatic correspondence concerning the republic of Texas—1836–46, **46-478**

The British emigrant's advocate: being a manual for the use of emigrants and travellers in British America and the United States, **37-158**

The British farmer and his competitors, **88-2662**

British industries and foreign competition, **94-2995**

The British mechanic's and labourer's hand book, and true guide to the United States, **40-264**

British merchant seamen in San Francisco, 1892–1898, **99-3165**

British North American boundary commission, **75-2096**

The British North American colonies. Letters to the Right Hon. E.G.S. Stanley, M.P., upon the existing treaties with France and America, **34-90**

British opinion of the American contest, **62-1216**

British opinions of the American colonization society, **33-34**

British sympathy in the American crisis, **63-1377**

British versus American civilization, **73-2006**

The British versus the American system of national government, **91-2824**

Brook Farm: the amusing and memorable of American country life, **59-1060**

Brother Jonathan; or, the "Smartest nation in all creation." Sketches of American life and manners, selected from the papers of Mr. Hugo Playfair, **41-314**

Brother Jonathan, sketched by himself, in the Yankee notions he has of his own importance as a nation, **56-960**

The Brotherhood of the new life and Thomas Lake Harris, **93-2929**

The Brownings and America, **61-1165**

Burning Canadian questions. Inter-provincial communication, Atlantic ports, development of natural resources, labor and capital, immigration, and prohibition, **92-2892**

By canoe and dog-train among the Cree and Salteaux Indians, **90-2797**

By land and ocean; or, The journal and letters of a young girl who went to South Australia with a lady friend, then alone to Victoria, New Zealand, Sydney, Singapore, China, Japan, and across the continent of America to home, **78-2244**

By ocean, prairie and peak, **96-3035**

By sea and by land; being a trip through Egypt, India, Ceylon, Australia, New Zealand, and America, **74-2060**

Caird's slanders on Canada answered & refuted!, 59-1064

Calcutta to Liverpool, by China, Japan, and America, in 1877, **78-2241**

California, **69-1831**

California: a handbook of useful and reliable information, **96-3038**

California: a history of Upper and Lower California from their first discovery to the present time, **39-218**

California and its gold mines: being a series of recent communications from the mining districts, upon the present condition and future prospects of quartz mining, **53-800**

California and its resources. A work for the merchant, the capitalist, and the emigrant, **58-1052**

California and the gold mania, **52-753**

California as a field for emigration for the farmer, labourer, and mechanic; and paramount advantages over Australia, **71-1906**

California broadsides, **50-676**

California: its climate and prospects for emigrants, **87-2613**

California: its gold and its inhabitants, **56-973**

California: its life and climate, with an account of the prospects of fruit-growing, **93-2904**

California: its past history; its present position; its future prospects; containing a history of the country from its colonization by the Spaniards to the present time, **50-660**

California: its present condition and future prospects; with an interesting account of the gold regions, **50-653**

The Californian Crusoe; or, The lost treasure found. A tale of Mormonism, 54-881

Californian homes for educated Englishmen. A practical suggestion for a model colony, **75-2081**

Californian sketches, **98-3123**

The Californians, **76-2138**

Campaign echoes. The autobiography of Mrs. Letitia Youmans, **93-2953**

The campaign in Virginia, May and June, 1864, 91-2828

The campaign of Fredericksburg, Nov.–Dec. 1862, **86-2583**

The campaigns in Virginia, 1861–62, **91-2828**

Camps in the Rockies. Being a narrative of life on the frontier, **82-2382**

Can Canada be coerced?, **91-2845**

Can we enter into treaty with the new slave trading Confederacy?, **61-1135**

Canada, a battle ground; about a Kingdom in America, **62-1277**

Canada. An essay, **55-923**

Canada and her commerce, from the time of the first settler to that of the representative men of to-day, **94-2974**

Canada and invasion, **63-1324**

Canada and the Canadian question, **91-2841**

Canada and the Canadians, in 1846, **46-467**

Canada and the Crimea; or, Sketches of a soldier's life, **62-1267**

Canada and the empire, **73-2032**

Canada and the States; recollections, 1851 to 1886, **87-2650**

Canada and the United States: [A letter] to the editor of the National Intelligencer, **49-643**

Canada and the United States compared, with practical notes on commercial unions, unrestricted reciprocity, and annexation, **89-2719**

The claims to the Oregon territory considered, **44-427**

Class despotism, as exemplified during the four years struggle for freedom in the United States of America; and the evils of individual wealth considered, as reflecting the well-being and lives of the mass of a people, **67-1736**

The clergy of America: anecdotes illustrating the life and labour of ministers of religion in the United States, **69-1818**

The climax of protection and free trade, capped by annexation, **49-604**

The clockmaker; or, The sayings and doings of Samuel Slick, of Slickville, 51-703

Closest trade relations between the United States and Canada, **92-2895**

The coal-fields of Great Britain: their history, structure, and duration. With notices of the coal-fields of other parts of the world, **61-1171**

The Cockney Columbus, **98-3125**

The collected remarkable travels of George Pitt, (accompanied by his wife), round and over the world, **86-2591**

A collection of speeches, delivered in America, by the Right Hon. Sir Henry Lytton Bulwer, G.C.B., her Majesty's envoy and Minister plenipotentiary to the United States, **62-1227**

Colonial policy, with hints upon the formation of military settlements. To which are added observations on the boundary question now pending between this country and the United States, **35-98**

The colonies of Colorado in their relation to English enterprise and settlement, **74-2038**

The colonies of England: a plan for the government of some portion of our colonial possessions, **49-629**

Colonization, **55-921**

Colorado, **72-1969**

Colorado for invalids, **80-2328**

Colorado: its agriculture, stockfeeding, scenery and shooting, **79-2285**

Colorado: its resources, parks, and prospects as a new field for emigration, **69-1811**

Colorado: United States, America. Its history, geography, and mining, **69-1842**

Columbia and Canada: notes on the Great Republic and the New Dominion, **77-2198**

The Columbian exposition and World's fair. Chicago, 1893, **93-2940**

Columbian sketches, **95-3017**

A comic history of the United States, **76-2143**

The coming struggle among the nations of the earth, **53-847**

The coming struggle in America. Laws of nations, privateering and blockades, and the laws of neutral trade, **61-1156**

The coming struggle in the United States and Canada and its origin, **97-3087**

A commentary on criticisims [sic] concerning American v. English locomotives, with testimony by English engineers, **80-2312**

Commerce between the United States & Canada, **92-2869**

Commercial and financial legislation of Europe and America; with a pro-forma revision of the taxation and the customs tariff of the United Kingdom, **41-309**

Commercial blockades, considered with reference to law and policy, **62-1291**

Commercial law, its principles and administration, **52-765**

The commercial policy of the British colonies and the McKinley tariff, **92-2864**

Commercial statistics. A digest of the productive resources, commercial legislation . . . of all nations, 47-548

Commercial statistics of America: a digest of her productive resources, commercial legislation, etc., 47-548

Commercial tarriffs and regulations of the several states of Europe and America, 47-548

Commercial union, a study, **89-2713**

The day-star of the world's freedom; or, the British lion trampling on the neck of slavery, **34-81**

Death and funeral of Abraham Lincoln, with some remarks on the state of America at the close of the civil war, **65-1596**

Death of President Garfield, **81-2345**

The debasing and demoralizing influence of slavery on all and on everything connected with it, **47-542**

Declaration of the objects of the Newcastle Upon Tyne Society for abolishing slavery all over the world, **36-140**

Dedication of the Holley memorial, New York, October, 1890, **92-2858**

The deer of all lands, **98-3120**

The default of the United States government, **77-2191**

Defence of Canada considered as an imperial question with reference to a war with America, **65-1633**

Defence of Canada. 1st. General character of country—strength of militia—lake district from Lake Superior downwards to the Falls of Niagara . . . . , **62-1229**

Defence of the American ecclesiastical statistics, put forth by the Voluntary Church Magazine, **33-40**

The defences of England. Nine letters, **62-1275**

The defense of Great and Greater Britain, **80-2305**

Deliverance of the Reformed Presbytery of Edinburgh on American slavery and church-fellowship with slave-holders, **45-438**

Democracy and liberty, **96-3052**

Democracy in the Old world and the New, **84-2477**

Democracy. Its influence on liberty, property, and social happiness, **35-99**

Democracy vindicated, **67-1730**

Democracy: what is it? Let us inquire!, **59-1066**

The Denver & Rio Grande railway of Colorado, **77-2170**

The Denver Pacific railway: its present position and future prospects, **70-1865**

Description and price of improved farms in the state of Tennessee, United States of America, for sale by the East Tennessee land proprietors, **71-1912**

Description of a view of the city of New York, now exhibiting at the Panorama, Leicester square, **34-70**

Description of improved farms in the state of Tennessee, in the United States of America, **43-390**

Description of new coniferous trees from California, **55-938**

A description of south-western and middle Texas, **77-2184**

Description of the mammoth tree from California, now erected at the Crystal Palace, Sydenham, **57-1000**

Description of the Wisconsin territory, and some of the states and territories adjoining to it, in the western parts of the United States of America, **43-366**

Descriptions of Niagara; selected from various travellers; with original additions, **47-533**

A descriptive hand-book to "The two lands of gold," or, the Australian and Californian directory for 1853, **53-811**

Descriptive sociology; or, Groups of sociological facts, **78-2247**

The deserters; a narrative founded on facts of recent occurrence, **47-561**

Despatch from Lord Lyons respecting the obstruction of the Southern harbours, 65-1610

Despatch from Lord Lyons respecting the reciprocity treaty, 65-1610

The despotism at Richmond. The Confederate loan in England. The Slave Power and its supporters, **62-1230**

The emigrant's friend; a true guide to the emigrant proceeding to New York, Boston, Philadelphia or the Canadas, **64-1525**

The emigrants' friend; or, Hints on emigration to the United States of America, addressed to the people of Ireland, **53-850**

The emigrant's guide; containing practical and authentic information, and copies of original and unpublished letters from emigrants, **32-9**

The emigrant's guide for 1883, **82-2394**

The emigrant's guide; or Sketches of Canada, with some of the northern and western states of America, **67-1719**

The emigrant's guide to the colonies, **50-675**

Emigrants' guide to the United States and the Dominion of Canada, **72-1954**

The emigrant's guide to the United States. Who should, and who should not, emigrate; being plain practical advice to intending emigrants, **49-608**

The emigrant's guide to the western states of America; or, Backwoods and prairies, **52-782**

Emigrant's guide: where, when & how to emigrate, **82-2415**

The emigrants' hand-book and guide to the United States; or England and America contrasted, **49-609**

Emigrants' hand book to the United States, **48-572**

The emigrants' handbook: being a guide to the various fields of emigration in all parts of the globe, **52-747**

The emigrant's handbook of facts, concerning Canada, New Zealand, Australia, Cape of Good Hope, etc., with the relative advantages each of the colonies offers for emigration and practical advice to intending emigrants, **43-371**

The emigrants' informant; or, A guide to upper Canada, containing reasons for emigration, who should emigrate, necessaries for outfit, and charges of voyage, travelling expences, manners of the Americans, **34-73**

Emigrants' letters: being a collection of recent communications from settlers in the British colonies, **50-657**

The emigrant's manual. British America and the United States of America, **51-695**

The emigrant's manual: particularly addressed to the industrious classes and others who intend settling abroad, **40-274**

An emigrant's narrative; or, A voice from the sterrage [sic]. Being a brief account of the sufferings of the emigrants in the ship India, on her voyage from Liverpool to New York, in the winter of 1747 i.e.,1847 –8, **50-681**

The emigrant's newest guide to the United States, **51-696**

The emigrant's reverie and dream: England and America, **56-966**

Emigration; an address to the clergy of England, Ireland, Scotland and Wales, on the condition of the working classes, with a few suggestions as to their future welfare. Also, an address to persons about emigrating to America, **45-455**

Emigration by colony for the middle classes, **85-2555**

The emigration circular; or, Complete hand-book and guide to the United States; being England and America contrasted, **48-573**

Emigration considered; or, A general description of the leading countries most adapted to emigration, **53-818**

Emigration, emigrants, and know-nothings, **54-887**

Emigration fields. North America, the Cape, Australia, and New Zealand; describing these countries, and giving a comparative view of the advantages they present to British settlers, **39-227**

Emigration for the millions: directions where to go, and how to get there, **48-574**

Emigration from Ireland, **83-2426**

England's western, or America's eastern shore? Old Ireland a new state? With their various complexities and perplexities discussed, **51-697**

The English angler in Florida, **98-3137**

An English colony in Iowa, **79-2266**

The English colony in Iowa and Minnesota, U.S.A, **82-2405**

The English colony in Iowa: with a list of vacancies, **81-2362**

The English cricketers' trip to Canada and the United States, **60-1114**

English criticism on President Lincoln's anti-slavery proclamation & message, **63-1444**

The English in America, **51-703**

English institutions and the American rebellion, 64-1531

English notes for American circulation. (With apologies to Charles Dickens), 80-2330

English opinion on the American rebellion, **61-1138**

The English party's excursion to Paris, in Easter week 1849. To which is added, a trip to America, **50-648**

An English settler in pioneer Wisconsin: the letters of Edwin Bottomley, 1842–1850, **50-649**

The English sportsman in the western prairies, **61-1143**

English sympathies and opinions regarding the late American civil war, **66-1684**

English versus American cupolas. A comparison between Capt. Coles's & Capt. Ericsson's turrets, **64-1466**

An English view of American Quakerism, 77-2200

English views of American investments. American railways, **92-2861**

An Englishman in the American Civil War; the diaries of Henry Yates Thompson, 1863, **63-1433**

An Englishman's Arizona; the ranching letters of Herbert R. Hislop, 1876–78, **78-2233**

The Englishman's duty to the free and enslaved American, **53-870**

An Englishman's thoughts on the crimes of the South, and the recompence of the North, **65-1561**

An Englishman's travels in America: his observations of life and manners in the free and slave states, **53-805**

An Englishwoman in America, **48-579**

The Englishwoman in America, **56-958**

An Englishwoman's experience in America, **53-821**

Enquiry into the circumstances that have occasioned the present embarrassments in the trade between Great Britain and the United States of America, **37-160**

Episodes before thirty, **99-3147**

Episodes in a life of adventure; or, Moss from a rolling stone, **87-2633**

An epitome of anti-slavery information: or, A condensed view of slavery and the slave-trade, **42-331**

Equality; a discourse, **86-2595**

An errand to the South in the summer of 1862, **63-1387**

An essay on cotton growers and cotton workers: an account of the culture of the plant and the manner of its manufacture, **64-1487**

An essay on Negro slavery, **64-1530**

An essay on the Oregon question, written for the Shakespeare club, **46-498**

Essays by ministers of the Free Church of Scotland, **58-1040**

Essays from reviews, **93-2942**

Essays in military biography, **74-2043**

Essays in political and moral philosophy, **79-2269**

Essays in politics, wherein some of the political questions of the day are reviewed from a constitutional and historical standpoint, **91-2822**

Free and friendly remarks on a speech lately delivered to the Senate of the United States, by Henry Clay, of Kentucky, on the subject of the abolition of North American slavery, **39-219**

Free blacks and slaves. From the Christian reformer for August 1853, **53-810**

Free blacks and slaves. Would immediate abolition be a blessing?, **53-807**

Free Church alliance with manstealers. Send back the money. Great anti-slavery meeting in the city hall, Glasgow, 46-519

The Free church and American slavery. Slanders against the free church met and answered, **46-496**

The Free church and her accusers in the matter of American slavery; being a letter to Mr. George Thompson, **46-472**

The Free church and her accusers: the question at issue, **46-519**

The Free church of Scotland and American slavery. Substance of speeches delivered in the Music hall, Edinburgh, during May and June 1846, **46-520**

The free coinage of silver in the United States, **86-2577, 96-3042**

"Free grazing." A report to the shareholders of the Powder river cattle Co., **83-2434**

Free labour cotton: it can be had, **62-1240**

The free school system of the United States, **75-2076**

Free town libraries, their formation, management, and history; in Britain, France, Germany, & America, **69-1823**

Free trade & the cotton question with reference to India, being a memorial from the British merchants of Cochin, to the Right Hon. Sir John Hobhouse, **47-534**

Free trade and free enterprise, **73-2001**

Free trade and protection. An inquiry into the causes which have retarded the general adoption of free trade . . . , **78-2228**

Free trade and protection. Considered with relation to Canadian interests, **78-2242**

Free trade and the European treaties of commerce, **75-2092**

Free trade for the people. Protection for the favored few, **78-2230**

Free trade v. reciprocity, **81-2349**

Free trade versus fair trade, **82-2395**

Free trade versus protection: being a series of papers illustrative of what protection has done for "The United States of America" and for "Russia," and of what free trade has done for "Switzerland", **64-1482**

Free trade versus protection in the United States, **92-2894**

Free trade versus reciprocity, **81-2369**

The freedmen in America. Speeches . . . . at a meeting held at the Wesleyan mission house, June 9, 1865, **65-1587**

Freedom and slavery: an explanation of the principles & issues involved in the American conflict; and the duty of the people of Britain in relation to that momentous struggle, **63-1421**

Freedom and slavery in the United States of America, **63-1403**

Freedom in America; its extent and influence, **54-910**

Freedom or slavery in the United States, being facts and testimonies for the consideration of the British people, **62-1274**

A freehold farm of 25 acres, a free passage to America, a dwelling house, and other advantages, secured for £30, payable in weekly instalments [sic] to the artizans and labourers of Great Britain and Ireland, **48-582**

French domination, **49-613**

Friendly international addresses recommended, being a brief narrative of the origin and early progress of an already rapid movement in the cause of national arbitration, unfettered commerce, and universal peace, **46-482**

A friendly mission; John Candler's letters from America, 1853–1854, **54-879**

The friendly remonstrance of the people of Scotland, on the subject of slavery, **55-920**

Friendly sketches in America, **61-1192**

A friendly voice from England on American affairs, **62-1222**

A friendly warning to the Latter-Day Saints, or Mormons; in which the character of the Mormon missionaries is plainly set forth by one who was of that community, and a resident in Salt Lake, **60-1108**

From Ceylon to England by way of China, Japan & the United States, **91-2812**

From cowboy to pulpit, **99-3154**

From Edinburgh to Vancouver's island, **84-2502**

From England to California. Life among the Mormons and Indians, **68-1780**

From England to Virginia, **72-1943**

From Glasgow to Missouri and back, **78-2229**

From golden gate to golden horn, and many other world wide wanderings, **92-2879**

From home to home: autumn wandering in the Northwest, **85-2538**

From life. (Recollections and jottings), **91-2837**

From Liverpool to St. Louis, **70-1875**

From Montreal to San Francisco across Canadian territory, **87-2636**

From New Zealand to Lake Michigan, **89-2745**

From ocean to ocean, being a diary of a three months' expedition from Liverpool to California and back, from the Atlantic to the Pacific by the overland route, **71-1918**

From pillar to post, **90-2777**

From Saranac to the Marquesas and beyond, **88-2698**

From shadow to sunlight, 67-1707

From the Clyde to California, with jottings by the way, **82-2376**

From the yearly meeting of the religious Society of Friends held in London, fifth month 1863, to Friends in North America, **63-1352**

From the yearly meeting [of the Society of Friends], held in London . . . . to Friends in North America, **61-1163**

From wealth and happiness to misery and the penitentiary, **93-2899**

The frontier schoolmaster: the autobiography of a teacher, an account not only of experiences in the schoolroom but in agricultural, political, and military life, **80-2331**

Frost and fire. Natural engines, tool marks and chips, with sketches taken at home and abroad, **65-1566**

Froth and bubble, **99-3172**

The fruit industry of California, **95-3007**

Fruit Vale irrigation colony, Rio Puerco Valley, New Mexico, **93-2922**

The fugitive slaves in Canada, **58-1055**

Fur brigade to the Bonaventura; John Work's California expedition, 1832–1833, for the Hudson's bay company, **33-66**

The fur hunters of the far West; a narrative of adventures in the Oregon and Rocky mountains, **55-946**

Further observation on the Devonian plants of Maine, Gaspe, and New York, **63-1336**

The future government of Canada: being arguments in favor of a British American independent republic, **64-1535**

The future of British America. Independence! How to prepare for it . . . . shall the constitution of the United Provinces of British America be formed after the model afforded us by the constitution of the United Kingdoms or that of the United States?, **65-1568**

The future of the United States, **84-2498**

The future trade relations between Great Britain and the United States, and the World's Columbian exposition to be held at Chicago in 1893, **92-2873**

G. T. T. Gone to Texas; letters from our boys, **84-2492**

"G.G.", **98-3116**

The gallery of geography; a pictorial and descriptive tour of the world, **64-1501**

The Gallynipper in Yankeeland, **82-2397**

Galveston Island; or, A few months off the coast of Texas: the journal of Francis C. Sheridan, 1839–1840, **40-276**

The gaming table: its votaries and victims, in all times and countries, **70-1892**

Garrisonian infidelity exposed: in two letters from the Rev. John Guthrie, Greenock, in reply to George Thompson, **51-702**

General Grant: an estimate, **87-2605**

General hints to emigrants: containing notices of the various fields for emigration, with practical hints on preparation for emigrating, outfit for the voyage, the voyage, landing, obtaining employment, purchase and clearing of land, etc., **66-1676**

A general history of humming-birds, or the Trochilidae, **52-771**

A general plan for a mail communication by steam between Great Britain and the eastern and western parts of the world; also to Canton and Sydney, westward by the Pacific, **38-198**

The gentleman emigrant: his daily life, sports, and pastimes in Canada, Australia, and the United States, **74-2069**

Geographical & mineralogical notes, to accompany Mr. Wyld's map of the gold regions of California, **49-644**

The geographical distribution of mammals, **66-1690**

The geography of America and the West Indies, **41-308**

The geography of North America: a brief hand book for students, **94-2969**

Geological report of an examination made in 1834 of the elevated country between the Missouri and Red rivers, **35-100**

Geological sketches at home and abroad, **82-2398**

George Macdonald and his wife, **73-2018**

George Stanley: or, Life in the woods. A boy's narrative of the adventures of a settler's family in Canada, **64-1484**

Germanization and Americanization compared, **96-3062**

Gipsy Smith; his life and work, by himself, **96-3063**

Gleanings and reminiscences by Thomas Ellison, 58-1036

Gleanings from western prairies, **82-2420**

Gleanings of past years, 1843–78, **79-2263**

A glimpse at the great western republic, **51-694**

A glimpse at the United States and the northern states of America, with the Canadas, comprising their rivers, lakes, and falls during the autumn of 1852; including some account of an emigrant ship, **53-849**

A glimpse of America, **86-2599**

Glimpses in America; or, The new world as we saw it, **75-2077**

Glimpses of American life and scenery, sketched in letters and diary of a tour in the United States and Canada, during the summer and autumn of 1872, **73-1998**

The great Mormon fraud; or, The church of Latter-Day Saints proved to have had a falsehood for its origin, **85-2541**

The great Northwest and the great lake region of North America, 99-3166

The great republic, **84-2482**

The great theme of the age; a poem of the confederation of the British American provinces, **66-1660**

The great tree on Boston common, **55-952**

Great waterfalls, cataracts, and geysers, described and illustrated, **87-2621**

Greater America; hits and hints by a foreign resident, **87-2623**

Greater Britain: a record of travel in English-speaking countries during 1866 and 1867, **68-1764**

The greater half of the continent, 91-2845

Green pastures and Piccadilly . . . in conjunction with an American writer, 76-2159

The Greville diary, including passages hitherto withheld from publication, **59-1071**

Grierson raids, and Hatch's sixty-four days march, with biographical sketches, **65-1640**

Grimes's trip to America, **77-2180**

Grover Cleveland, **96-3071**

Guide to California. (With a map.) Containing an account of the climate, soil, and natural productions of upper California, with authentic particulars respecting the gold region, derived from the official documents of the government of the United States, **49-615**

A guide to mechanics and working men wishing to emigrate to the United States of America, **37-172**

A guide to the emigration colonies: including Australia, Tasmania, New Zealand, Cape of Good Hope, Natal, Canada, and the other British possessions of North America, also the United States and California, **51-698**

A guide to the gold country of California. An authentic and descriptive narrative of the latest discoveries in that country, **49-645**

Guide to the gold regions of Upper California. With a map, and scientific designs of native gold, mode of working, &c., &c., **49-638**

"Guilty or not guilty?" A few facts and feelings regarding the religious bodies of America in the matter of slavery, **55-912**

Gun, rod, and saddle. Personal experiences, **69-1826**

Habitual drunkenness and insane drunkards, **78-2222**

Half hours in the wide west over mountains, rivers, and prairies, **75-2102**

Half hours in woods and wilds. Adventures of sport and travel, **75-2103**

Hand book to the Pacific and California, describing eight different routes, by sea, Central America, Mexico, and the territories of the United States, **49-637**

A hand-book of Newport, and Rhode Island, **52-781**

A hand-book of the cotton trade; or, A glance at the past history, present condition, and future prospects of the cotton commerce of the world, **58-1036**

Hand-book to Canada and the United States, with descent of Niagara and the St. Lawrence, **54-895**

Handbook of commercial union, **88-2656**

Handbook of republican institutions in the United States of America, **87-2607**

A handbook of the history of the United States; including the discovery and European settlement, the colonial period, the War of Independence, the Constitution, and history to the present time, **62-1270**

A handbook to the industries of the British Isles and the United States, **82-2383**

Handy book of ornamental conifers and of rhododendrons and other American flowering shrubs suitable for the climate and soils of Britain, **75-2098**

A handy-book for investors; comprising a sketch of the rise, progress, and present character of every species of investment, British, colonial, and foreign, **69-1808**

Hard life in the colonies, and other experiences by sea and land, **92-2868**

Hardscrabble; or, The fall of Chicago. A tale of Indian warfare, 42-353

Harvard college, by an Oxonian, **94-2975**

Hearts of oak, **89-2748**

Hebrew servitude and American slavery: an attempt to prove that the Mosaic law furnishes neither a basis nor an apology for American slavery, **63-1376**

Hell upon earth; the doctrines & practices of the "Latter-Day Saints" in Utah, **87-2628**

Henry Irving in England and America 1838–84, **84-2463**

Henry Irving's impressions of America, narrated in a series of sketches, chronicles and conversations, **84-2487**

Henry Vincent's visit to Mt. Lebanon, Columbia county, New York, **68-1800**

Henry; or, the juvenile traveller. A faithful delineation of a voyage across the Atlantic, in a New York packet; a description of a part of the United States—manners and customs of the people . . . , **36-121**

Herbert Spencer on the Americans and the Americans on Herbert Spencer, **83-2458**

The hermit of Westminster on the tramp among the western states of North America, **85-2554**

Hesperos; or, Travels in the West, **50-665**

Hesperothen: notes from the West; being a record of a ramble in the United States and Canada in the spring and summer of 1881, **82-2416**

The highway of the seas in times of war, **62-1251**

Hints to emigrants on the purchasing and clearing of land in America, with some observation on the manner of living in the United States and Canada, **66-1661**

Hints to emigrants; or, Incidents in the emigration of John Smith of Smith-town, designed & etched by Percy Cruikshank, **49-605**

Hints to emigrants to the United States of America, **78-2218**

Historic doubts relative to the American war, **62-1279**

A historical account of the neutrality of Great Britain during the American civil war, **70-1855**

Historical and philosophical essays, **65-1631**

Historical essays and studies, **66-1651**

History and progress of the temperance reformation, in Great Britain and other countries of the globe, **54-878**

The history and topography; of the United States, **32-13**

The history of a cotton bale, **63-1364**

A history of American compromises, **56-975**

The history of ancient America, anterior to the time of Columbus; proving the identity of the aborigines with the Tyrians and Israelites, **43-381**

The history of banking in America: with an inquiry how far the banking institutions of America are adapted to this country, **37-162**

History of British Columbia from its earliest discovery to the present time, **94-2956**

History of Chicago from 1833 to 1892, 82-2388

History of federal government, from the foundation of the Achaian league to the disruption of the United States, **63-1450**

History of Grant's campaign for the capture of Richmond (1864–1865), with an outline of the previous course of the American civil war, **69-1814**

History of merchant shipping and ancient commerce, **76-2149**

A history of slavery and serfdom, **95-3014**

Lectures on America. Delivered in the Mechanics' institute, Dublin, November, 1859, **59-1085**

Lectures on Canada, illustrating its present position, and shewing forth its onward progress and predictive of its future destiny, **63-1308**

Lectures on the labour question, **78-2220**

Lectures on the United States, **41-310**

Lectures to American audiences, 83-2433

Legal view of the "Alabama" case, and ship building for the Confederates, **63-1409**

Legislation on gold . . . The question of money—how it will be affected by large imports of gold from California, **49-599**

The lessons of history, **88-2674**

Letter addressed to Elisha Bates, esq., minister of the Society of Friends, **33-61**

A letter addressed to Michael Thomas Sadler, Esq., M.P. on the subject of emigration, **32-23**

A letter addressed to the anonymous author of "England and America", **34-89**

The letter bag of the Great Western; or, Life in a steamer, 51-703

Letter favoring the political union of the United States and British America, **98-3114**

Letter from a tradesman, recently arived from America, to his brethren in trade, **35-106**

A letter from Anthony Trollope describing a visit to California in 1875, **75-2123**

Letter from Lauchlan Donaldson to John Boyd on commercial and reciprocal trade between the United States and the British provinces, **65-1581**

Letter from Mr. Cobden, M.P., to Henry Ashworth, esq., president of the Manchester chamber of commerce, upon the present state of international maritime law, as affecting the rights of belligerents and neutrals, **62-1223**

Letter from the inhabitants of Bridgewater, Somersetshire, England, to the inhabitants of Bridgewater, Massachusetts, New-England, America, dated Sept. 10, 1846, **47-547**

Letter of the Hon. John Young, (Member of the Provincial parliament of Canada), on the postal and passenger communication between Great Britain & North America, **56-987**

Letter on American slaveholding, with remarks, by the Belfast anti-slavery committee, **46-473**

Letter on free trade, and navigation of the St. Lawrence, addressed to the Earl of Elgin and Kincardine, governor-general of Her Majesty's North American possessions, **46-471**

Letter on jetties at the passes of the Mississippi, **75-2104**

A letter on the American colonization society, addressed to the editor of the "Herald of Peace", **32-25**

Letter on the lands of the Illinois Central Railway Company, **59-1063**

A letter on "Uncle Tom's Cabin", **52-759**

Letter to a member of the Congress of the United States of America, from an English clergyman, **35-107**

A letter to a Whig member of the Southern independence association, **64-1528**

Letter to His Grace the Duke of Newcastle, upon a union of the colonies of British North America, **60-1109**

Letter to Lord [John] Russell on belligerent rights, with reference to merchant shipping; and the reply thereto, **63-1383**

Letter to Lord Stanley, on the dearth of cotton, and the capability of India to supply the quantity required, **63-1446**

A letter to Mr. Bright on his plan for turning the English monarchy into a democracy, **58-1034**

A letter to such professing Christians in the Northern states of America, as have had no practical concern with slave holding, and have never sanctioned it by defending it, **44-400**

The making of the American nation; or, The rise and decline of oligarchy in the West, **66-1692**

A man adrift: being leaves from a nomad's portfolio, **99-3177**

Man and his migrations, 50-671

The 'manifest destiny' of the American union, **57-1014**

Manitoba and the North-west of the Dominion, its resources and advantages to the emigrant and the capitalist, as compared with the western states of America, **71-1935**

Manitou, Colorado, U.S.A., its mineral waters and climate, **75-2121**

Mann's emigrant's complete guide to the United States of America: containing a description of the country and the several states, **50-673**

Manstealing by proxy; or, The guilt of our countrymen in upholding slavery and the slave trade, by the purchase of slave grown produce, **50-659**

A manual of geography; being a description of the natural features, climate, and productions of the various regions of the earth, **61-1174**

A manual of recent and existing commerce, from the year 1789 to 1872, **72-1994**

A manual of the ornithology of the United States and of Canada, **34-82**

Maple leaves; being the papers read before the National club of Toronto, **91-2830**

Maple leaves from Canada, for the grave of Abraham Lincoln, **65-1611**

The maple-leaf and the union Jack: a brief study of British connection, **91-2820**

The Mapleson memoirs, 1848–1888, **88-2687**

Mapping the frontier. Charles Wilson's diary of the survey of the 19th parallel, 1858–1862, **62-1294**

Marie Tempest, **93-2901**

Maritime capture. Shall England uphold the capture of private property at sea?, **62-1257**

Maritime law and belligerent rights, **62-1224**

The maritime rights & obligations of belligerents, as between themselves, their allies and neutrals, as recognized by English maritime courts, **62-1244**

Martin Chuzzlewit, 42-339

Martin county, and the other border counties of southern Minnesota, and upper Iowa, **76-2162**

The martyr age of the United States, **39-225**

Mason's handbook to California; its gold and how to get it; a description of the country, etc., **50-674**

The Maxwell land grant, situated in Colorado and New Mexico, United States of America, **70-1866**

Medical education. A letter adressed to the authorities of the Johns Hopkins Hospital, **79-2253**

Medical education and practice in all parts of the world, **80-2315**

Meeting the sun: a journey all round the world, through Egypt, China, Japan, and California, **74-2068**

Melodies and memories, **96-3055**

Memoir and letters of Sidney Gilchrist Thomas, **91-2844**

Memoir, extracts of speeches, diary of a journey to America, &c., **66-1674**

Memoir of a mechanic. Being a sketch of the life of Timothy Claxton, written by himself, **39-213**

A memoir of Abraham Lincoln, president elect of the United States of America, his opinion on secession, extracts from the United States Constitution, &c., **61-1145**

A memoir of Duncan Wallace, being a narrative of his voyages, shipwrecks, travels and battles by sea and by land, during a period of eighty-three years, **62-1247**

A memoir of Edward Askew Sothern, **89-2735**

A memoir of John Conolly, M.D., D.C.L., comprising a sketch of the treatment of the insane in Europe and America, **69-1817**

A memoir of the life of John Tulloch, **88-2692**

Memoir of W. H. Harvey, M.D., F.R.S., etc., etc., late professor of botany, Trinity College, Dublin. With selections from his journal and correspondence, **69-1828**

Memoirs of a professional lady nurse, **73-2033**

Memoirs of a reformer, **93-2936**

The memoirs of Admiral Lord Charles Beresford, **99-3145**

Memoirs of an ex-minister; an autobiography, by the Right Hon. the Earl of Malmesbury, **84-2497**

Memoirs of an old parliamentarian, **90-2784**

Memoirs of Charles Mathews, comedian, **39-226**

Memoirs of David Nasmith: his labours and travels in Great Britain, France, the United States, and Canada, **44-398**

Memoirs of Henry Richard, the apostle of peace, **89-2703**

Memoirs of P.R. Jarvis, **45-447**

Memoirs of the life and correspondence of Henry Reeve, **98-3119**

Memoirs of the life and gospel labours of the late Daniel Wheeler, a minister of the society of Friends, **42-361**

Memoirs of the life and work of Philip Pearsall Carpenter, **80-2302**

Memoirs of travel, sport, and natural history, **95-3006**

Memoirs of William Forster, **65-1586**

Memorandum and articles of Association, **77-2209**

Memorandum on the commercial relations, past and present, of the British North American provinces and the United States of America, **74-2059**

The memorial & petition of the people of Rupert's land and North-west territory, British America, to his excellency, U. S. Grant, **70-1882**

Memorial from the Glasgow emancipation society, in public meeting assembled, to the general assembly of the Free church of Scotland, regarding Christian fellowship with slaveholders, **46-484**

Memorial presented to the Right Hon. the Earl of Aberdeen, by the committee of the British and foreign anti-slavery society, on the 22nd of February, 1843, **43-365**

Memorial to the Commercial convention in Detroit, **65-1564**

Memorials of Albert Venn Dicey, being chiefly letters and diaries, **98-3111**

Memorials of John Curwen, **82-2390**

Memories, **73-2026**

Memories and adventures, **94-2963**

Memories and notes, **98-3117**

Memories of a labour leader; the autobiography of John Wilson, **87-2652**

Memories of a musical career, **78-2246**

Memories of America, and Reminiscences at home and abroad, **39-209**

Memories of fifty years, **72-1984**

Memories of four continents, **81-2353**

Memories of half a century, a record of friendships, **63-1380**

Memories of sport and travel fifty years ago, from the Hudson's bay company to New Zealand, **79-2256**

Memories of the southern states, **65-1573**

Men and manners in America, **33-46**

Men and manners in Britain; or, A bone to gnaw for the Trollopes, Fidlers, &c. being notes from a journal, **34-87**

The new Virginians, **80-2292**

New world heroes: Lincoln and Garfield, **84-2491**

New world notes: being an account of journeyings and sojournings in America and Canada, **75-2091**

The new world: being a story of ten thousand miles travel on the North American continent, in the summer of 1890, **91-2831**

The new world; or, Recent visit to America, **71-1907**

New York industrial exhibition. General report of the British commissioners, **54-893**

New York to Niagara, 1836. The journal of Thomas S. Woodcock, **36-151**

The New Zealander abroad in England, America and the Highlands of Scotland, **88-2685**

Newell's notes on Abraham Lincoln, President of the United States of America, with extracts from his speeches on slavery, secession, and the war, **64-1506**

Newell's notes on tar and feathers, and the atrocities of lynch law in the slave states of America, **64-1507**

Newell's notes on the cruel and licentious treatment of the American female slaves, **64-1508**

Newman Hall in America. Rev. Dr. Hall's lectures on temperance and missions to the masses; also, an oration on Christian liberty, **68-1771**

Niagara. Glacial and post-glacial phenomena, **75-2080**

A night with the Yankees: a lecture delivered in the town hall, Cambridge, on March 30, 1868, **68-1777**

Nine years in America . . . in a series of letters to his cousin, Patrick Mooney, a farmer in Ireland, **50-677**

A nine years' residence, and a nine months' tour on foot, in the states of New York and Pennsylvania, for the use of labourers, farmers and emigrants, **41-293**

No fellowship with slaveholders: a calm review of the debate on slavery, in the full assembly of 1846, **46-494**

No mistake; or, A vindication of the negotiators of the treaty of 1783, respecting the north eastern boundary of the United States, **42-343**

No war with America. A lecture on the affair of the Trent, **61-1169**

No war with America. An address to his countrymen, by an Englishman, **56-977**

North America, **62-1283**

North America viewed as to its eligibility for British emigration. Giving ample details to meet the inquiries of all classes, **48-581**

The North American sylva; or, A description of the forest trees of the United States, Canada, and Nova Scotia, **49-628**

"North and South." Letters to "The Guardian", **63-1365**

The North Atlantic telegraph, via the Faroe islands, Iceland, and Greenland, **61-1176**

North Carolina: its resources and progress, **75-2116**

The Northern kingdom, by a colonist, **64-1472**

Notes and letters on the American war, **64-1455**

Notes and observation on America, and the Americans: including considerations for emigrants, **39-232**

Notes and sketches during an overland trip from New York to San Francisco, **69-1852**

Notes by a wanderer from Demerara, in the United States, **85-2560**

Notes from a journal in North America in 1883, **84-2467**

Notes of a journey from Toronto to British Columbia, via the Northern Pacific railway, **84-2470**

Notes of a journey round the world: made in 1875, **76-2136**

Notes of a journey through Canada, the United States of America, and the West Indies, **38-197**

Notes on the distribution of gold throughout the world, including Australia, California & Russia, **52-799**

Notes on the geography of North America, physical and political, **73-2022**

Notes on the legalized reclamation of fugitive slaves from the free states of America, according to a recent decision of the Supreme Court, **57-1002**

Notes on the new reformation in Germany, and on national education, and the common schools of Massachusetts, **45-436**

Notes on the river navigations of North America, **63-1359**

Notes on the slaveholders' mission to England, **60-1103**

Notes on the slave-trade, etc., 32-19

Notes on the United States, **41-294**

Notes on the United States of North America, during a phrenological visit in 1838–40, **41-289**

Notes on upper California: a journey from Monterey to the Colorado river in 1832, **32-6**

Notes upon Californian trees, **60-1124**

Notes upon Canada and the United States of America: in the year MDCCCXXXV. By a traveler, **35-117**

Notes upon the south western boundary line of the British provinces of Lower Canada and New Brunswick, and the United States of America, 38-205

Observations of a ranchwoman in New Mexico, **98-3105**

Observations on American slavery, after a year's tour in the United States, **52-745**

Observations on professions, literature, manners, and emigration, in the United States and Canada, made during a residence there in 1832, **33-43**

Observations on railroads in the United States, **77-2192**

Observations on the effect of the Californian & Australian gold: and on the impossibility of continuing the present standard, **52-769**

Observations on the financial position and credit of such of the states of the North American Union as have contracted public debts, **39-240**

Observations on the Niagara railway suspension bridge, made during a recent tour in America, **60-1097**

Observations upon the Treaty of Washington, signed August 9, 1842; with the treaty annexed, **43-377**

Occasional paper of the Anglo-American church emigrants' aid society, **59-1057**

Ocean echoes: an autobiography, **99-3186**

The ocean waves: travels by land and sea, **75-2089**

Oceana; or, England and her colonies, **86-2578**

Odger's monthly pamphlets on current events, etc. No. 1. Republicanism versus monarchy, **72-1975**

O'er many lands, on many seas, **84-2515**

The officer's memorandum book for peace and war, **77-2179**

The official correspondence on the claims of the United States in respect to the 'Alabama', **67-1746**

The old country and the new, **87-2642**

Old England and New England, in a series of views taken on the spot, **53-808**

Old recollections of an old boy, **69-1845**

The Old world and the New, 32-28, **84-2464**

Old-world questions and New-world answers, **84-2505**

On coal at home and abroad with relation to consumption, cost, demand, and supply and other inquiries of present interest, **73-2016**

and philanthropists of the United States of North America, for the extirpation, by our aid, of that slavery which we introduced into those states, **41-318**

The operations of war explained and illustrated, **66-1677**

Opinion pronounced by Mr. Edmund Hornby, the British commissioner, in the case of the Florida bonds, **55-924**

Opinions of the English and the United States press on Catlin's North American Indian museum, **41-287**

Opuscula. Essays chiefly philological and ethnographical, **60-1113**

Oranges and alligators: sketches of south Florida life, **86-2581**

Oration of Ernest Jones on the American rebellion, **64-1489**

Oregon botanical expedition, **53-832**

The Oregon hand-book and emigrants' guide, **73-2021**

Oregon indemnity. Claim of chief factors and chief traders of the Hudson's Bay company, **92-2877**

Oregon: its resources, climate, people, and productions, **78-2239**

The Oregon question, **45-457**

The Oregon question. A glance at the respective claims of Great Britain and the United States to the territory in dispute, **46-511**

The Oregon question, as it stands, **46-512**

The Oregon question determined by the rules of international law, **46-524**

The Oregon question examined, in respect to facts and the law of nations, **46-522**

The Oregon question: or, A statement of the British claims to the Oregon territory, in opposition to the pretensions of the government of the United States of America, **45-440**

The Oregon territory: a geographical and physical account of that country and its inhabitants, with outlines of its history and discovery, **46-503**

The Oregon territory. Claims thereto of England and America considered; its conditions and prospects, **46-515**

The Oregon territory, consisting of a brief description of the country and its productions; and of the habits and manners of the native Indian tribes, **46-504**

Oregon: the claim of the United States to Oregon, as stated in the letters of the Hon. J. C. Calhoun and the Hon. J. Buchanan, (American secretaries of state,) to the Right Hon. R[ichard] Pakenham, Her Britannic Majesty's plenipotentiary, **46-505**

Oregon: there and back in 1877, **78-2240**

The organization of the Empire, **66-1680**

Orient and Occident: a journey east from Lahore to Liverpool, **88-2689**

Origin and progress of the American republic and the war, **64-1518**

Origin and traditional history of the Wyandotts, and sketches of other Indian tribes of North America, **70-1860**

The origin of civilization and the primitive condition of man. Mental and social condition of savages, **65-1552**

Other countries, **72-1942**

Other days, **93-2928**

The other side, how it struck us, **80-2296**

The other side the herring pond. (American notes), **69-1837**

Our "Constitutional rights" vindicated; or, An argument for the legal prescription of the traffic in alcoholic beverages, **54-880**

Our American cousins at home, **73-2017**

Our American cousins: being personal impressions of the people and institutions of the United States, **83-2421**

The Red River country, Hudson's Bay, and North-west Territories, considered in relation to Canada, **69-1844**

Reflections from sunny memories of a tour through Canada, British Columbia, and the United States of America, **95-2999**

Reflections on some of the results of the late American war, **66-1656**

Reflections on the domestic and foreign policy of Great Britain since the war, **33-55**

Reflections suggested by a second visit to the United States of America, **67-1749**

The refugee: being the life of political exiles in Europe and the United States, **58-1039**

The refugee in America, 32-28

Refutation of fallacious arguments anent the American question, **63-1412**

Rejoinder to Mrs. Stowe's reply to the address of the women of England, **63-1330**

Relation of the Free Church to the American churches: speeches delivered in the Free synod of Angus and Mearns, on Tuesday the 28th April 1846, **46-510**

The relations between America and England, an address delivered before the citizens of Ithaca . . . May 19, 1869. A reply to the late speech of Mr. Sumner, **69-1847**

The relations of the industry of Canada, with the mother country and the United States, **64-1460**

Religion and education in America: with notices of the state and prospects of American Unitarianism, popery, and African colonization, **40-266**

The religion of organisation, **92-2871**

Religious movement in the United States, **58-1050**

Remarks occasioned by strictures in the Courier and the New York Enquirer of December, 1852, upon the Stafford-House address, **53-853**

Remarks on a war with America, and its probable consequences to that country, **40-265**

Remarks on emigration to Jamaica: addressed to the coloured classes of the United States, **40-244**

Remarks on reciprocity and the [Sir Edward] Thornton-Brown memorandum, **74-2065**

Remarks on the colony of Liberia and the American colonization society, with some account of the settlement of coloured people, **32-26**

Remarks on the disputed north-western boundary of New Brunswick, bordering on the United States of North America, **38-208**

Remarks on the extension of reciprocity between Canada and the United States, **55-935**

Remarks on the historical mis-statements and fallacies of Mr. Goldwin Smith. . . in his lecture, "On the foundation of the American colonies," and his letters "On the emancipation of the colonies", **66-1697**

Remarks on the policy of recognizing the independence of the southern states of North America, and on the struggle in that continent, **63-1413**

Remarks on the statistics and political institutions of the United States, with some observations on the ecclesiastical system of America, her sources of revenues, **32-19**

Remarks on the United States of America, with regard to the actual state of Europe, **33-41**

Remarks on the western states of America or valley of the Mississippi: with suggestions to agricultural emigrants, miners, &c., **39-233**

Remarks upon the disputed points of boundary under the fifth article of the Treaty of Ghent, **38-186**

Remarks upon the proposed Federation of the provinces, **64-1498**

A reminiscence of the Union Pacific railroad, containing some account of the discovery of the eastern base of the Rocky mountains, **73-2030**

Shall we emigrate? A tour through the states of America to the Pacific coast of Canada, **85-2552**

"Shall we recognize the Confederate States?" The question considered in three letters with reference to our national interest and duty, and to slavery as illustrated in the history of our West Indian possessions, **63-1314**

The shame and glory of the American Baptists; or, Slaveholders versus abolitionists, **60-1120**

Shifting scenes; or, Memories of many men in many lands, **65-1606**

The shoe and canoe; or, Pictures of travel in the Canadas, **50-647**

Shooting Niagara: and after?, **67-1712**

A short account of our trip to the Sierra Nevada mountains, **84-2510**

A short American tramp in the fall of 1864, **65-1567**

A short and interesting account of America. By English settlers, **35-116**

A short history and description of the Ojibbeway Indians now on a visit to England, **44-424**

A short history of the Episcopal church in the United States, **84-2468**

A short history of the Mormonites; or, Latter-Day Saints. With an account of the real origin of the Book of Mormon, **50-662**

Short journal of a visit to Canada and the states of America, in 1860, **61-1188**

Short notes of tours in America and India, **69-1838**

Short stalks; or, Hunting camps, north, south, east, and west, **92-2851**

A short tour through the United States & Canadas, October 10th to December 31st, 1832, **32-5**

Should the Free church hold fellowship with slave-holders? And, should the money lately received from slave-holding churches be sent back?, **46-513**

The shrines and sepulchres of the Old and New world. . . .including notices of the funeral customs of the principal nations, ancient and modern, **51-718**

Sights and sounds: the mystery of the day: comprising an entire history of the American "spirit" manifestations, **53-860**

Silvanus Phillips Thompson, his life and letters, **93-2944**

Silver in its relation to industry and trade: the danger of demonetizing it. The United States monetary commission of 1876, **80-2300**

Silver in the Fifty-third Congress, **93-2921**

Silver mines and incidents of travel, **93-2943**

The silver question, **77-2193**

The Silverado squatters, **83-2453**

Silverland, **73-2015**

The sinfulness of maintaining Christian fellowship with slave-holders. Strictures on the proceedings of the last general assembly of the Free church of Scotland, regarding communion with the slave-holding churches of America, **47-540**

Sinners and saints. A tour across the states, and round them; with three months among the Mormons, **83-2450**

Sir Arthur Sullivan: life-story, letters, and reminiscences, **99-3179**

Sir Charles G. D. Roberts; a biography, **97-3089**

Sir James Douglas and British Columbia, **59-1086**

Sir Wilfrid Laurier at Washington, **99-3181**

Sir William Gregory, K.C.M.G., formerly member of Parliament and sometime Governor of Ceylon. An autobiography, **94-2971**

A sister's memorial; or, A little account of Rebecca Farrand, **57-1004**

Six happy weeks among the Americans, **76-2157**

A six months exploration of the state of Texas, **78-2249**

Six months in America, **32-29**

Speech of Thomas Clarkson, esq., as originally prepared by him in writing, and intended to have been delivered at the opening of the general anti-slavery convention, **40-250**

Speech of Viscount Palmerston, in the House of Commons, on Tuesday the 21st of March, 1843, on the Treaty of Washington, **43-388**

Speech on arbitration between Great Britain and the United States, **94-2966**

Speech on Canada's tariff. Trade relations with the United States, **93-2908**

Speech on reciprocity with the United States, **88-2670**

Speech on the divisions among American abolitionists, delivered at the annual meeting of the Glasgow Emancipation Society, 2d. Aug., 1841, **41-321**

Speech, at Birmingham, Jan. 26, 1864, **64-1457**

Speeches and addresses chiefly on the subject of British-American union, **65-1603**

Speeches and addresses [of Edward Henry Stanley, Earl of Derby], **94-2961**

The speeches and public letters of Joseph Howe, **72-1962**

Speeches delivered at the anti-colonization meeting in Exeter hall, July 13, 1833, **33-58**

The speeches delivered at the soiree in honour of George Thompson, esq., in the Renfrewshire Tontine Inn, Paisley, on the evening of Wednesday 25th January, 1837. With an appendix, containing a remonstrance on the subject of slavery, **37-179**

Speeches of Daniel O'Connell and Thomas Steele, on the subject of American slavery, delivered before the Loyal national repeal association of Ireland, **43-386**

Speeches of John Bright, M.P., on the American question, **65-1559**

Speeches on the public affairs of the last twenty years, **69-1813**

The sphagnaceae or peat-mosses of Europe and North America, **78-2219**

The spirit of a public school, 66-1673

Spirit rapping in England and America; its origin and history, **53-861**

Spiritual wives, **68-1765**

Spiritualism in America. With fac-similes of spirit drawings and writing, **61-1155**

Sport and adventures among the North- American Indians, **90-2782**

Sport and photography in the Rocky mountains, **80-2335**

Sport and travel east and west, **98-3131**

Sport in many lands: Europe, Asia, Africa and America, **77-2186**

Sporting adventures in the far West, **79-2274**

Sporting adventures in the Pacific, whilst in command of the "Reindeer", **76-2147**

A sportsman of limited income; recollections of fifty years, **60-1100**

The St. Albans raid. Investigation by the police committee, of the City Council of Montreal, **64-1537**

The St. Albans raid; or, Investigation into the charges against Lieut. Bennett H. Young and command, for their acts at St. Albans, Vt., on the 19th October, 1864, **65-1555**

St. Lawrence and Atlantic rail-road, **46-500**

St. Louis' Isle, or Texiana; with additional observations made in the United States and in Canada, **47-544**

Standard time. Letter to the President of the American society for the advancement of science, on the subject of standard time for the United States, **82-2396**

Stars and stripes, or American impressions, **56-968**

A start in life. A journey across America. Fruit farming in California, **91-2809**

State aid and state interference, **82-2380**

Statement as to the iron trade of Scotland, and the exports of iron to foreign parts, particularly with reference to the United States of America, **50-682**

Statement of the principles and proceedings of the Edinburgh emancipation society, instituted in 1833, **47-537**

Suggestions on the military resources of Canada, and the means of organizing a small provincial army, **53-855**

A summer in prairie-land. Notes of a tour through the northwest territory, **81-2371**

A summer on the Rockies, **98-3127**

Summer suns in the far West; a holiday trip to the Pacific slope, **90-2753**

Sunbeams from a western hemisphere, **74-2047**

A Sunday at Coney Island, **82-2379**

Sundays spent about the world, **75-2106**

The sunlit hours. A record of sport and life, **97-3076**

Sunny lands and seas. A voyage in the S.S. 'Ceylon', **83-2457**

Sunways: a record of rambles in many lands, **78-2217**

Supplement . . . containing drawings to explain the construction of the rolling stock in use on the American railways, 57-1005

The supply of cotton from India, **63-1318**

Synopsis of lecture on the importance of the American war of 1861–65 as a strategical study, **92-2878**

A system of geography, popular and scientific, or a physical, political, and statistical account of the world and its various divisions, **32-3**

Systematic colonization. Speech of Charles Buller, esq., M.P., in the House of Commons, on Thursday, April 6, 1843, **43-370**

Systems of land tenure in various countries. A series of essays published under the sanction of the Cobden club, **70-1863**

Tables shewing the progress of the shipping interest of the British Empire, United States, and France, compiled from parliamentary papers and other sources, **44-395**

A tangled yarn: Captain James Payen's life log, **91-2833**

Tapscott's emigrants' travelling guide through the United States & Canada, **45-460**

The tariff hand-book, shewing the Canadian customs' tariff, with the various changes made during the last thirty years; also the British and American tariffs, **78-2236**

Tariff re-adjustment. Canada's national policy, **78-2224**

The tariffs of the United States in relation to free trade, **90-2787**

Technical education. Report of a visit to the schools of Massachusetts, and opinions on the subject of technical education, **99-3188**

"Tell It All": the story of a life's experience in Mormonism. An autobiography, **74-2070**

Temperance legislation in America, **88-2696**

The temperence problem and social reform, **99-3197**

Ten letters on the church and church establishments; addressed to the Hon. W. H. Draper, M.P.P., **39-239**

10,000 miles by land and sea, **76-2160**

Ten thousand miles in fifty days: being an account of a flying visit to the Dominion of Canada and the northern and southern states of America, **77-2171**

Ten thousand miles of travel, sport, and adventure, **69-1851**

Ten years in the United States; being an Englishman's view of men and things in the North and South, **62-1264**

Ten years on a Georgia plantation since the war, **83-2444**

Ten years' wild sports in foreign lands; or, Travels in the eighties, **89-2740**

A tenderfoot in Colorado, **74-2073**

The tenderfoot in New Mexico, **85-2557**

Teresina in America, **75-2111**

Teresina peregrina; or, Fifty thousand miles of travel round the world, **74-2058**

A trip to the tropics and home through America, **67-1707**

A trip to the United States and Canada: in a series of letters, **52-796**

A trip to the United States in 1887, **87-2609**

A trip west and back, **91-2817**

The Trollopiad; or, Travelling gentlemen in America, **37-174**

Trottings of a tenderfoot; or, A visit to the Columbian fiords, **84-2504**

The troubled aspect of affairs, etc., **52-793**

Troublous times in Canada, a history of the Fenian raids of 1866 and 1870, **70-1878**

The true commercial policy for Greater Britain, **88-2664**

The true history of the Emma Mine, **73-2024**

The true interpretation of the American civil war, and of England's cotton difficulty; or, Slavery, from a different point of view, shewing the relative responsibilities of America and Great Britain, **63-1405**

The true origin of the American rebellion, **65-1554**

A true picture of emigration; or Fourteen years in the interior of North America, **48-564**

The true state of the American question. Reply to Mr. Thurlow Weed, **62-1236**

The true way to abolish slavery, **55-929**

The truth about America, **86-2590**

The truth about America. The electoral system of the United States: its mechanism and workings, **60-1121**

The truth of the American question: being a reply to the prize essay of Mr. [J.C.] Rowan, **64-1490**

The twelve days' campaign. An impartial account of the final campaign of the late war, **66-1665**

Twelve lectures on primitive civilizations, and their physical conditions, **69-1836**

Twelve milestones: being the peregrinations of Ethel Knight Kelly, **99-3176**

Twelve years in America; being: observations on the country, the people, institutions and religion; with notices of slavery and the late war; and facts and incidents illustrative of ministerial life and labor, **67-1748**

Twenty years of my life, **91-2840**

Twenty-five years in the secret service; the recollections of a spy, **92-2849**

The two Americas; an account of sport and travel. With notes on men and manners in North and South America, **77-2197**

Two health-seekers in Southern California, **97-3079**

The two hemispheres: a popular account of the countries and peoples of the world, **82-2387**

Two journals of Robert Campbell, Chief Factor, Hudson's Bay Company, 1808 to 1853, **33-35**

Two lectures delivered at Newcastle-upon-Tyne, on the constitutions and republican institutions of the United States . . . from data procured on a visit to that country, **40-268**

Two lectures on a short visit to America, **76-2148**

Two lectures on America: being a few jottings made during a tour in the United States of America, **71-1926**

Two lectures, on the poetry of Pope, and on his own travels in America, by the right honourable the Earl of Carlisle, **50-654**

Two lectures on the present American war, **61-1144**

Two letters of Thomas Nye, relating to a journey from Montreal to Chicago in 1837, **37-168**

Two months in the Confederate states; including a visit to New Orleans under the domination of General Butler, **63-1333**

A two months' tour in Canada and the United States, in the autumn of 1889, **89-2718**

The wanderings of the hermit of Westminster between New York and San Francisco in the autumn of 1881, **82-2417**

The war in America: a sermon preached on Sunday, August 18th, 1861, at St. Peter's church, Congleton, **61-1147**

The war in America: its origin and object, **61-1186**

The war in America: Negro slavery and the Bible, **62-1290**

The war in Cuba; the experiences of an Englishman with the United States Army, **99-3144**

War of 1812. First series. Containing a full and detailed narrative of the operations of the right division, of the Canadian army, **42-353**

The war of 1812 in connection with the army bill act, **92-2888**

The war of 1812–13–14 between Great Britain and the United States, **99-3152**

The war of American independence, 1775–1783, 66-1686

The war of parties and waste of the national resources, with a peep into the policy of European cabinets. . . .in a series of dialogues between John Bull and Brother Jonathan, **53-869**

War or slavery, **62-1261**

The war upon American commerce; by subjects of Great Britain, **64-1542**

War, waves, and wanderings, **81-2350**

A warning voice from America to Victoria, **74-2074**

Warships for the Southern Confederacy, **63-1442**

Washington: a drama in five acts, 86-2600

Washington and other great military commanders: a series of biographical sketches, 76-2124

Washington and the mother country, **97-3085**

Waterways and water transport in different countries, **90-2766**

Wau-nan-gee; or, The Massacre at Chicago. A romance of the American Revolution, 42-353

Wayfaring notes. Second series. A holiday tour round the world, **76-2165**

The weakness and inefficiency of the government of the United States of North America, **63-1393**

Welcome to Goldwin Smith, regius professor of modern history in the University of Oxford, England, by citizens of New York, **64-1543**

The Welsh in America, **95-3001**

The West and North-west. Notes of a holiday trip, **80-2320**

The West Indies and the Spanish Main, **59-1088**

A westerly trend, being a veracious chronicle of more than sixty years of joyous wanderings, mainly in search of space and sunshine, **99-3204**

The western Avernus; or, Toil and travel in further North America, **87-2638**

The western farmer of America, **80-2321**

Western life, and how I became a bronco buster, **91-2836**

Western skies, a narrative of American travel in 1868, **70-1854**

Western wanderings; a record of travel in the evening land, **74-2040**

Western wanderings; or, A pleasure tour in the Canadas, **56-974**

Western woods and waters: poems and illustrative notes, **64-1449**

The Western world; or, Travels in the United States in 1846–47: exhibiting them in their latest development, social, political and industrial; including a chapter on California, **49-620**

The western world. Picturesque sketches of nature and natural history in North and South America, **74-2057**

The western world revisited, **54-881**

West-nor' west, **90-2790**

Westward by rail: the new route to the East, **70-1888**

"Westward Ho!" Sights on sea and land, rail and river; being an account. . . of a recent trip to America, **85-2537**

What I did in "The long." Journals home during a tour through the United States and Canada, **81-2340**

What I heard in Europe during the "American excitement"; illustrating the difference between government and people abroad in their hostility and good wishes to the perpetuity of the great republic, **64-1536**

What I saw in Texas, **72-1993**

What is contraband of war, and what is not. Comprising all the American and English authorities on the subject, **61-1175**

What is the matter? A political address as delivered in Masonic hall, October 28th, 1838, **38-187**

What shall we do with the Hudson's bay territory?, **66-1696**

What the South is fighting for, **62-1215**

The wheat problem, **99-3158**

White and black; the outcome of a visit to the United States, **79-2257**

The white chief: a legend of Northern Mexico, 55-943

White conquest, **76-2134**

Whittlings from the West. By Abel Log, **48-577**

Who are the canters?, **63-1323**

Who began the Frontier troubles? Who broke the Treaty? To the Hon. members of the Senate and House of Representatives in Congress, **40-267**

Who is to blame? or, Cursory review of "American apology for American accession to Negro slavery", **42-341**

Whom do English Tories wish elected to the Presidency?, **64-1478**

Why I have not gone to the South, **58-1051**

Why not have reciprocity? An easy, wise, and practicable method of settling the outstanding disputes between Canada and the United States, **90-2762**

Why without cotton?, **62-1235**

Wickets in the West; or, The twelve in America, **73-2010**

The wigwam in the wilderness, 66-1670

Wild adventures in wild places, 84-2515

Wild Beasts and their ways; reminiscences of Europe, Asia, Africa and America, **90-2751**

Wild life in Florida, with a visit to Cuba, **75-2122**

Wild sports of the world. A boy's book of natural history and adventure, **62-1242**

The wilderness and its tenants: a series of geographical and other essays illustrative of life in a wild country, **97-3083**

William Black, novelist: a biography, **76-2159**

William Bollaert's Texas , **44-396**

William Clark: a collection of his writings, with a biographical sketch, **99-3156**

William King, friend and champion of slaves, **44-416**

William Overend Simpson, Methodist minister and missionary, **86-2570**

William Sharp (Fiona Macleod): a memoir, **97-3092**

Winter and summer excursions in Canada, **94-2980**

A winter in the West Indies, described in familiar letters to Henry Clay, of Kentucky, **40-259**

Winter studies and summer rambles in Canada, **38-192**

Wit and humour: poems from Punch, **75-2085**

With Mr. [Joseph] Chamberlain in the United States and Canada, 1887–88, **88-2688**

With pack and rifle in the far south-west, **86-2573**

With Thackeray in America, **93-2913**

With the border ruffians; memories of the Far West, 1852–68, **68-1804**

A woman's example: and a nation's work. A tribute to Florence Nightingale, **64-1479**

A woman's wanderings in the western world: a series of letters addressed to Sir Fitzroy Kelly, M.P., by his daughter, **61-1148**

A word on behalf of the slave; or, A mite cast into the treasury of love, **48-592**

Wordsworth & Reed; the poet's correspondence with his American editor: 1836–1850, **50-686**

Work and wages; or, The penny emigrant's guide to the United States and Canada, **54-890**

Work and wages practically illustrated, **72-1945**

Working men in America, a lecture to workingmen in England, **72-1950**

The working men of Manchester and President Lincoln, **63-1447**

Working-class emigration, **76-2156**

The working-class movement in America, **88-2660**

Workmen and wages at home and abroad; or, The effects of strikes, combinations, and trades' unions, **67-1752**

A workshop paradise and other papers, **87-2640**

The world: round it and over it, **81-2352**

A world tour: being a year's diary, written 1884–85, **86-2594**

The world's fair, at Chicago, 1893. Information for travellers, **93-2911**

World's fair, Chicago, 1893: souvenir, **93-2952**

The world's highway, with some first impressions whilst journeying along it, **94-2965**

Wreck and ruin; or, Modern society, 60-1101

The wrongs and claims of Africans, **63-1325**

Yankee humour, and Uncle Sam's fun, **53-833**

Yankee land and the Yankees, being notes of a journey to and from the World's fair, **93-2906**

Yankeeland in her trouble. An Englishman's correspondence during the war, **64-1526**

A year in the great republic, **87-2608**

A Yorkshireman's trip to the United States and Canada, **92-2887**

Young Canada's reply to "Annexation", **88-2663**

The young emigrants, **53-871**

The young man of God: memories of Stanley Pumphrey, **82-2409**

A young traveller's journal of a tour in North and South America during the year 1850, **52-798**

Younger American poets, 1830–1890, 91-2840

The youthful travels and adventures of George Samuel Cull, a deaf and dumb cripple . . . including a sketch of seventeen years' residence in England, and five years' travelling through Canada and the United States, **63-1335**

Yr American, yr hwn sydd yn cynnwys Nodau ar daith o ddffryn Ohio i Gymru, Golweg ar dalaeth Ohio; Hanes sefydliadau Cymreig yn America, **40-249**

Zanita; a tale of the Yo-semite, 74-2058

Zigzag travels, **95-3020**

The zoology of the voyage of H. M. S. Sulphur, under the command of Captain Sir Edward Belcher . . . during the years 1836–42, **44-413**